German Legal System & Laws

German Legal
System & Laws

··

Nigel G. Foster, BA, LLM, Dip German

Senior Lecturer in Law, Cardiff Law School,
University of Wales
Director, Law and German Degree

Satish Sule, Assessor, LLM (Eur)

DAAD-Fachlektor, Cardiff Law School
University of Wales

Foreword by Dr. Axel Boetticher
Richter am Bundesgerichtshof (Judge at
the Federal Court of Justice)

OXFORD
UNIVERSITY PRESS

OXFORD
UNIVERSITY PRESS

Great Clarendon Street, Oxford OX2 6DP

Oxford University Press is a department of the University of Oxford.
It furthers the University's objective of excellence in research, scholarship,
and education by publishing worldwide in

Oxford New York

Auckland Cape Town Dar es Salaam Hong Kong Karachi Kuala Lumpur
Madrid Melbourne Mexico City Nairobi New Delhi Shanghai Taipei Toronto

With offices in

Argentina Austria Brazil Chile Czech Republic France Greece
Guatemala Hungary Italy Japan South Korea Poland Portugal
Singapore Switzerland Thailand Turkey Ukraine Vietnam

Oxford is a registered trade mark of Oxford University Press
in the UK and in certain other countries

Published in the United States
by Oxford University Press Inc., New York

© N. Foster, 1993
© N. Foster and S. Sule, 2002

The moral rights of the authors have been asserted

Database right Oxford University Press (maker)

First Edition, 1993
Second Edition, 1996
Third Edition, 2002
Reprinted 2003, 2005 (twice)

British Library Cataloguing in Publication Data

A cataloguing record for this book is available from the British Library

ISBN 0-19925-483-4

Typeset by RefineCatch Limited, Bungay, Suffolk
Printed in Great Britain
on acid-free paper by
Biddles Ltd., King's Lynn, Norfolk

OUTLINE CONTENTS

PART I **Introduction to the German Legal System**

1 German legal history and legal development   9

2 Sources of German law   36

3 Legal institutions   66

4 Legal education and legal personnel   80

5 The operation of justice   110

PART II **Substantive German Law**

6 Public law I: constitutional law: principles and institutions   145

7 Public law II: basic rights and the Federal Constitutional Court   204

8 Public law III: general administrative law   248

9 Public law IV: criminal law   295

10 Private law I: the German Civil Code   364

11 Private law II: business and labour law   482

Appendix: Extracts from the German Constitution   549
Glossary   563
Index   573

DETAILED CONTENTS

Foreword to the Third Edition   xxi
Foreword to the Second Edition   xxv
Foreword to the First Edition   xxvii
Preface   xxix
Table of Legislation   xxxiii
Table of Cases   lv
Abbreviations   lix

PART I   Introduction to the German Legal System

1 Introduction *3*
2 Historical influences *3*
3 The classification as a civil law country *3*
4 The division of public and civil (private) law *4*
5 Code and statute-based law *5*
6 Sources of law *5*
    6.1 Statute (*Gesetz*) *6*
    6.2 Custom (*Gewohnheitsrecht*) *6*
    6.3 The role of the courts, judiciary, and precedence *6*
    Further reading *7*

1   German legal history and legal development   9

1 Introduction *9*
2 Early developments *9*
3 The *Fränkisch-Deutsche Reich* *10*
4 Charlemagne *12*
5 The middle- to late-middle ages *13*
6 Early modern times: renaissance and reformation *16*
    6.1 The reception of Roman law into Germany *17*
7 Post-medieval developments *21*
    7.1 School of Natural Law *22*
    7.2 Historical School of Law *23*
    7.3 Commerce and unification *24*
    7.4 The civil code (*Bürgerliches Gesetzbuch*: BGB) *26*
8 Legal developments in the twentieth century *27*
    Further reading *34*

2   Sources of German law   36

1 Introduction *36*
2 Sources of law *37*
    2.1 The constitution: the "basic law" (*Grundgesetz*) *37*
    2.2 Statute (*Gesetz*) *37*

2.3   Customary law (*Gewohnheitsrecht*) 38
2.4   Judicial law-making (*Richterrecht*) 39
2.5   European Community law 42
2.6   International law 56
2.7   Natural law as a source of law? 57
2.8   Summary 57
3   Legal method 58
3.1   Hierarchy of legal provisions 58
3.2   *Subsumtion* 59
3.3   Gaps of legislation and analogies 59
3.4   Statutory interpretation (*Auslegung von Gesetzen*) 61
Further reading 64

3   Legal institutions   66

1   The courts and court structure: introduction 66
2   Decentralization 66
2.1   The federal courts (*Bundesgerichte*) 67
2.2   Courts of the *Länder* (*Gerichte der Länder*) 67
3   Specialization 67
3.1   Courts of ordinary jurisdiction 69
3.2   Administrative courts (*Verwaltungsgerichte*) 72
3.3   Labour courts (*Arbeitsgerichte*) 73
3.4   Social courts (*Sozialgerichte*) 74
3.5   Tax or revenue courts (*Finanzgerichte*) 75
3.6   Conclusion 75
4   The situation in the new federal regions (*Bundesländer*) 75
5   The Federal Constitutional Court 76
6   The *Länder* Constitutional Courts 77
7   The Justice Ministries 78
7.1   The Federal Ministry of Justice (*Bundesministerium der Justiz* (*BMJ*)) 78
7.2   The Justice Ministries of the *Länder* (*Landesjustizministerien*) 78
Further reading 79

4   Legal education and legal personnel   80

1   Legal education 80
1.1   Introduction 80
1.2   University entrance 80
1.3   Legal education 83
2   The judiciary and legal professions 88
2.1   Introduction 88
2.2   The judiciary 89
2.3   Lawyers 92
2.4   Additional legal occupations 100
2.5   Rights allowed non-German attorneys 104
2.6   The position of EC attorneys 104
3   Lay participation in the legal system 106
Further reading 108

5   The operation of justice   110

1   Legal advice and legal aid *110*
   1.1   Legal representation *110*
2   Litigation costs *111*
   2.1   Court costs *111*
   2.2   Fees for legal representation *112*
3   Legal aid *113*
   3.1   The Legal Advice Act (*Beratungshilfegesetz*: BerHG) *113*
   3.2   Legal aid for representation in court (*Prozeßkostenhilfe*) *115*
4   Legal publications, reporting, and citation *116*
   4.1   Official publications *116*
   4.2   Private reporting and publication *119*
5   Academic legal opinion *121*
6   Aspects of civil procedure *122*
   6.1   Introduction *122*
   6.2   General principles of civil procedure *123*
   6.3   General considerations of procedure *126*
   6.4   The civil law action *128*
   6.5   Special procedures *133*
   6.6   Appeals (*Rechtsmittel*) *133*
   6.7   Enforcement of judgments (*Zwangsvollstreckung*) *134*
   Further reading *135*

PART II   Substantive German Law

A Outline of subject areas   139

1   Public and civil (private) law *139*

B Public law   139

1   *Staatsrecht* *139*
2   Administrative law *140*
3   Judicature and procedural law *140*
4   Criminal law *141*
5   Tax law *141*
6   Social law *141*
7   The law of economic administration and labour law *142*
   7.1   The law of economic administration *142*
   7.2   Labour law *142*

C Civil law   143

1   The civil code (*Bürgerliches Gesetzbuch*: BGB) *143*
2   Commercial law *143*

6   Public law I: constitutional law: principles and institutions   145

1   Historical development *145*
   1.1   Constitutional developments until unification *145*
   1.2   Changes made to the *Grundgesetz* following unification *147*
   1.3   Content *148*
   1.4   Constitutions of the *Länder* *149*
2   The supreme position of constitutional law *149*
   2.1   The priority of constitutional provisions *149*
   2.2   Interpretation of the constitution *150*
   2.3   Distinction: interpretation in the light of constitutional law *151*
   2.4   Position of international law *152*
3   The basic principles of state *153*
   3.1   Republicanism *154*
   3.2   Democracy *155*
   3.3   *Rechtsstaat* *163*
   3.4   Principle of the social state (*Sozialstaatsprinzip*) *173*
   3.5   Principle of the federal state (*Bundesstaatprinzip*) *174*
   3.6   Environmental protection (Art. 20a GG)—a new principle? *180*
4   Organization of the state *181*
   4.1   *Bundestag* (Federal Parliamentary Assembly, Arts 38–49 GG) *181*
   4.2   Federal government (*Bundesregierung*, Arts 62–69 GG) *186*
   4.3   The Federal President (*Bundespräsident*, Arts 54–61 GG) *189*
   4.4   The Federal Council (*Bundesrat*, Arts 50–53 GG) *192*
   4.5   Functions of the state *194*
5   Protection of the constitution *198*
   5.1   Amendments of the constitution *198*
   5.2   Defending the free democratic basic order *199*
   Further reading *203*

7   Public law II: basic rights and the Federal Constitutional Court   204

1   Basic rights (*Grundrechte*) *204*
   1.1   General principles *205*
2   The individual rights *214*
   2.1   Article 1: The protection of human dignity (*Schutz der Menschenwürde*) *214*
   2.2   Article 2: The right to personal freedom (*Allgemeines Persönlichkeitsrecht*, Art. 2 I GG), right to life (*Recht auf Leben*), and physical integrity (*köperliche Unversehrtheit*, Art. 2 II GG) *216*
   2.3   Article 3: Equality before the law (*Gleichheit vor dem Gesetz*) *219*
   2.4   Article 4; The freedom of faith, conscience, and creed (*Glaubens-, Gewissens- und Bekenntnisfreiheit*) *222*
   2.5   Article 5 I GG: Freedom of communication; freedom of expression, information, press, broadcasting, and film (*Kommunikationsgrundrechte*) *224*
   2.6   Article 5 III GG: Freedom of artistic expression and science (*Freiheit von Kunst und Wissenschaft*) *227*
   2.7   Article 6: Marriage and family, children born outside marriage (*Ehe, Familie, Nichteheliche Kinder*) *227*
   2.8   Article 7: School education (*Schulwesen*) *228*
   2.9   Article 8: Freedom of assembly (*Versammlungsfreiheit*) *228*
   2.10   Article 9: Freedom of association (*Vereinigungsfreiheit*) *229*
   2.11   Article 10: Privacy of correspondence, posts, and telecommunications (*Brief-, Post- und Fernmeldegeheimnis*) *229*
   2.12   Article 11: Freedom of movement (*Freizügigkeit*) *230*
   2.13   Article 12: Free choice of occupation or profession, prohibition of forced labour (*Berufsfreiheit*) *230*

2.14 Article 13: Privacy of the home (*Unverletzlichkeit der Wohnung*) *232*
2.15 Article 14: Property, inheritance, expropriation (*Eigentum, Erbrecht, Enteignung*) *233*
2.16 Article 15: Public ownership (*Sozialisierung*) *234*
2.17 Article 16: Citizenship, extradition (*Ausbürgerung, Auslieferung*) *234*
2.18 Article 16a: Asylum (*Asylrecht*) *235*
2.19 Article 17: Right of petition (*Petitionsrecht*) *235*
2.20 Article 17a: The restriction of the basic rights for members of the armed forces and the alternative service in the civil sector *236*
2.21 Articles 18 and Article 19 I–III *236*
2.22 Article 19 IV: Procedural basic rights (*Prozeßgrundrechte*) *236*
2.23 Article 19 IV: Recourse to the courts (*Rechtsschutzgarantie*) *236*
2.24 Article 101 I GG: Right to a lawful judge, prohibition of exceptional courts (*Recht auf den gesetzlichen Richter, Verbot von Ausnahmegerichten*) *236*
2.25 Article 102 GG: Abolition of death penalty (*Abschaffung der Todesstrafe*) *237*
2.26 Article 103 I GG: Right to legal hearing (*Anspruch auf Rechtliches Gehör*) *237*
2.27 Article 103 II GG: *nulla poena sine lege* *237*
2.28 Article 103 III GG: *ne bis in idem* *238*
3 The Federal Constitutional Court and constitutional procedural law *239*
  3.1 The Federal Constitutional Court (*Bundesverfassungsgericht, BVerfG*) *239*
4 Constitutional procedural law (*Verfassungsprozessrecht*) *240*
  4.1 Abstract review of statutes (*Abstrakte Normenkontrolle*, Art. 93 I No. 2, §§ 13 No. 6, 76 et seq. BVerfGG) *241*
  4.2 The submission procedure (*Vorlageverfahren, Konkrete Normenkontrolle*, Art. 100 I GG, §§ 13 No. 11, 80–82 BVerfGG) *241*
  4.3 Constitutional complaint (*Verfassungsbeschwerde*) *242*
  4.4 Constitutional courts of the *Länder* *245*
Further reading *245*

8 Public law III   **248**

A General administrative law   **248**

1 Introduction *248*
  1.1 Different types of administration *248*
  1.2 Administrative law as part of public law *249*
  1.3 Influence of European law *250*
  1.4 General and specific administrative law *250*
2 Sources of administrative law *251*
  2.1 The *Grundgesetz* *251*
  2.2 Federal and *Länder* statutes (*Bundes- und Landesgesetze*) *251*
  2.3 Delegated legislation (*Rechtsverordnungen*) *251*
  2.4 Bye-laws (*Satzungen*) *251*
  2.5 Administrative guidelines (*Verwaltungsvorschriften*) *252*
  2.6 EC law *253*
3 Administrative bodies *253*
4 Basic principles of administrative law *254*
  4.1 Impact of constitutional law *254*
  4.2 Discretion (*Ermessen*) *255*
  4.3 Margin of appreciation (*Beurteilungsspielraum*) *256*
  4.4 Subjective public right (*Subjektives Öffentliches Recht*) *258*
5 Types of administrative action *258*
  5.1 The *Verwaltungsakt* (administrative act) *259*
  5.2 Public law contract (*öffentlich-rechtlicher Vertrag*, § 54 VwVfG) *264*

5.3 Plan and planning *264*
5.4 Other instruments *264*
6 Enforcement by the authority *265*
7 Judicial review *265*
7.1 Informal remedies (*formlose Rechtsbehelfe*) *265*
7.2 Formal remedies: *Widerspruchsverfahren* (§§ 68–73 VwVfG) *265*
7.3 Formal remedies: types of action *266*
8 Claims for damages *271*
Further reading *271*

B Particular adminstrative law (*Besonderes Verwaltungsrecht*)   272

Further reading *272*

C Social law   273

1 Introduction *273*
2 Sources of social law *273*
3 The aims and basic principles of social law *274*
4 The administration and distribution of social aid *275*
5 Social welfare provision *275*
6 Breaches of duty by social bodies *277*
7 Persons eligible for social assistance *277*
Further reading *277*

D The law of economic administration (*Wirtschaftsverwaltungsrecht*)   278

1 Introduction *278*
2 The scope of the law of economic administration *278*
3 The economic system *279*
4 State promotion of the economy (*Wirtschaftsförderung*) *280*
5 The general regulation of business *280*
5.1 The Trade Act (*Gewerbeordnung*: GewO) *280*
5.2 Particular trade law (*Besonderes Gewerberecht*) *281*
6 Consumer protection law (*Verbraucherschutzrecht*) *281*
6.1 Safety legislation *282*
6.2 Identification and labelling *282*
6.3 Advertising legislation *283*
6.4 Sale of goods laws *283*
6.5 Warranty and liability legislation *284*
6.6 Other areas of consumer law *284*
6.7 Enforcement *284*
Further reading *285*

E Environmental law (*Umweltrecht*)   285

1 Sources *286*
2 General principles *287*
2.1 The preventative or precautionary principle (*Vorsorgeprinzip*) *287*
2.2 The principle that the polluter pays (*Verursacherprinzip*) *288*

2.3   The co-operation principle (*Kooperationsprinzip*) *288*
2.4   The protection of the existing position principle (*Bestandsschutzprinzip*) *288*
3   Principal legislative enactments *288*
3.1   The Water Resources Act (*Wasserhaushaltsgesetz*: WHG) *288*
3.2   The Federal Emissions Control Act (*Bundesimmissionsschutzgesetz*: BImSchG) *289*
3.3   The Waste Act (*Abfallgesetz*: AbfG) *289*
3.4   The Federal Nature Conservation Act (*Bundesnaturschutzgesetz*: BNatSchG) *290*
3.5   The Environmental Information Act (*Umweltinformationsgesetz*: UIG) *290*
3.6   The Ozone Act (*Ozongesetz*: OG) *290*
3.7   The Federal Building Code (*Baugesetzbuch*: BauGB) *291*
3.8   The Packaging Act (*Verpackungsverordnung*: VerpackV) *291*
4   Liability and enforcement following environmental damage *291*
4.1   Civil law *291*
4.2   Criminal sanction *292*
4.3   Public law *293*
5   Public enforcement of environmental law *293*
Further reading *293*

---

9   Public law IV   295

A   Criminal law   295

1   Introduction *295*
2   History of criminal law *296*
3   Structure of the criminal code *297*
4   Applicability of german criminal law (§§ 3–9 STGB) *298*
5   Leading principles of German criminal law *298*
5.1   The principle of legality (*Gesetzlichkeitsprinzip*) *298*
5.2   The principle of the protection of legal rights (*Rechtsgüterschutzprinzip*) *299*
5.3   The principle of guilt (*Schuldprinzip*) *299*
6   General concepts in criminal law *300*
6.1   Forms of criminal offences *301*
6.2   Structure of the criminal offence (*Aufbau der Straftat*) *301*
6.3   Negligent offences (*Fahrlässigkeitsdelikte*) *320*
6.4   Offences of omission (*Unterlassungsdelikte*) *321*
6.5   Attempt (*Versuch*) *325*
6.6   Different forms of participation: *Täterschaft und Teilnahme*, §§ 25–31 *330*
6.7   Legal consequences: punishment and other measures *335*
7   The individual or substantive offences *336*

B   Criminal procedural law   337

1   Introduction *337*
2   Historical aspects *338*
3   Sources *339*
4   Principal stages of procedure *339*
4.1   The pre-trial procedure *339*
4.2   The interim proceedings (*Zwischenverfahren*) *340*
4.3   The main proceedings (*Hauptverfahren*) *340*
4.4   Appeal *340*
5   Leading principles of procedural law *340*

5.1   Principles on commencing the procedure 340
5.2   Principles concerning the implementation of the procedure 342
5.3   Principles concerning evidence 344
5.4   Principles concerning the form of proceedings 345
6   The pre-trial preliminary investigation (*Vorverfahren*) 346
6.1   The investigation (*Ermittlungsverfahren*) 347
6.2   Powers of state prosecution and police during pre-trial investigation 347
7   The role of the defence attorney (*Verteidiger*) during pre-trial investigations 351
7.1   Right to a defence attorney 351
7.2   Rights and duties of the defence attorney 352
8   The interim proceedings (*Zwischenverfahren*) 352
8.1   The choice of court 352
8.2   Result of interim proceedings 353
9   Structure of the main proceedings (*Hauptverfahren*) 353
9.1   The role of the judge 354
9.2   The main proceedings: the oral trial (*Hauptverhandlung*) 354
10   The law of evidence 355
10.1   Principles of the law of evidence 355
10.2   Forms of proof (*Beweismittel*) 356
10.3   The prohibition of evidence (*Beweisverwertungsverbot*) 357
11   The conclusion of the trial 359
12   The accelerated procedure (*Beschleunigtes Verfahren*, §§ 417–420 StPO) 359
13   The summary procedure (*Strafbefehlsverfahren*, §§ 407–412 StPO) 359
14   Means of legal redress (*Rechtsmittel*) 360
14.1   Common rules on ordinary means of legal redress 360
14.2   Forms of appeal 360
14.3   The re-trial (*Wiederaufnahme des Verfahrens*) 362
Further reading 362

10   Private law I: the German Civil Code   364

A Introduction   364

1   The structure of the BGB 366
2   Method of addressing private law problems: finding the claim
(*Anspruchsgrundlage*) 367
3   Major principles 369
3.1   Freedom of contract (*Vertragsfreiheit*) 369
3.2   The principle of abstraction (*Abstraktionsprinzip*) 370
3.3   Possession and ownership (*Besitz und Eigentum*) 371
3.4   *Verpflichtungs- und Verfügungsgeschäfte*: Two different categories of legal transaction 372

B Book One: the general part   374

1   Introduction 374
2   *Rechtssubjekte* (holders of subjective rights) 374
2.1   Natural and legal persons (*Natürliche und Juristische Personen*) 375
2.2   Different forms of legal capacity 375
3   The legal transaction (*Das Rechtsgeschäft*) 379
3.1   Declaration of intent (*Willenserklärung*) 379
3.2   The "real act" (*Realakt*) 382

3.3 The legal transaction (*Das Rechtsgeschäft*) *383*
3.4 The contract (*Der Vertrag*) *383*
4 Interpretation rules (*Auslegung*) *387*
  4.1 Paragraph 133 *387*
  4.2 Paragraph 157 *388*
  4.3 Paragraph 242 *388*
  4.4 The application of § 242 *389*
5 Void legal transactions (*Nichtige Rechtsgeschäfte*) *390*
  5.1 Breach of formal requirements (§§ 125–129 BGB) *391*
  5.2 Breach of a law or good morals (§§ 134, 138 BGB) *391*
  5.3 Defect of declaration of intent (*Willensmängel*) *393*
  5.4 The concept and consequences of the void legal transaction *398*
6 Agency (*Stellvertretung*) *398*
  6.1 Types of agency *399*
  6.2 Agency authority (*Vollmacht*) *400*
  6.3 The scope of agency powers *400*
  6.4 Legal consequences of agency *401*
  6.5 Lack of authorization *401*
  6.6 Prohibition of self contracting (*Verbot des Insichgeschäfts*) *402*
7 Limitation *402*
Further reading *403*

C Book Two: the law of obligations: general part   404

1 Introduction *404*
2 The obligational relationship (*Das Schuldverhältnis*)—general principles *404*
  2.1 Types and the creation of obligational relationships *405*
3 Content of the obligational relationship *406*
  3.1 Primary and secondary duties (*Primär- und Sekundärleistungspflichten*) *406*
  3.2 Main and ancillary duties (*Hauptleistungspflichten und Nebenleistungspflichten*) *406*
  3.3 Performance of individual and generic obligations (*Gattungs- und Stückschuld*, §§ 243) *406*
  3.4 Time and place of performance (*Leistungsort und -zeit*, §§ 269, 270, 271) *407*
  3.5 Passage of risk in performance *408*
  3.6 Standard form contracts and general conditions of business (*Allgemeine Geschaftsbedingungen*, §§ 305–310 BGB) *408*
  3.7 Third parties to contracts *410*
  3.8 Extinction of an obligational relationship (*Erlöschen des Schuldverhältnisses*) *411*
4 Irregularities in performance *412*
  4.1 Basic provision for liability: the new § 280 BGB *412*
  4.2 Impossibility (*Unmöglichkeit der Leistung*) *413*
  4.3 Delay (*Verzug*) *415*
  4.4 Positive breach of obligation/contract (*Positive Forderungsverletzung/Vertragsverletzung*) *417*
  4.5 Problems in pre-contractual relations (c.i.c.) *419*
  4.6 Collapse of foundation of contract, § 313 (*Wegfall der Geschäftsgrundlage*) *420*
  4.7 Rescission, §§ 323–326, 346–349 (*Rücktritt vom Vertrag*) *421*
5 Assessing damages and compensation *421*
  5.1 Types of damage *422*
  5.2 Fault (*Verschulden*) *423*

D Book Two: the law of obligations: special part   424

1 Law on contracts of sale (*Kaufrecht*) *424*
  1.1 Duties of seller and buyer *425*

1.2 Passage of risk *425*
1.3 Remedies for delivery of defective goods (*Gewährleistungsrechte*) *426*
1.4 Limitation periods *428*
1.5 Consumer protection *429*
2 Unjustified enrichment (*Ungerechtfertigte Bereicherung*) *429*
2.1 The enrichment of the obligor *430*
2.2 The performance of the creditor *430*
2.3 The absence of a legal basis *430*
2.4 Enrichment in other ways (§ 812 I 1 2nd alternative) *431*
2.5 Performance by a third party *432*
2.6 The scope of the obligation to return possession *432*
3 Tort law (*Unerlaubte Handlung*) *433*
3.1 The duty to compensate for damage *433*
3.2 The infringement of a protective law *435*
3.3 Intentional damage *435*
3.4 Other provisions of delictual liability *436*
3.5 Vicarious liability (*Haftung für den Verrichtungsgehilfen*) *436*
3.6 Strict liability (*Gefährdungshaftung*) *436*
3.7 Product liability *438*
3.8 Buildings and occupiers' liability *438*
3.9 Liability of the state *438*
3.10 Compensation *438*
3.11 Limitation periods *439*
Further reading *439*

E Book Three: property law (*Sachenrecht*)   440

1 Introduction to the scope and sources of property law *440*
2 Definitions and general principles of property law *441*
2.1 Real rights (*dingliche Rechte*) *441*
2.2 Principles of property law *441*
3 Possession (*Der Besitz*) *443*
3.1 Direct and indirect possession *443*
3.2 Exclusive and joint possession *443*
3.3 Complete and partial possession *444*
3.4 The possessor's agent (*Besitzdiener*) *444*
3.5 The acquisition and loss of possession *444*
3.6 The protection of possession *445*
4 Ownership (*Das Eigentum*) *445*
4.1 The acquisition and loss of ownership *447*
4.2 The acquisition and loss of real estate *447*
4.3 The acquisition and loss of movable property *451*
4.4 Good faith acquisition *451*
5 Acquisition of ownership by other means *453*
5.1 Appropriation (*Aneignung*) *453*
5.2 Prescription (*Ersitzung*) *453*
5.3 Union or combination (*Verbindung*) *453*
5.4 Mixing (*Vermischung*) *454*
5.5 Manufacturing or processing (*Verarbeitung*) *454*
5.6 Found objects *454*
5.7 Separation of objects *455*
5.8 Succession (*Gesamtrechtsnachfolge*) *455*

6 The protection of ownership *455*
    6.1   The claim for return (*Herausgabeanspruch*, § 985) *455*
    6.2   Rights under §§ 987 et seq. (*Eigentümer-Besitzer-Verhältnis*) *456*
    6.3   Interference with ownership (*Unterlassungsanspruch*) *457*
    6.4   Other claims under private law *457*
    6.5   Judicial review *458*
7 Other types of property rights *458*
8 Property finance and security (*Sicherungsrechte*) *458*
    8.1   Security interests in land (*Grundpfandrechte*) *459*
    8.2   Securities over movables *461*
    Further reading *463*

F Book Four: family law (*Familienrecht*) 464

1 Introduction *464*
2 The scope of family law *465*
3 Matrimonial law (*Eherecht*) *465*
    3.1   Engagement (*Verlöbnis*) *465*
    3.2   The act of marriage (*Die Eheschließung*) *466*
    3.3   Non-existent and voidable marriages (*Nichtehen und aufhebbare Ehen*) *466*
    3.4   Legal consequences and the obligations of marriage *467*
    3.5   Marital property (*Ehegüterrecht*) *467*
    3.6   Divorce (*Scheidung der Ehe*) *468*
4 Relationship (*Verwandtschaft*) *470*
    4.1   The legal relationship between parents and children *470*
    4.2   Adoption (§§ 1741–1772) *471*
5 Guardianship (*Vormundschaft*), curatorship (*Pflegschaft*), and care and control (*Betreuung*) *171*
    Further reading *472*

G Book Five: the law of succession (*Erbrecht*) 472

1 Introduction, sources, and scope *472*
2 The basic principles of succession *473*
    2.1   The principle of universal succession (*Gesamtrechtsnachfolge/Universalsukzession*) *473*
    2.2   Automatic inheritance (*Vonselbsterwerb*) *473*
    2.3   Capacity *473*
    2.4   Testamentary and intestate succession *473*
3 The acquisition of the inheritance *474*
    3.1   Acceptance *474*
    3.2   Repudiation of the inheritance *474*
4 Rights and liabilities in succession *474*
5 Heirs *475*
6 Intestate succession (*gesetzliche Erbfolge*) *475*
7 Testamentary succession (*gewillkürte Erbfolge*) *476*
    7.1   The will (*Das Testament*) *476*
    7.2   The succession contract (*Erbvertrag*) *477*
    7.3   The ineffective or invalid will *477*
8 Compulsory portion (*Pflichtteil*) *477*
9 The execution of the estate *478*
    Further reading *478*

H Private international law/conflict of laws 478

1 International civil procedural law (*Internationales Zivilverfahrensrecht, IZVR*) *479*
2 International private law (*Internationales Privatrecht*) *480*
   Further reading *481*

11 Private law II: business and labour law 482

A Commercial law and the law of business association 482

1 Introduction *482*
2 Commercial law *483*
   2.1 History *483*
   2.2 The structure of the HGB *483*
   2.3 HGB Book One *484*
   2.4 Book Two: partnerships under the commercial code *488*
   2.5 Book Three: business accounts *489*
   2.6 Book Four: commercial transactions *489*
   2.7 Commercial arbitration *491*
3 The law of business association *492*
   3.1 Introduction *492*
   3.2 Partnerships *493*

B Company law (*Gesellschaftsrecht*) 498

1 The private limited liability company *498*
   1.1 Formation *498*
   1.2 Capital *499*
   1.3 Registration *499*
   1.4 Pre-incorporation status (vor-GmbH) *500*
   1.5 The rights and duties of shareholders (*Gesellschafter*) *500*
   1.6 Management (*Geschäftsführung*) *501*
   1.7 General meetings *502*
   1.8 The supervisory board (*Aufsichtsrat*) *503*
   1.9 Alterations to the articles *503*
   1.10 Dissolution and liquidation (*Auflösung*) *503*
   1.11 Company restructuring, mergers, and acquisitions *503*
2 The joint stock corporation *504*
   2.1 History *504*
   2.2 Formation *505*
   2.3 The board of management (*Vorstand*) *506*
   2.4 The supervisory board (*Aufsichtsrat*) *507*
   2.5 The general meeting of the shareholders (*Hauptversammlung*) *508*
   2.6 Shares *508*
   2.7 Minority protection *509*
   2.8 Accounting provisions *509*
   2.9 Dissolution (*Auflösung*) *509*
   2.10 Acquisition and mergers *510*
3 Limited stock partnership/association limited by shares *511*
4 The law of groups of companies (*Konzernrecht*) *512*
   Further reading *514*

C Competition law and anti-trust law — 515

1   Introduction *515*
2   Competition law (*Wettbewerbsrecht*) *516*
   2.1   The general prohibition *516*
   2.2   Particular prohibitions *518*
   2.3   Remedies *519*
3   Anti-trust law (*Kartellrecht*) *519*
   3.1   Horizontal agreements between undertakings *520*
   3.2   Vertical agreements *521*
   3.3   Dominant positions and mergers *521*
   Further reading *522*

D Labour law (*Arbeitsrecht*) — 523

1   Introduction and history of German labour law *523*
2   Categories of labour law *525*
   2.1   Individual labour law (*Individualarbeitsrecht*) *525*
   2.2   Worker protection laws (*Arbeitschutzrecht*) *525*
   2.3   Collective labour law (*Kollektives Arbeitsrecht*) *525*
   2.4   Procedural law *525*
3   Sources of labour law *526*
   3.1   Constitutional law *526*
   3.2   Civil law *526*
   3.3   Case-law *527*
   3.4   Contractual agreements *527*
4   Labour law institutions *528*
   4.1   Unions and employers' associations *528*
   4.2   The works council (*Betriebsrat*) *529*
   4.3   The supervisory board (*Aufsichtsrat*) *529*
   4.4   Labour law courts *529*
5   Individual labour law *530*
   5.1   The employment relationship *530*
   5.2   The formation of contracts of employment *531*
   5.3   Works councils and hiring employees *533*
   5.4   General terms of contracts *533*
   5.5   Ending the employment relationship and dismissal *535*
6   Worker protection laws *537*
7   Collective labour law *539*
   7.1   Industrial conflict law *540*
   7.2   Worker representation and co-determination *541*
8   Procedural law *546*
   8.1   Individual disputes *546*
   8.2   Collective disputes *547*
   8.3   Judicial investigation *547*
   Further reading *548*

Appendix: Extracts from the German Constitution 549
Glossary 563
Index 573

FOREWORD TO THE THIRD EDITION

It has already been six years since the appearance of the second edition of the book *German Legal System and Laws*, written by Nigel Foster. Meanwhile, we not only have a second editor of the book, who is a German lawyer, but we have also witnessed vivacious changes in EC law and, in consequence, in the national German Legal System. Today we have many political and economic problems in further integrating Europe. We are, however, on a silent and straight path to a further legally unified Europe, with the ambitious aim of harmonising the legal systems of the EU member states.

The primary laws of the European Treaty, after which came a flood of secondary Community Law and decisions in the European Court of Justice, have more and more influence not only in the law-making of the *Bundestag* but also in the parliaments of the *Länder*. No interpretation of the German Constitutional or Federal Law is possible without proving whether EC law has already regulated the matter. Furthermore, the standards of the European Convention for the Protection of Human Rights and Fundamental Freedoms (ECHR)—the rules of which have the same rank in Germany as any other Federal Law (*Bundesgesetz*)—have great influence in the use and the interpretation for example of the Criminal Procedural Law and national Criminal Sentence Enforcement Law. Thus, it is very helpful that the book now has a much wider view upon the sources of German Law. In Chapter II we can see the development of the Basic Law towards a unified Europe since the famous decisions of the *Bundesverfassungsgericht* called *Solange I* from 1974 and *Solange II* from 1987. In 1992 there was clearer acceptance of EC law by introduction of new Art. 23 (the European Article) in the *Grundgesetz*. At the end there came the historic decision of 1993, the *Maastricht Urteil*. Sovereign powers can now be transferred to the European Union as long as the EC law still complies with the requirements of Art. 79 II and III of the Basic Law. The *Bundesverfassungsgericht* has accepted the Treaty of Maastricht (now developed by the Treaties of Amsterdam and Nice). This acceptance is conditional upon widening protection against the acts of Community institutions by reviewing them in the light of the Grundgesetz protections. The Court emphasised that its review of EC law would be exercised in 'cooperation' with the European Court of Justice. The *Bundesverfassungsgericht*'s declaration shows that there will be other Courts in Europe who interpret German law in the light of EC law. This link has become increasingly important since the release of the first draft of the Charter of fundamental rights of the European Union, in September 2000. These fundamental rights open the way for a further step by a new Community legal order, which stands in competition with the national legal orders of the member states. The Charter is not yet legally binding, but it expresses its generally recognised principle in Article 41: 'Every person has the right to have his or hers affairs handled impartially, fairly and within a reasonable time by the institutions and bodies of the Union'. This can only mean that Community law will gain much more supremacy over the national German law.

Not only as a consequence of 11 September 2001, we also have, in addition to the development of the Treaty, intensive intergovernmental cooperation in the fields of asylum and anti-terror legislation. The struggle against organised crime made it possible to build up first standards of European criminal law for offences like sexual crimes against children, slave trade, drug trafficking, corruption and fraud, and money laundering. We have new constructions like a European Corpus Juris and ideas of European institutions like EUROJUST or EUROPOL. All these examples of common activities have asked for reactions in the German legal system. Not only did the constitutional law have to be adapted on the European level but also several national special Acts had to be changed in respect for a number of European Directives, which Germany had to transpose into the national legal system.

How quickly and intensively the order to transpose European law can change the national legal system is shown by the 2001 reform of the Law of Obligation (*Schuldrechtsreform*), which came into force on 1 January 2002. Several directives on the field of freedom of trade made it necessary that central parts of the Civil Code were matter of an intensive reform after one hundred years of validity with only few amendments. EC law provided the occasion to change important parts of the BGB such as the rules of irregularities in performance (*Leistungsstörungen*, §§ 280 ff. BGB) and the rules for the limitation are completely regulated from new (*Verjährung*, §§ 194–218 BGB). The general period of limitation is in respect for European standards and is now three years, but there are numerous exceptions. Importantly, specific laws outside the BGB, such as the Standard Contracts Act of 1976 (*AGB-Gesetz*) or the Package Tour Contracts Act of 1979 (*Reisevertragsgesetz*), which have modified the application of the BGB, have now been incorporated within the Code. The book gives an introduction in the 2001 reform and gives advice for further interpretation. The BGB was not the only matter for reform: the code on civil procedure of 1877 (*Zivilprozeßordnung*; ZPO) was the subject of one of the biggest revisions of the last thirty years. The central aims of this reform are a new structure of the proceeding before the *Amtsgericht* and new forms of appeal. The first appeal (*Berufung*) is no more a complete second instance to prove all the facts again in front of a higher court, but is now only an instance of judicial control to avoid severe judicial mistakes. The second appeal, the revision to the Federal Court, is no longer dependent on a minimum value. The Court must accept appeals only if they are of fundamental importance or can help to save the further development of the law or the unity of the jurisdiction. As some more reforms have taken place, in criminal law for example, the basis and the sources of national German law have changed to a high degree.

Last but not least, the *Bundestag* has just decided a new Act for Legal Education. This Act encourages young law students to have a look outside Germany, to learn foreign languages, and to study the sources of the laws of other countries, especially European law. I had the honour to be External Examiner at the University of Surrey for four years, and was deeply impressed by the engagement of young law students from Great Britain and many countries from all over the world, many of whom practised in Germany, and learned the German language and legal system. They wrote remarkable dissertations on various matters and they discussed their works in German in their vivas. Those young law students are the real Europeans, because they do not care about political, judicial and linguistic frontiers. They are just curious, and set out to study German legal tradition and practice. Many of them were exceptionally lucky to have the aid of the book by Nigel Foster, and now by Satish Sule.

Dr. Axel Boetticher, Karlsruhe
Judge at the Federal Court of Germany

FOREWORD TO THE SECOND EDITION
by The Rt. Hon. Lord Hoffmann

English law has recently emerged from a long period of insularity. It was not always thus. In creating our commercial law, that jewel in the crown of English jurisprudence, Lord Mansfield drew upon the law merchant of the whole of Europe. In the nineteenth century, no one thought it eccentric for judges to go to Pothier or Dumat, or even to the Digest of Justinian, for principles of the law of contract. Decisions of the courts and writers of the United States were cited with respect. But in the twentieth century, the fog around our shores descended. The only foreign cases which judges were sometimes prepared to read were, curiously enough, those from Australia. Europe was assumed to have nothing to offer.

During the last twenty years, our membership of the European Union has required English judges to undergo a compulsory education in continental legal thinking. In having to deal with the European treaties and subordinate legislation, they have been exposed to statutory provisions which are abstract, general and open-textured; a style of legislation far from the finely crafted precision of Parliamentary draftsman, but familiar enough to practitioners in a codified system of law. And with the continental style of legislation has come continental methods of construction, which allow a freedom to mould language almost sinful to puritan English sensibilities, and continental legal concepts such as good faith, proportionality and the rights of man.

English judges have on the whole risen to the challenge. They have welcomed the draughts of continental air which have been let into their legal system. And acquaintance with Community law, its methods and its doctrines, has given rise to an interest in the domestic laws and legal systems of our European partners. As a result, they have discovered German law, which until recently was more or less *terra incognita*. Again, it was not always thus. When John Austin was appointed professor of law at the newly established University College, London in 1829, he went to Heidelberg to prepare himself for his lectures. It seemed the obvious place to go for any serious study of the law. It was certainly not happening at Oxford or Cambridge, then the only other English universities. But time and change brought about a withdrawal into common law self-sufficiency which is only now coming to an end. Now it is possible for an English judge in the House of Lords to urge upon his colleagues the adoption of the German principle of *Schadensverlagerung*, if not with success, at least without the astonished incomprehension which would have greeted the proposal fifteen years ago.

For judges and advocates in our higher courts who want to see whether the German solution to a problem offers a new insight into how English law might develop, the second half of this new edition of Nigel Foster's successful book provides a lucid, though necessarily compressed, summary of the principal doctrines of German law over a wide field. It is a point of departure to the wider reading which is helpfully listed in a bibliography at the end of each chapter. But this is a minority and self-regarding view of the value of this part of the book, which is not of course aimed at English appellate judges as its principal audience. If it were, very few copies would be sold, because one of the most fascinating pieces of information in the first part of the book (to which I shall return) is how very few full time judges we have in England compared with the 20,000 or so in Germany. No, the book is mainly intended for English practitioners, barristers and solicitors, who need to know something about German law because their clients have dealings with Germany, and for the increasing number of students who are including a systematic study of German law in their courses in English universities. For both of these categories, the second half of the book concentrates on those areas of German law which are likely to be of practical interest to English lawyers: public law, contract and tort, property, commercial and company law and some family law.

I have left until last, however, what is to me the most fascinating and original part of this book. That is its first part, dealing with the origins and structure of German law, the organisation of the German judiciary and legal profession and the German constitution. Unlike the second part on substantive law, which is organised so that the reader may confine himself to the subject in hand, the first part repays reading at a continuous sitting. It gives one the flavour of the contemporary German legal system; the questions which are debated and controversial as well as those which are settled by history and tradition; the attitudes and expectations which inform the relationship between a German and the law. There too, an English lawyer and even a non-lawyer has much to learn. It is for example difficult not to feel embarrassment at the contrast in intellectual levels between the debate over closer European integration in the United Kingdom and in Germany. Here we often have sentimentalism on one side of the argument and barely concealed xenophobia on the other. In Germany, the agenda of debate on the real issues of democracy, parliamentary control and regional autonomy has been set by the terms of the Constitution and articulated in the judgment of the Constitutional Court in the Maastrict case. Then there are other important contemporary issues, such as the organisation of the legal profession and the cost of litigation, where the first part of this book provides remarkable facts and figures which will surprise English lawyers. Generally speaking, it gives me the impression that litigation in Germany is less expensive than in England, partly because more of the work is done by judges and less by the lawyers employed by the parties and partly because the lawyers are not so highly remunerated. By the iron law that talent follows money, the consequence is that litigators in Germany are on the whole not as experienced or intellectually gifted as their counterparts in England. But whether the English litigating public would prefer to pay less and take their chance with the results is another matter. On these and many other questions, this book has much to offer.

Leonard Hoffmann

FOREWORD TO THE FIRST EDITION

Many of my colleagues in Luxembourg had a remarkable knowledge of the structure of the English legal system and of the principles of the common law. It was remarkable not because it was complete but by contrast with what most English lawyers (and I include myself) knew of the structure of Continental legal systems and the laws they applied. The gap in our knowledge has been lessened by an increasing awareness of what happens in France—due partly to the more extensive teaching of comparative law, partly to an interest in the Conseil d'État as judicial review has developed in the United Kingdom, partly to a self-questioning as to whether accusatorial methods are necessarily better than inquisitorial methods of trial, partly due to newspaper coverage of French criminal trials, partly to books such as Professor Neville Brown's editions of *Amos and Walton* on French law.

It is by contrast no less remarkable that, although much has been written in English and in German about German law, that was largely for the specialist and the subject, as I see it, is far less widely known in the United Kingdom and, indeed, by common lawyers generally. Our membership of the European Economic Community and the influence which contemporary German law has had on other legal systems—Japan, Greece and Turkey, Austria and Switzerland, several countries of Central and South America—make it necessary or at least desirable that in the United Kingdom we should know more about it.

Nigel Foster's book has made a great contribution to reducing our ignorance. He was right to begin with an historical introduction—even though it had inevitably to be brief and made one wish to have more—and to show the way in which customary law and Roman law came together in Germany, how the Holy Roman Empire gave way to the German monarchy and to the Weimar Republic and then, following the Nazi period, to a reconstruction of both the legal system and the law after 1945.

The early difference in approach of the German courts—eyes firmly fixed on general principles and influenced far more than in the United Kingdom by the opinions of university professors, and also affected by the differences between the procedures and the laws of the regions of Germany—from the approach of English judges, has had an important influence on that development. At the same time the establishment of new rules of law by statute—in labour law, in environmental law, in business and economic law—find their parallels in this country. The post war change in the attitude of the German judges, the influence of the all important Bundesverfassungsgericht, and other factors have contributed to reducing the differences between the way our two systems operate. Yet the differences at still considerable; the existence of a Basic Law, a constitution, a 'Grundgesetz' has to be understood to appreciate at any rate some of these differences.

To try to say whether one system overall is better than another is a futile exercise since so much depends on the historical context. But it is of great value to consider the differences when changes are being considered here. The author thinks that the high degree of specialisation amongst German courts means that 'there should be a better quality of judicial application for the individual'. He may be right in theory but I wonder whether it follows. He also writes, 'The highly specialised and decentralised court system in Germany is considered to have made justice, certainly at the lower levels, much more accessible and a much quicker process'. That may be so at the lower levels; the length of time which had passed before many cases reached the European Court of Justice makes me also wonder if this is so overall. The conflict of jurisdictions, of competence, which does not exist here, but which seems to create difficulties in some countries, the author considers not to be a problem in Germany. The vast number of German judges, even excluding the many lay members involved in specialised courts is, however, striking when one compares this system. Are so many really necessary? Perhaps they are and the system benefits from it.

Different chapters of this book will have particular interest for different readers—criminal law, the Civil Code, the law of obligations, property law, family law, succession, company law, public law—and each chapter usefully recommends further specialised reading. But the analysis of the task of judges who are supposed in theory to apply law rather than to create it but who do in fact considerably influence the development of the law and who, if they do not have a doctrine of precedent, do clearly regard existing decisions, particularly those of higher courts, as having an authority which can amount to a practice if not a principle of 'precedent' is of general interest. So also sections on methods of interpretation, the training of judges and lawyers, legal aid and advice, the principles of judicial review and the elucidation of general principles of law should be of interest to all lawyers. Indeed many of the chapters in the first part of the book are highly relevant to our sense of disquiet as to what subsidiarity really means, whether 'federation' is necessarily an abhorrent concept since it means transferring more power to the centre, whether it makes sense to adopt the European Convention of Human Rights as part of domestic law. And a lot more.

I said that this is a necessary book; in my opinion it is also an excellent book with a wealth of detailed information which has required extensive and careful research. Even though particular legal issues will drive the practitioner to the primary sources of the law there is a valuable survey not only of the whole but of particular parts. It is no less, a very readable book.

Slynn of Hadley

PREFACE

As can be seen from the cover, this third edition of German Legal System and Laws is now a co-authored publication but as it is a continuation of the publication written originally solely by Nigel Foster, some of the comments made by him in the prefaces to the first two editions have been reproduced here.

This book provides a comprehensive introduction to the German legal system and a number of areas of the substantive law of Germany. Hopefully, it will serve both as an accessible reference source for the professions and others who wish to obtain fundamental information about the German legal system and German law and as a text for the many undergraduate and postgraduate students who study the German legal system or aspects of German law as a part of a university or college course. It may also be of interest to those on multidisciplinary European Legal Studies degrees and Politics, History, Economics, and Business Studies courses which have included the study of aspects of German law and legal system. The chapters on historical legal development, constitutional law, sources of law, legal professions, legal education, and the administration and implementation of justice would appear to be particularly relevant to those groups.

The initial impetus to write this book arose as a direct result of teaching a course on the German legal system at Cardiff and much of the initial research and work was originally done for this purpose. This book includes elements which might be found in an English legal system course such as historical legal development, the legislative process, the administration of justice, court structure, judiciary, legal professions, legal aid, legal education, sources of law, the function of the judiciary, precedent, and basic criminal and civil law procedure. In Part Two, the book provides digests of the principal areas of substantive and procedural German law as detailed in the Table of Contents. In covering a breadth of topics a degree of overlap is inevitable and it is hoped that this will not only be tolerated but appreciated as enhancing its usefulness as a source of reference. The book cannot, considering the constraints, provide an in-depth analysis of certain or indeed all aspects of German substantive law. Similarly, this book is not really intended for those whose proficiency in German allows them to read the original German source material. It is intended as an introduction to ease those, who wish to know more, into the subject and terminology of German law. It was considered appropriate to include the relevant German legal terminology and English translations in the appropriate places in the text. The most popular German terms and those widely understood will appear, after the first appearance, only in the original German, and will no longer translated into English: for example, *Grundgesetz*, *Bundestag*, and *Länder*. In other cases, translations will be repeated but for the majority of terms only the English will subsequently be given. The German terms will be included in a separate index. General and more specialized information on the subject matter of each chapter will be listed under "Further reading" at the end of each chapter.

German writers customarily use many more abbreviations than English language law texts, due largely to the inordinate length of some words and phrases, therefore a list of abbreviations is included. Those included are the German as there seems little sense in using a convoluted set of English initials instead of a convoluted set of German initials, thus, for example, the *Bundesverfassungsgericht* (Federal Constitutional Court) will be abbreviated as "BVerfG" and not FCC. Our apologies to those who find the constant need to refer to the abbreviations list at the start of the volume to look up "BVerfG"; they might, however, have also had to do so for FCC and others. We have made considerable changes to this third edition. Apart from thoroughly checking the validity of the material contained in the second edition and making numerous revisions to all of the chapters, we have taken the opportunity to both re-order some of the material and expand considerably the substantive law chapters.

In the first part of the book, Chapters 2 and 3 have been re-ordered. The material on state institutions has been moved into Chapter 6 and the chapter on sources of law has been expanded to include legal methodology. The rest of Part I has been updated and revised as necessary, notably in Chapter 5 to include the changes to civil procedural law. Part II has been considerably expanded and extensively revised. Chapter 6 on public law has been increased to such an extent that we have considered it helpful to split it into three chapters dealing in turn with constitutional law, basic rights and then other aspects of public law with the exception of criminal law, which is now to be found in expanded form in Chapter 9. The German civil code and the much heralded reform of the law of obligations can be found in an expanded Chapter 10.

The degree of change was intended both to reflect the increase in German law taught in the United Kingdom, or at least the trend to provide more specialist German law courses or those dealing with substantive law subjects rather than just a general introduction, and also to make the volume more useful as a teaching and reference aid. For teaching purposes we have visually accentuated summaries of cases and examples. Note that when using examples we adhere to the German textbook principle of labelling the persons involved with capital letters (*A, B, C*) instead of giving them proper names. The glossaries and abbreviations have also been updated and revised to reflect the changed material in the book and further additions have been made to the *Grundgesetz* extracts included, which were taken from translations published by the Press and Information Office of the Federal Government in Bonn, and we acknowledge with thanks the permission to reproduce these.

We would like to thank those who took the time and trouble to provide us with advice, corrections, and suggestions for the improvement of the first and second editions and are grateful to those who took the time to do so either by letter or formal reviews of the volumes. These are too numerous to mention individually.

For helpful advice and/or assistance in the process we would like to thank Herr Bijan Fateh-Moghadam (Ludwig-Maximilians-Universität München), Dr. Wolfgang Hau (Universität Trier), Dr. Ulrich Stelkens (Universität des Saarlandes,

Saarbrücken), Prof. Herbert Bethge (Universität Passau), Herr Wolfgang Meyer (Universität Trier), and Herr Nikolaus Assfalg (Universität Konstanz).

Whilst the updating and introduction of material was undertaken individually, we have also considered and commented on each other's work in progress. Chapters 2, 6, 7, 8 (in part), 9, and 10 were completed by Satish Sule and Nigel Foster attended to the Introduction, Chapters 1, 3, 4, 5, 8 (in part), and 11. We bear, however, joint responsibility for any errors or omissions in the material. Where spotted we would be extremely grateful to be informed or indeed to receive any form of comment or criticism of the book and its contents or omissions.

Nigel Foster & Satish Sule,
Cardiff, March 2002.

TABLE OF CASES

BAGE (Decisions of the Federal Labour Court)
BAGE 1, 185 ... 209
BAGE 1, 291 ... 540
BAGE 34, 230 ... 546
BAG DB 1987, 2106 ... 533
BAG NJW 1959, 356 ... 539
BAG NJW 1964, 883 ... 540
BAG NJW 1964, 1921 ... 231
BAG NJW 1967, 843 ... 540
BAG NJW 1968, 1903 ... 539
BAG NJW 1970, 487 ... 536
BAG NJW 1971, 1668 ... 541
BAG NJW 1977, 1079 ... 540
BAG NJW 1980, 1642 ... 541
Berlin Constitutional Court (BerlVerfGH) NJW 1993, 515 (*Honecker case*) ... 215
BGH (Decisions of the Federal Court of Justice)
BGH NJW 1951, 513 (*Fall der Massentötung von Geisteskranken*) ... 318
BGH NJW 1952, 514 (*Pfeffertüten-Fall*) ... 326
BGH NJW 1973, 255 (*Brusttaschenfall*) ... 308
BGH NJW 1978, 1206 (*Zahnarzt-Fall*) ... 311
BGH NJW 1980, 1759 ... 326
BGH NJW 1983, 1665 ... 41
BGH NJW 1984, 2279 ... 380–1
BGH NJW 1986, 188 ... 512
BGH NJW 1996, 984 ... 64
BGH NStZ 97, 83 ... 326
BGH NStZ 1987, 172 ... 308
BGH NStZ 1995, 80 (*Behandlungsabbruchsfall*) ... 312
BGH VersR 1979, 225 (*Dienstfahrt*) ... 249–50
BGHSt 1, 332 ... 302
BGHSt 2, 20 (*KZ-Fall*) ... 302–3
BGHSt 4, 24 ... 310
BGHSt 5, 290 ... 349
BGHSt 5, 332 ... 348
BGHSt 9, 184 (*Lilo-fall*) ... 329
BGHSt 11, 1 (*Lastwagen-Fall*) ... 321
BGHSt 11, 20 (*Kartoffelschäler-Fall*) ... 313
BGHSt 11, 268 (*Verfolgerfall*) ... 333
BGHSt 13, 197 ... 310
BGHSt 14, 358 ... 348
BGHSt 18, 87 (*Staschynski-Fall*) ... 330–1

BGHSt 21, 381 ... 315
BGHSt 25, 325 ... 348
BGHSt 26, 35 (*Gaststättenfall*) ... 324
BGHSt 26, 201 (*Tankstellenfall*) ... 326
BGHSt 26, 256 (*Boxer-Fall*) ... 309
BGHSt 32, 38 (*Sirius-Fall*) ... 332–3
BGHSt 32, 68 ... 349
BGHSt 32, 367 (*Fall Wittig*) ... 323–4
BGHSt 33, 295 (*Schläfenschuss-Fall*) ... 328
BGHSt 34, 53 (*Anfahr-Fall*) ... 307
BGHSt 34, 362 ... 348
BGHSt 35, 246 ... 311
BGHSt 35, 246 (*Sterilisationsfall*) ... 313
BGHSt 36, 1 (*AIDS-Fall*) ... 306
BGHSt 37, 106 (*Lederspray-Fall*) ... 324
BGHSt 37, 289 ... 331
BGHSt 38, 214 ... 348
BGHSt 39, 1 ... 238
BGHSt 39, 133 ... 316
BGHSt 39, 349 ... 348
BGHSt 40, 218 (*Fall des Nationalen Verteidigungsrats*) ... 334–5
BGHSt 42, 235 (*Grenzenübergangsfall*) ... 315–16
BGHSt 45, 321 ... 343
BGHSt 56, 37 ... 348
BGHZ 2, 90 ... 409
BGHZ 6, 270 ... 61
BGHZ 21, 319 (*Hamburger Parkplatz Fall*) ... 385–6
BGHZ 21, 378 ... 505
BGHZ 23, 157 ... 233
BGHZ 26, 349 (*Herrenreiterfall*) ... 434
BGHZ 40, 272 ... 430
BGHZ 51, 91 (*Hühnerpestfall*) ... 435
BGHZ 73, 20 (*Stern case*) ... 434
BGHZ 80, 129, NJW 1981, 1373 ... 500
BGHZ 91, 324 ... 380–1
BGHZ 92, 143 ... 291
BGHZ 95, 330 (*Autokran*) ... 514
BGHZ 105, 140 ... 60
BVerfG NJW 1979, 2607 ... 135
BVerfG NJW 1988, 191 ... 96
BVerfG NJW 1988, 1456 ... 47
BVerfG NJW 1988, 1459 ... 47

BVerfG NJW 1988, 2173 ... 47

BVerfG NJW 1990, 974 ... 47

BVerfG NJW 1991, 2549 ... 541

BVerfG NJW 1992, 1613 ... 97

BVerfG NJW 1994, 36 ... 392–3

BVerfG NJW 1994, 1614 ... 97

BVerfG NJW 2001, 591 ... 517

BVerfGE (Decisions of the Federal Constitutional Court)

BVerfGE 1, 14 ... 175

BVerfGE 1, 97 ... 243

BVerfGE 1 BvQ 23/01 ... 238

BVerfGE 2, 1 (*SRP-Urteil*) ... 199

BVerfGE 2, 266 ... 230

BVerfGE 2 Bvl 1/97 (*Bananenmarktverordnung* case) ... 55

BVerfGE 3, 407 ... 177

BVerfGE 4, 7 ... 279

BVerfGE 5, 85 (*KPD*) ... 200

BVerfGE 6, 32 (*Elfes case*) ... 216, 218, 230

BVerfGE 6, 55 ... 227

BVerfGE 6, 70 ... 222

BVerfGE 6, 84 ... 158

BVerfGE 6, 124 ... 115

BVerfGE 7, 198 (*Lüth case*) ... 210, 224

BVerfGE 7, 377 (*Apothekenurteil*) ... 232, 279

BVerfGE 8, 89 ... 343

BVerfGE 9, 259 ... 343

BVerfGE 10, 136 ... 234

BVerfGE 12, 45 ... 224

BVerfGE 12, 205 (*1. Fernsehurteil*) ... 177, 178, 240

BVerfGE 13, 54 ... 175

BVerfGE 14, 121 (FDP) ... 158, 160, 161

BVerfGE 18, 14 ... 158

BVerfGE 20, 156 (*Parteienfinanzierung I*) ... 161, 162

BVerfGE 20, 175 ... 225

BVerfGE 25, 256 (*Blinkfuer case*) ... 225

BVerfGE 25, 269 (*NS-Verbrechen*) ... 168

BVerfGE 27, 195 ... 228

BVerfGE 28, 104 ... 228

BVerfGE 29, 166 ... 228

BVerfGE 30, 1 ... 229

BVerfGE 30, 173 (*Mephisto*) ... 151, 207, 213, 214, 227

BVerfGE 31, 173f ... 45

BVerfGE 32, 54 ... 233

BVerfGE 32, 98 ... 222

BVerfGE 33, 303 (*Numerus Clausus case*) ... 81, 232

BVerfGE 34, 269 (*Soraya case*) ... 40, 42, 63, 217

BVerfGE 35, 202 (*Lebach case*) ... 172, 213, 226–7

BVerfGE 36, 1 (*Grundlagevertrag*) ... 146

BVerfGE 36, 323 ... 252

BVerfGE 37, 271 (*Solange I*) ... 44, 45, 153

BVerfGE 39, 1 (*Schwangerschaftsabbruch I*) ... 218–19

BVerfGE 39, 276 ... 81

BVerfGE 39, 302 ... 273

BVerfGE 39, 334 (*Extremisten*) ... 201

BVerfGE 40, 121 ... 228

BVerfGE 43, 213 ... 273

BVerfGE 43, 391 ... 81

BVerfGE 44, 308 ... 183

BVerfGE 45, 187 ... 215

BVerfGE 46, 160 (*Schleyer case*) ... 206–7, 218

BVerfGE 48, 127 ... 224

BVerfGE 49, 89 (*Kalkar*) ... 166, 167

BVerfGE 50, 234 ... 225

BVerfGE 50, 290 279, ... 545

BVerfGE 52, 131 ... 222

BVerfGE 52, 369 (*Hausarbeitstag*) ... 221

BVerfGE 53, 257 ... 233

BVerfGE 55, 159 (*Falknerjagdschein*) ... 171

BVerfGE 56, 31 ... 232

BVerfGE 57, 134 ... 39

BVerfGE 58, 1 (*Eurocontrol I*) ... 47

BVerfGE 58, 35f ... 44

BVerfGE 58, 300 ... 233, 234, 289

BVerfGE 59, 231 ... 225, 231

BVerfGE 61, 15 ... 252

BVerfGE 62, 1 ... 188

BVerfGE 64, 87 ... 273

BVerfGE 65, 1 (*Volkszählung*) ... 172, 217, 218, 242

BVerfGE 69, 1 ... 224

BVerfGE 69, 315 (*Brokdorf case*) ... 229

BVerfGE 72, 300 ... 252

BVerfGE 72, 330 (*Finanzausgleich II*) ... 179

BVerfGE 73, 118 ... 225

BVerfGE 73, 339 (*Solange II*) ... 46, 55, 153

BVerfGE 73, 374 ... 45

BVerfGE 74, 51 ... 45

BVerfGE 75, 40 ... 228

BVerfGE 75, 244 ... 45

BVerfGE 76, 83 ... 233

BVerfGE 76, 171 ... 96

BVerfGE 77, 84 ... 233

BVerfGE 80, 74, NJW 1990, 974 ... 48

BVerfGE 80, 137 (*Reiten im Walde*) ... 206, 216

BVerfGE 80, 188 (*Wueppesahl case*) ... 185, 240

BVerfGE 81, 347 ... 115

BVerfGE 82, 126 (*Kündigungsfristen von Arbeitern und Angestellten*) ... 220–1, 536

BVerfGE 82, 159 ... 237

BVerfGE 82, 322 (*Gesamtdeutsche Wahlen*) ... 158, 159

BVerfGE 83, 37 (*Ausländerwahlrecht Schleswig-Holstein*) ... 155

BVerfGE 83, 238 ... 225

BVerfGE 84, 34 ... 257

BVerfGE 85, 191 ... 221

BVerfGE 85, 264 (*Parteienfinanzierung III*) ... 162

BVerfGE 88, 203 (*Schwangerschaftsabbruch II*) ... 218–19

BVerfGE 89, 155 (*Maastricht judgment*) ... 36, 42, 46, 51–4, 153, 156, 243

BVerfGE 90, 27 (*Parabolantennen*) ... 210–11, 225

BVerfGE 90, 241 ... 224

BVerfGE 90, 286 (*Auslandeinsätze der Bundeswehr*) ... 157, 240

BVerfGE 92, 203 ... 179

BVerfGE 92, 277 (*DDR-Spione*) ... 168

BVerfGE 93, 1 (*Kruzifix*) ... 212, 223

BVerfGE 94, 49 ... 235

BVerfGE 94, 82 ... 224

BVerfGE 94, 307 (*Weinprämierung*) ... 257–8

BVerfGE 95, 15 ... 255

BVerfGE 95, 96 (*Mauerschützen*) ... 238

BVerfGE 95, 335 ... 182

BVerfGE 96, 27 ... 236

BVerfGE 99, 216 ... 228

BVerfGE 100, 313 ... 230

BVerfGE JZ 2001 ... 93

BVerfGE NStZ 1997, 94 ... 343

BVerfGE ZUM 2001, 220 ... 345

BVerwG NJW 1995, 2648 ... 181

BVerwGE (Decisions of the Federal Administrative Court)

BVerwGE 1, 159 (*Fürsorgepflicht*) ... 173, 258

BVerwGE 8, 272 ... 257

BVerwGE 11, 95 ... 258

BVerwGE 14, 323 ... 259

BVerwGE 21, 127 ... 257

BVerwGE 26, 135 ... 256

BVerwGE 28, 145 ... 261

BVerwGE 52, 122 ... 258

BVerwGE 60, 144 ... 261

BVerwGE 64, 274 (*Peep-Show case*) ... 215

BVerwGE 91, 211 ... 257

BVerwGE 92, 81 ... 264

BVerwGE 97, 203 ... 257

BVerwGE 99, 74 ... 257

Emden AG NJW 1975, S.1363 (*Hoteldoppelzimmer*) ... 62

Hamm OLG WoM 1981, 257 ... 135

Koblenz OLG NJW 1978, 54 ... 469

München LG NJW 2000, 1051 (*Compuserve*) ... 324

RGSt (Decisions of the Supreme Court of the German Reich in Criminal Cases)

RGSt 1, 373 ... 302

RGSt 2, 160 ... 330

RGSt 29, 111 ... 61

RGSt 30, 25 (*Leinenfänger-Fall*) ... 321

RGSt 79, 49 ... 322

RGZ (Decisions of the Imperial Court)

RGZ 54, 98 (*Gravel case*) 39, ... 417

RGZ 66, 289 (*Poisonous horse fodder case*) ... 418

RGZ 78, 239 (*Linoleumrollefall*) ... 419

RGZ 99, 147 (*Haakjöringsköd-Fall*) 387, ... 395

RGZ 100, 130 ... 29

RGZ 105, 101 ... 497

RGZ 107, 78 29, 64, ... 389

RGZ 108, 380 ... 29

RGZ 131, 274 ... 389

RGZ 161, 330 (*Venusberg case*) ... 389

RGZ 167, 40 ... 513

European Court cases

Amministrazione delle Finanze dello stato v Simmenthal [1978] ECR 629, [1978] 3 CMLR 263 ... 42

Commission v Germany ECJ [1991] I–2567 ... 252–3

Costa v ENEL [1964] ECR 1251 ... 42

Fratelli Costanzo SpA v Commune di Milano [1989] ECR 1839 ... 250

Hellmut Marschall v Land Nordrhein-Westfalen [1997] 1 CMLR 547 ... 26

Hoechst AG v Commission ... 233

Internationale Handelsgesellschaft case [1974] 2 CMLR 540 ... 45

Kalanke v Freie Hansestadt Bremen [1995] ECR–I 3052 ... 221

Kloppenburg case [1988] 3 CMLR 1 ... 47

Re Lawyers Services: EC Commission v Germany (Case 427/85 [1989] 2 CMLR 677) ... 93

Re Patented Foodstuffs case [1989] 2 CMLR 902 ... 47

Rheinland-Pfalz v Alcan ECJ [1997] I-1591 ... 263

Tanya Kreil v Bundesrepublik Deutschland NJW 2000, 497f ... 221

VAT Exemption case [1989] 1 CMLR 113 ... 47

Wünsche Handelsgesellschaft case [1987] 3 CMLR 225 ... 46, 153

European Court of Human Rights

Eckle v Germany 125, ... 344

Klaas v Germany ... 230
König v Germany ... 125, 344

Niemitz v Germany ... 233

Vogt v Germany ... 202

TABLE OF LEGISLATION

Accession Act (1986) ... 49

Accession Act to the Treaty on European Union (1992) ... 51, 53

Accession Act to the Treaty of Rome (1957), art.2 ... 49

Administrative Courts Act (VwGO) ... 72, 251
  para.5 ... 73
  para.5 III ... 107
  para.9 ... 73, 107
  para.10 ... 73
  para.11 ... 73
  para.35 ... 73
  para.36 ... 73, 100
  para.37 ... 73
  para.40 ... 72, 249, 267
  para.40 I ... 265
  para.40 II ... 271
  para.41 ... 127
  para.42 ... 266
  para.42 I ... 266
  para.42 I 1 ... 268
  para.42 I 2 ... 269, 270
  para.42 II ... 268
  para.43 ... 270
  para.45 ... 73, 267
  para.46 ... 73
  para.47 ... 73, 270
  para.47 II ... 271
  para.47 VI ... 41
  para.48 ... 73
  para.50 ... 73, 267
  para.52 ... 267
  para.53 III ... 267
  para.57 ... 266
  para.58 ... 266
  para.61 ... 267
  para.67 ... 111
  para.68 ... 73, 268
  para.74 I ... 269
  para.80a 73
  para.81 ... 269
  para.113 ... 269

Administrative Enforcement Act (VwVG) ... 265

Administrative Offences Act ... 295

Administrative Procedure Law (VwVfG) ... 249, 251
  para.1 ... 259
  para.10 ... 261
  para.11 ... 261
  para.13 ... 261
  para.24 ... 261
  para.25 ... 261

Administrative Procedure Law – continued
  para.26 ... 261
  para.28 ... 261
  para.29 ... 261
  para.30 ... 261
  para.31 ... 262
  para.32 ... 262
  para.35 ... 259
  para.35 I ... 260, 266
  para.37 ... 261
  para.39 ... 261
  para.42 I ... 266
  para.43 ... 262
  para.44 I ... 262
  para.44 II ... 262
  para.45 ... 262
  para.48 ... 253, 262
  para.48 I ... 263
  para.48 II ... 263
  para.49 ... 262
  para.49 I ... 263
  para.49 II ... 263
  para.49 III ... 263
  para.49 III 1 ... 263
  para.49 VI ... 263
  para.54 ... 264
  para.61 ... 264
  para.62 ... 264
  para.68 ... 265
  para.73 ... 265

Agricultural Disputes Procedural Act (LwVG), para.2 II ... 107

Air Traffic Act ... 437

Applications Statute (1993) ... 50

Assemblies Law (VersG) ... 228
  para.15 II ... 255, 256

Bavarian Penal Code 1813 ... 296

Bills of Exchange Act 1848 ... 24

Brussels Convention ... 127

Building Code (BauGB) ... 291
  para.8 ... 264
  para.9 ... 291

Care and Control Act ... 471

Carolingian Penal Code 1532 ... 296, 338

Chemical Substances Act (ChemG) ... 291

Child Allowance Act ... 276

Child Law Reform Act ... 464, 470, 475

Child Support Act ... 464

Civil Code (BGB) ... 13, 23, 26–7, 29, 31, 143,
   310, 364–481, 488, 526
 para.1 ... 127, 366, 375
 para.2 ... 466
 para.13 ... 429
 para.14 ... 429
 para.21 ... 127, 160, 376, 493
 para.22 ... 376
 para.55 ... 493
 para.77 ... 391
 para.79 ... 376
 para.80 ... 376
 para.88 ... 376
 para.90 ... 441, 446
 para.90a ... 441
 para.93 ... 441, 447, 453
 para.94 ... 447
 para.95 ... 441
 para.104 ... 376, 377, 402, 466
 para.105 ... 398
 para.106 ... 377
 para.107 ... 377, 378
 para.108 ... 378
 para.108 II ... 378
 para.109 ... 377, 378
 para.109 I ... 378
 para.110 ... 378
 para.112 ... 379
 para.113 ... 377, 379
 para.115 ... 376
 para.116 ... 379, 393, 394
 para.116 I ... 393
 para.117 I ... 393, 398
 para.117 II ... 394
 para.118 ... 393, 394
 para.119 ... 393, 394, 396, 397, 398, 420
 para.119 I ... 395, 396, 401, 431
 para.119 II ... 396
 para.120 ... 393, 394, 396, 397, 398,
   399
 para.121 ... 397
 para.121 I ... 397
 para.121 II ... 397
 para.122 ... 394, 422
 para.122 II ... 398
 para.123 ... 393, 394, 397
 para.123 I ... 397
 para.124 ... 397
 para.124 III ... 397
 para.125 ... 390, 391, 398
 para.126 ... 370, 391
 para.127 ... 391
 para.128 ... 391
 para.129 ... 370, 391
 para.130 ... 382, 384
 para.130 I ... 382, 383, 384, 427
 para.133 ... 387, 388, 395
 para.134 ... 391, 398, 424

Civil Code – *continued*
 para.138 ... 29, 216, 391, 392, 398, 408, 424,
   463, 491
 para.138 I ... 62, 63, 391, 392
 para.138 II ... 283, 392, 393
 para.139 ... 398, 409
 para.140 ... 398
 para.141 ... 398
 para.142 ... 397, 431
 para.142 I ... 374, 394
 para.142 II ... 394
 para.143 ... 397
 para.144 ... 379
 para.145 ... 384
 para.146 ... 384
 para.147 I ... 383, 384
 para.147 II ... 384
 para.150 I ... 384
 para.150 II ... 384, 387
 para.151 ... 38, 385
 para.154 ... 386
 para.154 I ... 386
 para.155 ... 386
 para.156 ... 385
 para.157 ... 29, 38, 387, 388, 420, 424
 para.161 ... 493
 para.161 I ... 463
 para.164 ... 398, 494
 para.164 I ... 399
 para.164 I 1 ... 401
 para.164 II ... 401
 para.164 III ... 399
 para.165 ... 399
 para.166 I ... 401
 para.166 II ... 401
 para.167 I ... 399, 400
 para.167 II ... 400
 para.168 ... 400
 para.170 ... 400
 para.173 ... 400
 para.177 I ... 401
 para.178 ... 401
 para.179 ... 401
 para.179 II ... 401
 para.179 III 2 ... 401
 para.181 ... 398, 402
 para.182 ... 378
 para.183 ... 378
 para.184 ... 378
 para.185 II ... 463
 para.194 ... 402
 para.194 I ... 367, 402
 para.195 ... 402, 439
 para.197 ... 402
 para.197 I ... 428
 para.199 I ... 439
 para.199 II ... 439
 para.199 III ... 439

Civil Code – *continued*
  para.214 ... 402
  para.218 ... 402
  para.228 ... 310
  para.240 ... 366
  para.241 ... 366, 405, 418, 420
  para.241 I ... 405, 406
  para.241 II ... 417, 419
  para.242 ... 29, 216, 370, 387, 388–90, 392,
    395, 406, 408, 420, 424, 425
  para.242 II ... 406
  para.243 ... 406
  para.243 I ... 407
  para.243 II ... 407, 408, 413
  para.249 ... 422, 438
  para.252 ... 422
  para.253 ... 63, 64, 422
  para.254 ... 422, 423, 439
  para.267 ... 407
  para.269 ... 407, 408
  para.269 III ... 407
  para.270 ... 407, 408
  para.271 ... 407
  para.273 ... 408
  para.275 ... 413, 414
  para.275 I ... 413, 414, 415
  para.275 II ... 413, 414
  para.275 III ... 414
  para.275 IV ... 414
  para.276 ... 413, 434, 435, 489
  para.276 I ... 423
  para.276 II ... 423
  para.278 ... 419, 423
  para.279 ... 423
  para.280 ... 412, 413, 414, 415, 416, 418, 421,
    422, 427, 428
  para.280 I ... 414, 415, 416, 418, 420, 426, 427,
    428
  para.280 I 1 ... 412
  para.280 I 2 ... 412
  para.280 II ... 412, 426, 427
  para.280 III ... 414, 416, 418
  para.281 ... 413, 416, 418, 422, 427, 428
  para.281 I ... 418
  para.281 II ... 416, 419
  para.281 IV ... 416
  para.282 ... 413, 420
  para.283 ... 413, 414, 415, 422, 427
  para.284 ... 414
  para.285 ... 414, 415
  para.286 ... 416, 426, 427
  para.286 I ... 416, 428
  para.286 II ... 416
  para.286 III ... 416
  para.288 I ... 416
  para.293 ... 417
  para.294 ... 417
  para.295 ... 417

Civil Code – *continued*
  para.297 ... 417
  para.298 ... 417
  para.299 ... 417
  para.305 ... 283, 408, 409, 410, 424
  para.305 I ... 409
  para.305 I 3 ... 409
  para.305 II ... 409, 410
  para.305 III ... 410
  para.305b ... 409
  para.305c I ... 409
  para.306 ... 409
  para.307 ... 409
  para.308 ... 410
  para.309 ... 410, 427
  para.310 ... 283, 408, 409, 410, 424
  para.310 I ... 410
  para.310 IV ... 410
  para.311 ... 98
  para.311 I ... 405
  para.311 II ... 420
  para.311a ... 413, 414, 427
  para.311b I ... 370, 390, 394, 398, 448
  para.312 ... 98, 410
  para.312d ... 410
  para.313 ... 98, 390, 391, 420, 421
  para.313 III ... 421
  para.314 ... 419
  para.317 I ... 378
  para.320 ... 408
  para.323 ... 419, 421, 427, 428
  para.323 I ... 421
  para.323 I 1 ... 416
  para.325 ... 415
  para.326 ... 414, 421
  para.326 II ... 415
  para.326 IV ... 415
  para.328 I ... 410
  para.331 I ... 410
  para.343 VI ... 421
  para.346 ... 412, 415, 421, 427, 428
  para.347 ... 421
  para.349 ... 421, 427, 428
  para.362 ... 411
  para.364 ... 411
  para.368 ... 411
  para.372 ... 411, 412
  para.387 ... 411
  para.388 ... 412
  para.398 ... 411, 412, 461, 463
  para.399 ... 412
  para.414 ... 411
  para.432 ... 366
  para.433 ... 366, 371, 405, 424, 425
  para.433 I ... 405, 406, 425
  para.433 I 1 ... 368, 373
  para.433 II ... 373, 406, 425, 428
  para.434 ... 418, 426, 427, 428

Civil Code – *continued*
para.434 I ... 426, 427
para.434 II ... 427
para.434 III ... 427
para.435 ... 426
para.437 ... 427, 428
para.438 ... 402
para.438 I 3 ... 428, 429
para.439 ... 427
para.440 ... 427, 428
para.441 ... 427
para.442 ... 427
para.444 ... 427
para.445 ... 427
para.446 ... 408, 425
para.447 ... 415, 425, 426
para.448 ... 425
para.448 I ... 407
para.449 ... 426
para.453 ... 425
para.455 ... 458, 462
para.459 ... 387, 418
para.460 ... 490
para.463 ... 60, 397, 418
para.465 ... 427
para.467 ... 387
para.474 ... 429
para.474 I ... 415
para.474 II ... 426
para.474 III ... 429
para.475 I ... 427
para.475 I 1 ... 429
para.475 II ... 429
para.475 III ... 427
para.476 ... 429
para.478 ... 429
para.479 ... 424, 429
para.480 ... 428
para.491 ... 283, 410
para.504 ... 283, 410
para.516 ... 405
para.518 ... 370
para.518 II ... 398
para.535 ... 405
para.550 ... 370
para.564 ... 284
para.598 ... 405
para.604 ... 368
para.606 ... 405
para.611 ... 526, 531, 533, 535
para.611a ... 531, 533
para.612 ... 533
para.613 ... 533
para.613a 503, 534, 537
para.613a IV ... 537
para.614 ... 533
para.615 ... 534
para.616 ... 534

Civil Code – *continued*
para.618 ... 534
para.622 ... 220, 527, 530, 535, 536
para.622 V ... 535
para.623 ... 535
para.626 I ... 536
para.626 II ... 536
para.628 ... 535
para.630 ... 526, 531
para.631 I ... 373
para.634a 402
para.651a 284
para.652 ... 488
para.705 ... 95, 404, 493
para.706 ... 493
para.707 ... 493
para.708 ... 493
para.709 ... 493
para.709 I ... 494
para.709 II ... 494
para.710 ... 494
para.711 ... 493
para.713 ... 494
para.716 ... 494
para.717 ... 494
para.718 ... 494
para.719 ... 494
para.719 I ... 446
para.721 ... 494
para.722 ... 494
para.723 ... 494
para.728 ... 494
para.730 ... 494
para.735 ... 494
para.736 ... 494
para.737 ... 494
para.741 ... 446
para.765 ... 458
para.766 ... 370, 391, 398
para.812 ... 394, 405, 424, 429, 443
para.812 I ... 374, 429, 430, 431
para.816 ... 452
para.816 I ... 431
para.816 II ... 431
para.817 I ... 431
para.817 II ... 431
para.818 II ... 431
para.819 ... 431
para.819 II ... 431
para.823 ... 284, 291, 397, 405, 419,
    422, 424, 433, 434, 441, 457, 541
para.823 I ... 375, 433, 434, 435, 445,
    457
para.823 II ... 433, 435
para.824 ... 433, 436
para.826 ... 210, 370, 433, 435
para.827 ... 376, 436
para.828 ... 436

Civil Code – *continued*
  para.828 I ... 436
  para.828 II ... 436
  para.829 ... 376
  para.830 I ... 438
  para.830 I 2 ... 438
  para.831 ... 419, 436
  para.831 I ... 436
  para.831 I 2 ... 436
  para.833 ... 436
  para.833 I ... 437
  para.833 II ... 437
  para.834 ... 437
  para.836 ... 438
  para.836 I 2 ... 438
  para.838 ... 438
  para.839 ... 271, 277, 438
  para.842 ... 438
  para.843 ... 438
  para.847 ... 422, 438
  para.848 ... 438, 457
  para.851 ... 438
  para.853 ... 366, 424
  para.854 ... 367, 440, 443
  para.854 I ... 371, 443, 444
  para.854 II ... 444
  para.855 ... 444, 453
  para.856 I ... 445
  para.858 ... 444, 445, 456
  para.858 I ... 445
  para.858 II ... 445
  para.859 ... 443
  para.859 I ... 445
  para.859 II ... 445
  para.859 III ... 445
  para.861 ... 445
  para.862 ... 291, 445
  para.862 I ... 445
  para.864 ... 444
  para.866 ... 443
  para.868 ... 443, 444, 451, 461
  para.869 ... 443
  para.870 ... 444, 456
  para.872 ... 443
  para.873 ... 447, 448, 450, 459
  para.875 ... 447
  para.878 ... 450
  para.879 ... 450
  para.883 ... 450
  para.883 II ... 450
  para.888 I ... 450
  para.891 I ... 450
  para.891 II ... 450
  para.892 ... 450, 452
  para.894 ... 450, 452
  para.899 ... 452
  para.900 ... 453
  para.903 ... 233, 371, 440, 445, 446, 447, 448

Civil Code – *continued*
  para.904 ... 310
  para.905 ... 448
  para.906 ... 291, 447, 448
  para.907 ... 448
  para.908 ... 448
  para.923 ... 448
  para.925 ... 448
  para.925 II ... 448
  para.928 ... 447
  para.929 ... 371, 382, 431, 443, 447, 451, 461, 462
  para.929 I ... 373
  para.930 ... 451, 461
  para.931 ... 451
  para.932 ... 394, 401, 431, 452
  para.932 II ... 452, 456
  para.933 ... 452
  para.934 ... 452
  para.935 ... 444, 452, 453
  para.935 I ... 372, 452
  para.936 ... 452
  para.937 ... 453
  para.937 II ... 453
  para.946 ... 453, 454
  para.947 ... 454
  para.947 I ... 454
  para.947 II ... 454
  para.948 ... 454
  para.950 ... 454, 462, 463
  para.951 ... 457
  para.951 I 1 ... 454
  para.953 ... 455
  para.954 ... 455
  para.958 I ... 453
  para.958 II ... 453
  para.959 ... 447, 453
  para.965 ... 454
  para.973 ... 454
  para.985 ... 443, 455, 456, 458
  para.986 ... 455, 456
  para.987 ... 456, 457
  para.987 I ... 456
  para.987 II ... 456
  para.989 ... 456
  para.990 I ... 456
  para.992 ... 456, 457
  para.993 I ... 456, 457
  para.994 ... 456, 457
  para.994 I ... 457
  para.994 II ... 457
  para.1001 I ... 457
  para.1002 ... 457
  para.1004 ... 291, 455, 457, 458
  para.1004 II ... 457
  para.1008 ... 446, 454
  para.1018 ... 458
  para.1030 ... 458

Civil Code – *continued*
para.1036 ... 458
para.1060 ... 458
para.1085 ... 458
para.1094 ... 458
para.1104 ... 458
para.1113 ... 442, 459
para.1116 ... 460
para.1116 I ... 459
para.1116 II ... 459
para.1116 II 1 ... 460
para.1117 ... 460
para.1120 ... 459
para.1136 ... 459
para.1147 ... 459, 460
para.1153 I ... 460
para.1154 II ... 460
para.1160 ... 460
para.1161 ... 460
para.1181 ... 459
para.1190 ... 442, 459
para.1191 ... 459, 460
para.1192 ... 460
para.1199 ... 459
para.1199 I ... 460
para.1201 ... 460
para.1204 ... 461
para.1205 ... 461
para.1228 ... 461
para.1258 ... 461
para.1273 ... 461
para.1278 ... 461
para.1280 ... 461
para.1296 ... 367, 440
para.1297 ... 367, 464, 465
para.1297 I ... 465
para.1298 ... 465
para.1301 ... 465
para.1301 I ... 466
para.1303 ... 466, 467
para.1303 I ... 466
para.1303 II ... 466
para.1304 ... 466, 467
para.1306 ... 466, 467
para.1308 ... 466
para.1309 ... 466
para.1310 ... 466
para.1311 ... 398, 466, 467
para.1312 ... 466
para.1312 I ... 466
para.1313 ... 467
para.1314 ... 467
para.1314 I ... 467
para.1314 II ... 467
para.1318 I ... 467
para.1353 ... 467
para.1353 I 1 ... 467
para.1356 I ... 467

Civil Code – *continued*
para.1356 II ... 467
para.1357 ... 467
para.1360 ... 467
para.1360b ... 467
para.1361 ... 467
para.1363 ... 467, 468
para.1365 ... 468
para.1366 ... 468
para.1369 ... 468
para.1371 ... 468, 475
para.1372 ... 468
para.1378 ... 468
para.1408 ... 467
para.1410 ... 467
para.1414 ... 468
para.1416 ... 468
para.1417 ... 468
para.1418 ... 468
para.1419 I ... 446
para.1478 ... 468
para.1558 ... 467
para.1564 ... 468
para.1565 ... 468
para.1565 II ... 469
para.1566 ... 469
para.1566 I ... 469
para.1566 II ... 469
para.1567 I ... 469
para.1568 ... 468, 469
para.1569 ... 469
para.1570 ... 368
para.1572 ... 469
para.1573 ... 469
para.1579 ... 470
para.1587 ... 469, 470
para.1588 ... 367, 465
para.1589 ... 367, 465, 470
para.1601 ... 471
para.1602 I ... 471
para.1615l ... 470, 471
para.1615o ... 470, 471
para.1616 ... 470
para.1626 ... 377, 398, 399, 402, 471
para.1627 ... 471
para.1628 ... 471
para.1629 ... 377, 398, 399, 402
para.1629 I 1 ... 471
para.1666 ... 471
para.1667 ... 471
para.1671 ... 471
para.1698b ... 470
para.1705 ... 470
para.1711 ... 470
para.1741 ... 471
para.1752 I ... 471
para.1754 ... 471
para.1755 ... 471

Civil Code – *continued*
para.1767 II ... 471
para.1770 ... 471
para.1772 ... 367, 465, 471
para.1773 ... 367, 465, 471
para.1774 ... 471
para.1895 ... 471
para.1909 ... 472
para.1909 I ... 472
para.1921 ... 367, 464, 465, 471, 472
para.1922 ... 367, 455, 472, 473, 475
para.1922 I ... 376, 473
para.1923 I ... 473, 475
para.1923 II ... 375, 473
para.1924 ... 474
para.1931 ... 475
para.1931 III ... 475
para.1933 ... 475
para.1934d 476
para.1936 ... 474, 475
para.1941 ... 476
para.1942 ... 474
para.1942 I ... 474
para.1943 ... 474
para.1943 II ... 474
para.1944 I ... 474
para.1945 I ... 474
para.1945 III ... 400
para.1950 ... 474
para.1953 ... 474
para.1954 ... 474
para.1954 I ... 474
para.1957 ... 474
para.1966 ... 473
para.1967 ... 474
para.1967 I ... 474
para.2031 ... 474
para.2032 ... 473
para.2064 ... 398, 476
para.2077 ... 477
para.2086 ... 476
para.2229 ... 476
para.2229 II ... 476
para.2229 III ... 476
para.2229 IV ... 476
para.2231 ... 98
para.2232 ... 476
para.2233 I ... 476
para.2247 ... 370, 382, 391, 476
para.2249 ... 476
para.2251 ... 476
para.2253 I ... 476
para.2254 ... 476
para.2255 ... 476
para.2256 ... 476
para.2258 ... 476
para.2264 ... 476
para.2265 ... 477

Civil Code – *continued*
para.2273 ... 477
para.2274 ... 366, 398, 477
para.2290 ... 477
para.2302 ... 473, 477
para.2303 ... 477
para.2325 ... 477
para.2326 ... 477
para.2333 ... 477
para.2338 ... 477
para.2353 ... 478
para.2385 ... 367, 472
Civil Code (East Germany; ZGB)
... 365–6
Civil Procedure Code (ZPO) ... 25, 41, 93, 113,
122–3
para.1 ... 112
para.2 ... 127
para.9 ... 127
para.12 ... 127, 480
para.13 ... 127
para.15 ... 128
para.17 ... 127
para.20 ... 127
para.23 ... 127, 128
para.29 ... 128
para.29b ... 128
para.32 ... 127
para.37 ... 128
para.38 ... 128
para.39 ... 128
para.40 ... 128
para.41 ... 126
para.49 ... 126
para.50 ... 127
para.51 ... 127
para.52 ... 127
para.55 ... 127
para.71 ... 127
para.72 ... 93, 127
para.78 ... 93, 128
para.78 I ... 110
para.78 II ... 110
para.79 ... 128
para.80 ... 110
para.85 ... 124
para.90 ... 110, 128
para.91 ... 111
para.91 II ... 112
para.92 ... 112
para.114 ... 113, 114, 115
para.115 ... 115
para.116 II ... 115
para.117 ... 116
para.119 ... 127
para.123 ... 116
para.127 ... 113, 116
para.128 ... 124

Civil Procedure Code – *continued*
para.128 I ... 125
para.133 ... 127
para.136 ... 124
para.137 ... 125
para.138 ... 124, 132
para.138 I ... 124
para.139 ... 124, 126, 130
para.140 ... 93
para.141 ... 124, 130
para.142 ... 130
para.143 ... 130
para.144 ... 124
para.157 ... 103, 111
para.253 ... 129
para.253 V ... 129
para.261 ... 129
para.271 ... 128
para.272 ... 125, 128, 129, 130
para.273 ... 125, 130
para.273 II ... 130
para.274 ... 130
para.275 ... 129
para.275 IV ... 130
para.276 ... 127, 129, 130
para.276 III ... 130
para.277 ... 130
para.278 ... 128, 130, 131
para.279 ... 128, 130
para.282 ... 124
para.282 II ... 130
para.286 ... 125, 132
para.288 ... 124
para.290 ... 132
para.294 ... 132
para.296 ... 125
para.300 ... 133
para.307 ... 129
para.308 ... 124
para.309 ... 125
para.310 ... 129
para.319 ... 133
para.330 ... 130
para.331 ... 129, 130
para.348 ... 70
para.349 ... 129
para.355 I ... 125
para.361 ... 125
para.371 ... 132
para.373 ... 132
para.375 ... 125
para.391 ... 132
para.392 ... 132
para.393 ... 132
para.397 ... 132
para.398 ... 132
para.402 ... 132
para.415 ... 132

Civil Procedure Code – *continued*
para.445 ... 132
para.511 ... 134
para.511a 70
para.513 ... 134
para.520 ... 134
para.524 ... 71
para.527 ... 125
para.536 ... 124
para.538 ... 134
para.539 ... 134
para.540 ... 134
para.541 ... 134
para.542 ... 134
para.543 II 1 ... 134
para.559 ... 124
para.566 ... 134
para.567 ... 134
para.577 ... 134
para.592 ... 133
para.605a ... 133
para.606 ... 465
para.606a I ... 480
para.617 ... 124
para.640a II ... 480
para.644 ... 465
para.688 ... 133
para.700 ... 133
para.703d ... 133
para.704 ... 129, 134, 135
para.739 ... 135
para.753 ... 135
para.764 ... 69
para.764 I ... 134
para.766 ... 69
para.775 ... 135
para.776 ... 135
para.788 I ... 135
para.794 ... 135
para.803 ... 135
para.829 ... 135
para.857 ... 135
para.859 ... 494
para.864 ... 135
para.871 ... 135
para.887 ... 69
para.888 ... 69
para.890 ... 69
para.916 ... 133
para.945 ... 133, 134
para.1025 ... 491
para.1027 ... 72
para.1029 ... 491
para.1030 ... 491
para.1031 ... 491
para.1033 ... 491
para.1042 ... 491, 492
para.1055 ... 492

Civil Procedure Code – *continued*
  para.1059 ... 492
  para.1060 ... 492
  para.1066 ... 491
Coal and Steel Industry Co-determination Act
  ... 544
  para.12 ... 544
  para.13 ... 544
Co-determination Act (MitbestG) ... 529, 545
Collective Agreements Act (TVG) ... 524, 539
  para.1 ... 539
  para.2 ... 539
  para.5 ... 540
Combating Environmental Criminality Act
  ... 292
Commercial Code (1861) ... 24
Commercial Code (HGB) ... 24, 365, 458, 482,
  483–91, 526, 530
  para.1 ... 487, 494
  para.1 I ... 484
  para.1 II ... 484
  para.2 ... 484, 487, 494
  para.3 ... 485
  para.5 ... 485
  para.8 ... 485
  para.13 ... 485
  para.13c ... 485
  para.15 ... 485
  para.15 II ... 485
  para.16 ... 485
  para.17 II ... 485
  para.18 ... 485
  para.19 ... 485, 486
  para.21 ... 482
  para.29 ... 485
  para.30 ... 486
  para.31 ... 485
  para.35 ... 485
  para.37 ... 485, 486
  para.49 ... 486
  para.49 II ... 486
  para.50 ... 486
  para.52 ... 486
  para.53 ... 485, 486
  para.54 ... 486
  para.55 ... 487
  para.56 ... 486
  para.59 ... 486, 534
  para.60 ... 534
  para.61 ... 534
  para.63 ... 534
  para.74 ... 534
  para.75 ... 534
  para.75h ... 486
  para.83 ... 534
  para.84 ... 487
  para.86b ... 487

Commercial Code – *continued*
  para.87c ... 487
  para.88 ... 482
  para.88a ... 487
  para.89 ... 487
  para.89a ... 487
  para.89b ... 487
  para.89b II ... 487
  para.90 ... 487
  para.90a ... 488
  para.91 II ... 487
  para.93 ... 488
  para.94 ... 488
  para.105 ... 493, 494, 495
  para.106 ... 485, 494
  para.112 ... 494
  para.113 ... 494
  para.114 ... 494
  para.115 ... 494
  para.117 ... 494
  para.118 ... 494
  para.120 ... 494, 496
  para.121 ... 494, 496
  para.123 ... 494
  para.124 ... 494
  para.125 ... 494
  para.128 ... 494
  para.129 IV ... 494
  para.130 ... 494
  para.131 ... 494
  para.135 ... 495
  para.145 ... 495
  para.158 ... 495
  para.161 ... 495
  para.162 ... 485, 496
  para.164 ... 486, 496
  para.165 ... 496
  para.166 ... 496
  para.167 ... 496
  para.170 ... 496
  para.171 ... 496
  para.230 ... 493, 496
  para.231 ... 496
  para.232 ... 496
  para.233 ... 496
  para.234 ... 496
  para.237 ... 496
  para.238 ... 485, 489
  para.242 ... 482
  para.267 ... 502
  para.339 ... 489
  para.343 ... 489
  para.343 I ... 490
  para.344 ... 489
  para.346 ... 385, 489
  para.347 ... 489
  para.350 ... 489
  para.352 ... 489

Commercial Code – *continued*
para.353 ... 489
para.355 ... 490
para.357 ... 489
para.362 ... 385
para.362 I ... 490
para.363 ... 490
para.365 ... 490
para.369 ... 490
para.372 ... 489, 490
para.373 ... 490
para.376 ... 490
para.377 ... 490
para.383 ... 399, 490
para.400 ... 488
para.406 ... 490
para.407 ... 491
para.416 ... 491
para.420 ... 491
para.421 ... 491
para.425 ... 491
para.429 ... 491
para.431 ... 491
para.452 ... 485
para.453 ... 491

Competition Code (KO) ... 24

Competition Law (GWB)
... 488
para.1 ... 520
para.2 ... 520, 521
para.3 ... 521
para.4 ... 520, 521
para.5 II ... 521
para.6 ... 521
para.7 ... 521
para.8 ... 520, 521
para.9 ... 520
para.10 ... 520
para.14 ... 521
para.15 ... 521
para.16 ... 521
para.17 ... 521
para.18 ... 521
para.19 ... 521
para.19 II ... 521
para.19 IV ... 521
para.20 ... 521, 522
para.21 ... 522
para.22 II ... 521
para.23 ... 521
para.26 ... 520
para.32 ... 520
para.33 ... 520
para.35 ... 521
para.39 ... 521
para.41 ... 521
para.42 ... 521
para.81 ... 520

Competition Law – *continued*
para.86 ... 520
para.91 ... 491

Condominium Act (WEG) ... 451
para.1 II ... 451

Constitution (*Grundgesetz*) ... 6, 32, 43, 116, 140,
251, 279, 296
art.1 ... 57, 151, 154, 204, 205, 214–16, 310,
549
art.1 I ... 63, 64, 153, 164, 173, 199, 204,
214, 215, 216, 227, 237, 348, 351, 358,
392
art.1 I 1 ... 208, 216, 218
art.1 I 2 ... 218
art.1 III ... 37, 163, 164, 204, 209, 210, 214,
255, 481
art.2 ... 151, 216–19, 310, 516, 549
art.2 I ... 63, 64, 114, 163, 166, 171, 205, 206,
209, 216, 218, 227, 229, 254, 268, 269, 279,
310, 357, 358, 369, 392, 393
art.2 II ... 167, 171, 207, 208, 211, 218, 237,
310
art.2 II 1 ... 207
art.2 II 3 ... 218
art.3 ... 114, 206, 219–22, 273, 279, 526, 530,
549
art.3 I ... 161, 209, 219, 220, 255, 369, 535
art.3 II ... 219, 221, 464
art.3 II 2 ... 221
art.3 III ... 220
art.4 ... 205, 208, 213, 222–4, 227, 549
art.4 I ... 212, 222–4
art.4 II ... 208, 222–4
art.4 III ... 224
art.5 ... 157, 209, 224, 229, 517, 550
art.5 I ... 151, 172, 202, 205, 214, 224–7, 345
art.5 I 1 ... 163, 210, 211
art.5 I 2 ... 225
art.5 I 3 ... 226
art.5 II ... 212–13, 226, 227
art.5 III ... 151, 181, 202, 208, 210, 213, 224,
227
art.6 ... 166, 209, 227–8, 464, 550
art.6 I ... 227, 228, 268, 269, 464, 466
art.6 II ... 464, 465, 470
art.6 IV ... 206, 227
art.6 V ... 219, 464, 470
art.7 ... 166, 209, 228, 550
art.7 I ... 223, 224, 228
art.7 IV ... 228
art.8 ... 157, 202, 207, 228–9, 550
art.8 I ... 163, 205, 228, 229, 256
art.8 II ... 212
art.9 ... 157, 202, 207, 229, 279, 526, 551
art.9 I ... 376
art.9 II ... 201, 229
art.9 III ... 209, 229, 524, 526, 539, 540, 545
art.9 III 2 ... 229

Constitution – *continued*
art.10 ... 229–30, 551
art.10 I ... 229
art.10 II ... 213, 229, 230
art.11 ... 207, 230, 526, 551
art.11 I ... 230
art.11 II ... 230
art.12 ... 55, 81, 170, 202, 207, 230–2, 279,
 516, 526, 551
art.12 I ... 208, 212, 230–2, 243
art.12 I 1 ... 211
art.12 I 2 ... 211, 213
art.12 II ... 232
art.12 III ... 232
art.12a ... 232
art.12a II ... 224
art.12a VI ... 221
art.13 ... 232–3, 235, 551–2
art.13 I ... 232
art.13 II ... 233
art.13 III ... 233
art.13 V ... 233
art.13 VI ... 233
art.14 ... 14, 45, 55, 170, 202, 209, 233–4, 270,
 273, 279, 446, 458, 552
art.14 I ... 205, 208, 211, 213, 233, 270, 440,
 445, 455, 472
art.14 I 1 ... 233, 445
art.14 I 2 ... 233, 446
art.14 II ... 234, 270, 440, 446, 447
art.14 III ... 61, 271, 446
art.14 III 2 ... 234
art.14 III 3 ... 234
art.14 III 4 ... 234
art.15 ... 234, 279, 446, 552
art.16 ... 234–5, 552
art.16 II ... 297
art.16a ... 235, 552–3
art.16a I ... 235
art.16a II ... 235
art.16a III ... 235
art.17 ... 185, 235, 553
art.18 ... 202, 553
art.19 ... 204, 205, 206, 553
art.19 I ... 212, 213
art.19 II ... 212, 213
art.19 III ... 208
art.19 IV ... 114, 164, 172, 208, 236, 257, 265
art.19 VI ... 236
art.20 ... 50, 51, 57, 150, 164, 180, 198, 204,
 526, 554
art.20 I ... 48, 52, 150, 153, 155, 156, 158, 159,
 163, 173, 175, 273
art.20 II ... 48, 52, 150, 153, 154, 155, 156,
 159, 163, 164, 348, 351
art.20 III ... 37, 40, 63, 64, 150, 153, 154, 155,
 163, 164, 165, 191, 251, 254, 348, 351, 357
art.20 III 2 ... 164

Constitution – *continued*
art.20 IV ... 199, 205
art.20a ... 154, 180, 286, 554
art.21 ... 150, 157, 159, 160, 184, 229, 554
art.21 I ... 160, 161
art.21 I 4 ... 161, 162, 163
art.21 II ... 160, 199, 200, 240
art.21 III ... 160, 176
art.23 ... 42, 44, 49, 50, 51, 54, 152, 153, 164,
 179, 193, 235, 554–5
art.23 I ... 50, 156, 179
art.23 II ... 50
art.23 III ... 50
art.23 IV ... 50, 179
art.23 VI ... 50, 179
art.24 ... 43, 44, 46, 48, 51, 233, 555
art.24 I ... 54, 152
art.24 I ... a 51
art.24 II ... 157
art.25 ... 43, 56, 57, 152, 555
art.28 ... 150, 153, 154, 164, 526, 555
art.28 I ... 149, 150, 173, 175, 178, 273
art.28 I 1 ... 175
art.28 I 3 ... 156
art.28 II ... 155, 251, 254
art.29 ... 155
art.29 I ... 175
art.30 ... 175, 176, 177, 556
art.31 ... 15, 37, 150, 177, 556
art.32 I ... 179
art.33 ... 205, 219
art.33 II ... 201, 206
art.34 ... 164, 271, 277, 438
art.35 II ... 178
art.35 III ... 178, 189
art.37 ... 178
art.38 ... 51, 52, 53, 157, 181, 556
art.38 I ... 52, 156, 158, 159, 208
art.38 I 1 ... 181, 205, 219
art.38 I 2 ... 150, 104, 105
art.38 III ... 182
art.40 I ... 182
art.42 I ... 183
art.42 II ... 183
art.43 I ... 185
art.44 ... 183
art.45 ... 50, 183, 556
art.45a ... 157, 183
art.45b ... 157
art.45c I ... 185
art.46 I ... 183
art.46 II ... 184
art.48 III ... 184
art.49 ... 181
art.50 ... 51, 178, 193, 556
art.51 I ... 192
art.51 II ... 192
art.51 III ... 192

Constitution – *continued*
art.52 I ... 193
art.52 III ... 51
art.53 ... IIIa 193
art.53a ... 183, 194
art.54 ... 189
art.54 I ... 189
art.54 II ... 189
art.54 II 2 ... 189
art.55 ... 190
art.55 I ... 190
art.56 ... 190
art.57 ... 190, 193
art.58 ... 190, 191
art.59 ... 556
art.59 I ... 57, 190
art.59 II ... 47, 56, 179, 213
art.60 I ... 190
art.60 II ... 190
art.61 ... 189
art.61 I ... 192
art.62 ... 186
art.63 ... 164, 185, 186
art.63 I ... 186
art.63 II ... 186
art.63 III ... 186
art.63 IV ... 186, 191
art.63 IV 3 ... 186
art.64 I ... 186, 188, 190
art.65 I ... 188
art.65 III ... 189
art.66 ... 186
art.67 ... 556–7
art.67 I ... 187
art.68 ... 187, 557
art.68 I ... 187, 188
art.69 ... 186
art.69 II ... 187, 188
art.70 ... 48, 176, 177, 194, 557
art.70 I ... 54
art.71 ... 47, 176, 557
art.72 ... 48, 557
art.72 I ... 176
art.72 II ... 176
art.73 ... 47, 176, 177, 194, 286, 557–8
art.74 ... 48, 273, 276, 286, 558–9
art.74 I ... 176
art.75 ... 176, 177, 194, 286
art.76 ... 185, 194, 559
art.76 I ... 193, 194
art.77 ... 560
art.77 I ... 194
art.77 II ... 193, 195
art.77 II 4 ... 196
art.77 III ... 193, 195
art.78 ... 185, 195, 196, 560
art.79 ... 150, 560
art.79 I ... 212

Constitution – *continued*
art.79 I 1 ... 198
art.79 II ... 44, 50, 198
art.79 III ... 47, 50, 52, 57, 153, 175, 180, 198, 204, 214
art.80 ... 164, 196, 251, 560–1
art.80 I ... 157, 165
art.82 ... 191, 194
art.82 I ... 196
art.82 II ... 196
art.83 ... 165, 177, 197, 251, 253, 254
art.84 ... 197
art.84 I ... 193
art.84 III 1 ... 197
art.85 ... 197
art.85 III 1 ... 197
art.86 ... 177, 197
art.87 ... 197
art.87 I ... 177
art.87a ... 197
art.87a I 2 ... 157
art.87b ... 197
art.87c I ... 191
art.88 ... 197
art.90 ... 177
art.91 ... 253
art.91a ... 253
art.92 ... 66, 67, 77, 178, 197, 239, 561
art.93 ... 77, 150, 178, 197, 561
art.93 I ... 240
art.93 I 1 ... 163, 185, 240
art.93 I 2 ... 41, 178, 241
art.93 I 3 ... 48, 178, 240
art.93 I 4 ... 178
art.93 I ... 4a 56, 163, 243
art.94 ... 77, 197, 239, 562
art.94 I ... 92, 194
art.94 I 1 ... 41
art.95 ... 66, 67, 75, 178, 198
art.95 II ... 89
art.95 III ... 41, 75
art.96 ... 67
art.97 ... 89, 172, 197
art.97 I ... 40, 107, 339
art.99 ... 77, 197
art.100 ... 77, 172, 197, 562
art.100 I ... 41, 46, 55, 241
art.101 ... 46, 47, 126, 149, 164, 197, 204, 206, 352, 562
art.101 I ... 236–7, 337
art.102 ... 126, 218, 237, 562
art.103 ... 126, 149, 205, 206, 296, 562
art.103 I ... 114, 237, 339, 343
art.103 II ... 167, 168, 169, 237–8, 298, 299, 315, 339
art.103 III ... 339
art.104 ... 164, 172, 197, 205, 206, 339
art.104 II 1 ... 350

Constitution – *continued*
    art.104 III ... 350
    art.107 II ... 179
    art.109 ... 279
    art.112 ... 189
    art.115a ... 194
    art.115g ... 77
    art.116 ... 207
    art.116 I ... 155
    art.118 ... 175
    art.118a ... 175
    art.137 I ... 223
    art.140 ... 222
    art.143 ... 148
    art.146 ... 148, 199, 562

Constitution of the Second Empire
    (*Reichsverfassung*) ... 25, 145, 204

Constitution of the Weimar Republic (WRV)
    ... 30, 145, 146, 204, 222
    art.25 ... 30, 189
    art.41 ... 30, 189
    art.42 ... 30
    art.43 ... 30
    art.47 ... 189
    art.48 ... 30, 31, 189
    art.53 ... 189
    art.54 ... 30
    art.76 ... 30
    art.109 ... 30
    art.137 III ... 222
    art.165 ... 30, 541

Consumer Credit Act (VerbrKrG) ... 283

Copyright Act ... 522

Court Costs Act (GKG) ... 111, 112
    para.11 ... 111

Criminal Code (StGB) ... 25, 295, 297, 299
    para.1 ... 297, 298
    para.2 ... 298, 299
    para.3 ... 298
    para.4 ... 298
    para.5 ... 298
    para.6 ... 298
    para.7 ... 298
    para.7 II 1 ... 298
    para.10 ... 297
    para.12 ... 295
    para.13 ... 297, 301, 322, 323
    para.15 ... 301, 320
    para.16 ... 306, 319
    para.17 ... 300, 306, 318, 319, 320, 325
    para.19 ... 300, 313
    para.20 ... 300, 313, 314, 315, 316, 320
    para.21 ... 313, 314
    para.22 ... 325, 333
    para.23 ... 333
    para.23 I ... 325

Criminal Code – *continued*
    para.23 III ... 327
    para.24 ... 320, 330
    para.24 I ... 319, 327
    para.24 I 1 ... 327, 328
    para.24 I 2 ... 328
    para.24 II ... 327, 329
    para.25 ... 330
    para.25 I 1 ... 330, 331, 332
    para.25 I 2 ... 330
    para.25 II ... 330, 333
    para.26 ... 330, 333
    para.27 ... 330, 333, 335
    para.29 ... 334
    para.30 I ... 334
    para.30 II ... 335
    para.32 ... 307, 308
    para.33 ... 316
    para.34 ... 309–10, 317
    para.35 ... 317, 320
    para.35 II ... 318
    para.36 ... 319, 320
    para.37 ... 297
    para.38 ... 297, 335, 336
    para.38 II ... 300
    para.39 ... 336
    para.40 ... 336
    para.40 I ... 336
    para.43a ... 336
    para.44 ... 336
    para.45 V ... 158
    para.46 ... 299–300, 336
    para.46 I ... 313
    para.49 ... 325
    para.49 I ... 314
    para.60 ... 335
    para.61 ... 336
    para.62 ... 336
    para.67 I ... 336
    para.72 ... 336
    para.76a ... 297, 335
    para.78 ... 297
    para.79b ... 297
    para.80 ... 297, 336
    para.154 ... 330
    para.211 ... 260, 306, 318, 323, 333
    para.211 II ... 318
    para.212 ... 306, 314, 323
    para.218 ... 218
    para.218a 218, 219
    para.222 ... 315, 320, 321
    para.223 ... 435
    para.223 II ... 325
    para.228 ... 310–11
    para.242 ... 301, 435
    para.242 I ... 59, 60, 325
    para.258 VI ... 319
    para.259 ... 391

Criminal Code – *continued*
  para.315c ... 315
  para.316 ... 315
  para.323a ... 301, 314, 316
  para.323c 3... 22, 323
  para.324 ... 292
  para.325 ... 292
  para.326 ... 292
  para.327 ... 292
  para.328 ... 292
  para.329 ... 292
  para.330 ... 292
  para.330d ... 292
  para.358 ... 297, 336

Criminal Procedure Code (StPO) ... 25, 99, 296, 338, 339
  para.48 ... 356, 357
  para.51 ... 357
  para.52 ... 357, 358
  para.53 ... 357, 358
  para.53 I 2 ... 352
  para.54 ... 357
  para.55 ... 357
  para.60 ... 357
  para.70 ... 357
  para.71 ... 356
  para.72 ... 356
  para.73 ... 357
  para.74 ... 357
  para.81a ... 349
  para.81b ... 349
  para.81e ... 349
  para.81f ... 349
  para.85 ... 356
  para.86 ... 356, 357
  para.90 ... 341
  para.93 ... 356
  para.94 ... 349
  para.95 ... 349
  para.97 ... 349
  para.99 ... 229
  para.100 ... 349
  para.100c ... 358
  para.100c I ... 349
  para.100d II ... 349
  para.101 ... 349
  para.102 ... 233, 349
  para.103 ... 349
  para.104 II 1 ... 350
  para.110 ... 233
  para.112 ... 350
  para.112 I ... 349
  para.112 II 1 ... 350
  para.112 II 2 ... 350
  para.112 II 3 ... 350
  para.112 III ... 350
  para.112a ... 350

Criminal Procedure Code (StPO) – *continued*
  para.113 I ... 350
  para.114 ... 350
  para.114b I ... 350
  para.115 II ... 350
  para.116 ... 350
  para.117 ... 350
  para.121 ... 350
  para.121 II ... 350
  para.123 ... 341
  para.127 ... 350
  para.127 I 2 ... 350
  para.127 II ... 350
  para.128 ... 351
  para.133 ... 347
  para.133 I ... 347
  para.136 ... 350, 356
  para.136 I ... 347
  para.136 I 1 ... 347
  para.136 I 2 ... 347
  para.136a ... 347, 348, 349, 357, 358
  para.136a I ... 349
  para.136a III ... 349
  para.136a III 2 ... 348
  para.137 ... 350
  para.138 ... 111
  para.139 ... 351
  para.140 ... 115, 351
  para.140 I ... 110
  para.140 II ... 110
  para.141 ... 110
  para.142 I 1 ... 351
  para.142 II ... 351
  para.145 ... 351
  para.147 ... 352
  para.147 II ... 352
  para.148 I ... 352
  para.151 ... 340, 341
  para.152 ... 340, 346, 347
  para.152 I ... 341
  para.152 II ... 341, 346
  para.153 ... 342
  para.153 I ... 342
  para.153a I ... 342
  para.154e ... 342
  para.155 II ... 342
  para.157 ... 347
  para.158 ... 346, 347
  para.160 ... 99, 340, 346
  para.160 I ... 346
  para.160 II ... 347
  para.161 ... 99, 346, 347
  para.162 ... 346
  para.163 ... 346
  para.163 III 1 ... 347
  para.163a ... 347
  para.170 I ... 341, 347
  para.172 ... 341

Criminal Procedure Code (StPO) – *continued*
para.199 ... 345
para.200 ... 345
para.201 ... 353
para.203 ... 353
para.204 ... 353
para.206 ... 353
para.207 ... 353
para.210 ... 353
para.212 ... 344
para.213 ... 353
para.226 ... 344, 355
para.227 ... 344
para.229 ... 343
para.238 ... 354
para.238 I ... 354
para.239 ... 354
para.240 ... 357
para.240 II ... 343, 354
para.243 ... 354
para.243 I ... 354
para.243 II ... 356
para.243 III ... 354
para.243 IV ... 354, 356
para.243 IV 1 ... 356
para.244 ... 354, 356
para.244 I ... 354, 356
para.244 II ... 342, 355
para.244 III ... 356
para.244 IV ... 356
para.244 VI ... 356
para.245 ... 356
para.246a 336
para.247a 355
para.249 ... 345, 354, 355, 356, 357
para.250 ... 344, 355
para.250 II ... 355
para.251 ... 344, 345, 355
para.252 ... 345, 358
para.254 ... 345
para.256 ... 356
para.257 ... 343
para.257 I ... 354
para.257 II ... 354
para.258 ... 359
para.258 II ... 359
para.260 ... 345, 359
para.261 ... 344, 355, 356
para.263 I ... 359
para.264 II ... 342
para.267 ... 359
para.268 ... 359
para.270 I ... 353
para.271 ... 345
para.274 ... 344, 361
para.275 ... 345, 359
para.296 ... 360
para.296 II ... 360

Criminal Procedure Code (StPO) – *continued*
para.297 ... 351, 360
para.300 ... 360
para.304 ... 362
para.311a 362
para.312 ... 360
para.314 I ... 360
para.323 ... 361
para.323 III ... 361
para.324 ... 361
para.325 ... 361
para.326 ... 361
para.327 ... 361
para.331 I ... 360
para.332 ... 360
para.333 ... 361
para.337 ... 361
para.337 I ... 361
para.338 ... 361
para.341 ... 361
para.344 ... 361
para.344 I ... 360
para.345 ... 361
para.349 II ... 361
para.351 ... 361
para.358 ... 361, 362
para.358 II ... 360
para.359 ... 360, 362
para.362 ... 362
para.366 ... 362
para.368 ... 362
para.369 ... 362
para.370 ... 362
para.370 II ... 362
para.372 ... 362
para.373 ... 362
para.374 ... 341
para.407 ... 359
para.407 II ... 359
para.408 II ... 359
para.408 III 1 ... 359
para.408 III 2 ... 359
para.410 I ... 359
para.410 III ... 359
para.411 I 2 ... 359
para.412 ... 359
para.417 ... 359
para.464 ... 112
para.465 ... 112
para.467 I ... 112

Disabled Persons Act (SchwBG) ... 538

Drinking Water Act 289

EC Treaty
art.17 ... 156
art.18 ... 156
art.30 ... 282

EC Treaty – *continued*
art.39-art.55 ... 230
art.81 ... 519
art.82 ... 519
art.83 ... 250
art.87 ... 253, 263
art.88 ... 263
art.130i ... 49
art.149 IV ... 49
art.151 V ... 49
art.152 IV ... 49
art.153 IV ... 49
art.175 III ... 49
art.203 ... 51
art.234 ... 46, 47, 242
art.234 II ... 237
art.249 II ... 250
art.249 III ... 250, 252
art.280 ... 297
art.308 ... 54

Educational Grants Act (BAföG) ... 275, 276

Employees Insurance Act (AVG) ... 274, 530

Employment Protection Law ... 365

Enabling Act 1933 ... 31

Enforcement of Criminal Sentences Act
(StVollzG) ... 295

Environmental Code ... 287

Environmental Impact Assessment Act (UPVG)
... 287

Environmental Information Act (UIG) ... 290

Environmental Liability Act (UmweltHG)
... 291–2, 437
para.1 ... 292
para.4 ... 292
para.5 ... 292
para.6 ... 292
para.8 ... 292
para.10 ... 292

European Convention on Human Rights (ECHR)
... 56–7, 152, 242
art.1 ... 213
art.6 ... 343
art.6 I ... 348
art.6 II ... 344
art.10 ... 202
art.11 ... 202
art.13 ... 230

European Convention on Jurisdiction and
Enforcement of Judgments in Civil and
Commercial Matters ... 479

Federal Child Benefit Act (BKGG) ... 276

Federal Constitutional Court Act (BVerfGG)
... 77, 91, 239, 240
para.1 ... 77, 92

Federal Constitutional Court Act (BVerfGG) –
continued
para.2 ... 77, 239
para.3 ... 91
para.3 I ... 91
para.3 II ... 91
para.4 ... 91, 239
para.5 ... 92, 163
para.6 ... 239
para.7 ... 239
para.13 ... 77, 150
para.13 VI ... 241
para.14 ... 77
para.15 ... 77
para.15 III 2 ... 240
para.15 III 3 ... 240
para.15 IV 3 ... 182
para.16 ... 77, 239
para.23 ... 244
para.30 II ... 240
para.31 ... 77, 90
para.31 I ... 41
para.31 II ... 41, 240
para.32 ... 240
para.46 III ... 200
para.63 ... 163
para.76 ... 241
para.80 ... 241
para.82 ... 241
para.90 ... 163, 242, 243
para.90 II 1 ... 244
para.90 II 2 ... 244
para.92 ... 244
para.93 I ... 244
para.93 II ... 244
para.95 II 2 ... 244
para.95 III 1 ... 244

Federal Elections Act (BWahlG) ... 158
para.1 II ... 182
para.4 ... 182
para.5 ... 182
para.6 ... 182
para.6 III ... 182
para.6 V ... 182
para.6 VI ... 158, 159, 182

Federal Emissions Control Act (BImSchG) ... 289
para.1 ... 287, 289
para.52 ... 293
para.54 ... 289
para.58 ... 289

Federal Law on Notaries (BNotO) ... 98, 99
para.3 ... 98
para.5 ... 98
para.7 ... 98
para.10 ... 98
para.11 ... 98
para.14 ... 98
para.19 ... 98

Federal Nature Conservation Act (BNatSchG)
... 290
  para.1 ... 290
  para.5 ... 290
  para.7 ... 290
  para.12 ... 290
  para.15 ... 290
  para.20 ... 288, 290
Federal Social Assistance Law (BSHG) ... 274,
276
  para.1 ... 276
  para.4 I ... 258
  para.9 ... 275
  para.12 ... 275, 276
  para.21 ... 275, 276
  para.96 ... 275
Federal Staff Representation Act ... 543
Federal Statute on Attorneys (BRAO) ... 25, 92,
94, 112
  para.1 ... 92, 351
  para.2 ... 96
  para.3 ... 93, 112
  para.4 ... 92
  para.6 ... 93
  para.11 ... 112
  para.17 ... 93
  para.18 ... 93
  para.23 ... 112
  para.25 ... 93
  para.26 ... 112
  para.27 ... 93
  para.28 ... 94
  para.29a ... 94
  para.30 ... 112
  para.31 ... 112
  para.43 ... 96
  para.43b ... 96
  para.43c ... 96
  para.46 ... 100
  para.49b ... 97
  para.49b II ... 97
  para.59a ... 95
  para.59a II ... 95
  para.59c ... 96
  para.59m ... 96
  para.60 ... 93
  para.92 ... 95
  para.161a ... 95
  para.175 ... 93
  para.177 II ... 94
  para.191 ... 93
  para.206 ... 104
  para.209 ... 104
  para.225 ... 93
  para.226 ... 93
  para.227 ... 93
Federal Vacation Act ... 538

Food and Consumer Goods Act (LMBG) ... 282,
283
  para.8 ... 282
Foreigners Law (AuslG) ... 295
  para.45 I ... 266, 269
  para.48 ... 269
Formation of Marriage Act ... 464, 466
Frankfurt Constitution (1849) ... 145, 204, 239
Free Gifts Regulation ... 518

General Conditions of Business Act (AGBG)
... 283, 285, 369, 409, 488
  para.13 ... 410
  para.24a 410

Hague Conventions ... 480
Higher Education Framework Act (HRG) ... 81
Housing Benefit Act (WoGG) ... 276

Imperial Compulsory Liability Act 1871 ... 25
  para.1 ... 437
Imperial Constitution (*Reichsverfassung*) ... 25,
145, 204
Imperial Insurance Ordinance (RVO) ... 273, 274
Imperial Penal Code ... 296
Instalment Sales Act ... 283
Insurance Contracts Act (VVG) ... 283
Introductory Act to the Civil Code (EGBGB)
... 364
  art.2 ... 38
  art.3 ... 480
  art.4 I ... 481
  art.6 ... 481
  art.27 ... 480
  art.28 ... 480
  art.28 II ... 480
  art.29 ... 481
  art.30 ... 481
  art.46 ... 480
  art.230 ... 366
  art.231 ... 366

Joint Stock Corporation Act (AktG) ... 492,
504–5
  para.1 I 1 ... 376
  para.2 ... 505
  para.4 ... 505
  para.7 ... 505
  para.8 ... 505
  para.10 ... 505, 508
  para.15 ... 512
  para.16 ... 512
  para.17 ... 512
  para.18 ... 513
  para.19 ... 512, 513

Joint Stock Corporation Act (AktG) – *continued*
para.20 ... 510, 512
para.20 VII ... 513
para.23 ... 505
para.23 I ... 505
para.23 III 2 ... 507
para.24 ... 508
para.27 ... 505
para.30 ... 505
para.30 I ... 507
para.30 II ... 507
para.30 IV ... 505
para.31 ... 507
para.32 ... 506
para.33 ... 506
para.36 ... 505, 506
para.36 II ... 505
para.36a ... 505
para.38 ... 506
para.39 ... 506
para.41 ... 505, 506
para.41 I 2 ... 506
para.41 II ... 506
para.46 ... 505
para.71 ... 508
para.76 ... 506
para.76 II ... 506
para.78 ... 399, 506, 507
para.78 II ... 506
para.80 ... 506
para.81 ... 506
para.82 ... 507
para.84 ... 506
para.84 III ... 506
para.86 ... 506
para.87 ... 506
para.88 ... 507
para.89 ... 507
para.90 ... 507, 512
para.90 I 2 ... 512
para.91 ... 507
para.92 ... 507
para.93 ... 507
para.94 ... 506
para.95 ... 507
para.100 ... 507
para.101 ... 507
para.102 ... 507
para.105 ... 507
para.111 ... 507
para.112 ... 507
para.116 ... 507
para.117 ... 509
para.117 II ... 509
para.118 ... 508
para.119 ... 508
para.122 ... 508, 509
para.124 ... 508

Joint Stock Corporation Act (AktG) –
continued
para.128 ... 508
para.131 ... 508, 512
para.133 ... 508
para.139 ... 508
para.141 ... 508
para.142 ... 509
para.142 II ... 509
para.147 ... 509
para.160 ... 506, 512
para.179 ... 508
para.181 ... 508
para.186 ... 508
para.222 ... 508
para.262 ... 509
para.263 ... 509
para.264 ... 509
para.265 ... 509
para.266 ... 509
para.273 ... 509
para.278 ... 505, 511
para.278 II ... 511
para.285 ... 511
para.290 ... 511
para.291 ... 512, 513
para.293 ... 513
para.294 ... 513
para.302 ... 513
para.304 ... 513
para.305 ... 513
para.309 ... 513
para.311 ... 513
para.311 II ... 513
para.312 ... 510
para.317 ... 513
para.320 ... 513
para.323 ... 513
para.324 ... 513
para.328 ... 512, 513
para.339 ... 510
para.361 ... 510

Judiciary Law (DRiG) ... 83, 86, 87, 89
para.4 I ... 40
para.5a ... 83
para.5a II ... 84
para.5a III ... 84
para.5b ... 86
para.5b I ... 85
para.5d ... 87
para.5d III ... 85
para.21 ... 89
para.45 I ... 107
para.69 ... 91
para.70 ... 91
para.122 I ... 99
Juvenile Courts Act ... 295

Juvenile Courts Act (JGG)
  para.3 ... 313
  para.33 ... 353
  para.40 ... 107, 353
  para.41 ... 107

Labour Courts Act (ArbGG) ... 73, 525
  para.2 ... 74, 546
  para.3 ... 74
  para.4 ... 546
  para.8 ... 74
  para.10 ... 74
  para.11 ... 74, 111
  para.11 I ... 546
  para.11 II ... 546, 547
  para.12a ... 547
  para.13 ... 547
  para.14 ... 74
  para.16 II ... 107
  para.31 ... 74
  para.33 ... 74
  para.35 II ... 107
  para.39 ... 74
  para.40 ... 74
  para.41 II ... 107
  para.45 ... 74
  para.48 ... 68, 127
  para.64 ... 74, 547
  para.72 ... 74
  para.101 ... 546
  para.154 ... 547

Land Register Act (GBO) ... 449
  para.12 ... 449
  para.13 ... 449
  para.19 ... 449
  para.45 ... 450

Legal Advice Act (BerHG) ... 113–15
  para.1 ... 115
  para.1 I ... 114
  para.2 II 1 ... 115
  para.3 ... 114
  para.8 ... 115
  para.14 I ... 114
  para.14 II ... 114

Legal Advice Act (RBerG) ... 102
  para.1 ... 93, 110
  para.1 I ... 102

Legal Aid Law (PKHG) ... 113, 115

Legal Services Act (RPflG) ... 103

Limited Liability Company Act (GmbHG)
  ... 376, 492, 498, 500
  para.1 ... 498, 499
  para.2 ... 499
  para.2 I ... 499
  para.3 ... 499
  para.4 II ... 499
  para.5 ... 499, 500

Limited Liability Company
  Act (GmbHG) – *continued*
  para.5 III ... 498
  para.6 ... 499, 501
  para.7 ... 499
  para.7 II ... 499
  para.8 ... 499
  para.10 ... 501
  para.11 ... 499
  para.11 I ... 499
  para.11 II ... 500
  para.12 ... 499
  para.13 ... 500
  para.15 I ... 500
  para.15 III ... 500
  para.15 IV ... 500
  para.15 V ... 500
  para.22 III ... 500
  para.24 ... 500
  para.26 ... 500
  para.27 ... 500
  para.29 ... 501, 502
  para.30 ... 500
  para.32a ... 501
  para.32b ... 501
  para.34 ... 501
  para.35 ... 501
  para.35 I ... 399
  para.37 II ... 501
  para.37 III ... 499
  para.38 ... 501
  para.38 II ... 501
  para.39 ... 501
  para.40 ... 500, 501
  para.41 ... 502
  para.42 ... 502
  para.43 ... 502
  para.43a ... 502
  para.45 ... 499, 502
  para.46 ... 502
  para.47 ... 502
  para.48 ... 502
  para.48 II ... 502
  para.50 ... 502
  para.51 ... 502
  para.51a ... 503
  para.51b ... 503
  para.52 ... 501, 503, 544
  para.53 ... 502, 503
  para.55 ... 500, 503
  para.58 ... 503
  para.59 ... 503
  para.60 ... 503
  para.60 I ... 503
  para.60 I 4 ... 503
  para.61 II ... 503

Limited Liability Company
  Act (GmbHG) – *continued*
  para.65 ... 503
  para.66 II ... 503
  para.77 ... 503
Lugano Convention on Jurisdiction and
  Enforcement of Judgments in Civil and
  Commercial Matters ... 479

Maastricht Treaty on European Union ... 44, 50,
  51–3, 153
  art.F3 53
Managerial Employees Committee Act (SprAuG)
  ... 529
Marriage Act ... 466
Missing Persons Act ... 376

Nationality Act (StAG) ... 207
Nuclear Energy Act ... 293, 437
Nuclear Substances Act (AtG) ... 291
  para.7 ... 167
  para.7 I ... 167
  para.7 II ... 167
  para.19 ... 293

Organization of the Courts Act (GVG) ... 25, 41,
  66, 106, 296, 339
  para.1 ... 40, 89
  para.13 ... 69
  para.17 ... 127
  para.23 ... 126
  para.23 II ... 69
  para.23b ... 69
  para.24 ... 352, 353
  para.25 ... 352, 353, 359
  para.25 III ... 69
  para.26 ... 107
  para.28 ... 69, 353
  para.29 ... 69, 353
  para.29 I ... 107
  para.32 ... 107
  para.35 ... 107
  para.45 ... 107
  para.46 ... 107
  para.71 ... 70
  para.72 ... 70
  para.74 ... 70, 107, 353
  para.74 II ... 107, 353
  para.74b ... 107
  para.74c ... 70
  para.75 ... 70
  para.76 ... 70, 107, 353
  para.76 II ... 353
  para.93 ... 70
  para.95 ... 129
  para.105 I ... 107
  para.119 ... 70, 71
  para.120 ... 71, 353

Organization of the Courts Act (GVG) –
  continued
  para.121 I ... 1a 71
  para.121 I ... 1b 71
  para.121 I ... 1c 71
  para.122 ... 71, 353
  para.132 ... 41, 71
  para.139 ... 71
  para.141 ... 99
  para.150 ... 99
  para.152 ... 99
  para.169 ... 124, 345
  para.169 II ... 124, 345
  para.170 ... 124
  para.171a ... 345
  para.171b I 1 ... 345
  para.172 ... 124
  para.194 ... 359
  para.197 ... 107
Ozone Act (OG) ... 290–1

Package Tour Contracts Act ... 365
Packaging Act (VerpackV) ... 291
Part Time and Fixed Term Contracts Act (TzBfG)
  ... 532
  para.7 ... 532
  para.8 ... 532
  para.9 ... 532
  para.14 ... 533
  para.14 I ... 532
  para.14 II ... 532, 533
  para.22 ... 533
Partnership Law (PartGG) ... 96, 497
  para.1 I ... 497
  para.1 II ... 497
  para.2 ... 497
  para.4 ... 497
  para.5 ... 497
  para.7 ... 498
  para.8 ... 498
Passport Law (PassG), para.7 1a ... 216
Patent Act (PatG) ... 522
  para.100 ... 72
  para.110 ... 72
Pharmaceutical Act ... 282, 437
Political Parties Act (PG) ... 162
  para.2 I ... 160
  para.25 I 5 ... 162
Price Information Act ... 519
Product Liability Act (ProdHaftG) ... 282, 284,
  291, 438
  para.1 ... 438
Promotion of Employment Act (AFG) ... 274
  para.100 ... 277
Protection from Dismissal Act (KSchG) ... 535,
  536, 538

Protection from Dismissal Act (KSchG) –
    continued
    para.1 ... 536
    para.1 II ... 536
    para.1 III ... 536
    para.4 I ... 537
    para.7 ... 537
    para.12a 547
    para.15 ... 537
    para.23 ... 536
Protection of Working Mothers Act (MuSchG)
    ... 538
Prussian Common Law Act 1794 ... 296
Pub Licensing Law (GaststättenG), para.4 I 1
    ... 257

Radiation Protection Regulation (StrSchV)
    ... 291
Rebate Act ... 518
Regulation on Auditors ... 101
Regulation of the National Labour Act ... 524
Regulation on Patent Attorneys ... 102
Religious Education Act, para.5 ... 208
Rent Act (MHG) ... 284
Restraints of Competition Act (GWB) ... 519
Revenue Courts Act (FGO) ... 75
    para.33 ... 75
    para.34 ... 127
    para.35 ... 75
    para.36 ... 75
    para.40 ... 75
    para.115 ... 75, 111
    para.118 ... 111
Road Traffic Act (StVG) ... 196
    para.3 I ... 254
    para.7 ... 437
    para.7 I ... 437
    para.7 II 2 ... 437

Sick Pay Act ... 538
Social Courts Act (SGG) ... 74, 273
    para.7 ... 74
    para.12 I ... 107
    para.27 ... 74
    para.28 ... 107
    para.29 ... 74
    para.33 ... 74, 107
    para.39 ... 75
    para.40 ... 107
    para.41 ... 75
    para.52 ... 127
Social Law Code (SGB) ... 274, 275–6
    para.1 ... 274, 276
    para.4 ... 275, 541
    para.10 ... 276

Social Law Code (SGB) – *continued*
    para.13 ... 111, 276
    para.15 ... 276
    para.18 ... 275
    para.29 ... 275
    para.31 ... 276
    para.39 ... 276
    para.40 ... 276
    para.60 ... 277
    para.64 ... 112
    para.86 ... 275
    para.91 ... 275
    para.94 ... 275
    para.129 ... 277
    para.143 ... 275
    para.191 ... 277
Specialist Lawyers Act (FAO) ... 96
    para.4 ... 96
    para.5 ... 96
Stability Act (StabG) ... 280
Standard Contracts Act (AGB-Gesetz) ... 365
Standing Orders of the Bundestag (GeschOBT)
    para.10 I ... 183
    para.36 ... 183
    para.38 ... 183
    para.75 ... 194
    para.76 ... 194
Standing Orders of the Federal Government,
    para.24 ... 189
Statute on Attorney's Fees (BRAGO) ... 97
    para.3 V ... 98
    para.97 ... 351
Statutes of Peace ... 16
Stock Corporation act ... 541
Strict Liability Act ... 437

Trade Act (1869/1891) ... 523, 541
Trade Act (GewO) ... 280–1, 526, 530, 534
    para.139b ... 528
Transformations Act (UmwG) ... 504, 510
    para.9 ... 510
    para.12 ... 510
    para.46 ... 510
    para.59 ... 510
    para.60 ... 510
    para.65 ... 510
    para.66 ... 510
    para.68 ... 510
    para.69 ... 510
    para.72 ... 510
    para.73 ... 510
    para.77 ... 510
    para.78 ... 510, 511

Unfair Competition Act (UWG) ... 283, 285, 488,
    516, 518–19

Unfair Competition Act (UWG) – *continued*
para.1 ... 516, 517, 518
para.3 ... 517, 518, 519
para.4 ... 519
para.4 I ... 517
para.6 ... 517, 519
para.7 ... 519
para.7 III ... 518
para.8 ... 519
para.8 I ... 518
para.12 ... 518
para.13 ... 519
para.13a ... 519
para.17 ... 519
para.19 ... 519
para.20 ... 519
para.20a ... 519
para.37 ... 283

Unification Treaty ... 33, 66, 148, 159, 281, 297, 524, 527

University Framework Act (HRG) ... 232

Vienna Convention on Contracts for the International Sale of Goods ... 480

War Victims Benefits Act ... 276

Washing and Cleaning Products Act ... 289

Waste Act (AbfG) ... 289–90
para.2 ... 290
para.2 II ... 290
para.3 ... 289
para.4 ... 289
para.9a ... 290
para.11 ... 293
para.13 ... 290
para.18 ... 293

Waste Water Charges Act (AbwAG), para.1 ... 289

Water Management Act (WHG) ... 286, 288–9, 437
para.1 ... 287
para.2 ... 288
para.6 ... 288
para.19 ... 289
para.21 ... 293
para.22 I ... 289

Wine Law (WeinG), para.12 ... 257

Witnesses and Experts' Expenses Law (ZSEG) ... 112

Working Time Act (ArbZG) ... 533, 538
para.3 ... 538

Works Constitution Act (BetrVG) ... 524, 529, 541, 542, 544
para.1 ... 542
para.2 ... 542
para.5 ... 531
para.5 III ... 542

Works Constitution Act (BetrVG) – *continued*
para.38 ... 542
para.40 ... 543
para.47 ... 545
para.54 ... 545
para.76 ... 544
para.80 ... 532
para.87 ... 543
para.93 ... 533
para.95 ... 532, 533
para.99 ... 533, 543
para.102 I ... 537
para.103 ... 537
para.106 ... 543, 546
para.111 ... 543
para.112 ... 543
para.113 ... 543
para.130 ... 543

Works Constitution Reform Act 530–1, 542

Works Councils Act 523, 541

Youth Employment Protection Act (JArbSchG) 538

European Legislation

Cigarette Packet Warnings Directive (1989) ... 47

Consumer Sale Contracts Directive (99/44) ... 429

Environmental Impact Assessment Directive (85/337) ... 287

Environmental Information Directive (90/313) ... 290

Equal Treatment Directive (76/207) ... 221–2

Jurisdiction Regulation 2001/44 ... 127

Lawyers (Provision of Services) Directive 77/249 ... 104

Lead in Air Directive (80/779) ... 252–3

Mutual Recognition of Diplomas Directive 89/48 ... 104

Package Tour Directive ... 284

Product Liability Directive ... 284

Single European Act ... 49

Television Broadcasting Directive (89/552) ... 48, 54

Transfer of Undertakings Directive (77/187) ... 534

Working Time Directive (93/104) ... 538

ABBREVIATIONS

AbfG	Abfallgesetz	Waste Act
AbwAG	Abwasserabgabegesetz	Waste Water Charges Act
a.d.	anno domini	in the year of our Lord
AG	Aktiengesellschaft	Public Company / Stock Corporation
AGBG	Allgemeine Geschäftsbedingungengesetz	General Conditions of Business Act
AFG	Arbeitsförderungsgesetz	Promotion of Employment Act
AGG	Arbeitsgerichtsgesetz	Labour Courts Act
AktG	Aktiengesetz	Joint Stock Corporation Act
AnwBl	Anwaltsblatt	
ArbGG	Arbeitsgerichtsgesetz	Labour Courts Act
AOK	Allgemeine Ortskrankenkassen	Health Insurance Offices
ArbZG	Arbeitszeitgesetz	Working Time Act
AtG	Atomgesetz	Nuclear Substances Act
AuslG	Ausländergesetz	Law on Foreigners
AVG	Angestelltenversicherungsgesetz	Employees Insurance Act
BAföG	Bundesausbildungsförderungsgesetz	Educational Grants Act
BAG	Bundesarbeitsgericht	Federal Labour Court
BAGE	Entscheidungen des Bundesarbeitsgerichts	Decisions of the Federal Labour Court
BauGB	Baugesetzbuch	Building Code
BayObLG	Bayerisches Oberstes Landesgericht	Bavarian Supreme Court
BDA	Bundesvereinigung der deutschen Arbeitgeberverbände	Confederation of German Employers
Bd	Band	Volume
BerHG	Beratungshilfegesetz	Legal Advice Act
BetrVG	Betriebsverfassungsgesetz	Works Constitution Act
BFHE	Entscheidungen des Bundesfinanzhofs	Decisions of the Federal Tax Court
BGB	Bürgerliches Gesetzbuch	Civil Code
BGBl	Bundesgesetzblatt	Federal Law Gazette
BGH	Bundesgerichtshof	Federal Court of Justice
BGHSt	Entscheidungen des Bundesgerichtshofes in Strafsachen	Decisions of the Federal Court of Justice in Criminal cases
BGHZ	Entscheidungen des Bundesgerichtshofes in Zivilsachen	Decisions of the Federal Court of Justice in Civil cases
BGSE	Entscheidungen des Bundessozialgerichts	Decisions of the Federal Social Court
BKartA	Bundeskartellamt	Federal Cartel Office
BKGG	Bundeskindergeldgesetz	Federal Child Benefit Act
BImSchG	Bundesimmissionsschutzgesetz	Federal Pollution Protection Act
BMJ	Bundesjustizministerium	Federal Ministry of Justice
BNatSchG	Bundesnaturschutzgesetz	Federal Nature Conservation Act
BNotO	Bundesnotarordnung	Federal Notary Act
BRAGO	Bundesrechtsanwaltsgebührenordnung	Federal Statute on Attorney's Fees
BRAK	Bundesrechtsanwaltskammer	Federal Chamber of Attorneys
BRAO	Bundesrechtsanwaltsordnung	Federal Statute on Attorneys
BSHG	Bundessozialhilfegesetz	Federal Social Welfare Act
BtMG	Betäubungsmittelgesetz	Drug Act
BVerfG	Bundesverfassungsgericht	Federal Constitutional Court

BVerfGE	Entscheidungen des Bundesverfassungsgerichts	Decisions of the Federal Constitutional Court
BVerfGG	Bundesverfassungsgerichtsgesetz	Federal Constitutional Court Act
BVerwG	Bundesverwaltungsgericht	Federal Administrative Court
BVerwGE	Entscheidungen des Bundesverwaltungsgericht	Decisions of the Federal Administrative Court
BWahlG	Bundeswahlgesetz	Federal Elections Act
CDU	Christlich Demokratische Union	Christian Democrat Party
ChemG	Chemikaliengesetz	Chemicals Act
CSU	Christlich Soziale Union	Christian Social Party
DAG	Deutsche Angestelltengewerkschaft	German Office Workers Union
DAV	Deutscher Anwaltsverein	German Association of Attorneys.
DB	Der Betrieb	
DDR	Deutsche Demokratische Republik	German Democratic Republic
DGB	Deutscher Gewerkschaftsbund	German Confederation of Trade Unions
DKP	Deutsche Kommunistische Partei	German Communist Party
DRiG	Deutsches Richtergesetz	German Law of the Judiciary
DriZ	Deutsche Richter Zeitung	
EC	European Communities	
ECHR	European Convention for the Protection of Human Rights and Fundamental Freedoms	
ECJ	European Court of Justice	
EG	Europäische Gemeinschaften	The European Communities
EGBGB	Einführungsgesetz zum BGB	Introductory Act to the Civil Code
EheG	Ehegesetz	Marriage Act
EMRK	Europäische Konvention zum Schutze der Menschenrechte und Grundfreiheiten	
EuGRZ	Europäische Grundrechte Zeitschrift	
EuZW	Europäische Zeitschrift für Wirtscahftsrecht	
e.V.	eingetragener Verein	Registered association
EVO	Eisenbahnverkehrsordnung	Railways Regulation
FAO	Fachanwaltsordnung	Specialist Lawyers Act
FDP	Freie Demokratische Partei	Liberal Democrats
FernAbG	Fernabsatzgesetz	Distance Sales Act
FGG	Freiwilligengerichtsbarkeitsgesetz	Non-contentious Jurisdiction Act
FGO	Finanzgerichtsordnung	Revenue Courts Act
GaststättenG	Gaststätten Gesetz	Public House Licencing Act
GBl	Gesetzblatt	Law Gazette
GBO	Grundbuchordnung	Land Register Act
GDR	German Democratic Republic	
GewO	Gewerbeordnung	Trade Act
GeschOBT	Geschäftsordnung des Bundestages	Standing Orders of the Bundestag
GG	Grundgesetz	Basic Law / Constitution
GKG	Gerichtskostengesetz	Court Fees Act
GmbH	Gesellschaft mit beschänkter Haftung	Limited Liability Company
GmbHG	Gesellschaft mit beschänkter Haftung Gesetz	Limited Liability Companies Act

GVG	Gerichtsverfassungsgesetz	Organization of the Courts Act
GWB	Gesetz gegen Wettbewerbsbeschränkungen	Act against Restraints of Competition
HaustürWG/ HwiG	Haustürwiderrufsgesetz	Doorstep Sales Act
HGB	Handelsgesetzbuch	Commercial Code
HRG	Hochschulrahmensgesetz	University Framework Act
ILO	International Labour Organisation	
JA	Juristische Arbeitsblätter	
JAG	Juristenausbildunggesetz	Legal Training Law
JAPO	Juristische Ausbildungs- und Prüfungsordnung	Legal Training and Examinations Regulation
JGG	Jugendgerichtsgesetz	Juvenile Courts Act
JR	Juristische Rundschau	
Jura	Juristische Ausbildung	
JuS	Juristische Schuling	
JZ	Juristen Zeitung	
KG	Kommanditgesellschaft	Limited Partnership
KGaA	Kommanditgesellschaft auf Aktien	Partnership limited by shares
KostO	Kostenordnung	Fees Act
KPD	Kommunistische Partei Deutschlands	Communist Party of Germany
KSchG	Kündigungsschutzgesetz	Protection from Dismissal Act
LG	Landgericht	Regional Court
LMBG	Lebensmittel- und Bedarfsgegenständegesetz	Food and Consumer Goods Act
LwVG	Landwirtschaftsverfahren Gesetz	Agricultural Disputes Procedural Act
MDR	Monatsschrift für deutsches Recht	
MHG	Miethöhegesetz	Rent Act
MitbestG	Mitbestimmungsgesetz	Co-determination Act
MuSchG	Mutterschutzgesetz	Protection of Working Mothers Act
NATO	North Atlantic Treaty Organisation	
NJW	Neue Juristische Wochenschrift	
NPD	Nationaldemokratische Partei Deutschlands	National Democratic Party of Germany
NSDAP	National Sozialistische Deutsche Arbeiter Partei	National Socialist German Workers Party
NZtS	Neue Zeitschrift für Strafrecht	
OG	Ozongesetz	Ozone Act
OHG	Offene Handelsgesellschaft	General Partnership
OLG	Oberlandesgericht	Regional Appeal Court
ParteienG	Parteiengesetz	Political Parties Act
PartGG	Partnerschaftgesellschaftsgesetz	Partnership Company Act
PatG	Patentgesetz	Patent Act
PKHG	Gesetz über Prozesskostenhilfe	Law on Legal Aid
ProdHaftG	Produkthaftungsgesetz	Product Liability Act
RAF	Rote Armee Faktion	Red Army
RabattG	Rabattgesetz	Rebate Act

RBerG	Rechtsberatungsgesetz	Legal Advice Act
RG	Reichsgericht	Supreme Court of the German Reich
RGBl	Reichsgesetzblatt	Statute book of the German Reich
RGSt	Entscheidungen des Reichsgerichts in Strafsachen	Decisions of the Supreme Court of the German Reich in criminal cases.
RGZ	Entscheidungen des Reichsgerichts in Zivilsachen	Decisions of the Supreme Court of the German Reich in civil cases
RPflG	Rechtspflegergesetz	Legal Services Act
RVO	Reichsversicherungsordnung	Imperial Insurance Code
SchwBG	Schwerbehindertengesetz	Disabled Persons Act
SGB	Sozialgesetzbuch	Social Law Code
SGG	Sozialgerichtsgesetz	Social Courts Act
SPD	Sozialistische Partei Deutschland	Social Democrat Party
SprAuG	Sprecherausschußgesetz	Managerial Employees Comittee Act
SRP	Sozialistische Reichspartei	Socialist Imperial Party
StAG	Staatsangehörigkeitsgesetz	Nationality Act
StGB	Strafgesetzbuch	Criminal Code
StPO	Strafprozessordnung	Criminal Procedure Code
StrSchG	Strahlensschutzverordnung	Radiation Protection Regulation
StVG	Strassenverkehrsgesetz	Road Traffic Act
StVollzG	Strafvollzugsgesetz	Criminal Sentence Enforcement Act
TEU	Treaty on European Union	
TVG	Tarifvertragsgesetz	Collective Agreements Act
TzBfG	Teilzeit- und Befristungsgesetz	Part time and Fixed Term Contracts Act
UIG	Umweltinformationgesetz	Environmental Information Act
ULA	Union Leitender Angestellte	Union of Managerial Employees
UmweltHG	Umwelthaftungsgestz	Environmental Liability Act
UmwG	Umwandlungsgesetz	Transformation Act
UrhG	Urhebergesetz	Copyright Act
UVPG	Umweltverträglichkeitsprüfungsgesetz	Environmental Impact Assessment Act
UWG	Gesetz gegen den unlauteren Wettbewerb	Unfair Competition Act
VAG	Versicherungsaufsichtsgesetz	Insurance Supervision Act
VerbrKrG	Verbraucherkreditgesetz	Consumer Credit Act
VerpackV	Verpackungsverordnung	Packaging Act
VersG	Versammlungsgesetz	Public Meetings Act
VVaG	Versicherungsvereine auf Gegenseitigkeit	Insurance associations
VVG	Versicherungsvertragsgesetz	Insurance Contracts Act
VwGO	Verwaltungsgerichtsordnung	Administrative Courts Act
VwVfG	Verwaltungsverfahrensgesetz	Law of Administrative Procedure
VwVG	Verwaltungsvollstreckungsgesetz	Administrative Judgments Enforcement Act
WEG	Wohnungseigentumsgesetz	Condominium Act
WHG	Wasserhaushaltsgesetz	Water Management Act
WoGG	Wohngeldgesetz	Housing Benefit Act
WRV	Weimarer Reichsverfassung	Constitution of the Weimar Republic
WV	Weimarer Verfassung	Constitution of the Weimar Republic
ZPO	Zivilprozessordnung	Civil Procedure Code
ZRP	Zeitung für Rechtspolitik	

ZSEG	Gesetz über die Entschädigung von Zeugen und Sachverständigen	Witnesses and Experts Costs Act
ZDF	Zweites Deutsche Fernsehen	Second German Television Channel
ZVS	Die Zentralstelle für die Vergabe von Studienplätzen	Central Admissions Office for the distribution of University places

PART I

Introduction to the German Legal System

1 Introduction

This section is intended to provide a concise introduction to the nature of the legal system and laws in Germany and to highlight their distinctive features.

2 Historical influences

The distinctive features of the German legal system arise in large part from the relatively comprehensive and rapid assimilation of Roman principles of law in the middle ages, the codification of the nineteenth century, in part influenced by codification in France, and more recently the changes introduced as a result of the restructuring of Germany following the Second World War. At the turn of the last century it was true to say that a vast difference existed between the German and English legal systems. For a number of reasons these systems are now coming closer together. This is in part due to the increasing importance of case law in Germany, the consolidation of statute in the UK and the membership of both countries of the European Union.

3 The classification as a civil law country

The German legal system belongs to the central European family of legal systems, broadly classified as civil law countries. German law contrasts, at least in theory and in basic principles, quite strongly with the UK legal system.

The term 'civil law country' is not a very useful term but unfortunately is in widespread usage. One of its basic features is that a country which has adopted the civil law tradition will usually have as the core of its legal system five codes, normally including civil law in the roman law definition, criminal law, civil procedural law, criminal procedural law, and commercial law. This is in fact just what the German legal system has, although it is adding to these. The Germanic type of legal system, which includes German, Austrian, and Swiss legal systems, has influenced, to a large extent, Turkish, Greek, Japanese, and Brazilian law amongst others, and more recently the former eastern bloc countries such as the Czech Republic.

4 The division of public and civil (private) law

The term 'civil law' is also used to describe a particular division of law. Despite the fact that all German laws, at least in theory, have an equitable status within a unified system of law, the German legal system has been influenced by the roman legal system division between civil and public law. Criminal law is sometimes also accredited as being a separate division on its own but because it is provided and upheld solely by the state, to whom citizens must answer for breaches of criminal law, it must be regarded as a specialized part of public law.

Public law is concerned with the legal relationships between the citizen and the state, or the manifestations of the state in the form of public authorities. Most of the public law actions take place in the administrative courts.

Civil law (*Privatrecht*) contains the concentration of legal principles concerned with the regulation of civil life, i.e. the affairs between individuals as private individuals. Transactions undertaken between a public body and an individual which concern civil law are governed by civil law and not public law rules. The classical roman formulation of civil law includes the laws of obligations (contact and tort), succession, family law, and property law, but has been extended in the modern setting to further include commercial law, company law, and labour law. Labour law has, however, been subject to such considerable state influence, and now contains extensive public law elements, that it is difficult strictly to regard it as civil law any longer.

The division would have been more distinct in the past. The greater power of the state inherent in public law is a major reason for the distinction between public and private law. Public law was as a result more rigid and insisted on a stricter relationship of rights between the state and the citizen. Civil law, concerned with equals, could afford to be based on much more flexible foundations and was left very much to the parties to determine exactly how their relations should be governed. This greater emphasis on the classification or division into private and public law subject areas had and still has an influence on the organization of the courts, the form and style of legal education and, to some extent, on the legal professions of Germany but no great effect on the law itself and how it is applied in individual circumstances.

Areas of law within public law are primarily constitutional law and administrative law and, amongst others, criminal law, procedural law (applicable in both public and civil jurisdictions), international law, law governing the public authorities, courts and public professions, social law, electoral and political parties law, and revenue law. As the concern and the influence are manifested in ever more regulation, the boundaries and intervention of the state in areas of law becomes ever more great. This is resulting (and will continue to result) in the erosion of the reasonably clear boundaries between civil and public law seen in the past. The clearest example of this can be observed in the birth and development of the law of economic administration (*Wirtschaftsverwaltungsrecht*) which is entirely concerned with the state's intervention in the economy and thus the civil and commercial affairs of individuals. This hybrid area of law will without doubt grow as exampled by environmental law. Environmental law is another area of law which although having its roots firmly in public law, nevertheless has significant impact on civil law relations. An example of a similar development but coming from the opposite direction would be consumer law, essentially and indeed still a civil law development, but which is now subject to increasing state and international legislative intervention.

5 Code and statute-based law

The high degree to which German laws are contained in codifications and in statutory form originally distinguished them from the UK system with its predominant base in common law. This has allowed the description of a 'written law country' to be applied. A number of major codes exist, most notably the civil and criminal codes amongst the original five, but the process of codification continues. Codification is more than simple assimilation or compilation or, as in the UK, the consolidation of a number of statutes in particular areas of law. It is the presentation of these laws in a complete and systematic form, free from contradiction and complete with general and specific principles. The very many statutes and case decisions that exist in a particular area of law are completely reviewed, and the general principles that exist are filtered out and presented at the beginning of the code with the specific rules in following books of the code. The style of codified law differs greatly from UK law. It is an attempt to present an area of law as a unified whole, to contain not only the specific rules but also the general and abstract rules and principles which apply to all of the specific circumstances. Thus in the German legal system the codes contain what at first seem to be vague legal concepts but which can be applied to new legal problems to achieve a result. The codes can be used to interpret everyday problems and agreements without the need for going into great detail in the agreements themselves. To a limited extent, codification continues with, further additions to the social law code and various proposals, although as yet, no firm action for the codification of environmental and labour law.

6 Sources of law

Only two sources of law are formally recognized in the German legal system—statute and customary law—although other influences do without doubt have an impact.

6.1 Statute (*Gesetz*)

Statute, translated above as *Gesetz*, as a source of law includes the German Constitution of the present Republic; the *Grundgesetz*,[1] the comprehensive codes and amending or additional individual statutes of both the Federation (*Bund*) and individual states (*Länder*): *Gesetz* in a wider sense may further encompass legal acts, which could be equated to the term 'secondary legislation', of the Federation, Ministries of the Federation, *Länder* and other law-making bodies under public law and all of which constitute normative acts in that they are abstract and general. Predominantly these include regulations and bye-laws (*Verordnungen* and *Satzungen*). The internal rules promulgated by the local authorities do not have the force of law or the same status as *Gesetz*.[2]

6.2 Custom (*Gewohnheitsrecht*)

This includes all regular and general public practice recognized as binding. There is no strict time requirement for customary law in Germany and it is now a very limited source of new law.

More recent legal developments, although not formally acknowledged as sources of law, must undoubtedly include the case-law of the courts. Another recent influence is the membership of the European Communities. Another equally, if not more, profound influence and source of considerable law is membership of the European Communities. This will be discussed in more detail in Chapter 2.

6.3 The role of the courts, judiciary, and precedence

The courts and case law in the modern German legal system play no formal part as a source of law. In Germany, judges are supposed only to apply law and not to create it. However, this view is increasingly regarded as unrealistic, and the role judges do play is clearly far greater than legal theory permits and is quite extensive as interpreters and developers of law. The German courts need to interpret law, hence there is plenty of scope for judicial creativity and legal development.[3] The judiciary in Germany do, however, clearly play a far more active role in the administration of court proceedings than in the UK.

In theory, precedence in the common-law countries is a strictly applied principle, but in practice the ability to distinguish a case means that precedence can be circumvented when it suits the purposes of the court. In Germany, the theory is that with no system of binding precedence the judges are completely free to decide every case on its merits and not be hindered by previous decisions. In practice

---

[1] The term *Grundgesetz* will be used throughout the text to mean 'Constitution', which words are intended to be synonymous and interchangeable. The term 'basic law' will not be used but will be found in many texts on German law. The reasoning behind this will be found in the section on constitutional law in Chapter 6.

[2] The further meanings of the term *Gesetz* are discussed in Chapter 2.

[3] Judicial law-making (*Richterrecht*) is discussed more fully in Chapter 2.

previous decisions are observed and considered. There are also exceptions to the basic rule that there is no system of *stare decisis* in Germany, as will be seen in the section on judicial law making in Chapter 2. The clearest example is in the case of the decisions of the Federal Constitutional Court (*Bundesverfassungsgericht*: BVerfG) which are binding rules of law. Generally, decisions of higher courts are studied carefully and consistency is maintained wherever possible. Indeed, major or radical changes proposed by the courts to principles of law must be sanctioned by special senates of the Federal Court of Justice. However, courts increasingly pay a great deal of attention to previous decisions, especially those of higher courts. German courts, in contrast to those in the UK, have adopted the practice of giving greater respect to more recent decisions. Additionally, the writings of academics and jurists command considerable persuasive authority, especially if a dominating opinion (*herrschende Meinung*) appears to exist. There is thus a much greater influence of legal theory and private legal research.

FURTHER READING

This section lists books and articles of general concern, some of which may be included in the specialized bibliographies at the end of each section or chapter.

J. Baumann, *Einführung in die Rechtswissenschaft: Rechtssystem und Rechtstechnik*, 8th ed. (1989: C.H. Beck, Munich).

F. Baur and G. Walter, *Einführung in das Recht der Bundesrepublik Deutschland*, 6th ed. (1992: C.H. Beck, Verlag, Munich).

E.J. Cohn, *Manual of German Law*, vols I & II (1968: Institute of Comparative Law).

Droste, Killius and Triebel, *Business Law Guide to Germany*, 3rd ed. (1991: CCH Editions, Bicester).

W. Ebke and M. Finkin (eds.), *Introduction to German Law* (1996: Kluwer, The Hague).

Freckmann and T. Wegerich, *The German Legal System* (1999: Sweet & Maxwell, London).

Horn, Kötz and Leser, *German Private and Commercial Law* (1982: Clarendon Press, Oxford).

A. T. von Mehren and J. R. Gordley, *The Civil Law System: An Introduction to the Comparative Study of Law*, 2nd ed. (1977: Little, Brown and Company, Boston).

J.H. Merryman, *The Civil Law Tradition: An Introduction to the Legal Systems of Western Europe and Latin America*, 2nd ed. (1985: Stanford University Press, Stanford, California).

O. Model & C. Creifelds, *Staatsburger Taschenbuch*, 30th ed. (2000: C.H. Beck, Munich).

G. Robbers, *Einführung in das deutsche Recht*, 2nd ed. (1998: Nomos Verlag, Baden-Baden).

G. Robbers (Translated by M. Jewell), *An Introduction to German Law* (1998: Nomos Verlag, Baden-Baden).

I. Sartorius (ed.), *Verfassungs- und Verwaltungsgesetze der Bundesrepublik* (C.H. Beck, Munich).

H. Schönfelder (ed.), *Deutsche Gesetze: Sammlung des Zivil-, Straf- und Verfahrensrechts* (C.H. Beck, Munich).

H. Simon and G. Funk-Baker, *Einführung in die deutsche Rechtssprache* (1999: C.H. Beck, Munich).

1

German legal history and legal development

1 Introduction

This chapter covers the principal developments in German legal history. In essence this history spans the transition from an unwritten, *ad hoc* and localized dispute settlement to a formal, largely codified, and highly organized and prescribed system for the administration of justice. As a result, Germany, or the constituent and varying German states through the centuries has evolved one of the most codified legal systems in the world.

The most outstanding feature of this history is the comprehensive adoption of roman law and canon law in the late-middle ages in preference to the indigenous Germanic and largely customary laws. Other important features are the systematic organization of many areas of German law into general and specific rules, the organization of state, government, and the courts, and the changes imposed on them and the legal system in the aftermath of each of the two world wars. The status of legislation has emerged as paramount to the almost total exclusion of other formal sources of law. European Community law must, however, be acknowledged as an extremely important and growing present day source of law.

2 Early developments

The first records of Germanic laws arise from the observations of the Roman authors, notably Caesar and from the *Germania* of Tacitus, otherwise there is little evidence. Germanic culture was spoken rather than written, as were the language and customary law. The oldest reported written German is alleged to be the *Abrogans*, a Germanic-Latin dictionary from AD 770. As a result of the migratory nature of the Germanic tribes, there was no fixed or united homeland—so much so, that some authors regard it as too much of an unnecessary abstraction to try to speak of a single Germanic law or people, while others approach German legal history from the angle of the observation of the Germanic people's constant search for a German identity, homeland, and the laws to reflect that. The prevailing social structure was very hierarchical, at the apex of which were the kings and princes, through various levels of nobleman to the freemen and slaves.

The type of law employed by the tribes was a form of customary law, and this simple unwritten law was communally established in a democratic manner by a general open air assembly (*Volksversammlung*) of the freemen of the tribe approving, as the occasion demanded, customary rules. Legal proceedings were based on the same assembly, described as either a *Thing*, *Ding* or a *Gau* depending on the particular tribe and matter at trial, but little other formal organization of the administration of justice seems to have taken place. The law was based on the collective of persons as the originator of rules rather than individual rights or laws based on a particular area or property. Courts were established only when needed and the leader of the tribe, by whatever title, was usually the spokesman who expressed the finding of the assembly. Developments to this form of dispute resolution included the setting aside of a particular day or days on a regular basis to resolve disputes, for example at the time of full or new moon. However, this is not to say that there was a universal pattern throughout the Germanic tribes for dispute resolution, and many variations existed with varying levels of democratic participation.

3 The *Fränkisch-deutsche Reich*

This period, later titled the Salic Frank period (*Fränkische Zeit* or the *Fränkisch-deutsche Reich*), covers the era of the southern and western movement of the various Germanic tribes, in particular the Franks. This migration had started from northern Germany many centuries previously but was far more noticeable in the second to fifth centuries AD when lands occupied by the Romans were acquired. The most notable date in this movement is the fall of the western arm of the Roman Empire to the Germanic tribes in AD 476.

The migrating tribes were for the most part settlers, rather than invaders and destroyers of Roman cities. There were, of course, many conflicts and battles with the receding Roman legions, but the period did not witness the complete rout of civilisation, as sometimes popularly depicted. These settlers brought with them their own customary rules and informal system of legal administration as they moved south.

The regions in which they settled were largely inhabited by Roman citizens or those who were previously under rule from Rome and used roman law. Each of the settling tribes continued to apply their own customary laws, the Salic Frank kingdom being subject to Salic customs, the Burgundian kingdom to Burgundian customs. These ethnic customs were not imposed on the Roman or Gallo-Roman inhabitants of the various kingdoms. Instead, the tribes usually allowed roman law to be retained for the use of the local native populace and Roman citizens, at least in respect of private law matters, whereas Germanic customary law was retained for the settled conquerors. In other instances a mix of roman law and their own customary law would take place or provisions of roman law might be applied directly, particularly some of the procedural rules and especially in the area of criminal law. Many of the tribes had been converted to Christianity and had, to a limited extent, incorporated within their customary law, laws of the church which were based on canon and roman law. There was, however, no overall fixed pattern of legal system equally applicable or body of laws applicable throughout the whole, or even parts, of the areas of Germanic domination.

The example of the written roman law seems to have prompted some of the barbarian rulers to write down their own customary laws to clarify them or to ensure the survival of their own customs against the roman law, e.g., the Visigoth customs (*Codex Euricianus*) by Euric the West Goth in AD 480. The Salic laws (*lex salica*) were thus codified during the reign of Clovis (482–511), the Burgundian customs (*lex barbara burgundionum*) by Gundobad (474–516), and the Edict of Theodoric the Ostrogoth (*edictum theodorici*). Such codified Germanic law was not, however, superior to the remaining unwritten customary law of the Germanic nations. As a counter to preserve the rules applicable to the Roman and Gallo-Roman population, there were also codifications of the law applying to these subjects, which included amongst others the Burgundians (*lex romana burgundionum*) and the Visigoths (*lex romana visigothorum* (also known as Breviary of Alaric), drawn up by Alaric II in 506); the latter was in time recognized as applying to all Gallo-Romans, and indeed proved to be the major source of roman law until the late-eleventh century.

The term *lex* (law), used in conjunction with the written customary laws, is not equivalent to legislation in the modern sense. Germanic custom did not recognise the power of the king to legislate without the approval of the assembly. The *lex salica* was not promulgated by a royal ordinance of King Clovis but, as with all the forms of the customary law, was approved at the assemblies by the Salic Frank freemen.

Germanic law clearly incorporated the personal principle of law, which meant that a member of the particular tribe was subject to the customary law of his ethnic group of origin. There was no territorial aspect to this law and if the tribe settled elsewhere, the established inhabitants of the new homeland would not then be subject to the occupiers' customary law. Only specifically recognised strangers would be subject to the tribal law. Hence in the occupied lands more than one system of law could apply to the inhabitants.[1]

In the case of conflict between the laws of different tribes and the Germanic and roman laws, the personal law of both parties would be given effect wherever possible. However, if the personal rules had been introduced but had led to conflict, then the law could be chosen, if acceptable to both parties. Otherwise an overriding principle that the dominating interest should prevail came into play. The dominating interest was determined by the nature of the contract and the strength of the

---

[1] A full treatment of the principle of the personality of law is given by Guterman, noted in 'Further reading' below.

parties involved. It was always applied in favour of the weaker party. It could be applied according to the clause in question and a contract could have different laws applying to different clauses. The personal rule or principle of law was, however, progressively abandoned as the various ethnic groups (and hence their customs) became intermingled through marriage and migration. An exception was canon or ecclesiastical law, common to both and was given priority because of the power and strength of the church in this period, which enjoyed a virtual monopoly over education, particularly legal education which was almost entirely based on roman law.

There is greater knowledge of the development of law in the regions in which the Germanic tribes settled than in the original lands from which they came because these developments were recorded in writing. Much of this stemmed from the fact that many transactions between Roman and Germanic subjects were subject to the superior procedural recording by the Roman notary, regardless of which law applied. Hence the influence of Roman procedural law was very great due to the absence of such qualified Germanic scribes. In the original homelands or territories the tribes continued to use their own unwritten customary laws. These were subject to only limited influence from principles of roman law and mixed Romano-Germanic law which occurred under the influence of the church.

4 Charlemagne

By reason of fratricide and alliances, the Merovingian dynasty of the Franks was succeeded by the Carolingian dynasty, which led to the re-establishment of the Western Roman Empire with the papal recognition and coronation by Pope Leo III in AD 800 of Charles the Great (Charlemagne) as Emperor of the Romans, and thus the origin for the establishment of the Holy Roman Empire was achieved.

During his reign, Charlemagne was able to benefit from the gradual strengthening of the power and influence of the kings in the Merovingian dynasty. He sought to establish his imperial authority by promulgating edicts (*Kapitularen*) in an attempt to regulate affairs on an equal footing for the whole of the empire which purported to apply to all subjects of the empire, regardless of their ethnic origin. He relied on the Roman emperors' right to legislate and attempted the reformation of the existing law by trying to reduce to writing the customary laws of the various regions and tribes. This attempt to unify law in the empire led inevitably to conflicts of law. Imperial laws enacted by the Emperor were to prevail, but as they were largely based on roman and canon law they conflicted with Germanic law. While Charlemagne lived his personal power was strong enough to ensure priority in matters of general application—in other words, to try to impose a territorial law over the principle of personality of law. This was not always the case due to the very well-established principle of the personality of law, and it was necessary for Charlemagne to allow the priority of personal law to continue and for the tribes to keep priority of law in their own matters. This endeavour to re-establish imperial power after the Roman model did not last long. Charlemagne's success was limited and achieved no lasting effect, primarily due to the lack of continuity of imperial policy by those emperors who succeeded him. The attempt at this stage to unite the peoples of the Empire under one rule of law had failed. The unity of the empire could not be maintained, and following the death of Charlemagne and the death of Louis the Pious, his son, it was formally brought to an end in AD 843 when the Treaty of Verdun divided the Empire, under the prevailing customary law of split inheritance (*Pflichtteilsrecht* or *Erbteilung*) into three parts. (This particular law has been a thorn in the side of legal development in Germany even with the drafting of the Civil Code in the late-nineteenth century.) The separate kingdoms were ruled by different kings (the grandsons of Charlemagne). They were *Francia Occidentalis* (roughly equivalent to the western part of modern France, excluding Britanny, but including part of Belgium, Pamplona and Catalonia); *Germania*, also referred to as East Franconia (modern Germany); and *Lotharingia* (Benelux, Provence, and Lombardy).

Legal development following this period was fragmented, and there was more emphasis on the tribal and regional distinctions. The emperors ruled a federation of areas or realms rather than a united realm. The imperial rule that had previously taken place had established one broad principle which was to some extent retained as Germany, and Europe generally, drifted into feudalism. This principle was that laws could be made at a central or higher level and be imposed on the citizens rather than be made by the populace itself. Although this had no direct or lasting effect at the imperial level, it was the recognized basis of feudal power in that local and regional rulers could become the source of law rather than people themselves. Thus the law-making assemblies disappeared from the legal horizon and a shift from law of the people to law over the people took place.

The Carolingian emperors found themselves unable to exercise effective authority over the empire and increasingly, in order to preserve any semblance of unity, had to abdicate real power and control over the regions to the counts and dukes and other noblemen who defended territories from the invading incursions from the north and east. Imperial rule was forced to give way to a resurgence of the old Germanic groupings, where allegiance was given primarily to the ethnic group.

5 The middle- to late-middle ages

The transition of East Franconia to the German Reich began in AD 911 after the demise of the Carolingian dynasty. From the tenth century it was established as the Holy Roman Empire[2] and much later becoming established as the Holy Roman Empire of the German Nation. It was not a smooth or straightforward progression,

---

[2] The formal beginning of the Holy Roman Empire is attributed to the reigns of both Heinrich I in 919 and Otto I in 962, see the histories cited in further reading at the end of the chapter.

and this period between AD 900 and 1300 witnessed severe and often violent changes in the fortunes of the imperial rule in terms of the power and authority of the Germanic kings and emperors, especially in their relations with the prince electors (*Kurfürsten*) and the church. Although there was a period of relative stability in which the kings of the empire had been able to exert at least enough authority to hold the empire together as a federation of states, the investiture contest with the Catholic Church led to extremely serious repercussions from which the empire was not able to recover for a very long time. From the eleventh century, the unity of the empire was in decline, in contrast with the position in Britain where a single ruler reigned over a united realm and centralized government was able to increase its strength and influence throughout the whole nation. In Germany, instead of a national attempt to develop a centrally organized legal system, the only significant legal developments taking place were of local law in the form of customary and feudal laws. This allowed a strong diversity of local customary law to develop, as most of the attention given to law was at the local rather than the national or federal level. The limited centralizing influence that roman law had previously had, was simply never established strongly enough to have any long-lasting influence outside of that in the church. The increasing attention paid to the task of establishing the empire in the eyes of the church and the lack of a clear and regular succession based in one city or town or area were the main reasons for the failure to establish a fixed capital where a central administration or legal centre could be established.

Local customary laws, outside of those collections previously mentioned, remained largely unwritten but retained a status equal to and often greater than that of the written law. Regional laws became more important than the imperial law and, correspondingly, as the tribes established themselves in particular areas, territorial law rather than personal law became the applicable law in cases of conflict, i.e. the law of where a person was, rather than the law of the migrating ethnic group. There was still a limited unifying influence on the content of local laws by the church which, because of its power, could withhold its approval if the local laws offended church law.

Customary law in this period was largely administered and developed by the law-finders (*Schöffen*) who determined what the law was from the inherited body of law of the ethnic group. They did not actually pronounce the judgment; that task fell to the judge who was usually, as in the past, the local lord. The decisions reached sought to render justice in the particular case rather than attempting to develop general and rational principles of law. The nature of Germanic customary law meant it was often known only to the law-finders. At first these law-finders were chosen from the freemen on a case to case basis, or were asked to act on the regular basis of the meeting of the assembly. In the developing towns their services were increasingly required on a permanent basis, and specific individuals were called upon time and again to decide cases. This led to long-term and eventually life appointments, usually of prominent local merchants or those connected with the local ruler and who had some local land holding.

In the towns and in commercial matters other independent legal developments were taking place, influenced by the volume of trade in Europe at the time, including that of the law merchant, the maritime and commercial rules, and special laws for the towns and fairs. The various forms of commercial laws all had their own, more advanced forms of courts, arbitrators and administrators which had developed independently of other local and regional legal judicial and administrative developments. These specific laws took precedence over the local law, which in turn prevailed over more general customary laws. The more specialized or localized the law, the greater the priority it had. This is the free translation of legal sayings of the time, two examples of which are: '*Stadrecht bricht Landrecht, Landrecht bricht allgemeines Recht*' and '*Willkür bricht Stadtrecht, Stadtrecht Landrecht, Landrecht Reichsrecht*'. Other similar examples exist and continue to this day, such as the rule that specialist rules apply first, in the absence of which general rules must be sought. See also Chapter 2 and statutory interpretation. Contrast, however, the rule in Art 31 *Grundgesetz*, which gives federal law priority over regional law.

A contemporary legal development, but not yet one influencing the application of laws at the local or court level, was the resurrection of the study of roman law (in particular the Justinian *corpus iuris civilis*, which until then had been unknown in the Western Empire). In the eleventh and twelfth centuries this commenced in the first European universities, primarily at the Pavia Law School which had cultivated the comparative study of Lombardian law and roman law, but principally through the work of the Glossators at Bologna. This beginning, which was to have far-reaching consequences, was itself a remarkable event.[3]

There were, however, in the Germanic regions from the thirteenth century examples of attempts to rationalize or codify the customary and local laws in order to organize their development. The most notable example is the *Sachsenspiegel* of the law-finder Eike von Repgow. This consisted of the fairly comprehensive collection and partial codification of Saxon customary law. It has been argued that this was a deliberate attempt to keep out roman law by providing a viable local alternative, although this assumes that Eike von Repgow had a fairly complete knowledge of what was taking place in the other regions in Germany and the influence that roman law was having or was to have in these places. Other notable examples of early collections and attempts to codify are the *Deutschenspiegel* and the *Schwabenspiegel*. The decisions of the law-finders were often collated into a number of volumes of written records, known under numerous titles, including the *Weistum* (font of knowledge) and the *Systematisches Schöffenrecht* (the systematic laws of the law-finders). The laws of the towns were also issued in written form, often taking their lead from the original grant of power which was given in written form by the regional ruler. For the most part, however, Germanic laws remained unwritten and uncodified.

Following the collapse and fragmentation of the quite loosely controlled Holy

---

[3] For further details see U. Wesel, *Juristische Weltkunde: Eine Einführung in das Recht* (1984: Suhrkamp), pp. 64–5 and A. Laufs, *Rechtsenwicklungen in Deutschland*, 4th ed. (1991: Walter de Gruyter, Berlin), pp. 42–57.

Roman Empire of Germany under Frederick II, a central legal system had little chance to come into existence. Even limited imperial law-making, such as the Statutes of Peace, which were attempts to rein in the anarchy of the time and put a stop to feuding, or the constitutional agreements determining the relative powers between the emperor and the princes, such as the *Goldene Bulle* of 1356, was subject to constant alteration and revision and did not have a normative or lasting effect. The stronger Hapsburg dynasty under Emperor Maximilian I established centralized organs in an attempt to extend central power and influence. The *Kammergericht* of the fifteenth century was concerned with the settlement of disputes between the *Fürsten* and kings and emperors, and its successor, the central Imperial Court of Appeal (*Reichskammergericht*) of 1495 was established following the settlement of Worms to resolve disputes between the prince electors and also between the landed estates and the princes. The *Reichskammergericht*, which used roman and canon law, was rarely used because it would not recognize local customary law and thus was of little use to potential litigants, but it does signify the imperial recognition of roman law as the common German law and thus helped promote its general reception throughout the empire over local laws. The emperor's position was not powerful enough to ensure a compulsion to use its jurisdiction, and its rulings were mostly secret and of little or no use in the territories where local law prevailed. The *Reichstag*, which was also set up at this time, enjoyed little or no effective national power or authority and could legislate only in very few areas of common interest to both the Kaiser and all the prince electors (*Kurfürsten*). The prince electors enjoyed their own sovereign rights over the areas they ruled. Rather than submit dispute settlement to outside courts, they retained the business themselves and disputes could only be settled locally. To support this, the rule that local law took priority applied.

6 Early modern times: renaissance and reformation

This period marks the change from the old to the new world order and roughly covers the existence of the Holy Roman Empire of the German Nation at its zenith. After the enforced abdication of Charles V (1519–1556) the empire was again divided. Reformation and counter-reformation led to the Thirty Years War (1618–1648).

In this period the study of law in the universities was further developed as a discipline in its own right. The remarkable figure of 10,000 law students from all over Europe studying in Bologna in the year 1200 is given.[4] Intense and extensive legal study of the Roman laws led to the production of glossaries on Roman law which were extremely influential and authoritative. This systematic study of roman and canon law was to form the basis of the academic training of would-be

[4] U. Wesel, op. cit., p. 65.

continental lawyers, and would prove to be of importance because it made them willing to refer to roman law concepts when customary law was lacking and firmly established Roman law as the legal subject of study rather than customary law.

The separate development of local and commercial laws continued until about 1500, after which roman law was adopted to a very great and rapid extent in Germany. It filled the gap left by the absence of the central organisation of national law or a national legal system, but was not an organised or planned introduction. The reception occurred for a number of reasons, and Roman law almost completely overwhelmed German customary law. This fairly rapid assimilation of Roman law, although still taking a couple of centuries, is considered below.

6.1 The reception of Roman law into Germany

The reception of Roman law can be introduced by loosely dividing it into two phases: that of the theoretical, which can be considered as providing a form of infrastructure, and that of the practical, providing the superstructure. It must be stated that the divisions are far from watertight.

6.1.1 *The influence of the church*

Roman law had already influenced to a very great extent the cannon law used as ecclesiastical law by the strong and centrally organised church in Germany, and had been applied in the ecclesiastical courts over hundreds of years. These church courts using written Roman procedural, and to a lesser extent substantive, law, provided clear and reasonably certain dispute resolution. They became very popular as a legal forum and their jurisdiction was much wider than purely church or strictly religious matters. If a question concerning a dispute in the law was framed in such a way as to introduce an element of concern to the church, it could then morally and lawfully claim jurisdiction. For example, an offending clause in a contract could be presented as a sinful question for the church court to resolve. This popularity was largely because the legal procedure, based on canon and Roman law, was more certain and attractive to litigants and the church courts commanded a higher authority.

The church's study, understanding and use of roman law was highly developed and was instrumental in making people familiar with Roman law principles and preparing the ground for the later full-scale adoption of Roman law.

6.1.2 *The continuity of the Holy Roman Empire*

German kings and emperors had allowed the indigenous inhabitants of the regions in Italy to continue to use roman law for dispute settlement, and because roman law was favoured by some of the emperors, they decreed that roman law should also apply to the settled Germanic tribes. Some regarded the position of emperor as direct successors to the Imperial Roman Caesars and the German empire as a continuation of the Roman empire, and viewed roman law as the natural choice for imperial law and tended to prefer its use. However, their direct influence was fairly limited due to the paucity of imperial law-making on a level which had any effect for the majority of the citizens. The preference of these emperors constituted a progressive example to the princes and other noblemen rather than any form of direct instruction to adopt roman law.

6.1.3 *The universities*

The tradition of the study of law in the German universities was inherited from the Italian universities where the study of roman law was paramount. Initially this was for religious purposes (canon law), but also because the developed roman law was the prevailing law in Italy. German scholars at first studied at Italian universities, and as they set up or taught in the new German universities in the sixteenth century, roman law was their natural choice. Furthermore, many of the German universities were first set up as theological colleges where canon law, based on roman law, was the basis of legal instruction. Thus all learned scholars in Germany were trained in roman law and not local customary law, regardless of the area of Germany from which they came. Customary law was not regarded as a suitable object of study, or indeed a necessary object of study, because of its very nature as customary law. It was concerned more with everyday rules rather than the broader principles of roman law.

The German universities which were being established, continued to take their lead in legal studies from the longer established Italian universities, partly because of the continuing prestige and partly because the professors were trained in Italy. University study and the revival and concentration of study predominantly of roman law led to the intellectualization of law, whereby lay understanding and application of this law were impossible. This marked a shift to the professionalism of law, and the wider this new law spread the greater the requirement for jurists trained in Latin and roman law.

6.1.4 *The absence of a central legal system*

The influence of the church and the universities, and the continuity of the Holy Roman Empire basically are the theoretical reasons for the adoption of roman law in the German territories. There are, however, practical reasons for its reception too.

The fragmentation of power in Germany resulted in there being no strong central legal system. There was very little imperial law-making having a general effect on all parts of the empire and little in the way of an organized administration of justice. Instead, numerous independent legal developments had taken place, and although there were some written laws and partial codification, laws were, for the most part, uncodified and, at the local level, unwritten.

In contrast to England and Wales, where the strong build-up and development of a national common law could resist, or in fact did not require, roman law, there was less resistance in Germany to the input of new laws. There was no fixed or distinct German capital around which to base an indigenous legal movement or a definitive, and thus effective, imperial or central court. Some emperors had little interest or too many other problems to concern themselves with legal or judicial reform;

others lived in Italy, further undermining any chance to promote national German legal developments.

Classical roman law had, in contrast, already been the subject of considerable refining, codification and gloss, possible in the unitary Roman state and through long application by the church courts and study in the universities.

There was little national resistance to roman law, but the question that needs to be addressed is why the various territories with their own local Germanic customary law adopted roman law. Notably, Saxony, with its *Sachsenspiegel*, was less affected by roman law because a considerable part of its law was written and codified, including, as mentioned, some of the decisions of the law-finders. In the other regions, however, there was little in the way of written Germanic law, and particularly important was the fact that Germanic procedural law differed amongst the regions and was also predominantly unwritten. Inevitably this caused considerable difficulties to parties wishing to plead. Roman procedural law was written and codified and thus easier to plead, and was therefore welcomed by parties to the German courts.

6.1.5 *The unsuitability of customary law to a changing world*

The fragmented local customary law became increasingly unsuitable to commercial development in Germany, and the courts, staffed by the law-finders (*Schöffen*), were not able to cope with the changing conditions or the increasing introduction of roman law.

In trade between two areas or towns, or litigation between parties from two different areas, the question arose of whose law would apply. The parties or the courts in the different areas would often deny the priority or validity of the other's laws. In addition to this, German law was not coping or able to compete with the growing universality of trade laws taking place in Europe; local law priority destroyed any chance of this. Germanic customary law dispute settlement was very uncertain and unsuited to the needs of the time. Decision-making was based on tradition, the applied wisdom and the perceptions of the law-finder of the case in hand. It often lacked rationality and reasoning, and there was no framework to determine the path of German law development. Most decisions were unpublished, and litigants were unable to assess their chances on the basis of past decisions as there was no precedent of past cases to rely on.

Roman law, on the other hand, provided the certainty of a procedural and substantive law framework and adaptability to new circumstances. Many of the developing commercial towns in the fifteenth century saw the benefits of roman law and deliberately worked it into their town law.

6.1.6 *The courts*

In 1495, Emperor Maximilian reformed the Imperial Court (*Reichskammergericht*) to promote certainty in dispute settlement. In order to attract litigants to the court, it first adopted ecclesiastical law and written procedures. As it became increasingly desirable and necessary, roman procedural and substantive law was adopted.

Despite the limited success of this example, in terms of a direct influence on the laws of Germany, the princes in the regions saw the advantages of the reforms adopted by the court. They also favoured the use of canon and roman law in their revised courts, both because of the clear advantages of these laws and their attractiveness to litigants.

The lower regional courts set up by the emperor were required to follow the decisions of the *Reichskammergericht*. These also proved more attractive to litigants than the local courts, which continued to be staffed by the law-finders as opposed to the new professional judges emerging from the universities to staff the emperors' and princes' courts.

These facts worked together to promote the reception of roman law. Due to the high degree of uncertainty, local courts became increasingly less attractive to litigants, who required much more predictable dispute resolution. They turned instead to the ecclesiastical courts. In order to compete with this development, the emperor and the prince electors revised their courts and procedures by reserving business in their areas, denying outside appeal and adopting Roman legal principles and procedure. In order to staff these new courts the authorities had to turn to the universities for trained jurists. These were at first only available from the Italian universities trained in roman law, and later from the fledgling German universities. The demand for jurists promoted further and greater study of roman law in the universities to produce the necessary staff.

As the use of roman law spread in the courts, the practice was adopted in the local courts by the law-finders, who lacked expertise in roman law, of turning to legal advisers or referring to the university professors for legal opinion on points of law or on how to decide cases, known as the *Aktenversendung*. This practice may have led to a further slump in confidence in the local courts and had the effect of further advancing the status of university legal study and opinion. Graduates easily found work in the courts, increasing further the influence of roman law. The law-finders were gradually replaced by a professional judiciary or reduced to the role of a jury. This change is now reflected in the current composition of the judiciary in Germany, i.e. for the most part, professional judges with less use of lay judges. The change also meant that the judiciary became bound by the law, unlike the law-finders who decided what the law was and how it should apply to suit the case in hand.

The enhanced status gained at that time by the doctors of law, university law professors, and generally the German law faculties is still relevant today, in that legal theory and private opinion are highly regarded in the German legal system and in court decision-making. Those who had received a university legal education were much sought after and obtained positions at all levels—judicial and other administration—as remains the case today. The law professors in particular were in high demand to provide legal opinion and also to argue in the courts. This may account for the longer courses in legal instruction which were, and are still, deemed to be necessary in the German universities. The professors were so involved in other duties, legal instruction took second place. The status accorded to the professors can also be observed by considering the rights of appearance and representation accorded university law professors in the courts. This system of referral was viewed as allowing the development of a learned, impartial and rational law, but of roman law and not Germanic customary law, which was pushed into the background and could only be pleaded if proved. As it was mostly unwritten, it was therefore unprovable and viewed as a closed and limited set of rules. Roman law thus had priority, except in Saxony where, as noted above, the presence of the *Sachsenspiegel* enabled the region to resist the input of roman law. As referral increased, the university law faculties published their opinions and decisions and a new common doctrine of law developed, based largely on roman law but with some of the Germanic customary law rules worked in. This was the *usus modernus pandectarum*, which was the modernised or developed roman law not the classical roman law. The universities were thus established in the influential role of producing highly analysed and structured studies of how the law stood.

By the seventeenth century the whole of Germany had become to a greater or lesser extent subject to the reception of roman law, which had overwhelmed Germanic law rather than modified it. What took place later was simply a confirmation and refinement of the process. During the period of reception there had been attempts to codify certain parts of the law on a national basis and a handful of imperial laws had been issued, but these attempts met with very little success. The most notable example was the criminal law codification of Charles V in 1532. Although this particular code was influenced by roman procedural and substantive law principles, it admitted the priority of the criminal laws of the individual states as insisted upon by the prince electors, and therefore was undermined as a national law.

7 Post-medieval developments

This period covers the time from the effective collapse of the Holy Roman Empire of the German Nation in 1648 following the Thirty Years War, up to the establishment of the Second Reich in 1871. The Peace of Westphalia in 1648 included the cession of territories to France and Sweden and the withdrawal of The Netherlands and parts of present-day Switzerland from the German Reich. It left the institutions of the central Reich sovereign, however, in respect of both religious and political matters. This period is noted for the rise in the importance of the individual states to the detriment of the Reich and for the increase in power and influence of particular states, notably Prussia, Austria, and Bavaria.

The formal dissolution of the empire took place in 1815 following the claiming and appropriation of lands by France and the foundation of the Confederation of Rhine States (*Rheinbund*) under Napoleonic protection in 1806. This and the formation of the Federation of German States (*Deutscher Bund*) set the political order of the period with the confirmation of the sovereignty of the individual German states and the real ineffectiveness of the empire. A loose association or Federation of states was formed which only had a weak *Bundestag* as a centralized organ and no central court.

The First Empire effectively had been dissolved by Napoleon, who had imposed the French civil code in those German states under French protection. Even the territorial settlement established by Napoleon was retained by the Federation of German States in 1815.

Thus any moves towards codification at this time are to be seen as untimely in view of the prevailing political situation. However, the influence was nevertheless felt of the imposition of a codified legal system by the French.

7.1 School of Natural Law

One of the prevailing intellectual views in Germany at the time for codification was influenced by the codification that had taken place in France and was taking place in Italy. It was represented by the School of Natural Law and took its lead from the Dutchman Hugo Grotius, and Puffendorf and Leibnitz, two of the most influential exponents of the school in Germany. It was a product of the law faculties of the German universities which had experienced a long unfettered period of criticism and analysis of law.

The basic precept of this school was a study of what law was perceived to be or what it should be, and not, in contrast to the views of the School of Historical Law, law as the historically determined product of civilisation.

Those influenced by this natural school of thought considered how law had been applied in the past and sought to abstract general principles of what law should be, in an attempt to develop reasoned universal or rational laws. This reasoning seemed logically to give rise to the ordering or systemization of the abstracted principles. In other words, the general rules discovered could be seen to make up an orderly an comprehensible system. Although there was no necessity to choose roman law, those principles appeared to natural law scholars as good examples of how natural law principles should be, and thus much of their study concentrated on roman law.

The development of this school of thought also increased the desire to go beyond revision and the systemization of existing law to the creation of comprehensive codes applicable at a practical level.

To a limited extent this age of reason or natural law did lead to some codification of the existing law material. However, prior to the later attempts to codify, this academic or juristic reasoning had limited immediate effect on the overall development of law in Germany. The most notable codifications of this period were the attempts of create codes for the states of Bavaria and Prussia and the codification which took place in Austria. The Prussian code (*Das Allgemeine Landrecht für die preußischen Staaten*) was embarked upon in 1714 but not finalized until 1794. The Bavarian code, which was narrower in scope than the general regional law for the Prussian states, was completed in 1756. Although the impetus for both these codes was provided by the school of natural lawyers and should not have relied so much on roman law, the codes were nevertheless largely based on developed and systemized roman law principles, the *usus modernus pandectarum* as noted above, and as such were criticized by the movement of the German nationalist jurists. They did, however, incorporate some of the more particular rules of Germanic customary law, and they both reflected the requirements of a law of reason in that they were written in German and not Latin. The codes, especially the Prussian code, were also criticized as being too detailed and hence too complex. No interpretation of these very complete statements of legal life was allowed, which meant that there was no room for manoeuvre to suit changing circumstances or times. Despite the criticisms, the Prussian code remained in force, replacing all previous laws in the areas of its application until 1900 when the civil code (BGB) came into force.

Natural law, then, had led towards codification but only on the level of single states. Codification could not realistically be entertained comprehensively until unification of the German states had taken place with a single central organization under a ruler and leaders who also desired legal reform.

One of the main protagonists for codification was Thibaut (1772–1840) who argued the unifying effect of laws which would be common to all the German states and that these should be in the form of a legislative code universally available and understandable to Germans. Ideally, therefore, this should not be too reliant on roman law principles, which historically were established at a time and in conditions quite alien to those relevant to the German states.

Thibaut's ideas were considered as untimely by Savigny (1779–1861)[5] who was the leading member of the Influential Historical School of Law. He argued they did not take into account the reality of the present state of law, or indeed the present state of German politics and state. Prior to unification this was probably a correct view.

7.2 Historical School of Law

The title 'Historical School of Law' is not the most accurate that could be used. 'Historical' could really be read as 'empirical', although followers of this school did undertake the study of historical as well as socially existent law, but nevertheless concentrated their study on roman law. Therefore, this school paradoxically strengthened even further the influence and reception of roman law in Germany, despite its ideals. The two schools were thus not diametrically opposed, which is the popular impression, due to the common history of study in the German universities.

The basic precept of the historical school was the study of the evolutionary jurisprudential development of law as the historically determined product of civilisation and not, in contrast to the views of the natural lawyers, what it was perceived

---

[5] A complete issue of the *American Journal of Comparative Law* has been devoted to the work, writings and influence of Savigny. See Am J Comp L vol. 37, No. 1, Winter 1989, pp. 1–169.

to be. This view is described as that of legal positivism which, presented crudely, is concerned with what the law is and not what it should be, although there has been a great deal of debate as to whether the historical school and legal positivism were academically and theoretically compatible.[6] Hence the argument that the school was in fact misnamed.

Although attention should also have been given to German customary law, the historical school concentrated instead on a study of the classical law of Ancient Rome and the digest or pandect of Justinian, which in turn produced the offshoot Pandectist School. This was subject to the criticism that the development of the German legal system by the importation of classical Roman and Justinian principles divorced legal theory, as perceived in the universities, from the practice in the local courts throughout the German states. It was argued that, as Roman law had been comprehensively received in the German states, it was now in fact part of the tradition of German law and must therefore be accepted as such.

Extensive development of purely Germanic legal principles received little support as they were considered too set in the past; but more to the point, German law lacked influence, especially in law-making. There were no influential lawyers who practised German law, which was mainly limited in its application in the local courts.

Criticisms of the approach of this school were that there was no recognition of the changing political, social or economic climate or the adoption of any principles to take account of this, and that there was an overconcentration on the authority of statute law or on written principles of law. Ironically, the German customary law, which had largely been rejected, was law which was capable of rapid and continual change to suit the circumstances of the time, and indeed of the very case at hand. However, the conceptual jurists in Germany then, as now, were very influential and their views held sway. They were easily able to spread their ideas through the universities, and these concepts of law became established as a common scheme accepted throughout Germany.

The moves to comprehensive codification had now been abandoned. The legal principles finally adopted by the German scholars and jurists were neither purely classical roman law nor the *corpus iuris* of Justinian, but a modern adaptation of Roman law suitable for application in German states.

7.3 **Commerce and unification**

Both schools of thought were influential in evolving German law to the point when the greater part of codification took place. Commercial requirements first dictated the move to legal codification on a national level, and to a limited extent also foresaw a greater demand for national political unity, with common provisions for the Customs Union 1833 (*Zollverein*), the Bills of Exchange Act of 1848 and the General German Commercial Code of 1861. The 1848 revolution and the

---

[6] See John (1989), pp. 84–102.

subsequent National Assembly and constitution were premature evidence of the desire for German unity. The failure to agree put the clock back until Bismarck and the Prussians were able to lead the way with their form of unification.

Codification was desired by Bismarck and supported by the emperor, who regarded it as important, and even central, to the unification of the German states. The creation of the civil code both helped and was helped by moves towards German unification. Following the defeat of France by Prussia in 1870, re-awakening nationalism led again to a desire for German unity, which this time was finally realized. The southern German states joined the confederation of the northern German states and the Second Reich was officially established from 1 January 1871. In reality the new German state was really a mix of a Federation, represented by the various German states in the second chamber (*Bundesrat*), and a unitary state emphasized by the central powers of the emperor (*Kaiser*), the chancellor (*Reichskanzler*) and the *Reichstag*.

Even though the new German constitution was designed as a federal one, central powers of the Reich outweighed those of the *Länder*. The latter were involved in legislation through their participating rights in the *Bundesrat*. These rights however were only few compared to those of the *Reichstag*. Furthermore, due to its population and votes in the *Bundesrat* one of the states played the leading role: Prussia, Supreme executive powers were exerted by the emperor and the Chancellor. The latter was appointed by the emperor without any participation from the democratically elected *Reichtstag*. Finally, it is noteworthy that the constitution of 1871 did not include a catalogue of basic rights. Following the establishment of the new Reich there was considerable legislative activity in order to try to achieve legal as well as political unity. Amongst the most important enactments of the time are the 1871 penal code (*Reichsstrafgesetzbuch*: StGB), the code of criminal procedure (StPO) and the code of civil procedure (ZPO) 1877, the Organisation of the Courts Act (GVG), the Law on Attorneys (BRAO) and the commercial (HGB) and competition (KO) codes of 1879. Much of the theoretical work on the unification of law had already been undertaken in the universities prior to the unification of the German states, which is why so much was achieved in a relatively short space of time. This period also saw, despite the individualism of the time practised by the German states, the first interventions by the Reich on behalf of weaker elements in society, notably the child labour protection laws, and also evidenced by the Imperial Compulsory Liability Act of 1871 (*Reichshaftpflichtgesetz*) which imposed no fault liability for damage on parties in control of sources of danger, notably on the developing railway companies. The most influential legislative action taken by Bismarck was the comprehensive enactment of a social security system (*Sozialversicherungsgesetzgebung*). It was designed to protect against typical risks of modern working environment such as accidents, illness and, disability but also included retirement pensions. Based on equal contributions by employers and employees and the idea of self-administration of the public insurance companies Germany's system of social security has survived until today.

The new Courts Act in 1879 introduced a decentralized system of courts which, was essential because of the federal form of state in the Reich, but it did establish a hierarchy of appeal to the Reich courts. This was an essential preliminary step for the reform and harmonization of law in Germany, in that the necessary procedural provisions were in place so that the unity of Reich law was maintained. At the same time the specialization of the courts was also being achieved by the establishment of a hierarchy of administrative courts, followed by specialist business or industrial courts (*Gewerbegerichte*) to deal with the growing mass of industrial law of the period. These were staffed with lay representatives from employers and employees.

In reforming the courts, a much more formal role was imposed on the legal profession and it assumed a greater importance in this period. The new laws concerning the training of the judiciary and the legal profession, which gave the state the sole right to determine these matters, set the mould which has largely remained to the present day.

Arguably, the single most important development of this time was the new civil code to replace the various applicable laws in the different German regions.

7.4 The civil code (*Bürgerliches Gesetzbuch*: BGB)

Codification involved not only an historical approach, which respected existing local and Germanic interests, but also had regard to the requirements of the legislator and German unification. The latter requirements reflect the change in legal positivism, which was being heavily influenced by nationalist considerations and led to the desire for a reform in the law on the basis of legal nationalism and national sovereignty. The approach also involved a consideration of the jurisprudence of the German courts so that the codes might not become too far removed from the realities of life.

Work began in 1874 on the civil code, and the first draft reflected the prevailing ideology of individualism, popularly reflected in the terms *laissezfaire* or the Manchester Doctrine. The freedom of the individual, expressed as the autonomy of the will, was regarded as paramount and is still regarded as an important concept within the civil code. This concept was pursued to such an extent that the results have become extremely difficult to grasp. The prime example of this is the principle of abstraction (*Abstraktionsprinzip*) which has resulted in a very obtuse application of roman legal principles in civil code paragraphs.

A continuing criticism has been that the provisions of the codes did very little to reflect the social and economic concerns of the day or subsequent changes. Despite the changing economic and political climate throughout Europe in the late-nineteenth century, the drafting largely excluded such considerations.

The style and type of reform which took place left too much to the lawyers' views of how reform and codification should be achieved. The code still depended too heavily on the extremely abstract pandectist roman arrangement of laws and legal principles. The whole idea of preceding the specific rules on obligations with a substantial section containing all the general principles of law pertaining to all forms of obligations, was a reflection of the way civil law had been developed from roman principles and taught in the universities.

Following criticisms of the first draft, a second Commission was formed, drawn from a wider background than the first. Nevertheless, due to the pressures of time it was asked only to redraft the existing draft code. It resulted in little change, due to the disunity of its critics and the fact that the lawyers in the Commission still took the leading role. This was partly because of the obtuseness of the legal style of the code and partly because of the high absenteeism of other members. Furthermore, the Commission's work was prepared by a sub-commission which was part of the Reich's Judicial Office, and there were intense pressures not to spoil the unity of the code which had political consequences for the unity of the Reich. Similar considerations applied when the code came before the *Reichstag* and the *Bundesrat* and resulted in little change to the draft. Thus unity of the code and the unity of the Reich had won the day. After some twenty years' work, the civil code was adopted in 1896 and came into force on 1 January 1900. It remains the basis of German civil law today.[7]

The style of codification has influenced other countries, and the study of German law (especially the civil code) may prove useful in the study of the laws of these other legal systems. It has proved to be a major influence in the following systems: Austria, Switzerland, Hungary, Greece, Japan, Turkey, Brazil, Mexico, and Peru, and once again now in the former communist eastern European countries which have replaced their socialist laws with those based on the German and Austrian legal orders.

How the codes have survived despite their dogmatic style and the criticisms of their extremely limited social conscience, may be considered by a brief review of modern German legal developments.

8 Legal developments in the twentieth century

For the most part, changes and the position of law in the twentieth century are dealt with in the chapters on substantive German law. Consequently, this section will simply provide an overview of the principal influences.

The codification of the nineteenth century largely replaced existing law, although in principle it remained possible for regional variations to persist. The application of the civil code in the courts became the focus of attention as there was a now clearly defined code which the courts were expected simply to apply and not to interpret. The nineteenth century and the early part of the twentieth century saw a massive increase in legislation which served to undermine further the role of customary law.

The universities and professors had less scope for comment because there was less

---

[7] An extremely good study of the whole of the process of the drafting of the civil code (*Bürgerliches Gesetzbuch*) is M. John, noted in 'Further reading'.

need for the courts to refer to them for opinions. When the code was established the universities' role was generally reduced to commenting on the provisions of the code, and they had no further need to engage in the search for general principles as before. In other words simply to provide glosses on the code or the modern day equivalents, the commentaries, which are really quite limited in their scope.

The function of the courts and the judiciary had now been reduced, from the complete freedom of the earliest forms of courts to the simple application of the law and nothing more. This view of the function of the courts and judiciary is one that has prevailed far longer and far more strongly in Germany than in the UK and it is still the current theoretical position. The courts are required to apply the clear principles of law neutrally and not to engage in judicial law-making. However, with such abstract and, at times, rigid codes containing little social conscience, their application had to be subject to further reasoning in order for them to cover novel situations and developments in society. Legislation taking account of the social needs of the time was enacted under the lead of Kaiser Wilhelm II. This included the sickness, accident and disability insurance laws and pension laws of the 1880s and the pension legislation of 1911.

Although the codes are highly technical and fairly extensively detailed, designed to reflect all aspects of legal life as they stood in the mid- to late-nineteenth century, they have proved to be flexible and have been considerably adapted by the courts, to apply them to new situations. Such extensive adaptation has been forced on the courts as a result of the radical changes that have taken place in Germany since the codes were first enacted. It is not just the severity of the changes that is remarkable, but also the number and rapidity of changes that have occurred, including most notably two world wars. The codes have simply had to be adapted to meet the new conditions.

One of the reasons for the willingness to allow changes to the codes is because of the First World War. The individual legal rights established in the BGB had to be curtailed or adapted by the state in many circumstances because of the demands of the state in wartime. These included the restrictions of personal residence, proscription of undesirable organizations, a ban on public assemblies, censorship, and the curtailing and alteration of civil law rights. It became clear both during and after the war that the BGB worked in favour of stronger parties and that there had to be either new laws to protect the weaker parties in society or a more generous application of existing laws. Laws protecting workers' jobs and security benefits were introduced during the First World War.

The political situation in the twentieth century rapidly changed in the aftermath of the First World War. Following the military, political, and constitutional collapse, there was a short-lived parliamentary monarchy, and then the ill-fated parliamentary democracy of the Weimar Republic, which only seemed capable of producing unstable governments—twenty in fourteen years. It attempted to change radically the basis of the German state and government, from the autocracies of the past and heavy reliance on the centralized monarchical state, and to remove the domination of either Prussia or an emperor. Clear principles of republicanism and democracy were laid down in the constitution. The aims of the Weimar Republic were little different from those of the Bonn Republic following the Second World War. Both were formed out of the chaos of defeat in a devastating world war and sought to establish a democratic federal republic guaranteeing rights to prevent war again, and both set up a dualist division of powers in government. However, the new constitutional framework for government under the Weimar Republic marked no radical shift of power from the pre-war forces in Germany. The Western allies actually welcomed this state of affairs, partly because of their fear, in the light of the Russian revolution, of Bolshevism taking hold in Germany—the old forces were preferable to Communism. However, the governments were often too weak, and the opposition both within and outside of Parliament was too strong and too vocal, for stability to be established. The political situation led to consequences which made very heavy demands on the legal system.

The BGB, having been rationalized to meet the demands of the war, was set to be adapted in the future as was deemed necessary. Wider interpretation of laws was required to cope with the many social problems which arose in the 1920s and 1930s. For example, the revaluation of debts in order to offset the unfairness of the hyperinflation of the early 1920s. The civil code had not envisaged a situation whereby a contract might have to be reinterpreted because its demands were unfair in the circumstances of hyperinflation, therefore, in order to offset the unfairness of such contracts, fairly radical decision-making was necessary in the courts. The code itself actually had the means within it, in the form of the general paragraphs (§§ 138, 157) and the most extensively used paragraph requiring good faith (§ 242), to take account of changing circumstances. The general paragraphs allowed the more specific or rigid paragraphs to be neutralised. A change in the attitude of the judiciary to give a wider interpretation to the paragraphs of the code was also required. In doing so the judiciary were able to give judgments to offset the harshness of the contracts (see RGZ 100, 130; 107, 78 and 108, 380). At the time there was much debate as to whether, if indeed a new source of quasi law had been established, it was acceptable. Regardless of the outcome of this discussion, this judge-found law (*Richterrecht*) helped push customary law further into the background.

The period of the Weimar Republic is also notable for its state paternalism, in that the state involved itself further in the relations of individuals. Further reform of the many laws regulating labour relations and the composition of companies was undertaken, including a complete review and setting up of a separate hierarchy of labour courts in 1927 in order to avoid the conflict with the provisions of the BGB in the courts of ordinary jurisdiction. The BGB was based on a liberal philosophy and did not have the presumptions of labour law which was interventionist. In addition, there were many more tax and rent laws enacted to more clearly define the respective rights of the state and individuals, social insurance laws, laws for the protection of young persons, and housing and health laws. All of these, because of the potential clash with the individualist outlook of the BGB, required specialist hierarchies of courts to administer them.

The problems of the Weimar Republic were caused by a number of factors. The constitution required a system of pure proportional representation under Art 17, which led to a fragmentation of party representation and political splinter groups, with up to thirty-five parties represented in the *Reichstag* at one stage. The *Reichstag* could operate only by majority, and had to do so with weak coalition governments more often than not lacking effective or working majorities. In the last fourteen years of the Republic there was never a single party majority. The political vacuum which arose as a result of this situation came to be filled by the President.

The constitution was silent on the form and aims political parties could adopt Consequently, extremely radical and, by present standards, unconstitutional parties could exist, such as the Communist KPD and Nazi NSDAP, whose aims were to overturn the constitutional order. Basic rights were catalogued in Articles 109–165, but were expressed in terms of principles rather than inviolable rights. They were not entrenched, and Article 76 allowed all provisions of the constitution to be changed by a two-thirds majority in both houses of Parliament.

Article 54 provided for votes of no confidence, which often led to the enforced resignation of the Chancellor or cabinet ministers in the event of a lost vote. The government was dissolved frequently as a result of the strong, destructive majority coalitions which voted to bring them down. New governments could be formed only with the support of anti-republican factions. The unstable governmental situation was exacerbated by the problem of the dual executive of the Chancellor and President, both of whom could exercise power. This is regarded as the chief flaw of the constitution. Article 43 provided for the direct election of the President for seven-year periods of office and resulted in the election of the monarchist Hindenburg in 1925 and 1932, whose position was protected under Article 41 by a very limited ability to remove the President.

Article 25 gave the President the power to dissolve the *Reichstag*, and Article 53 provided the power to pick and dismiss Chancellors, both of which were necessary to overcome the frequent dissolutions of Parliament. This led to a strengthening of the role of the President to the detriment of Parliament. Article 42 gave powers of emergency to the President to defend the German people. Of all the powers given, Article 48 was the most far-reaching and eventually subversive. The President could step in to make laws in cases of emergency under Article 48, but only to defend the constitution and constitutional rights. It empowered the President to take any step necessary to restore public security or order. This provision was never properly defined and was therefore open to wide interpretation by the President. He used this power over fifty times in 1932, and in effect supplanted the power and role of the parliamentary legislature. This abuse of Article 48 led to the erosion of checks and balances in government and effectively removed democracy. The provision was supposed to balance extremes but in fact led to them. It has been described as the 'suicide clause' of the Weimar Republic.

There is one other factor which, if different, might have led to another view being formed of the state form of the Weimar Republic. A stable economic period following the war may have allowed political stability. Instead, various economic problems blighted Germany. The depressions of the 1920s and 1930s, the burden of war remuneration repayments and the resultant hyperinflation all added to the economic and political misery experienced by the Germany of the Weimar Republic. Without a stable government to cope with the crises, legislation could in the end only be enacted by the President under Article 48.

The problem of weak minority governments and their inability to get legislation through the *Reichstag* was often circumvented by the request of the Chancellor to the President to enact legislation previously rejected. The problems of the Weimar Republic eventually allowed Hitler's rise, due to paralysis of successive governments.

The rather peculiar circumstances occurring under National Socialism can be dealt with only in passing here, because the changes made to the law in this period mark such a radical departure from otherwise normal legal development. There was no new constitution enacted in the period of Nazi rule but the existing one was substantially reworked or simply ignored; it was still in force in name but was in effect suspended. The basic rights were easy to ignore in cases of conflicting legislation, such as Hitler's Enabling Act of 23 March 1933 (*Ermächtigungsgesetz*) which allowed him to change the constitution at will. Article 1 of this Act allowed the Reich cabinet to enact law and § 2 allowed deviations from the constitution, which included the Communist party ban of 14 July 1933. It is noteworthy that the majority in Parliament (444 members of 647) voted for the 'Enabling Act' including conservative and centre democratic parties. Only the ninety-four social democrats present voted against it. The missing twenty-six Social Democratic and eighty-one Communist members of Parliament were already imprisoned or had left the country. Parliament was thus deprived of authority and a secured Nazi majority ruled. The state assemblies were abolished, and with them federalism. Natural law and basic rights were largely abandoned. On 2 August 1934, the roles of President and Chancellor were combined in the *Führer*.

During the course of the Third Reich, laws were radically changed to suit the Third Reich and to fit in with the far greater centralism of the form of National Socialist state. The Nazi view was that all laws should work in favour of the state and that the *Führer's* law was supreme. Law was conceived now no longer in terms of the rights of the individual but as the rights of the people as determined by the state. Whatever was good for the state was to be achieved, regardless of the right or morals of it. The main changes were in the areas of criminal law, and administrative and constitutional law. Derogations from the civil code, especially in the area of marriage laws, were made in favour of the totalitarian state and the members of the NSDAP (Nazi Party). Remedies in the administrative courts were severely curtailed and judicial process was frequently entirely ignored. In short, where thought desirable, law and justice were perverted to the aims of the Nazi state.

In this respect the judiciary and attorneys were also required to serve the ideals of the state, and had been purged of all elements unsympathetic to the Nazi regime well before the Second World War. The top judicial positions in the Ministries of Justice were then filled with party members. Those who were able to remain in post earned an extremely bad reputation for themselves by the willingness they showed to pervert the cause of justice in favour of the Nazis.[8] The changes and perversion of the criminal justice system were the most extreme. Law and justice became another weapon in the hands of the state against all the elements in society it found undesirable. However, to concentrate too much on the wrongs to the legal system and justice at this time is to ignore the greater atrocities which took place entirely outside of the law or any legal process. The abuse of the legal system is in contrast a lesser evil.

Despite the original plans of the allies in post-war Germany to erect a demilitarized but unified German state, Germany was in fact divided and certain territories ceded to Poland and the Soviet Union. After the war there was no wholesale reshaping of the legal system. It was not necessary to revise all laws individually as the problem mainly concerned the arbitrary application of the law, although there were Nazi laws *per se*. Following the capitulation of the German state and nation, the allies repealed all of the Nazi laws and the rest were subject to the no discrimination rule. This was a rule of interpretation to the courts that required that no rule of law should cause injustice or discrimination by favouring the Nazis or discriminating against any others by reason of race, nationality, religion or moral belief.

Court restaffing and general de-nazification to weed out Nazis met with only limited success. The experiences of Nazism and military laws greatly influenced the provision, after the war, of laws and the administration of justice in the three western zones of occupation which formed the earlier Federal Republic. The further details of this are dealt with more appropriately in the section on constitutional law in Chapter 6.

Many of the pragmatic principles of the Weimar Republic have found better legal expression and success in the Federal Republic. Hence the basic law or constitution (*Grundgesetz*) has an extensive provision of human rights. In civil law, legal development has been restored, according to views[9] to the position it had reached in 1933.

The period following the Second World War also saw a consolidation of social laws and the further decentralization and specialization of the court structure. A significant change, however, was in the strength of the Federal Constitutional Court which is able to overrule all other laws which may be in breach of the basic law. This has provided the greatest development of law in the post-war period, particularly in the clear constitutional law-making role the judges of this court have. Another of the significant changes brought about by the constitutional court, which is having a limited influence on other areas of German law, is with regard to the development of a body of case law and rules developed from case law. This is more akin to the common law, and has even gone so far as to make incursions into civil law, especially in the area of labour law. In this way the German legal system is moving closer to a common-law system, with the necessity to rely on case law to be able to reach the correct result to a problem.

---

[8] For further details on this period see, amongst others, Marsh, 'Some aspects of the German legal system under National Socialism' (1946) LQR 367–74.

[9] See E. J. Cohn, *Manual of German Law*, 2nd ed. (1968: Oceana Publications, New York).

Another relatively new influence on the legal system is the membership of the European Communities. The new constitution envisaged the transfer of some sovereign rights to international organizations, and the reception of Community law in Germany, although not entirely without its problems, has been relatively straightforward. See Chapter 2 for details.

Other legal developments include the relatively new area of law which considers the impingement of the state on the economy—in other words the rules which have been created by the state to regulate its participation in economic affairs, until recently administered entirely under private law, notably the civil and commercial codes. A new body of law has been established which, although it is concerned with the economy, stems from the public sector. A new public law subject, known as public business law (*öffentliches Wirtschaftsrecht*) or, more frequently, the law of economic administration (*Wirtschaftsverwaltungsrecht*), is recognized. The latter name, albeit clumsy, is probably the most descriptive, as this area of law concerns precisely the way in which the state administers business economic decisions. This can be defined extremely widely, and thus incorporates antitrust law and parts of criminal law, taxation, administrative law, trade and industry laws, environmental protection. A narrower definition is preferred which does not annexe legal areas previously quite independent.

A second, relatively new legal development is the establishment of environment law (*Umweltrecht/Umweltschutzrecht*) as a distinct area under the umbrella of public law, although, again, it has been regarded by some writers as just another subcategory of the law of economic administration. Although the laws have largely been derived from many pre-existing statutes and regulations, they have nevertheless been drawn together and have been recognized as such, and the process of codifying this area has commenced.

In conclusion, the German legal system is certainly dominated by legislation, particularly in the form of comprehensive codes. Although these are highly detailed, they are open to rational application, especially now in the light of the basic law—for example, about one-third of the provisions of the civil code have been the subject of revision, repeal, amendment, or addition. The German system nevertheless still relies primarily on the application of these codes of law and statutes which contain general principles and concepts, but subject to the comments made in respect of case law.

The final paragraphs of this chapter must be devoted to a brief overview of the changes brought about by the rejection of Communism in East Germany and the unification of the two parts of Germany in 1990. The events that took place have been called in some quarters the only true revolution in the history of the German nations. The constitutional method of unification and changes to the *Grundgesetz* subsequent to that are considered in Chapter 6.

In most areas the law of the Federal Republic was adopted wholesale into the new *Länder*. In some cases there were particular problems to overcome, as in the case of abortion and § 218 of the criminal code, and other exceptions as noted in the following chapters and found in the annexes to the Unification Treaty. Property law in East Germany and the transformation of the East German economy have proved particularly problematic and have been separately considered in the sections on the law of economic administration in Chapter 8 and in the section on property law in Chapter 10.

The unification with the German Democratic Republic has now determined the final shape of Germany, and outside of deeper integration in the European Community and the consequent changes of unification, all radical changes to the legal system of the Federal Republic of Germany are those of the past.

FURTHER READING

General histories

G. Barraclough, *The Origins of Modern Germany* (1988: Basil Blackwell, Oxford).

J. Fleckenstein, *Early Medieval Germany* (1978: North-Holland, Amsterdam).

H.W. Koch, *A Constitutional History of Germany in the Nineteenth and Twentieth Centuries* (1984: Longman, London).

F. Owen, *The Germanic People* (1960: Bookman Associates, New York).

E.A. Thompson, *The Early Germans* (1965: Clarendon Press, Oxford).

M. Todd, *The Northern Barbarians 100 BC–AD 300* (1987: Basil Blackwell, Oxford).

Legal histories

Bundeszentrale für politische Bildung (ed.), *Deutsche Verfassungsgeschichte*.

H. Conring, *Der Ursprung des deutschen Rechts*, (1643) Translated by I. Hoffmann–Meckenstock (1994: Insel Verlag, Frankfurt-om-Main). *1849–1919–1949* (1989: Bonn).

U. Eisenhardt, *Deutsche Rechtsgeschichte* 3rd ed. (1999: C. H. Beck, Munich).

W. Frotscher/B. Pieroth, *Verfassungsgeschichte*, 2nd ed. (1999: C.H. Beck, Munich).

S.L. Guterman, *The Principle of Personality of Laws in the Germanic Kingdoms of Western Europe from the Fifth to the Eleventh Century* (1990: Peter Lang, New York).

R. Huebner, 'A history of Germanic private law', *Rothman Reprints: A 1968 Re-print of a General Survey of Continental Legal History* (1968: Rothman Reprints, New York) which includes translations of the works of very many German academics, including Savigny.

M. John, *Politics and the Law in Late Nineteenth-century Germany: The Origins of the Civil Code* (1989: Clarendon Press, Oxford).

G. Köbler, *Bilder aus der deutschen Rechtsgeschichte* (1988: C. H. Beck, Munich).

G. Köbler, *Deutsche Rechtsgeschichte*, 4th ed. (1990: Vahlen, Munich).

K. Kroeschell, *Deutsche Rechtsgeschichte 1 (bis 1250)*, 11th ed. (1999: Westdeutscher Verlag, Opladen).

K. Kroeschell, *Deutsche Rechtsgeschichte 2 (1250–1650)*, 7th ed. (1989: Westdeutscher Verlag, Opladen) (new edition in preparation).

K. Kroeschell, *Deutsche Rechtsgeschichte 3 (seit 1650* 3rd ed.), (2001: Westdeutscher Verlag, Opladen).

Mitteis and Lieberich, *Deutsche Rechtsgeschichte*, 19th ed. (1992: C.H. Beck, Munich).

A. Laufs, *Rechtsenwicklungen in Deutschland*, 4th ed. (1991: Walter de Gruyter, Berlin).

Robinson, Fergus and Gordon, *An Introduction to European Legal History*, 3rd ed. (2000: Professional Books, Abingdon).

I. Ward, *Law, Philosophy and National Socialism* (1992: Peter Lang, Bern).

U. Wesel, *Geschichte des Rechts* (1997: C. H. Beck, Munich).

J. Whitman, *The Legacy of Roman Law in the German Romantic Era* (1990: Princeton University Press, Princeton, New Jersey).

F. Wieacker (Translated by T. Wein), *A History of Private Law in Europe* (1995: Clarendon Press, Oxford).

D. Willoweit, *Deutsche Verfassungsgeschichte*, 3rd ed. (1997: C.H. Beck, Munich).

Articles

H. Coing, 'German *Pandektistik*' in its relationship to the former "*ius commune*" ' (1989) 37 Am J Comp L 9–15.

K. Mollnau, 'The contributions of Savigny to the theory of legislation' (1989) 37 Am J Comp L 81–93.

N. Marsh, 'Some aspects of the German legal system under National Socialism' (1946) 62 LQR 366–74.

J. Rückert, 'The unrecognized legacy: Savigny's influence on German jurisprudence after 1900' (1989) 37 Am J Comp L 121–37.

2

Sources of German law

1 Introduction

The term 'sources of law' describes the various elements or influences which contribute to the totality of laws present in a legal system. It can therefore refer to the historical source of law, as discussed above in Chapter 1, but also to current influences. Discussion in this chapter concentrates on the latter.

Only two sources are formally acknowledged in the German legal system: statute (*Gesetz*) and customary law (*Gewohnheitsrecht*). However, to accept this statement entirely would not disclose an accurate picture of the position in Germany today, and it must be stated that other influences do have an impact. Furthermore, the formal position, if applied strictly would seriously hinder or restrict judges in deciding cases as they would be unable to look further for assistance than the two acknowledged sources of law. Additional factors, although not formally sources of German law, have had a strong influence on the past development and present position of German law. These are the general influences of legal history, notably the roman and Germanic laws, legal philosophy, general constitutional and legal theory, sociology of law, and comparative law.

It is now arguable that two further sources have developed. These are the decisions reached in the courts by the judiciary, which are not a simple application of existing law, and the application of European Community law. An alternative argument is that both of these more recent sources fall within the existing sources because of their incorporation into the legal system by statute.

A constitutional ranking of laws is generally accepted. At the apex, constitutional law, followed by *Bundesgesetz* in the formal sense of federal statutes and codes promulgated by a parliament, delegated legislation (*Rechtsverordnungen*), the bye-laws of federal organs (*Satzungen*), and then the equivalents at the level of the *Länder* and other bodies established under public law. The place of EC law at the apex of this hierarchy is still disputed, especially in view of the latest statement of the BVerfG on the subject.[1] This chapter will first outline the sources of German Law and then turn to the subject of legal method, briefly examining different methods by which the law is applied.

---

[1] See BVerfGE 89, 155, (Maastricht Judgment) also reported in JZ 1993, 1100 et seq. and further details in sec. 2.5 below.

2 Sources of law

2.1 The constitution: the "basic law" *(Grundgesetz)*

The constitution (*Grundgesetz*) as supreme source of German law states the leading principles of the state, its organization, and the individuals' basic rights.[2] Its supreme position is emphasized by Article 1 III GG, declaring all state authorities bound by the basic rights and Article 20 III GG subjecting even the legislature to the constitutional order. Thus any source of law below the constitution has to comply with the *Grundgesetz*. Whether EC law, a source of law of the supranational bodies, the European Community, prevails over constitutional law as a higher-ranking source of law still remains disputed at least to a certain extent. This will be discussed below.[3]

2.2 Statute *(Gesetz)*

The term *Gesetz* includes all enacted and written rules of law which in legal systems today are the main source of law, including the comprehensive legislative codes and amending or additional single enactment from both the Federal and *Länder* legislatures and their executives endowed with law making powers. "*Gesetz*" is, however, used in two different senses in the German legal system. In the narrow sense it refers to a form of law which has been promulgated by a parliamentary process and is thus termed *Gesetz im formellen Sinn* indicating that a particular procedure has been followed resulting in a specific form of law. This is clearly closest to an understanding of a Statute as an Act of Parliament. In this sense in the German legal system both statutes of federal and *Länder* parliaments are included. Law-making (*Gesetzgebung*) will be examined in the chapter on constitutional law.[4]

The term *Gesetz*, used in its wider sense as a source of legal rule (*Gesetz im materiellen Sinn*), can include any form of law which has been enacted by an authority competent to do so. Thus it includes provisions of the constitution itself, the general codes, individual statutes enacted by the Federal Government, and the legislation enacted by the *Länder*. Furthermore, it includes the various forms of secondary legislation of general application, which have the force of law (the *Rechtsverordnungen* and *Satzungen* of general application issued by legal persons under public law).[5]

It has to be noted that within Germany's federal system federal laws, including regulations on a federal level, prevail over laws of the *Länder* (Art 31 GG).

Finally, administrative rules or orders (*Verwaltungsverordnungen* or *Verwaltungsvorschriften*) are only applicable as internal rules of the administration in the form of guide lines and codes of practice for the benefit of the administrators. In strict

---

[2] The most frequently cited provisions of the *Grundgesetz* have been included in an Appendix at the end of the volume.
[3] See below, sec. 2.5.
[4] See below, Chapter 6, sec. 4.5.1.
[5] Conditions for delegated legislation are mapped out in Chapter 6, sec. 4.5.1.

terms they do not constitute *Gesetze* but may help the authorities put into practice the requirements of a statute or complete the obligation of a statute at the practical level.

2.3 Customary law (*Gewohnheitsrecht*)

This has little influence now, but includes regular and general public practice recognized as binding. It is almost vestigial as a source of German law. Historically, once the only source of law for the German tribes it has little influence now as the written and enacted forms of law have constituted, since the reception of Roman law, by far the greatest source of law. Although customary law continues to be recognized by the courts, it has to be proved, a task, which is extremely difficult. The nineteenth century drive to codification led to the promulgation of imposing quantities of legislation. The uncertainty of the Weimar Republic and the dictatorship of the Third Reich meant that *Gesetz* dominated legal sources to the almost total exclusion of customary law. From 1949 the re-organization of the state led to a renewed legislative programme which further eclipsed customary law. Therefore due to the increasing regulation of daily life by enacted laws, true customary law is understandably a very limited source of new law and has practically no relevance to the study of law.

Customary law nevertheless still finds a place, albeit an ambiguous one, in the German legal system. It has, for instance, been recognized by the introductory law to the civil code,[6] which states that, for the purposes of the civil code, law is any normative rule of law.

One way to define it would be to distinguish it from the other source of law: *Gesetz*. Customary law cannot be a part of *Gesetz* and cannot arise as the result of *Gesetz* or from the state. Additionally, in strict legal theory, it cannot arise by the input of the legal profession, in particular the judiciary. However this is questionable, since it is the judiciary that has to decide, which rules it accepts as customary law.[7] In legal theory it must arise from an existence entirely of its own as a custom amongst the populace.

Furthermore, it is not to be confused with usage (*Verkehrssitte*) in the sense recognized by the BGB § 151 "Acceptance without notification may be valid if according to common practice and § 157 "interpretation according to practice". It is often difficult to distinguish the two. Both customary law and common usage have their origins in a continued or extended and recognized practice, but one has the force of law and the other does not. The problem is determining when custom ends and customary law begins. Inevitably those called upon to decide are the judiciary, as the real test of what is customary law and which are mere customs is whether it is enforceable before the courts. Thus the question of the recognition of customary law becomes inextricably linked with that of judicial function.

---

[6] *Einführungsgesetz zum Bürgerlichen Gesetzbuch* (EGBGB) § 2, "*Gesetz im Sinne des Bürgerlichen Gesetzbuchs und dieses Gesetzes ist jede Rechtsnorm*".
[7] B. Rüthers, *Rechtstheorie* (1999: München), pp. 130–131.

The Federal Constitutional Court has defined customary law as an unwritten rule or practice, which has arisen as the result of a consistent and constant general application over many years (*langandauernde Übung*) and a widespread conviction or recognition that it is a valid and binding rule of law.[8] Although not all must believe in its validity, a majority in the particular sphere of operation must do so, as in the geographic area or trade, if a trade rule.

It is suggested, that customary law now plays a much more general role in providing the judiciary with a reason by which they can introduce general principles of law to fill gaps in legislation and to overcome ambiguities in a *Gesetz*, as evidenced by an example from the civil law. In a civil case in 1902, the principle of the positive breach of contract was given a place in German contract law by the *Reichsgericht*.[9] Alternatively, it may be argued that judge made law (*Richterrecht*) has replaced customary law as a source of law in the German legal system. The notion of unwritten principles of customary law is a very vague term and can arguably include any rule of law or general principle, which satisfies the above definitions and customary law could be equated with the term "general principles of law".[10] The difference is that customary law must be brought to the court to be approved by the judiciary whereas judge made law may arise from within the case, from legislation, or introduced by the court itself.

2.4 Judicial law-making (*Richterrecht*)

Following the reception of Roman law and codification, the decisions of the courts and case law in Germany have played no part as a formal source of law. However, it must be acknowledged that the courts play a distinct role as interpreters and developers of law. The extent to which they actually make law or simply interpret and apply it, is the decisive factor in determining whether it ranks as a modern day source.

2.4.1 Historical aspects

The theoretical or formal function of the judiciary, which has developed in the German legal system, is that judges simply apply law and should not create it, therefore case law cannot stand as a source of law. Any decisions, which are reached in a case are applicable to that case only and do not have any general binding effect in other cases. This view is widely supported but is not entirely without contention or refinement.[11] The courts clearly play a very important role as interpreters and developers of law—in particular, the Federal Constitutional Court, in interpreting the constitution, notably the provisions for human rights, has often overruled

---

[8] BVerfGE 57, 134.

[9] The case is known as the Gravel case, RGZ 54,98. This has now developed into the legal principle of *positives Vertragsverletzung*. See the details on this case in Chapter 10.

[10] See, *inter alia*, D. Schmalz, *Methodenlehre für das juristische Studium*, 2nd. ed. (1990: Nomos Verlag, Baden-Baden), Zippelius, *Juristische Methodenlehre*, 5th ed. (1990), pp. 8–10, 60 & 75–76, R. Haase and R. Keller, *Grundlagen und Grundformen des Rechts*, 7th ed. (1986: Kohlhammer Stuttgart), p. 35.

[11] For critical evaluation see Rüthers, above, n 7, pp. 132–146.

Federal *Gesetze* which were found to be inconsistent with the constitution. Labour law court decisions have added to and reinforced the phenomenon of case law in Germany.[12] It is the extent to which it can be argued the judiciary interpret and apply law or create law, which is decisive in determining whether it should now rank as a source. It was the reception of Roman law and the codification of the nineteenth century, which formally denied the judiciary a role in law creation. Prior to this, law had developed from the unwritten Germanic customary law, which was perceived and applied to the case by the law finders. Thus in the history of German law a complete about turn has taken place and the position at the end of the nineteenth century, when positive law theories were at their zenith, was that the heavily codified and statute law was sufficient to provide for all legal situations. The judiciary should be not only denied a role but would have no need to create law. Since this period further arguments have arisen for and against judicial law making. Recent historical objections to judicial law-making arise from the experience of the judiciary in the Weimar Republic and the abuses by the judiciary in the Third Reich.[13] Therefore a reluctance to ascribe any law making power to the judiciary, which by its very definition conflicts with the exclusive right of the legislators and thus the principle of the separation of powers, is understandable.

2.4.2 *The constitutional position*

Germany's constitutional position is a strict adherence to the principle of the separation of powers. The *Grundgesetz* did not give a law-making role to the judiciary, with the exception of the Federal Constitutional Court, and guaranteed the independence of judiciary as an arm of the state bound only by the law. They should not create law because the independence from the law making division of power would be lost. See Articles 20 III and 97 I *Grundgesetz* and § 1 GVG (*Gerichtsverfassungsgesetz*). The main principle is that judges are bound by statute and law (*Gesetz und Recht*). Here the term *Gesetz* is used in its material sense to include not only statute but constitutional law and secondary legislation. Furthermore, § 4 I of the German Law of the Judiciary (*Deutsches Richtergesetz*, DRiG) denies the judiciary the ability to undertake the competence of the legislature or the executive.

2.4.3 *The effect of court decisions*

Formally, precedent (*Präjudizien*) does not exist in Germany, except in the limited circumstances given below, therefore court decisions do not have any effect in future cases and only bind the parties to the case. Prior decisions do have some temporal effect. But in contrast to the UK the older the statute, the weaker it is in terms of its persuasiveness and conversely the more recent a judicial decision is in relation to an older statute, the greater its persuasive authority.[14] Decisions of the superior courts do have a greater temporal effect and newer decisions reached are

---

[12] See H. Brox and B. Rüthers, *Arbeitsrecht*, 14th ed. (1999: Stuttgart), pp. 34–36.
[13] See E.J. Cohn, *Manual of German Law, Volume I*, pp. 27–30 and N. Marsh, "Some Aspects of the German Legal System under National Socialism", (1946) 62 LQR 366–374.
[14] BVerfGE 34, 269, 288.

taken into account by scholars, practitioners, and judges alike. The general requirement of legal certainty in a legal system also demands consistency in court decisions. The judges in the lower courts are certainly aware of the decisions in the higher courts and are likely to follow these using them as a sort of persuasive authority for their own decisions. It has even been held that an attorney may be liable in damages by neglecting precedents of higher courts.[15]

Exceptions to the rule of non-binding precedent include one formal exception and procedural divergencies :

(a) Decisions of the Federal Constitutional Court are the formal exception. These are—according to § 31 I BVerfGG—binding on all organs of the constitution and all courts and legislative and executive authorities. They have the force of statute (according to § 31 II BVerfGG) which refers to the force of law (*Gesetzkraft*) in the circumstances outlined in the paragraph. The constitution provides for it in Article 94 I 2 GG. These decisions can invalidate Federal Statutes, see Articles 93 I 2 and 100 I GG.

The following cases outline the procedural divergencies from the strict rule.

(b) Decisions of the Senates of the Federal Court of Justice (*Bundesgerichtshof*) are not generally binding on other senates. However, to deviate from previous established decisions of the Civil or Criminal Senates of the same court a senate must refer the question to the Great Senate (*Großer Senat*) for either civil or criminal matters in a process known as the *Divergenzvorlage*. This special senate, or the combined Great Senate (*Vereinigter Großer Senat*), deals with contradictions in the law between the criminal and civil senates or for changes of a general principle of law. The Senate first has to sanction any change which then becomes binding on the Federal Court of Justice senates unless reversed again by the Great Senate (see § 132 GVG). Furthermore, Article 95 III GG requires a Common Senate of all the highest federal courts to oversee the development of law and to head off any inconsistencies being introduced into the legal system as a result of differing decisions in the different hierarchies of courts.[16]

(c) Decisions of the "Courts of Appeal" or "Higher Regional Courts" (*Oberlandesgerichte*) where they deviate from previous decisions of other higher regional courts. First, however, the deviation must be sanctioned by the Federal Court of Justice whose decision on the matter must be followed regardless of the outcome but only in the case and not generally. This is another form of *Divergenzvorlage*. See GVG and § 47 VI VwGO § 28 II FGG, § 121 II for administrative courts and the BVerWG.

(d) An appeal on a point of law referred to a higher court and in particular the Federal Court of Justice. If the higher court reverses the decision of the

---

[15] BGH NJW 1983, 1665.
[16] This is the *Gemeinsamer Senat der obersten Gerichtshöfe* introduced by the *Gesetz zur Wahrung der Einheitlichkeit der Rechtsprechung der obersten Gerichtshöfe des Bundes vom 19. Juni 1968* (BGBl I S. 661).

lower court, the lower court is obliged to apply that decision in the particular action. This latter exception therefore fits in with both lines of argument in that the higher decision is binding but only in the singular appeal action.

Apart from these situations, there is no effect in future cases and a binding rule of law does not come into existence, therefore it is argued that it is impossible to talk of law-making but only of decision-making. It may also be argued that the above cases do not support the view that judicial law making constitutes a separate source of law as arguably all of the above rules have been enacted in statute form.

2.4.4 *Conclusion*

It is still heavily disputed whether judicial law making can be regarded as a source of law. Those who argue that judges are merely interpreting statutes cannot satisfactorily explain the handling of cases, which expose gaps in statutory regulation. Furthermore, if a court starts interpreting a law against its wording, as had happened in the *Soraya* case,[17] the line between interpretation and creating new law is blurred. The strong impact of the higher courts' decisions can be seen in less codified areas of law, as for example in labour law. Finally, the lower courts must take the above-mentioned exceptions to the rule of non-binding precedent in the German legal system into account. Thus, bearing in mind all these aspects, it seems very difficult to completely deny judicial law making as a source of law.[18]

2.5 **European Community law**

As with all Member States, the Community position on the relationship of Community and national law is that Community law has supremacy over all inconsistent national law which should be put aside side by the judiciary in favour of applying Community law.[19] This would make it a source of law, supreme even to the constitution, the *Grundgesetz*. However, the position of Community law in Germany has given rise to much debate especially in respect of its relationship with the German constitution. Without any express provisions regulating this problem the starting points to turn to are Article 23 GG and the case law of the BVerfG culminating in the famous "*Maastricht Urteil*".[20]

2.5.1 *Historical aspects*

At times the implementation of Community law in the Member States has been contentious, especially in respect of secondary Community law. But before the particular problems of German membership are considered, a brief review of the historical development of German membership will be provided.

Democratic Germany, which evolved from the aftermath of the Second World War, was, with France, directly instrumental in the foundation of the European

---

[17] Considered below in sec. 3.
[18] Rüthers, above, n 1, p. 145.
[19] See, *inter alia*, Case 6/64 *Costa v ENEL* [1964] ECR 1251 and Case 106/77 *Amministrazione delle Finanze dello stato v Simmenthal* [1978] ECR 629, [1978] 3 CMLR 263.
[20] BVerfGE 89, 155 and discussed in detail below.

Community. The precise impetus for the Community came in the form of the plan proposed in 1950 by the French Foreign Minister Robert Schuman[21] to link the French and German Coal and Steel industries. This proposal was welcomed by the German Chancellor Konrad Adenauer and was extended to include the participation of the Benelux nations and Italy. That such a form of supranational co-operation could be fully entered into by Germany is due in large part to the German Constitution, the *Grundgesetz,*which embraced the ideal of a United Europe within its preamble and contained Articles specifically allowing for the transfer of state power to international organizations. From such positive beginnings, Germany and the EC worked well for each other. Germany was a strong and enthusiastic member and the Community provided the economic environment, which assisted the rapid and successful economic growth in Germany.

The discussion from the German point of view lies essentially with the relationship of international law and in particular the membership of the Community, to the provisions of the *Grundgesetz*. Traditionally, Germany adopted a rather dualist approach to the reception of international law whereby some form of transformation or adoption of international law was necessary in order for it to have any direct effect in the state. In practical terms it meant that there had to be a process of incorporation by statute. Once incorporated, a law would simply rank as with other *Gesetze* and if a later law was in conflict with an earlier law, the latter law would prevail. Following Articles 24–25, and the fact that Community law is not simply another form of international law, it is argued that there has been a shift to a monist approach.[22]

The *Grundgesetz* Articles 24 and 25 provided for the peaceful co-operation of the German state with international organizations. Article 24 GG allows for membership of international organizations and a transfer of powers to them and was used to establish membership of the European Communities. Article 25 declares **general rules** of public international law to be an integral part of federal law and to take precedence over national statutes. It is silent as to all other sources of international law such as treaties. The commentaries and texts describe Article 25 GG as being "International Law friendly" (*völkerrechtsfreundlich*).[23] However, neither Article 25 nor Article 24 GG was specifically formulated with membership of the European Community in mind and neither provides a clear statement as to whether all forms of Community law should be accorded a status of priority over German law or over the German Constitution itself. Article 25 was not relied on or cited in respect of the impact of Community law in the German legal order, therefore Article 24 had been the provision considered in this context. The academic debate has raged as to whether priority of

---

[21] Based on the research plans of Jean Monnet.

[22] Refer to the chapter by M. Hilf, "General problems of Relations between Constitutional Law and International Law" in Starck (ed.) *Rights, Institutions and Impact of International Law according to the German Basic Law* (1987: Nomos Verlag, Baden-Baden).

[23] See, *inter alia*, M. Herdegen in: T. Maunz and G. Dürig (ed.): *Grundgesetz Kommentar* (2001: München), Art. 25, paras 1–10; G. Brockmeyer in: Schmidt-Bleibtreu and Klein (eds.), *Kommentar zum Grundgesetz*, 9th ed. (1999: Luchterhand), pp. 616–622; R. Streinz in: M. Sachs (ed.), *Grundgesetz Kommentar*, 2nd ed. (1999: München), Art. 25, paras 8–21.

Community law included Regulations and Directives and whether these laws take precedence over all forms of German law, including constitutional law or just over federal and *Länder* laws.

The particular problems encountered with Article 24 are that, despite the fact that it could facilitate the transfer of wide ranging powers from Germany, which clearly result in constitutional consequences or changes, it does not specify how this is to be done, or whether the process should conform to the constitutional requirements for such changes imposed by Article 79 II GG, that alteration of the provisions of the *Grundgesetz* requires two-thirds majorities in both the *Bundestag* and *Bundesrat*. The BVerfG has held that transfers of sovereignty do not permit the basic structure of the *Grundgesetz* to be altered[24] and that any transfer of sovereignty under Article 24 must be authorized by a statute. Such transfers are to be regarded in the same way as laws seeking to make changes to the Constitution,[25] i.e., by requiring a special majority to be achieved in both houses of the German Parliament.

Article 24 does not appear to allow the complete transfer of sovereign powers from Germany, in effect the dissolution of the German state by abdication of all state power and the transfer of the power to establish further powers to another body. Until recently this point had not been developed as it was generally accepted that a complete transfer of powers could not be envisaged. However, the Maastricht Treaty on European Union has now opened up such an eventual possibility, and consequently the debate about the scope of Article 24 intensified. A consequence was that a new Article 23 was inserted to regulate the transfer of powers to the European Union.

2.5.2 The constitutional difficulties caused by community membership

Issues resulting from Community membership included the question whether Article 24 allows the transfer of *Länder* powers; the previous human rights position in the EC; the democratic deficit in the Community; and its impact on German Federalism. The latter is threatened because the EC has ignored the internal political make up of Member States and the division of state power and competences in federal states. It recognizes only the central or federal state level and has been described as blind to the regions (*länderblind*).[26]

As with other Member States, theoretical and academic opinions do not constitute the real test of legislation, which only arises when the courts are faced with the application of Community law. The view of BVerfG is paramount because of its constitutional position in the German state, therefore the case law of this court must be considered. Previously, German courts had been divided as to the effect of Community law, however the great majority now give preference to all forms of

---

[24] BVerfGE 37, 217, 279. (Decisions of the Federal Constitutional Court, Vol. 37, at p. 217 with the relevant material at p. 279).
[25] BVerfGE 58, 35f.
[26] See H.P. Ipsen, "Als Bundesstaat in der Gemeinschaft", in *Festschrift für W. Hallstein* (1966), p. 248 at p. 256.

Community law. Occasionally a court may not recognize a certain aspect or rule of Community law which happens in all Member States to some extent and which poses no significant problem within the German legal system due to the absence of a system of precedent. More emphasis can be placed on the rulings of the BVerfG on this matter, which has held that:

(i) all Community law is valid in the German legal order and applicable in the German courts,[27]

(ii) provisions of the Treaties take priority over both earlier and later national law,[28] and

(iii) secondary Community law Regulations are directly valid in Germany and supreme over federal law.[29]

We will now look at the constitutional issues involved in detail.

(a) *The protection of fundamental rights*
Two leading cases concerning the relationship between the basic rights provision of EC law and the *Grundgesetz* effectively summarize the developing position of the Court.

BVerfGE 37, 271 Solange I[30]

In this case a German import-export company had obtained an export license for a certain amount of maize meal under EC law. This license expired before the company had exported the whole amount of the product. According to the relevant EC regulation the deposit compulsory for obtaining the license was forfeit as soon as the license expired. Claiming back the deposit and questioning the EC regulation the company brought the matter before the German administrative court. It claimed breaches of basic rights such as the right to carry commercial activity (based on Art 14 GG) and constitutional principles, e.g. the principle of proportionality. After the ECJ in a preliminary ruling had rejected this argument, thus guiding the German administrative court to reject the claim, the company brought on a constitutional complaint before the BVerfG. This court then basically stated that **as long as** (in German: *"solange"*) **the recognition of human rights in the EEC had not progressed as far as those provided for by the *Grundgesetz*, German courts retained the right to refer questions on the constitutionality of secondary Community law to the BVerfG with the possible result that Community law may be ignored if it did not have sufficient regard for basic rights.**

---

[27] BVerfGE 31, 173f.
[28] BVerfGE 75, 244 in connection with BVerfGE 31, 173.
[29] BVerfGE 73, 374 & BVerfGE 74, 51.
[30] Also known as the *"Internationale Handelsgesellschaft"* case [1974] 2 CMLR 540.

This position changed by the ruling in the *Wünsche Handelsgesellschaft* decision[31] thirteen years later, also known as *Solange II*:

BVerfGE 73, 339 Solange II

This time it was the import license system of the European Community that was challenged. The applicants again claimed a violation of their basic rights under the *Grundgesetz*. However, in this case the BVerfG accepted that Community recognition and safeguards of fundamental rights through the case law of the ECJ were now sufficient and of a comparable nature to those provided for by the *Grundgesetz*. It held that as long as Community law ensured the effective provision of fundamental rights the BVerfG would not review Community law in the light of the rights provisions of the Constitution. It also stated that it would not be prepared to accept constitutional complaints from lower courts under Article 100 I GG on this basis.

Provided that Community rights are in fact as good as German rights this means Community law overrules the German constitution itself. However, it is argued that a reservation is still inherent in the ruling.[32] The basis for the decision was not, however, the inherent supremacy of Community law but the fact that Article 24 GG allowed a transfer of powers to the Community and the subsequent accession Act obliged the German courts to accept the supremacy of Community law. This seems to indicate that the dualist approach to international law is still the one favoured by the BVerfG and means that there is still some form of barrier which must be overcome in some way for the supremacy and direct effect of Community law to be recognized in Germany. In its *Maastricht decision* the BVerfG introduced the idea of a relationship of co-operation between the ECJ and the BVerfG claiming to retain a reservation to review EC Acts including a review in order to protect fundamental rights.[33]

There had also been some difficulties in German courts in the past regarding references to the ECJ under the preliminary ruling procedure, Article 234 (ex 177) of the EC Treaty, and at times courts had refused to make a reference thus denying the parties to the case the chance to see whether EC law would have affected the outcome of the case. In the *Solange II* decision the BVerfG pointed out that the ECJ was a court within the meaning of Article 101 GG. This provision guarantees individuals the right to have access to a lawful, as in regular state appointed, judge, thus within limits the right to have access to the ECJ as well. This effectively means that German courts can no longer refuse to make references in last instance to the ECJ as

---

[31] *Wünsche Handelsgesellschaft* [1987] 3 CMLR 225.
[32] See M. Schweitzer, *Staatsrecht III*, 6th ed. (1997: Heidelberg), p. 28; Cornils in J. Menzel (ed.), *Verfassungsrechtsprechung* (2000), pp. 239–241 with further references; T. Jakob, "The Rule of Law", in Starck (ed.), *Rights, Institutions and Impact of International Law according to the German Basic Law* (1987: Nomos Verlag, Baden-Baden).
[33] The decision is considered below sec. 2.5.4.

had happened in the case of *Kloppenburg*.[34] In this case the Federal Tax Court refused to recognize direct effects of Community law. The BVerfG held in *Re: VAT Exemption*[35] the follow up to the *Kloppenburg* case, and in the separate case of *Re Patented Feedstuffs*,[36] that German courts, which are courts of last instance in terms of Article 234 (ex 177) of the EC Treaty would be in breach of the German constitution if they failed to refer to the ECJ when necessary. Therefore German courts of last instance are obliged to make a reference where a dispute as to interpretation or application of Community law exists. The *Kloppenburg* case also held that acts of Community law must be given precedent by German courts even if they conflict with national legislation. Applications to the BVerfG to question the constitutionality of Community legislation have been declared to be inadmissible because the Court considered that such acts are not acts of German public authorities within the scope of the *Grundgesetz* and cannot thus be complained of to the BVerfG.[37]

Following these cases there would seem to be no procedural difficulty in getting Community rights at least considered in the proper forum in Germany. Any court which refuses either to follow a previous ruling of the ECJ or make an Article 234 ruling may be subject to the review of the BVerfG for an arbitrary breach of Article 101 I GG.

(b) *The legislative roles of the* Länder *and the Federation*
Article 79 III GG guarantees the federal state form and thus the division between the Federation and the *Länder*. It also guarantees the legislative role of the *Länder* in federal law making. As the Community developed, and particularly as it expanded its competence in existing areas or into new areas, partly the result of judicial interpretation, e.g., in the area of training and education, but more significantly through Treaty amendments, the focus of attention for the constitutional implications of Community membership shifted to the effect that membership was having on the *Länder* in the *Bundesrat* in the legislative process and on the division of power between the Federation and the *Länder*.[38] While Article 59 II 1 GG requires statutory approval for a transfer of powers by any bodies responsible for federal legislation in respect of international treaties relating to matters which come within the competence of the *Länder*, it does not question the right of the Federation to propose this transfer in the first place, thus concentrating the political impetus in respect of the EC in the *Bundestag*.

Within Germany, legislative competence is divided into areas of exclusive competence of the Federation, with the *Bundestag* and thus the German government in the leading role (Arts 71 and 73 GG), concurrent competence with the *Länder* who

---

[34] NJW 1988, 1459, [1988] 3 CMLR 1.
[35] NJW 1988, 2173, [1989] 1 CMLR 113.
[36] NJW 1988, 1456, [1989] 2 CMLR 902.
[37] See BVerfGE 58, 1, 27, known as the *Eurocontrol I* decision, and the Judgment of the 12 May 1990, NJW 1990, 974 concerning the enactment of the Cigarette Packet Warnings Directive ([1989] O.J. C 124/5). For further details see BVerfG 12 May 1989, NJW 974, Nicolaysen in 24 EuR (1989) pp. 215–225 and Roth 28 C M L Rev (1991) 137–182 at 144.
[38] For discussions of this see, *inter alia*, Kirchener and Haas, "*Rechtliche Grenzen für Kompetenzübertragungen auf die Europäische Gemeinschaft*", *Juristen Zeitung* 1993, 760–771, von Münch, *Staatsrecht*, op. cit.

are represented within the *Bundesrat* in Parliament (Arts 72 and 74 GG) and a residual area of competence exclusive to the *Länder* (Articles 70 and 30 GG). Increasingly, concern had been expressed that, because the Community is given legislative competence by the Member States, the decision-making process is located in the Council of Ministers. The German government was only represented in the Council of Ministers by a member from the *Bundestag*, regardless of the subject matter. On matters which are domestically the responsibility of the *Länder*, this arrangement effectively conceded legislative power to the Federation and beyond: it is the Federal Government which participates in the Council of Ministers in the Community and not the *Länder*. Thus, as more and more power was transferred from the national level to the Community and as the Community expanded its competences, as under the SEA and the Maastricht Treaty, federal democracy in Germany and the position of the *Länder* within the national system had been threatened. A good example is in the area of broadcasting in which a competence of the *Länder* was undermined as a result of implementation of an EC Broadcasting Directive.[39] The Directive imposes a quota on European productions and regulates advertising and thus directly concerns the powers of the *Länder*. The main question raised in a case (*Bund-Länder-Streit* Article 93 I 3 GG) before the BVerfG[40] was whether the Federation had violated the *Grundgesetz* in the manner it handled the transfer of competences in broadcasting to the EC when it was the right of the *Länder* to regulate this area of law. In the previous case of *Land Bayern v Bund, Re the EC Broadcasting Directive*,[41] Bavaria applied for an injunction against a vote of Germany in Council on a Directive on Transfrontier Television. The injunction was denied but the BVerfG expressed the view that where appropriate Community law would be reviewed to see if it did in fact infringe the *Grundgesetz*. It was held that the Federation can transfer powers of the *Länder* under Article 24 GG but not core powers. This has inevitably raised the question of what is meant by core powers.[42]

(c) *Democracy and sovereignty*

The question arises whether the democratic principle enshrined in Article 20 I GG has been undermined by deepening Community membership. Under Article 20 II GG, state authority (Sovereignty or *Staatsgewalt*) can only be exercised with the direct legitimization of the people. A transfer of powers to the EC breaks that chain of legitimization because the transfer of power to the EC from the national and regional parliaments is made to the Council of Ministers, which meets behind closed doors and does not enjoy direct legitimization from the people. The view may be taken that the EC has not closed this gap effectively enough, even with a democratically elected European Parliament because of its legislative weakness.

---

[39] Directive 89/552 of 3 October 1989 [1989] O.J. L298/23.
[40] The case, an application to the BVerfG by Bavaria, had been lodged with the FCC since 1989. Case no 2 BvR 1/89.
[41] Judgment of the BVerfG of 11 April 1989, BVerfGE 80, 74, NJW 1990, 974.
[42] For a general consideration of the difficulties experienced as a result of the Community-German conflict in Broadcasting law see K. Hesse, "*Rundfunk zwischen demokratischer Willensbildung und dem Zugriff der EG*", Juristen Zeitung, 1993, 545 and generally in respect of media law in Germany: F. Fechner, *Medienrecht*, 2nd ed. (2001: Mohr Siebeck) Tübingen, pp. 126–148.

2.5.3 *Procedures enacted to redress the balance*

Initially, the concerns about the assault on the principles of the *Grundgesetz* were partially counteracted by measures to increase the participation of the *Länder* in the scrutiny and consideration of Community proposals prior to a decision being taken in the Council of Ministers, including the setting up of a European chamber (*Europakammer*) in the *Bundesrat* to review European legislative proposals.[43] Subsequently, Article 2 of the Act assenting to the SEA, provided that the federal government, when dealing with EC matters exclusively within the legislative competence of the *Bundesrat* or matters of essential interest of the *Länder*, must take account of the opinion given by the *Bundesrat*. If, however, the matter impinged on the exclusive legislative competence of the *Länder*, then the government could only ignore their opinion in cases concerned with external policy or integration matters. It further provided that, when demanded but only when practically possible, a *Länder* representative should be invited to attend working committees of the Commission and Council in the EC.[44] However, this was not regarded as an effective answer, as most decisions were taken in the Council of Ministers without the participation of the *Bundesrat*.

In the run up to the agreements reached in Maastricht, it was realized that the problem would be exacerbated as a result of the extension of Community competence into the newer areas, particularly those previously within the joint or exclusive competence of the *Länder*.[45] It was agreed that because ratification of the Maastricht Treaty would require *Bundesrat* approval, changes to the *Grundgesetz* to put membership of the EU and transfers of powers on a new constitutional basis would be both desirable and necessary. These changes gave the opportunity to the *Bundesrat* to extend its participation and obtain constitutional guarantees for future changes, which affected German sovereignty and the balance of legislative power. These benefits would arguably compensate for the drift of competences engendered by Maastricht.

2.5.4 *Constitutional amendments*

A new Article 23 GG (the *Europa Artikel*)[46] was added and amendments were made to other key provisions. Article 23 provides that sovereign powers (*Hoheitsrechte*) can be transferred to the European Union provided the transfer has the approval of

---

[43] See Art. 2 of the Accession Act to the Treaty of Rome (*Zustimmungsgesetz*) of 27 July 1957, BGBl. 1957 II, S.753, which required the federal government to keep the *Bundestag* informed and allowed the *Bundesrat* to give a non binding opinion on the Community measure proposed in a process known as the *Zuleitungsverfahren*. In 1979 an informal agreement was achieved between the Chancellor and the Heads of Governments of the Länder which led to a more formal procedure for the SEA.

[44] Accession Act of 19 December 1986, BGBl 1986 II, S.1102.

[45] Examples are: incentives (Art. 149 VI EC), incentive measures to promote education policies (Art. 149 VI EC), incentive measures to promote action by member states in public health (Art. 152 IV EC), action in respect of consumer protection (Art. 153 IV EC), general programmes on the environment (Art. 175 III EC), incentives on culture (Art. 151 V EC), a programme for research and development under Art. 130i EC and generally in the areas of economic and monetary union.

[46] Contained in *Gesetz zur Änderung des Grundgesetzes* of 21 December 1992, BGBl. I S. 2086. See, Liebholz, Rinck, and Hesselberger, *Grundgesetz Kommentar an Hand der Rechtsprechung des Bundesverfassungsgerichts*, 7th ed. (1993), and for a discussion on Art. 23, see Schotten, *"Das Grundgesetz nach Maastricht"*, Verwaltungsrundschau, 1993, pp. 89 et seq. at p. 94.

the *Bundestag* and *Bundesrat*. Joint approval is also required for the ratification of the European Union Treaty and for any future changes affecting the contents of the *Grundgesetz*. Any such changes must, however, still comply with the requirements of Article 79 II, III GG that, a two-thirds majority must be obtained in both chambers (Art. 23 I GG). This ensures that a complete parliamentary process is observed with the full participation of the *Länder* and that the fundamental principles of state set out in Article 20 GG are also observed before any transfer of powers can take place.

Article 23 II–IV GG introduces formal parliamentary scrutiny procedures for Community legislative proposals, which go further than the previous provisions. First, the *Bundestag* and the *Länder* in the *Bundesrat* shall take part in discussion of all matters relating to the European Union. The federal government has a duty to keep both the *Bundestag* and *Bundesrat* informed in good time and is required to give the *Bundestag* the chance to give an opinion prior to its participation in the formal decision making process in the European Union. This is achieved by the establishment of a new *Bundestag* committee (under Art. 45 GG) which can be empowered to oversee new laws resulting from the application of the new Art 23 GG. However, no legal requirement to follow the opinion of the *Bundestag* is placed on the government.[47]

The federal government is required to take account of the opinion of the *Bundesrat* in matters, which impinge on the exclusive legislative competence of the *Länder* (Art. 23 V GG). Different rules apply to the participation of the *Bundesrat* according to the subject matter. This has now been further regulated by an Applications Statute.[48] Essentially, where a matter impinges on the interests of the *Länder*, where represented by the *Bundesrat*, the federal government is only obliged to take account of the opinion of the *Bundesrat*. It is not binding. This applies also to areas of usual competence of the *Bundestag* and in areas of concurrent legislative competence. Where the matter concerns the legislative competence of the *Bundesrat* affecting *Länder* authorities or administrative procedures, the view of the *Bundesrat* should prevail. However, in cases of conflict between the government and *Bundesrat*, the Application Statute provides a special process whereby the view of the *Bundesrat* will prevail if secured by at least a two-thirds majority.[49]

Finally, in cases of conflict in areas of the exclusive legislative competence of the *Bundesrat* (Art. 23 VI GG), not only should the view of the *Bundesrat* prevail, but it shall also have the right to represent the Federal Republic of Germany in the EU.[50] A representative of the *Bundestag* additionally has the right to participate in EU level

---

[47] *Gesetz über die Zusammenarbeit von Bundesregierung und Deutschem Bundestag in Angelegenheiten der Europäischen Union* of 12 March 1993, BGBl I, S. 311.

[48] *Gesetz über die Zusammenarbeit von Bund und Ländern in Angelegenheiten der Europäischen Union* 12 March 1993, BGBl I, S. 313. This Statute repealed at the same time Art. 2 of the Statute on the SEA, see above.

[49] § 5 II *Gesetz über die Zusammenarbeit von Bund und Ländern in Angelegenheiten der Europäischen Union* 12 March 1993, BGBl I, S. 313.

[50] For further and more general considerations of the new Art. 23, see U. Di Fabio, *Der Neue Artikel 23 des Grundgesetzes, Der Staat* (1993), pp. 191 et seq.

discussions. Both must work in co-operation and take into account the expressed opinion of the government.[51]

An amended Article 50 GG extends the powers and tasks of the *Bundesrat* into matters of European Union and gives it a co-legislative role. Article 52 III a GG formally institutionalizes the *Europakammer*, which was previously established to assist the *Bundesrat* in participation in European matters relevant to it. Decisions of this Committee count as decisions of the *Bundesrat* itself in the German legislative process. An addition to Article 24 is made to formalize the requirement that the approval of the *Bundesrat* is required in decisions which transfer powers affecting the *Länder* (Art. 24 I a GG).

The German Accession Act to the Treaty on European Union was passed by the German Parliament in December 1992.[52] However, as a result of considerable criticism that there had been no real debate on Maastricht in Germany and that a referendum had not been held to test public opinion on further integration, constitutional complaints were made to the BVerfG by a former German EC Commission official (Manfred Brunner) and four German MEP's of the Green Party acting in individual capacities.

Due to the importance of this case for the subject of Germany and the EU, it will be considered in some detail.[53]

2.5.5 *The Maastricht judgment*[54]

BVerfGE 89,155 Maastricht Urteil

The grounds of challenge focused on the threat to the constitutionally guaranteed principles of German democracy and national sovereignty posed by accession to the Maastricht Treaty, in particular to Article 20 GG, the requirement that Germany be a democratic state, and under Article 38, the right to take part in elections to select a government and its policies as well as the right of the MPs to effectively take part in democratic decision-making. The complaints were also aimed at the Act amending the *Grundgesetz*,[55] notably Article 23 GG. As a consequence, the formal confirmation (*Ausfertigung*) by the German President to complete the process for parliamentary approval was delayed until the constitutional case had been decided.

---

[51] This is approved by new Articles 203 EC as an accepted representative at the ministerial level who can act with binding force on behalf of the government of the Member State.

[52] *Gesetz zum Vertrag vom 7. Februar 1992 über die Europäische Union* of 28 December 1992, BGBl II S. 1251.

[53] Further detail can be found in N. Foster, "The German Constitution and EC Membership", Public Law, Autumn 1994, pp. 392–408.

[54] *Bundesverfassungsgericht* 12 October 1993. Cases 2 BvR 2134/92 and 2BvR 2159/92. English translation; [1994] 1 CMLR 57. For considerations of the judgment in German legal literature see, *inter alia*, Götz JZ 1993 1081–1086, Schachtschneider, *Recht und Politik*, 1994, 1–9; Schwarze, *Neue Justiz*, 1994, 1–5; Ipsen, EuR, 1994, 1–21; and Herdegen, "Maastricht and the German Constitutional Court: Constitutional Restraints for an Ever Closer Union" (1994) 31 CML Rev 235–249.

[55] *Gesetz zur Änderung des Grundgesetzes* of 21 December 1992, BGBl I S. 2086, noted above.

Of the various grounds cited in the constitutional complaint only a complaint in respect of Article 38 I showed the possibility of infringement and all others were dismissed as inadmissible.[56] It was argued that ratification of the Maastricht Treaty would undermine the right to participate in the exercise of state power, guaranteed by Article 20 II GG, 2nd sentence, by transferring power to the Community and away from democratic representatives in the *Bundestag* and the *Länder* representatives in the *Bundesrat*. The personal right to vote to influence the exercise of state power was alleged to have been damaged.

While BVerfG agreed that the transfer of power to the EC had the consequence of the *Bundestag* reducing its authority over certain policy areas and in turn of the voters losing their influence in those areas, Article 38 would only be infringed if the transfer of powers to the EC resulted in the minimum requirements of Article 20 I and II no longer being observed. It is notable in the case that despite restricting itself to the merits of the one ground it held to be admissible, the BVerfG in fact reviewed the whole process of accession and the content of the Maastricht Treaty. For example, the BVerfG considered that there would be a wider protection of German fundamental rights after the entry into force of the Maastricht Treaty and that it would provide protection against the acts of Community institutions by reviewing them in the light of the *Grundgesetz* protections. However, it emphasized that its review of EC law for compatibility with the fundamental rights provision of the *Grundgesetz* would be exercised in co-operation with the European Court of Justice. It emphasized that as the ECJ guaranteed basic rights for the whole of the EC in individual cases, the BVerfG would restrict itself to a general guarantee of basic rights standards.[57]

In its judgment, the BVerfG ruled that the Accession to the Maastricht Treaty under the terms agreed by the German Federal Parliament and the subsequent transfer of powers were compatible with the principles of the *Grundgesetz* requiring democratic legitimation and were thus constitutional. The Court considered that the constitutional principle of democracy and the right to vote in parliamentary elections under Article 38 *Grundgesetz* do not prevent the Federal Republic from transferring part of its power to supranational institutions such as the European Community.[58] However, Article 38 GG would prevent such a transfer if the democratic content of the right under Article 38 GG is reduced to such an extent as to become meaningless and thus contrary to Articles 79 III and 20 I GG.[59] The Court suggested that substantial powers can be transferred and exercised by supranational institutions if constitutionally legitimized via the

---

[56] Breaches of the following articles of the *Grundgesetz* were alleged: Arts 1(1), 2(1), 5(1), 9(1), 12(1), 20(4) in connection with 93(4a), 21(1), 14(1), 38(1) and 38(2). For details of the procedure for constitutional complaints see the Law on the federal Constitutional Court (Bundesverfassungsgerichtsgesetz BVerfGG) Arts 90–95, especially Art. 93a and Articles 38–39 of the Rules of Procedure of the Federal Constitutional Court.

[57] See the judgment, at B 2.b. [1994] 1 CMLR 57 at 79, paras 12–13, EuGRZ 1993, pp. 434–5. The FCC referred back to its judgments in the two *Solange* cases. It seems this case has re-opened the potential for conflict or even extended the potential scope for conflict, especially as the previous position maintained by the BVerfG was that it would not accept direct complaints against Community legislation, BVerfGE 58, 1.

[58] See the judgment, at C I 2. a-b., [1994] 1 CMLR 57, at 85–6, paras 36–38.

[59] ibid., at C I 1., [1994] 1 CMLR 57 at 84, para. 34.

Bundestag but that Article 38 GG would be violated if the German Accession Act did not state with sufficient clarity the scope of those transferred powers. The Court further considered that, Article 38 does not allow a general transfer of powers.[60] This has the consequence that if the European Union institutions applied or developed the Treaty in a manner which is not compatible with the Accession Act, any European legal instruments would not be binding within German territory and German state organs would be prevented constitutionally from applying such legal instruments. The Court therefore reserved the right to review legal instruments issued by the European Union with a view to determining whether or not they were compatible with the powers transferred. In other words the Community legal order is subject to the approval of the BVerfG.[61] But the BVerfG considered that as the EU cannot act beyond the powers given to it by the Member States (as "Masters of the Treaties" (*Herren der Verträge*)), it does not deprive national parliaments, including the *Bundestag*, of any further powers than those already democratically and constitutionally ceded. Hence it held that the transfer does not offend the *Grundgesetz*.[62] The BVerfG also considered carefully Article F3 TEU[63] and concluded that there had been no transfer of power to create powers by the enactment of Articles F3[64] and, having made all of these observations, the Court concluded that, the Accession Act and the Maastricht Treaty were constitutional.[65]

Finally, the Court held that the ratification of the Treaty does not automatically lead to the establishment of a currency union,[66] which may have undermined the constitutional principles, but provides for controlled integration, step by step, each step being subject to further requirements which are either known to the German Parliament at this date, or which depend on further consent by the federal government by participation in future intergovernmental conferences, and which can be influenced by the German and other parliaments.[67] Therefore there had been no breach of Article 79 III GG and the principle of democratic legitimacy.

It would seem that both the amendment of the *Grundgesetz* and the ruling of the BVerfG should satisfy most of the concerns raised that the constitution was been breached by deeper European integration. On the one hand, the BVerfG may be regarded as legitimately substantiating a supervisory role over future proposals for integration and securing greater transparency in parliamentary debate of

---

[60] ibid., at C I 3., [1994] 1 CMLR 57 at 88–9, para. 48.
[61] ibid., at C I 3., [1994] 1 CMLR 57 at 89, para. 49.
[62] ibid., at C II 1.a., [1994] 1 CMLR 57 at 90–1, paras 52–56.
[63] Which states: "The Union shall provide itself with the means necessary to attain its objectives and carry through its policies".
[64] No *Kompetenz-Kompetenz* as it is referred to and understood in German. See the Judgment, at C II 2.b. 1–5, [1994] 1 CMLR 57 at 94–5, paras 59 and 65–68.
[65] ibid., at C II 2.c., [1994] 1 CMLR 57, at 97, para. 78.
[66] ibid., at C II 2.d.5., [1994] 1 CMLR 57 at 101 para. 87. The BVerfG seemed very concerned with the role played by the DM because it has upheld economic and thus political stability. It considered it vital that moves to monetary union be subject to clear control as this was a condition precedent for German participation and continued membership.
[67] ibid., at C II e-f., [1994] 1 CMLR 57 at 101–02, paras 89–91.

Community proposals. On the other hand, it has also been argued that the democratic ideals of European Union were upheld by the Court in preference to the democratic reality of the *Grundgesetz*.[68] The decision does not block further progress to European integration because it confirms that the new Article 23 GG is the proper basis for further integration. Ultimately, the effectiveness of the procedures adopted by the German *Bundesrat* and *Bundestag* in reviewing Community proposals and the level of participation allowed the *Bundesrat* and *Bundestag* representatives at the European level may determine whether concerns about the participation of the *Länder* will be resolved. Article 23 *Grundgesetz* may, however, hinder the development of the EU by imposing a cumbersome and interruptive legislative procedure in Germany, which may hold up the EU decision making process. A further difficulty caused by the judgment may be that encouraged by the pronouncements of the BVerfG, lower courts may well consider that the BVerfG needs to be made aware of possible infringements of the *Grundgesetz* by EC law and to be given the chance to adjudicate on them. Having made the statements in the present case, it must be assumed that the BVerfG is prepared to undertake the functions it has reserved for itself. These are, to review Community law in the light of the fundamental rights provision of the *Grundgesetz*, to review legal instruments of the EC to see if they are compatible with the extent of the powers transferred, and, presumably, to be prepared to adjudicate on complaints that either the institutions of the Community under Article 308 (ex 235) EC Treaty or the ECJ has gone too far in developing Community law. The Court's conclusion that the Accession Act was compatible with the *Grundgesetz*, by its suggestion that the BVerfG reserve to itself a review function over these three areas, seems only to give rise to possible future conflicts between Community law and the *Grundgesetz* or between the ECJ and the BVerfG—even if the BVerfG likes to declare its relationship to the ECJ as a cooperative one (*Kooperationsverhältnis*).

The Television Directive case, noted above, was decided against the government but appears to represent no further complication for German-EC relations. It was held that the federal government had breached the rights of the *Länder* arising from Article 70 I GG in connection with Article 24 I GG and a constitutional principle (*Grundsatz des bundesfreundlichen Verhaltens*) because it failed in its duty to properly or adequately work with and consult the *Länder* in a EC matter which infringed on the legislative competence of the *Länder*. It was, however, further held that, the Directive itself could not be declared inadmissible because the right to enact or repeal Directives was that of the Community and not the German government or parliament.[69]

2.5.6 *Further development*

After the Maastricht judgment the relationship between ECJ and the BVerfG remains unclear. Even though the BVerfG claims that fundamental rights will be

---

[68] See *Der Spiegel*, 42/1993, pp. 28–32.
[69] The full text of the judgment of 22 March 1995 can be found in EuGRZ 1995 at pp. 125–137.

protected and upheld by a relationship of co-operation between both courts, it does not clearly explain how this protection will work in practice. It seems that the BVerfG has accepted the standard of basic rights protection provided by ECJ but reserves a right to review EC acts that would evidently infringe basic rights under the *Grundgesetz*, if the ECJ does not offer protection. So far this has been a theoretical case. The lengthy "banana battle" however did not culminate in a decision defining when exactly the BVerfG is willing to use its reserved power to review EC acts, despite the anticipation of many academics:

BVerfG–2 BvL 1/97- Bananenmarktverordnung[70]

In 1993 the new EC regulation on the banana market aimed at benefiting ACP-bananas. Quotas and duties were put on the import of other bananas, mainly those from Latin American countries (*Dollarbananen*). An import company in Germany that for several years used to import about 100,000 t of these bananas p.a. was only allowed a quota of 150 t to be imported under a preferential duty for the year of 1994 according to the new regulation. Special circumstances in favour of the company had not been taken into account. The company challenged the quota and implicitly the regulation before the Administrative Court (VG) in Frankfurt/a.M. asking for interim measures. Together with other importers in a similar situation they claimed a breach of their basic right to carry commercial activity, property, and profession (Arts 12, 14 GG), as the new quota was about to ruin their business. The administrative court submitted the EC regulation to the BVerfG according to Article 100 I GG in order to decide on its compatibility with basic rights under the *Grundgesetz*. According to the *Solange II* decision such a submission would be inadmissible as long as the ECJ provides a sufficient protection of basic rights, which has generally been accepted. But in this case the VG Frankfurt argued that recent case-law of the ECJ showed a less effective protection of individual's basic rights, especially when weighing them against measures of Common Agricultural Policies. Furthermore, the ECJ had already upheld the EC regulation on bananas in a previous case, when Germany had challenged it because of violations of WTO law and basic rights. After having granted the interim measures to avert the company's financial ruin[71] the BVerfG finally decided that the complaint of the main procedure was inadmissible. It held that the plaintiff had failed to show a decline of the standard of protection of basic rights in ECJ case law. It also pointed out subsequent amendments to the regulation as well as the ECJ's decision of 1996 requiring the Commission to provide for transitory hardship clauses.

Furthermore, because of several parts contradicting WTO law the regulation had been partly revised. The case shows the ECJ as well as the BVerfG prefer an exchange of views through their decisions resulting in co-operation of the courts

[70] Of 7 June 2000.
[71] BVerfG EuZW 1995, 126.

rather than open confrontation.[72] Whether the BVerfG at some point will admit a constitutional complaint due to a decline in the ECJ's protection of basic rights remains even more doubtful after this decision.[73]

2.6 International law

Treaties under public international law have to be transformed into national law in order to become effective on a national level. Article 59 II GG requires the consent and participation of the legislative institutions, namely *Bundestag* and *Bundesrat*. General rules of international law, however, are given direct effect by the general transformation clause of Article 25 GG. This provision declares all general rules of international law an integral part of federal law, directly creating rights and duties for the inhabitants of the federal territory. They rank above federal laws but below the constitution.

2.6.1 *The position of the ECHR (EMRK)*

An example for an international treaty transformed into national law is the European Convention for the Protection of Human Rights and Fundamental Freedoms (ECHR: *EMRK*). It was signed and ratified by the Federal Republic in 1952 and transformed into federal law in the same year.[74] The transformation into federal law meant that the European Convention ranks equally with other federal *Gesetze* and is binding on all authorities and courts and overrules inconsistent law of the *Länder* and prior inconsistent federal legislation. However, the exact status of the Convention in the German legal order is far from undisputed. Opinions vary from according the individual rights of the Convention a status the equivalent of the *Grundrechte* in the *Grundgesetz* to, treating them as a guide for the interpretation of the *Grundrechte* or as an analogy for the interpretation of the *Grundgesetz*, to the majority view that it ranks equally with any other *Bundesgesetz* and that consequently any later *Gesetz* in conflict should be accorded priority. Alternative opinions suggest that later laws should be interpreted in conformity with the Convention as it has assumed the status of a special law.[75] The most unfortunate consequence of the adopted method is that a complaint that one of the rights protected by the Convention has been breached cannot be raised as a constitutional complaint before the BVerfG because the rights protected do not give rise to a right of action under Article 93 I 4a GG.[76]

It was originally considered that because the *Grundgesetz* provision of human

---

[72] As expressly noted by the BVerfG, 2 BvL 1/97, para. 68.

[73] For further discussion see also H.-W. Arndt, *Europarecht*, 4th ed. (1999: C. F. Müller Heidelberg), pp.77–80; Oppermann, *Europarecht*, 2nd ed. (1999: C. H. Beck, Munich) pp. 571–573, T. Stein, "*Bananen-Split?*", 1998 EuZW 261 et seq.

[74] BGBl 1952 II S. 685.

[75] For a full discussion of the various opinions and theories of the position and status of the ECHR in the German Legal system refer to B. Schmid, *Rang und Geltung der EMRK in der Vertragsstaaten*, (1984: Helbing & Lichtenhahn, Basel), pp. 23 et seq. in respect of Germany and W. Kleeberger, *Die Stellung der Rechte der Europäischen Menschenrechtskonvention in der Rechtsordnung der Bundesrepublik Deutschland* (1992: Verlag V. Florentz, Munich).

[76] BVerfGE 10, 274.

rights was so extensive that would be no need to rely on the ECHR but this has not always proved to be the case, as exemplified by the telephone tapping and length of proceedings cases amongst others.[77]

2.7 Natural law as source of law?

Typical questions of legal philosophy such as "Why does law exist?" and "Why is it binding?" offer two answers—in a nutshell: either because man has set it as law or because there is a natural source of law and justice. Whereas the first possibility only accepts as law rules that have been positively set up by the state the second possibility refers to a source of law independent from law-making mechanisms. In German history the perversion of law by the Third Reich showed that the law enacted by the state could be manifestly unjust, for example the Nuremberg race laws, which openly discriminated against Jews. But when referring to a source of law or justice above the law set by man the difficulty of determining this source arises. Theological principles as well as principles of common sense have been used in the history of legal philosophy leaving unanswered the question of who was to define the exact scope of such sources of law. Immediately after the Second World War natural law had been used as a source of law in several German court decisions, especially when dealing with cases where people had acted lawfully under the previous law of the Third Reich.[78] However, towards the end of the fifties natural law no longer appeared in German court decisions.

Natural law has **not** been recognized as a source of law in Germany. Instead, fundamental values (e.g., Human Dignity) and principles have been included in the constitution as "eternal" law, exempt from any constitutional amendment (Art. 1, 20, 79 III GG).

2.8 Summary

To conclude the hierarchy of these sources of law is mapped out below. It has to be borne in mind that although EC law as supranational law prevails over any national law, this relationship is not entirely clear, where EC Law infringes basic rights guaranteed by the *Grundgesetz*.

According to general opinion judicial decisions do not constitute sources of law, although this is disputed.[79] International law only becomes source of law directly applicable when it is transformed into national law either at the same level as federal laws (Acts of Parliament, Art. 59 II GG) or above them but below constitutional law (Art. 25 GG).[80]

---

[77] *Klass v West Germany*, European Court of Human Rights, Judgment of 6 September 1978 and *König v Germany*, 1978 and *Eckle v Germany*, 1982.
[78] See Rüthers, above, n. 7, pp. 248–249. For natural law and the "*Radbruch'sche Formel*" in decisions of the Federal Supreme Court and the Federal Constitutional Court see below, Chapter 6, sec. 5.2, Articles 103 II.
[79] See above, sec. 2.4.
[80] See above, sec. 2.6 and below, Chapter 6, sec. 2.4.

German Legal System: Hierarchy of Sources of Law

(1) **Supranational law**: EC law/EU law
  (a) primary legislation: EC Treaties of the European Communities, Treaty of the European Union, accession treaties, etc.
  (b) secondary legislation: e.g. EC directives, EC regulations (Art. 249 EC)
(2) **National law**:
  (a) Federal law (*Bundesrecht*)
    (i)   (federal) constitution (*Grundgesetz*)
    (ii) federal laws: Acts of Parliament (*Bundesgesetze*)
    (iii) federal laws: delegated legislation (*Rechtsverordnungen des Bundes*, Art. 80 I GG)
    (iv) bye-laws of federal institutions
  (b) Law of the *Länder* (*Landesrecht*)
    (i)   constitutions of the *Länder* (*Länderverfassungen*)
    (ii) laws of the *Länder*: acts passed by parliaments of the *Länder* (*Landesgesetze*)
    (iii) laws of the *Länder*: delegated legislation (*Landesrechtsverordnungen*)
    (iv) bye-laws
  (c) customary law

---

3 Legal method

When applying the law the lawyer is required to observe the systematic order of the legal system as well as certain methods. This section will briefly look at the methods by which law is applied such as *Subsumtion*, drawing analogies and rules of interpretation.[81]

3.1 Hierarchy of legal provisions

Obviously the hierarchy of laws or legal provisions has to be observed when applying them, as a higher-ranking provision prevails over a lower-ranking one. This hierarchy has been mapped out above. Among legal provisions of equal rank the following rules apply:

  (i) Later provisions prevail over older ones (*lex posterior derogat legi priori*),
  (ii) More specific provisions prevail over general ones (*lex specialis derogat legi generali*).

---

[81] See generally on this topic Rüthers, above, n 7, Chapter 4, pp. 364–547.

3.2 *Subsumtion*

Applying the law means finding the apt legal provision that fits the individual case. The lawyer will have then have to apply this (general) legal provision (*abstrakter Rechtssatz*) to this concrete case (*konkreter Sachverhalt*) examining whether the facts of the case match the abstract conditions named in the provision. This examination is called *Subsumtion*. The term derives from the Latin word *subsumere* meaning "to draw something under something". Here the lawyer has to draw the concrete facts of the case under the wording of an abstract provision.

Example: Satish has always longed enviously for Nigel's posh *Cardiff Law School* pen. One day during a chat in Nigel's office Satish takes the pen and slips it into his pocket without Nigel noticing it. If only German Criminal law was applicable in Nigel's office, would Satish have committed a theft?

The relevant provision of the German Criminal Code could be § 242 I StGB, a rough translation of this provision being: "Whoever **takes away a mobile thing** from **someone else** with the **intention** of **unlawfully appropriating** it or giving it to someone else, shall be punished by imprisonment up to five years or a fine". *Subsumtion* now requires comparing the facts of the case with the elements of § 242 I StGB:

The pen is a **mobile thing** not belonging to Satish. By slipping the pen into his pocket Satish has removed it from Nigel's possession, in other words he has **taken it out of someone else's area of control**. It does not matter that he is still in Nigel's office, because Nigel no longer exerts any control over the pen. Satish also did this with the **intention of appropriating** it, as he wanted to own the pen. This appropriation is also **unlawful** as he is not entitled to it. Thus as all conditions of §242 I StGB have been fulfilled, Satish has committed a theft (it would be different if Nigel had previously sold the pen to Satish but subsequently refused to hand it over. The contract of sale would then have entitled Satish to the pen even before having become lawful owner).

3.3 **Gaps of legislation and analogies**

The previous example dealt with a rather straightforward case of theft. It becomes more problematic where *Subsumtion* is not that simple. Difficulties arise where elements of a legal provision cannot be easily interpreted or where the facts of a particular case do not exactly match the conditions of the legal provision. The latter will be the case where the legislative has not foreseen a particular case as a consequence of which a gap in legislation appears. Two examples will illustrate this:

Example 1: *A* sells *B* a car malevolently feigning good acceleration as special characteristic. According to the former[82] § 463 S.2 BGB the buyer has a claim to compensation, if the seller malevolently conceals a fault of the object of sale. Could this provision be applied by analogy?

Example 2: Without intention to pay for it *A* extracts electrical energy from the electrical supply for his own private purposes. Has he committed a theft? If not, is § 242 I StGB at least applicable by analogy?

Analogies have been generally accepted as instruments to fill out legislative gaps.[83] The two main conditions for applying a legislative provision in an analogous way are:

(i) An unintended legislative gap (*planwidrige Gesetzeslücke*),

(ii) A comparable relation of interests involved (*vergleichbare Interessenlage*).

Thus a lawyer, especially the judge, does not only have to determine whether the particular case bears sufficient resemblance to other cases that are clearly covered by a legal provision. He furthermore has to decide whether the legislature overlooked the gap by accident. In some cases the legislature might have decided not to regulate a certain set of cases. Exceptionally, analogies are not permitted in criminal law where they would disadvantage the individual as this would breach the principle of legal certainty. In our examples this leads to the following results:

Example 1: The former § 463 S.2 BGB provides only for the malevolent concealment of faults of an object of sale. The malevolent feigning of a beneficial characteristic is not provided for. The legislature did not foresee this as a source of litigation. However, the situation is comparable. The Federal Court of Justice has held that feigning characteristics of an object of sale is as detrimental as concealing them and that in both situations the seller misuses the buyer's ignorance in order to induce him to conclude the contract.[84] Note that this provision has been deleted by the reform to the law of obligations.[85]

Example 2: The problem in this—authentic—case was that electric energy did not constitute a **mobile thing**. As we have seen the theft provision only covers mobile things. Thus the question arose whether § 242 I StGB could be used in an analogous way. The situation seemed to be comparable to the usual cases of theft. However, as

---

[82] This provision has now been deleted by the reform of the law of obligations, however, it may still serve as an example for analogies.

[83] Palandt-Heinrichs, *Bürgerliches Gesetzbuch*, 59th ed. (2000: München, Einleitung), para. 40; B. Rüthers, above, n 7, pp. 489–493; H. Brox, *Allgemeiner Teil des BGB*, 23rd ed. (1999: München), pp. 39–42.

[84] BGHZ 105, 140.

[85] For details on the new law on contracts of sale, see below, Chapter 10, sec. D.

> criminal law provides for the most restricting possible legal consequences an individual must face, its terms must be well defined. This principle of legal certainty prohibits any analogy to the detriment of the individual. Thus a conviction for theft was impossible.[86]

Other instruments to fill out gaps are the ***argumentum a fortiori*** (*Erst-recht-Schluss*) and **teleological reduction** (*Teleologische Reduktion*). The latter will be examined in the next section. An example for the *argumentum a fortiori* is the interpretation of Article 14 III GG by the Federal Court of Justice: This provision provides for compensation in cases of lawful expropriation. The Court held that it follows that unlawful expropriations have to be compensated even more so.[87]

3.4 Statutory interpretation (*Auslegung von Gesetzen*)

Where the application of the legal rule to the facts is not obvious or the factual situation is not one clearly envisaged by the legal rule, more than a straightforward application of the law is required on behalf of the judge. The first step taken by the judge is then to interpret the law. If no relevant provision by interpretation can cover the case, then a gap in the legislation becomes apparent and the judge might turn to gap filling methods such as analogies, etc.[88] Although this progression seems logical in theory, in practice such a clear procedure is not always upheld. Rather it seems that interpretation is used for gap filling and the line between interpreting the law and creating new law is often blurred.[89]

There are two approaches to interpretation: the **objective interpretation**, which considers what the statute requires, and the **subjective interpretation**, which concentrates on the purpose and intent of the law from the point of view of the legislator. In spite of academic disputes about objective and subjective interpretation[90] it is commonly accepted that the aim of any interpretation is to find the purpose or aim of the provision.[91] The judges often employ a combination of both general approaches to legal problems along with the following more precise techniques of interpretation. These techniques have developed not too differently from the rules of legislative interpretation employed in the U.K. Briefly they are:

(a) The grammatical interpretation (*grammatische* or *philologische Auslegung/ Auslegung nach dem Wortlaut*), which gives the words used their literal meaning or attempts to respect the internal sense of the words and sentence in their ordinary or common legal usage and is the equivalent of the literal rule in the United Kingdom.

---

[86] RGSt 29, 111.
[87] BGHZ 6, 270. For Articles 14 GG see below, Chapter 7, sec. 2.2.
[88] See previous section.
[89] See above, sec. 2.4, on judicial law-making.
[90] See below.
[91] Palandt-Heinrichs, above, n 79, *Einführung*, para. 34; Brox, above, n 79, p. 36; Rüthers, above, n 7, p. 403–405.

(b) The logical (*logische Auslegung*) and systematic (*systematische Auslegung*) interpretations are sometimes considered separately but together form a kind of contextual rule to interpret the provision in the context or light of the system of rules or the provision as a whole.

Should these rather objective rules fail to render a clear decision possible the following subjective rules are employed:

(c) The historical rule (*historische Auslegung*) considers the state of affairs at the time the provision was drafted in order to determine what the draftsman or legislator wanted or was seeking to protect or correct.

(d) The teleological rule (*teleologische Auslegung*) aims to determine the meaning of the provision in the light of the purpose or aim of the provision or provisions. This, however, should not distract from the fact that all interpretation must strive to find the aim or purpose of the law.

In order to apply these subjective rules of interpretation it is quite in order for the judge to look at the source of the subjective intent and thus the preparatory legislative material, which is evidence of this intent. Therefore a wide range of materials is available to the German judiciary to assist them, including parliamentary minutes, Commission minutes, or any other form of official statement in respect of the legislation.

Among these rules grammatical interpretation takes priority. This, however, may pose problems, where vague general clauses come into play offering a range of possibilities of interpretation. Thus § 138 I BGB declares void all contracts that contravene "good morals" (*gute Sitten*). What a judge will regard as a violation of good morals will probably depend on views held in society at the time of the decision. Then again there might not be a homogenous view in society on the morals of a particular subject as the following example shows:

AG Emden NJW 1975, S. 1363 Hoteldoppelzimmer

In 1975 the *Amtsgericht* (Lower Court) *Emden* held void a contract of booking a double hotel room on the basis of § 138 I BGB. It had only turned out after the booking of the room for a couple, i.e., on their arrival, that they were not married. The hotel owner considered it immoral to let a room to an unmarried couple and thus refused to hand out the keys. The couple brought an action for performance. The court agreed with the defendant regarding the contract as contravening good morals, although arguably by 1975 there was no longer a clear majority within society detecting anything immoral about the couple's behaviour.

Instead of restricting judges to a simple unrealistic application of statutory rules the German legal system, through these general legal rules or clauses, allows some form of judicial interpretation applying the law to fit present social, economic, and political circumstances. Thus the law remains open to changes in society allowing or interpretations the original legislator had not even thought of. Even though the *AG Emden* still upheld the view of the legislator enacting the original § 138 I BGB of 1900 a court nowadays would most probably take a different view. In other words: legislation turns out to be wiser than its legislator. This objective interpretation of the law is favoured by general opinion because it enhances flexibility of the law.[92] However, there are minority views drawing attention to the disadvantages. It is argued that this objective approach gives too much legislative power to the judiciary thus infringing the principle of separation of powers. It then becomes increasingly difficult to distinguish the application of law from judicial law making.[93]

A classical example showing the blurring of the line between interpretation and judicial law making is the famous *Soraya* case.

BVerfGE 34, 269 Soraya

The case deals specifically with the ability of the courts to extend legal protection to the general right of personality beyond that formally provided by legislation. It concerned an action for damages for defamation by the ex-wife of the Shah of Iran against "*Die Welt*" newspaper. Although the behaviour leading to the claim was a criminal offence, it would not, under the existing German laws, constitute a civil ground for obtaining damages, as § 253 BGB only allows compensation for immaterial damages where the law explicitly says so. The Federal Court of Justice was nevertheless able to make an award on the basis that the protection of the personality by the *Grundgesetz*[94] was a reflection of the changed values of society, which should in turn be reflected by the judgments of the courts. Thus the Court's interpretation went expressly against the wording of Article 253 BGB. The judgment was contested before the Federal Constitutional Court (BVerfG) on the grounds that the judges had gone beyond their formal and constitutionally allowed function. The BVerfG reasoned that the traditional view, that judges were entirely bound by statute and statute only, had now changed and that the *Grundgesetz* had specifically sanctioned that change by the words "*Gesetz und Recht* (law and justice)" in Article 20 III GG. The Court acknowledged that there were gaps in legislation which had to be filled by the judiciary, who must resort to sources other than statutory. Thus the judge must be able to rely on common sense views of what the solution should be, sometimes referred to as the sense of justice (*Rechtsgefühl*), and from general principles of justice as established by society.

---

[92] See Palandt-Heinrichs, above, n 79, *Einführung*, para. 34 with further references.
[93] Rüthers, above, n 7, pp. 448–449. *Rüthers*, however, seems to accept the fact that judicial law making may be required, as changes in society demand a new application of the laws. But as a consequence this should be openly labelled as "judicial law-making" instead of disguising it as "interpretation". It would then put judges under higher pressure to support their decisions by clear, logical and convincing reasoning, ibid., p. 453.
[94] Articles 2 I in connection with Articles1 I GG, see also below, Chapter 7, sec. 2.2.

Other examples of the judicial establishment of legal principles are the treatment of the hyper-inflation cases of the 1920's[95] and decisions in the area of Labour law. Here the traditional role of the judiciary has been questioned in the light of the leading role played by the courts and role given to the Federal Labour Court to develop labour law.[96]

The Soroya Case indicates that legal development is not only an accepted part of judicial function but also an encouraged part. The *Grundgesetz*, Article 20 III GG determines that the judiciary shall be bound by "law and justice". When applying § 253 BGB the Federal Court had employed the measure of "**teleological reduction**". This means the court when interpreting the provision "reduced" its scope to achieve an inherent aim. This aim was the effective protection of a right to personality. Although it was not mentioned in § 253 BGB it was derived from Article 2 I and Article 1 I GG, a higher-ranking source of law. Thus § 253 BGB was interpreted in the light of the *Grundgesetz*. What remained questionable was the fact that the Court had interpreted the provision against its wording (*contra legem*). Although the decision was heavily disputed,[97] it became accepted as general approach to damages claims against infringements of personality rights. This approach has recently been confirmed when assessing the appropriate sum to compensate for violations of personality rights by the press, stressing its punitive effect.[98]

FURTHER READING

R. Alexy and R. Dreier, 'Statutory Interpretation in the Federal Republic of Germany' in D. N. MacCormick and R. S. Summers (eds.), *Interpreting Statutes: A Comparative Study* (1991: Dartmouth, Aldershot), pp. 73–121.

K. Engisch, *Einführung in das juristische Denken*, 5th. ed. (1997: Kohlhammer, Stuttgart).

R. Haase and R. Keller, *Grundlagen und Grundformen des Rechts: Eine Einführung*, 9th ed. (1992: Kohlhammer, Stuttgart).

A. Pizzorusso (ed.), *Law in the Making* (1988: Springer Verlag, Berlin).

B. Rüthers, *Rechtstheorie* (1999: C.H. Beck, Munich).

W. Schreckenberger et al. (eds.), *Gesetzgebungslehre* (1986: Kohlhammer, Stuttgart).

D. Schmalz, *Methodenlehre für das juristische Studium*, 3rd ed. (1992: Nomos Verlag, Baden-Baden).

R. Zippelius, *Juristische Methodenlehre*, 6th ed. (1994: C.H. Beck, Munich).

The Reception and Status of Community Law

H.-W. Arndt, *Europarecht*, 4th ed. (1999: C.F. Müller, Heidelberg), pp. 77–81.

P. Craig/G. Burca, *EU Law*, 2nd ed. (1998: Oxford University Press, Oxford) pp. 268–276.

P.M. Lutzeler, *Western Europe in Transition: West Germany's Role in the European Community*, (1986: Nomos Verlag, Baden-Baden).

---

[95] RGZ 107, 78.

[96] See M. Weiss, *Labour Law and Industrial Relations in the Federal Republic of Germany* (1987: Kluwer), p. 34.

[97] For critical analysis and further reference see T. M. Spranger in J. Menzel (ed.), *Verfassungsrechtsprechung*, (2000: Tübingen), pp. 205–213.

[98] BGH NJW 1996, 984—Caroline von Monaco.

T. Oppermann, *Europarecht*, 2nd ed. (1999: C.H. Beck, München).

C-C. Schweitzer and D. Karsten, (eds.), *The Federal Republic and EC Membership Evaluated* (1990: Pinter Publishers, London).

M. Schweitzer, *Staatsrecht III*, 6th ed. (1997: C.F. Müller, Heidelberg), pp. 10–3.

Starck (ed.), *Rights, Institutions and Impact of International Law according to the German Basic Law* (1987: Nomos Verlag, Baden-Baden).

Articles

N.G. Foster, "The New Conciliation Committee under Article 189b EC" (1994) 19 E L Rev 185–194 (a comparison with the German *Vermittlungsausschuß*).

N.G. Foster, "The German Constitution and EC Membership", Public Law, Autumn 1994, pp. 392–408.

C. Fulda, "Prospective Overruling of Court Decisions in Germany and the United States", (1964) 13 Am J Comp L 438–41.

A. Greifeld, "Requirement of the German Constitution for the Installation of Supranational Authority as posited in the Eurocontrol Decisions by the Constitutional Court" (1983) 20 CML Rev 87–95.

C.W.A. Timmermans, "German Unification and Community Law" (1990) 27 CML Rev 437–449.

W.-H. Roth, "The Application of Community Law in West Germany: 1980–1990" (1991) 28 CMLR 137–182.

C. Tomuschat, "A United Germany within the European Community" (1990) 27 CML Rev 415–436.

B. Vitanayi, "Some Reflections on Article 25 of the Constitution of the German Federal Republic" (1978) 24 NILR 578–588.

3

Legal institutions

1 The courts and court structure: introduction

The German court structure is complex. This is mainly due to two principles in the ordering of the court system. These are the principles of specialization and decentralisation which have evolved due to the federal nature of Germany and the historical development and codification of German law, and the present system thus represents a compromise between maintaining the independence of the *Länder* in legal and court matters and the desire for legal unity. Unification meant a significant restructuring of the court system in the former East Germany in order that the general structure of the German court system be introduced into the new *Bundesländer*. The Unification Treaty required the incorporation of the existing courts and judges into the federal model,[1] a process which is mostly completed, with the exception of one or two moves for federal courts which is taking more time. Brief details of the changes are considered below.

The principal piece of legislation for the courts is the Organization of the Courts Act (*Gerichtsverfassungsgesetz*: GVG),[2] but it is not the only Act concerned with court organization, as will be indicated in the following text.

2 Decentralization

Decentralization arises largely from the division between the federal and *Länder* courts, primarily governed by Article 92 *Grundgesetz*, which states that judicial power is exercised only by the judiciary in the BVerfG, the federal courts and courts of the *Länder*. This is known as the judicial monopoly (*Rechtsprechungsmonopol*). Article 95 *Grundgesetz* states that at the head of each of the five named judicial branches, the Federation is responsible for the highest courts, the federal courts of last instance.

---

[1] Appendix One, Chapter Three, Subject Area A, Parts One to Three and also now the *Gesetz zur Anpassung der Rechtspflege im Beitrittsgebiet vom 30.06.1992* (RpflAnG) BGBl I S. 1147.
[2] This is also translated as the Judicature Act and the Constitution of the Courts Act.

2.1 The federal courts (*Bundesgerichte*)

To a much greater extent than with governmental functions, there is a division between the Federation and the *Länder* in the administration of justice under the *Grundgesetz*, Articles 92 and 95–96. At the head of each of the hierarchies of court there is a federal court. The main duties of these courts are to act as final appeal courts for the *Länder* courts and to ensure the uniform interpretation and development of law in Germany.

The federal courts at the head of the five hierarchies are: the Federal Court of Justice (*Bundesgerichtshof*) in Karlsruhe, the Federal Administrative Court (*Bundesverwaltungsgericht*) in Berlin but which is due to move to Leipzig by the end of 2003, the Federal Labour Court (*Bundesarbeitsgericht*) in Kassel but which is moving to Erfurt, the Federal Social Court (*Bundessozialgericht*) in Kassel, and the Federal Tax Court (*Bundesfinanzhof*) in Munich. Additional courts of the Federation are noted below.

2.2 Courts of the *Länder* (*Gerichte der Länder*)

Each *Land* is set up with its own court structure, according to the general model prescribed by the *Grundgesetz*, and is responsible for its own administration of justice, jurisdiction, and procedure. The new *Länder* are also now required to conform to the same court structure.[3]

The *Länder* maintain responsibility for the staffing, payment, and maintenance of the courts in their region. However, the overall structure and procedure of the courts is almost exclusively federally ordered. There is also a constitutional court in all the *Länder*, with the exception of Schleswig-Holstein and Mecklenburg-Vorpommern which refers constitutional conflicts to the BVerfG, to solve disputes between the organs of the *Land*, to consider questions concerning the validity of *Länder* legislation and to consider questions of the breach of constitutionally protected rights, according to the constitutions of the *Länder* and the *Grundgesetz*.[4]

3 Specialization

To a greater degree than has happened in France and the UK, the German courts have been set up to deal with specialized subjects. Thus five different hierarchies of courts with their own specific jurisdiction have been established. Article 95 *Grundgesetz* also provides the confirmation of the division of the hierarchy of the courts. These hierarchies are:

---

[3] See above, n 1.
[4] In this last respect refer to Prof. Kunig, 'Die Rechtsprechende Gewalt in der Länder und die Grundrechte des Landesverfassungsrechts', NJW 1994, 687 et seq., which considers amongst other matters conflicts in the interpretation of basic rights provisions by the *Länder* constitutional courts and the BVerfG.

(a) *Ordentliche Gerichte*—courts of ordinary or regular jurisdiction;

(b) *Verwaltungsgerichte*—administrative courts;

(c) *Arbeitsgerichte*—labour courts;

(d) *Sozialgerichte*—social courts; and

(e) *Finanzgerichte*—revenue or finance courts.

There is also the jurisdiction of the constitutional courts in the *Länder* and the BVerfG to consider, which does not represent a hierarchy but which does provide a control over the courts of the other jurisdictions in the respective areas of the *Länder* and the *Bund*.

One of the advantages of this division is that disputes and matters of a particular kind can be considered by a court set up specifically for this purpose. The judges will have specialist knowledge and experience in such matters, and therefore there should be a better quality of judicial application for the individual. The more specialized judges should therefore also be aware of the sometimes different principles of law which have been developed in particular areas of law. Disadvantages are the problem of choosing the correct division in cases where the legal matter may overlap the jurisdictions of two or more court hierarchies, the development of differing and even conflicting legal principles, and the consequences of this for the unity of law. In individual cases, this can add to cost and introduce delay to the overall settlement of the case. This is partially overcome by the rule that once a court of ordinary jurisdiction has admitted a case as falling within its material competence, the courts of the other divisions cannot accept the case and, vice versa, if it does not accept the case, the other courts are bound in the last resort to accept it—the so-called positive and negative conflicts of competence or jurisdiction. Many of the potential difficulties have been foreseen in the legislation so that problems are not commonplace. See, *inter alia*, §§ 48 ArbGG (Labour Courts Act: *Arbeitsgerichtsgesetz*) and 17V GVG. Furthermore, the Common Chamber (*Gemeinsamer Senat*) of the federal courts was designed to help alleviate the possibility of conflicting decisions being reached on the same facts by different courts.[5]

Thus, due to the division of courts between the Federation and *Länder*, and the division into five separate hierarchies of jurisdiction and the *Länder* and federal constitutional courts, there are many courts in Germany spread throughout the country.

The jurisdiction of the various courts and routes of appeal are very complex, and only a simplified explanation is given here as an overview. Further details may be found in the sections on procedure and substantive law areas. In particular recently, reform measures have been enacted for civil justice and proposed for criminal justice. The main aspects of these will be noted here where they affect the overall picture of the court system and further details will be given in later chapters where they affect civil and criminal procedural law.

---

[5] For details refer to the Act to protect the unity of decision making from the Highest Courts of the Federation (*Gesetz zur Wahrung der Einheitlichkeit der Rechtsprechung der obersten Gerichtshöfe des Bundes*: RsprEinhG of 19 June 1968 (BGBl I 661)).

3.1 Courts of ordinary jurisdiction

These are primarily concerned with civil actions between citizens and criminal actions between the state and citizens as determined by § 13 GVG. They cover the bulk of legal work in Germany and constitute by far the largest of the court hierarchies. This type of court also has the widest jurisdiction of the five, in that it deals with all matters outside the other specialist courts, including contested actions in all civil matters and non-contentious civil law matters, the so-called *Freiwillige Gerichtsbarkeit*, such as the registration of land and property, procedural aspects of guardianship, wills, and registration of certain legal documents.[6] It also maintains the Commercial Register, which involves the court in considerable work in the registration, alteration, and removal of all forms of commercial association and the details of their management, shareholding, and annual reports. The enforcement of judgments (*Zwangsvollstreckungsverfahren*) may also be carried out by these courts.[7]

This hierarchy of courts is also the most decentralised, with three levels within the *Länder*.

3.1.1 The local court (Amtsgericht)

This is the lowest level of court and can be found in some of the smallest towns (693 in total).[8] It deals with civil disputes of a low value as a small claims court, to a current maximum of DM 10,000 (§§ 23 I 23 II, 23b GVG), although in family law and landlord and tenant matters this limit does not apply in order that local, and thus informed, settlement can be achieved. The specialist chambers dealing with family law matters are termed *Familiengerichte*. In civil law matters, a single judge presides.

The local court also deals with the least serious criminal matters before a single judge where the sentence for the crime, if proven, is expected to be no more than one year. This applies to both types of offence (*Vergehen* and *Verbrechen*).[9] Criminal matters with an expected penalty of up to four years' imprisonment can be tried by a specialist criminal chamber of the *Amtsgericht* consisting of one professional judge (*Berufsrichter*) and two lay judges (*Laienrichter/Schöffen*) and called the (*Kleines*) *Schöffengericht*. In complex matters where the assistance of a second professional judge is considered necessary an *Erweitertes* or *Großes Schöffengericht* can be established (§§ 28–29 GVG). For further details refer to criminal procedure section in Chapter 9 and the section on lay participation in Chapter 4. In a small town a single judge may deal with all these matters. These courts, since they are so

---

[6] For details refer to the *Gesetz über die Angelegenheiten der Freiwilligen Gerichtsbarkeit* (FGG) and for a concise overview of the area, to the student text D. Knöringer, *Freiwillige Gerichtsbarkeit*, 2nd ed. (1995: C.H. Beck, Munich).

[7] The principal authority for enforcement is the *Gerichtsvollzieher* (Court Bailiff) but see ZPO §§ 764, 766, 887–8 and 890 for instances when the ordinary courts undertake this function.

[8] One is allocated per local administrative area (*Landkreis*). The figures for all court numbers are taken from the *Bundesjustizministerium* and are as of 1 January 2001, see the website reference below.

[9] For a consideration of the distinction please refer to the section on criminal law in Chapter 7. Refer also to § 25 III GVG.

numerous, do have distinct advantages, especially in the large cities where there may be dozens of judges specializing in different divisions. They are very accessible and provide simple and speedy solutions. For an appeal in civil matters, the previous minimum appeal value (*Berufungssumme*) of DM 1,500 (€ 0) (§ 511a ZPO) is abolished with effect from 1 January 2002[10] and an appeal without value limit lies, from this court to the regional court as last instance. However, an appeal committee can now refuse appeals which appear hopeless so that issues can no longer be dragged through the appeals procedures merely on account of their value and regardless of their merits, which was often the case previously. In family matters the appeal goes to the higher regional Court of Appeal (§ 119 GVG). In criminal matters appeals from a single judge go to the *Kleine Strafkammer* (small criminal court) and those from the *Schöffengericht* go to the *Große Strafkammer* (large criminal court) of the *Landegericht*.

3.1.2 *The regional court (Landgericht)*

There are 116 regional courts in Germany, based in larger towns and cities. Apart from hearing appeals from the *Amtsgerichte* (§ 72 GVG), the *Landgerichte* are also courts of first instance for all civil matters and commercial matters not tried by the *Amtsgericht* (§ 71 GVG) where the value of the matter in dispute is more than € 5,000 and for more serious criminal matters (§ 74 GVG).

The courts are split into chambers of special jurisdiction for civil, commercial, criminal, family and juvenile matters, according to which the membership of the chamber differs. For civil matters three judges staff the chamber, headed by a president (*Vorsitzender*) of higher status and salary (§75 GVG). However, where a case is relatively straightforward a single judge presides (§ 348 ZPO) and following the reform from 1 January 2002, single judges will hear all first instance cases and will also be able to hear appeals from the *Amtsgericht*.

In the commercial chamber (*Kammer für Handelssachen*) where established, one judge is assisted by two lay judges (*Handelsrichter*), commercial persons who act as temporary judges of equal status and power (§§ 93 et seq. GVG). In the cities these commercial chambers can be split into highly specialized divisions for expert decisions and are noted for their extremely high standard.

The criminal courts can be constituted as a small chamber (*Kleine Strafkammer*) with one professional and two lay judges, which hears appeals from the *Amtsgerichte*, and a large chamber (*Große Strafkammer*), which tries serious criminal offences, not tried by the Amtsgericht or the higher appeal courts, at first instance and is staffed by three professional and two lay judges. For the most serious criminal matters, such as unlawful killings, a similarly constituted *Schwurgericht* is established (§§ 74–76 GVG). There are also specialist chambers to hear cases involving juveniles, and the possibility of establishing a chamber to hear cases of serious commercial or economic offences (*Wirtschaftsstrafkammer*), including competition, fraud, share dealings and, property offences (§ 74c GVG).

---

[10] By *Das Gesetz zur Änderung der Zivilprozessordnung* passed by the Bundestag on 17 May 2001.

From these courts appeals are allowed to the highest courts of the *Länder* and sometimes to the *Bundesgerichtshof*. In civil matters, the appeal value limit has now been abolished but appeals can be rejected which show no prospect of success.

3.1.3 *Higher regional courts of appeal (Oberlandesgerichte)*

There are now 24 higher regional courts of appeal situated in the larger cities.[11] The courts are concerned mainly with the hearing of first instance appeals (*Berufungsinstanz*) in both civil and criminal jurisdictions (§§ 119 and 121 I 1a and 1c GVG) and of second instance appeals (*Revisionsinstanz*: § 121 I 1b GVG) from the *Landgericht* in criminal matters, and also act as courts of first instance for the most serious criminal cases, for example, treason (§ 120 GVG).

For most cases these courts are last instance courts, as there are appeals only in limited circumstances to the Federal Court. Bavaria has an alternative highest court of appeal, the *Bayerisches Oberstes Landgericht* (BayObLG) for matters of ordinary jurisdiction not involving Federal Law. The higher regional courts of appeal are constituted with senates of three judges (§ 122 GVG) unless in civil actions the parties agree that a single judge hear the trial (§ 524 ZPO).[12]

Thus, although there are four levels of courts of ordinary jurisdiction, individual cases proceed through no more than three instances. The appeal route from the *Amtsgericht* to *Landgericht* is known as the *Berufung*, the first appeal on points of law and fact. A second instance appeal known as the *Revision* can be made on points of law only. The further complex details on appeal routes in the civil and criminal jurisdictions are considered in the appropriate procedural sections below. The final court to consider in the hierarchy of ordinary jurisdiction is the Federal Court of Justice.

3.1.4 *The Federal Court of Justice (Bundesgerichtshof: BGH)*

The Federal Court of Justice situated in Karlsruhe[13] hears an appeal from the *Oberlandesgericht* only if that court has consented and the appeal involves a novel principle of law or deviates from a previous BGH decision.

The BGH has twelve civil and five criminal senates, and eight senates for specialized legal areas, including cartel law and the law applicable to the various legal professions, each senate comprising four federal judges (*Bundesrichter*) and one senate president (§ 139 GVG). In addition there are two special great senates (*Großer Senat*), to consider important changes of law and legal unity in civil and criminal matters consisting of the President and one judge from each of the civil senates and the President and two judges from each of the criminal senates. There is also a combined great senate (*Vereinigter Großer Senat*) to oversee changes and disunity in the law between the civil and criminal jurisdictions (§ 132 GVG). The BGH is considerably overworked, thus there are serious delays in appeals to this court.

---

[11] In Berlin, this is called the *Kammergericht*.
[12] This is allowed by §§ 8–9 *Einführungsgesetz zum Gerichtsverfassungsgesetz* (EGGVG). Bavaria is the only *Land* to have taken advantage of this.
[13] With the exception of the five criminal senates which are now located in Leipzig.

There are other specialist courts which do not have a hierarchy of their own but do have a final appeal to the BGH. These are considered below.

3.1.5 *Federal Patent Court (Bundespatentgericht)*

Although this court falls within the courts of ordinary jurisdiction division, it is not a part of the hierarchy and only appears at the level of the Federation. Apart from considering cases for the withdrawal or cancellation of patents and licences, the court hears appeals from the Federal Patent Office. An appeal lies to the *Bundesgerichtshof* on points of law (§§ 100 and 110 et seq. of the Patent Act (*Patentgesetz*) Pat G[14]).

3.1.6 *Professional courts and arbitration tribunals*

A number of specialist courts exist to hear cases arising from public service matters. These Federal professional courts deal with civil servants (*Bundesdisziplinargericht*), the army, and questions of service and discipline in the legal professions for example, the Disciplinary court for Judges (*Bundesdienstgericht*).[15]

Mention must also be made of the arbitration tribunals (*Schiedsgerichte*) for the private resolution of legal disputes, which are used extensively in commercial law. These are subject to the provisions of the ZPO and to judicial review of the legality of their decisions (§§ 1027 et seq. ZPO and see Chapter 11).

3.2 **Administrative courts (*Verwaltungsgerichte*)**

These courts deal with matters relating to public law but outside purely constitutional matters and the other specialist hierarchies dealing with social law and taxation (§ 40 VwGO). Administrative courts were first introduced piecemeal in some of the larger states in the late-nineteenth century with other reforms aimed at the administration of justice. Their complete introduction throughout Germany and on a much wider subject matter basis was achieved only with the coming into force of the *Grundgesetz* in 1949. They deal with the area of law concerned with disputes between the public authorities and individuals arising from the exercise of public authority. This includes natural persons and legal persons. They are regulated by the Administrative Courts Act (*Verwaltungsgerichtsordnung*: VwGO). Any dispute which arises from an administrative decision which may affect a person's rights may be challenged before these courts. All areas of public life are covered: planning law, trade and professional licensing, police, water, school regulations, roads, and the civil service. The courts can consider constitutional elements in a case unless a matter of the constitutional validity of a statute is at stake.

Before these courts can be approached a preliminary administrative procedure of objection (*Widerspruchsverfahren*) must be undertaken, in which the complainant states the objection to a committee (*Beschwerdeausschuß*) and the public authority

---

[14] 23 March 1961 (BGBl I 274).
[15] The details of these are really beyond the remit of this book. See M. Wolf, *Gerichtsverfassungsrecht Aller Verfahrensweige*, pp. 111–15 or E. Schilken, *Gerichtsverfassungsrecht*, 2nd ed., pp. 291–296.

concerned can review and perhaps correct its action. The process attempts to avoid court action by settling things at a more informal level. If the authority sticks to its original action, the applicant then has one month to file a court action (see generally §§ 68–80a VwGO). For further details on administrative review process refer to the section on administrative law in Chapter 8.

The administrative courts operate on three levels. The first instance court for most actions is the *Verwaltungsgericht*, consisting of three professional judges and two lay judges, although there are different rules applying in Bavaria and Baden-Württemburg (§ 5 VwGO).[16] They are not nearly as decentralized as the courts of ordinary jurisdiction; there are now fifty-two such courts in larger towns and cities.

Appeals from the decisions of the *Verwaltungsgerichte* are heard by the Administrative Appeal Court (*Oberverwaltungsgericht*) (16 in total and referred to in some *Länder* as *Verwaltungsgerichtshof*), which sits in senates of three professional judges, and in some *Länder* may include two lay judges. Appeals may be made both on questions of law and fact (§ 46 VwGO), hence the inclusion of lay members of the court in most *Länder* at this level of court (§ 9 VwGO).

A restricted appeal from the lower courts may be made on points of federal law only, to the Federal Administrative Court (*Bundesverwaltungsgericht*) in Berlin and Munich but is due to move to Leipzig in 2003. This sits in senates of five professional judges, but in special cases a great senate of seven will preside to consider legal unity (§§ 10–11 VwGO).

Although most administrative law is *Land* law, the *Bundesverwaltungsgericht* is exceptionally busy because it deals with questions concerning general principles of administrative law which are so well established they are treated as federal law, a sort of common law.

Attached to the Federal Administrative Court are state attorneys (*Oberbundesanwalt*) as representatives of the public interest (*Vertreter des öffentlichen Interesses*) whose function is, as the title suggests, to help guide legal development along the lines of the public interest (§§ 35–37 VwGO). The *Länder* courts may have a *Landesanwalt* attached, attorneys appointed by the local authorities to represent the public interest because at this level the concern is with provisions of *Land* law and not federal law (§ 36 VwGO).

A *Großer Senat* of the *Bundesverwaltungsgericht* has been established to oversee legal unity and the development of administrative law (§ 11 VwGO).

3.3 Labour courts (*Arbeitsgerichte*)

Although labour law is a part of civil law, specialized courts were set up in 1926 under pressure from the unions to deal with disputes arising from labour relations; amongst others, collective bargaining, pay, conditions, dismissal, and worker participation. These courts were organized into a distinctly separate hierarchy in 1953 and are governed by the Labour Courts Act (*Arbeitsgerichtsgesetz*: ArbGG).

---

[16] In exceptional circumstances the *Oberverwaltungsgerichte* or the *Bundesverwaltungsgericht* replace the *Verwaltungsgericht* as court of first instance, see §§ 45, 47, 48, and 50 VwGO.

The labour courts are also less decentralized than the courts of ordinary jurisdiction (123 in total). The first instance courts are the *Arbeitsgerichte*, staffed by one professional judge and two lay judges selected from employers' and employees' organizations (§§ 2–3, 8 and 14–31 ArbGG).

Legal representation is allowed on all three levels of these courts but is not compulsory before the *Arbeitsgerichte*. Some form of representation is required before the *Landesarbeitsgerichte*, but this can be by a union or employers' representative or adviser (§§ 10–11 ArbGG).

An appeal on law and fact lies to the regional labour courts (19 in total) (*Landesarbeitsgerichte*) which have the same composition as the lower courts (§§ 8, 33–39 and 64). In matters of collective agreements between unions and employers, both levels of court have four lay judges instead of two.

A final restricted appeal on points of law only lies to the Federal Labour Court (*Bundesarbeitsgericht*) which sits in Kassel but is due to move to Erfurt (§§ 8, 40–45 and 72). This sits in senates of three professional judges and, despite hearing points of law only, still retains the lay element of two judges. Representation by a lawyer is compulsory before this court.[17]

A *Großer Senat* of the *Bundesarbeitsgericht* has been established to oversee legal unity and the development of Labour law (§ 45 ArbGG).

Further details on procedure can be found in the section on labour law in Chapter 9.

3.4 Social courts (*Sozialgerichte*)

The three levels of this court deal exclusively with matters relating to social insurance payments, unemployment payments, benefits for illness, accidents, invalidity and pensions, child benefits, health insurance, and other state-organized or administered benefits such as war victims compensation. They are governed by the Social Courts Act (*Sozialgerichtsgesetz*: SGG). Access to these courts also requires the completion of a less formal procedure to get the relevant authority to review the matter in dispute.

The *Sozialgerichte* (sixty-nine in total) are divided into specialist subject matter chambers and are staffed by one professional judge and two lay judges (§§ 7–27 SGG). Lay members are selected from a variety of organizations depending on subject matter, and may include doctors, social workers, employers, employees, and insurance officials, amongst others. An appeal lies to the *Landessozialgericht* (sixteen in total) which has three professional and two lay judges (§§ 29 and 33 SGG).

A final restricted appeal on points of law lies to the Federal Social Court

---

[17] Note that for an indefinite time, some former rules from the DDR still apply in the new *Bundesländer*. The *Gesetz über die Errichtung und das Verfahren der Schiedsstellen für Arbeitsrecht* of 29 June 1990 (GBI, DDR 505) provides that in businesses with more than 50 employees, it is compulsory that an arbitration panel must consider a matter before resorting to the courts. Appeals against the decision can be made to the Labour court.

(*Bundessozialgericht*) in Kassel, which has twelve divisions. Two lay judges sit with three professional judges in the Federal Social Court (§ 39 SGG). This also has a great senate to decide on matters of legal unity in this jurisdiction (§ 41 SGG).

3.5 Tax or revenue courts (*Finanzgerichte*)

Set up after the First World War but formally being established as a separate hierarchy only in 1965, these courts deal with disputes arising from tax, revenue, succession, and customs law (§ 33 FGO), governed by the Revenue Courts Act (*Finanzgerichtsordnung*: FGO). There are only two levels of these courts, because a first complaint must go to the relevant administrative authority, such as the local tax office committee (*Steuerausschuß*), which hears the complaint and issues a decision which must then be challenged at first instance before the *Finanzgericht* (§ 35 FGO).

The finance court (nineteen in total) consists of chambers of three judges and two lay judges (§ 40 FGO). Appeals on important questions of law only lie to the *Bundesfinanzof* in Munich (§ 36 FGO), which is composed of senates of five judges (§ 115 FGO).

3.6 Conclusion

Despite the potential for conflicting legal decisions and developments by reason of having five different hierarchies of courts, this has not transpired to any great extent. A common senate of the highest federal courts (*Gemeinsamer Senat*) was established,[18] consisting of the presidents and chairmen of the federal courts, to discuss and decide on points of law and to avoid inconsistency in important legal principles and conflicting decisions (*Grundgesetz* Article 95 (3)).

The highly specialized and decentralized court system in Germany is considered to have made justice, certainly at the lower levels, much more accessible and a much quicker process. Final courts are well distributed throughout the country, thus avoiding an overcentralisation of legal affairs in one city.[19]

4 The situation in the new federal regions (*Bundesländer*)

Prior to unification there was only one hierarchy of courts in East Germany, divided into 233 local (*Kreisgerichte*) and fourteenth regional (*Bezirksgerichte*) courts, which were adopted, and centralized appeal courts, which were not adopted, into the court structure in the new Germany. The highest Federal Appeal Courts named in Article 95 *Grundgesetz* have now replaced the former highest courts of appeal. In

---

[18] By the *Gesetz zur Wahrung der Einheitlichkeit der Rechtsprechung der obersten Gerichtshöfe des Bundes vom 19.6.1968* (RsprEinhG) (BGBl I S. 661).
[19] The figures for the numbers of courts are taken from the BMJ Website, 2001.

Berlin the adjustment was made easier by the extension of the jurisdiction of the West Berlin courts in all five hierarchies to the area of East Berlin. Additionally, Berlin now has its own *Land* constitutional court.[20] In the other new *Länder* the process was not so straightforward.

5 The Federal Constitutional Court

While there is no direct historical predecessor to the BVerfG, largely because its powers and functions are far greater than those given to any previous court, there have been a number of courts in German legal history which have exercised forms of constitutional review. Examples can be found from a surprisingly early date, but these forms were concerned only with the rights of organs of power or government between themselves and not the right of ordinary citizens in relation to the organs of state, now the major role of the BVerfG. The *Hofgericht* of 1235 and the *Kammergericht* of 1415 were both concerned with the settlement of disputes between the *Fürsten* and kings and emperors. In 1495, the *Reichskammergericht* was established following the settlement of Worms, to resolve initially the essentially political disputes between the various ruling elements in the empire. These included the Kaiser, the Prince Electors, the landed aristocracy and estates, and the church. Its judicial role, however, broadened over the years to include more ordinary matters of jurisdiction if indeed, 'witch trials', amongst other processes, can be regarded as ordinary. Also fulfilling a judicial role was the Imperial Council (*Reichhofsrat*) which included a constitutional judicial role, although its main role remained that of an executive organ of the state, ensuring that the will and thus laws of the Kaiser were put into effect and as it developed its ordinary jurisdiction was also much wider than the *Reichskammergericht*. These early constitutional court examples were dissolved when the *Reich* was dissolved and direct constitutional review by a court, rather than political review by a state organ (*Bundesversammlung, Reichsrat* or *Bundesrat*), was not re-established until the setting up of the *Staatsgerichthof* of the Weimar Republic which sat only on limited and infrequent occasions. The *Staatsgerichthof* was able to consider violations of the constitution by organs of state, disputes between the states and between the states and the *Reich*. Its membership was appointed by the legislature, a feature retained in the BVerfG. It shared a constitutional competence with the *Reichsgericht*, which decided on the compatibility of *Länder* law with laws of the *Reich*. Neither was able to hear complaints by citizens that rights under the constitution had been violated by an organ of state.

The BVerfG was established under the *Grundgesetz* as a state institution of the constitution, independent from both other state organs and the courts. As such it ranks equally with the President, *Bundestag, Bundesrat,* and Government. It is

---

[20] Unification Treaty, Appendix One, Chapter Three, Subject Area A, Part Four.

governed by Articles 92–4, 99, 100 and 115g *Grundgesetz* and the Federal Constitutional Court Act (*Bundesverfassungsgerichtsgesetz*: BVerfGG).

The BVerfG consists of two senates of eight judges which have different jurisdictions and act almost as two different courts. The first senate considers cases involving basic rights (Arts 1–20 GG), and the second the more overtly political actions involving inter-institutional, electoral, international law, political party questions, and governmental disputes. Both senates are the BVerfG for the purposes of rendering decisions. The quorum for a decision is six judges. Exceptionally, the BVerfG may sit in plenum of both senates when one senate wishes to depart from a ruling of the other. For further details refer to §§ 1, 2 13–16 BVerfGG.

The court's main function is that of guardian of the *Grundgesetz*, which involves interpreting the *Grundgesetz* to ensure uniformity and consistency for all other courts and organs of the state and government. Thus it has far-reaching competence and, as with many other features of the present Constitution in Germany, the experiences of history, in particular the excesses which were allowed to take place in the Weimar Republic and the Third Reich, place it in a strong position.

It has jurisdiction over all disputes concerning the authority and obligations of the various constitutional bodies arising under the *Grundgesetz*, and the resolution of disputes between Federation and *Länder* and between the *Länder* themselves. It can review the legislation of the Federation and the *Länder* to ensure it is in conformity with the *Grundgesetz*, and can overrule legislation if found to be unconstitutional. The court upholds and protects basic rights and can hear directly complaints by individuals that their rights may have been infringed contrary to the human rights provisions of the constitution. All government agencies may be taken to task for human rights infringements. See generally § 13 BVerfGG for a catalogue of its jurisdiction. Its decisions are binding on all lower courts and Government agencies and have the force of law (§ 31 BVerfGG).

The court can declare political parties unconstitutional. Decisions are made on the basis of a simple majority or a two-thirds majority for a party ban. Further details of the powers and membership of this court can be found in Articles 92–94 *Grundgesetz*, BVerfGG and in Chapters 4 and 7.

6 The *Länder* Constitutional Courts

These are either termed *Ländesverfassungsgerichte* or *Staatsgerichtshöfe* and play a similar role to the BVerfG but in respect of the Constitutions that each *Land* has enacted in adjudicating disputes between public bodies in a *Land* and testing the constitutionality of *Land* legislation. Not all *Länder* have established their own constitutional court and two have taken advantage of Article 99 GG, which allows them to transfer jurisdiction over questions concerned with their own Constitutions to the BVerfG. Schleswig-Holstein and Mecklenburg-Vorpommern are the only *Länder* to have done this. The BVerfG enjoys a control jurisdiction over questions decided by the *Länder* constitutional courts.[21]

The Ländesverfassungsgerichte are staffed by part-time judges, normally serving in other *Länder* courts.

7 The Justice Ministries

Justice Ministries have been established at both the level of the Federation and the *Länder*.

7.1 The Federal Ministry of Justice (*Bundesministerium Der Justiz (BMJ)*)

This is headed by the Minister of Justice, and the head of the civil service in the Ministry is the *Staatssekretär*. It is divided into eight departments with different responsibilities concerned with legal administration (the courts and the professions), European and international law and legal development, civil law, criminal law, commercial, and economic law, public law, human rights questions and a department concerned with the internal personnel and financial administration of the Ministry. It is responsible for the drafting of bills concerned purely with constitutional matters, procedural laws, the courts, and legal professions. Appointment of the federal judiciary is also a function of this Ministry, as is the review of the drafts of other ministries for their conformity with the law. The Justice Ministry was also made responsible for overseeing the legal integration of the former East Germany into the present day German state and in particular the integration of criminal law and dealing with the vexed questions of property ownership and claims. It also has an extremely useful and informative website, noted below, containing all manner of information and statistics.

7.2 The Justice Ministries of the *Länder* (*Landesjustizministerien*)

At the level of the *Länder*, the Justice Ministries do not play such an extensive role as their federal counterpart, but are generally responsible for the equivalent matters at the *Länder* level unless a particular matter is within the competence of the federal Ministry. They are concerned with the appointment of judges for the particular *Land* and with the training of the legal professions, with a special examinations office for this purpose.

---

[21] Further limited details can be found in *Handbuch der Justiz*, (G. Schenck, ed.) (1994: R. v Deckers Verlag Köln).

FURTHER READING

Bundeszentrale für politische Bildung (ed.), *Grundlagen unserer Demokratie* (1988, Bonn).

Bundeszentrale für politische Bildung (ed.), *Deutsche Verfassungsgeschichte 1849–1919–1949* (1989: Bonn).

O. Akalin (ed.), *Law on the Federal Constitutional Court*, (a translation of the BVerfGG), with an introduction by G. Wöhrmann (1982: Inter Nationes, Bonn).

W. Heyde, *Die Rechtspflege in der Bundesrepublik Deutschland*, 5th ed. (1990: Bundesanzeiger, Köln).

W. Heyde, *Justice and the Law in the Federal Republic of Germany* (1994: C. F. Müller, Heidelberg) (English translation and update of the above).

O. R. Kissel, *Gerichtsverfassungsgesetz: Kommentar*, 2nd ed. (1994: C.H. Beck, Munich).

D. P. Kommers, *Judicial Politics in West Germany: A Study of the Federal Constitutional Court* (1976: Sage, Beverly Hills, California).

D. P. Kommers, *Constitutional Jurisprudence of the Federal Republic of Germany* (1990: Duke University Press, Durham, North Carolina).

O. Model, C. Creifelds and G. Lichtenberger, *Staatsbürger Taschenbuch*, 30th ed. (2000: C.H. Beck, Munich).

E. Schilkin, *Gerichtsverfassungsrecht*, 2nd ed. (1994: C. H. Beck, Munich).

K. Schlaich, *Das Bundesverfassungsgericht*, 4th ed. (1997: C. H. Beck, Munich).

P. Schwacke, E. Stolz and G. Schmidt, *Staatsrecht: mit Allgemeiner Staatslehre und Verfassungsgeschichte*, 3rd ed. (1993: Kohlhammer Verlag, Köln).

H. Seidentopf, C. Hauschild & K-P. Sommermann, *Implementation of Administrative Law and Judicial Control by Administrative Courts* (1998: Forschungsinstitut für öffentliche Verwaltung, Speyer).

C. J. Whelan (ed.), *Small Claims Courts: A Comparative Study* (1990: Clarendon Press, Oxford).

M. Wolf, *Gerichtsverfassungsrecht aller Verfahrensweige* (1987: C.H. Beck, Munich).

Articles

G. Robbers, 'Die Historische Entwicklung der Verfassungsgerichtbarkeit', *JuS* 1990, 257–63.

Useful Website addresses

The Federal Ministry of Justice, Bundesministerium der Justiz:
www.bundesjustizministerium.de/

4

Legal education and legal personnel

1 Legal education

1.1 Introduction

Education in Germany largely is organized and administered by the education ministries of the *Länder*. The universities are in theory independent in their own administration but are nevertheless dependent on the *Länder* for finance and where the examination of subjects is nationally regulated. Most of the regulations governing the universities are therefore *Land* regulations but these are similar amongst the *Länder*.

In terms of the general academic freedom regarding the content of curricula, it is certainly true to say that the universities enjoy independence; however, the organization and content of legal education is a considerable departure from this general position, and the content and examination of legal training is regulated by federal and *Länder* rules and regulations.

As well as considering the general background and structure of legal education in Germany, this chapter will also consider the long-standing debate taking place in Germany with regard to the reform of legal education. Many factors have contributed to this debate, latterly not least the influence exerted by European Community Directives concerning the practice of the legal professions and the consequences of the accession of the territory of the former German Democratic Republic to the Federal Republic of Germany. These supplement domestic demands for reform which have been around for many decades and are part of the process of reform which has been in train since the first national regulation of the judiciary, and hence judicial training, in 1851. Before details of this form of training are considered, the route and entry to a university will be briefly outlined.

1.2 University entrance

It is most likely that those entering German law faculties will have come through secondary education in a *Gymnasium*, the equivalent of a grammar school. At present some forty-one German universities have law faculties Candidates will have (probably) obtained their *Abitur* after thirteen years at school, at around the age of nineteen to twenty. The *Abitur* is the completion examination taken by those who have attended the schools of higher academic ability and is the equivalent of 'A' levels in the UK and also acts as a school leaving certificate. Entry ages to university are usually nineteen for females and twenty-one to twenty-two for males, because of the requirement to undertake either National Service in the forces or service in a civil occupation.

Historically, the holding of the *Abitur* conferred the right to attend the course and university of one's choice. However, due to the considerable increase in the numbers of those leaving *Gymnasium* with an *Abitur*, some restrictions have been placed on this right in certain subjects, most notably medicine and business degrees and from time to time in law. The numbers leaving school with the *Abitur* has risen considerably in the last few years so that demand for a university place has increased ten-fold. Even the considerable expansion in the universities in the 1960s and 1970s, when more than twenty universities were established, could not keep pace with the demand for places. Demand for some subject areas was so high that some universities and faculties restricted entry or required entrants to have reached a certain standard in their final exams for their *Abitur*, a restriction or quota which is termed the *numerus clausus* or *Aufnahmesperren*. This *numerus clausus* was challenged because it appeared to infringe the basic right of university attendance under Article 12 *Grundgesetz*, the right to choose training (education). For further details see also Chapter 7 on basic rights. The BVerfG, however, in two cases declared the restriction to be constitutionally acceptable, provided it was forced upon the university because of economic and physical exigency—that no further places were available for the study of a particular subject in the university and that no more money was forthcoming to provide them. The restrictions selected must nevertheless be according to objective criteria such as exam performance. In the first case, the Bavarian rules, which gave priority on the basis of residence in Bavaria, were held to be unconstitutional.[1] These court cases led to the establishment of a Central Office for the distribution of university places (*Die Zentralstelle für die Vergabe von Studienplätzen*: ZVS), similar to UCAS in the UK, to which all applications for university places go in the first instance. The BVerfG was also requested to review the workings of this office (BVerfGE 39, 276), the result of which was that there is now a greater federal and judicial involvement in higher education, largely through the Higher Education Framework Act (*Hochschulrahmengesetz*: HRG) in 1976 which itself was subject to review by the BVerfG, (BVerfGE 43, 391) Entry requirements and competition to get into certain faculties and universities is very high. The ZVS worked originally on the basis that the applicants with the best grades were sent to the faculty and university of their choice. If a faculty or university is not subject to the centralized application procedure, the candidate can make a direct application to matriculate into the university and faculty. Others have to see where there are remaining places. The participation of law faculties in

---

[1] For further details see BVerfGE 33, 303 and Kommers, *The Constitutional Jurisprudence of the Federal Republic of Germany*, pp. 295–304.

the system has been irregular, with partial participation by some *Länder* at various times to a decision in December 1991 that all law faculties rejoin the system to cope with the increased number of applications to law following unification. Since then, the numbers have stabilized again and not all law faculties impose a *numerus clausus*. Figures from the applications for 2001 reveal that overall, 14,866 applicants applied for 13,645 places in the law faculties. Both the asking requirements of the *numerus clausus* and the criteria applied by the ZVS for the allocation of study places has changed over the years and today, following a further change which came into effect in 2001, a fixed percentage of places (17.5) are allocated on the basis of merit per law faculty and the rest allocated according to a list of social criteria, such as disabilities or family circumstances, but also taking into account the applicant's desire to study locally, where this is the case.[2]

Prior to unification, German universities were producing an excess of qualified jurists and there were many unemployed jurists in Germany. As a result, all the legal professions were able to demand very high grades in the law final examinations. To some extent this excess was absorbed by the requirements of the new *Länder* as they converted to the new legal system. However, it seems that there will again be surpluses given the number of students studying and qualifying in law from the universities.[3] In 1992/93 there were an estimated 1,600,000 students in Germany, of whom about 100,000 study law,[4] the largest law faculties being Berlin, Munich, Cologne, Bonn, Bochum, Hamburg, Münster, Heidelberg, Aachen, Frankfurt, Göttingen, and Hannover.

Students in Germany are not required to follow such a formal or fixed system as exists in the UK. Although, for the most part, required subjects are determined by the legislation, students can create their own scheme of study and follow and attend any courses of their choice. Having attained the required entry standard, German students are able to attend any and as many universities as they wish. They are not restricted to one university, and traditionally students moved universities to attend the lectures of the most respected professors. To a growing extent the similar organization for state exams in all the *Länder* has undermined this as a reason to move, and the exercise of this freedom is very limited. In order to give themselves a fair chance of success in the exams, most (about 85%) students attend just one or two universities. Practical and personal considerations, such as the setting up of a new home in each city and family and friendship ties, rule out frequent change.

---

[2] The full and now somewhat convoluted details of the process are beyond the remit of this book but details of the applicants per university, those faculties imposing a *numerus clausus*, and the decision criteria can be found at the ZVS website which is: **www.zvs.de**.

[3] Since the effects of unification are now stabilized there has been a considerable increase in those leaving the Universities and figures provided by the *Bundesministerium für Justiz* for 1999 of those taking and passing the first state examinations are 17,023 and 12,099 respectively. Further details are given in the appropriate sections below.

[4] A figure which has remained fairly constant since then see S. von Elsner.

1.3 Legal education

The general form of legal education in Germany is characterized by a combination of the teaching of legal theory and the provision of a period, or in reality a number of periods, of practical experience.[5]

In order to qualify as lawyers, students must pass two sets of state examinations set by professors of the university in collaboration with judges of the *Land* and the officials from the *Land* Education and Justice Ministries. These exams are taken following two distinct phases of training which consist of university study and practical training. While the overall form of university instruction is governed by the German Law on the Judiciary (*Deutsches Richtergesetz*: DRiG),[6] the details vary from *Land* to *Land* as they each have their own regulations for the instruction and examination of lawyers. Such regulations are called, amongst other formulations, *Juristenausbildunggesetz* (JAG), or *Juristische Ausbildungs-und Prüfungsordnung* (JAPO). The Law on the Judiciary may seem an odd source for rules regarding legal training but the aim of German legal training is to produce a complete lawyer, who is known after training as a *Volljurist*—a lawyer qualified in all the traditional major aspects of the law and legal system, someone who is capable of working in any legal profession. Provided the requirements for admission to the judiciary have been fulfilled, the requirements for all legal professions have also been fulfilled.[7]

1.3.1 *Part one: the first state examinations (Referendarexamen)*

The first phase, leading to the first state examinations, consists of a notional three and a half years' (with an absolute minimum of two years university study, but generally no maximum period for study (§ 5a DRiG). In practice it takes usually not less than nine semesters, or four and a half years. Most law students take their time to ensure they are thoroughly prepared for the final exams, and a survey in *Juristische Schulung* (JuS) showed ten semesters as the preferred number to complete the first state exams but the average was almost twelve semesters (six years). Figures for 1999 from the BMJ-*Ausbildungsstatistik* pages show that the average time taken has dropped nationally to about 10 semesters (five years) but that 21% of candidates still take longer, even for a first attempt and that 8% take fifteen semesters or more to finally successfully complete the first state examinations.[8]

Subject choice is more extensive than in the past however, certain subjects must

---

[5] For a full discussion of this form and its historical basis and development refer to M. Braun and R. Birk, Historical Roots of German Legal Education, (1981) 5 Comp. Law Yearbook, pp. 69–82.

[6] Deutsches Richter Gesetz (DRiG), BGBl I S 2026 as last amended on 6 August 1998, Schönnfelder, No. 97.

[7] A full look at the history of this can be found in Hattenhauer, JuS, 1989, 513ff. Refer also for details to G. Zacharias, *Wie finde ich meinen Studienplatz?*, 2nd ed. (1992: Lexika Verlag) and K. H. Bock, *Studien und Berufswahl 1994/95* (Bund-Länder-Kommission für Bildungsplanung und Forschungsförderung und Bundesanstalt für Arbeit, Bonn).

[8] Figures from the BMJ for 1999 reveal that just 0.38% of candidates successfully passed the first state examinations on the first attempt within four to six semesters, i.e. below the statutory notional minimum time requirement.

be studied, as laid down in DRiG § 5a II. Civil law, criminal law, public law and procedural law, including that of the European Community, as well as a general introduction to legal history, legal philosophy and jurisprudence (*BGB, StGB, Öffentliches Recht, Verfahrensrecht* and *Allgemeine Rechtswissenschaftliche Methoden- lehre*) are prescribed as core subjects but the Act leaves the exact details to the regulation of the *Länder*. In addition, optional subjects may be studied and counted towards the qualifications for judicial office. Most *Länder* offer the usual array of options, including administrative law, labour law, company law, commercial law, criminology, etc. In practice, however, the core subjects occupy students to such an extent that little time is devoted to the optional subjects, thus a quite narrow range of subjects is usually studied. The Act also requires that before the first state exams can be taken, three periods of one month must be spent receiving practical training, for example with *Rechtsanwälte* (DRiG § 5a III).

The study of law predominantly adopts the form of individual research with a high emphasis on problem-solving. In stark contrast to the UK, there is far less reliance on case law and a greater reliance on the text of the law and the commen- taries on this, which reflects the inductive tradition of German law. However, as the wealth of case decisions which interpret or add to the codes increases, so the reli- ance on case law increases and the German attorney must apply those reasoned decisions to new factual circumstances as they arise, particularly in the areas of constitutional and labour law. In the past little close or small group teaching was given and students largely were left to personal study. This is now changing and tutorial groups are more frequently organized, known as *Arbeitsgemeinschaften* but the numbers in them are still much higher than in the UK and can reach sixty or more, allowing little time or chance for personal instruction.

During the course of study, students must undertake a number of assignments in order to advance to the first state exams (*Erstes Staatsexamen*) which conclude the university part of legal training. This work varies between the *Länder* but popularly consists of written assignments (*Hausarbeiten*) and examinations in each of the three core areas of civil law, criminal law, and public law to attain the required proficiency level for beginners (*Kleiner Schein*). A *Hausarbeit* would usually involve the setting of a more difficult case for which a full explanation is required, and an extended period of time of four to six weeks is allowed for the preparation and written submission of an answer which must closely follow a distinct style. Addition- ally, in some *Länder* a *Großer Schein* (or *Übung*), at an advanced level, in the three core subjects must also be achieved before admittance to the first state exams is granted. For the optional subjects, it is also possible that a seminar paper may be written.

The first state exams also vary between the *Länder* in respect of the number of exams to be taken, but up to eight five-hour exams in the space of two weeks, followed at some later stage by an oral exam, would not be unusual. The students may be allowed the use of statute texts in the examination but not commentaries or case decisions. The correction of scripts and the notification of results is notoriously slow and heavily criticized, because it frequently results in the students wasting considerable time waiting for results before they can progress to the next stage of their education and training. In some *Länder* notably in the Northern and North Eastern *Länder*, course work (also in the form of a *Hausarbeit*), may count towards the final examination result. The exams may be retaken only on one further occasion in the event of failure, with the exception of the *Freischuß*, noted below. Of the estimated 15,000 students per year commencing law studies, a figure which has remained fairly constant, those taking and passing the first state examinations over the last ten years has increased from only some 7,500 to 12,000.[9] The failure rate remains also fairly level at around 25–30% but with regional variations. The success or failure is observed to be proportional to the quality of the *Abitur*.[10]

1.3.2 Part two: the second state examinations (Assessorexamen)

If successful in the first state examinations, students may then proceed to the second part of their training—the professional part or *Referendarzeit*—which takes place between the first and second state exams. Known as *Referendar*, they have the status of temporary civil servants and are provided with a state organized and paid period of comprehensive training. This period of training, for two years (DRiG § 5b I), consists of four compulsory placements (*Stationen*) of a minimum of three months and up to nine months. If there is a surplus of candidates over the finite number of places, candidates are selected according to a number of criteria including exam results, time spent waiting, and social considerations. These are attached to a court of regular jurisdiction in the civil division, in either a criminal court or with a public prosecutor, with a public authority and with an attorneys' office. In addition four to six months must be spent gaining experience in a placement of the candidate's choice in a court or public body, with a notary, a trade union, in business, or gaining experience in a placement in another legal jurisdiction. This period of training is supervised by the *Land* education and administration authorities and by the office of the president of the local *Landgericht*.

Finally the candidates are given the opportunity to return to a university for a short period in preparation for the second state examination. This is particularly demanding and tests the candidate on the whole period of study (DRiG § 5d (3)). It can consist of up to twelve exams of between three to eight hours' duration, being mainly written but also oral examinations and case presentations and in some *Länder* a further *Hausarbeit*. More so than the first state examinations, the form and content varies between the *Länder*. The overall candidate numbers have also increased for the second state exams both candidates and pass numbers,[11] although approximately 13% of candidates fail the second state examinations at the first attempt. The second state exams can be repeated once, even if passed first time.

Once a candidate has passed the second state examination, he or she is known as an *Assessor* or a *Volljurist*, a fully-fledged lawyer. He can now follow whichever

---

[9] In 1999, nationally, of 17023 candidates for the first state examinations, some 71% (12,099) passed. Figures taken from the BMJ Ausbildungsstatistik: **www.bundesjustizministerium.de**
[10] S, von Elsner, op cit., p. 13.
[11] According to BMJ figures in 1999, of the 12,374 candidates presenting, 10,710 passed at the first attempt.

branch of the legal profession he chooses, be it as judge, public prosecutor, attorney, notary, civil servant, or in outside employment. In 1999, over 25,000 were undertaking the *Referendar* training and 11,417 had found employment that year, although the destinations were not revealed by the figures. It is estimated that the courts and various public authorities only have demand for about 1,000 *Assessoren* per year which leaves a lot to be soaked up by the other professions, noted below.

Despite views expressed elsewhere, it has been noted that there is hardly any difference in the chances of employment and the quality of candidates' results in any of the principal legal professions of judge, attorney, notary or public prosecutor.[12]

1.3.3 *Criticisms*

The most constricting factor, and the one subject to the most debate and criticism, is that all those who wish to pursue a legal profession are required to follow similar legal training as laid down by the DRiG, despite the fact that only about 10% of them will go on to be judges. The original grounds for having a state or nationally organized set of exams for lawyers seem to a large extent to have been omitted from the texts, however, it would seem to be quite plausible that a nationally organized system of training for lawyers, laying down broad but fairly precise details of what is required would fit in with the general reforms of the legal system in the late-nineteenth century. At this time there was a push for the unification of the German state and legal system—each would aid the other. Therefore, it seems entirely within this rationale to ensure that the exponents of this national legal system and law are trained in the same laws and in the same way in order to ensure the continuing unity of a national legal system, hence the requirement for all lawyers to be trained up to the standard of the requirements for judicial office. In the same way, European harmonization can only be achieved if all member states' courts apply the same law in the same way. Each German *Land* cannot be allowed a separate legal development which includes the form of training. If there was no national training, each *Land* would be able to go its own way, which would hinder national legal development. Once the law becomes nationally established it is very difficult for the *Länder* to change it.

Legal training in Germany has also been criticized as being too strict and too long. The length can cause severe financial hardship to those who do not have sufficient means and who often have to work part-time to finance their training. This in turn often further extends the time required to complete the training with an average age of about twenty-eight on completion which is much higher than the european average. There is also criticism that there is, despite the plan, insufficient integration between the university study and the practical training in the second part. Hence, there were some reforms to the DRiG § 5b which allowed the *Länder*, for an experimental period between 1971 and 1981, with a short extension to 1984, to blend as they wished the theoretical and practical elements of the training into a

---

[12] S von Elsner, op. cit., pp. 13–14.

one-part system. This single phase method of legal education has not been continued and the structure of legal education remains essentially the same as it was when the present law was enacted in 1961. The form of legal education that was again approved by the German Parliament in 1984, aims to provide jurists with as complete a knowledge of German law as possible and to have regard for the system of German laws as a whole. The form of education also serves to give the qualified lawyers the widest choice between legal and other professions.

A further criticism is that many students (up to 90 per cent in some Universities)[13] feel forced to resort to the use of private crammer tutorials (*Repetitorium*) for up to eighteen months before the examinations in order to stand a good or better chance of success which they feel is not provided by the university instruction or, which is simply in preference to attending University lectures and seminars.

1.3.4 *Reform*

Largely due to the influences and pressure of the European Community market in legal services, but also continuing the internal debate which has continued for decades, the whole matter of legal training has been subject to considerable debate. The pages of the German legal press, such as the NJW, JuS and other leading journals, frequently feature discussions on the most recent suggestions for reform. The form of training is regarded as too long, as too general and as lacking the specialist training required of some careers. Therefore, amongst the latest suggestions for reform are for the introduction of a phase in which the student can qualify in a particular chosen legal profession. Minor changes have been made to the requirements of the DRiG to allow an early attempt at the first state examinations and a reduction in the *Referendarzeit* to a two-year maximum. A number of *Länder* have already amended their legislation as permitted by § 5d DRiG, to allow for an extra 'free go' (*Freischuß/Freiversuch*) at the first state examinations after only two and a half years to encourage quicker completion. Candidates still have two further attempts and are allowed to resit the examination even if they have passed to attempt to improve their grade.[14] There are suggestions that a fixed training period lasting no more than six years in total should be introduced, which appears to be the European average for legal training, and that a period abroad should be the norm for German law students. A new three-phase system would consist of the traditional university first part, fixed at three and a half years; the second part would be a reduced practical section, fixed at one and a half years the third would consist of specialized training for the profession the jurist has chosen (as a judge, *Staatsanwalt*, lawyer in public administration or an attorney (*Rechtsanwalt*)). According to other sources, the content and the form of exams within the existing

---

[13] S. von Elsner, op cit., p. 64.

[14] BMJ statistics show that in 1999, 40% of all candidates for the first state examinations attempted a *Freiversuch* and, more interestingly, of those, 80% passed, which is 10% higher than the percentage for all candidates. Furthermore, just over half of those taking the *Freiversuch*, achieved a grade higher than the lowest grade of 'sufficient' (*Ausreichend*), i.e. 65% of those passing. This compares with 56% achieving better than the lowest grade of all first state exam candidates in 1999. It may, tentatively, be suggested that this result reflects the fact that only the more able candidates attempt the *Freiversuch*.

two-phase system should be overhauled. The latest proposals for reform have now (or at last) come before Parliament. The main changes proposed include a much greater emphasis on optional subjects to allow both the faculties to build on their specializations and the students to engage much more in their own interests. Legal education is to be orientated not just to the judiciary but also to other legal professions. The core by which this reformed system is delivered remains the existing two-phase, state examined *Einheitsjuristen* model.[15]

A different suggestion is that the first state exams should be recognized as an academic qualification in their own right, so that those who wish to may seek work after this stage of education and training, with a generally recognized qualification. At the moment it is regarded as failure if students abandon their training, for whatever reason.

2 The judiciary and legal professions

2.1 Introduction

The legal professions in Germany include the following separate career paths: attorney (*Rechtsanwalt*), judge (*Richter*), notary (*Notar*) and state prosecutor (*Staatsanwalt*). The lay personnel involvement in the legal system will be considered at the end of this chapter. Other careers exist outside of the strict definition of the legal system, employing large numbers of legally qualified graduates, which, in the course of the employment, entail a high involvement with law. These are in regional and local government and in commerce and industry. There is not a single career progression from attorney to judge, creating in effect a hierarchical structure across the professions. Those legally qualified enter either as one of the types of lawyer or as a judge, and then follow different career paths. The term 'attorney' has been used generally to describe the single legal profession (*Rechtsanwalt*) which combines the functions of both barristers and solicitors in the UK.

All legal professions are entered at the same level of qualification, when the common legal training laid down in federal legislation, consisting of the first and second state examinations, has been completed. Once a career is chosen it would be extremely rare to change to another legal profession—for example, an attorney to transfer to become a judge—although this remains possible. Formally, all the legal professions in Germany are accorded equal status; however, partly because of the security of position and income and perhaps, more importantly, because of the stricter requirements of the judicial authorities of the *Länder*, entry into the judiciary is only really open to those with better grades in the second state examinations.

---

[15] For further details and technical details of how it is proposed the system will change see: Hommelhoff and Teichmann, Forum: Modernisierung in Kontinuität—die Revolution der Juristenausbildung, JuS 2001, Heft 9, pp. 841–845.

In addition to the more formal legal professions introduced above, there is a small number of other forms of occupation concerned with the administration of justice, legal advice and, to a limited extent, representation in the courts. The two most popular of these are the *Prozessagenten* and the *Rechtsbeistände*, considered below. Also considered briefly is the alternative of an academic legal career.

The system in Germany has not established a clearly distinct legal profession but a number of legal professions, and more than half of those legally qualified work outside of the strictly defined legal system. Other openings for the legally qualified are as independent attorneys, in-house company lawyers, or in positions in the federal, regional, and municipal administrations.

2.2 The judiciary

2.2.1 *Länder and federal courts*

In Germany the judiciary is a separate career, embarked upon by professionally qualified lawyers after educational and practical legal training; it is not entered after a number of years' practice as an attorney. Judges are initially appointed to a court of first instance after fulfilling the training requirements of the German Law on the Judiciary (DRiG). This is usually between the ages of twenty-six and thirty-two. The judiciary is a particular public service office and career which is formally independent of the employing executive authority and which has a separate pay scale. The initial appointment to a local court (*Amtsgericht*) or regional court (*Landgericht*), will be on a temporary basis (*Probezeit*), for three to five years depending on the *Land*, as a probationary judge (*Gerichtsassessor*), after which the position may be confirmed (see §§ 10–24 DriG for the full details on appointment and dismissal).

Appointments and promotions are made by the Ministers of Justice of the *Länder* and additionally, in some regions, with the agreement of the Committee on Judicial Appointments (*Richterwahlausschuß*), composed of members of parliament of the *Land*, judges and attorneys. Promotion to higher courts, such as the regional court of appeal (*Oberlandesgericht*), may only take place after ten years' service in the courts of first instance. As in any career service, promotion is not automatic and depends largely on good service and seniority. Those promoted may either become associate judges in the regional court of appeal or presiding judges in one of the divisions of the regional court.

At the federal courts level, members of the two Houses of the Parliament are involved in appointments with the Federal Justice Minister and *Länder* Justice Ministers, or the relevant ministers in respect of appointments to the specialised federal courts (Art. 95 (2) *Grundgesetz*).

Once the permanence of their position is confirmed, the appointment is full-time, with a guaranteed salary. Judges are guaranteed complete independence under Article 97 *Grundgesetz* and are formally bound only by *Gesetz* as confirmed by § 21 DRiG and § 1 GVG. The Statute on the Judiciary requires judges to act in a manner so as not to impair confidence in their ability and independence. Judges cannot be sacked unless it is by judicial order following a judicial hearing. They are not bound by decisions of higher courts, except those of the Federal Constitutional Court (BVerfGG § 31) and in other exceptional instances, and they are not formally subject to orders from superior judges. However, as in any career hierarchy where promotion is largely dependent on the views and good reports of superiors in the same hierarchy, advice from seniors will no doubt be carefully considered. Refer further to the sections on the status of court decisions and judicial decision-making in chapter 2.

In Germany, the number of the judiciary is far higher (c. 21,000) than in the UK, due in large part to the civil legal system which is judge led and the greater use of senates of three or more judges. This has the result that it is not an occupation which often catches the public eye, and judges rarely become either famous or infamous. For the most part, they do not have the same level of experience or reputation as UK judges, and there are simply far more of them in society. In contrast to the generally high regard for the professions, and in particular for judges, that there is in society, a number of comments have been expressed which may or may not reflect an objective view of the positions and status of the German judiciary:

(a) The much lower age, and therefore inexperience, at the start of their judicial career may not inspire the parties and attorneys appearing before a court to have a great deal of confidence.

(b) They are sometimes regarded as ordinary civil servants by the public. This view may be encouraged because a judge plays a much more 'down to earth' role in the actual proceedings in the court and in case preparation. The judge determines which witnesses and experts will appear, questions them and the parties and deals with much of the preparatory work of the court. These functions would be undertaken by other individuals, such as the Master, Registrar or court officials, in the relevant UK courts.

(c) Under the civil law system, the promotion system and the fact that judges are appointed at a comparatively young age would appear to encourage conservatism. A judge therefore is far more likely simply to apply law and is usually very conservative, especially in the lower courts. Judges are in any case given less scope by the civil law system because of the legacy of codification. They are expected only to apply law and not to develop legal principles themselves. At this level it could not really be argued that they are creators of law.[16]

(d) Lastly, the greater numbers of courts and far greater scope and amount of work carried out by the judges in Germany means that many more of them are required than in the UK. Germany has been described as having a judge-oriented or judge-led system, as opposed to the UK which has an attorney-led

---

[16] See for an expanded critique of this point, J. H. Merryman, *The civil law Tradition: An Introduction to the legal systems of Western Europe and Latin America*, 2nd ed. (1985: Stanford University Press, Stanford, Calif), pp. 109–10.

system. The German judiciary comprising in total of c. 20,500 *Länder* judges and c. 1000 federal judges compares to the 500 full-time judges and the c. 1000 part-time recorders and district judges in the UK plus around 30,000 magistrates. Although there is no direct equivalent of a magistrate in Germany, numerous lay-judges do take part in the decision-making in a number of German courts, particularly the specialist courts, as discussed below.

2.2.2 *The judges of the Federal Constitutional Court*

Quite distinct from the above court and career hierarchy is the Federal Constitutional Court (*Bundesverfassungsgericht*: BVerfG). This does not form part of the career ladder of the judiciary, although judges from the federal courts, and occasionally the courts of the *Länder*, may be appointed to the Federal Constitutional Court.

The judges of this court are not civil servants or to be likened with the other 'ordinary' *Länder* or federal judges. They are the guardians of the constitution in a special court designed for that purpose. They have a status in law corresponding to that of the highest state officials. The president of the court receives a salary equivalent to that of a Cabinet Minister and occupies the fifth highest position in the constitutional hierarchy of Germany: the President; the Chancellor; the president of the *Bundestag*; the president of the *Bundesrat*; and the president of the Federal Constitutional Court.

The high salaries of these judges ensure economic independence, and they have complete independence in other matters such as the administration and rules of the court. Once appointed they are virtually irremovable. In order to qualify for this court judges must possess qualifications for judicial office (BVerfGG § 3 II). This is a fairly recent change, as previously some had been appointed who were not legal qualified but had political experience. The legal qualification does not, however, present a problem to selection from a wider base than from the judiciary. Many of those who are legally qualified do not become judges or attorneys, and anyone who has passed their second state examination is eligible for appointment. They are also formally required to be at least forty years of age and be eligible for election in the *Bundestag* (BVerfGG § 3 I).

Once appointed the judges cannot hold any other office, with the exception of law professor at a university, in order to avoid positions of conflict with other political appointments (BVerfGG § 3). Those judges who are also university professors are required to put their judicial requirements first. This judicial office is often seen as a reward for sound political service in the *Bundesrat*, *Bundestag* or in the political parties. The judges serve for a fixed period of twelve years and are not eligible for re-election (BVerfGG § 4), a factor which also helps to ensure independence in office. Retirement at the age of sixty-eight is compulsory. Unlike all other courts, the judges in the BVerfG are allowed to publish dissenting opinions. Full details regarding the rules of this court are to be found in the Statute on the Federal Constitutional Court (*Gesetz über das Bundesverfassungsgericht*: BVerfGG) and the *Deutsches Richtergesetz* (DRiG §§ 69–70).

The selection procedure of this court is that each of the Houses of Parliament elects, by a two-thirds majority, half the judges to each of the two senates of the court (Art. 94 (1) *Grundgesetz* and BVerfGG §§ 5–7). At least three of the judges in each of the senates must have been judges who have served in one of the federal courts (BVerfGG § 1). The election process is viewed as giving democratic legitimacy to what is clearly a political appointment and really results from party negotiation rather than open competition. Most of these judges come from judicial backgrounds, closely followed by civil servants, legislators, professors, teachers and other lawyers.

The removal of judges of the BVerfG can only be by the Federal President on a motion by the court itself and not by political impeachment or removal by Parliament (BVerfGG § 5).

2.3 Lawyers

2.3.1 *Attorneys (Rechtsanwälte)*

At present there are about 104,000[17] practising attorneys in the Federal Republic.

Attorneys, historically and theoretically, were considered as an independent profession in that they were self-employed and were not in the pay of an employer or the state. Independence is guaranteed under § 1 of the Federal Statute on Attorneys (*Bundesrechtsanwaltsordnung*: BRAO[18]). Attorneys in Germany are also said to belong to a unified profession, in contrast to the position in the UK where there is a division of the profession into solicitors and barristers. However, the following specialist lawyers must also be considered: notaries public (*Notare*) and state prosecutors (*Staatsanwälte*). Attorneys may be unified in the sense that they have all completed the same legal training, whether they take part in court work, litigation, or advisory work. They are required by § 4 BRAO to be qualified for judicial office. There is not, however, a single unified market in which attorneys can appear in any court in Germany. Their freedom to practise their profession as and where they wish is severely restricted and is closely regulated by the BRAO, amongst others.[19]

2.3.1.1 *Rights of audience*

German attorneys have had exclusive rights of representation and audience before some courts and, with the exception of the limited rights allowed the *Rechtsbeistände* and the other exceptions noted below, a near monopoly of work in the remaining courts, as German law requires representation before all courts except the local ordinary, labour, tax courts, or the *Länder* administrative courts or any of the social courts. In criminal matters before the local courts, all offences carrying a penalty of more than one year's imprisonment require representation. There are no

---

[17] This figure also includes the c. 9,000 Anwaltsnotare who combine the functions of attorney and notary public and is considered further below. Figures from 1 January 2000, courtesy of BMJ.

[18] Of 1 August 1959 (BGBl I 1959, 565 in the latest version of 27 July 2001)

[19] BRAO, *Strafprozeßordnung* (StPO), *Zivilprozeßordnung* (ZPO), *Arbeitsgerichtsgesetz* (ArbGG), *Gerichtskostengesetz* (GKG), *Bundesgebührenordnung für Rechtsanwälte* (BRAGO), *Beratungshilfegesetz* (BerHG), *Rechtsberatungsgesetz* (RBerG), (GVG).

such restrictions on giving legal advice outside court work and an attorney can do so in any part of Germany, provided it is not on a permanent basis. This near monopoly over legal advice and representation is confirmed by statute (see RBerG § 1 and BRAO § 3).

2.3.1.2 *Restrictions on professional practice*

Since the last edition of this work, the considerable restrictions which were imposed on German attorneys as soon as they seek to enter into practice have been considerably lightened. After qualification an attorney must first be admitted to a local Bar chamber (*Rechtsanwaltskammer*) and to the jurisdiction of the local regional court by the Justice Ministry or Administration (*Landesjustizverwaltung*) of the *Land* (BRAO §§ 6–17). Membership of the law chambers is in fact compulsory under public law, (BRAO §§ 60 et seq.). They must apply to the regional court for audience rights and are granted limited rights to appear before the local court (*Amtsgericht*), sometimes in combination with the regional court (*Landgericht*). Prior to legislative amendment of both the BRAO and the Law of Civil Procedure (ZPO) and judgments of the BVerfG, a combination of rules severely restricted the freedom of lawyers to appear before particular courts. ZPO §§ 72, 78 and 140 make legal representation compulsory in certain courts, and is known as the *Anwaltszwang*. There was, however, also a requirement that in civil law matters, attorneys were required to live in the area close to the court (known as the *Lokalisierungsgebot* or *Lokalisierunsprinzip* (BRAO §§ 18 and 27). Furthermore, lawyers were only admitted to represent clients, in some cases, before one court only (referred to as *Singularzulassung*). Only after a number of years' practice, usually five, could a limited number of attorneys be elected to appear before the regional appeal courts (*Oberlandesgerichte*). In some *Länder* they would then lose their rights of appearance before the lower courts (BRAO § 25 and §§ 225–227). The net result was that only specifically admitted attorneys were allowed audience rights to a certain court or courts which meant that there was very often a very limited choice of lawyer for individuals. However, both the *Lokalisierungsgebot* and the *Singularzulassung* have now been repealed, greatly opening up the exercise of the profession of attorney. In the Federal Court of Justice (*Bundesgerichthof*) the number is still strictly regulated by law, which provides that audience rights can be granted only by the Federal Minister of Justice following selection by a Committee (*Wahlausschuß*).[20] A Federal Association of Attorneys (*Bundesrechtsanwaltskammer:* BRAK), required by law (BRAO §§ 175–191), exists to regulate both locally and nationally the conduct of attorneys and provides a useful forum for the discussion of topics affecting the profession. It is concerned with the reform of both the profession and the training

---

[20] See for further details on these wide sweeping changes, Henssler, *Anwaltszulassung in der Rechtsmittelinstanz* JZ 2001, 337–342 and the BVerfG judgment at JZ 2001, 350. For the BGH, see §§ 162–171 BRAO and the case of *Re Lawyers Services: EC Commission v Germany* (Case 427/85) [1989] 2 CMLR 677, in which the figure of twenty-two was cited by the German Government in its pleadings. Elsewhere the figure is given as slightly higher, twenty-six cited by Eidenmüller in 'Deregulating the market for legal services in the European Community: freedom of establishment and freedom to provide services for EC lawyers in the Federal Republic of Germany' (1990) 53 MLR pp. 604–08 and 25 cited in F. Wooldridge, 'The German rules governing the professional conduct of Rechtsanwälte', (1990) 39 ICLQ 683–90.

for the profession. This forum determines the additional rules of professional conduct, which is sanctioned by § 177 II BRAO.

Although in theory, and certainly after the form of legal training, German attorneys are regarded as generalists, they often specialize in a particular area or appear only before that specialized division of court. Tax is the most notable example but this may also apply in family, juvenile, civil, commercial, or criminal law matters.[21]

Attorneys may appear before all levels of the criminal division of the courts of ordinary jurisdiction.

The restrictions, the requirement of local residence and representation only before local courts were arguably originally imposed to instil in the attorneys a sense of local community, to ensure better and easier communication between attorney, client, and court, and to help guarantee the independence of the attorney as a provider of legal help for the citizen. Additional reasons are the historical connection of the attorneys to the courts of the prince electors, who would be admitted only if known to the court, and more recently, the protection of smaller practices, thus guaranteeing the provision of legal services at all local levels. These reasons sheltered under the umbrella of being in the best interests of the administration of justice. Whether this was ever achieved remains an open question.

2.3.1.3 *Reform*

There has already been extensive revision of the Federal Statute on Attorneys.[22] The home residence requirement for the provision of services has, as with the prohibition on having two offices, already been removed for EC attorneys as a result of ECJ rulings.[23] It remains to be seen whether this will result in similar changes in favour of domestic attorneys, although in exceptional circumstances this is now possible domestically, see BRAO § 28 and it is allowed to have a second office outside Germany (BRAO § 29a). The most important change has been easing the restriction on court audience rights. This remains, however, an area in need of reform.

2.3.1.4 *Disciplinary action*

As it is the right of all those who have qualified to practise as an attorney, it is only possible to exclude an attorney on the basis of a serious wrong proved against him or her. Disciplinary proceedings for a breach of the rules are undertaken at first instance in a tribunal called the Attorneys Tribunal (*Anwaltsgericht*), consisting of three senior attorneys, and at appeal level in the Attorneys Appeal Tribunal (*Anwaltsgerichtshof*) of the OLG, additionally with two local judges. Sanctions can be, a warning, a reprimand, a fine up to 25,000 Euro, a restriction on being able to

---

[21] Specialization is considered further below.

[22] Given that the law will not change until at least then and its entry into force can be delayed in any case until 2005, no further details will be provided at this time. For further details, however, see *Gesetz zur Neuordnung des Berufsrechts der Rechtsanwälte und der Patentanwälte vom 02.09.1994* (BGBl I S. 2278).

[23] *Van Binsbergen* (Case 33/74) [1974] ECR 1299, [1975] 1 CMLR 298 (see Plender and Usher op. cit., p. 347 and *Ordre Des Advocats au Barreau De Paris v Klopp* (Case 107/83) [1984] ECR 2971, [1985] 1 CMLR 99. See also the recently revised § 29a BRAO. See Foster (1991) 40 ICLQ 623.

represent clients to ultimately being struck off the register of attorneys and thus, no longer being able to practice. See generally for details of the disciplinary proceedings BRAO §§ 92–161a.

2.3.1.5 *The form of professional practice*

For the most part German attorneys used to practise as individuals, or in shared offices (*Bürogemeinschaft*) of two to four attorneys or in relatively small civil law partnerships under § 705 BGB (*Kanzlei* or *Sozietät*). Today, following considerable merger activity between Kanzlei, both within Germany and with firms outside Germany, and changes in the legal forms available to attorneys, this is no longer the case and most attorneys practice in some form of society or firm with other attorneys.[24] Frankfurt, Düsseldorf, Hamburg and Munich are the cities containing the largest concentrations of attorneys and the largest law firms in Germany, and recently larger firms are becoming more common, with *Kanzlei* of up to 100 or more attorneys appearing on the scene. At the same time most large companies, insurance brokers, and banks employ their own equally qualified and specialized in-house attorneys who conduct all the litigation on behalf of the company. The localization restrictions and the ban on second branches would appear to have restricted growth. This has been overcome by the use of the so-called 'correspondence attorneys', whereby company attorneys prepare the material which is merely rubber stamped by the local attorney who is admitted and entitled to appear before the relevant *Landgericht*. This is risky because the stand-in attorney may not be able to answer questions raised by the court on the material presented.

A more significant development to overcome the very restrictive rules in Germany is the association agreements between firms of attorneys, both regionally and nationally. Known in German as *überörtliche Rechtsanwaltssozietäten*, they have finally found statutory approval after their legal admissibility was the subject of considerable dispute both in legal literature and before the courts, although they were approved of by the BVerfG subject to certain conditions.[25] As a result of the court pronouncements, there was considerable activity, especially in the new *Länder*, in reaching supraregional association agreements and a considerable number of this type of merger took place creating much larger firms than previously witnessed in Germany.

The new § 59a BRAO allows attorneys to cooperate with other attorneys or firms of attorneys (*Kanzlei*) or indeed with other professional groups, locally, regionally, nationally, or internationally. Liability is imposed on at least one member for the whole association (§ 59a II BRAO). Additionally, the possibility of entering into a

---

[24] See further below and Steinkraus and Schaaf, *Zur Einführung: Das Berufsrecht der Rechtsanwälte* JuS 2001, 167 et seq., 275 et seq., and 377 et seq.
[25] Refer to M. Heintzen, *Die überörtliche Rechtsanwaltssozietät* (1990: Schäffer Verlag, Stuttgart), P. Hanau et al., *Deutsches und europäisches Anwaltsrecht: Festschrift für Walter Kolvenbach* (1992: Deutscher Anwaltverlag, Bonn). Case-law considering this is, *inter alia*, BGH NJW 1981, 2477, BVerfG NJW 1989, 2611, BGHZ 108, 290 = NJW 1989, 2890, BGHSt 37,200 = NJW 1991, 49, BGH, NJW 1993, 196.

new form of partnership has been established for all of the liberal professions including attorneys, by a new Partnership Law.[26]

Furthermore, lawyers can now form limited liability companies, both private and public, as the legal basis for a practice (*Rechtsanwaltsgesellschaft mit beschränkter Haftung* (RA-GmbH) *Anwalts-Atkiengesellschaft* (Anwalts-AG)). These were both initially approved of by the Bavarian Regional Court of Appeal after considerable debate as to the validity of such forms. The RA-GmbH was confirmed by an amendment to the BRAO (see §§ 59c-m).[27] The company itself must seek admittance to the local bar and be approved by both the Land Justice Ministry and the chamber of the local Bar There remains, in any case for an attorneys' private company, a minimum insurance cover of 2.5 million Euro. As yet statutory rules have still to be developed for the Anwalts-AG.

2.3.1.6 *Fachanwalt*

A further development which has been gaining ground recently is that of the specialized lawyer (*Fachanwalt*). This is catered for in § 43c BRAO and the Specialist Lawyers Act (*Fachanwaltordnung* FAO) which provide that a lawyer may hold him or herself out to be a specialist in one of a number of designated areas providing that the lawyer has been active as an attorney for at least three years, is able to demonstrate to the local BRAK particular knowledge and experience in that area and have received tuition in that area of at least 120 hours and have dealt with cases in that specialization (§§ 4–5 FAO).

2.3.1.7 *Advertising*

The advertising of attorneys' services is more restrictive than that allowed in the UK and is subject, at least in practice if not statutorily, to severe restrictions. The restriction is referred to as the *Werbeverbot*, which stems from the cryptic sentence in § 2 of BRAO, '*seine Tätigkeit ist kein Gewerbe*' which is loosely translated as 'their activities do not constitute a trade'. The ban has been translated into a professional rule by BRAK, who issued Standing Rules for Attorneys (*Grundsätze des anwaltlichen Standesrechts, Richtlinien der BRAK*, § 2 (2)). As with a number of aspects of the profession and practice of the professions in Germany, this is at the moment subject to change. A past case criticized this rule as uncertain, and refused the ability or right of the BRAK to base it and other rules of professional conduct on federal legislation such as § 43 BRAO (BVerfGE 76, 171, NJW 1988, 191). Amendments to the BRAO have now been made whereby for the first time the BRAO itself, in § 43b, regulates the ability of attorneys to advertise. The new paragraph, however, has not brought about a new legal situation and basically reproduces the prior legal rules as

[26] *Partnerschaftsgesellschaftsgesetz* (PartGG) *vom 25.7.1994* (BGBl I S 4744) which is in force from 1 July 1995. It resembles the OHG, see Chapter 9 for details on partnerships. For details of this change and the others made to the BRAO, see M. Kleine-Cosack, 'Neuordnung des anwaltlichen Berufsrechts', NJW 1994, 2249–2258, see also Prütting in *Integritätsprobleme im Umfeld der Justiz*, noted in Further reading, and K. Schmidt, 'Die Freiberufliche Partnerschaft', NJW 1995, 1–7. See more recently Steinkraus and Schaaf, ibid., p. 278.
[27] RA-GmbH-BayObLG, ZIP 1994, 1868. *Gesetz zur Änderung der Bundesrechtsanwaltsordnung* of 7 September 1998, BGBl 1, 2600 and Anwalts-AG, BayObLG, ZIP 2000, 835. For further details of this development, see Steinkraus and Schaaf, ibid., pp. 278–279.

developed from professional rules and judicial interpretation. Advertising is allowed only where it provides true and factual information. While the ability to represent clients in specific circumstances cannot be advertised, attorney may generally inform by way of adverts their usual areas of service, such as contract law or commercial law. The BVerfG has already decided that the ban on a complete freedom to advertise is constitutionally acceptable (see BVerfG NJW 1992, 1613 & NJW 1994, 1614). Attorneys' practices in Germany are not allowed to carry the name of deceased partners, with the intention of preventing them trading on past reputations which may no longer be valid.

2.3.1.8 *Fees*

Attorneys' fees for litigation are strictly controlled by BRAO § 49b and a Statute on Attorneys' Fees (*Bundesrechtanwaltsgebührenordnung*: BRAGO) on a claim value scale for civil matters and by fee guidelines for criminal work (§§ 7–11 and Appendix). The fee set out in the schedule of the statute is based on the value of the claim and must be paid not just once but up to four times, depending on the type of work undertaken or the stage of proceedings reached. One fee is payable for each of the filing of the action, representation at the court hearing, the hearing of evidence at court, and at the stage of the conclusion of the matter.[28] Contingency fees and discounts from the statutory amounts are, under BRAO § 49b II, illegal and void. This has some undesirable effects, in that for most attorneys it limits their income, especially in the lower courts where claims are of lower value.

The fixed scale of fees is criticized on a number of grounds. It can mean that the same amount is earned by attorneys, regardless of a number of factors. For example, the amount of pre-trial work undertaken can vary enormously, depending on the complexity of the subject matter and the conscientiousness of the attorney. The fixed scale takes no account of the ability of the client to pay, although obviously this statement must be qualified by the provision of legal aid in certain approved circumstances, considered in full in the section on legal aid in the next chapter. Nor does it take account of the experience of the attorney or whether or not the case was successful. It does, however, have the advantage of allowing a potential litigant to know, with a fair degree of accuracy, how much his legal fees will be in advance and ensures that some form of proportionality applies to fees. All fees are in any case recoverable on the successful outcome of the case. The system of fees can often mean that attorneys must try to balance the low income from a number of low-value cases with a large fee from a high-value case. Set fees apply most strictly to litigation and representation but also to outside court work conducted by

---

[28] Anlage zn § 11 BRAGO, see also Schönfelder No. 117. The following figures are taken from the statutory table and indicate the unit fee payable per value of claim for range of amounts:

Value in Euro	Unit fee in Euro
300	25
2,500	160
5,000	300
25,000	715
50,000	1,065
200,000	1,865
470,000	2,990

attorneys. However, attorneys have more control over fees charged out of court by deciding the value of the substance of the work themselves, or by charging a package amount or agreeing an hourly figure in advance with the client (termed *Gebührenvereinbarung*). These charges can be lower than the statutory charges (see § 3 V BRAGO).

The actual work performed by attorneys in litigation is also different to that in common-law countries. The attorney plays a far more restricted role in court litigation. Generally he would not check the accuracy of the client's statements or witnesses' statements. In both cases it is the function of the court and presiding judge to do this. This is generally the result of the inquisitorial system in civil law countries, in that there is less confrontation and greater neutrality in German courts in contrast to the confrontational system in the common-law courts. The attorney's role is mainly restricted to the preparation and the submission of written pleadings, more usual in civil law courts, plus some oral representation in the main court proceedings. In court, cross-examining of witnesses is far less extensive than in the UK and most questions are put by the presiding judge. The dynamic of court-room exchanges in common-law countries is almost non-existent in Germany. Litigation is thus often regarded as low-paid and dull work and is mainly left to the junior members and less experienced attorneys of a practice. The senior and more experienced attorneys prefer to take the better paid consultancy and advisory work.

2.3.2 The notary (Notar)

The office of the notary is one of the specialist legal professions in Germany, largely regulated by the Federal Law on Notaries (*Bundesnotarordnung*: BNotO) of 1961. Notaries are appointed by the *Land* Justice Department (*Landesjustizverwaltung*) to exercise their profession in a particular area, after they have served an obligatory three-year probation period as a *Notarassessor* (§§ 7 and 10–11 BNotO). At least five years' experience as an attorney is also demanded where the offices of *Notar* and *Rechtsanwalt* are combined (§§ 3 and 5 BNotO).

The work of a notary is essentially non-contentious work. For a number of transactions and changes in the law to be legally valid, authentication by a notary is required, who for that purpose is performing a public function. It is, for example, compulsory for real estate sales (BGB §§ 311–313) and for all sales of shares to be attested. Additionally, most wills are authenticated by a notary (BGB § 2231). One of the largest sources of work for a notary is commercial work, and in particular the attestation of the decisions of the general meetings of public companies. Notaries have a monopoly over this type of work and may undertake other work as well, such as advising on legal drafting. The notary is supposed to act as an impartial adviser to all parties and represent a fair, impartial public interest in an important transaction (BNotO § 14). Notarial attestation is not supposed to be a rubber stamp of an agreement but provides an explanation to the parties of the legal consequences of their actions. There is an imposed public duty to take care of the inexperienced, and if this duty is breached damages may be payable (BNotO § 19).

Depending on the *Land* the notary can work purely as a notary (*Nur-notar*), either as an independent professional in private office but fulfilling a public function, as in Hamburg and Bavaria, or as a state official (*Amtsnotar* or *Bezirksnotar*), in Baden-Württemburg. In other *Länder* one can work both as notary and as a *Rechtsanwalt* (*Anwaltsnotar*). About 8,900 notaries combine professions, with about 1,700 pursuing the profession of *Nur-notar*. Regardless of the actual situation in each of the *Länder*, the number of notaries is strictly regulated by the public authorities and the BNotO. Thus, with a monopoly of work, limited numbers and fees fixed by statute on a value basis, this is an extremely lucrative and secure position, and a considerable waiting list exists, of up to fifteen years, for an appointment.

2.3.3 *State attorneys or public prosecutors (Staatsanwälte)*

In Germany all prosecutions are carried out by a separate prosecution service set up by the state which is independent from the police. The functions and procedure of state attorneys are governed by the Organization of the Courts Act (GVG) §§ 141–152 and the Code of Criminal Procedure (StPO). State attorneys are independent of the judiciary and courts (GVG § 150) and are public officials (*Beamten*), but their functions are closely allied to the judiciary because of their public duty as an organ of the administration of justice.

Every court must have a state attorney's department attached to it (§ 141 GVG), and there are about 4,900 state attorneys in Germany. They are appointed by the Federal Minister of Justice and the *Land* Justice Ministers. State attorneys are civil servants in a career profession with its own promotion hierarchy: *Staatsanwalt, Erster Staatsanwalt, Oberstaatsanwalt and Generalstaatsanwalt*. At the Federal level there is also the *Bundesanwaltschaft* of which there are about 80, This is an independent hierarchy leading up to the *Generalbundesanwalt* who do not have a supervisory role over the state attorneys in the *Länder*. Only some 20% are involved in court appearances, and the rest are concerned with investigation of possible criminal offences or general investigations into areas of crime such as the rising economic or white-collar crimes.

The professional requirements for this position are the same as for judicial office (DRiG § 122 I) and high grades in the state examinations are demanded of those seeking to join the profession, which may account for the fact that transfers between the judiciary and *Staatsanwaltschaft* are more common than between other legal occupations.

The state attorney undertakes criminal investigations, collecting evidence both against and for the accused, and has the discretion to prosecute on information passed on from the police and other sources. The decision to prosecute or not comes close to deciding in fact, if not in law, the guilt of the parties. The police can appeal against a decision not to prosecute.

State attorneys have wide powers to investigate crime, to arrest suspects, search, secure and subpoena witnesses, etc. They have rights to call on the police to assist in the investigation of possible offences (StPO §§ 160–161), and most investigation is in fact carried out by the police because of their greater access to forensic experts. See also Chapter 6 and the section on criminal procedure for additional details.

Legal opinion in Germany debates the true role of the state attorney, in that the powers to investigate are unfilled because of the better ability of the police and the fact that the police pass on information usually only when they are fairly certain conviction will ensue, rather than at the stage of their suspicions. Hence it is suggested that state attorneys are now no more than state prosecutors, on behalf of the police, a title by which they are also known. This is ironic, because it is precisely the reason they were established in the first place, to avoid the suggestion that prosecutors simply acted for the police.

During the main trial it is the task of the state attorney to ensure that the correct procedure is being observed as a part of the general task of representing the public interest. The state attorney is involved in the execution of sentence, imprisonment, and with the possibility of a retrial or the granting of a pardon.

2.3.4 *Public authority attorney (Amtsanwalt/Landesanwalt)*

These are specialized legal representatives (c. 900) of the regional authorities, whose role it is to represent the public authorities in actions before the *Länder* administrative courts (VwGO § 36). They are concerned with the general development and application of the law in actions taking place between the public authority and citizens and representatives of the public interest (*Vertreter des öffentlichen Interesses*).

2.4 **Additional legal occupations**

Apart from the specific professions discussed above, qualified lawyers play a greater role in positions in the municipal, regional and federal administrations; in other public institutions and bodies; and in industry and commerce, in total in far greater numbers than in the traditional legal professions.

2.4.1 *Lawyers in commerce and industry (Juristen in der Wirtschaft)*

There are more than 20,000 qualified lawyers who are in full-time employment in commerce and industry, both as ordinary employees and also as specialist legal advisers, employed either by a company or on a fee basis for regular representation, known in turn as *Syndikusanwälte* or *Justitiare*. About 9,000 of these were first self-employed attorneys. They are, as the result of their employment by some other person, denied court audience rights for the employer under § 46 BRAO. They can nevertheless undertake all other legal work on behalf of their employers and are still required to register with the local court.

In addition to the varied number of industries who employ qualified lawyers in their legal and personnel departments amongst others, the insurance companies and banks stand out as substantial employers.

2.4.2 Public authorities and bodies (Juristen in der Verwaltung)

Over 35,000 qualified lawyers are currently employed in public administration. This level of experienced administrators trained in the law has made them particularly qualified to obtain positions in the bureaucracies of international organisations, especially the European Communities.

Particularly large employers are the federal, *Länder* and local government administrations, the area, town and community administrations, and the legal departments of the many government departments and bodies established under public law such as the Foreign Service (*Auswärtiger Dienst*), the Post Office (*Bundespost*), the Federal Bank (*Bundesbank*), the Federal Railways (*Bundesbahn*), the Customs Service (*Zolldienst*), or the Tax Office (*Steuerverwaltungsdienst*). Some of these occupations offer an entry level after the first state examinations only have been achieved.

A further specialized form of public body legal employment for those possessing both state examinations are as officials in the Enforcement of Judgments Service (*Strafvollzugsdienst*) which employs about 2,000 jurists at the Federal level alone. Additional possibilities in the Police Enforcement Service (*Polizeivollzugsdienst*) exist for those having passed only the first state examination.

2.4.3 Tax advisers (Steuerberater)

A tax adviser may be either an independent adviser, or part of a partnership with other tax advisers or other professional services. The profession is governed by the Tax Advice Act (*Steuerberatungsgesetz*)[29] and can be conducted either independently, with limited court audience rights before the finance courts only, or in combination with the profession of *Rechtsanwalt*. Separate training and examinations are necessary in addition to the state examinations in law. There are an estimated 44,000 tax advisers, of whom about 1,000 combine the profession with that of *Rechtsanwalt*.[30]

2.4.4 Auditor (Wirtschaftsprüfer)

This occupation has the exclusive rights of auditing company accounts and is governed by the Regulation on Auditors (*Wirtschaftsprüferordnung*)[31] It requires a separate five-year practical training and the successful passing of the examinations for auditors. It can also be exercised in combination with work as a *Rechtsanwalt*, something undertaken by about 500 of the 7,500 auditors.[32]

2.4.5 Patent lawyer (Patentanwalt)

This is an independent profession specializing in patent law matters and belonging to a separate organization of patent lawyers (*Patentanwaltschaft*), but with limited court audience rights before the lower patent courts and the Patent

---

[29] BGBl 1961 I S 1301.
[30] See Kreizberg, cited in 'Further reading', p. 232.
[31] BGBl 1961 I S 1049.
[32] Kreizberg, op. cit., p. 232.

Senate of the BGH. It is governed by the Regulation on Patent Attorneys (*Patentanwaltsordnung*).[33]

2.4.6 Academic career (Hochschullehrer)

An academic career with the goal of university professor, although prescribing no strict career pattern, usually goes as follows. After the second state examination, both a higher degree (*Promotion*) and a *Habilitation* are required in ordinary circumstances. Those pursuing this career are usually assistants to established professors, who undertake teaching and research on behalf of the professor while working towards a higher degree (*Promotion*[34]) the *Habilitation* required for appointment to a chair (*Lehrstuhl*) themselves. Then they must wait for an opening at one of the universities. Considerable extra opportunities were afforded by the expansion of the education system, and in particular by the increase in the numbers of law faculties in the former East Germany. This eastward movement of academics then opened up gaps in the older universities.

Once established, full professors can also serve as part-time judges or as the representatives of clients before the *Länder* and federal courts. Salary is determined according to a statutory scale. Further career enhancement is often achieved by movement from one university to another to get on to a higher scale.[35]

An alternative academic career is afforded by the *Fachhochschule* for which the writing of a *Habilitation* is not required but instead more practical experience of the law might be expected.

2.4.7 The legal adviser (Rechtsbeistand)

Individuals who are not fully legally qualified have been allowed to act as legal advisers (*Rechtsbeistände*) in limited circumstances as quasi attorneys. Although the role, or indeed many forms of less formal legal adviser, existed prior to the period of the Third Reich, it was in this period that the position was rationalized. In 1935, the Statute on Legal Advice (*Rechtsberatungsgesetz*: RBerG), or as first enacted the Statute for the Protection against Misuse in giving Legal Advice (*Rechtsberatungsmißbrauchgesetz*), gave German attorneys exclusive audience rights in the courts to give advice and represent clients in German law matters. The statute considerably tightened up the previous regime in respect of audience rights. Non-lawyers were allowed to provide services, but this was limited to giving specific advice concerning, for example, tax matters. At first most *Rechtsbeistände* were granted full competence (*Vollrechtsbeistand*), but this has been restricted by law now, and only a partial competence (*Teilrechtsbeistand*) is granted for a specific area such as tax, old age pensions, rent or international, foreign and EC Law (RBerG § 1 I). Persons who were recognised for this purpose were allowed to adopt the title of *Rechtsbeistand*.[36]

---

[33] BGBl 1966 I S 557.

[34] The equivalent of a Master's Degree by Research.

[35] See the *Bundesbesoldungsgesetz* (BBesG) latest version from 3 December 1998 (BGBl I 3434 and amended to 17 August 2001 (BGBl I 2144), §§ 33–36, Anlagen II & IV. This is also the statute in which the salaries of public servants can be found, and those of judges and state attorneys.

Rechtsbeistände must obtain permission to represent clients from the presiding judge of the *Amtsgericht* or *Landgericht* in the area from which they wish to practice.

Foreign attorneys could, upon application, be given a general permission by the competent authority to represent clients in matters of foreign law. Following the war, the legally experienced *Rechtsbeistände* with full competence were allowed to become attorneys in an attempt to phase out this role, which is still an aim. However, the need for foreign attorneys to have audience rights in German courts has continued, particularly since EC membership. This is considered in the section below on the rights of non-nationals to practise as attorneys in Germany.

Prozeßagenten are legal advisers who are admitted to represent clients in the oral proceedings of the administrative and social courts only (ZPO § 157). They are, however, usually required to be an admitted *Rechtsbeistand* and, like the attorneys, are also restricted, usually to one court.

2.4.8 Court officials (Rechtspfleger)

The term *Rechtspfleger* is a generic term for court officials—legally trained civil servants (*Beamte des gehobenen Justizdienstes*), who have their own training of at least three years' duration at one of the *Fachhochschule/Verwaltungshochschule*. They play an increasingly important role in the conduct of the administration of justice and the tasks of the court. Those who have passed the first and second state exams are exempted part or all of the training requirements. As of 1998, there were 11,224 employed in the old *Bundesländer* and 2,711 employed in the new *Bundesländer* with an additional 167 employed in federal institutions such as the *Bundesgerichthof* and the Federal state attorney's office.

These court officials mainly deal with the non-contentious business of the court, for which they have independent powers of decision-making entrusted to them by the *Rechtspflegergesetz* (RPflG). They also have the authority to conduct, in terms of German court procedure, the less important oral proceedings of the court involving, for example, the taking of statements of witnesses and testimonies of experts. They deal with the applications for legal aid and matters in respect of the registration of property, the commercial register, and enforcement of judgments. It is compulsory for each court of ordinary jurisdiction and each labour court to appoint at least one *Rechtspfleger*, in practice all courts employ one or more.

Decisions of a *Rechtspfleger* can be appealed to a judge. There is no question of a progression to judge from the position of *Rechtspfleger*.[37]

---

[36] See also Dr H. Schorn, *Die Rechtsberatung* (1967: Fachverlag Stoyscheff, Darmstadt) pp. 106–07 & 160–61 and see for full details of the statute, *Rechtsberatungsgesetz* (RBerG): *Kommentar von Altenhoff, Busch & Chemnitz*, 10th ed. (1993: Aschendorff, Münster).

[37] Further and fuller details can be found in Greffiers (ed.), *Rechtsstellung und Aufgaben der Rechtspfleger: Vergleichsstudie EUR*, 2nd ed. (1989: Gieseking, Bielefeld).

2.5 Rights allowed non-German attorneys

The basic position in Germany is that there is no discrimination against non-Germans but audience rights are granted only on the same basis as to Germans, thus the applicant must have been qualified in the same way as German attorneys. Therefore, in order to provide services in the German courts or establish oneself as an attorney in Germany, it is first necessary to take and pass the necessary state exams for attorneys, as discussed in full under the section on legal education and training.

The only alternative to this was provided by the law on the *Rechtsbeistand*, as discussed above. This was adapted so that non-German attorneys were allowed to provide legal services, but they were limited to giving legal advice on non-German law and, additionally, the discretionary permission of the president of the local regional court was required. In order for a foreign attorney to become fully established to represent and advise on German law in the courts, it was still necessary to take the state examinations as required according to each *Land*. Therefore, under the present law, but subject to the comments on Community law following, German attorneys have an almost total monopoly on private legal services.

2.6 The position of EC attorneys

The rights of attorneys from the EC Member States to practise in Germany is determined by the way in which Germany has implemented the Diplomas Directive and other Legislation[38] Previously, EC attorneys had been recognized as having rights similar to the *Rechtsbeistand* to appear in German courts to represent clients, but only in matters of international and foreign law (BRAO § 206). However, the local residence requirement for the provision of services has already been removed for EC attorneys as a result of an ECJ ruling on the implementation in Germany of the EEC Directive 77/249 (see BRAO § 209). As a result of this ruling, EC attorneys have the right to represent clients before German courts without the need for local residence and without the support of a German attorney in courts where representation is not required by law.

The implementation of the Mutual Recognition of Diplomas Directive in Germany (BGBl 1990, I S 1349) basically sets up a regime of mutual acceptance of professional qualifications from other Member States. In Germany, other member state attorneys will be required to pass an aptitude test which will be administered by the same authorities who administer the second state examinations which is usually the Ministries of Justice in the individual *Länder*. The examination will consist of an obligatory paper in civil law, two optional subjects and a paper on the

---

[38] Council Directive 89/48 on a general system for the recognition of Higher Education Diplomas on completion of Professional Training of at least three years' duration (OJ 1989, No. L19/16). Foster, *EC Legislation*, 12th ed. (2001), Blackstone Press, London, p. 336. Lawyers (Provision of Services Directive 77/249 [1977] OJ L78/17 (Foster, ibid., p, 334) and the Lawyers Home Title Directive 98/5 [1998] OJ L77/36 (Foster, ibid., p. 364).

particular area of law in which the candidate has specialized. The optional subjects are chosen from two groups consisting of five subjects from public law and criminal law to include a further area of civil law, but not one previously covered by the obligatory exam; commercial law; labour law; public law; and criminal law. This is not a light requirement, as the obligatory paper in civil law can cover any topic in the civil code and candidates will have to be prepared to answer questions on the equivalents of any of the following: contract, tort, property, family and succession law (§ 5). The exams, according to § 5 II, can include questions about the key legislative provisions in both obligatory and optional subjects, aspects of the pertinent procedural law, including basic aspects of the law of the constitution of the courts, and basic elements of criminal procedure and insolvency. Paragraph 6 provides that the exams will consist of supervised written papers in the obligatory subject and one of the optional subjects. In addition, there is also an oral exam to which entry is allowed only when the requirement has been met that at least one of the supervised papers has been successfully completed. The oral consists of a short presentation talk and a discussion. Topics covered are the other optional subject and the area of usual practical experience of the candidate. In addition, if one of the papers has been failed this will also be orally examined. Paragraph 8 provides that the entire examination can be repeated.

A completing *Verordnung* (administrative regulation)[39] has been issued by the Minister of Justice which gives further details on the test including the very important decision to grant exemptions in certain circumstances. Paragraph 3 II 1 requires that the application to take the examination must include a curriculum vitae submitted in one's own handwriting. Although it is silent as to the consequences of not complying, the presumption must be that an application form failing to comply will be rejected. There are also requirements under §§ 3 II, 6 and 7 for the applicant to give an assurance that an application has not been made elsewhere and to give details of any previous, unsuccessful attempts. Exemptions from the relevant exams will be granted where applicants can prove, by means of a diploma or certificate, that they have already reached the required standard of knowledge of substantive and procedural law (§ 5).

The obligatory written paper in civil law can cover the general part of the civil code, the law of obligations and property law, all the applicable procedural law (including the Organization of the Courts Act) and basics of enforcement and insolvency law. The exam on public law can cover basic rights, general administrative law and general procedural law, basic building law, the law of public security and public order, and court and legal procedural laws (§§ 6 and 7). Each of the written papers is five hours in length and will usually consist of one question, without choice, on any aspect of the subject under examination. The oral presentation and exam cover the subject of practice of the applicant. Two hours' preparation time is given for an exam lasting some forty-five minutes and for a

---

[39] *Verordnung über die Eignungsprüfung für die Zulassung zur Rechtsanwaltschaft*, 18 December 1990, BGBl I S 2881.

fifteen-minute presentation. Paragraph 12 allows a retake on two subsequent occasions. Finally, if successful, the candidate is then admitted and can use the title of *Rechtsanwalt* in Germany.

These reforms and those prompted by national discussions, have already and may result in further considerable change to the practice of the professions in Germany over the next few years. It would be too speculative to spend time here trying to guess the eventual outcome of further reforms, particularly as a survey of recent literature demonstrates that many aspects, including those already amended, are still subject to debate and proposals for change.

3 Lay participation in the legal system

Germany not only has a considerable history of lay participation in the dispensation of justice but there is also a considerable current lay element in a wide variety of courts and legal situations.

Historically, the *Schöffengericht* and the *Schwurgericht* stand out as the principal examples of courts with lay participation. The *Schöffengericht* certainly had its origins in the participation of members of a local assembly in dispute resolution, initially on an *ad hoc* basis, although this could be over an extended period of time. The head of the court, the *Richter*, took no part in the decision-making but presided over the proceedings. The reception of roman law meant that the law-finders (*Schöffen*) were either replaced by a professionally trained judiciary or themselves became qualified in the law, although variations of the *Schöffengericht* existed in Germany until the nineteenth century.

The jury court (*Schwurgericht*) was a later arrival to criminal proceedings and was introduced in the territories under Napoleonic occupation. It was retained following the overthrow of French rule and, due to its popularity, the jury trial spread throughout the German states. In a pure form the jury court did not last long and was replaced by the mixed court of professional and lay members, also known as *Schöffengericht* but with the professionals and the lay members judging the merits of the case, applying the law and determining sentence.

In 1879, the reforming Statute on the Organisation of the Courts (*Gerichtsverfassungsgesetz*: GVG) laid the foundation for the organization of court structure which remains essentially the same today. It introduced the *Schöffengericht*, and the *Schwurgericht* for serious crimes, for the whole of the *Reich*. There were, however, some considerable changes during the period of the Weimar Republic and the Third Reich, including the abolition of juries.

The present criminal courts are no longer full jury courts but, as reintroduced in the Federal Republic, are mixed courts consisting of professional judges and lay judges (called *Laienrichter* or *Ehrenamtliche Richter*). To confuse matters further the lay participants of criminal courts are called *Schöffen*. In the commercial courts the lay judges are called *Handelsrichter* and in all other instances, honorary judges

(*Ehrenamtliche Richter*) (§ 45a DRiG). The participation of the lay judges in the criminal courts alone amounts to over 40,000 persons.[40]

In the criminal courts, at the level of the *Amtsgericht*, minor offences for which the penalty is less than one year's imprisonment are tried before a single judge. More serious offences at first instance are heard before the *Schöffengericht*, composed of one professional and two lay members (GVG § 29 I) and sometimes known as the *kleines Schöffengericht*. Decisions in the *Schöffengerichte* are based on a two-thirds majority with the lay members being required to cast their votes first (GVG § 197). The *Landgericht* sits as a *kleine Strafkammer* with one professional and two lay members, and hears appeals from the single *Amtsgericht* judge (GVG §§ 74 II and 76). Secondly, it sits as an appeal court from the *Schöffengericht* (known as the *grosse Strafkammer*) with a membership of three professional and two lay judges (GVG § 74). Lastly, it sits as a *Schwurgericht* with two professional and three lay members at first instance for the most serious crimes. Special juvenile courts (*Jugend-schöffengericht*) of the *Amtsgericht* have a lay presence of two members to one professional judge for serious offenders (JGG § 40). A *Jugendstrafgericht* in the *Landgericht* hears the most serious offences and appeals from the *Amtsgericht* in juvenile cases (JGG § 41, GVG §§ 26 and 74b).

Participation in civil cases is less extensive, with lay members sitting in the commercial senates of civil courts (GVG § 105 I) and in agricultural disputes at the *Amtsgericht*, *Oberlandesgericht* and BGH levels (LwVG § 2 II).

In the specialized court divisions, lay participation is more extensive. In the labour courts at the level of the *Amtsgericht* and *Landgericht* one professional and two lay members sit, and in the Federal Labour Court there are three professional and two lay members (ArbGG §§ 16 II, 35 II and 41 II). The lay judges are taken equally from amongst employers and employees or their organizations.

In the first instance administrative and revenue courts there are three judges and two lay judges VwGO § 5 III, FGO § 5 III. In the administrative *Landesgericht* there are three professional and two lay judges but only in some *Länder* (VwGO § 9). They also sit on the disciplinary court and the court for other professions.

The social courts have one judge and two lay members, and on appeal three to two in both the *Landessozialgericht* and the *Bundessozialgericht* (§§ 12 I, 28, 33 and 40 SGG).

Lay judges are selected on the basis of a list of local citizens from a professional and social cross-section of society, which is drawn up by the local authority every four years and presented to the local *Amtsgericht*. A committee consisting of an elected judge, a court official and ten elected citizens then selects lay judges from the list by a two-thirds majority vote. Their term of office is for four years. They are required to serve for at least twelve sessions per years, for which they are paid expenses and a small fee (GVG §§ 32–35 and 45–46).

Lay members are equally independent and serve under the same conditions as the professional members (Art. 97 (1) *Grundgesetz* and DRiG § 45 I).

---

[40] Wolf, op. cit., p. 227.

FURTHER READING

Useful Website addresses The Federal Ministry of Justice, Bundesministerium der Justiz: **www.bundesjustizministerium.de/**

Legal education

M. Braun. and R. Birk, 'Historical roots of German legal education' (1981) 5 *Comparative Law Yearbook*, pp. 69–82.

H. Giehring et al (eds.), *Juristenausbildung- erneut überdacht* (1990: Nomos Verlag, Baden-Baden).

A. Gleiss, *Soll ich Rechtsanwalt werden?*, 3rd ed. (1992: Sauer-Verlag, Heidelberg).

Hommelhoff and Teichmann, Forum: *Modernisierung in Kontinuität—die Revolution der Juristenausbildung* (2001) JuS Heft 9, pp. 841–845.

S. Krüger-von Elsner, *Studienführer Rechtswissenschaft*, 3rd ed. (1997: Lexica Verlag, Munich).

J. Lonbay, *Training Lawyers in the EC* (chapter 4 on Germany) (1990: Law Society, London).

JuS-Redaktion (ed.), *JuS-Studienführer*, 3rd ed. (1991: C. H. Beck, Munich).

Recht und Politik 1/2000. *Schwerpunktthema: Reform der Juristenausbildung*, pp. 7–22.

A. Rinken, *Einführung in das juristische Studium*, 2nd ed. (1991: C.H. Beck, Munich).

D. Schmalz, *Methodenlehre für das juristische Studium*, 2nd ed. (1990: Nomos Verlag, Baden-Baden).

Legal personnel

M. Bohlander and C. Latour, *The German Judiciary in the Nineties: A Study of the Recruitment, Promotion and Remuneration of Judges in Germany* (1998: Shaker Verlag, Aachen).

E.J. Cohn, *Manual of German Law*, vol. I (1968: Institute of Comparative Law).

H. Eidenmüller, 'Deregulating the market for legal services in the European Community: freedom of establishment and freedom to provide services for EC lawyers in the Federal Republic of Germany' (1990) 53 MLR 604–08.

N. Foster, 'European Community Law and the freedom of lawyers in the United Kingdom and Germany' (1991) 40 ICLQ 607–34.

Embassy of the FRG, Lawyers and courts: the German legal profession (1989: Federal Republic of Germany).

G. Hartstang, *Der deutsche Rechtsanwalt: Rechtsstellung und Funktion in Vergangenheit und Gegenwart* (1986: Müller, Heidelberg).

W. Heyde, *Die Rechtspflege in der Bundesrepublik Deutschland*, 5th ed. (1990: Bundesanzeiger, Cologne).

W. Heyde, *Justice and the Law in the Federal Republic of Germany* (1994. C. F. Müller, Heidelberg) (English translation and update of the above).

D. P. Kommers, *The Constitutional Jurisprudence of the Federal Republic of Germany* (1990: Duke University Press, Durham, North Carolina).

K. Kreizberg, *Die Juristen in den Organisationen der deutschen Wirtschaft* (1994: Wirtschaftsverlag Bachem, Cologne).

H. Prütting (ed.), *Die deutsche Anwaltschaft zwischen heute und morgen* (1990: Heymanns, Cologne).

E. Schilkin, *Gerichtsverfassungsrecht*, 2nd ed. (1994: C.H. Beck, Munich).

T. Rasehorn, *Der Richter zwischen Tradition und Lebenswelt* (1989: Nomos Verlag, Baden-Baden).

H. Prütting, 'Die Rechtliche Organisations der Rechtsberatung aus deutscher und europäische Sicht' in P. Schlosser (ed.), *Integritätsprobleme im Umfeld der Justiz*, pp. 1–31 (1994: Gieseking, Beilefeld).

Dr H. Schorn, *Die Rechtsberatung* (1967: Fachverlag Stoyscheff, Darmstadt).

Dr W.B. von Schweinitz, *Rechtsberatung durch Juristen und Nichtjuristen, inbesondere durch Wirtschaftprüfer* (1975: Duncker & Humblot, Berlin).

Steinkraus and Schaaf, *Zur Einführung: Das Berufsrecht der Rechtsanwälte*, JuS 2001, 167 et seq., 275 et seq., and 377 et seq.

A. Tyrrell and Z. Yaqub (eds.), The Legal Professions in the New Europe, Chapter 9: The Legal Professions in Germany by G. Manz and S. Padman-Reich, pp. 130–153 (1992: Blackwell Publishers, Oxford).

F. Wooldridge, 'The German rules governing the professional conduct of Rechtsanwälte' (1990) 39 ICLQ 683–90.

Lay participation

G. Casper and H. Zeisel, 'Lay judges in the German criminal courts' (1972) 1 J Legal Stud 135–91.

J.P. Richert, *West German Lay Judges* (1983: University Press of Florida, Tampa).

5

The operation of justice

This chapter brings together a number of related topics concerned with the operation of the legal system in Germany. It includes details of the courts before which legal representation is either required or not, the costs of litigation, the provision of financial assistance for both legal advice and legal representation, the assistance available in studying or understanding the laws of Germany by the provision of published and electronic works and, lastly, aspects of civil law procedure. Aspects of criminal law procedure are considered alongside the general system of criminal law in Germany.

1 Legal advice and legal aid

1.1 Legal representation

1.1.1 *Courts of ordinary jurisdiction*
The principle of compulsory representation (*Prinzip des Anwaltszwangs*) applies in many of the courts in Germany. Legal representation is compulsory before all courts and all chambers of the courts of civil jurisdiction above the level of the *Amtsgericht*. In the family division of the *Amtsgericht* in marital and divorce settlements and where the interest of children is concerned, representation is also required (see ZPO § 78 I and II 1–3). The only exceptions to this in civil litigation are the increased rights now enjoyed by EC attorneys and the limited rights of representation granted to *Rechtsbeistände* and *Prozeßagenten* (see § 90 ZPO, § 1 RBerG and further details in Chapter 4). The attorney must formally prove his right to represent his client before the case can commence (§ 80 ZPO).

In the criminal courts, in the main proceedings of a case of first instance before the *Landgericht* or *Oberlandesgericht*, § 141 and § 140 Abs. 1 StPO require a defence attorney to be appointed by the court if the accused does not have one, or in certain other circumstances where the penalty would be for more than three months or when concerned with serious crime, or if it was obvious the accused would not be able to defend themselves properly (§ 140 II StPO). The representative can be, according to § 138 StPO, a *Rechtsanwalt* admitted to any court in Germany or a university law professor.

1.1.2 *Other courts*

Before the labour courts, representation by an attorney is compulsory only before the *Bundesarbeitsgericht*, although some form of representation is required before the *Landesarbeitsgericht*, which can be by a qualified representative of the union or employers organization (see § 11 ArbGG).

In the tax courts it is only before the *Bundesfinanzhof* that representation is compulsory, but this can be by a specialized tax adviser (*Steuerberater* or *Wirtschaftsprüfer*). Hence this is *Vertretungszwang* rather than *Anwaltszwang* (FGO §§ 115–118).

In the administrative courts representation is not compulsory before the lower or *Länder* courts but it is required before the Federal Administrative Court by either a *Rechtsanwalt* or a university professor (VwGO § 67).

There is no compulsion to have professional representation before any of the social courts (§ 13 SGB X).

For further details refer to the appropriate substantive law chapters.

In those courts where attorneys are not compulsory, the litigant or defendant may conduct his own case or engage the help of a non-legally qualified adviser who may be allowed or admitted by the court. A particular form of *Rechtsbeistand*, known as *Prozeßagent*, may appear in the proceedings at the discretion of the court (new § 157 ZPO) as an exception to the general prohibition on non-qualified legal representatives (for further details see chapter 4 above on legal personnel).

2 Litigation costs

2.1 Court costs

Fees for court litigation are payable to both the representative attorney and the courts and are largely determined by reference to the statutory scales (the Court Costs Act (*Gerichtskostengesetz*: GKG) and others).[1] Civil court costs rise on a scale depending on the value of the claim, which is not uniformly proportional and is referred to in Germany as a reclining scale (*regressiv*). As of 1994 and unchanged to 2001, a subject value of € 3,000 would attract a unit court fee of € 10,000, € 196; and € 110,000, € 856. See § 11 GKG and the second annex to the Act which reproduces a table of costs.

Costs in the civil courts are determined initially by § 91 ZPO, on the basis that the loser pays for all court costs, costs of the winner's attorney, and those of witnesses and experts when necessary. The other party's attorney's costs are limited to the

---

[1] 15 December 1975 (BGBl I 3047) amended to 10 December 2001 (BGBl I 3422) and see VwGO, KO, FGO, KostO, ArbGG.

statutorily provided levels (§ 91 II ZPO). Partial success will result in the proportional apportionment of costs (§ 92 ZPO).

The civil divisions of the ordinary courts, administrative and tax courts apply the schedule of costs statutorily provided according to the value (*Streitwert*) of the matter disputed (§ 1 ZPO). Labour court costs are lower (§ 1 ZPO), and costs for actions in the social courts are only payable by the public authorities (§ 64 SGB X). Payments for court costs are made on a unit basis according to the type of proceedings and at various stages of the proceedings, partly in advance and partly on judgment, and the unit fee may be divided into fractions (full details in GKG annex 1). A case which goes to final judgment will result in the payment of three full units at first instance, three and a half at second instance and four at third instance.

In criminal law proceedings the burden of costs is laid down by the StPO §§ 464 et seq. Basically, if the accused is convicted he is liable for his own costs and court fees but not those of the state attorney prosecuting (§§ 464–5 StPO). These may be reduced, in part or in whole, by the court where an order for costs would be unjust. If acquitted, the state pays for all fees and costs (§ 467 I StPO).

2.2 Fees for legal representation

Attorneys' fees for litigation work in civil law are regulated by the Federal Statute on Attorneys' Fees (*Bundesrechtsanwaltsgebührenordnung*: BRAGO), which details schedules of the statutory fees payable on a claim value basis and payable in stages following the commencement of the action, the oral hearing and at judgment (§§ 23 and 31). The unit fees work in the same way as those for the court, and a completed case would require the payment of three unit fees, or four if a settlement was reached purportedly to take account of the increased amount of work necessary. See § 11 BRAGO and the appendix giving a table of fees. A subject matter of the value of € 3,000 will attract a unit fee of € 189; € 10,000, € 486; and € 10,000, € 1354.[2]

Fees for out of court work are more flexible but, may still be determined on a sliding scale according to the value of the work undertaken. The client and attorney can, however, agree on a price outside of the fees scale, provided it is not lower and that it is in writing (§ 3 BRAGO). See the section on fees in Chapter 4.

In addition to the unit fees for the court and attorneys, there would also be the additional expenses (disbursements) of the attorney, detailed in §§ 26–30 BRAGO, and the costs of witnesses and experts who give evidence. These are regulated by the Law relating to Witnesses and Experts' Expenses (*Gesetz über die Entschädigung von Zeugen und Sachverständigen* (ZSEG)).[3] A matter with a subject value of € 3,000, for example, would cost a minimum of € 1500 in court and attorneys' fees for the losing party, plus additional expenses for attorneys and witnesses, which could well reach the value of the subject matter in total. Thus actions in pursuit of

---

[2] Figures last effectively increased 24 June 1994. See also Chapter 4.
[3] Of 1 October 1969, BGBl I S 1756, but with the fees tables amended 24 June 1994.

subject value below this must either be very certain to be worthwhile or be assisted by legal aid.

3 Legal aid

Even in the courts where self-representation is possible, the complexity of both the material and procedural law makes representation virtually a necessity. The high cost of litigation and legal advice can result in injustice if no provision is made for poorer members in society. This situation is aggravated in Germany by the fact that legal representation by a qualified attorney or adviser is compulsory before many of the courts. Without the provision of legal aid, the basic right of equality in the law and its application for all would be in serious danger. This concern was given statutory expression when the administration of justice was overhauled in the second half of the last century. The basis for the law as it stands today was included in the Law on Civil Procedure (ZPO) in 1877. Formerly known as *Armenrecht*, it is now known as *Prozeßkostenhilfe*.

The provision of legal advice and legal aid for representation before the courts is now catered for by two provisions: the Legal Advice Act (*Beratungshilfegesetz*: BerHG) and the Law on Legal Aid (*Gesetz über Prozeßkostenhilfe*: PKHG, an unofficial acronym) both of 13 June 1980, with the latter being incorporated into the ZPO §§ 114–127.[4]

3.1 The Legal Advice Act (*Beratungshilfegesetz*: BerHG)

This Law concerns help to get legal advice and legal assistance outside litigation. Over the last century there has been a number of private legal advice schemes provided by attorneys' associations, or state schemes promoted and established by the public authorities. The latter were, however, restricted in general to the larger towns and cities.

The legislative origins of assistance can be found in the rules contained in the code on civil procedure on the rights of the poor. They were provided as a result of the concern that, certain members of society would be deprived of legal rights due to the prohibitive costs of legal representation. Whilst a court action may be the necessary final step for many disputes or problems, it is by no means the only answer, and help may be more usefully provided by other forms of legal assistance or advice outside of court actions. Legal advice is an essential precondition for an action, therefore it may be more important to provide legal aid for this aspect than only for court actions.

Discussion has more recently taken place within the framework of the provisions of the *Grundgesetz* for the guarantee of procedural rights to protect basic material

---

[4] 13 January 1980, BGBl I 677 and 689. The latest version of which was last amended 13 July 2001, BGBl I S 1542.

rights. See Articles 2(1), 3, 19(4), 103(1) *Grundgesetz*. The view arose that, in respect of persons who are unable to provide for themselves either the knowledge or financial means to assert or defend their actual or perceived legal rights, it is the duty of the state to provide these as a part of the principles of a democratic and social *"Rechtstaat"*. This discussion resulted, in the mid-1970s, in the experimentation in some of the *Länder* of models for legal advice.

Two main models arose. The first is the attorney model where, following a form of interview to determine both the strength of the claim and need for legal help by a means test, a person would be given a certificate to engage the help of an attorney of his or her choice. The second model is described as the public authority or social model (*Öffentliche Rechtsberatung*), whereby a Legal Advice Centre, staffed by attorneys, would be established from which help could be sought by those within the qualifying means test. Some *Länder* combined these two models, so that an advice centre acted either as a filter before the attorneys or gave legal advice to all except the cases which required further legal action.

The Law on Legal Advice was passed on 21 June 1980 and came into force on 1 January 1981. For the most part the *Länder* adopted the attorney model and excluded from the scope of aided legal advice the areas of labour law, social security law and, to a large extent, tax law. The Law did, however, allow the city states of Hamburg, Bremen and Berlin to adopt a social model and include advice from individual attorneys where necessary. Where *Länder* wished to do so, they could extend the scheme to the areas omitted by the federal legislation. The application of legal aid therefore varies considerably between the old *Länder*. Generally it covers civil law, administrative law, constitutional law, criminal law, non-criminal penalties and, to an extremely limited extent, tax matters. In Hamburg and Bremen they have set up Public Legal Advice Centres instead of providing legal aid through attorneys (§ 14 I BerHG) and Berlin has set up both and allows a choice (§ 14 II BerHG). Bavaria, Lower Saxony, Rhineland-Palatinate and Saarland have all included labour and social law matters in their own *Land* legislation, and Bavaria alone has extended it to tax matters. Changes introduced in 1994 have extended the scheme generally to social matters and allowed the new *Länder* to extend it also to labour law.[5]

To obtain help, applicants can either apply to the *Amtsgericht* to appoint an attorney or go directly to an attorney (§ 3 BerHG). It has to be shown that the person seeking advice is unable to afford it from his own personal and financial means (§ 1 I BerHG). It was originally dependent on the amount of net disposable income and the number of persons legally reliant on that income, but has been changed[6] so that it is now based on the amount of monthly disposable income after certain deductions have been made. Full details of what is to be considered income, the deductions which should be made and deductions which can be made for a spouse and dependants are now provided in § 114 ZPO. Property and savings are

---

[5] See BGBl 1994 I S 2323.
[6] By the *Gesetz zur Änderung von Vorschriften über die Prozeßkostenhilfe vom 10.10.1994* (PKHÄndG), BGBl I S 2954.

also to be taken into account. Only those with less than 15 Euro disposable monthly income will be relieved of the entire burden of payment. Those with greater amounts remaining will be required to pay according to a sliding scale, for example, those with 50 Euro remaining would be required to pay 15 Euro and those with 500 Euro remaining 175 Euro.[7]

It must be proved that there is a matter which falls outside court action, that no other means exist to obtain legal advice and that the assertion of rights is reasonable (§ 1). It is, however, sometimes hard to define where advice on court action becomes part of the preparation for court action and thus subject to the rules on legal aid.

Legal advice provision also applies in civil law, for example, when entering into contractual relations, where explanation of the conditions or general explanation of the contracts is required, or in order to determine the duties in certain occupations, especially the self-employed (§ 2 II 1).

A fee of 10 Euro is payable regardless, as long as the provision of some sort of advice has taken place. This was an attempt to discourage time-wasters but attorneys may waive this (§ 8 BerHG).

This Law can apply to natural and legal persons and to foreigners.

3.2 Legal aid for representation in court (*Prozeßkostenhilfe*)

The provision of legal aid was reconsidered in the light of the rights guaranteed by the *Grundgesetz* at the same time as the Legal Advice Act, and has been confirmed by the BVerfG as a guaranteed basic right stemming from the principle of the *Rechtsstaat* (BVerfGE 6, 124 and 81, 347). The Law on Legal Aid (*Gesetz über Prozeßkostenhilfe*: PKHG) made significant changes to the code on civil procedure.[8] Due to the high and rising costs of the scheme, the law has been changed on a number of occasions.

The underlying basis of the provision of legal aid is that the undertaking by a person of an action or defence to preserve rights must not materially damage the position of the applicant or his family (§ 114 ZPO). The basis of assessment is the same as for legal advice, considered above (§ 115 ZPO).

Legal aid may be applied for in most civil law proceedings, with the notable exceptions of the application procedure itself and arbitration, and by all persons. In criminal law, special rules apply whereby the accused must have a representative appointed (see StPO §§ 140 et seq.). It also applies correspondingly to labour law courts, social security courts, tax courts, and administrative law courts, and even to foreign legal actions. It applies to natural persons, foreigners and, in limited circumstances to legal persons (§ 116 II ZPO).

If an applicant wishes to obtain legal aid, he may approach a court or, in practice, any attorney (not just those on a panel or list). The attorney will then submit a

---

[7] For full details refer to §§ 114 et seq. ZPO and generally on the reformed law on legal aid, W. Friedrich, '*Wie erhalte ich Prozeßkostenhilfe?*', NJW 1995, pp. 617–20.
[8] See ZPO §§ 114–127, BRAGO §§ 121–130.

written petition to the court for legal aid along with the statement of claim for the dispute matter (§ 117 ZPO).

The court to which application is made, which is the same court that will hear the action itself, is called the *Prozeßgericht* and will decide on the basis of three main criteria:

(a) A strict means test, essentially to determine whether the applicant (as plaintiff or defendant) would endanger his maintenance or that of his family if he had to pay himself and is thus deserving in terms of legal aid.

(b) A *prima facie* case exists in which the applicant would be successful either as a plaintiff or defendant.

(c) The action must be reasonable and not an action for a very small amount or where it would be unlikely that the successful award could be obtained.

If it allows legal aid, then the court grants a provisional exemption from court and attorney fees according to the financial position of the applicant and the case can be conducted. If the court refuses legal aid, this decision can be appealed against just once to a higher court (see § 127 ZPO).

As in the UK in civil actions, the loser must pay the cost and fees of the winner as well as his own. In comparison to the UK small claims are more expensive and large claims are cheaper to litigate. If the assisted party wins the case the opponent pays all the costs, as he would in any normal case, and the assisted party's court and attorney's costs will be settled by the losing party. If the assisted party loses, the *Land* treasury will pay the attorney (§ 123 ZPO). Should the applicant's position improve he would be expected to repay the costs.

4 Legal publications, reporting, and citation

Legal publications or the writings of judges and academics may be important enough to be considered as a quasi source of law, although they are not formally recognised. The historical section emphasized the important role played by the universities in the development of the German law, and so today German legal literature plays a much greater role than in common-law countries.

4.1 Official publications

The most important publication is undoubtedly the *Grundgesetz* which is available in many forms including the official texts, those issued by the *Bundeszentrale für politische Bildung* in Bonn and available in German and English, and the many examples published by the private publishing houses. See, amongst others: *Grundgesetz, Beck Texte im dtv* (C. H. Beck, Munich), *Textbuch staats- und verwaltungsrechtlicher Gesetze* (C. F. Müller, Heidelberg).

Secondly, there are the major codes—the civil code (BGB), code of civil procedure

(ZPO), commercial code (HGB), criminal code (StGB), code of criminal procedure (StPO), and the social code (SGB), which are only officially published as first enacted. They have not been officially amended but have been updated by various official enactments and supplementary laws (*Nebengesetze*). All forms of law must be published in an official journal before they can take effect. For federal *Gesetze*, this is the Federal Law Gazette (*Bundesgesetzblatt*: BGBl). This is published in three parts. The first volume includes all important federal legislation of daily concern and the second contains less important federal legislation and international agreements, it is cited, for example, as BGBl 1986 I S. 654. Part III contains collections of laws by subject matter but it is not up-to-date, although new consolidations are planned.

Particular legislation or parts thereof carry the following abbreviations: § = Paragraph (*Abschnitt*), Abs = a section of a paragraph (*Absatz*). S or s = *Satz* = Sentence (this can also mean *Seite*). There is supposed to be a distinct, correct way of referring to provisions of legislation, as follows: §. 12 I. S.2. BGB: but often abbreviated to § 12 1.2 Unfortunately, as in the UK, a wander through legal literature will reveal that not only do different authors and publishers have their own forms of citation, but also they often declare them to be the officially recognized form. For example, *Jura Extra: Studium und Examen* (1981: de Gruyter), p. 60, gives the following recommended form of citation: § 40 Abs. 2 S. 1, using arabic numerals for paragraphs, subparagraphs and sentences. Köbler, *Das Studium des Rechts*, 3rd ed. (1982: Vahlen), p. 134, disagrees and cites § 812I 1 BGB, Art 73 Nr. 2 Grundgesetz, § 220 a I Nr. 5 StGB. This appears to be the most common form, using arabic, roman and arabic for paragraphs, sub-paragraphs and sentences respectively. The *Grundgesetz* is also cited using arabic numerals throughout only and in combination with roman sub-paragraphs.

For secondary legislation the name of the official collection varies from *Land* to *Land*, but there is a collection of the laws of the Federation and the *Länder*, the *Sammelblatt* (Sabl). The *Länder* have in addition their own Official Gazettes of legislation, and laws made by the *Länder* can be found in each of the relevant official public collections, carrying various titles such as, *Gesetzblatt* or *Verordnungsblatt* or *Amtsblatt*.

Additionally, there are published collections of ministerial directions issued by the Federal and *Länder* Ministers or Ministries, for example, the *Bundesarbeitsblatt, -steuerblatt* or *zollblatt* or the various *Ministerialblätter* or *Amtsblätter*. They are useful guides to Ministry practice, the reasons behind the enactment of new legislation and movements on new issues. In this context the official publications of the *Bundestag* and *Bundesrat* are also important (*Drucksachen, Berichte, Entwürfe* and *Begründungen*).

Lastly, as far as official publications are concerned, there are official reports. All Federal Supreme Courts and the BVerfG publish their own series of reports. Most higher courts of the *Länder* also publish reports. These are the court's own official collection of decisions. This is in contrast to the UK where official transcripts are for internal use and reporting is almost entirely private. Most reports are cited simply by adding E (*Entscheidungen*: Decisions) after the appropriate abbreviation for the court, hence the references are usually very concise: BVerfGE 40, 141 = *Entscheidungen des Bundesverfassungsgerichts*, vol. 40, p. 141.

Most, but not all, of the Federal Supreme Court Civil Senate reports are cited BGHZ (*Entscheidungen des Bundesgerichtshofes in Zivilsachen*). Decisions of the civil courts for the years 1880–1945 appear in the *Entscheidungen des Reichsgerichts in Zivilsachen* (RGZ).

BGHSt   *Entscheidungen des Bundesgerichtshofes in Strafsachen* (Decisions of the Federal Court of Justice in Criminal Cases).

RGSt   *Entscheidungen des Reichsgerichts in Strafsachen* (Decisions of the Supreme Court of the German Reich in Criminal Cases).

BVerwGE   *Entscheidungen des Bundesverwaltungsgerichts* (Decisions of the Federal Administrative Court).

BGSE   *Entscheidungen des Bundessozialgerichts* (Decisions of the Federal Social Court).

BAGE   *Entscheidungen des Bundesarbeitsgerichts* (Decisions of the Federal Labour Court).

BFHE   *Entscheidungen des Bundesfinanzhofs* (Decisions of the Federal Tax Court).

Most texts, and most other commentaries, carry a table of abbreviations at the front (as does this book) and reflect the greater practice of this in Germany.

The reports do not usually make any reference to the names of the parties, and cases are seldom referred to in this way. Cases are distinguished by the date of judgment and reference citation. This is not a particularly easy way to remember notable cases. Most texts in fact simply give the case citation, for example, BGHZ 51, 91, 102, i.e. volume 51 of the civil case reports of the Federal Court of Justice, starting at p. 91, with the relevant material to be found on p. 102. As case law in some subject areas is cited more readily and often in court, the most notable cases are referred to by subject matter for easier recollection. This does not happen all that frequently and references are often very bland, as the following cases from civil law demonstrate: the Fowl Pest case (*Hühnerpestfall*), the Roll of Linoleum case (*Linoleumrollenfall*), or the Hamburg Parking Place case (*Hamburger Parkplatzfall*). Less frequently, a case becomes known by the name of one of the parties, as happens occasionally in cases arising under consideration of provisions of the *Grundgesetz*, as in the *Soraya* case or the *Lüth* decision; and in many constitutional law cases, a name is given by the case commentators and used generally thereafter, for example, the *Solange* judgments, the *Mephisto* case or the Maastricht judgment.

The official case reports are not complete and at the lower court levels contain only what are considered to be the most important and/or necessary cases. Publication of the reports is also very slow and there are considerable delays in reporting and publication. There is, however, as in the UK, a large number of private reports of court decisions as described below.

4.2 **Private reporting and publication**

4.2.1 *Legislation collections*

As noted above, there are officially produced texts of the civil codes and legislation but these are not published in an amended or consolidated form. Therefore, the private publishing houses have stepped in to fill the gap. They produce straight-forward versions of the legislation which are updated, and also annotated versions. The best known unannotated collections are *Schönfelder Deutsche Gesetze, Sammlung des Zivil-, Straf- und Verfahrensrechts* and *Sartorius Verfassungs- und Verwaltungsgesetze der Bundesrepublik* both published by C. H. Beck, Munich. These have been joined by three annual companion publications of Nomos Verlag containing the most important statutes in the broad areas of public, civil and criminal law.

4.2.2 *Commentaries*

The text of commentaries basically follows the structure of the codes and enact-ments. The style is forced upon them by the greater reliance on codes in Germany. Written by leading academics, judges, and practitioners, they are readily quotable in court. They follow a legal code or statute paragraph by paragraph and try to provide a complete statement of the law with many references to court decisions and other literature which has considered the particular provision. They are referred to first by the name of the editor, as many people usually contribute to a commentary, and then to the author's name if a particular passage is cited. They very considerably in size between *Großkommentare, Handkommentare* and *Kurz-kommentare*. Notable commentaries on the *Grundgesetz* are the *Bonner Kommentar* of 11 volumes published by C. F. Müller, the *Alternativkommentar* of two volumes (c. 3,500 pages), *von Münch* of three volumes and the smaller *Schmidt-Bleibtreu* and *Jarass & Pieroth*. Two notable commentaries on the civil code are *Münchener Kom-mentar zum Bürgerlichen Gesetzbuch* in seven volumes and *Staudinger: Kommentar zum Bürgerlichen Gesetzbuch mit Einführungsgesetz und Nebengesetzen* in 25 volumes. These, as might be expected, consider the paragraphs of the civil code in some considerable detail and include all the latest case references. Much more manage-able is *Palandt: Bürgerliches Gesetzbuch*, which is updated and published every year. Citation of other references and legislation in commentaries is by § (paragraph) number or Rdnr (*Randnummer*: marginal) number.

A rough equivalent to these in the UK would be either the annotated statute collections of Halsbury or Statutes in Force, although there is far more detail and analysis in the German versions.

4.2.3 *Textbooks and casebooks*

Textbooks are known in German as *Lehrbücher, Kurzlehrbücher* and *Handbücher*, and as with the commentaries they vary greatly in size and reputation. They aim to present a systematic consideration of a particular area of law, but are criticized for employing an often inaccessible abstract style. Very many of them have been cited in the further reading sections at the end of each of the chapters in this book so individual mention of them will not be made here.

In addition, there are now smaller introductory textbooks, termed *Lernbücher*, which introduce the main elements of a particular legal area and are aimed at students preparing for the first state examinations. The major legal publishers have a series covering at least the core subjects.

Casebooks, as the name suggests, are books containing a number of the leading decisions of particular courts or areas of law, some with and some without comment or explanation. They are a relatively new phenomenon in German legal literature and thus bear witness to the growing importance of past case decisions in the German legal system. Constitutional law is particularly well catered for in this respect. See also the further reading sections.

4.2.4 Legal periodicals

Partly because of the above reasons, delay and incompleteness, and partly due to the historical tradition of private law reporting, as in the UK, there exists a wide range of private court reports. These are more up-to-date and report more decisions than the official reports. By far the most notable and widely taken in Germany of these is the *Neue Juristische Wochenschrift* (NJW), which is published weekly and reports the important decisions and cases from all the hierarchies of courts. It is often cited by textbook writers alongside the official citation, and sometimes on its own when there is no official report of a case. It is frequently cited in courts or used to refer to previous cases. This publication is not just a series of law reports in the standard UK format but also contains shorter articles, commentaries, annotations on both cases and legislation, as well as case reports and book information, reviews, and general information. It is an all-rounder. Cases in it are cited as, e.g. NJW 1988, 2089, simply providing the year and page number, and in some citations it is preceded by the abbreviation of the court whence the case comes, e.g. BGH NJW 1988, 2089. There are many other private reports but they are nowhere near as comprehensive and widely used as the NJW, which runs annually to 2,000–4,000 pages.

Examples of other periodicals are: *Juristenzeitung* (JZ), a monthly publication aimed more towards academics and containing lengthier articles and discussions; *Monatsschrift für deutsches Recht* (MDR), which mainly carries case reports; and the *Juristische Rundschau* (JR), designed for practitioners. Three legal periodicals specifically produced for students are *Juristische Schulung* (JuS), *Juristische Arbeitsblätter* (JA) and *Juristische Ausbildung* (JurA). Periodicals aimed more at specific professions are: *Deutsches Richter Zeitung* (DRiZ) and *Anwaltsblatt* (AnwBl).

4.2.5 Electronic material

Along with the general growth of electronic and digitally stored material, there has also been an exponential growth in the amount of legal information available at the stroke of a few keyboard keys. Both public and private databases provide gateways to huge amounts of material on German law including statutes, cases, statute and case comments and articles. There are so many now, that it is only possible here to provide the addresses of a select few but which are themselves excellent conduits to further information. There is no better starting point than the website of the Federal Ministry of Justice. This provides easy access to other government departments and all their material but also to the most important statutes. The Federal Ministry of Justice, Bundesministerium der Justiz: **www.bundesjustizministerium.de/**

4.2.6 *Other internet resources*

Cardiff Law School German Law: **www.cf.ac.uk/claws/german_law/**
German embassy: **www.german-embassy.org.uk/**
    Oxford   University: **units.ox.ac.uk/departments/enrocomplaw/gla/ index.html**
    www.jura.uni-sb.de/jurpc/ is the homepage address of the Jurpc on-line computer law journal of the University of Saarbrucken.
    University of Bayreuth Jurweb (Legal Information in the Internet): **www.unibayreuth. de/students/jurweb/jurweb-home-engl.html**
    Medien-/OnlineRecht **www.zurecht.de/xonline.htm**
    Strömer Rechtsanwälte Online- und Multimediarecht: **www.netlaw.de/ team@online-recht.de www.online-recht.de/es.html**
    Chritsopher Kuner, Attorney, Law of Electronic and Internet Commerce in Germany: **www.kuner.com/**
    Frhr. v. Gravenreuth & Syndikus Rechtsanwälte: **www.gravenreuth.de/**
    A database of legal material was established by the state under the title *Juris* (*juristisches Informationssystem*). It contains federal statutes, administrative regulations (particularly in the area of tax law), court decisions of the federal courts, and details or summaries of legal articles and books. As a result of its expense, its use is not widespread and in any case much of the material stored by it is available more easily in other websites, such as the BMJ, cited above. Alternatively, many legal periodicals and collections of court decisions have been made available on CD-ROM, for example the NJW, to name just one.

5 Academic legal opinion

Academic legal opinion and, in general, legal publication and literature hold a much more influential position in Germany than in the UK. The historical section emphasized the much more important role played by the universities in the analysis, development, and systemization of German law. Therefore, today German legal literature plays a much greater role than is the case in the UK, which is partly to do with the system by which the courts would refer to the professors in the universities for an opinion on a particular case, known as the *Aktenversand*. In the UK it is only rarely that the work of academic writers will be referred to by counsel in a case, and even rarer that a judge or the court will refer to discussion in a legal textbook. In those cases it will have to be a very well-established textbook and author; however, it is thankfully no longer the case that to be able to be cited the author must be dead before the jurisprudential merits of his opinions are recognized. In Germany the position is very different, in that legal academic writing is quoted keenly in courts of all levels, from *Amtsgericht* to BVerfG.[9] The work of highly reputable authors can carry considerable persuasive authority. This authority is particularly enhanced when it forms part of the dominant view of a number of texts or legal writers (*herrschende Meinung*). So much so that it would even serve to overrule previous decisions on the matter. Courts frequently refer to and discuss the views of writers, and more so, in fact, in the higher courts when novel points of law are under discussion.

A comprehensive guide to the legal materials of Germany can be found in C. Szladits, *Guide to Foreign Legal Materials: German* (1990: Oceana Publications), pp. 55–146 and in Hirte, noted in 'Further reading' below. Further individual items are listed in the further reading sections at the end of each of the chapters on German substantive law in Part Two of this book.

6 Aspects of civil procedure

6.1 Introduction

Although strictly part of public law and thus really belonging to Part Two of this volume, this topic has been included in this chapter because of its close affinity to other topics in Part One, and in providing an introductory volume to German law it would appear sensible to deal with the subject here.

Civil procedure is regulated largely by the code on civil procedure (*Zivilprozeßordnung*: ZPO) of 30 January 1877, reissued in 1950. As with other nineteenth-century legal measures, it was designed to standardize the law throughout the new German state. Reflecting the times in which it was drafted, it also promoted liberal and individual values, and in its first appearance gave the parties to a legal dispute a great deal of freedom in how they conducted it. They could determine the context of the pleadings, the time of submissions, and thus the length of proceedings. New arguments and evidence could be introduced even up to the stage of the oral hearing, which inevitably meant further delays to give the other party time to respond. (This freedom of control over the proceedings by the parties is reflected in the principle *Grundsatz der Parteiherrschaft*, considered below.) The system was thus open to abuse by the parties and was in large part responsible for the very long proceedings for which Germany became notorious. The code has been amended a number of times since its inception, and many of the amendments were introduced to try and speed up the proceedings and to shift the balance of the proceedings from exclusively party-led to court-led. Just recently, in June 2001, it has been subject to

---

[9] A browse through the court reports will reveal this to be the case, see for example BGHZ, 124, 128, 137, BGHZ 124, 298, 302, and BVerfGE 90, 145, 178–181.

the biggest series of revisions for some thirty to forty years. Whilst many of the reforms are relevant to the specialized procedures of marital, family proceedings, and arbitration and so will not be considered here, it is the proceedings before the *Amtsgericht* and the appeals procedures which have been given most attention and will be considered where appropriate, either here or in the substantive law chapters in Part Two of this volume. Most of the reforms came into force on 1 January 2002.

The ZPO concerns actions between private parties before all the courts of ordinary jurisdiction. Recourse to the courts can lawfully be excluded by the parties by agreement, and it would be usual to agree to arbitration to resolve disputes in such cases. However, whether the courts or arbitration are used, the ZPO applies. The code lays down certain principles, some of which represent rules of natural justice, generally understood and accepted in many legal systems, and some principles specific to the German legal system, for example the right of oral presentation of evidence and more relaxed rules on the admissibility of evidence to the court.

The ZPO is divided into 10 Books. Book One contains the general rules; Book Two the procedure in courts of first instance, the *Amtsgericht* and *Landgericht*. The code then deals with the appeal procedures in Book Three, retrials in Book Four, special procedures and family law matters in Books Five to Seven, enforcement in Book Eight; cancellation of rights proceedings in Book Nine and arbitration in Book Ten.

The differences in procedure between the UK and Germany reflect the historical developments of their legal systems. In Germany, the absence of a jury in any civil litigation had consequences for the way in which proceedings and trials are conducted. A fundamental and significant difference is that in the English legal system, the trial procedure is concentrated in the day at court or series of days where most of the fact-finding takes place, originally required by the presence of a jury. In Germany, where there was no jury, and hence no need for a single trial of the issues, the development of the process allowed it to take place over a number of separate days, spread out over weeks or months, and often longer. Courts in the UK require elaborate preparation, whereas German courts prepare as they go along and frequently adjourn until information is supplied as required. Shorter procedures have been introduced in Germany which will be discussed below. In contrast there is, however, greater lay participation in civil proceedings in Germany, considered in the section on lay participation in Chapter 4.

6.2 General principles of civil procedure

Some of the principles of civil procedure derive from the more extensive development of these principles in criminal procedure. Those presented here are an attempt to consolidate the astonishing variety of principles to be found in the German literature on the subject.

6.2.1 *The principle of publicity (Grundsatz der Öffentlichkeit)*

Publicity of the proceedings is regarded as desirable for a number of reasons, not least to inform the public generally about the administration of justice so that it is not a closed world and thus to remove the myths of the law. How far this succeeds is uncertain because of the simple fact that the law is such a complex process that, even when visible, it is often seemingly inexplicable to the public. The principle also incorporates the provision for public access to the courts and requires judgments to be read out in open court. Those presented here are an attempt to consolidate the astonishing variety of principles to be found in the German literature on the subject.

The publicity requirement is laid down in the GVG, §§ 169 et seq., and the basic rule is that the proceedings are public except in prescribed circumstances. Paragraph 169 II does not include the admittance of radio or television within the basic definition of open publicity. Pictures may be taken during recesses, however, if permitted by the judge, and the usual forms of reporting are allowed, i.e. the taking of notes and drawings (§§ 169–175). There are exceptions to this principle in the interests of public order, safety of the state or to protect commercial secrets (§ 172 GVG), and more extensively in family law matters (§ 170 GVG).

6.2.2 The principle of party control (Grundsatz der Parteiherrschaft)

Originating under the liberal philosophy of the nineteenth century, this principle reflects the general freedom of contract enjoyed by the parties. It is they who must be left to decide the timing, manner and form of legal process. Further aspects of this principle are that it is the parties who should lead the proceedings (*Dispositionsmaxime*) unless, exceptionally, public interest demands the state determines the process (*Offizialmaxime*, see ZPO § 617) and that the parties be left to decide what matters or facts should be brought before the court for a decision (*Beibringungsmaxime*). This latter aspect is both well supported by aspects of civil procedure (for example §§ 85, 282, 288) and subject to a considerable number of exceptions imposed on it by the ZPO (§§ 138 I, 139, 141–144). Also very closely connected to the above principles, if not indeed a sub-principle, is the principle of party presentation (*Verhandlungsgrundsatz Parteimaxime*), which holds that it is for the parties to decide what information they present to the court, including which facts and evidence support their claim (§§ 308, 536 and 559 ZPO). In support of this, it is not for the court to decide to introduce facts or evidence, nor to make an award which was not claimed. A further principle that is also applicable here is the duty of the parties to tell the truth (*Wahrheitspflicht*) (§ 138 ZPO) and, furthermore, the court retains a right, and indeed even a duty to ask questions to ensure that all matters considered are clear to both parties (§§ 136 and 139 ZPO). The freedom of the parties to control the procedure is now more generally restricted by a greater responsibility imposed on the court to conduct proceedings, partly to maintain the unity of the law. Some of the following principles reflect this change.

6.2.3 The right to oral proceedings (Mündlichkeitsprinzip)

This ensures the parties have the chance to present the facts, evidence and arguments orally in court (§ 128 ZPO). It has, however, largely been overshadowed by both the right to written presentation (*Schriftlichkeitsprinzip*) and the practice by attorneys of providing written documentation for everything, as to make oral presentation largely superfluous. Parties can agree, however, to rely on written statements only (§137 ZPO).

6.2.4 *The principle of directness (Unmittelbarkeitsgrundsatz)*

This guarantees that the parties are able to present their cases directly to the court and judge who both hears the evidence and decides the case and not to an intermediate party (see ZPO §§ 128 I, 309, and 355 I). There are specific exceptions to this rule (see §§ 361 and 375).

6.2.5 *The unity of the oral or main proceedings (Einheit der mündlichen/Hauptverhandlung)*

This principle underlines the attempt to try to achieve a consistent and coherent trial with as few interruptions as possible and, in theory, in one go. However, as the whole of the written and oral proceedings were previously considered to be the main proceeding, the principle did not mean the speedy conclusion of a legal matter. Until the reform of the law, German civil law proceedings became very extended, as witnessed by the cases reaching the European Court of Human Rights.[10] This was mainly due to the fact that everything was written and sent to the court and the other party with ample opportunities for both parties to introduce new material. There were inevitable delays in the transfer of information in this way. In the new procedures this principle has more application, although it would still be a rarity for a case to be handled in one hearing unless it was particularly straightforward and of low value.

6.2.6 *The principle of concentration efficacy (Konzentrationsmaxime/Beschleunigungsprinzip)*

Allied to the above principle, the concentration of the proceedings aims to keep the trial as short as possible (see ZPO §§ 272–273). This demands the avoidance of a protraction of the proceedings and provides for sanctions if a party deliberately delays an action (§ 296 ZPO and in appeal ZPO § 527).[11] The further details of how this works is considered on the section on civil law proceedings below.

6.2.7 *Freedom of evidence (Freie Beweiswürdigung)*

The rules of evidence are much more relaxed in German civil courts, and the court has wide discretion to decide what evidence to accept and the weight it attaches to admissible evidence (§ 286 ZPO). This aspect of procedure is thus one of the most notable in the German system and contrasts with other legal systems, notably common-law systems. Evidence is considered further below.

There are further principles which equate to principles of natural justice in common-law countries, including the right to have a dispute considered by the

---

[10] For example, the *Konig* v *Germany* case of 1978 and the *Eckle v Germany* case of 1982 where periods of 10 and 17 years were involved!

[11] Unless otherwise stated, all § references in this section will be to the *Zivilprozeßordnung*: ZPO.

courts, the equality of arms,[12] and the right to reply to allegations made by the other party. All of these aspects can be determined from the general principles of the right to a hearing according to the rule of law, the right to be heard by a lawful judge and the right to a fair procedure (*Grundsatz des rechtlichen Gehörs, Anspruch auf einen gesetzlichen Richter* and *Anspruch auf ein faires Verfahren*) which are generally reflected in constitutional law in Arts 101–103 *Grundgesetz* and considered in Chapter 7.

6.3 General considerations of procedure

As an example of civil process the basic procedure before a *Landgericht* will be considered, which is similar to the procedure in the lower *Amtsgericht*. The normal court of first instance would be the regional court, unless the matter concerns a value of less than 5,000 Euro as from 1 January 2002 (§ 23 GVG), in which case the action would be heard before the *Amtsgericht*. Further details on the court structure can be found in Chapter 3 above.

The information that follows is only in respect of a general civil procedure. Details of peculiarities of labour law or of other court procedures in the administrative or social courts can be found in the appropriate chapters.

Actions heard by the courts of ordinary jurisdiction can be for contractual performance (*Leistungsklage*), a demand for payment or delivery (usually the most frequent), a declaration (*Feststellungsklage*) or for a constitutive change of a legal situation (*Gestaltungsklage*), as in the change of membership of a partnership or company amongst others.

6.3.1 The role of the judges

The judges in a civil action decide on the basis of the laws provided by the legislature, in the absence of decisions by the parties on particular points. Judges must be independent from any parties in a dispute, and a motion (*Ablehnungsgesuch*) can be made under §§ 41–49 to disqualify a judge who, in the view of one of the parties, has not acted independently.

In comparison to the common law, the judges take a more active and involved role, partly because they are under a duty to assist the parties (§ 139) to clarify the information presented by the parties, to point out irrelevant material, and to indicate more relevant requirements of both fact and law. This includes a duty to point out any special circumstance which may lead to a surprise result or which a party may not have realized applied. The parties must be given a chance to reply to the special circumstance.

The judge undertakes much of the work carried out by the court officials in the English legal system. He determines and obtains initial evidence from witnesses

---

[12] The principle of the equality of arms is part of the expression *audi alterem partem* and seeks to ensure that both parties have equal opportunity to present their case and comment on the presentation of the other party's case. See also Chapter 7.

and experts, and is also required to attempt to get an early settlement of the problem.

The style of proceeding, with the emphasis placed on the judge to lead proceedings and questioning, is considered to be unbiased. The system is referred to as inquisitorial, rather than adversarial as in common-law systems, although in reality it is a mix, in that the proceedings are commenced by the parties who decide the contents of the pleadings.

6.3.2 The parties to the proceedings

Any person with legal capacity, as defined by the BGB (§§ 1 and 21), can be a party to a civil process (*Parteifähigkeit*). This includes natural and legal persons. Foreign legal persons are covered by § 55 ZPO.

Paragraph 50 ZPO states that capacity to be a party includes those with legal capacity. In private and public companies this usually covers only the directors and any specifically empowered agents or those with powers of attorney. For further details, see the sections on Book One of the BGB and commercial law below.

The capacity to pursue a particular action in the courts (*Prozeßfähigkeit*) must then be determined by the applicable substantive law, generally the disputed contract (see §§ 51–52).

6.3.3 Jurisdiction of the court

A precondition for the judicial acceptance of a writ is concerned with the factual and geographical jurisdictions of the court.

6.3.3.1 Subject matter (sachliche Zuständigkeit)

This concerns the matter under consideration, which must be relevant to the jurisdiction of the courts of ordinary jurisdiction. In cases of uncertainty, rules are provided so that the matter must in the last resort be heard by a court (details of this are also considered in Chapter 3 and § 17 GVG, § 276 ZPO, § 48 ArbGG, § 41 VwGO, § 52 SGG, § 34 FGO). The value of the subject matter is also relevant to the level of the court before which the matter is heard, as noted above. Paragraphs 2–9 ZPO provide rules for the court to adjudge the value of the dispute for the purposes of determining the level of court. For civil law jurisdiction, see further §§ 23, 71–72, 119 and 133 GVG.[13]

6.3.3.2 Geographic jurisdiction (Gerichtsstand/örtliche Zuständigkeit)

The general rule is that the court for an action is determined according to where the parties have their legal residence or domicile (*Wohnsitz*) (§§ 12–13) and, in the case of legal persons, the registered office, usually the headquarters (§ 17 ZPO). Other possibilities are: the present place of residence of the one of the parties (§ 20); in delict cases, where the harm was caused (§ 32); in contract cases, where a

---

[13] Also relevant to a consideration of jurisdiction is the Brussels Convention on Jurisdiction and the Enforcement of Judgments in Civil and Commercial matters as now updated and replaced by the EC Jurisdiction Regulation (2001/44) [2001] OJ L12/1. The EC Regulation is applicable in Germany as in the UK directly and without transformation into a national law.

performance was or is to be rendered (§ 29); and, with property and real estate law cases, where the property is situated (§§ 23 and 29b). The ZPO is quite flexible, however, and allows for other venues (see §§ 15–37).

Where both the parties have merchant status or are legal persons under public law their agreement for another particular court, or the local court of the branches of the enterprise rather than the headquarters, will be accepted; unless the case concerns real estate, in which case it must be at the court of jurisdiction where the property is situated (see §§ 38–40 et seq.).

6.3.4 Representation in court

In the regional courts and in all higher courts, the parties must be represented by a *Rechtsanwalt* admitted to practice before the specific court (§ 78). Before the *Amtsgericht*, a party can conduct his own case (§ 79 ZPO) or with the assistance of a *Beistand* (§ 90 ZPO). Full details are given above.

6.3.5 Costs

Fees are payable in stages both to the court and to the representing lawyer, and are also considered in greater detail above.

6.4 The civil law action

Civil procedure consists of a number of phases:

(a) The opening phase (*Eröffnungsphase*), when a claim is made by the plaintiff (*Kläger*) which is forwarded to the defendant and a decision is made by the judge as to which of the possible preliminary proceedings is to be adopted (§§ 271–272).

(b) The preparation stage (*Vorbereitungsphase*), consisting of the collection of material and evidence of witnesses and parties for the main stage of the proceedings. This phase may take different forms depending on the complexity of the case and the procedure adopted by the judge. Under the new reforms of 2001, the judge must be satisfied that a friendly settlement of the matter has either been attempted or appears to be completely hopeless. The judge is again obliged to ensure that both parties are fully aware of all the factual and legal circumstances of their dispute and to ask questions if required. A settlement can be agreed either outside the court or within court oral proceedings for which the judge may order the appearance of the parties who both have the right to be heard. (§§ 272 and 278). If no settlement is achieved the proceedings must move on immediately to the early hearing or the main proceedings (§ 279).

(c) The main hearing (*Haupttermin*), in which the parties present their respective cases and evidence is taken in court (§ 279) and usually after which the decision in the case is made, but usually at a later date, although in more straightforward cases, this can be immediately after the main hearing.

(d) The consideration of the case by the court (*Überprüfungsphase*) followed by the formal legal judgment (*Endurteil*) (§ 310).

(e) The enforcement of the judgment (*Vollstreckungsverfahren*) (§ 704).

6.4.1 *The issue of a claim (Erhebung der Klage)*

The action commences with the issue of a claim (*Klage/Klageschrift*) by the plaintiff (*Kläger*), which must be registered with the court (§ 253 V). The claim contains the names of the parties, the grounds, legal rules in support of the claim and the amount in dispute (§ 253). The amount may well be adjusted later in the light of replies from the defendant. This is particularly important, as it is the amount of the claim or dispute that determines the level of court and *Rechtsanwälte* fees (see further above).

It is at this stage that the court considers the admissibility of the claim. It is the duty of the court to ascertain that the issue is justiciable and that there is a point of law or genuine legal dispute to resolve, and that the claim appears conclusive. If the facts appear to warrant a claim and the proper court has been selected, the court will accept the claim.

If the dispute involves merchants or commercial partnerships or companies, or commercial reasons listed in § 95 GVG, or competition law or membership of a company, the matter must then be dealt with by the commercial law chamber of the regional courts, in courts where a commercial chamber has been established. The duties of that chamber are listed in § 349 ZPO.

If the court is satisfied and the statement of claim has been served on the defendant the matter becomes legally pending (*Rechtshängigkeit*) (§ 261). The court has discretion as to the next move in terms of the procedure adopted (§ 272). Two forms of procedure are available to the court:

(a) a written preliminary procedure (*schriftliches Vorverfahren*) (§ 276), which can result in a longer process; or

(b) a procedure which involves an early oral hearing (*Früher erster Termin*) to determine the issues in contention, and thus may either conclude the matter by settlement or speed up the preparation for the main trial.

The choice largely depends on the complexity of the subject matter and an early view of the likely result of the case (refer generally to §§ 272, 275–276). Both alternatives are, however, designed to bring about the quickest conclusion of the matter. The court retains the discretion to decide which procedure to adopt.

6.4.2 *'Written' proceedings (Schriftliches Vorverfahren)*

The scope of the dispute and evidence is determined by the court from reading the written submissions of both parties. The court can then decide what further action is necessary, or can bring the matter to a conclusion where the action is not contested or if the defence fail or choose not to respond (*Anerkenntnisurteil* (§ 307) or *Versäumnisurteil* (§ 331)).

The objective pursued to achieve a successful main trial is the thorough preparation for this event. Parties are coerced into compliance by the fact that time limits will be imposed, after which the submission of new material or evidence will be refused.

6.4.3 The 'early' hearing procedure

The preliminary or early first hearing will be chosen by the court on the basis of the claim received (§ 272). For example, matters which are more easily dealt with orally, or where no further facts will be presented by the plaintiff, or where both parties are not represented by an attorney or where the court is required to make rulings on points of law to progress the case further. The date will be set and the defendant will be given at least two weeks to prepare his defence. It is usual for a written reply to be prepared in addition (§ 274).

This hearing can result in a settlement or final judgment if the issues in the case allow it, and is not necessarily just a preparation for the main trial. Even if it is, it enables the court to determine what further information and evidence is necessary to decide the matter, and the court can order the production of these and defence statements subject to strict time limits (§ 273).

6.4.4 The preparation for the main trial

Regardless of which procedure is adopted, because both are simply alternative ways of allowing the court to determine what further material it needs to decide the matter, the preparation for the main trial is conducted by the court in much the same manner.

The court requires the defendant to inform the court in writing within two weeks whether the action will be contested. If it is to be contested, a written statement of defence (*Klageerwiderung*) must be forwarded to the court within another 14 days (§§ 274–277). A counterclaim (*Widerklage*) is an action brought in the court of the claim against the person making the original claim and involves related issues (and not defences) which are an attempt to offset the claim in respect of the same subject matter.

If necessary the court will request the parties to supply further pleas, to define for the court the scope or subject matter of the dispute, procedural motions specifying the value of the disputed matter and, in the view of counsel, the applicable law, although it is of course ultimately for the court to decide this. Time limits for the submission of these documents may be set by the court (§ 275 IV and § 276 III), but they are often extended by the request of the parties with good cause. Failure to respond, or to make any reply or attend hearings in any of the procedures described above, will result in a judgment in default. There is a period of two weeks in which a party may object to this and cause the proceedings to continue where they left off (see §§ 276 and 330–331).

The parties themselves decide which material to present to the court. Under German law there is no general pre-trial discovery of documents by the declaring and showing of all evidence to the other party. Parties may wish to do this to get a speedier and cheaper resolution of the dispute, but they cannot be forced to do so, only the court can do this. Parties therefore have considerable freedom to decide what information should be withheld or presented to the court, subject to the overriding right of the judge to determine the relevance of evidence and to request specific items, although the failure to submit is not enforceable. The court may, however, determine that evidence for the court hearing withheld at this stage may not later be accepted (§§ 142–143). Correspondingly, the parties are obligated by § 282 I to submit all the relevant material and any material, a party wishes to include should be submitted at the earliest possible time. Documents which require a response must be submitted in good time (§ 282 II). Late submissions may not be accepted (§ 296). The pleadings tend to be very detailed and very long, including all material thought relevant even if it subsequently proves not to be. The statements and allegations made need not be supported by proof at this stage. All documents are sent to the court and forwarded by the court to the parties, although it is the practice for attorneys to send copies directly to the attorney of the other party.

Motions and rulings may be made as the case progresses and areas of agreement and disagreement are identified. A number of meetings may take place between the parties, *Rechtsanwälte* and judge on the direction of the judge (§ 273 II), which can take place in open court or in closed sessions in which witnesses and experts may give evidence or may present other forms of evidence. The evidence and all materials will be referred to at the main hearing.

As noted above, the court is now under a much higher duty to both explain the consequences of the facts and legal situation to the parties, including the results of the taking of evidence, and to ensure that all possible has been done to try to achieve a friendly settlement of the dispute. The court may summons the parties to try to reach a compromise (*Vergleich*) if this is likely from the case as it progresses, as required by § 278–279 in connection with § 141.

6.4.5 The main hearing (Haupttermin)

As the case proceeds, the court determines what is necessary to decide the issue. When it has enough evidence it will declare this in court and the main hearing will take place which usually lasts no more than one day. At this oral hearing there is a general duty imposed on the court under § 139 fully to discuss the details of the case and to ensure that the parties are aware of all relevant legal aspects and generally to ask the parties questions and clarify the proceedings, especially in the *Amtsgericht* for parties not represented (termed the "*richterliche Frage-und Auf-klärungspflicht*). The court summarizes the factual and legal issues and the arguments of the parties by reference to the written submissions, and any legal points not raised by the parties (§ 279). The parties are given the opportunity to comment on this. Fresh arguments may not be accepted at this stage.

Paragraph 278 imposes a duty on the judge to attempt a compromise settlement before the witnesses or experts are heard, and the judge may inform the parties of the difficulties of an outright win by either party or their relative chances. The compromise has the same weight as a final judgment and may be conditionally accepted by the lawyers, subject to an objection by their clients within a specified period. If no compromise is possible the evidence is heard by the court. The 2001 reforms have considerably strengthened the judge's ability to try to achieve a settlement at the time of the oral proceedings or to refer the case to a procedure outside of the court system (new § 278).

6.4.6 The evidence (Beweismittel)

Overreliance on the oral evidence on the day in court is viewed as too biased and thus unreliable, and the written and unbiased evidence of neutral parties is much preferred in the German legal system. The process of the piecemeal collection of written evidence over a period of time makes extensive oral examination unnecessary. The means of proving facts are the hearing of witnesses (*Zeugen*), expert evidence (*Sachverständige*), the court's inspection (*Augenschein*), documents (*Urkunde*) and the questioning of the parties (*Parteivernehmung*), all of which are subject to the discretion of the judge and are conducted first by the judge. Evidence may be taken earlier by the judge in private and put into writing for the *Rechtsanwälte* to consider to be represented to the court. The burden is on the party alleging a certain point to prove it if it is disputed and considered crucial by the court.

The judge's decision on numbers of witnesses and experts is final. The judge will hear all the evidence, including hearsay, and decide what weight to accord it (§§ 286, 290 and 294 ZPO).

Inspections by the court are regulated under §§ 371 et seq.

In contrast to the English legal system, oaths are not always required of the parties, witnesses or experts (§§ 391–393). However, one of the amendments introduced into the proceedings in the 1933 reform, was the duty of the parties to make and provide full and truthful statements (§ 138), which effectively replaces the oath.

Witnesses (§§ 373 et seq.) are summoned to appear, subject to fines and a warrant for failure to do so. Close personal relatives are excepted. All witnesses are entitled to compensation for expenses and loss of earnings, which is added to the court fees. Witnesses are not usually interviewed by *Rechtsanwälte* before they have been questioned by the judge.

Experts are the experts of the court and do not appear in support of one of the parties, indeed they could be disqualified if they even appeared to favour one of the parties (§§ 402 et seq.).

There is a right for the *Rechtsanwälte* to question experts and witnesses after the judge but this is usually only cursory. Objections to these questions can be made by the other party (§§ 397–398).

The parties' testimony and documentary evidence is regulated by §§ 445 et seq. and §§ 415 et seq. The parties must attach documentary evidence to their pleadings. Parties have the right to attend the hearings of evidence but not as witnesses in their own case. This prohibits company representatives, directors or legal representatives (*Prokuristen*) from appearing in the case of their company. The testimony of the parties is ranked below the other forms of evidence mentioned.

The hearings are concluded by the opportunity to sum up orally. This consists only of a reference to all the pleadings and defence previously considered and a final plea on behalf of the client, and does not detain the court very long.

6.4.7 Termination of the law suit (Endurteil)

If the case is not withdrawn or settled beforehand, either in or out of court, a final judgment may be made at this stage if possible, but it is more likely a date will be set, usually within three weeks, for the reading of the judgment. Judgment is given orally after all evidence has been heard and the oral hearing closed. The judges retire to decide on the basis of a simple majority and the court will be recalled for the oral judgment to be read out. On request, the detailed and reasoned written decision is given, subject to the payment of additional court fees. The written judgment is required to form the basis of a decision to appeal. See generally in respect of judgments, §§ 300–319 ZPO.

6.5 Special procedures

A summary procedure for the collection of specific debts (known as the *Mahnverfahren*) exists which is used in cases where it is not expected that the claim for the debt will be disputed (§§ 688–703d). This is made by application to the local court, following which a default summons for a summary payment order (*Mahnbescheid*) is issued against the respondent. This may, however, be challenged by a written objection (*Widerspruch*), in which case the proceedings continue as if a normal case. If not challenged, the decision is made in favour of the applicant and an enforcement order (*Vollstreckungsbescheid*) can be issued under § 700, which becomes final within two weeks unless objected to.

A documentary proceeding (*Urkundenprozeß*) (§§ 592–605a) for claims on bills of exchange and cheques is considered by a judge, who usually gives immediate judgment if the claim is in order. If the defendant wishes to dispute the claim, only allowed on the basis of the monetary instrument itself, a preliminary judgment is issued which is subject to the commencement of normal proceedings.

Injunctions are available in the form of attachments (Arrest like a Mareva injunction) for money claims and, for others, in the form of interlocutory injunctions (*einstweilige Verfügung*) (§§ 916–945).

6.6 Appeals (Rechtsmittel)

The appeal system has been considerably revised under the 2001 reforms and additionally in the third book concerned with appeals, many paragraphs have been renumbered. The essential points to note are that the value restriction has been removed but the higher court can now dismiss much more easily appeals which are hopeless. Appeals at the lower levels are no longer just the concern of the parties and the lower appeals courts now may also refuse appeals unless the appeal is fundamentally important or that new points of law are at stake.

Ordinary appeals at first instance (*Berufung*) can be made on fact and law, and at second instance (*Revision*) on points of law only. Both have the effect of suspending the enforceability of the previous judgment and seising the superior court of the case. There is also the complaint (*Beschwerde*) which is an appeal against an order other than a judgment (§§ 511, 542, and 567 et seq.).

To be admissible, appeals must be made in the proper form, i.e. in writing, within the time limits (normally two months from formal judgment or five months from the oral judgment) and show the reason for the appeal (§ 520). Appeals may be on part or all of a judgment.

6.6.1 *Berufung*

A first appeal allows the introduction of new facts in very restricted circumstances (§ 513). There is no longer a minimum value but hopeless appeals may be dismissed by the decision of single appeal court judge. The appeal court may allow or dismiss the appeal (§ 538–40). Referral will only take place where judgment was preliminary or where serious mistakes were made by the lower court. Refer generally to §§ 511–541.

6.6.2 *Revision*

A second appeal will not be allowed on preliminary or interlocutory judgments, but now, following the reforms in 2001 is no longer dependant on a minimum value (new § 543 II 1). Instead the BGH will accept appeals only where they are of fundamental importance and they develop a point of law or help secure the unity of the law (new § 543 II 1). The time limit for appeals has been increased from one to two months. The leap-frog appeal (*Sprungrevision*), under § 566 ZPO has been extended to the *Amtsgericht*, where there was no appeal, on procedural points or an error in the law. Here there is a minimum value of 600 Euro imposed. Likewise the BGH can refuse to accept appeals unless they fulfil the criteria outlined above. No further evidence is taken and the facts are accepted as proved by the lower court. Refer generally on *Revision* to §§ 542–566.

6.6.3 *The complaint (Beschwerde)*

The detailed rules on the procedural complaint and complaints on law have been extensively revised by the 2001 reform. There is a two week limit on complaints and a minimum value imposition of 100 Euros for immediate complaints and 50 Euros for all other forms of complaint. Full details new in §§ 567–577.

6.7 Enforcement of judgments (*Zwangsvollstreckung*)

Enforcements legally realize the creditors' rights, and the details of regulation are contained in Book Eight of the ZPO (§§ 704–945). Whilst the enforcement court (*Vollstreckungsgericht*) is the *Amtsgericht* (§ 764 I), enforcement is conducted by the *Rechtspfleger* in that court, who will issue a certificate of enforcement (*Vollstreckungsklavsel*) to enable the court or the bailiff to act upon it. Bailiffs

(*Gerichtsvollzieher*) are the official agents of enforcement most frequently employed. Applications to them may be made by the person who is seeking enforcement of a judgment (§ 753).

Basic principles require that there must be no infringement of basic rights in the execution of a judgment. The BVerfG quashed a decision for the eviction of a tenant because it was alleged that his ill health would deteriorate further (BVerfGE 3 October 1979, 1979 NJW 2607).

An application must be made under § 754, for all final decisions (§§ 704 and 794), to certify the final judgment. Service of the judgment is effected by the court or the bailiff. Costs of enforcement normally are to be borne by the debtor (§ 788 I).

There are no time limits to enforcement proceedings but the courts have allowed pleas by the debtor that thirty years have passed and the judgments are no longer enforceable. In some instances, and depending on the subject matter, the court may regard a judgment as stale, and hence unenforceable, after a much shorter period of time. For example, the decision of the Hamm *Oberlandesgericht* of 1 October 1981 (WoM 1981, 257), in respect of eviction judgment which was not enforced for two years whilst rent was being accepted, was held to be unenforceable at that late stage.

A stay of execution is available on both a temporary and final basis in cases where the debtor has paid security in to the court or been given a respite by the creditor (§§ 775–776).

Enforcement orders against money, against movable property, and details of the bailiff's right to seize property, can be found in §§ 739 et seq. and §§ 803 et seq. Enforcements can also attach to money claims of the debtor (§§ 829 et seq.), claims for recovery or delivery of goods (§§ 846 et seq.) and other property rights (§§ 857 et seq.).

Enforcement against immovable property is regulated under §§ 864–871. The debtor has certain rights of protection against the removal of necessary items etc.[14]

FURTHER READING

Legal representation, legal aid and legal citation:

Books

Council of Europe, *Procedures Facilitating Access to Justice* (1980: Strasbourg).

H. Hirte, *Der Zugang zu Rechtsquellen und Rechtsliteratur* (1991: Heymanns Verlag, Cologne).

E. Kalthoener and H. Buttner, *Prozeßkostenhilfe und Beratungshilfe* 2nd ed. (1999: C.H. Beck, Munich)

R. Künzl and J. Koller, *Prozeßkostenhilfe* (1993: Verlag Recht und Wirtschaft, Heidelberg).

H. Prütting (ed.), *Die deutsche Anwaltschaft zwischen heute und morgen* (1990: Heymanns, Cologne).

---

[14] For an extensive overview of the considerable reforms to the ZPO, especially to the Berufung, Revision and Beschwerde, see the Hartmann article, cited below.

A. Schoreit and J. Dehn, *BerHG/PKH Kommentar*, 6th ed. (1998: C. F. Müller, Heidelberg).

C. Szladits, *Guide to Foreign Legal Materials: German* (1990: Oceana Publications).

H. Thomas and H. Putzo, *ZPO Kommentar*, 22nd ed. (1999: C.H. Beck, Munich)

H. Vallender, *Beratungshilfe* (1990: Heymanns Verlag, Cologne).

Articles

J. Gordley, 'The meaning of equal access' (1977) 10 Cornell Int'l LJ 220–30.

H. A. Hirte, 'Access to the courts for indigent persons: a comparative analysis of the legal framework in the United Kingdom, United States and Germany' (1991) 40 ICLQ 91–123.

R. Schlesinger, 'The German alternative: a legal aid system of equal access to the private attorney' (1977) 10 Cornell Int'l LJ 213–19.

Civil procedure:

Books

Zivilprozeßordnung, Beck-Texte im DTV, 32nd ed. (2000: C.H. Beck, Munich).

Baumbach et al., *Zivilprozeßordnung Kommentar*, 59th ed. (2000: C.H. Beck, Munich).

F. Baur and W. Grunsky, *Zivilprozeßrecht*, 10th ed. (2000: Luchterhand, Neumied).

Business Transactions in Germany (M. Bender, New York and C.H. Beck, Munich), vol. I, chs 5 and 6.

S. Goren (translator), *The Code of Civil Procedure rules of the Federal Republic of German of 30 January 1877* (1990: F. B. Rothman, Littleton, Colorado). H. Koch & F. Diedrich, *Civil Procedure in Germany* (1998: C.H. Beck, München & Kluwer, The Hague).

H. Koch & F. Diedrich, *Civil Procedure in Germany* (1998: C.H. Beck, München & Kluwer, The Hague).

H.-J. Musielak, Grundkurs ZPO, 5th ed. (2000: C.H. Beck, München).

R. Oberheim, *Zivilprozeßrecht*, 2nd ed. (1994: Werner Verlag, Düsseldorf).

S. O'Malley and A. Layton (eds), *European Civil Practice* (1989: Sweet & Maxwell, London), ch 51, Federal Republic of Germany, pp. 1282–1320.

H. Thomas and H. Putzo, *ZPO Kommentar*, 22nd ed. (1999: C.H. Beck, Munich).

C.J. Whelan (ed.), *Small Claims Courts: A Comparative Study* (1990: Clarendon Press, Oxford).

W. Zeiss, *Zivilprozeßrecht*, 9th ed. (1997: Möhr, Tübingen).

Articles:

P. Hartmann, *Zivilprozess 2001/2002: Hunderte wichtiger Änderungen* (2001) 36 NJW, 2577–2598.

F. Reuschle, *Das Zivilprozessreformgesetz: Synoptische Darstellung der Rechtsänderungen in ZPO, EGZPO und GVG* (2001) *Beilage zu Heft* 36 NJW, 1–63.

PART II
Substantive German Law

A Outline of subject areas

This section introduces the main subject areas and divisions of German substantive law, some of which will be considered in greater detail later. The particular division of areas of German law derives from the primary division imposed on it by the classification into public law and civil law.

1 Public and civil (private) law

While this has been considered in the introductory chapter, only the principal aspects will be repeated here. Public law is concerned with the legal relationships between the citizen and the state, or the manifestations of the state and public authorities, whereas civil law (*Privatrecht*) contains the laws concerning legal relations between individuals. Previously there was no overlap between public and civil law.

Public law includes constitutional law and administrative law foremost, and criminal law, procedural law as applicable in public and civil jurisdictions, international law, laws governing the public professions, social law, and revenue law.

Increasingly, newer legal developments and developing areas of law do not observe the division so closely and often straddle both categories, thus serving to weaken the previously clear distinction. European law is such an example, as is the law of economic environment, both of which originate in public law but produce laws which clearly concern civil law activities.

B Public law

1 *Staatsrecht*

Öffentliches Recht is the overall category for public law. It includes all constitutional and administrative law. Its scope is much wider than in the UK, partly because of the provision of a written constitution. Even within the area of public law, a division can be identified between the state's relations with other states and international bodies (*Völkerrecht*), the relations of the organs of the state *inter se* and the state's relations with the subjects of the state the constitutional rights of individuals and the rights and obligations of constitutional state bodies

(*Staatsrecht*). The document which straddles both of these areas of public law is the most fundamental in Germany, the *Grundgesetz*. This was previously translated as the 'basic law' and less frequently as 'constitution', for reasons which will be explained in full in the section on constitutional law below. The *Grundgesetz* provides two main forms of provision, one part concerned with Governmental powers and the powers of other state bodies, and the second with basic rights.

Whilst the *Grundgesetz* overrides any other form of law in Germany, it is not a complete statement of constitutional law and has been supplemented by numerous other enactments. Some of the more notable statutes in public law are: the constitutions of the *Länder*, the Federal Constitutional Court Act (*Gesetz über das Bundesverfassungsgericht*: BVerfGG), the Federal Elections Act (*Bundeswahlgesetz*: BWahlG), the Political Parties Act (*Parteiengesetz*: PartG), the Accession Act to the EEC Treaty (*Vertrag zur Gründung der Europäischen Wirtschaftsgemeinschaft*: EWGV), and the ECHR (*Europäische Konvention zum Schutze der Menschenrechte und Grundfreiheiten*: EMRK).

Many other enactments in the sphere of public law concern the relations between the state and individuals and are classified under administrative law (*Verwaltungsrecht*).

2 Administrative law

Administrative law (*Verwaltungsrecht*) concerns the application and procedure of law which, for the most part, is implemented by the various *Länder* public authorities. However, the general principles of administrative law, especially procedural administrative law, are now been catered for on a federal basis. There has not been a complete codification in this area but the most important enactments are: the Administrative Courts Act (*Verwaltungsgerichtsordnung*: VwGO), the Administrative Procedure Act (*Verwaltungsverfahrensgesetz*: VwVfG), and the Enforcement of Administrative Judgments Act (*Verwaltungsvollstreckungsgesetz*: VwVG).

Additionally, there are numerous special administrative laws dealing, amongst other topics, with building regulations, the police and roads, which, for the most part, are governed by *Länder* legislation.

3 Judicature and procedural law

Within the division of public law are areas of law dealing with the organisation of judicial bodies and areas of law which, although affecting purely private or civil rights, are enacted on a federal level within public law.

These enactments include the code of civil procedure (*Zivilprozeßordnung*: ZPO), the Organization of the Courts Act (*Gerichtsverfassungsgesetz*: GVG), the Non-contentious Jurisdiction Act (*Gesetz über die Angelegenheiten der Freiwilligen Gerichtsbarkeit*: FGG), the Administration of Property Act (*Zwangsversteigerungsgesetz*: ZVG), the German Law on the Judiciary (*Deutsches Richtergesetz*: DRiG), the Federal Attorneys Act (*Bundesrechtsanwaltsordnung*: BRAO), the Federal Notaries Act (*Bundesnotarordnung*: BNotO), the Legal Services Act (*Rechtspflegergesetz*: RPflG), the Court Costs Act (*Gerichtskostengesetz*: GKG), the Fees Act (*Kostenordnung*: KostO), and the Federal Statute on Attorneys' Fees (*Bundesrechtsanwaltsgebührenordnung*: BRAGO).

Despite the fact that many of the enactments above, particularly the law of civil procedure, are public law rules and should therefore be considered within the part of the book on substantive law, the majority of the topics to which they relate are best introduced and understood within the context of the legal system itself. They have therefore been considered under Part One of this book. In particular, civil procedure is considered in Chapter 5.

4 Criminal law

Despite the separation and teaching of these subjects in the universities as a self-contained subject area, criminal law and criminal procedure are also in the public law division and include two major codes, the criminal code (*Strafgesetzbuch*: StGB) and the code of criminal procedure (*Strafprozeßordnung*: StPO), and additionally the Criminal Sentence Enforcement Act (*Strafvollzugsgesetz*: StVollzG) and the Juvenile Courts Act (*Jugendgerichtsgesetz*: JGG).

5 Tax law

The major enactments in this area are the Internal Revenue code (*Abgabenordnung*: AO) and Revenue Courts Act (*Finanzgerichtsordnung*: FGO).

6 Social law

This area of law is initially governed by a code, the social law code (*Sozialgesetzbuch*: SGB), which is still in the process of completion; therefore many other single enactments apply, including the Federal Social Welfare Act (*Bundessozialhilfegesetz*: BSHG) and the Social Courts Act (*Sozialgerichtgesetz*: SGG).

7 The law of economic administration and labour law

These two areas of law fit uncomfortably within the division of public and civil law. The first belongs to public law but has most effect in the private sector, and the second arose out of private law but is increasingly regulated by public law. Both can therefore be regarded as quasi public/private law subjects.

7.1 The law of economic administration

This area is made up of such a number of diverse laws and statutes affecting so many areas of the economy, it would serve no purpose attempting to identify the principal enactments. The most prominent areas of law in terms of legislation within this heading are environmental law, with its roots in general administrative law, consumer law and competition law. Details can be found in Chapter 8.

7.2 Labour law

Labour law was originally contained within civil law, but now falls between private and public law and is regarded as a distinct branch of law (confirmed BVerfGE 7, 342, 348). Numerous enactments regulating labour relations exist in addition to many general rules arising from the civil code (BGB) and commercial code (HGB), amongst others. Notably, the Labour Courts Act (*Arbeitsgerichtgesetz*: ArbGG), the Collective Agreements Act (*Tarifvertragsgesetz*: TVG), the Business Organization Act (*Betriebsverfassungsgesetz*: BetrVG), the Trade Act (*Gewerbeordnung*: GewO), and the Co-determination Act (*Mitbestimmungsgesetz*: MitbestG). It is an area which may be codified in the future.

c Civil law

The following subject areas are classified within civil law. They are predominantly, but not exclusively, concerned with the relations between individuals.

1 The civil code (*Bürgerliches Gesetzbuch*: BGB)

The BGB deals with many areas of law which would have separate classifications in common law, and includes contract, quasi-contract, tort, property, family, and succession law.

The BGB is the most comprehensive code in Germany, but has been subject to supplementary statutes and many updating and amending enactments, notably the Land Register Act (*Grundbuchordnung*: GBO).

2 Commercial law

The final major code to be identified is the commercial code (*Handelsgesetzbuch*: HGB), supported by the Act against Restraints of Competition (*Gesetz gegen Wettbewerbsbeschränkungen*: GWB), the Unfair Competition Act (*Gesetz gegen den unlauteren Wettbewerb*: UWG), the Bills of Exchange Act (*Wechelgesetz*: WG), the Cheques Act (*Scheckgesetz*: ScheckG), and the Bankruptcy Act (*Konkursordnung*: KO).

Commercial law also includes the specialist statutes relating to specific forms of business association, notably the Stock Corporation Act (*Aktiengesetz*: AktG) and the Limited Liability Companies Act (*Gesetz über die Gesellschaft mit beschränkter Haftung*: GmbHG).

6

Public law I: constitutional law: principles and institutions

1 Historical development[1]

1.1 Constitutional developments until unification

Although German constitutional law is today based on a written constitution which came into being after the Second World War its historical roots reach back further than that[2]. Roots of German federalism, for example, can be traced back to the last 300 years of the Holy Roman Empire of German Nation when Germany was made up of several territorial states of different size and influence. Ideas of federalism, seperation of powers, and basic rights are set out in the "Frankfurt Constitution" (*"Frankfurter Reichsverfassung"* or *"Paulskirchenverfassung"*) of 1849 incorporating ideas of the American and the French constitutions of the preceding century. Even though the "Frankfurt Constitution" never came into existence it nevertheless had a strong influence on the Weimar Constitution of 1919 as well as on the *"Grundgesetz"* (Basic Law) of 1949. The protection of federalist interests was also provided for in the constitution of the second German Empire of 1871, even though Prussia played a clearly dominant role.

Finally, the inadaquacies of the Weimar Constitution were of significant impact for current German constitutional law. After the catastrophe of the Weimar Republic yielding to the Nazi totalitarian dictatorship, the weaknesses within the Weimar constitution concerning defence mechanisms against undemocratic movements became obvious. Thus the Weimar Constitution could be used as a "negative blueprint" for the Basic Law of 1949 indicating which particular provisions should be left out or improved. When formulated the constitution was envisaged as a temporary and provisional set of laws for the areas of allied occupation, but not including the Soviet zone. The creation of one German state according to Western democratic principles including all occupied zones was obstructed mainly by the USSR.[3] As a consequence the three Western Allies promoted the formation of a Western German state with its own constitution. It was intended that this

[1] For a concise history of German constitutional law see H. Maurer, *Staatsrecht, München* (1999: C. H. Beck, München), pp. 33–115.
[2] For further details on German Legal History see Part One, Chapter 1.
[3] But also France was sceptical towards the full "territorial reestablishment" of its neighbour.

constitution would one day lose its validity when a new constitution came into force following the free determination of the German people and which would take place following unification (see preamble and Art. 146 of the pre- 1990 constitution).[4]

The name adopted was *"Grundgesetz"* rather than *"Verfassung"*, "the Basic Law" as opposed to "Constitution", underlining its provisional character. It was designed under the influence of the Western allies to have adequate central authority but balanced by the *Länder*, to protect the rights of the constituent states and individuals and most importantly not to stand in the way of re-unification. This latter requirement was known as the *Wiedervereinigungsgebot* which meant that all organs of the Federal Republic of Germany were obliged not to hinder unification but in fact to pursue policies which encouraged this aim. This was confirmed by the Constitutional Court in the case of the *Grundlagenvertrag* in 1973:

BVerfGE 36, 1 (Grundlagenvertrag):

Here the Court approved a treaty with East Germany (or the German Democratic Republic, GDR) designed to clear the complicated relations between both German states. It acknowledged the factual recognition of East Germany as a state under Public International Law but **reminded the Government of the duty to aim for the goal of unification**. The Court held that the German Empire had not ceased to exist after capitulation at the end of the Second World War but that the two "new" German states (Federal Republic of Germany and German Democratic Republic) were now both partly identical with the former Empire. As a consequence the latter still existed as a subject of Public International Law but lay merely "dormant" for the time being since it lacked capacity to act. This meant that from the viewpoint of each German state the other state could not be a "foreign country". Thus their relationship had to be different from the usual "inter-state" relationships. The treaty in question (*Grundlagenvertrag*) aimed at clarifying this relationship and provided for mutual respect for internal and external affairs.

One of the major concerns of the new constitution was to design something which would avoid the inadequacies of the Weimar Constitution. Those mainly concerned the political parties, representation, the protection of basic rights, and the powers of the President and *Länder*. Although even a perfect constitution would not prevent a dictator from gaining power, it is widely considered the weaknesses of the Weimar Constitution helped the process by which Hitler was able to rise to power. Therefore, although the *Grundgesetz* adopted the parts of the old Weimar Constitution which were considered acceptable, it made major changes to other parts and introduced basic principles to ensure that the basic rights could not be weakened or

---

[4] Extracts from the *Grundgesetz* are contained in an appendix at the end of this volume.

removed under the present structure. These principles underpin the constitutional existence of Germany.

Despite the supposedly transitory term of *"Grundgesetz"* it was often and clearly acknowledged to have become a complete and competent constitution for the former Federal Republic of Germany. A body of opinion had been established that the *Grundgesetz* was the equivalent of a constitution designed for a permanent state, as noted in the introductory chapters and comments on the Preamble in commentaries on the *Grundgesetz*.[5] This is not a surprising conclusion to reach, especially if it is considered that even up to October 1989, the changes which took place following the fall of the Berlin Wall in November 1989 were hardly thought possible.

One of the problems with the *Grundgesetz* is that there were doubts as to whether the German people had themselves decided on the form of state and constitution, as stated in the Preamble, because they were given no chance at the time to vote on the issue. It was rather accepted by the regional Parliaments within the allied zones.

The same argument applies to the *Grundgesetz* as amended in 1990, in that the German people as a body did not have the chance to vote on the issue but that it was merely accepted by the *Bundestag*. It can however be argued, as it has been for the original *Grundgesetz*, that voting in general elections after the event can constitutionally sanction what has already happened and retroactively validate the product of political agreement of the regions or, in the latest case, the agreement of the Federal Republic of Germany and the German Democratic Republic, by the first democratic elections in East Germany and the all-German general election in December 1990.[6]

1.2 Changes made to the *Grundgesetz* following unification

The method by which East Germany could accede to the Federal Republic was relatively straightforward, if not entirely without contention, by the simple accession of the regions from the former East Germany into the Federal Republic under the pre-1990 Article 23 of the *Grundgesetz* rather than by a referendum of the whole population prior to unification.[7] The changes made were the minimum necessary for the unification of Germany, rather than all those necessary for the establishment of the new Germany on a much revised constitutional basis. They concerned the amendment of the *Grundgesetz* to take account of the accession of East Germany and to confirm the united status of the new Federal Republic. This was achieved by the removal of some of the references to the transitional nature of the *Grundgesetz* and the revision of others. Those aspects which were removed were those relating to the territorial uncertainty of Germany following the division after the war. Those revised related to its provisional or temporary nature.

The second paragraph of the Preamble now states that the unity of Germany has

---

[5] *See*, e.g., M. Sachs (ed.), *Grundgesetz Kommentar*, 2nd ed. (1999: C. H. Beck, München) Präambel, para. 5 *or* Maunz in T. Maunz and G. Duerig, *Grundgesetz Kommentar*, vols 1–5 (July 2001: C. H. Beck, München), (Präambel), para. 6.

[6] See H. Maurer, *Staatsrecht*, München (1999: C. H. Beck, München), p. 92f.

[7] This "old" Art. 23 GG has been repealed as provided for by Art. 4 II of the of the Unification Treaty.

been achieved, and disposes of the thorny problem regarding the territory, in particular the Eastern frontiers of the united Germany. The signing of the Treaty between Germany and Poland on 14 November 1990 and ratified in January 1992 re-confirmed the Oder-Neisse border.

The Unification Treaty inserted a new Article 143 into the *Grundgesetz*, a transitional provision to allow amendments in the application of the *Grundgesetz* in the area of the former East Germany. Here derogations were possible under certain conditions in order to adapt the new regions to the *Grundgesetz*. But since 1995 the *Grundgesetz* is fully applicable in the new *Länder*.[8]

Providing the final aspect of the legal and territorial consideration of the temporary validity of the original *Grundgesetz* is Article 146. The Article has been revised to read "This Basic Law, *which following the achievement of the unity and freedom of Germany is valid for the entire German people*, shall cease to be in force on the day on which a constitution adopted by a free decision of the German people comes into force". Words added by the unification Treaty are those in italics. The *Grundgesetz* still regards itself therefore as a provisional and transitory constitution until the German people decide to replace it with another constitution. The possibility of a referendum to decide this was specifically included in the Unification Treaty Article 5. Whether to have a new constitution is not now one of the questions on the political agenda, but until a new constitution is enacted the *Grundgesetz* remains, at least technically, a transitory instrument, as evidenced by Article 146. A constitutional Council (*Verfassungskommission*) comprising members of both houses was established to review changes to the present constitution and a number of changes were made to the *Grundgesetz*, as noted in the text below. Any substantial changes face the difficult political hurdle of finding sufficient supra party support to change the present constitution which requires a two-thirds absolute majority in both houses.[9] Hence, the situation now is that the *Grundgesetz* has the validity and acceptance as a true consitution for the German state.

1.3 Content

The *Grundgesetz* regulates and guarantees two main sets of rights. One set dealing with the rights of the various governmental organs, the organization of state, and the relationship between the different organs of state (Arts 20–146 GG). The other set concerned with the rights of individuals in relation to governmental organs, essentially a bill of rights (Arts 1–19 GG). These basic rights are presented before the other chapters to underline their importance in the new German Constitution in contrast to the position given to them at the end of the Weimar Constitution. As developed by the BVerfG, they supplement the provision of rights in the *Grundgesetz* itself. Nevertheless some basic rights can be found in subsquent chapters (for

---

[8] For more details see previous edition of this book, pp. 142, 144, and J. Ipsen, *Staatsrecht I (Staatsorganisationsrecht)*, 11th ed. (1999: Luchterhand, Neuwied), p. 10.
[9] Details of the considerations of the constitutional Commission can be found in BTDr. 12/6000 of 5 November 1993.

example those relating to basic procedural rights of the individual, Arts 101, 103 GG).

The fundamental constitutional provisions will be considered first as they are a prerequisite to an understanding of the basic rights.

1.4 Constitutions of the *Länder*

As the *Länder* have state quality they are entitled just as the federal state, to set up their own constitutions. Although this book will focus on federal constitutional law it is necessary to point out its relation to these "regional" constitutions. Their main purpose is to organize state institutions and functions **at the level of the Länder**, i.e. below the federal level. According to Article 28 I GG, however, their constitutions must comply with the principles of the republican democratic social "*Rechtsstaat*". Thus they have to mirror the basic principles of the federal state. As far as basic rights are concerned the constitutions of the sixteen German *Länder* often go beyond the standard of protection guaranteed in the GG for example by including social rights (right to social security, right to education). This is obviously compatible with the limits set up in Article 28 I GG. A restriction of the standard of basic rights protection on the other hand would be unacceptable. These basic rights limit powers of the state institutions of the *Länder* but not the federal state. It is the task of the Constitutional Courts of the *Länder* to guard them. Nevertheless, constitutional law of the *Länder* has hardly played a leading role. All major disputes of Constitutional law have been dealt with on a federal level.[10]

2 The supreme position of constitutional law

The *Grundgesetz* provides the most important or leading principles of the constitution and determines the form of state organization. It is not the only source of constitutional law in Germany and is supplemented by interpretation by the BVerfG.

2.1 The priority of constitutional provisions

The *Grundgesetz* has allowed the construction of a stable political community in Germany which is said to possess state unity. This is not to confuse it with a unified state as opposed to a federal state, it simply means to say that the Federal Republic of Germany has not been nor is likely to be torn apart by internal divisions as was the Weimar Republic.[11]

The ability to provide for this state unity is expressed in the basic principles (*Grundnormen* or *Grundsätze*) of the *Grundgesetz*. These norms have the greatest legal

---

[10] see E. Stein, *Staatsrecht* 16th ed.(1998: Mohr, Tübingen), pp. 146ff and Maurer, above, n l, pp. 161–169.
[11] see Chapter 1.

priority of all laws in the Federal Republic of Germany as confirmed by a consti-tutional ranking of laws. The *Grundgesetz* has the highest ranking of any law due to the source of its authority (Art. 20 I), the express statements to this effect (Art. 20 III) and because of the entrenchment of the basic principles and the difficulty of changing other provisions achieved by the effect of the combination of Articles 20 and 79.[12] It establishes a hierarchy of laws; *Grundgesetz, Gesetze* (Legislation), *Verordnungen* (Secondary legislation or executive laws), and *Satzungen*, other rules and laws. Article 20 (II and III) confirm that the hierarchy of legislation is protected and is binding on the courts and executive. Thus the priority of the constitution over other laws is confirmed, is binding on all other courts and can be enforced by the BVerfG, Article 93 GG and § 13 BVerfGG. Finally, despite being a federal state whose regions enjoy a significant degree of autonomy and which have their own constitutions, the constituent regions (*Länder*) are bound by the principles and norms of the *Grundgesetz* (Art. 28 (1)) and subject to the overriding priority of both the *Grundgesetz* and Federal law (Arts 28 and 31).

2.2 Interpretation of the constitution

The *Grundgesetz* and constitutional principles are subject to the normal rules of legislative interpretation as discussed previously in Chapter 2. With regard to the special political and notional values of the *Grundgesetz* and in respect of the cata-logue of basic rights (*Grundrechte*) the BVerfG has developed its own special rules of interpretation. This is also due to the vague phrasing of basic constitutional prin-ciples which constantly need to be given concrete meaning in "real (political and social) life". These special rules complement the traditional rules of legislative interpretation[13] and sometimes even replace them.

2.2.1 *The unity of the constitution*

The interpretation of a particular provision must not result in the introduction of contradictions within the *Grundgesetz*, therefore interpretation takes place with a view to the other provisions and requirements of the *Grundgesetz* and not in isol-ation.[14] At times this is difficult to observe. Article 21, for example, protects the (constitutional) status of political parties while Article 38 I 2 provides for autono-mous decision making of Members of Parliament. Where an MP's individual deci-sion conflicts with his party's policy the conflict of the two mentioned provisions becomes apparent.[15] Therefore additional rules of interpretation come into play.

2.2.2 *Harmonizing (praktische Konkordanz)*

In cases of a confrontation of rights, the BVerfG attempts to give both rights the greatest possible relative protection and to produce a result which does least harm

---

[12] For detailed discussion on this see below: Protection of the Constitution (sec. 5.1).
[13] See Chapter 2.
[14] BVerfGE 1, 14 (32). (Southwest State case).
[15] See below, sec. 4.1.3 for a more extensive discussion of this particular problem.

to any particular provision by attempting to harmonize the meaning or protection of the rights in conflict *(praktische Konkordanz)*.[16] A good example of this is the *Mephisto judgment*:

BVerfGE 30, 173 (Mephisto-Urteil)

In his novel "Mephisto" Klaus Mann described the career of a certain Hendrik Höfgen as an actor during the "Third Reich", marking him as a spineless opportunist. This person was clearly identifiable as the real person Gustaf Gründgens. Here freedom of expression and artistic expression contained in Article 5 I, III clashed with dignity and free development of the person protected by Articles 1 and 2. According to the principle of harmonizing it is not possible to generally attach more importance to one of the conflicting rights and then completely ignore the other interest. Thus in the *Mephisto judgment* the Court did not categorically declare protection of Gründgens' dignity and personality as supreme, totally neglecting Mann's right to free (artistic) expression. It rather considered both individual rights as human rights of fundamental value that influenced each other and had to be given the greatest possible effect. Ultimately **after having carefully balanced the two rights the BVerfG agreed that Gründgens' right to dignity could not be protected in any other way than to prohibit publication of the novel in question.**

2.2.3 Unity of the state

Any interpretation must go as far as possible to respect the basic rights, norms, or freedoms and integration of the state and not to isolate a particular organ of the state.

These rules have been held by the BVerfG not only to apply to it but to be binding on all courts and all organs of the state that are called upon to interpret the *Grundgesetz* and that the authority to define rights is held not just by the BVerfG but to all of the highest constitutional organs.[17] The BVerfG must, however, at the same time try not to hinder the constitutional political aims of the legislation passed by the government in Parliament.

2.3 Distinction: interpretation in the light of constitutional law

Rules of **interpretation of the constitution** have to be distinguished from the principle of **interpreting** parliamentary legislation **in the light of the constitution**. In the latter case courts are obliged to keep in mind constitutional principles and rights when construing other legal provisions. This is only logical as the constitution stands at the apex of all national legislation. As a consequence any legal

---

[16] This term was coined by K. Hesse, *Grundzüge des Verfassungsrechts der Bundesrepublik Deutschland*, new print of 20th ed. (1999: C. F. Müller, Heidelberg), para. 72.

[17] BVerfGE 62, 1.

provision below the *Grundgesetz* whether of criminal, private, or adminstrative law has to be interpreted "in line with" the constitution.[18] The principle is of paramount importance when several different interpretations are possible. Here the provision has to be construed in the light of the constitution—otherwise it would have to be repealed as unconstitutional.

A parallel of this technique on a European law level can be detected in the principle of "indirect effect" as applied by the European Court of Justice (*von Colson principle*).[19] According to that decision national courts must interpret national law in the light of supreme EC law, in particular EC directives.

2.4 Position of international law

There has been a considerable degree of debate in German legal literature as to whether Germany as a state conforms to the monist or dualist theories of the incorporation of international law into the domestic legal order. Neither the *Grundgesetz* nor the BVerfG explicitly favour the monist or dualist character of the state. Several variations within the two main theories are possible but practically it does not matter.[20] For the purpose of this book the most memorable rule is that international law has to be incorporated into domestic law through some state act of transformation. Thus **International Treaties** are not applicable under domestic law until they have been transformed into its legal system by an act of Parliament.[21] An example for this is the European Convention on Human Rights transformed into national law by the *Bundesgesetz*. As far as general rules of international law are concerned Article 25 provides a general instrument of transformation: This provision categorically declares them to be parts of domestic law. As a consequence they do not have to be transformed by specific acts of Parliament individually. According to Article 25 general rules of international law take precedence over statute and other laws but it is silent as to its effect on the constitution. Within the dispute on this effect the BVerfG takes the view that these general rules are above normal federal statutes but below the constitution.[22]

If a later *Gesetz* conflicts with the earlier implementation of an international treaty, the national rule will prevail[23] (*lex posterior* rule). Article 24 I allows for the transfer of sovereignty from the Federal Republic government and parliament to international governmental institutions. Initially this provision was the constitutional basis for transferral of powers onto the EC and NATO. As regards the European Union the new Article 23 is now applicable.

The position of international law in the hierarchy is of course a particularly acute

---

[18] See for an example of an administrative provision (§14 VersG) regulating demonstrations interpreted in the light of Art. 8 GG: BVerfGE 85, 69 (74).

[19] Case 14/83 *Von Colson and Hamann v Land Nordrhein-Westfalen* [1984] ECR 1891.

[20] For discussion of these theories see M. Schweitzer, *Staatsrecht III*, 6th ed., (1997: C. F. Müller, Heidelberg), pp.10–15.

[21] that is a *Bundesgesetz* enacted by *Bundestag* and/or *Bundesrat*—depending on the applicable procedure of legislation.

[22] BVerfGE 6, p. 309, 363; 37,p. 271, 279.

[23] BVerfGE 6, p. 309, 362ff.

question when membership of the EC and Community law is considered. The preamble to the *Grundgesetz* speaks of the desire of the Federal Republic of Germany to serve a United Europe. According to Community law and the ECJ, Community law is supreme even over constitutional law. In 1974, the BVerfG would not recognise this unless Basic Rights were guaranteed to the level of those in the *Grundgesetz*, the position in *Solange I*.[24] However, the 1986 decision in *Wünsche Handelsgesellschaft (Solange II)*,[25] suggests EC law takes priority over provisions of the constitution and will not be subject to constitutional review by the German courts, because the BVerfG accepts that, as long as the EC recognizes basic rights to the same extent as the *Grundgesetz*. The position has been thoroughly discussed since this earlier decision as a result of both the changes made to the *Grundgesetz*, namely inserting the new Article 23 in order to facilitate greater European integration and, the legal challenge to the ratification of the Treaty on European Union (the Maastricht Treaty) deliberated by the BVerfG in the Maastricht judgment.[26] There is, consequently, still a chance in the future that BVerfG will review Community law in particular cases.[27]

3 The basic principles of state

The key constitutional provisions are Articles 1 I and 20 I-III GG. As the most fundamental value Article 1 I GG declares human dignity as inviolable and provides for its obligatory protection by the state. This emphasizes the state's main philosophy: The constitution acknowledges each individual's dignity or "value". Thus the state exists to serve the individual not vice versa![28] To serve this purpose Article 20 I-III GG then outlines the basic constitutional principles relevant for state structure and actions.

Article 20 I *Grundgesetz* states "The Federal Republic of Germany shall be a democratic and social federal state". From this and Articles 20 II, III and 28, five principles are derived which are:

(a) republicanism,

(b) principle of democracy (*Demokratieprinzip*),

(c) *Rechtsstaatsprinzip* (often translated as rule of law),[29]

(d) principle of the social state (*Sozialstaatsprinzip*),

(e) principle of the federal state (*Bundesstaatsprinzip*).

All five principles are guaranteed by Article 79 III meaning they are exempted from

---

[24] BVerfGE 37, p. 271ff.
[25] BVerfGE 73, p. 339ff.
[26] BVerfGE 89, p. 155ff.
[27] For a detailled discussion of this see the section on Community law as a source of law in Chapter 2.
[28] Dürig in Maunz-Dürig, above, n 5, Art. 1, para. 15.
[29] This translation is somewhat inaccurate, see below, sec. 3.3.

any constitutional alterations. They are directly applicable and binding on all parts of the state by Articles 1 and 20 III. The principle *Rechtsstaatsprinzip*—comparable to the rule of law—is not expressly referred to in Article 20 but nevertheless can be derived from Article 20 II and III and expressly from Article 28. The latter Article requires that the *Länder*, which are guaranteed their independence, must nevertheless conform to the basic principles of republicanism, democracy, and social *Rechtsstaat*. Furthermore, the principles, with the exception of an express statement of republicanism, are repeated in the new Article 23. The German term *Rechtsstaat* will be retained because of the clarity and economy of expression. The principle of *Rechtsstaat* is similar to the requirement of a state based on and conforming to the rule of law.

These principles which form the constitutional framework of state and government have shaped the political and legal machinery of the Federal Republic of Germany and continue to play a part in the everyday workings of all parts of state. They influence the direction of all state tasks and give legitimacy to the use of state power and the exercise of government. As a final recourse they can be employed to prevent the misuse of State power. German governments cannot act unconstitutionally or beyond their powers or in other directions than those given to them by the *Grundgesetz*.

The additional principles of subsidiarity (*Grundsatz der Subsidiarität*) and protection of the environment have also been introduced to the *Grundgesetz* by Articles 23 and 20a respectively and are considered below.

3.1 Republicanism

The choice of a republican state form rather than any other stems more from negative reasons than positive. The term *"Republik"* simply implies an elected head of state instead of a monarch determined by dynastic criteria. This was fuelled primarily by the rejection of any form of state in which absolute power was vested in one person, or family. As opposed to safe monarchies, as for example of the UK or Sweden, in Germany there was fear that the German people may put too much faith and eventually power in one (non-elected) person. Thus, the choice of republic was entrenched in Article 20 I by Article 79 III GG.

It could be argued that further constitutional aspects could be derived from the republican principle—such as "government by the people" as the Roman definition *res publica* (*"public matter"*) suggests, however this is unnecessary as it is already covered by the principle of democracy.[30]

---

[30] Sachs, above, n 5, Art. 20, para. 10.

3.2 Democracy

3.2.1 *Government of the people (Art. 20 II GG)*

The term democracy is itself a very elusive term. It is politically extremely difficult to define with certainty and legally even more difficult to define. Thus the *Grundgesetz* does not attempt to outline a complete model or example of what democracy should be or consist of in state government. It does, however, require certain characteristics more normally associated with the presence of democracy.

The democratic principle in the Federal Republic of Germany can be found in the form of representative government. Legislative and executive decisions are taken by elected representatives of the people. Unlike the Weimar Constitution the *Grundgesetz* does not provide for any "plebescitary" elements except for cases of reorganizing the territory of the *Länder*. Here a plebiscite is necessary (Art. 29 GG). The reason for this general rule is that historical experience has shown the dangers of abusing plebiscites in order to obstruct the works of Parliament.[31] It is noteworthy though that most constitutions of the *Länder* allow plebiscitary decisions on statutes in certain areas.[32]

In a representative democracy supreme power is transferred **from the sovereign people** as recognized in Article 20 II GG. "All state authority is derived from the people". Who then are "the people"? The BVerfG had to address this question in 1990 when dealing with foreigners' rights to vote *(Ausländerwahlrecht)*:

BVerfGE 83, 37 Ausländerwahlrecht Schleswig-Holstein

One of the *Länder* (Schleswig-Holstein) had allowed foreigners to vote in local elections subject to certain conditions such as a minimum of five years residence in Germany. The BVerfG was called upon to decide whether this was compatible with the democratic principle enshrined in Article 20 II GG. According to Article 28 II GG all *Länder* have to respect the principles laid down in Article 20 I-III GG including the democratic principle. Furthermore, it was held that although the term "people" was not defined in the *Grundgesetz* it had to be interpreted as "people of the state" (*Staatsvolk*). The BVerfG relied on the **theory of "three-elements of state"** according to which a state consists of **power of state** being exercised by the **people of a state** on a defined **state territory**. Affiliation to the "people of the state" can only be established by an individual's citizenship of that state (in the sense of Art. 116 I GG). Thus foreigners were not part of the "people of the state". Consequently including them in voting rights—and thus in exercising state power—contravened the democratic principle of Article 20 I, II GG.

---

[31] see Chapter 1 above.
[32] For an overview see C. Degenhart, *Staatsrecht I*, 15th ed., 1999: C. F. Müller, Heidelberg, Paras. 29–44.

However, according to the amended Article 28 I 3 GG now there is an exception: Any citizen of an EC Member State is allowed to vote in Germany **as far as EC law requires this**. This amendment was necessary to comply with Article 17,18 EC Treaty which allows EC citizens a right to vote in local elections in EC Member States other than their own.

The development of European integration leads us on to the next constitutional problem: If the Federal Republic of Germany in certain areas transfers state powers to a supranational organization such as the EC or even to an organization (of unclear legal status) such as the EU, does this dilute or even eliminate the people's influence on state power? If so it would clearly contravene the democratic principle of Article 20 I, II GG. This question had to be decided when the BVerfG was called upon to review the act transforming the *Maastricht Treaty* into national law *(Maastricht judgment):*[33]

BVerfGE 89,155 "Maastricht-Urteil"

The facts of the case are outlined above.[34] With view to the democratic principle the BVerfG ruled that an accession to the Maastricht Treaty and a subsequent transferral of state powers onto the EU under the terms agreed by the Federal German Parliament were constitutional. It held that neither the democratic principle nor the citizen's right to vote in Parliamentary elections (Art. 38 I GG) prevented the Federal Republic from transferring part of its powers to the European Union or supranational organizations such as the European Community as long as the idea of democratic participation was not undermined and Article 38 I, 20 I GG did not become meaningless. Several conditions for further integration follow from this restriction: A **transferral** of such **state powers onto an international organization** needs **democratic authorization** in other words it must be linked to the national legislator. The act of Parliament approving of the Maastricht Treaty—mandatory according to Article 23 I GG—was held to be sufficient authorization. Furthermore, the BVerfG demanded sufficient **democratic authorization within the European Union** if the democratic principle was to retain its meaning. The BVerfG acknowledged a certain democratic impact of the European Parliament but also ascertained the European Council's dominant position. The latter consists of members of the national governments. These are only responsible to their own national Parliaments. Bearing in mind The European Parliament's weak position the BVerfG concluded that **substantial tasks and powers must rest with the national Parliament** (the *Bundestag*). It follows that a general transferral of power as well as transferral not clearly defining its scope would be incompatible with the democratic principle and thus unconstitutional. The BVerfG expressly reserved the right to review such acts of transferral.

---

[33] See above Chapter 2, sec. 2.5.5.
[34] Ibid.

This case illustrates the justaciability of general principles. The democratic principle is more than a vague declaration. It is a measurable principle that the BVerfG will use to review actions of the state organs.

A fundamental aspect of democracy is "parliamentary reservation" *(Parlamentsvorbehalt)*. Although it is acceptable that certain tasks of legislation can be delegated to the executive (government or individual ministers) as provided for by Article 80 I GG decisions of fundamental importance must remain with Parliament.[35] Such fundamental decisions generally include decisions affecting basic rights.[36] Parliamentary reservation does not necessary imply that an Act of Parliament is always required as can be seen in the case of deployment of the armed forces *(Bundeswehr)*:

BVerfGE 90, 286 "Auslandseinsätze der Bundeswehr"

In 1992 Germany sent a ship of her federal navy to the Adriatic in order to participate in monitoring the international embargo against Yugoslavia. This was part of a NATO action authorized by the UN. As the ship was sent by the executive without Parliament's consent the question arose whether this breached the principle of parliamentary reservation. The BVerfG held that putting units of the armed forces—the *Bundeswehr*—at NATO's disposal was constitutional as Article 24 II GG provided for Germany to join systems of collective security. But then the court went on to outline the manner of such a deployment. By referring to several constitutional provisions (Art. 45 a. 45 b, 87a I 2 GG) the Court pointed out that parliamentary control of the armed forces was a general rule of the constitution. It follows that deployment of the *Bundeswehr* is a matter of fundamental importance. Thus it requires parliamentary consent. However, the BVerfG held that **this would not have to be in form of a statute. A mere decision of the Bundestag** would suffice.

Although the *Bundestag*'s position cannot be characterized by parliamentary supremacy in the sense of UK constitutional law it becomes clear that the BVerfG is prepared to guard the *Bundestag*'s position as the most important representative organ of the people. This is merely a logical consequence of the democratic principle.

In addition to this basic principle the *Grundgesetz* guarantees other characteristics of democracy and basic rights of democratic participation which require free speech, press, free opinion, independent media, Article 5, freedom of assembly, Article 8, freedom of association, Article 9, political parties, Article 21, election rules, Article 38. Apart from being subjective democratic rights the individual can claim they also serve the purpose of safeguarding democracy. In a representative

---

[35] For a summary of the extensive case-law of the BVerfG on his topic see I. Richter, G. F. Schuppert, and C. Bumkeh, *Casebook Verfassungsrecht* 4th ed., (2001: C. H. Beck, München), pp. 315ff.
[36] BVerfGE 34, 165, 192f.

democracy this implies not simply a rule by the majority but also that the minority is protected and has a chance to succeed.

3.2.2 Election principles of Article 38 I GG

The election principles of Article 38 I GG allow these others a chance to succeed. The *Grundgesetz* limits itself to the institution of free elections and not to a specific election system such as proportional representation as in the Weimar constitution. This system itself is regulated by a special statute—the *Bundeswahlgesetz*. It illustrates a mixture of the proportional and the "relative majority" system and will be discussed further below.[37]

The democratic principle implies that choosing the representatives of the people is a free and fair process. Thus according to Article 38 I GG elections must be general, direct, free, equal, and secret. General elections mean a franchise of all German citizens above the age of eighteen (Article 38 II GG) allowing only for few exceptions as regards, for example, certain criminal offenders[38] or Germans residing abroad for more than twenty-five years.[39] Elections must be direct in that the voters themselves choose who sits in Parliament instead of choosing delegates to decide on this. Furthermore, voting must be free with no pressure or coercion. Recommendations by the church made in pastorals *(Hirtenbriefe)* before elections were held to be compatible with this rule as all groups of society—e.g. religious communities and trade unions—must be allowed to contribute to pre-election debates.[40] Secrecy of the ballot is an obvious precondition of free, unimpaired voting and does not need further explanation.

The final requirement of equality, however, deserves a closer look. It basically provides for an equal weight of each vote unlike, for example, in the election system of Prussia until 1918 where voters were divided into three classes according to their wealth *(Dreiklassenwahlrecht)*. As each class would elect a third of the members of Parliament, but there were fewer wealthier citizens, the "first class votes" easily outweighed the other classes. But even nowadays the concept of equal weight of votes is not strictly upheld in the Federal Republic as can be seen when looking at the limitations clause *(Sperrklausel)*.

The 5% limitation clause *(Sperrklausel)*—a feature of the German electoral system (§ 6 VI BWahlG)—was designed to keep small minority parties out of the *Bundestag*. As a consequence if a party accumulates less than 5% of the (second) votes these votes are ignored when distributing seats of the *Bundestag*. In other words these votes do not have any weight at all. This clause has been challenged several times before the BVerfG[41] as a breach of the principles of equality of votes (Art. 38 I GG) and the democratic principle (Art. 20 I GG). It was held to be constitutional though under the following reasons: the representation of numerous splinter parties in the

---

[37] See below, sec. 4.1.1.
[38] § 45 V StGB allows suspension of voting rights in cases of a few offences but can only be employed restrictively.
[39] §12 II Nr.3 BWahlG.
[40] BVerwGE 18, 14.
[41] BVerfGE 6, 84, 89; 14,121; 82,322.

Reichstag and the following coalitions of minorities were a contributory factor to the breakdown of democracy in the Weimar Republic. Thus to safeguard the ability of the *Bundestag* to operate effectively, the 5% clause was allowed and does not, according to the BVerfG, defeat the aims of the state as expressed by the *Grundgesetz*. Rather it helps the integrating function of elections. This reasoning was retained by the BVerfG in a case concerning the first German elections after Unification in 1990 although exceptions were made here:

BVerfGE 82, 322 Gesamtdeutsche Wahlen

Part of the Unification Treaty provided for retaining the 5% limitation clause of the election statute (§ 6 VI BWahlG). This was challenged on the grounds that it was extremely more difficult for former East German parties to get past the 5% mark. As the new Eastern *Länder* only made up a smaller part of the new Republic and those parties were not established in the old Western *Länder* yet they would have had to practically gain 20% in the East to get into the new *Bundestag*. When reviewing the 5% limitation clause the BVerfG—apart from the importance of equality of votes (Article 38 I GG)—expressly pointed out a necessity for strict equal treatment of political parties. Any derogations from such formal equal treatment could only be justified by pressing constitutional needs. The Court still upheld such a need of the clause for the sake of a functioning Parliament. However, it also acknowledged the special circumstances of this first election after unification and thus recommended a regional limitation clause of 3%.

Nevertheless this decision only applied to the election of 1990. The 5% limitation clause was applicable again in following elections. In academic debate its requirement and thus its proportionality are still heavily disputed.[42]

3.2.3 *Status of political parties*[43]

Although the democratic principle of Article 20 I, II GG is defined as government by the people in modern democracies an additional—practical—element has developed within the last decade: political parties. Nowadays they play a key role in phrasing the political will of the electorate by gathering individual interests and forming them into party programmes in order to realize these aspirations once they get sufficient support in the elections. As they play a clearly dominant role in Germany's democracy (*Parteiendemokratie*), they deserve a more detailed exposition.

The *Grundgesetz* has acknowledged the crucial role of political parties as mediator of the people's will in Article 21 GG, securing their position. This provision is the starting point of any legal discussion on political parties. As provided for in Article

---

[42] Compare for example Ipsen, above, n 8, p. 26 (in favour) and B. Pieroth and B. Schlink, *Staatsrecht II: Grundrechte*, 15th ed. (1999: C. F. Müller, Heidelberg), para. 464 (against).

[43] For detailed description see Maurer, above n 1, pp. 334–369; Ipsen, above, n 8, pp. 42–57.

21 III GG further details are regulated in a Statute on political parties *(Parteienge-setz).* Article 21 I GG states that they "shall participate in the formation of the political will of the people". It demands that their internal organization must "conform to democratic principles". Parties which seek to impair or abolish the democratic or constitutional order can be banned as unconstituional but only by the Federal Constitutional Court (Art. 21 II GG) which underlines their special status.[44]

As Article 21 GG offers political parties a certain degree of constitutional protection it is important to define what exactly a political party is. Such a definition cannot be found in the *Grundgesetz* but in § 2 I *Parteiengesetz.* This definition—also used by the BVerfG[45]—puts particular emphasis on elements such as permanent activity, the aim to be represented in either the federal *(Bundestag)* or a regional *(Landtag)* Parliament and a certain "seriousness".

Political parties have a somewhat ambivalent position: on the one hand, they are free private associations of citizens formed to realize political ideas. Thus they are founded according to the rules of the private law (§§ 21ff BGB) depending on which form they choose—as registered or unregistered organization *(eingetragener/nicht eingetragener Verein).* On the other hand, they take over a vital constitutional—thus public—task as a consequence of which they are granted certain constitutional privileges.

By trying to be represented in state institutions parties carry the political will of the people formed outside the state institutions into those institutions. Once a party is in power though the line between party and state is blurred. Still the BVerfG insists on this distinction, as can be seen in cases of the misuse of state resources for political advertisement campaigns for the party in power as opposed to legitimate public relations projects.[46]

What then are the consequences flowing from the singular constitutional status of political parties? One privilege is that although they can be banned if found to be unconstitutional they can only be banned by the BVerfG in a formal procedure instigated by one of the main constitutional organs *(Parteienprivileg).* By comparison other organizations could be banned by the *Bundesinnenminister.*[47]

Another principle derived from their status is the "principle of strict formal equality" *(formeller Gleichheitsgrundsatz).* Since the basic law *(Grundgesetz)* provides for a pluralistic system with competing parties it follows that the state must ensure a free competition of parties and as a consequence equal opportunities *(Chancengleichheit).* This means public authorities have to treat all parties equally if they decide to offer facilities and means for election campaigns, i.e. municipal halls, broadcasting opportunities, etc.[48] Still the BVerfG allowed exceptions. A good example for the court's jurisdiction on this principle is the *FDP* case of 1962 dealing with election broadcasts:

---

[44] For more details on party ban see below, sec. 5.2
[45] BVerfGE 24, 260, 263f.
[46] BVerfGE 44, 125ff.
[47] Equivalent to the Home Secretary.
[48] As has been put in concrete form in § 5 I *Parteiengesetz.*

BVerfGE 14, 121 FDP

Before elections in the *Land* of Northrhine Westphalia in 1962 the public broadcasting Channel WDR had alloted the Liberal Democrats (FDP) significantly fewer time for their campaign spots than the two major parties SPD and CDU. The allocated time mirrored the parties' importance and representation in Parliament. This was challenged by the FDP in a constitutional complaint. The complaint was rejected. The Court held that all parties had to be treated formally equal but exceptions were possible if absolutely necessary. As in the cases concerning the limititation clause the **court saw the functioning of Parliament as a reason allowing differentiation.** By limiting broadcasting times according to the real importance and support of political parties in the population the danger of too many splinter parties represented in Parliament was narrowed down. Thus formation of a government would not be obstructed as in the Weimar Republic. Nevertheless the BVerfG laid down safeguards for smaller parties: it held that a **mere determination of broadcasting times by the parties' success in the last election would reinforce the status quo and was thus unacceptable.** Other factors had to be taken into account as, for example, duration of the parties' existence or number of members. Furthermore, **no party could be totally excluded from using public institutions during election campaigns no matter how small.**

Note that the main legal provision for this principle of equality is not Article 3 I GG but **Article 21 I GG.**

The funding of political parties is also influenced by their constitutional role and has always been controversial.[49] It is not expressly regulated in the *Grundgesetz*. Article 21 I 4 GG merely states that the political parties have to publicly account for their assets, their sources, and the use of their funds. As a consequence there are numerous decisions by the BVerfG dealing with the two main funding sources: state funding and private donations. The problem of state funding will be looked at first:

BVerfGE 20, 156 Parteienfinanzierung I

From 1961 to 1965 the funding of political parties within the federal budget had increased from 5 million to 43 million DM. The BVerfG declared this general funding of political parties by the state unconstitutional. The main principle upheld was the independence of parties from state (*Staatsfreiheit*) since they were not parts of the state, but of society. It was reaffirmed that political will and power must be formed by the people via parties in order to control the state—not vice versa. A general state funding would allow parties to gradually sink into a dependancy on the state. Nevertheless the BVerfG allowed a partial restitution by the state of costs incurred by the parties during election campaigns.

---

[49] See Ipsen, above, n 8, pp. 50–53 and M. Morlok, "Spenden—Rechenschaft—Sanktionen" NJW 2000, pp. 761–769.

From this decision in 1965 it followed that a signficant part of party funding would depend on private donations. Under an altered version of the *ParteienG* private donators could benefit from tax advantages. Nevertheless the provision only favoured large donations and thus those parties that represented interests of the wealthier citizens. It follows that parties which represented the less well-off citizens—and consequently less generous donators—were at a disadvantage. This endangered equal opportunities within party competition. To compensate for this the *ParteienG* also added a minimum statefunding of parties. Against the background of bribery and donation scandals of the *Flick* affair, the BVerfG had to review the new version of the *ParteienG*:

BVerfG 85, 264 Parteienfinanzierung III

The essential element of this decision is the Court's modification of attitude towards general state funding. Although it upheld the principle of *Staatsfreiheit* it expressly departed from a mere restitution of costs incurred during election campaigns. Thus a partial funding by the state was held to be acceptable. Nevertheless such funding must be linked to the parties actual support within the population, i.e. to membership contributions, donations made, etc. It should induce parties to continue seeking the population's support. As far as donations were concerned the BVerfG reduced the tax deductability of donations significantly and declared tax advantages for donations by enterprises unconstitutional.

The case law of the BVerfG and subsequent alterations of the *ParteienG* leave us with the following principles of funding of political parties:

(a) Partial funding by the state is constituional but must be linked to the parties' real support, i.e. to membership contributions. It must not exceed other financial sources.

(b) donations to parties are legitimate and desired because they reflect the politically active participation of citizens. But there is a limit as to their tax deductibility. Large donations have to be publicly accounted for.

Against the background of the "CDU donation scandal" uncovered in 2000 the principle of tansperancy of political parties' means and sources becomes clear. It is the only aspect of funding mentioned in the *Grundgesetz* (Art. 21 I 4 GG). At its roots we again find the democratic principle: If state power is exercised by the people through the political parties they elect, then the people need to have all information about the aims, interests, and *possible dependencies* of the parties. In order to assess such dependencies the public must be able to identify where the financial means of a political party come from and how they are used. As a consequence anonymous donations of more than 1,000 DM may not be accepted (§ 25 I 5 *ParteienG*) and donations of more than 20,000 DM p.a. must be publicly accounted for by mentioning the name of the donor. As this interferes with the donor's constituionally protected rights (including privacy) derived from Article 2 I GG it can only be justified by a conflicting interest of constitutional importance. This can be found in the principle of funding transparency (Art. 21 I 4 GG) and the democratic principle (Art. 20 I, II GG).[50]

As far as procedural rights are concerned the political parties' ambiguous position offers several possibilities: in private law matters such as, for example, disputes over contracts on renting of rooms their rights as private entities under the law of civil procedure apply. Under constitutional law however political parties are offered two procedural remedies. As far as they claim infringements by the state of individual basic rights, as for example freedom of speech (Art. 5 I 1 GG) or assembly (Art. 8 I GG) they are entitled to constitutional complaints (Art. 93 I No. 4a GG, §§ 90 BVerfGG). But if they are infringed as regards particular constitutional rights of the party such as a right to equal treatment by the state the BVerfG recognizes their constitutional status and grants them *locus standi* in the special litigation procedure between constitutional institutions (*Organstreitverfahren*)[51] according to Article 93 I No. 1 GG, §5, §63ff. BVerfGG.

3.3 *Rechtsstaat*

The principle of *Rechtsstaat* is often translated as *rule of law*.[52] Although the core idea of the *Rechtsstaatsprinzip* is very similar to the British—in fact the Western—tradition of the *rule of law*, such a translation can be misleading. The term itself—*Rechtsstaat*—indicates the supremacy of law (*Recht*) within the state (*Staat*). Thus all state power is bound by the law. This principle is meant to offer protection against an abuse of power by the state. So far, this essence of the *Rechtsstaatsprinzip* seems to be similar to the one of the British *rule of law*.[53] But when looking at the components guaranteed by this principle—as has been decided by the BVerfG—it becomes apparent that the German concept is wider. This is due to the fact that the former idea of a formal (*formeller*) *Rechtsstaat* has been supplemented by that of the substantial (*materieller*) *Rechtsstaat*. The term *formeller Rechtsstaat* focuses on formal guarantees of supremacy of law and checks on state power, such as the formal Act of Parliament. But the experiences of the Third Reich have shown that formal Acts of Parliament do not necessarily safeguard against blatantly unjust and inhumane measures taken by the state against individuals. Thus the principle of *Rechtsstaat* now also includes a substantial element: According to Article 20 III state authorities such as, judiciary and the executive are not only bound by Acts of Parliament (*Gesetz*) but also "the law" (*Recht*) meaning "substantial rightness and justice"[54] as

---

[50] Morlok, above, n 49, p. 764. Compare this with the British emphasis on the right to privacy: E. Barendt, *An Introduction to Constitutional Law* (1998: Oxford), p. 157.
[51] See Chapter 7, sec. 2
[52] See S. Michalowski and L. Woods, *German Constitutional Law* (1999: Dartmouth) p. 25; K. Hailbronner and Hummel in W. Ebke and M. Finkin, *Introduction to German Law* (1996: The Hague) p. 47.
[53] As e.g. described by H. Barnett, *Constitutional and Administrative Law*, 2nd ed. (1998: London) p. 87.
[54] As expressed e.g. in BVerfGE 7, 89, 92.

expressed by fundamental constitutional values, namely the basic rights (Art. 1 III). It follows that Parliament itself is bound by the constitution (Art. 20 III). Again it becomes apparent that the German legislature is more restricted than British Parliament which—at least theoretically—can claim absolute sovereignty. Thus the *Rechtsstaatprinzip* somewhat restricts the principle of democracy.

While not expressly named in Article 20, the *Rechtsstaatsprinzip* is referred to in Articles 23 and 28. It is widely accepted that this principle although **not** explained in a **single** provision of the *Grundgesetz* must be derived from **several** fundamental provisions aiming at limiting state power in order to protect the citizen from arbitrary decisions. Some of these provisions are, e.g. the provisions on basic rights (Arts.1–19),the binding force of law (Art. 20 III) the separation of powers (Art. 20 II 2), the guarantee of legal protection by the courts (Art. 19 IV), the liability of the state (Art. 34) and procedural basic rights (Arts. 101–104).[55] It follows that the *Rechtsstaatsprinzip* comprises several principles all designed to protect the citizen against arbitrary decisions of the state and to uphold the supremacy of law. These components of the *Rechtsstaatsprinzip* were of paramount importance in several decisions by adminstrative courts and the BVerfG, especially when dealing with basic rights. The most important ones will be examined in greater depth.

3.3.1 *Basic rights (Grundrechte)*

Of paramount importance are the basic rights provisions when limiting the state's powers. Article 1 I GG, in particular, emphasizes the inviolability of human dignity as the key concept of the constitution. According to Article 1 III all three state powers are bound by the basic rights which are directly effective. It follows that they must also be legally protected in court. Basic rights and procedural mechanisms will be examined below.[56]

3.3.2 *The separation of powers*

One of the very important principles of the constitutional law and one of the basic requirements of a *Rechtsstaat* is the separation of powers *(Gewaltenteilung)*.[57] Article 20 II refers to the three arms of state authority: the legislature, the executive and the judiciary which should not overlap in the functions they perform. In some instances an overlap is inevitable and necessary in the modern and complex state.[58] Examples are the government as head of the executive emerging from the legislature (Art. 63 GG), the *Bundestag* or delegated legislation of the executive (Art. 80 GG).

However, the observation of this principle is very strong in the Federal Republic of Germany. A key feature of the separation of powers is the system of checks and balances of all three arms *(Gewaltenverschränkung, Machtbalancierungs-mechanismus)*. Judicial review is a good example for this: Administrative Courts can review whether adminstrative decisions of the executive are compatible with Acts

---

[55] Maurer, above, n 1, p. 210, see also Sachs, above, n 5, Art. 20 paras. 77–78 for further details.
[56] See Chapter 7.
[57] See, e.g. BVerfGE 34, 52, 58.
[58] Ibid.

of Parliament. Furthermore the BVerfG can review Acts of Parliament as to their constitutionality. Unconstitutional Acts will be declared void.[59]

Whereas all this shows the classical **horizontal** seperation of powers in a federal state like Germany there is also a **vertical** seperation of powers: that between the federal state and the *Länder*. Within the legislative procedure the *Länder* by participating through the *Bundesrat* can check on the actions of the federal state, namely the *Bundestag*. According to Article 83 ff GG not the federal state but the *Länder* execute federal laws in order to prevent a accumulation of power on the federal level by the state.

3.3.3 *Legality of administration (Gesetzmässigkeit der Verwaltung)* [60]

Since according to Article 20 III GG judiciary and executive are bound by Acts of Parliament and "the Law" *(Gesetz und Recht)* two main principles for administrative actions have been deduced. The first one, **Vorrang des Gesetzes** which could be described as a "priority of statute", means that administrative decisions must never contravene statutes, since the latter have been passed by a democratically elected body. Thus administrative actions are bound by the law and must be fully reviewable by the courts.

The second principle is called **Vorbehalt des Gesetzes** ("statutory reservation"). It requires a legal basis whenever the executive takes administrative action, especially when restricting the citizen's basic rights but also when granting rights to the individual. Thus, for example, a regional administrative authority could not grant subsidies to an individual without some legal basis, i.e. a legal provision clearly determining the conditions under which someone becomes eligible for this kind of funding. In other words, the principle of "statutory reservation" goes beyond the first principle: The executive is not only prohibited from contravening existing legal provisions when acting. Rather, it needs a legal basis to act in the first place. This principle is difficult to deduce from the phrasing of Article 20 III GG. Nevertheless it is generally accepted that it is one of the components of the *Rechtsstaatsprinzip* since all actions of the executive must be democratically justified and foreseeable by the citizen.[61] That is only possible if clear legal provisions for administrative action exist beforehand.

However, the term "*Vorbehalt des Gesetzes*" does not make clear which kind of legal provision is necessary. Does it have to be an act of Parliament or is delegated legislation sufficient? Here we have to distinguish between **statutory reservation** (*Vorbehalt des Gesetzes*) which covers delegated legislation (Art. 80 I GG) and **parliamentary reservation** (*Parlamentsvorbehalt*). In order to tackle this problem the BVerfG through its case law has developed a rule according to which **essential matters** have to be regulated by Parliament. This has been called the "*Wesentlichkeitstheorie*". As a consequence the more essential a matter is for the citizen and the

---

[59] See Chapter 7, sec. 2.
[60] For detailed and instructive description in H. Maurer, *Allgemeines Verwaltungsrecht* 12th ed. (1999: C. H. Beck, München), p. 106–121.
[61] Herzog in Maunz and Dürig, above, n 5, Art. 20 VII, para. 25; Sachs in Sachs, above, n 5, Art. 20, para. 114; Degenhart, above, n 32, para. 278.

public the more detailed Parliament's regulation has to be on this matter, leaving less discretion to administrative decisions when implementing the statute.[62] Although this leaves us with a vague term it has at least been generally accepted that matters which are of importance to the individual's enjoyment of basic rights are "essential matters". Therefore they must be decided upon by Parliament and cannot be left to delegated legislation. This has been decided by the BVerfG in several cases relating to reforms of the school system that were introduced by administrative authorities.[63] These reforms affected the public (public education, Art. 7 GG) and individual basic rights. An example of the latter was the introduction of sex education in schools in the 1970s which affected the pupil's right to personality (Art. 2 I GG) and the parental right to care and upbringing of children (Art. 6 GG).[64] The BVerfG held that such matters were "essential" and had to be decided by the legislature.

3.3.4 *Legal certainty (Rechtssicherheit)*

Any actions of the state affecting the individual must be foreseeable. The indidvidal needs **legal certainty** (*Rechtssicherheit*) in order to make arrangements that correspond with the law. From this fundamental principle of legal certainty other principles have been derived:

(a) *Bestimmtheitsgrundsatz*, and

(b) *Vertrauensschutz* (legitimate expectations) and based on this a ban of retroactivity (*Rückwirkungsverbot*).

Legal provisions must be sufficiently clear and precise for the citizen to. To ensure his actions are within the law. This has been coined as the *"Bestimmtheits-grundsatz"*. The more legal provisions affect individual rights the clearer and more precise they must be. This is of paramount importance for criminal law provisions as these offer the most drastic restrictions on the individual's freedom.

Example: If a criminal law provision penalized "actions that are detrimental to the environment" without further specification it would be very hard for the citizen to determine which actions would fall into this category and which would not. Consequently, he could not, be sure that his behaviour accorded with the demands of that law. Such an imprecise decision would contravene the *Bestimmtheitsgrundsatz* and thus the *Rechtsstaatsprinzip*. It would therefore be unconstitutional.

Nevertheless the *Kalkar* decision of 1978 shows how difficult it can be to determine whether a provision is sufficiently precise. It also adresses the problem of parliamentary reservation:

---

[62] Maurer, above, n 1, p. 219.
[63] For example: BVerfGE 41, 251; 45, 400; 64, 308.
[64] BVerfGE 47, 46.

BVerfGE 49, 89 Kalkar

According to § 7 I *AtomGesetz* (AtG) the construction of nuclear power stations requires approval by an administrative authority. § 7 II *AtG* lists several conditions for such an approval one being that "necessary precautions are made against any possible damage caused by the plant according to the latest standards of science and technology . . . ". As a new type of nuclear power station *(Schneller Brüter)* was to be introduced and built in Kalkar the question arose whether § 7AtG still covered this type. The BVerfG had to adress the question whether the possible dangers of this new type of nuclear power stations were so fundamental that only Parliament itself should decide on an approval and if so whether § 7 AtG was sufficiently clear and precise. It was held that there was no breach of the principle of parliamentary reservation *(Vorbehalt des Gesetzes* or more accurately: *Parlamentsvorbehalt).*[65] The use of approval procedures for nuclear power stations were held to be essential matters reserved for Parliament. But the BVerfG held that this matter had been already decided upon by enacting the AtG and that its wording included the new type of power stations. Furthermore, the Court held that § 7 AtG was sufficiently clear and precise. The main guidelines for the approval procedure were set out. Even though an approval of a station by the adminstrative authority could affect the citizen's basic rights (e.g. Art. 2 II GG right to bodily integrity) the statute offered sufficient protection. The use of vague terminology in § 7 II AtG ("precautions according to the latest standard of science and technology") did not amount to a breach of the *Bestimmtheitsgrundsatz* as it allowed flexible decision making by the authorities taking into account new scientific developments.

The other important principle to help maintain legal certainty is the concept of **legitimate expectations** *(Vertrauensschutz).* A citizen will have legitimate expectations that the legal framework for his actions will not change abruptly. Only this will allow him to make long term arrangements. This can best be explained when looking at the problem of retroactive laws. The principle of legitimate expectations demands that changes of the law cannot have retroactive effect if they are detrimental to the citizen, i.e. restrict his rights. This has been termed *Rückwirkungsverbot* **(ban of retroactive effect)** The most obvious consequence is common to most legal cultures: The ban of retroactive **penal laws** *(nulla poena sine lege).* It has furthermore been recognized as a general principle of European Community law by the ECJ.[66] German constitutional law expressly specifies it in Article 103 II GG. According to this provision an act may be punished only if it was defined by law as a criminal offence **before** it was committed. Only then the individual will be able to act accordingly. Two of the leading cases on Article 103 II GG which the BVerfG

---

[65] See above, sec. 3.3.2.
[66] Case 63/83 *R v Kent Kirk* [1984] 3 CMLR 522, para. 22.

decided are closely connected to modern German History and fundamental changes of the political system:

BVerfG 25, 269 NS-Verbrechen

In 1965 a federal law was passed which extended the limitation period for certain crimes committed during the time of the Nazi dictatorship. The reasons for this were (deliberate as well as unintentional) delayed investigation procedures after the war. This retroactive extension of limitation periods was challenged as a breach of the ban on retroactivity according to Article 103 II GG (and thus legitimate expectations). The BVerfG rejected this argument reasoning that Article 103 II GG bans retroactive legislation **creating an offence** but **not** legislation on the **procedural element** of limitation periods. It pointed out that legitimate expectations of the affected accused were not violated as the offences themselves had already been defined by law before they were comitted.

Another—heavily disputed—decision involving Article 103 II GG was the punishment of former East German spies after reunification in 1990:

BVerfGE 92, 277 DDR-Spione

The BVerfG had to decide whether after reunification East German spies could be punished for their activities directed against the former West German state under previously West German criminal law which was now applicable to the unified state. Their activities (e.g. eavesdropping, instructing agents in West Germany) had been conducted from the territory of the former East Germany. They argued that the extension of formerly West German criminal law to former East Germany was for them a case of retroactivity because under former East German Law their activities had—naturally—been lawful. The Court rejected this argument. Under West German law their activities had been defined as criminal offences before they had been committed. Thus no legitimate expectations were violated. The spies had merely relied on the expectation that they would never be prosecuted for their activities as long as they were sheltered by their state which—unfortunately for them—had disappeared after reunification. Article 103 II GG was thus not applicable. This was not a case of retroactivity of criminal laws. However, the Court acquitted some of the accused on the basis that a penalty would no longer be proportionate.

This reasoning left some academics with doubts as to its justice[67] whereas others

---

[67] E.g., P.-A. Albrecht and Kadelbach, "Zur strafrechtlichen Verfolgung von DDR-Aussenspionage", *Neue Justiz* 92, pp. 137–147.

were convinced by the Court's logical approach.[68] The debate shows that although the idea of non-retroactivity of criminal laws is generally accepted, different interpretations of this principle are possible in times of changes affecting a political system—often because the topic itself is a highly "political" rather than a strictly legal one.[69]

Beyond criminal law the question arises whether statutes can have some sort of **retroactive effect** even though they are of disadvantage to the individual as for example, when looking at tax law. Article 103 II GG is not applicable here. One rather has to resort to the general principle of legitimate expectations. The basic rule distinguishes between the following:[70]

(1) New statutes regulating actions/situtations that have already been concluded have retroactive effect. They generally breach legitimate expectations and are thus unconstitutional.

Example: A tax law amendment enters into force on 1 of May 2001. The new tax which it imposes is meant to be applicable for the tax year 1 January 2000 until 31 December 2000. But since this tax year has already concluded and tax for this period has already been paid the statute would retrospectively be regulating a concluded situation. Since the individual has already paid taxes for this period, he may safely assume that there will be no subsequent changes. This is a case of "real retroactivity" (*echte Rückwirkung*) which is banned.

Note though that such retroactivity can be constitutional in **exceptional cases**, such as when

(a) he should have known about an imminent change of the law[71] (debates in Parliament, news coverage),

(b) the current legal situation was unclear and confusing,[72]

(2) New statutes regulating actions/situations that have not yet been concluded do not produce retroactive effect. Since they interfere with an ongoing process the citizen could not build up any legitimate expectations. Such a case of "unreal retroactivity" (*unechte Rückwirkung*) is generally constitutional.

---

[68] K. Doehring, "Zur Ratio der Spionenbestrafung Völkerrecht und nationales Recht", ZRP 95, pp. 293–297.

[69] The easiest political solution for this problem would have been an amnesty clause for spies within the reunification treaty. See also B. Simma and K. Volk, "Der Spion, der in die Kaelte kam", NJW 1991, pp. 872–875, 874.

[70] For detailed exposition see Degenhart, above, n 32, paras. 311–318.

[71] BVerfGE 37, 363, 397.

[72] It could be argued that with German tax law this is always the case as it is changing constantly.

Example: The tax law amendment from the previous example is meant be applicable to the tax year 1 January 2001 until 31 December 2001. Since it enters into force in May 2001 it interferes with an ongoing process. Tax has not yet been paid. Here the individual could not expect the tax law to stay the same as the tax year has not yet concluded and the state needs some flexibility for example to adjust the budget. Thus it is difficult to speak of "real" retroactivity (unreal activity: *unechte Rückwirkung*).

However, *Unechte Rückwirkung* is unconstitutional if on balance the individual's interest outweighs the public interest.[73] This can be the case when basic rights of the individual are affected. In the previous example an unproportional tax throttling the individual's business would violate his right to carry a commercial business (Art. 12, 14 GG).

3.3.5 *The principle of proportionality (Grundsatz der Verhältnismässigkeit)*

The principle of proportionality (*Verhältnismässigkeitsgrundsatz* or *Übermassverbot*) has been acknowledged as one of the cornerstones of the *Rechtsstaatsprinzip*.[74] It demands that laws, actions, and measure, of public bodies do not go beyond that strictly required to achieve the legal purpose. It is based on the idea of basic rights and individual freedoms. If individual rights are to be taken seriously then the state may only impose restrictions that are justified by a legitimate purpose and absolutely necessary. This principle has also established itself as an important general rule in European Community law.[75] In German constitutional and administrative law it has been developped into a "three part test" that will allow to diligently scrutinize state actions. Such actions have to

(a) be suitable (i.e. efficient) to achieve the aim they are used for *(Geeignetheit)*,

(b) be necessary to achieve this aim *(Erforderlichkeit)*, **and**

(c) outweigh the individual's interest, i.e. basic right on a balance
     (*Angemessenheit or Verhältnismässigkeit i. e. S.*)

A classical fictional (crass) example will serve to explain this structure:

Example: A young boy steals an apple in the market and is just about to leave. A policeman having observed the theft reacts by drawing his pistol and shooting the boy. The legal (in fact legitimate) purpose to be achieved here was to prevent the theft from being completed. But was the policeman's action proportionate?

---

[73] BVerfGE 72, 200, 242.
[74] BVerfGE 19, 342, 348; 23, 133.
[75] See, e.g. Case 181/84 *R v Intervention Board, ex parte ED&F Man (Sugar) Ltd* [1985] ECR 2889. For further details see P. Craig and G. de Burca, *EU Law* 2nd ed. (1998), pp. 349–357.

1. Part: *Geeignetheit:* Shooting the boy was a suitable measure to (effectively) prevent the completion of the theft.
2. Part: *Erforderlichkeit:* However, the measure was not necessary. A less restrictive measure could have been used (e.g. arresting the boy). Thus the measure fails the proportionality test already in the second part and thus was disproportionate.
3. Part: *Angemessenheit:* **Alteration of example:** the policeman tries to grab the boy in order to arrest him but slips and falls to the ground. As he gets up again the boy has got already too much of a headstart to be caught. The only way to stop him now would be to shoot him. In this altered example the measure would be suitable and necessary, as no less strict measure could serve the purpose of preventing the theft. At this point the third part of the proportionality test works as a safety net: the two interests at stake have to be balanced: The boy's right to life (Art. 2 II GG) and the public's interest in preventing the theft of an apple. A diligent policeman will place the apple second. He has to let the boy go.

The BVerfG has applied the proportionality test in a number of cases especially when dealing with the protection of basic rights. The "falconry case" is a good example of how a provision can already fail the first part of the proportionality test:

BVerfGE 55, 159 Falknerjagdschein

A hunting law provision (§15 VII 1 BjagdG a.F.) required falconers to prove their knowledge of fire weapons in order to get a falconry licence. This was challenged as a disproportionate restriction of the falconer's basic right to freedom of action (Art. 2 I GG). Applying the proportionality test the Court looked at the purpose of the provision: A license requirement for falconers was to make sure falcons would be treated properly. Although this was a lgitimate purpose it was held that the requirement of a knowledge of firearms was not a suitable measure to serve this purpose (it would have made more sense to ask for knowledge of falcons and falconry itself). As a consequence the provision was disproportionate and declared unconstituional.

A failure of the second part of the proportionality test can be seen in the case of the heavily disputed census law of 1982 which will be looked at in more depth when dealing with data protection.[76]

---

[76] See below, Chapter 7, sec. 1.2.

BVerfGE 65, 1 Volkszählung

Within the census framework the highest federal authorities got wide access to personal data "in order to fulfil their tasks". These data were not truly anonymous as birthdays and addresses were still connected to them. Thus the authorities could easily link the data to their persons and potentially pass all data down to lower authorities. As the collection of data was restricting data protection and privacy rights its proportionality was questioned. The BVerfG held that it was not necessary for the highest authorities to have such a general access to personal data to fulfil their tasks. It would have been less restrictive to only name the few authorities in the statute which needed access and only to those data which were really relevant.

An instructive case for the third part of the proportionality test is the so-called *Lebach case*. It gives an idea of how the BVerfG balances two interests against each other and will be looked at when dealing with Article 5 I GG.[77]

3.3.6 *Right to judicial review (Rechtsweggarantie art. 19 IV GG)*

Judicial review, the citizen's right to legal protection against the state's unlawful restriction of his rights is a necessary complement to basic rights and the above-mentioned general principles. Otherwise those rights would not be worth the paper they are written on. There must be an independent judiciary to guarantee protection to the citizen. Thus Article 19 IV GG guarantees each individual whose rights have been violated recourse to the courts. It entails a **complete** and **effective** legal protection in the sense that no state action is exempt from judicial review. As a consequence even parliamentary statutes must be reviewable—albeit only by a special court, the BVerfG.[78] Effective legal protection means that procedural law allows review by as quick and uncomplicated mechanisms as possible.[79]

3.3.7 *Other elements of the Rechtsstaatprinzip*

The *Rechtsstaatsprinzip* is comprised of several other elements, e.g. the independance of the judiciary (Art. 97 *Grundgesetz*), fundamental procedural rights (Arts 100–104), and state liability. Some of these will be dealt with at a later stage.[80]

To sum up then, the *Rechtsstaatprinzip* demands a fixed and certain hierarchy of laws binding on all, the separation of powers, and the provision of accessible independent courts offering protection to the citizen, namely his basic rights. Principles of legal clarity and security of law and proportionality ensure that state actions are predictable and measurable.

---

[77] See below, Chapter 7, sec. 1.2.
[78] See below, sec. 7.
[79] For further details see Maurer, above, n 1, pp. 220–224.
[80] See: Sachs, above, n 5, Art. 20 paras. 77–78.

3.4 Principle of the social state (*Sozialstaatsprinzip*)

The requirement that the Federal Republic is also a social state (Arts 20 I and 28 I *Grundgesetz*) underpins the provision of social laws and the extensive involvement of the state generally in social welfare to provide the social element and balance or correct the unfortunate effects of a market economy. It does not, however, demand a certain economical (e.g. socialist) state form. The BVerfG has, on the contrary, upheld that the *Grundgesetz* itself is neutral as regards economic policy.[81] The principle of the social state rather focuses on remedying social inequality and protection of the socially weak. It imposes a legally binding obligation on the state for social welfare provisions and also for providing basic services to the public (water, electricity, transportation).[82] Although this principle seems to be a broad state aim to have general regard for social justice it does have specific values and uses, and as a self standing principle is equally binding on all organs of state to provide real benefits.[83] *Sozialstaat* is most often connected with the principle of the *Rechtsstaat* as the *sozialer Rechtsstaat*. The principle acts as a specific order or mandate to the legislature which must be observed and as a guide or a rule of interpretation for the executive and the courts for the construction of laws. However, it does oblige the legislature to take defined measures to achieve the aim of social justice. The choice of means is left at the legislator's discretion. The principle does not provide the citizen with enforceable subjective rights. The leading case on this question was decided by the highest German Administrative court (BVerwG).

BVerwGE 1, 159 Fürsorgepflicht

The claimant, who received benefits under a welfare statute, complained that these were too low as they only covered half of his rent. It was argued by the lower adminstrative courts that he did not have a claim to any assistance in the first place and thus could not complain about its amount. The BVerwG held that from several provisions of the *Grundgesetz*, namely the right to human dignity (Art. 1 GG) and the social state principle (Art. 20 I GG), the general idea followed that the individual had a claim against the state for a minimum of social assistance. However, such a claim can only be made in connection with existing legal social provisions as in this case the welfare statute in question. Thus the case is also a good example of interpreting statutes in the light of constitutional law (here Arts. 1 I, 20 I GG).[84]

The social state principle acts as a general legitimation and obligation for governments to develop a comprehensive social policy as, for example, social security provisions, illness, accident, unemployment, old age insurances and benefits,

---

[81] BVerfGE 50, 338.
[82] Maurer, above, n 1, pp. 243, 244.
[83] BVerfGE 1, 97.
[84] See above sec. 2.3.

legal aid and child payments amongst others. It has always been taken seriously by the government as the budget may show: in 1999, for example, 189.85 billion DM (= 40.8%) out of the federal budget was spent on social security.[85] But as has been pointed out this obligation of the state is not translateable into specific individual rights.[86] So far no specific law has been declared unconstitutional as a result of the application of the *Sozialstaatsprinzip* exclusively. Thus social rights depend on provision by the Government and are not guaranteed or absolute.

The boundaries of rights stemming from this are unclear and problematical and it is often discussed and reflected in a number of other basic rights including Articles 1, 3, 6, 7, 9, 12, 14 and 15 GG, the social basic rights.

3.5 Principle of the federal state *(Bundesstaatsprinzip)*

The remaining of the five main state principles according to Article 20 I GG is that of the federal state *(Bundesstaatsprinzip)*. Although it is mainly a concept of state organization it can have an impact on substantial constitutional law as well.

3.5.1. *General*

Federalism describes a state form according to which a state consists of several member states. The federal state as well as the individual member states have state quality. The main reason for a federalist state form is a desire to keep regional differences and protect certain regional interests while at the same time leaving tasks of common interest to be regulated on a common level. Centralized states (e.g. France, UK, Italy), on the other hand, tend to take all decisions at one level and leave it to lower territorial levels (regions, counties, districts) to implement them.

Regional distinctions are usually based on historical developments. As a consequence, federal state forms (e.g. USA, Germany, India, Switzerland) vary and may show surprising differences. Whereas in Germany, for example, criminal law and criminal procedural law are regulated by the federal state and thus applicable in all the *Länder*, in the USA the member states themselves decide upon these matters. It follows that criminal law and its sanctions may vary from state to state in the USA while they are the same in all of the German *Länder*. As a consequence in the USA it depends on each member state whether the death penalty is allowed. German (federal) criminal law does not provide for the death penalty. It follows that it cannot be found in any of the *Länder*.[87] This may show that a mere distinction between federalist and centralized states is too general when comparing state forms. Fundamental differences can be detected within both systems.[88]

---

[85] Taken from Ipsen, above, n 8, p. 262.

[86] BVerfGE 39, 302, 315.

[87] The death penalty has in fact been abolished by Art. 102 GG. Thus it is actually not regulated by criminal law but by the constitution itself. Nevertheless it is the **federal** constitution that regulates it and thus ensures a uniform approach on this matter.

[88] This applies of course as well to different centralized state forms. Compare devolution in the UK and the following rearrangement of legislative powers.

3.5.2 *Federalism according to the Grundgesetz*

Historical Roots of federalism in Germany can be traced back to the Holy Roman Empire of the German Nation. With the rise of numerous small principalities in the seventeenth century the power of the German emperor weakened. After abdication of the emperor in 1806 federations of German principalities followed.[89] A federalist structure was precondition to the forming or the second German empire. It was kept in the Weimar Republic then abolished by the Nazi dictatorship. Its re-establishment in the *Grundgesetz* after the Second World War was due to the insistence of the allies. They were determined to prevent accumulation of state power at a central level as had happened in the Third Reich.[90]

Article 20 I GG describes Germany as a federal state. It consists of two basic elements: the member states, called *"Länder"*, and the federal state itself (*"zweigliedriger Bundesstaat"*).[91] According to Article 28 I 1 GG the constitutional order of the *Länder* has to conform to the four leading principles of the *Grundgesetz*, which have been dealt with above (*Homogenitätsgebot*).[92] Thus Article 28 I GG acknowledges that the *Länder* have state quality but must adhere to certain principles. Their state quality is underlined by their own constitutions which basically deal with the organization of their instituions, e.g. the *Länderparlamente*, courts, and executive organs, but also contain a catalogue of basic rights.[93]

As federalism is guaranteed in Article 79 III GG as one of the "eternal constitutional principles" the Federal Republic of Germany will always consist of two state levels: a federal state and member states. However, this does not guarantee the existence of the *Länder* in their current form. Thus the territory of the *Länder* can be altered even allowing a merger of two or more *Länder* as it happened in 1951 when creating *Baden-Württemberg*.[94] Such a merger failed in the case of Brandenburg and Berlin in 1996 when the population of Brandenburg voted against it. Any territorial reorganization of the *Länder* requires a plebiscite according to the *Grundgesetz* (Art. 29 I GG).[95]

As state authority is exerted by the federation (*Bund*) and the *Länder* the most important aspect of federalism is the division of competences and tasks between them and their relationship.

3.5.3 *Competences of federation* (Bund) *and* Länder

The *Grundgesetz* provides a simple rule for the distribution of state authority between the federation and the *Länder* in **Article 30 GG**. The exercise of state power is a matter of the *Länder* **unless the *Grundgesetz* states otherwise**. Thus the

---

[89] *Rheinbund* (1806), *Deutscher Bund* (1815).

[90] It is noteworthy that East Germany's federal structure of 1949 was replaced by that of a centralized state in 1952.

[91] Generally accepted opinion, also by BVerfGE 13, 54, 77ff. For different theories on Germany's federalism see Stein, above, n 10 pp. 111–114.

[92] Obviously federalism is not a principle applicable within the member states but on the level of the federal state.

[93] For details see *Die Verfassungen der deutschen Bundeslaender*, 7th ed. (2001: C. H. Beck, München) with an introduction by C. Pestalozza.

[94] This lead to the first case to be decided by the BVerfG: E 1, 14.

[95] Arts.118, 118a GG in the two mentioned (special) cases.

general rule is that the *Länder* have to act, save for the exceptions the *Grundgesetz* has made empowering the federation in certain areas. These exceptions, however, are quite numerous as will be seen. The general rule of Article 30 GG can be found in more concrete provisions dealing with the legislative and executive tasks.

The division of legislative competence is outlined in Articles 70–75 GG. Article 70 GG points out that as a general rule the *Länder* have the right to legislate insofar as the *Grundgesetz* does not confer legislative power on the federation. The following provisions then enumerate numerous areas where the federation has a right to legislate. There are three types of the federation's ("exceptional") legislative competence: exclusive, concurrent, and framework legislation.

In areas of the federation's **exclusive legislation,** the *Länder* cannot legislate unless they are given (back) the power to do so by federal law (Art. 71 GG). Factually, it is an exclusive domain of the federation. Thus Article 71 GG is a reversal of the Article 70 GG rule-exception mechanism but only for exclusive legislation. Among the eleven subjects of exclusive legislation listed in Article 73 GG are, e.g. foreign affairs and defense (No. 1), citizenship (No. 2), currency (No. 4), postal and communications services (No. 7). These are matters that are naturally better dealt with at a federal level as they should be uniform in all *Länder*. Further subjects of exclusive legislation can be found throughout the *Grundgesetz*, as some constitutional provisions leave detailed regulations to federal statues (e.g. Art. 21 III GG statute on political parties).

In areas of **concurrent legislation** *Länder* only have a competence to legislate as long as the federation has not done so (Art. 72 I GG). Thus as soon as a federal law is passed in this area any statues of the *Länder* are automatically ineffective. A precondition to the Federation using this power is that an establishment of equal living conditions or maintainance of economic or legal unity through federal law is necessary (Art. 72 II GG). Subject to this rather flexibly-termed condition the federation may legislate on the twenty-six(!) subjects mentioned in Article 74 I GG. They include, for example, civil law and criminal law (No. 1), use of nuclear energy (No. 11a) and Labour law (No. 12).

Framework legislation according to Article 75 GG entitles the federation to lay down guidelines subject to the condition of Article 72 II GG. The core legislation here still rests with the *Länder*. Classical examples of framework legislation subjects are higher education (No. 1a), general legal relations of the press (No. 2) and hunting (No. 3).

Any subjects not listed in these three categories of Article 73–75 GG fall into the **exclusive domain of the Länder**. It follows that if the Federation wants to pass a law it must find a legal basis for it within Article 73–75 GG. Otherwise the statute can be reviewed and repealed by the BVerfG as unconstitutional on grounds of lack of competence. Examples for subjects of "exclusive *Länder* legislation" are mostly adminstrative law topics such as policing or planning law but also the law concerning organization of the counties and municipalities (*Kommunalrecht*).

BVerfGE 12, 205 1. Fernsehurteil

Until 1960 there had been only one TV channel (ARD). Its programme was put together by the different broadcasting companies of the *Länder*. Negotiations of the federal government and the *Länder* to set up a second TV channel proved to be difficult and ultimately broke down. Finally a federal channel was created in form of a private limited company (*Deutschland-Fernsehen GmbH*) run exclusively by the Federation. This was challenged by Hessen and Hamburg on constitutional grounds. The Court agreed with the *Länder* and declared the setting up and running of the TV channel by the federation as unconstitutional. One of the main reasons was that there was no competence of federal administration or legislation for it. The federal government had sought to rely on Article 73 No. 7 GG: "postal and communication services" as a matter of exclusive federal legislation and Article 87 I GG "federal post" as a matter of federal administration. This was rejected by the Court. It held that only the technical part of transmission and broadcasting was covered by Art. 73 No. 7 GG but not the whole of broadcasting. Only the technical preconditions were part of "communication service". Aspects of setting up a TV programme and organizing broadcasting companies were not mentioned as matters of federal legislation in the *Grundgesetz*. Thus the BVerfG held they fell into the scope of *Länder* legislation and administration according to the general rule of Article 30, 70, 83 GG.

It has to be noted that additional competences of the federation have been accepted by the BVerfG, for instance if they are closely linked to a subject of exclusive competence (*Bundeskompetenz kraft Sachzusammenhangs*).[96] For example, legislation on cultural institutions that are established abroad are closely linked to "foreign affairs" (Art. 73 No. 1 GG) and thus legislated on by the federation. However, these competences are not expressly mentioned in the *Grundgesetz* as required by Article 70 GG. It follows that this practice is at least questionable.[97]

This outline of the division of legislative competences shows that in spite of Article 70 GG emphasis has shifted from the *Länder* to the Federation. The Federation's dominant role is underlined by Article 31 GG ensuring that in cases of conflict between existing federal law and a law of a *Land* federal law will prevail and render the other ineffective (*"Bundesrecht bricht Landesrecht"*). This can be the case in areas of Article 75 GG if the framework legislation is contradicted by statutes of a Land.

When looking at the **execution of statutes**, however, it becomes apparent that the *Länder* are exercising most of the state powers. Article 83 GG again reflects the general rule of Art. 30 GG claiming that the *Länder* shall execute federal laws in their own right unless the *Grundgesetz* provides exceptions. This time there are only few exceptions in favour of the federation permitting the creation of only few federal authorities (Arts. 86–90 GG). Federal laws are, in general, executed by

---

[96] BVerfGE 3, 407, 421.
[97] Others are *Annexkompetenz, Kompetenz kraft Natur der Sache*. They cannot be examined here. For more information see Degenhart, above, n 32, pp. 44–46.

administrative authories of the *Länder*. The federation's possibilities of supervision in this area vary.[98]

Finally, it has to be pointed out that with the exception of the highest courts which are federal courts (Art. 95 GG) and the Federal Constitutional Court (*BVerfG*, Art. 93 GG) all courts are courts of the *Länder* (Art. 92 GG).[99]

3.5.4 *Relation between federation (Bund) and Länder*

Having defined the competences of Federation and *Länder* the question remains how the federation can influence the *Länder* and vice versa. The federation has several possibilities to influence the *Länder*. Federal laws have to be observed by the authorities of the *Länder*. Article 28 I GG sets the framework for the constitutions of the *Länder*. Furthermore, the federation may challenge legislation of the *Länder* before the BVerfG on grounds of lack of competence (Art. 93 I No. 2 GG) or interference with her powers (Art. 93 I No. 3, 4 GG). In cases of catastrophes the federation may intervene in order to uphold the free democratic order in a *Land* (Art. 35 II, III GG). If one of the *Länder* does not fulfil its obligations under the *Grundgesetz* the federal government may take steps to compel the *Land* to comply with its duties according to Article 37 GG. This includes drastic measures such as the draining of financial resources and the use of the *Bundeswehr*, the (federal) armed forces. However, in the history of the Federal Republic of Germany it has not been necessary to invoke Article 37 GG.

Although the *Länder's* possibilities to exert influence on the federation are fewer they are nevertheless important. The *Länder* have an effect on the federation's legislation through participation of the *Bundesrat* according to Article 50 GG. They can appeal to the BVerfG in cases of the federation interfering with their powers (Art. 93 I No. 3, 4 GG).

A non-written constitutional principle to ensure a fruitful cooperation of Federation and *Länder* is the idea of "***Bundestreue***", loyalty towards the Federation.[100] It demands mutual respect for the others interests and the federal state as a whole by the individual *Länder* and the federation. It is employed in cases of conflict that cannot be solved by the provisions of the *Grundgesetz*.

BVerfGE 12, 205 1. Fernsehurteil (s. above)[101]

After the breakdown of negotiations with the *Länder* about establishing a second TV channel the federal CDU-lead governement continued negotiations only with the *Länder* that were CDU-lead. Among other aspects this behaviour was criticised by the BVerfG as a violation of the principle of *Bundestreue* as the federal government had clearly discriminated against some of the *Länder* and tried to split them in their opinions in order to secure a better position in negotiations.

---

[98] See below, sec. 4.2.
[99] See above Part One, Chapter 3.
[100] Also described as "*Pflicht zum bundesfreundlichen Verhalten*".
[101] See above sec. 3.5.3.

The BVerfG has pointed out that *Bundestreue* is not only a supplementary principle of interpretation but an undelying rule of the whole principle of federalism. According to the financial provisions of the *Grundgesetz*, especially Article 107 II GG, a federal law shall redistribute revenue from taxation of the *Länder* in order to ensure reasonable equalisation of the disparate financial capacities of the *Länder*. In other words, financially stronger *Länder* will subsidize the weaker ones to a certain extent. This is called "horizontal financial equalization" (*horizontaler Finanzausgleich*). Naturally, this has lead to disputes as the "wealthier" *Länder* felt "financially exploited" and the "poorer" ones felt their situation was often not properly assessed.[102]

BVerfGE 72, 330 Finanzausgleich II

In this case several *Länder* challenged the constitutionality of a statute based on Article 107 II GG as some aspects of their financial burdens had not been taken into account. They succeeded on these grounds, which is not of further interest in this context. It is, however, noteworthy that the BVerfG in its decision outlined the meaning of the provisions of the *Grundgesetz* concerning the apportionment of tax revenue. It pointed out the significance of horizontal financial equalization as an important feature of the federal state. It underlines the necessity of solidarity within the federal state and the idea of "vouching for each other". In spite of the *Länder*'s individuality it obliges the wealthier to assist of poorer ones. Thus Article 107 II GG must be seen as a specification of the principle of *Bundestreue*.

Bundestreue, furthermore, puts the federation under an obligation to respect and protect the *Länder*'s rights and interests when preparing legal acts within the European Community.[103] According to Article 32 I, 59 II GG the federation is responsible for concluding international treaties. Where the *Länders*' legislative competence is at stake they may conclude international treaties themselves subject to approval of the federal government. However, as far as European integration is concerned the relevant provision is Article 23 GG. This integration process poses problems from the *Länders*' point of view. As Germany—i.e. the federation—may according to Article 23 I GG transfer sovereign powers to the EU the question of safeguarding the *Länder*'s interests arises. In these cases the *Bundesrat's* participation ensures their protection. As far as secondary community law is concerned, Article 23 IV–VI GG set out a complicated mechanism to ensure that the *Länder*'s interests are taken into account by the federation *before* its participation in the legislation of acts of the European Union. This mechanism basically provides close

---

[102] Financial provisions of the constitution are not examined in this book. Refer to Maurer, above, n 1, pp. 720–759, Stein, above, n 10, pp. 139–142.
[103] BVerfGE 92, 203, 230.

cooperation of federation and *Länder* focusing on opinions and participation of the *Bundesrat* as a representative of the *Länder*.[104]

3.5.5 Brief comment

There are several advantages to the federal structure as developped in Germany. A **vertical seperation of powers**—as the federation and the *Länder* both have legislative and executive powers—helps to prevent accumulation and a misuse of power at one level. Furthermore, the **distribution of tasks** between the two levels can effectively split up the work load. Finally, this federal structure is designed to maintain **regional interests and differences** that have traditionally evolved allowing harmonization only where it is necessary and of common interest. However, it has to be borne in mind that a significant portion of (legislative) power has steadily moved towards the Federation. As a consequence there is a uniform approach to numerous subjects throughout the *Länder* leaving only little room for regional differences. Consequently the *Länder* are determined to defend their remaining exclusive domains, namely by appealing to the BVerfG. When comparing state forms it has to be stressed that federalism is closely linked to the (traditionally evolved) needs of a territory. Thus it cannot abstractly be preferred to unitarian centralized state. In the case of Germany it has proven to be a valuable instrument of developing and sustaining a democratic state form.

3.6 Environmental protection (Art. 20a GG)—a new principle?

Environmental protection has been added under Article 20a GG. It is a constitutional guideline for the state but does not (yet) seem to have the same "constitutional strength" as most of the aforementioned traditional principles. Unlike the principles of Article 20 GG it does not enjoy the special protection of Article 79 III GG. Article 20a,[105] within the scope of the constitutional order, imposes on the three branches of state, a duty to protect the natural surroundings (*natürlichen Lebensgrundlagen*). Quite how this will be interpreted and how strict an imposition it will be will have to be awaited. It does not set out a programme or indeed a period in which to complete the duty. It is, however, an aim of state with some legally binding effect but only an objective duty and not one which can be enforced by individual citizens. It can, in this sense, be compared with the *Sozialstaatsprinzip*, in that alone it cannot be used to mount a constitutional complaint but only in connection with other substantive laws or rights. Furthermore, given that the requirement is imposed within the context of the whole constitutional order, it is not automatically superior to any other constitutional principles or rights. Thus in cases of conflict it has to be balanced with these.[106] In such a case the duty to protect

---

[104] See Schweitzer, above, n 20, pp. 115–120.
[105] Introduced by the amending law of 27 October 1994 (BGBl I S. 3146).
[106] See for further details Murswieck: in Sachs, above, n 5, Art. 20a, para. 58–72.

natural surroundings has already been held to restrict the basic right to freedom of art (Art. 5 III GG).[107]

4 Organization of the state

This section will briefly map out the constitutional organs and give an introduction to the (typical) functions of the state. The composition and functions of these organs are outlined in the *Grundgesetz* leaving more detailed regulation to federal legislation. The *Grundgesetz* names seven constitutional organs:

(a) *Bundestag* (Federal Parliamentary Assembly, Arts 38–49 GG),

(b) *Bundesrat* (Federal Council, Arts 50–53 GG),

(c) *Bundesregierung* (Federal Government, Arts 62–69 GG),

(d) *Bundespräsident* (Federal President, Arts 54–61 GG),

(e) *Bundesverfassungsgericht* (Federal Constitutional Court, Art. 93, 94 GG),

(f) *Gemeinsamer Ausschuss* (Joint Committee, Art. 53a GG),

(g) *Bundesversammlung* (Federal Assembly, Art. 54 GG).

Emphasis will be placed on the first four organs as the most important ones. The BVerfG will be dealt with in section 7 below.

4.1 *Bundestag* (Federal Parliamentary Assembly, Arts 38–49 GG)

This is the German national parliamentary assembly to which deputies (Members of Parliament) are directly elected as representatives of the people.

4.1.1 *Composition and electoral process*

The *Bundestag*—consisting usually of 656 members—is elected for a four year fixed period according to the election principles of Article 38 I 1 GG.[108] It is only in exceptional cases connected with failure to elect a Chancellor that premature elections can be called by the President.[109] Unlike the Weimar Constitution the *Grundgesetz* does not entitle parliament to dissolve itself.

The electoral system in Germany is a combined one of proportional representation *(Verhältniswahl)* and first past the post *(Mehrheitswahl)* and is referred to as personalized proportional representation. Whilst there was a deliberate move to avoid the type of system in the Weimar Republic, which was one of pure proportional representation and led to an damaging fragmentation of parties in the *Reichstag*, there is no specific system required by the *Grundgesetz*. The details of the

---

[107] BVerwG NJW 1995, 2648.
[108] See above, sec. 3.2.2.
[109] See below, sec. 4.2.

present system are left to the Federal Elections Act *(Bundeswahlgesetz)* according to Article 38 III GG.

This provides that electors cast two votes: the first one to elect constituency candidates on a first past the post basis (§§ 4–5 BWahlG). The second vote counts towards the election of candidates from party lists in each *Land* (§§ 4 and 6 BWG). The first votes directly elect 328 candidates from the 656 *Bundestag* seats. The second votes are counted and proportionately allocated to the parties from party lists on the basis of nationally combining all *Land* lists. They are allocated their proportional share of seats in the *Bundestag*. Subsequently the seats won in the constituencies are then subtracted from the seats allocated from the *Land* lists thus leaving 328 seats to be proportionately allocated to party candidates on the *Land* lists who were not directly elected. In the event that a party wins more direct seats than its proportional allocation would allow, it is allowed to retain these as supernumerary seats *(Überhangmandate)* and the total number of *Bundestag* seats is increased accordingly, § 6 III and V BWahlG. This is questionable when assuming that a party's proportional share of seats is basically determined by the second vote. However, an increase by sixteen seats was still held to be within acceptable limits and thus constitutional by the BVerfG, although it was a narrow decision.[110] Currently (2001) the SPD holds twelve supernumerary seats increasing the number of members of the *Bundestag* to 668.

Parties who receive less than 5% of the votes nationally from the *Land* lists will not be allocated any seats in the *Bundestag* unless they have won at least three constituencies (§ 6 VI BWahlG).[111]

The current number of 328 constituencies has been reduced to 299 for the next elections (§1 II BWahlG) thus reducing the total number of members of the *Bundestag* to 598 in future.[112]

4.1.2 *Organization*

According to Article 40 I GG the *Bundestag* elects its President *(Bundestagspräsident)* and the Vice-Presidents. The President exercises propriety and police powers on the premises of the *Bundestag*. He (or one of the Vice-Presidents) presides over debates ensuring conformity to the standing orders and represents the *Bundestag* legally. The business of the *Bundestag* is organized by the Council of Elders *(Ältestenrat)* whose membership is decided by party strength in the *Bundestag* and it is headed by the President of the *Bundestag*.

Article 40 I GG requires the *Bundestag* to set up standing orders *(Geschäftsordnung des Bundestages*, GeschOBT). The principle of "discontinuity" *(Diskontinuität)* recognizes the individuality of each elected *Bundestag*. This means that any procedures (of legislation or scrutiny by committees) instigated by one *Bundestag* will not be continued by the *Bundestag* of the next election period. It follows that the standing

---

[110] BVerfGE 95, 335. As there was no majority in favour of the claimant (four against four judges) a violation of the *Grundgesetz* could not be declared (§ 15 IV 3 BVerfGG).
[111] For discussion of the 5% clause see above, sec. 3.2.2.
[112] For detailed explanation of electoral process see Ipsen, above, n 7, pp. 28–32.

orders must be formally agreed upon at the beginning of each new election period. However, the *Bundestag* has practically always taken over the previous standing orders. They determine procedural matters, e.g. quorum and required majorities and are only internally binding. Thus a federal law cannot be challenged on procedural grounds because of lack of quorum.[113]

Although the main decisions are taken in public plenary sessions generally requiring a majority of the cast votes (Art. 42 I, II GG) substantial parts of the *Bundestag*'s tasks are dealt with in committees. Legislation is prepared and scrutinized here. The committees consist of members of the *Bundestag* reflecting the strength of the political parties represented within the *Bundestag*. As the committees are dealing with one particular area this allows for an effective distribution of workload as well as the development of expert knowledge by its members.

Furthermore, the *Grundgesetz* names some committees, e.g. for affairs of the European Union (Art. 45 GG), for foreign affairs and defense (Art. 45a GG), and fact-finding committees (Art. 44 GG).

Important institutions within the *Bundestag* are *Fraktionen*. They are only briefly mentioned in Article 53a GG. Yet they are of fundamental importance. They are the representation of a party within the *Bundestag*. § 10 I GeschOBT defines them as associations of members of the *Bundestag* that belong to the same party or at least parties that do not compete with each other in any of the *Länder*.[114] They must make up at least 5% of the members of the *Bundestag*. *Fraktionen* are granted several rights within the procedure of the *Bundestag* as well as before the BVerfG. Their organization allows the members to pool their resources and "to speak with one voice". *Fraktionen* should not be confused with the parties they usually represent. Political parties are private law associations enjoying a particular constitutional status and protection.[115] However, they have no direct influence on the *Fraktionen* and their decisions within the *Bundestag*.

4.1.3 *Status of the members of the Bundestag*

To ensure the functioning of the *Bundestag* its members are given special preroga-tives. Apart from the obvious rights such as rights to participation in plenary ses-sions, decisions, and elections, and a right to speak and question government members there is a right to indemnity and immunity.

Indemnity (*Indemnität*, Art. 46 I GG) provides a member with a protection against proceedings or other sanctions outside the *Bundestag* for his speeches or casting of votes within the *Bundestag*. Its purpose is mainly to ensure free debates in the *Bundestag*. Offensive remarks towards other members, however, will be sanctioned by the President within the *Bundestag* who presides over the debates (§§ 36–38 *GeschOBT*).

---

[113] BVerfGE 44, 308.
[114] The latter referring to the CDU/CSU that are not competing within Bavaria because of similar programmes.
[115] See above, sec. 3.2.3.

Immunity (*Immunität*, Art. 46 II GG), on the other hand, grants members of the *Bundestag* protection from prosecution for any criminal offences. Unlike in the case of indemnity this protection only lasts as long as the person affected is a member of the *Bundestag*. Furthermore, in cases of immunity the *Bundestag* may permit the arrest of a member.

Article 48 III GG entitles members of the *Bundestag* to remuneration adequate to ensure their independence. This has been a subject of public debate because it is difficult to determine the adaquacy of remuneration and because the *Bundestag* itself determines it by federal law. From 2002 on remuneration will be orientated to the salary of a judge at the highest federal court (§11 I AbgG).

An important aspect of the member's status is his position towards his *Fraktion*. What are the consequences if his views conflict with those of his *Fraktion* and thus (usually) his political party? He might have won his seat via the party's *Land* list. Thus not being directly elected he was arguably elected as a representative of his party. What if he does not adhere to general views of the party anymore and threatens to vote and act against the position of his *Fraktion*? And what happens if he is excluded from the *Fraktion* and the party or leaves them voluntarily? Such conflicts will have significant impact on his status within the *Bundestag* as it is through his *Fraktion* that the member is able to amplify his actions in the *Bundestag*, e.g. by pooling time of speech, being sent to a particular committee on behalf of his *Fraktion*, etc. The key provision to answer these questions is Article 38 I 2 GG providing that the members shall be representatives of the whole people, not bound by orders or instructions but only to their conscience. This suggests that the member cannot be restricted by his *Fraktion* and that any kind of pressure exerted on him would contravene Article 38 I 2 GG. On the other hand, Article 21 GG acknowledges the constitutional key role of political parties and thus *Fraktionen* as their representatives in the *Bundestag*. They are necessary to harmonize views within society, bundle them, and put them into a programme. As a consequence the *Fraktion* may exert a certain pressure (*Fraktionsdisziplin* or *Fraktionszwang*). The conflict between Article 38 I 2 GG and Article 21 GG is apparent. When interpreting the two provisions their purposes have to be balanced.[116] As a result party pressure on the member is allowed as far as it affects his status within the party (e.g. threat to withdraw him from a committee or even exclude him from *Fraktion* or party), in other words political pressure. This makes sense as the member has to ask himself whether he should still belong to a party whose main views he does not share anymore. It is noteworthy that in cases of sensitive personal decisions political parties often do not exert such pressure as has happened in decisions on regulating abortions. In any case a member will not lose his seat in the *Bundestag* even if being excluded from the *Fraktion* and party.[117]

---

[116] Or harmonized, see above, sec. 2.2.
[117] See also Degenhart, above, n 32, pp. 179–180.

BVerfGE 80, 188 Wueppesahl

In this case Wueppesahl, a member of the *Bundestag* and the Green Party (*Die Gruenen*) was excluded from his *Fraktion* after several disputes. He was also withdrawn from the committee of home affairs. The questions arising now were whether he could still claim a seat in a committee and had a right to speeches in plenary sessions. The BVerfG held that Article 38 I 2 GG granted a right to speeches in plenary sessions as a fundamental right of the member of the *Bundestag*. The length of speech must also be adaquate to represent his views because a mere mathematical allocation based on the numbers of members of the Bundestag (= 1 minute) would be ridiculous and a member without *Fraktion* (*fraktionsloser Abgeordneter*) does not have the possibilities to pool resources with his colleagues. Furthermore, Article 38 I 2 GG was held to grant a claim to a committee seat as the main parliamentary work was done there. However, it did not provide a claim choose a committee or vote within the committee as this would amount to an unproportional representation of his views.

4.1.4 *Tasks*

The main tasks of the *Bundestag* are to take the major part in law making (Arts 76–78 GG) and elect the Federal Chancellor (Art. 63 GG). The *Bundestag* also participates in electing the *Bundespräsident* and half of the judges of the BVerfG.[118] Further tasks of the *Bundestag* are the political control of the federal government, the representation and articulation of public feeling, and the explanation and dissipation of information to help build political awareness and consensus in society, i.e. an informative function.

Various rights can be exercised to control the government including the right of deputies to ask questions and obtain information and the right to set up a Committee of Investigation (*Untersuchungsausschuss*) at the request of at least 25% of members of the *Bundestag*. Although it may use the means provided in the Criminal Procedural Code, it does not give judgment on the investigated matter. Rather, it has to investigate the facts of alleged misuse of power (fact-finding committee) and deliver a report at the conclusion of its investigation. This is used mainly for publicity purposes. But as the number of investigation committees rise, and their work becomes more complicated and slow public interest diminishes thus rendering their effectiveness questionable.[119]

Deputies have the right under Article 93 I 1 *Grundgesetz* to approach the Federal Constitutional Court (*Bundesverfassungsgericht*) to adjudicate on disputes between the *Fraktionen* or between the *Fraktionen* of deputies and the government. The *Bundestag* committees have the right to call and question government ministers under Article 43 I *Grundgesetz* and the right to receive and deal with petitions sent in under Article 17 *Grundgesetz* (Art. 45c I GG).

---

[118] These subjects will be dealt with in the following sections.
[119] For detailed description of investigation committees see Maurer, above, n 1, pp. 451–463.

4.2 Federal government (*Bundesregierung*, Arts 62–69 GG)

The federal government consists of the federal Chancellor (*Bundeskanzler*) and the federal Ministers (*Bundesminister*, Art. 62 GG) and is usually supported by the members of the party, or parties, making up the government. The government is formally the head of the executive (see Arts 62–69 *Grundgesetz*).

4.2.1 Composition

Like in other systems of parliamentary government in Germany the Chancellor is elected by Parliament or rather the *Bundestag* (Art. 63 GG). Thus the election of the *Bundestag* indirectly determines the Chancellor. The usual process is the following: The Federal President will propose a candidate (usually the candidate of the strongest party) for election (Art. 63 I GG). If he receives the votes of the majority of the members of the *Bundestag* the President "shall" (= must) appoint him (Art. 63 II GG).

If, however, due to lack of a clear majority of one party the candidate is not elected Article 63 GG provides for two exceptional remedies: Article 63 III GG entitles the *Bundestag* to elect a Chancellor within the following fourteen days. Here the candidate has to be proposed by a quarter of the members of the *Bundestag*. If after this period no Chancellor has been elected the last remedy in Article 63 IV GG allows an election by the largest number of votes. In other words, in this case a Chancellor can be elected with relative majority supported only by a minority of the *Bundestag*. However, in this case the Federal President still has a right to decide whether to appoint this candidate or dissolve the *Bundestag* and call for new elections (Art. 63 IV 3 GG). Still these are only constitutional safeguards. So far the election procedures have been straight forward (Art. 63 I GG) based on solid majorities within the *Bundestag*.

Federal Ministers are appointed by the Federal President on proposal of the Chancellor (Art. 64 I GG). They can be members of the *Bundestag* but this is not a condition. Apart from that, neither Chancellor nor ministers are allowed to hold any other salaried offices (*Inkompatibilität*, Art. 66 GG). Due to the wording of Art. 64 I GG there has been debate as to whether the Federal President has a right to reject appointment of a candidate proposed by the Chancellor. Whereas in Article 63 II GG he "shall" appoint the Chancellor Article 64 I GG literally states that he "will" appoint the ministers.[120] This question has not been decided by the BVerfG as disagreements about ministers have always been solved at the political level.[121] The general opinion, however, is that the President has no discretion to reject a candidate proposed by the Chancellor as the latter must be able to put together a cabinet that will support his policies.[122] Furthermore, this interpretation corresponds with

---

[120] Here the necessity to look at the original language becomes apparent: contrast Art. 63 II GG:" . . . *ist* zu ernennen . . . " with Art. 64 I GG: " . . . *werden* . . . ernannt . . . ".

[121] E.g. in 1965 when President Luebke initially had doubts about appointing Gerhard Schroeder (**not to be confused with the Chancellor of 1998!**) as Minister for Foreign Affairs which he thought to be detrimental for the Franco-German relations.

[122] See Oldiges in: Sachs, above, n 5, Art. 64, paras. 15–16 with further reference.

the "neutral role" of the President.[123] He may only reject a candidate in cases of formal mistakes or evidence of the candidate endangering the constitutional order.

In the history of Germany since 1949, all governments have been the result of a coalition of parties. Coalition agreements are usually made between the strongest party in the *Bundestag* and a smaller one in order to obtain an absolute majority before the election of the Chancellor. Usually, a candidate of the smaller party will then be offered the post of Deputy Chancellor. Coalition agreements also set out agreements on the main politics to be implemented in the near future. Thus the parties are forced to come to compromises in several areas. It has to be pointed out though that they are informal political agreements that cannot be enforced in courts.[124] This political nature implies that a breakdown of the coalition cannot be judged upon by, say, the BVerfG but solely by voters in coming elections.

4.2.2 Removal of the government and Chancellor

Normally the tenure of office of the Chancellor and the ministers ends as soon as a new *Bundestag* convenes (Art. 69 II GG) thus linking the duration of government to each parliamentary period (usually four years). In exceptional cases, however, the Chancellor can be removed earlier.

The members of the *Bundestag* have the right, under Article 67 I GG, to demand a constructive vote of no confidence (*konstruktives Misstrauensvotum*) in the Chancellor and consequently the government. It is constructive because at the same time a successor must be named. This was deliberately included to avoid the situation in the Weimar Republic when Chancellors were voted out on the basis of objections to a particular policy without any constructive alternative or an alternative successor for the Chancellorship being suggested and which often led to the collapse of government and dissolution of Parliament (the *Reichstag*). Since 1949 this vote has only been instigated on two occasions and only once successfully, when in September 1982, Helmut Kohl was elected as Chancellor following the constructive dismissal of Chancellor Schmidt. In 1972 a similar attempt was made to replace Chancellor Brandt because of disagreement with his *"Ostpolitik"*—a new policy of approach towards Eastern European countries. It narrowly failed by two votes.

In the alternative, Article 68 I GG, allows the Chancellor to call for a vote of confidence in order to demonstrate the ability to continue governing with authority. If the Chancellor does not gain sufficient support Parliament may be dissolved by the President following a proposal from the Chancellor. This right elapses if the *Bundestag* elects another Chancellor within twenty-one days of the proposal. This was employed by Willy Brandt after the unsuccessful attempt to oust him in 1972. He used Article 68 GG with the intention of losing and was thus effectively able to resign to call new elections. The President had little choice but to call for an early election which Brandt went on to win. Helmut Schmidt successfully obtained a

---

[123] See below next section.
[124] For arguments against the perception of coalition agreements as contracts of private or public law see Maurer, above, n 1, pp. 474–479.

vote of confidence in February 1982 but he was ousted in September 1982 as mentioned. The use of Article 68 IGG has been subject of a constitutional law dispute:

BVerfGE 62,1 Bundestagsaufloesung

After the constructive vote of confidence establishing Helmut Kohl as chancellor in September 1982 the *Bundestag* was dissolved by President Carstens in December 1982 following Kohl's proposal. Just as Brandt in 1972 Kohl also used the provisions of Article 68 I GG in the likelihood of losing the vote in order to be able to ask for a dissolution of the *Bundestag*. This led to new elections by which he could seek to gain a greater majority. The dissolution was challenged as an unconstitutional use of Article 68 I GG before the BVerfG arguing that Chancellor Kohl had already had the necessary support of the *Bundestag* before the vote of confidence. The vote failed because several members of his party abstained from voting in order to enable dissolution of the *Bundestag*. The BVerfG, however, upheld the dissolution. Article 68 I GG is applicable in all cases of political instability. Whether there was a real case of political instability or whether it was probable to occur in future was held to be decided by the Chancellor. However, the BVerfG commented that the provision should not be used as a threat and should only be employed as a response to a genuine crises in government. Chancellor Kohl was re-elected in the subsequent elections with an increased majority for the coalition.

A federal Minister's tenure of office is dependant on the Chancellor. According to Article 69 II GG it ends as soon as the Chancellor ceases to hold office. Furthermore, the Chancellor can at any time propose the removal of a minister to the President (Art. 64 I GG).

4.2.3 *Tasks and internal organization*

The federal government's main task can be described as political leadership. It includes determining guidelines of policy, initiating legislation, and supervising the implementation of laws by the administration. Organization and distribution of tasks **within** the government are determined by the the the principles *Kanzlerprinzip*, *Ressortprinzip*, and *Kollegialprinzip*.

The term *Kanzlerprinzip* underlines the Chancellor's dominating role in determining the general guidelines of policy (Art. 65 S.1 GG) which must be followed by his ministers.[125] Thus the Chancellor is in a very strong political position in Germany and the phrase "Chancellor democracy" is often used in this context. It goes beyond Bagehot's classical description of the UK Prime Minister as being *primus inter pares*.

Although the Chancellor can in this way order or instruct the ministers they still conduct the affairs of their department on their own responsibility (= *Ressortprinzip*). An example of express competences allocated to a minister is Article

---

[125] Also described as "*Richtlinienkompetenz*".

112 GG requiring approval of the Federal Minister of Finance for expenditures in excess of budgetary appropriations.

According to the *Kollegialprinzip* the federal government has to decide collectively, i.e. in cabinet (*Bundeskabinett*) in cases of disputes (Art. 65 S.3 GG) and whenever the Grundgesetz refers to the federal government (e.g. Art. 35 III GG). Decisions are made according to standing orders of the federal government (§ 24 *Geschäftsordnung der Bundesregierung*) on a majority basis. The Chancellor's vote will decide in cases of a draw.

4.3 The Federal President (*Bundespräsident*, Arts 54–61 GG)

The Federal President is the formal Head of State. Formally, the role is politically neutral and the most prominent function is the representation of the German state in the international community.

The office has no significant political power now apart from the so-called "reserve function" discussed below. The powers of the President were deliberately diminished as a result of the experiences of the President in the Weimar Republic who enjoyed an immensely greater political authority due in large part to the direct election by the people (Art. 41 WRV[126]). He had a wide discretion to appoint and dismiss the chancellor (Art. 53 WRV), he could dissolve Parliament (the *Reichstag*), if he thought it necessary (Art. 25 WRV), he had command of the armed forces (Art. 47 WRV) and—the most notorious and important example of his powerful position—he had emergency legislative powers (Art. 48 II WRV). From 1930 on *Reichspräsident* Hindenburg in cooperation with his Chancellor(s) practically ruled on this basis without Parliament. When Hitler became Chancellor he used the President and his emergency powers in order to increase his power and finally destroy the democratic system of the Weimar Republic.[127] The Federal President's political powers by comparison are marginal nowadays, as will be seen.

4.3.1 *Election*

Article 54 I GG provides for the indirect election of the President without debate by an *ad hoc* Federal Convention (*Bundesversammlung*). It consists of the members of the *Bundestag* and an equal number of delegates nominated by the *Länder* parliamentary assemblies (*Landtage*, Art 54 II GG). These delegates need not be members of the *Landtage* but they can. The President's term of office is for five years and re-election for a consecutive term is only allowed once (Art. 54 II 2 GG). This wording suggests that a third presidency of the same person is possible but not in a consecutive term.

4.3.2 *The role of the Federal President*

As Head of State the President is mainly a representative figure. Although this implies only few political powers it is nevertheless a demanding role. The President

---

[126] *Weimarer Reichsverfassung* (= constitution of the Weimar Republic).
[127] See Chapter 1.

represents the state as well as its people including all elements of society. Thus in his acts he has to remain politically neutral but socially integrating. The latter means that he has to remind society of its fundamental values shared by most (ideally all) members of society. It follows that—amongst his tasks—he has to protect the constitutional values as is underlined by his oath of office (Art. 56 GG).

Article 55 GG indicates the activities held to incompatible with the office of President such as membership of the government or of the federal or *Länder* legislatures (Art. 55 I GG) or undertaking a salaried office, a business or the practice of a profession and belonging to the management or supervisory board or the of a business concern.

Although he is supposed to remain politically neutral this does not prevent him from being member to a political party like all presidents of the Federal Republic of Germany have been. Johannes Rau, the current President,[128] for example, is a member of the SPD. However, he may neither hold any party office[129] nor shall he take sides within political disputes. This can lead to complications, for example if he delivers a speech criticizing certain politics of the federal government. The general opinion believes that in these cases Article 58 GG is applicable.[130] It requires a countersignature of the Federal Chancellor or the competent federal minister for any order or directions of the Federal President. Even those academics that argue speeches and other non-legal acts are not covered by the terms "orders and directions" agree that the President is bound to coordinate his actions with the government because of the principle of loyalty between constitutional organs *(Verfassungsorgantreue)*.[131] President Weizsaecker's criticism of the German parties' "hunger for power" in a speech in June 1992 cannot be viewed as a violation of his neutrality as he warned of a danger to the common good emanating from *all* parties.[132]

In the event of death or illness or other incapacity the President of the *Bundesrat* stands in as President of the Federal Republic (Art. 57 GG).

4.3.3 Duties of office

The President's duties as a representative of state include representation on an international level, the conclusion of treaties with foreign states, and accrediting and receiving envoys (Art. 59 I GG).

Under Article 60 I GG the President formally appoints federal judges, civil servants and officers of the armed forces. He also exercises the right to pardon individual offenders on behalf of the federation (Art. 60 II GG). All of these acts require the counter signature of the Chancellor (Art. 58 GG).

The President possesses the formal right of nomination of the *Bundeskanzler* for the first vote of the *Bundestag* on the matter (Art. 64 I GG). In the event that a

---

[128] Elected for the period 1999–2004.
[129] Nierhaus in: Sachs, above, n 5, Art. 54, para. 9.
[130] See Degenhart, above, n 32, p. 206 with further references.
[131] Nierhaus in: Sachs, above, n 4, Art. 58, para. 19.
[132] See Degenhart, above, n 32, pp. 211–212.

candidate does not receive an absolute majority and the *Bundestag* then fails to elect a candidate, Article 63 (4) brings into play the "reserve function" whereby the President must decide according to his own political judgement whether to appoint the minority candidate or order a dissolution of Parliament. This is one of the few discretionary powers of the President allowing him to choose a way out of a parliamentary crisis. Unlike the Weimar system, however, he can only clear the way for other constitutional organs and not assume power himself.

There has been considerable dispute as to the President's powers in the legislative process. According to Article 82 I GG he gives formal assent to the laws enacted in the accordance with the provisions of the *Grundgesetz*. This wording has given rise to the question whether Article 82 I GG provides the President with a right to review the law as to its constitutionality. As Article 82 I GG mentions laws enacted in accordance with the provisions of the *Grundgesetz* it has been generally accepted that this allows a review on procedural grounds. Thus the President can check on formalities, i.e. the legislative competence of the federation or whether the *Bundesrat* has been included in the procedure *(formelles Prüfungsrecht)*.[133] Whether he may check on the law's compatibility with more substantial constitutional provisions, say basic rights, is a different question *(materielles Prüfungsrecht)*. Academics have tried to extract such a right from different provisions of the *Grundgesetz* such as the oath of office (Art. 58 GG). An important counter argument is that a constitutional review is the monopoly of the BVerfG. Bearing the few practical cases of the President's review in mind there now seems to be an acceptance that as one of the organs bound by the constitution (Art. 20 III GG) the President cannot be asked to give his formal assent to laws that—at least evidently—violate the constitution.[134] So far the BVerfG has not had to decide on the problem. Nevertheless there have been cases in which the President has exerted the right to refuse his formal assent.

Example: Fluglotsensicherung; One of the most recent noteworthy examples is President Weizsaecker's refusal to certify the federal law on privatization of air traffic control in January 1991. As the previous Article 87c I GG stated that "Air transport adminstration shall be conducted by the federal authorities" privatization was clearly not covered by the provision. After having communicated his reservations to the *Bundestag* a conflict could be prevented by changing the constitution as the necessary majority (across most parties) existed. A second sentence has been added to the previous Article 87c I GG leaving the decision of a private or public law organization of air traffic administration to implementation by federal law.

---

[133] Maunz: Maunz and Dürig, above, n 5, Art. 82, para. 2; Ipsen, above, n 8, p. 123 with further references.
[134] For discussions on this problem see Degenhart, above, n 32, pp. 208–209; Maurer, above, n 1, pp. 573–579; Ipsen, above, n 8, pp. 123–124.

4.3.4 *Actions against the President*

Under Article 61 I GG, the President can be subjected to a form of impeachment *(Präsidentenanklage)* if he has intentionally breached either the *Grundgesetz* or a federal statute. However, for this a majority of two-thirds in either the *Bundestag* or the *Bundesrat* is required. If a breach has been found by the BVerfG then it may declare that the President has forfeited his office.

4.4 The Federal Council (*Bundesrat*, Arts 50–53 GG)

4.4.1 *Nature*

The *Bundesrat* like its predecessors, the *Reichsrat* (1919–1934) and the *Bundesrat* of 1871–1919, represents interests of the *Länder* on a federal level. There is academic dispute whether it can be described as a second chamber.[135] This obviously depends on the definition of a "second chamber". The term usually implies a strong participation in the legislative process including the ability to scrutinize and block acts of the main legislative body, the "first chamber". Furthermore, a "second chamber" consists of representatives either of a certain class (e.g. the House of Lords) or in federal states of different regions (e.g. the US Senate).[136] As the *Bundesrat* does not have a strong participation in all areas, as will be seen, and as its members are not directly elected but are representatives of the governments of the *Länder* with strict directions as to voting, it should not be labeled a "second chamber".[137] Rather, the *Bundesrat* must be seen as a special constitutional organ to counterbalance centralist tendencies within the *Bundestag* and the *Bundesregierung*.

4.4.2 *Composition and procedure*

Article 51 I GG states that the *Bundesrat* consists of members of the governments of the *Länder*. According to their population the *Länder* have between three to six votes (Art. 51 II GG).[138] They may appoint as many members to the *Bundesrat* as they have votes. As a result the *Bundesrat* consists of sixty-nine members. The majority required for any decision is thirty-five votes. The members nominated by the governments of the *Länder* are usually members of the these government (i.e. ministers) but can also be represented by ministerial civil servants. They must vote on a block basis as required by the government of the *Land* from which they come (Art. 51 III GG).

Similar to the *Bundestag*, the *Bundesrat* has committees dealing with specific areas of legislation. Thus members of the *Bundesrat* will participate according to their expertise (e.g. the ministers of the *Länder* for home affairs will sit on the committee of home affairs). The committees merely prepare the decisions of the *Bundesrat*.

---

[135] In favour, e.g. C. Creifelds, *Rechtswoerterbuch* 15th ed. (1999: C. H. Beck, München), p. 1485.

[136] H. Barnett, *Constitutional and Administrative Law* 3rd ed. (2000: Cavendish, London), p. 633; R. Zippelius, *Allgemeine Staatslehre* 13th ed. (1999: C. H. Beck, München), p. 102.

[137] Degenhart, above, n 32, p. 186; Maurer, above, n 1, p. 531; Zippelius, above, n 136. BVerfGE 37, 363 takes the same view due to the *Bundesrat's* weak participation in the legislative process.

[138] e.g. Bremen: three votes; Bavaria: six votes.

However, decisions of the *Bundesrat's Europakammer* (Chamber for European affairs) have the same effect as the *Bundesrat's* decision (Art. 53 III a GG). This particular committttee was established following the introduction of a new Article 23 GG. As the *Länder* are guaranteed participation both nationally and at the European level in EU matters they needed an organ that could react quickly in urgent legislative matters concerning the EU.

According to Article 52 I GG the *Bundesrat* will elect its President for one year. Following an informal agreement of the *Länder* of 1950 *(Königssteiner Abkommen)* the head of governments of the *Länder* will take the presidency in turns following the size of their population. The President calls for and presides over plenary sessions of the *Bundesrat*. He also serves to stand in for the Federal President (Art. 57 GG).

Naturally, membership in the *Bundesrat* will depend on elections within the individual *Länder*. Thus party representation within the *Bundesrat* might be different than that in the *Bundestag*. Quite often the party in power in the *Bundestag* is in a minority in the *Bundesrat*.[139] Here the idea of vertical seperation of powers becomes apparent again. However, this does not necessarily mean that within the *Bundesrat* decisions are made according to the (federal) party line. Often the members of the *Bundesrat* rather try to protect *Länder* interests against the federation and here may find themselves in coalition with members from different parties.

4.4.3 *Tasks*

The *Länder* shall participate through the *Bundesrat* in legislation and administration of the federation according to Article 50 GG. After 1992 participation in European Union affairs was added.[140]

Within the legislative process the *Bundestag* has the right to initiate legislation (Art. 76 I GG) and to decide on it (Art. 77 II–III GG). This right is manifested in two types of co-decision depending on the type of statute: *Zustimmungsgesetze* (statutes requiring consent) demand an approval of the *Bundesrat* to become effective. *Einspruchsgesetze* (statutes subject to objection), on the other hand, only allow the *Bundesrat* to object to legislation within a certain time period. This objection can be overruled by the *Bundestag*. The *Grundgesetz* mentions expressly which sort of statutes are *Zustimmungsgesetze*, i.e. require approval. They cover areas that are of particular interest to the *Länder*. All other legislation can only be vetoed by the *Bundesrat*. Thus the *Grundgesetz* only allows strong participation of the *Bundesrat* as an exception to the rule of the *Bundestag* being the dominating legislative body.[141]

The *Bundesrat* also participates in issuing general administrative rules (Article 84 I GG). As it is the *Länder* administrations who are required to implement legislation, and they are better able to decide what is practically necessary, this has the result

---

[139] From 1991–98 the coalition of CDU/CSU and FDP had a majority in the *Bundestag* while the majority of the *Länder* were ruled by the SPD; hence an SPD-majority in the *Bundesrat*.
[140] See also above, sec. 3.5.4.
[141] See also BVerfGE 37, 363.

that the administration of government is exercised on a regional and thus more local basis.

Further powers of the *Bundesrat* can be found in Article 115a ff GG dealing with states of emergency but these cannot be covered here. In these cases another constitutional organ which can become important is the Joint Committee (*Gemeinsamer Ausschuss*, Art. 53 a GG). It consists of representatives of *Bundesrat* and *Bundestag* and can assume legislative powers in these cases but only subject to the conditions outlined in Article 115a GG.

The *Bundesrat* also participates in electing the judges to the Federal Constitutional Court (Art. 94 I GG).

4.5 Functions of the state

The basic functions of the state—relating to the classical three powers—are outlined in the *Grundgesetz*: legislation, administration, and the judiciary (Art. 70–104 GG).

4.5.1 *Legislation (Arts. 70–82 GG)*

The areas and the procedure of federal legislation are mapped out in Article 70–82 GG. It has already been pointed out that as a rule legislation is a matter for the *Länder* unless stated otherwise in the *Grundgesetz* (Art. 70 GG). We have also seen that the most significant part of legislation, however, has been taken over by the federation (Arts. 72–75 GG). Thus if a federal law is challenged on the grounds of "formal" irregularities the first aspect to look at is whether the federation had a mandate to pass legislation in the particular area under Article 73–75 GG. If the particular subject is not listed there then it falls into the *Länder's* scope of legislation. Consequently, such a federal law would be unconstitutional.[142]

The **legislative procedure** (for federal laws!) is described in Articles 76–82 GG. The formal parliamentary procedure is merely the tip of the iceberg, in that in order to reach this stage a considerable political process will have largely decided the eventual state of the legislation.

According to Article 77 (1) GG all federal statutes must be decided on by the *Bundestag*. All bills *(Gesetzentwürfe)* are introduced here (Art. 76 I GG) either by

(a) the *Bundesrat*, with the support of an absolute majority of the delegates,

(b) at least 5% of the members of the *Bundestag*[143], which constitutes the minimum requirement for a parliamentary faction, or

(c) the *federal government*.

It is the latter which introduces significantly the most bills to Parliament and succeeds in getting an even greater percentage enacted.[144]

---

[142] See above, sec. 3.5.3.

[143] This quorum is set out in §§ 75, 76 GeschOBT.

[144] Between 1949 and 1999 the government has introduced 4,912 bills. 4,181 have been successful. Contrast this with 2,954 bills of the *Bundestag* (adopted: 1,018) and 793 of the *Bundesrat* (adopted: 196); taken from Ipsen, above, n 8, p.63.

A governmental bill—after discussion within the government itself[145]—must first be referred to the *Bundesrat* for its opinion. This is the first opportunity for the *Bundesrat* to comment on the proposal and is in effect a continuation of the political process rather than strictly legislative (*"politischer"* or *"erster Durchgang"*). Whether an opinion is expressed by the *Bundesrat* or not, the proposal must be returned to the *Bundestag* after six weeks (Art. 77 II GG).

The parliamentary legislative process consists formally of three readings (*Lesungen*). The first reading is a plenary session of the *Bundestag* where in exceptional cases the bill is discussed but usually it is just formally introduced and then referred immediately to a standing committee. The bill's second reading takes place in plenary session for detailed discussion and adoption or otherwise of the positions decided on by the committee. The third and final reading concludes with a vote on the bill as a whole.[146]

After the final vote on the bill, which is now referred to as *Gesetzesbeschluß*, the legislative process shifts to the *Bundesrat* for the constitutionally required discussion. The procedure following now depends on whether the bill requires express approval (*Zustimmungsgesetz*) or only allows a right to objection (*Einspruchsgesetz*).[147]

Where an express approval of the *Bundesrat* is not necessary (*Einspruchsgesetz*), the following procedure applies: The *Bundesrat* agrees with the bill expressly or simply by not reacting within three weeks. It then becomes a valid law under Article 78 GG and only has to be certified by the President. If the *Bundesrat* disagrees it has the right to call the Mediations Committee (*Vermittlungsausschuß*). This committee, consisting of sixteen members from each of the two houses, representing party strength in the *Bundestag* and one permanent member for each *Land* in the *Bundesrat*, has the task of reaching a compromise solution where there is a difference of opinion and can usually facilitate an agreement. After the decision of the committee the bill is returned to the *Bundestag* to approve or reject the decision. In cases of rejection the *Bundesrat* can now raise a formal objection (*Einspruch*) but must do so within two weeks according (Art. 77 III GG). This objection can subsequently be overturned the *Bundestag* in the following way: If the *Bundesrat's* objection was based on a majority then a majority in the *Bundestag* is required. Likewise a qualified majority objection can only be overturned by a qualified majority in the *Bundestag*. Only if the *Bundestag* manages to overrule the objection the bill will be passed (Art. 78 GG).

Where *Zustimmungsgesetze* are concerned the *Bundesrat's* position is stronger. Here an express approval of the *Bunderat* is needed as the law will affect the interests of the *Länder*. If the *Bundesrat* consents to the bill it will be passed according to

---

[145] Most Government bills arise from the federal ministries which can present discussion bills (*Diskussionsentwürfe*) or ministerial bills (*Referentenentwürfe*) for the consideration of the *Bundesregierung*. The pre-parliamentary process consists of three broad stages in which the legislative proposal (*Referentenentwurf*) is prepared in the appropriate ministry or ministries, it is presented to the cabinet for consideration and if approved is formally adopted as a government bill (*Regierungsvorlage*).

[146] Refer generally to Arts 76–77 GG for details.

[147] See above, sec. 4.4.3.

Article 78 GG. If it disagrees, then either the *Bundesrat, Bundestag,* or the government may call upon the mediations committee to find a compromise (Art. 77 II 4 GG) which will be voted upon afterwards. It is parliamentary practice, where the decision in the committee was an agreed compromise, for the *Bundestag* and *Bundesrat* to vote in agreement. If an approval of the *Bundesrat* cannot be obtained the bill will fail.

Any bill passed according to the two mentioned procedures then requires the formal confirmation by signature of the Federal President that the bill has been correctly passed by Parliament and conforms with the *Grundgesetz*, known as the *Ausfertigung*. This process is not automatic and bills have been rejected on occasion, therefore political responsibility for bills is also required and is achieved by the counter signature of the Federal Chancellor and the relevant federal minister (Art. 82 I GG).[148] The President then transmits the approved law to the Federal Minister of Justice for promulgation (*Verkündung*) which consists of the printing and publication in the Federal Law Gazette (*Bundesgesetzblatt*). It becomes law on the fourteenth day thereafter if no date is specified in the Act (Art. 82 II GG).

Finally, **delegated legislation** has to be looked at. It is clearly defined by the constitution in Article 80 *Grundgesetz* which provides that law making powers can be transferred by *Gesetz*—meaning an Act of Parliament—to other bodies. The bodies to whom power is delegated are the Government, the various ministers and the governments of the *Länder*. The delegated legislation issued from these bodies may be called *Verordnungen* or *Rechtsverordnungen* (Regulations). The delegating *Gesetz* must state the content, objectives and scope of the delegated matter, e.g. rules relating to the conduct of road traffic are dealt with by *Straßenverkehrsordnung* (Road Traffic Regulations) which obtain their authority from the Road Traffic Act (*Straßenverkehrsgesetz*). Furthermore, the regulation must state its legal basis. These safeguards are a reaction to the wide discretion the President of the Weimar Republic had in enacting regulations without Parliament. The principle of democracy and the *Rechtsstaatsprinzip* require that essential matters cannot be regulated by delegated legislation but have to be dealt with by Parliament itself (*Parlamentsvorbehalt*).[149] The process of delegation is subject to the review of the administrative courts and finally the BVerfG.

Federal laws amending the constitution will be considered in the next chapter of this book.

4.5.2 *Administration (Arts 83–91 GG)*

The Administration of the state is largely a matter for the *Länder*. Laws of the *Länder* are obviously executed by their own authorities. But even when executing federal laws the *Länder* play the dominant role. There are, however, three different types of administration depending on the degree of the federation's involvement.

As a rule federal laws are executed by the *Länder* in their own right unless the

---

148 See above, sec. 4.3.3.
149 See above, secs. 3.2.1 and 3.3.3.

Grundgesetz permits otherwise (Art. 83 GG). This provision again reflects the main idea of the *Grundgesetz* that state power as a rule is exercised by the *Länder* (Art. 30 GG). This rule of executing federal laws in their own right (*Landeseigener Vollzug von Bundesgesetzen als eigene Angelegenheit*), mapped out in Article 84 GG, means that generally the *Länder* are responsible for the establishment of the authorities and their administrative procedure. It follows that the civil servants in these authorities are those of the *Länder* not of the federation. Furthermore, the federal government can only exercise oversight to ensure that the execution of federal laws are in accordance with the law (*Rechtsaufsicht*, Art. 84 III 1 GG). It does not have any powers to supervise the *Länder* as to usefulness or effectiveness of their decisions (which would be called *Fachaufsicht*). Thus the federal government cannot issue any directions or orders as to the "how" of executing the laws.

An exception is the execution of federal laws by the *Länder* on federal commission (*Bundesauftragsverwaltung*, Art. 85 GG). Although again authorities of the *Länder* are acting here, in these cases the competent federal minister can issue instructions as to how a law is implemented (*Fachaufsicht*, Art. 85 III 1 GG).

Finally, there are few areas where the *Grundgesetz* delegates administration to the federation (*Bundeseigene Verwaltung*, Arts 86, 87, 87a, 87b GG), e.g. for the federal border police authorities (*Bundesgrenzschutz*), armed forces (*Bundeswehr*), and federal office of crime investigation (*Bundeskriminalamt*). Often this includes not a hierarchical chain of authorities but rather a single authority that is subject to the competent ministry like in the case of the *Bundeskriminalamt*. In any case there must be a ministry responsible for each of the authorities and thus entitled to supervise them. The only exception is the Federal Bank (*Bundesbank*, Art. 88 GG) whose independence restricts the government's influence on currency policies.

4.5.3 Judiciary (Rechtsprechung, Arts 92–104 GG)

The *Grundgesetz* vests "judicial powers in the Judges" under Article 92 GG. Unlike in the two previous areas it does not set out the competences of *Länder* and federation. Mentioning the judges in the beginning puts particular emphasis on their independence and responsibility to uphold the law. This again must be viewed against the historical background of the Nazi dictatorship. Bearing in mind the atrocities of the Third Reich the authors of the *Grundgesetz* wanted to create a "*Rechtsstaat*" with an effective system of judicial remedies (including judicial review of state actions). Thus this part of the *Grundgesetz* is less concerned with a distribution of powers between federation and *Länder* but rather the independence of the judiciary (Art. 97 GG), substantial procedural rights of the citizen (Arts 101–104 GG),[150] and the establishment of a Federal Constitutional Court, the *Bundesverfassunggericht* (Arts 93, 94, 99, 100 GG).[151]

However, Article 92 mentions Federal Courts and Courts of the *Länder*. As a rule

---

[150] See below, chapter 7, sec. 2.
[151] Dealt with in chapter 7, sec. 2.

the courts are courts of the *Länder*. As an exception there are only five supreme federal courts (Art. 95 GG) and the Federal Constitutional Court.[152]

5 Protection of the constitution[153]

The collapse of the Weimar Republic and its constitution as well as the ease with which the Nazis rose to power and undermined all human values served the authors of the *Grundgesetz* as a warning in many ways. One of the most important consequences was the decision to establish a constitution capable of defending itself against inhumane and undemocratic tendencies. Unlike the Weimar constitution the *Grundgesetz* is not "politically neutral". It does not allow any alteration of the system solely on the basis that it is democratically legitimized. It rather determines a "free democratic order" as a fixed basis from which state and society must operate. Thus a fundamental change or even an abolition of the system from within the system—unlike in the Weimar Republic—is impossible or rather constitutionally prohibited. It remains of course factually (i.e. through revolution) possible—as in all systems. Furthermore, unconstitutional tendencies of individuals and associations will be monitored and fought once they become a threat to the system. This of course leaves the state with the difficult task to assess which political tendencies are still tolerable within a pluralistic society and where to draw the line. Obviously the stronger the population's support is for a system the more generous it can be towards opposing views.

5.1 Amendments of the constitution

Every constitution must show a certain degree of flexibility in order to adapt to social changes if a common conviction desires this. The German *Grundgesetz* allows this, albeit subject to certain conditions and within clear limits.

The *Grundgesetz* can be amended only by a law expressly amending or supplementing its text according to Article 79 I 1 GG. This precludes derogation from constitutional provisions through parliamentary decisions for individual cases. Any amendment must be general and identifiable. Furthermore, Article 79 II GG demands a two thirds majority within *Bundestag* and *Bundesrat* for such a law. Thus there has to be a broad consensus—usually enveloping both big parties—for the amendment.

However, Article 79 III GG has excluded fundamental constitutional principles from alteration: the five principles of Article 20 GG, the division of the federation into *Länder*, and the concept of human dignity in Article 1 GG must not be affected by any amendment. This has sometimes been described as "eternity clause" or "eternal guarantee". It has to be noted, however, that this guarantee will only

---

[152] For details on the court system see Chapter 3.
[153] For a more detailed examination of this topic see Ipsen, above, n 8, pp. 265–282 and Maurer, above, n 1, pp. 760–795.

protect the principles from changes within the system. Any abolition from the outside (e.g. a revolution) would render it useless. Article 20 IV GG though entitles every German to resist any person seeking to overthrow the constitutional order if no other remedy is available. Thus it creates a constitutional, basic right to resistance (*Widerstandsrecht*).

The *Grundgesetz* provides for one possibility to replace the constitution altogether in Article 146 GG. According to this provision the *Grundgesetz* "shall cease to apply on the day on which a constitution freely adopted by the German people takes effect". Historical background has already been discussed.[154] A replacement of the *Grundgesetz* seems improbable in the near future.

5.2 Defending the free democratic basic order

As the *Grundgesetz* is not politically neutral but has put certain values at its apex, namely the protection of human dignity (Art. 1 I GG) and the principles of Article 20 GG, it should not come as a surprise that it offers instruments to fight individuals and associations that strive to abolish these values. The key term in this context is the "free democratic basic order" (*Freiheitlich demokratische Grundordnung*). An aggressive attitude towards it will not be tolerated as has been emphasized by the BVerfG. A definition of the free democratic basic order was given in the *Socialist Reichsparty* decision in 1952:

BVerfG 2, 1 SRP-Urteil

In 1950 the SRP (= *Sozialistische Reichspartei*) a successor of the NSDAP gained political attention on a federal and a *Länder* level. After an anti-Israeli speech of one of its members in the *Bundestag*—who turned out to be a former Nazi functionary—the young German democracy was eager to show its renunciation from Nazism. The federal government applied for a party ban (Art. 21 II GG) in 1951 before the BVerfG. In order to find out whether the *SRP* endangered a "free democratic (thus constitutional) basic order" the court had to define this term. It held that such an order excluded violence and arbitrariness but manifested itself in a government based on self-determination of the people according to current majorities as well as freedom and equality. Its fundamental principles were held to be a respect for human rights as specified in the *Grundgesetz*, above all a right to life and self-determination, the sovereignty of the people, separation of powers, accountability of government, legality of administration, independence of the courts, the multi-party system, equal opportunities of all political parties, and their constitutional right to opposition.

The *SRP* was held to negate most of these principles and especially human rights and a democratic multiparty system. Its similarity to the NSDAP was difficult to overlook. Thus it was banned.

---

[154] See above, sec. 1.2.

5.2.1 Banning political parties (Parteienverbot)

Article 21 II GG claims that parties that seek to undermine or abolish the free democratic order or to endanger the existence of the Federal Republic of Germany shall be unconstitutional. As a consequence they will be banned (§ 46 III BVerfGG). As only the BVerfG is allowed to decide on a party's unconstitutionality and its ban Article 21 II GG has been called the "party privilege" (Parteienprivileg). It follows that no state authority is allowed to treat the party as unconstitutional as long as it has not been declared so by the BVerfG. Only two party bans have been enacted so far: the above-mentioned ban of the SRP and the ban of the KPD (Kommunistische Partei Deutschlands) in 1956.

BVerfGE 5, 85 KPD

Only a few days after the application for a ban of the SRP in 1951 the federal government applied for a second ban, this time of the communist party KPD. It obviously wanted to demonstrate a consistent line against unconstitutional parties from both sides. However, against the background of the Cold War and hopes of German reunification the ban of the Moscow-linked KPD implied political difficulties. This might have been the reason for the proceeding's length.[155] The decision banning the KPD was given in 1956. Whether the KPD in fact endangered the free democratic basic order by adhering to Marxist-Leninist programmes depended on how vigorously the party pursued these goals. It was held that the rather defensive nature of Article 21 II GG allowed a ban only if a party took an "active belligerent aggressive attitude towards the existing order obstructing it methodically in order to abolish it subsequently". On this basis the KPD was banned.

This ban has been viewed as more problematic as the BVerfG's own line of arguments seemed not entirely clear. Concrete proof indicating the KPD's methodical obstruction of the existing order, e.g. involvement in illegal activities was claimed to be missing by opponents of the decision.[156] It is remarkable, however, that no further party bans have been declared in the history of the Federal Republic. Only in 2001—against the background of increasing right-winged extremist violence especially in the new German Länder—the federal government, Bundestag, and Bundesrat have applied for a ban of the right-wing NPD (Nationaldemokratische Partei Deutschlands), putting emphasis on their contribution to spread racial hatred and incite violence. A decision is expected in 2002.

Applicants for such a ban are the federal government, the Bundestag, the Bundesrat, and the governments of the Länder. A ban entails a dissolution of the party, a ban on substitute parties, and loss of party mandates.[157]

---

[155] For background see Rensmann in J. Menzel (ed.), Verfassungsrechtsprechung (2000: Mohr Siebeck, Tübingen), p. 58.

[156] For discussion see Rensmann, above, n 155, pp. 61–63 and Michalowski and Woods, above, n 52, pp. 19–20.

[157] See §§ 43–47 BVerfG and § 46 BWahlG for details.

5.2.2 Banning associations (Art. 9 II GG)

Under Article 9 II GG associations whose aims are directed against the constitutional order shall be prohibited. Conditions are similar to those of a party ban with the exception that not the BVerfG but the executive, i.e. Minister for Home Affairs on federal or *Länder* level, is responsible for the ban. Thus associations do not enjoy the same protection as political parties. Such bans have been more numerous than party bans.

5.2.3 Loyalty of civil servants to the constitution (Verfassungstreue)

General opinion and the BVerfG demand a certain degree of loyalty towards the constitution from a civil servant.[158] It seems logical that a system which is not politically neutral but designed to uphold certain principles, like the free democratic basic order, will not allow enemies of this system to enter its institutions and abolish it from within. However, the rejection of applicants for civil service posts on grounds of their membership in extremist political parties in the 1970s triggered off a hefty public and academic dispute, the leading case being:

BVerfGE 39, 334 Extremisten

In 1975 a law graduate applied to be appointed "*Rechtsreferendar*" within the judicial state preparation service (*juristischer Vorbereitungsdienst*).[159] He was rejected on the grounds of lacking loyalty to the constitution as he had been member of a Communist student group at university. Ultimately, the BVerfG had to decide the case and upheld the view of the authorities. The Court's argument of rejecting the applicant was based on Article 33 II GG which among other qualifications for a public office demands "aptitude". According to the BVerfG this includes a loyalty to the constitution. Especially in times of crisis the state must have loyal civil servants identifying themselves with the system to protect it. The BVerfG held that a lack of such loyalty could be seen in the membership of extremist "anti-constitutional" parties.

The terminology used here is noteworthy: A party may be "anti-constitutional" (*verfassungsfeindlich*) but need not (yet?) be banned by the BVerfG. Thus it is not "unconstitutional" (*verfassungswidrig*). This provided the main argument against the decision of the BVerfG. If a party has not been banned by the BVerfG as unconstitutional but is tolerated within the system, why then should citizens of the state (including civil servants) be penalised for joining it? Questions arose whether at least it should be possible to distinguish between the different posts within the civil service. While it may be awkward to appoint an extremist to high official posts

---

[158] For a critical discussion see: Pieroth and Schlink, above, n 42, pp. 113–114 with further references; BVerfGE 39, 334, 348.

[159] For details on the German Legal education system see above, Chapter 4.

within the police or secret intelligence offices it should not endanger the system when allowing him to become a postman.[160]

In the case *Vogt v Germany*[161] the European Court of Human Rights has held Germany to be in violation of Articles 10 and 11 ECHR (freedom of opinion and association). Here a teacher was banned from her profession for being member of the *DKP*—a Communist party that has not been banned. Although the Court acknowledged the requirement of loyalty to the constitution as a legitimate principle it lacked an individual assessment of the complainant's case. Membership in extremist—not banned—political parties was too general a criterion for a professional ban.

5.2.4 *Forfeiture of basic rights (Grundrechtsverwirkung, Art. 18 GG)*

Individuals forfeit certain basic rights if they use them to combat the free democratic basic order. These rights are above all rights of communication as, for example, freedom of the press (Art. 5 I GG), freedom to teach (Art. 5 III GG), freedom of assembly and association (Art. 8 and 9 GG), but also other rights as, for example, those that guarantee the financial bases of such activities, freedom of profession, and freedom of property (Arts 12 and 14 GG). Because of the forfeiture's severe impact it can only be declared by the BVerfG and Article 18 GG is interpreted narrowly. The few applications for forfeiture (against right-wing extremists) have been rejected.[162]

5.2.5 *"Defensive" or "militant democracy"?*

Germany is the one of the few Western democratic systems providing for a party ban.[163] It has therefore been called a "militant democracy".[164] Most other democracies have chosen to deal with undemocratic parties at a political level, i.e. exposing their danger in public political debate leaving ultimate decisions to the common sense of the voter. The German instruments to fight unconstitutional tendencies, namely the party ban, can only be understood against Germany's historical background. Through (more or less) democratic elections the Nazi-party gained power and abolished the democratic system together with most fundamental values of human civilisation.

It has been questioned whether it is possible to secure a democratic order by undemocratic means such as the party ban and that a democracy should leave combating unconstitutional parties to the political arena.[165] This, however, implies that the people's common sense cannot be corrupted. While that might have been the case in the UK, Germany's history has proved otherwise. Not a decisive but certainly a contributing factor to the catastrophe of the Third Reich was the

---

[160] See Pieroth and Schlink, above, n 42, pp. 113–114, Michalowski and Woods, above, n 52, pp. 24–25.
[161] EGMR (= ECHR) NJW 1996, 375.
[162] Krueger in Sachs, above, n 5, Art. 18, para. 18.
[163] H.-W. Arndt and W. Rudolf, *Oeffentliches Recht*, 12th ed. (1998: Vahlen, München), pp. 49–50.
[164] Michalowski and Woods, above, n 52, p. 18.
[165] Michalowski and Woods, above, n 52, p. 23.

neutrality of the system based on the theory of "democracy's relativity".[166] Bearing this in mind a decision to protect certain concepts, such as human dignity and a democratic *Rechtsstaat*, seems reasonable. Even instruments provided by the constitution to defend itself including the party ban seem acceptable. It is rather the question of how these instruments are used, that triggered off discussion in Germany. The requirement of loyalty of civil servants, for instance, makes sense but the limits of this loyalty and its assessment on an individual basis must be assured. Any restricting measures have to be subject to the principle of proportionality. The state's actions must not go beyond what is necessary to protect the constitution. Under these circumstances the term "defensive democracy" seems more appropriate than "militant democracy" to describe Germany's system of proportionately *re*-acting to dangers to the constitution.

FURTHER READING

For list of further reading on constitutional law see the bibliography attached to Chapter 7.

[166] See also Maurer, above, n 1, pp. 778–779.

7

Public law II: basic rights and the Federal Constitutional Court

This chapter will deal with the basic rights (*Grundrechte*) as enshrined in the German constitution and their protection by the Federal Constitutional Court. Different remedies under constitutional procedural law will also be examined.

1 Basic rights (*Grundrechte*)

The *Grundgesetz* also provides substantive constitutional law in the form of a catalogue of basic rights, namely in Article 1–19 GG. The purpose of human rights—as developed by the philosophers of the age of enlightenment—was to limit arbitrary actions by an absolute monarch. This idea of protection against the state is still important but is no longer the only purpose.

The history of fundamental rights provisions in Germany is erratic. At no point until 1949 was there an efficient system of protecting them. The 1848 Constitution (*Paulskirchenverfassung*) included rights provisions but the constitution did not enter into force. The *Reichsverfassung* of 1871 did not provide for basic rights at all. An extensive catalogue of rights was contained in the 1919 Weimar Constitution. But these were rather guiding principles than rights enforceable in the courts. As they did not enjoy any specific protection they could easily be suppressed in the Third Reich.

The present constitution contains a significant catalogue of rights. Article 1 I GG provides that human dignity is paramount and that it is the duty of the state to uphold this. This points out that the constitution and the state system is there to serve the citizen, not vice versa. As a consequence Article 1 III GG states that the basic rights are binding on the legislature, the executive and the judiciary as enforceable law. This means that basic rights were not intended simply to be a catalogue of good intentions or empty words, which could be set aside when convenient. The "eternity clause" of Article 79 III GG,[1] expressly protecting Articles 1 and 20 GG from change or amendment, not only protects human dignity but also

---

[1] See above, Chapter 6, sec. 5.1.

the core substances of all other basic rights, according to general opinion.[2] In the context of the entrenchment of the rights this means regardless of the majority in Parliament the legislature cannot enact any effective conflicting law. They can be subject, however, to minor amendment. The catalogue of basic rights must not be too rigid, so as to be inflexible in changing circumstances or be able to fit new situations, nor too vague as to be too uncertain. Thus the rights in the *Grundgesetz* are clearly formulated but are capable of being interpreted to meet new circumstances.

As they stand at the apex of rights within German law, the basic rights have to be taken into account by the executive and the judiciary. Thus they play a considerable role in explaining and elucidating other laws and court decisions even where those appear on face value to conform to the *Grundgesetz*.

Before looking at some basic rights in detail their general principles have to be examined.[3]

1.1 General principles

1.1.1 Types of basic rights

The basic rights consist of the traditional rights of freedom and equality as found in other constitutions, notably the American and French, and newer general rights and positive rights of procedure and political involvement. The rights are largely contained in the form of a catalogue, in Articles 1–19 GG and in a number of other provisions of the *Grundgesetz*, e.g. Articles 20 IV, 33 and 38 I 1 (rights of political participation) and Articles 101 and 103–104 (a catalogue of procedural rights concerning the access to courts and rights of due process).

The rights of freedom (*Freiheitsgrundrechte*) and equality (*Gleichheitsrechte*) are collectively categorized as defensive rights designed to protect the individual from arbitrary state interference (*Abwehrrechte*).

It is important to distinguish between the general right (Art. 2 I GG) and the specific rights of freedom (e.g. Arts 4, 5 I, 8 I, 14 I GG). The latter protect specific areas of freedom, such as freedom of religion (Art. 4 GG), of speech, press, and broadcasting (Art. 5 I GG), of assembly (Art. 8 I GG) or of property (Art. 14 I GG). Art. 2 I GG is a general right of freedom to fall back on if the specific ones do not apply. It claims that "everyone shall have the right to free development of his personality . . . ". Thus it can be used as a defensive right against state actions if (but **only** if) these actions do not interfere with any of the specific rights of freedom. Hence Article 2 I GG is subsidiary to the other rights.

---

[2] Luecke in M. Sachs (ed.), *Grundgesetz Kommentar*, 2nd ed. (1999: C.H. Beck, München), Art. 79, paras. 30–35 with further references.

[3] This section only gives an outline of the German Basic Rights Doctrines. For a more detailed exposition refer either to the standard text book Pieroth and Schlink, *Grundrechte*, 15th ed. (1999: Heidelberg) or the English treatise on Basic Rights by Michalowsky and Woods, *German Constitutional Law* (1999: Dartmouth).

BVerfGE 80, 137 Reiten im Walde

A law protecting nature in Northrhine-Westphalia permitted horse-riding in forests only on specific tracks. Several horsemen felt restricted in their freedom to simply ride through forests without sticking to any paths. As they challenged the law as unconstitutionally restricting their rights to freedom personality and self-determination (Art. 2 I GG) the question arose whether horse-riding was an action which enjoyed protection under any basic right in the first place. It is not specifically mentioned as are the classic rights referring to freedom of religion or speech. However, the BVerfG held that Article 2 I GG offered a wide scope of protection. It protects "any form of human activity no matter how important this activity is for personality development". Thus such a restriction of Article 2 I GG even by statute must conform to the conditions set out in Article 2 I GG. The Court thus declared that Article 2 I offered protection for horse-riding. Within the possibilities of restriction, however, it held that the challenged statute pursued a legitimate purpose (protection of the forest grounds) and proportionality had been respected. Thus the complaint was rejected.

The rights of equality (*Gleichheitsgrundrechte*) providing for protection against discrimination are divided into general (Art. 3 GG) and specific rights (e.g. Art. 6 V, 33 II GG). Furthermore, the "modern" rights offer a claim to participation (*Teilhaberechte* or *Aktivbürgerrecht*) meaning a claim to participate in public affairs (e.g. elections) or demand certain actions by the state (e.g. claim to admission to universities or grants, *BAFöG*).[4] Procedural guarantees (*Prozeßgarantien*), under Articles 19, 101, and 103–104 GG are discussed in further detail below.

Additionally, basic rights also entitle the citizen to claim special state action from the state to protect his rights against intrusions from others. Thus the right to life and physical integrity not only protects against abuse by the state but also puts the state under an obligation to come up with instruments protecting the citizens from each other, namely a criminal code penalizing murder, manslaughter, grievous bodily harm, etc. The difficulty here lies in assessing what sort of action is required. According to the case-law of the BVerfG it seems that the individual may demand some state action but has no claim as to the type of action,[5] as the dramatic case of *Hanns Martin Schleyer* demonstrates:

BVerfGE 46, 160 Schleyer

The "second generation" of the left-wing *RAF* terrorism group had left a trail of blood through several assassinations in Germany between 1974 and 1977. Then in 1977

---

[4] Compare H. Maurer, *Staatsrecht, München* (1999: C.H. Beck, München), p. 274.
[5] See Pieroth and Schlink, above, n 3, pp. 23–26. This will be examined further when looking at Art. 2 II GG in sec. 1.2.

some members of the RAF kidnapped the President of the federal association of employees Hanns Martin Schleyer in order to obtain the release of other already captured terrorists. Against the background of numerous terrorist attacks on the state and a tense situation within the Federal Republic of Germany the Federal Government under Helmut Schmidt decided not to make any concessions to the terrorists but rather rely on the police authorities to find and free the hostage. After the drama had lasted for a month Schleyer's son handed in a constitutional complaint to the BVerfG against the government. He did so within an interim relief procedure on behalf of his father. He argued that Article 2 II GG which gave a right to life included an obligation for the state to do everything possible to protect his life. Thus the government was under an obligation to comply with the terrorists' demands and save Schleyer's life. In a decision—reached within seventeen hours after the complaint had been filed—the BVerfG rejected the complaint on the following grounds: It acknowledged the state's obligation to protect life according to Article 2 II GG. However, it was up to the executive authority to decide which measures should be taken to attain this goal. This choice was held to be within the government's discretion. The government's decision to rather try to find and free the hostage than submitting to terrorist threats thus taking a stand against terrorism was regarded as sufficient state action. Giving in to terrorists' demands would, furthermore, make the state's reactions predictable for terrorists and thus render effective protection of its citizens impossible.

Schleyer was found three days later in the trunk of a car, murdered.[6]

1.1.2 Rights holders (Grundrechtsträger)

In some cases the *Grundgesetz* differentiates between rights of German citizens, so called *Deutschenrechte*, and general rights for the protection of all. Those applying only to German citizens are, for example, assembly and association rights, rights of free movement, or freedom of profession (Arts 8, 9, 11, and 12). These reserved rights, especially free movement rights, may well offend EC provisions. German citizenship is determined by Article 116 GG and supplementary laws, in particular, the *Staatsangehörigkeitsgesetz (StAG)*.[7]

Basic rights can generally only be held by living human beings, i.e. they are held by them from the moment of birth until death. Death is generally accepted to have occurred as soon as the brain as a whole organ has irreversibly ceased to function.[8] However, there are exceptions: In the above mentioned *Mephisto case* it was held that a person's right to respect and dignity must be extended beyond his death.[9] The unborn child (*Embryo, nasciturus*) enjoys a right to life (Art. 2 II 1 GG) and

---

[6] Detailed information on the period of *RAF* terrorism can be found in S. Aust, *Der Baader-Meinhof-Komplex*, 2nd ed. (1997: Stern, Hamburg).

[7] From 22 July 1913, last amemdment 1 January 2000, *Sartorius*, No. 15.

[8] Pieroth and Schlink, above, n 3, p. 32.

[9] See above, sec. 2.2.2., Chapter 6.

human dignity (Art. 1 I 1 GG) according to the BVerfG.[10] Discussions on these decisions will be looked at below.

Another question is whether legal persons can be the holders of basic rights. Article 19 III GG provides that basic rights shall apply to domestic legal persons to the extent that the nature of such rights permits. Thus a private limited company can invoke freedom of property and freedom to carry on a commercial activity (Art. 14 I GG) but not a right to life and physical integrity (Art. 2 II GG). Legal persons under public law (*Körperschaften des öffentlichen Rechts*), in general opinion, cannot be holders of basic rights. Basic rights are mainly the defensive rights of the citizen against the state. As legal persons of public law form a part of the state, they should not be allowed to use them. Exceptions, however, have been admitted in those cases where there is a certain degree of independence from the state **and** the right in question is absolutely necessary for these legal persons to perform their tasks. Thus public broadcasting channels can rely on Article 5 I GG (freedom of broadcasting), universities on Article 5 III (freedom of science) and churches may rely on freedom of religion (Art. 4 II GG).[11]

1.1.3 *Capacity (Grundrechtsmündigkeit)*

The legal capacity to **bear** basic rights (*Grundrechtsfähigkeit*) is accorded by German law to every person including minors. Whether they can **exercise** these rights without assistance of their representatives, e.g. parents, is a different question and is determined according to the particular person's capacity. This will usually be linked to the particular age of majority required but it differs according to the legal right concerned. Thus those basic rights that are connected to business transactions and contracts in civil law (e.g. freedom of profession, Art. 12 I GG) will require majority according to the civil code. Article 38 I GG expressly puts the age limit at eighteen years for elections. Freedom of faith guaranteed by Article 4 GG can be exercised from the age of fourteen as specified in § 5 of the Law on religious education of minors.[12]

1.1.4 *The double character of basic rights*

The double character of basic rights (*Doppelnatur* or *Doppelcharakter der Grundrechte*) concerns the way in which rights can be invoked and is sometimes referred to as the multidimensional quality of the rights. Objective guarantees and subjective personal rights are contained at the same time in the basic rights provisions. This concerns the ability of general norms to be employed as positive rights in favour of individuals.

Subjective rights are the distinct rights of the recipient binding on all state authority and authorities, which will be upheld in favour of individuals by the courts. These are further protected by Article 19 IV GG, the ability to pursue and

---

[10] BVerfGE 39, 1; 88, 203.

[11] See J. Ipsen, *Staatsrecht II (Grundrechte)*, 2nd ed., (1998: Luchterhand, Neuwied), pp. 20–21, with further references.

[12] E. Stein, *Staatsrecht* 16th ed., (1998: Mohr, Tübingen), pp. 214, 215.

uphold rights by recourse to the courts and the distinct procedural rights, discussed below. Substantive rights are found in the form of defensive rights such as, for example, those of the freedom of opinion, and also those of equality or participation. They grant the citizen an individual claim against the state.

Objective guarantees, on the other hand, concern the general protection afforded by the basic rights. Those guarantees apply generally and not to specific instances in the form of a set of guidelines which provide for the authorities minimum standards to observe. They seek to protect certain revered values or institutions within democratic society (*institutionelle Garantien*) such as the institutions of freedom of the press and reporting (Art. 5); marriage and family (Art. 6 GG) education (Art. 7); and property rights (Art. 14). Thus there is a guarantee that the state does not abolish the institutions of marriage, public education, or a free press but in fact does everything to protect their existence.[13]

These rights mostly have a corresponding individual right, thus the objective rights can help to protect material individual rights. The legislature has to bear in mind basic rights as an objective value when enacting legislation.

1.1.5 Third effect of basic rights (Drittwirkung von Grundrechten)

The question **of the third effect** is whether provisions of the *Grundgesetz* can have effects between individuals to uphold a right contained in the *Grundgesetz* against another individual. There are arguments for and against such a proposition. On the one hand, it is suggested that the basic rights are only intended as a protection of individuals from the abuse of the state and state authorities and are not supposed to have an effect as between individuals. They are only supposed to bind the state authorities (Art. 1 III GG), and not be universal guarantees. They were designed to convey rights on individuals and not impose obligations on them. If a landlord, for example, were to be bound by Article 3 I GG (right to equal treatment), he could not enjoy the right to choose his tenant according to his liking. The same goes for the conclusion of any private law contract. This would infringe his right to self-determination (Art. 2 I GG). Furthermore, it is argued that because there are other forms of redress for individuals largely in civil law there does not need to be a form of third party rights arising from the constitution.

On the other hand, it is argued that the basic laws stand at the apex of Germany's legal system and thus influence relations between citizen and state as well as those between citizens. Also, some of the rights by their very nature should apply generally and some areas of law such as labour law rely on the applicability of these rights.[14] A clear and accepted example of a wider direct effect is Article 9 III GG. It guarantees the right to form associations to safeguard and improve working and economic conditions and declares all agreements—including private law agreements—that restrict this right void.[15]

---

[13] Pieroth and Schlink, above, n 3, p. 19, negating the press as a protected institution.
[14] The case of BAGE 1, 185, 191 is referred to in this respect as acknowledging the third effect but it is also argued that this is merely another form of the indirect effect discussed below. See Stein, above, n 9, p. 217.
[15] Pieroth and Schlink, above, n 3, p. 183.

General opinion including the BVerfG has rejected a direct effect of basic rights in relations between private individuals. But at the same time it has accepted that basic laws can create an indirect effect. Through general and equity clauses of private law legislation basic rights can influence a private law relationship. When applying the private law, especially when interpreting general provisions, the courts must bear in mind the basic rights of the individual parties and give effect to them. The classical case for indirect effect is the *Lüth* decision of 1958:

BVerfGE 7, 198 Lüth

Lüth called for a boycott of Veit Harlan's new film as Harlan had directed anti-Semitic films (such as *"Jud Süss"*) during the Third Reich. Harlan's film distributors (on his behalf) obtained a civil law judgment, which required Lüth to recall his boycott. This injunction was based on § 826 BGB because of "a tortuous act contrary to good morals" *(sittenwidrige Schädigung)*. The BVerfG held that when interpreting civil law provisions the civil court should have done this in the light of the basic rights affected. Thus when assessing whether Lüth's call for a boycott amounted to "a tortuous act contrary to good morals" the civil court should have borne in mind Lüth's right to freedom of speech (Art. 5 I 1 GG), the reason also being that the civil court as a part of the judiciary is bound by the basic rights (Art. 1 III GG). However, the court also had to bear in mind Harlan's basic rights such as a right to artistic expression (Art. 5 III GG). Thus it was required to balance the interest in the freedom of speech in calling for the boycott with the economic right to pursue a business and artistic right to display the film—a balance now struck by the BVerfG as the civil court had failed to do so. As Lüth had neither overstepped the line to slander nor exerted any direct coercion on the film companies or Harlan, the Court held that he had exercised his right to free speech within the usual limits of public discussion. The civil court had failed to assess this right properly when interpreting the civil law provision § 826 BGB.

This approach of "indirect effect" of the basic rights (*mittelbare Drittwirkung*) has been the permanent case-law of the BVerfG. Recent examples of it can be seen in the so-called "decisions on satellite dishes" (*Parabol-Antennenfälle*).[16]

BVerfGE 90, 27 Parabolantennen

In a dispute between Turkish tenants and German landlords on the erection of satellite dishes a civil court had to decide whether this was covered by the lease agreement. The decision that the tenant had no right under the agreement to put up a satellite antenna

---

[16] BVerfGE 90, 27. For further case reference see Spitzkatz in J. Menzel, *Verfassungsrechtsprechung* (2000: Mohr Siebeck, Tübingen), p. 532.

against the landlord's wish was overruled by the BVerfG. Again the BVerfG held that the court had failed to take into account the tenant's basic rights when applying the provisions on the law of leasing. It should have borne in mind the right of free access to information (Art. 5 I 1 GG). For a Turkish tenant relevant information on his state of origin could only be obtained via satellite dishes. Thus his right to information had to be balanced against the landlord's right to property (Art. 14 I GG). The Court held that in this particular case Article 5 I GG was more important.

1.1.6 *Structure of basic rights*

The structure of basic rights is not only important in order to understand their way of functioning and how to employ them. From a student's point of view it is also absolutely vital in order to answer problem questions correctly. Every basic right offers a "scope of protection" (*Schutzbereich*), which will determine who and which actions or situations are protected by it.

Example: Article 12 I 1 GG states that "all Germans have the right to freely choose their profession, their place of work and their place of training". Thus the scope of protection only covers Germans and the mentioned three elements connected with profession.

Basic rights, however, can be limited. Conditions for such "limitations" (*Schranken*) are usually found in the basic rights provision. These limitations usually call for a (parliamentary) law.

Example: Article 12 I 2 GG: "The practice of profession may be regulated by or pursuant to a law."

Such limitations though have to be constitutional. This means that they must not contravene leading constitutional principles, i.e. the principle of proportionality or non-retroactivity. Thus these principles "limit the limitations". As a consequence they are called "*Schranken-Schranken*".

It follows that an assessment of whether there has been a violation of a basic right by some state action will be conducted in three steps: First, it must be assessed whether the person affected and his curtailed action/behaviour are covered by the scope of protection.

> **Example:** A foreigner cannot rely on Article 12 I GG as it only applies to Germans. A thief could not rely on it either as stealing—even if it constitutes his maintenance—does not fall within the scope of protection of a "profession". In both cases no further analysis of Article 12 I GG will follow.

State action will then be scrutinized as to whether it amounts to an intrusion on the basic right (*Grundrechtseingriff*). This is not the case where the state action does not influence the rights holder.

> **Example:** In the *Kruzifix* case it was doubtful whether putting up a crucifix in class rooms by the state would practically affect the beliefs (and thus freedom of religion, Art. 4 I GG) of a non-Christian pupil.[17]

Finally, one has to assess whether the state's intrusion on the particular right was justified on a constitutional level. In other words, the intrusion must keep within the limits set by the constitution (i.e. parliamentary law, correct legislative procedure, proportionality, etc.) If this is not the case then the state's action amounts to a basic right's infringement (*Grundrechtsverletzung*).

1.1.7 *Limitations of basic rights (Grundrechtsschranken)*
The basic rights are not absolute and do have a number of limitations rather than being universally applicable. Individuals must therefore allow their freedoms to be limited at times but as a requirement of the principle of the *Rechtsstaat* any limitation must be legally sanctioned by a specific law and defined within the scope of the general principles of the constitution (Arts 19 I, II and 79 I GG). The limitations are found in a number of forms.

(a) *Constitutional limits (Verfassungsunmittelbare Schranken)*
Certain rights restrict themselves by the words used or contain a direct limitation. For example, Article 8 II GG allows for " . . . peaceful assembly without weapons", which automatically excludes from the protection of the right any armed assembly or one which is not peaceful.

(b) *Lawful limitations (Schranke des Gesetzesvorbehalts)*
Several basic rights allow for limitations by law. For example, Article 8 II GG states that with regard to open air meetings "the right to assemble peacefully" may be restricted by laws to be defined by the legislature. As a consequence there is a law on assemblies (*Versammlungsgesetz*)[18] dealing with limitations. See also Articles 2 II, 5

---

[17] The BVerfG decided it did. See below, sec. 1.2.
[18] *Sartorius* No. 435.

II, 10 II, 12 I 2, and 14 I GG. Note that such limitation always require a parliamentary law as they concern the restriction of basic rights and thus are essential matters.[19]

(c) *Limitations inherent to the constitution (Verfassungsimmanente Schranken)*
Some basic rights do not provide for any limitation at all such as, for example, the right to freedom of religion (Art. 4 GG) or the right to free artistic expression (Art. 5 III GG). But this obviously does not mean that each individual can enjoy them without any limits. Freedom of a basic right always ends where the freedom of someone else's right begins. This simplified rule has lead to the following generally accepted idea of limitations inherent to the constitution: Any basic right without express limitations must find them in a conflicting constitutional law, i.e. other basic rights or values of constitutional rank. Since there are no express limitations the only limitations acceptable must stem from the same source of law with the same rank, i.e. the constitution. Thus the freedom of artistic expression will find a limit when conflicting with the right to personality as the *Mephisto* case has shown.[20] However, when two interests conflict on the same level (constitutional law) they must be balanced against each other and harmonized.[21] A good example of balancing basic rights can be found in the *Lebach* case dealt with below.

(d) *General conditions for limitations*
The following general conditions have to be observed when limiting basic rights: Article 19 I GG demands that a basic right restriction by law or pursuant to law must be of general application and not only applicable to one individual case (*Verbot der Einzelfallgesetzgebung*). It furthermore requires the restricted basic right to be expressly named with an Article number in the restricting law. Finally according to Article 19 II GG no basic right may be affected in its essence.

1.1.8 *The European Convention of Human Rights*

Germany is party to the European Convention of Human Rights (ECHR). According to Article 1 ECHR the Member States secure the rights and freedoms of the Convention to anyone in their jurisdiction. This international treaty has been transformed into national law by an Act of Parliament (*Bundesgesetz*) according to Article 59 II GG.[22] As a consequence the content of the Convention is directly applicable in Germany. However, as a federal law it ranks below the constitution. Furthermore, the basic rights' scope of protection of the *Grundgesetz* often extends beyond that of the rights of the Convention. Thus although German courts have to take into account the rights of the Convention they often do so automatically when applying the basic rights of the *Grundgesetz*. If, however, an individual feels that his right under the Convention has not been protected by the national courts he can as a last resort turn to the European Court of Human Rights in Strasbourg.

---

[19] See above Chapter 6, sec. 3.3.3.
[20] See above Chapter 6, sec. 2.2.2.
[21] Ibid.
[22] BGBl 1952 II S. 685.

2 The individual rights

This section will briefly outline the scope of protection offered by the individual basic rights. They cannot be examined in detail.[23] Some of them, however, will be looked at more closely.

2.1 Article 1: The protection of human dignity (*Schutz der Menschenwürde*)

The primary position of this Article demonstrates the importance given to it and it is entrenched in the present order by Article 79 III GG. This is not surprising bearing in mind the experience of the atrocities under the Nazi dictatorship and the contempt with which human dignity had been treated in the Third Reich. At the same time Article 1 I GG is one of the most difficult provisions to come to grasp with because of its vagueness and its high aims. Thus question remains open as to whether Article 1 I GG provides subjective rights which can be claimed singularly or whether because it precedes Article 1 III GG which binds all state organs to the basic rights, it is simply an objective right and guideline for state action.

The jurisprudence of the BVerfG on this is not entirely clear. Although it has allowed complaints to succeed because of violations of human dignity, it usually did so in connection with other basic rights. Thus Article 1 I GG seems to be a central value statement which permeates the entire legal order and is not to be considered alone.

In this context the **scope of protection** includes all human beings including the unborn child, as decided in one of the *abortion decisions*[24] and deceased persons as decided in the *Mephisto* case.

BVerfGE 30, 173 Mephisto (cont.)[25]

It was the son of the deceased *Gründgens* who objected to the publication of the disputed novel on the ground that it damaged the name of his now deceased father. He obtained an injunction under private law to prevent further publication and distribution. The publisher filed a constitutional complaint that the freedom to publish (Article 5 I GG) had been infringed. The BVerfG was required to balance this right with the right of Article 1 I GG. Essentially, the BVerfG upheld the rights of the deceased actor because the right to be protected from attacks on human dignity under Article 1 I did not end with death.

---

[23] For more information refer to B. Pieroth and B. Schlink, *Staatsrechte II: Grundrechte*, 15th ed. (1999: C.F. Müller, Heidelberg or Michalowsky and Woods, above, n 3.
[24] BVerfG 39, 1, 41.
[25] See above, Chapter 6, sec 2.2.2.

But what exactly is protected by Article 1 GG is difficult to determine, as 2,500 years of occidental philosophy have not managed to define "human dignity" satisfactorily. It seems to comprise a respect for the value of a human being, as the word "*Würde*" (= dignity) is derived from "Wert" (= value). But who is to define what an individual's value is? Is there an objective common sense definition or does perhaps each individual decide for himself, what sort of actions infringe his dignity? For a long time general opinion adhered to a rather objective definition as coined by the constitutional lawyer Günter Dürig: "It would infringe Human Dignity if the state treated a human being as a mere object of its (the state's) actions" (*Objektformel*).[26]

Against the background of the Holocaust, which not only infringed the right to life but also negated respect for humans as individual beings, this formula makes sense. But applying it to everyday legal problems shows that it is too vague. Thus "human dignity" defies a single encompassing definition and is dependent on circumstances (*situationsabhängig*). Arguably, it might be difficult to define, but it is obvious when a violation of it occurs. Such typical violations are, e.g. slavery, torture, discriminations, brainwashing, and the refusal to individuals of a minimum support of existence.[27]

A case concerning life sentences[28] questioned the compatibility of life sentences with human dignity. The BVerfG upheld the right under Article 1 I GG as the highest value of the constitutional order but held it to be bound by concerns for the community. Thus the imposition of a life sentence would not itself offend the basic right. Life sentences in fact rarely, if ever, mean incarceration for the rest of a person's days and are reviewed in order to consider early release. Continuing with a criminal procedure against an accused who is terminally ill and will most probably not live to see the end of the trial has been held a violation of human dignity in the *Honecker* decision.[29]

Unlike the other basic rights there is **no possibility of justifying an intrusion** on the right to human dignity. It is "inviolable".

As the state is obliged to respect and protect human dignity the question arises whether it has to protect people against their will. This became a subject of discussion in the *Peep-show* case. The Federal Administrative Court (*BVerwG*) had to decide whether Article 1 I GG requires the state to prohibit peep-shows in order to protect the human dignity of the women involved.[30] As the women affected in such cases have chosen to work there themselves and might not even feel that their dignity was violated the issue is difficult to decide. The same problem occurs when people feel offended by "exhibitionary" television programmes such as "Big Brother" and call for a ban.[31] Again it would seem strange to "protect" against their

---

[26] Dürig in T. Maunz and G. Dürig (eds.), *Komm. z. GG* 8th ed. (1999), Art. 1 para. 34; also BVerfG 9, 167.

[27] For more extensive list see Pieroth and Schlink, above, n 3, p. 82.

[28] BVerfGE 45, 187, 227.

[29] BerlVerfGH NJW 1993, 515. Note though that this decision was made by the *Constitutional Court of Berlin*. It does not necessarily have to reflect the opinion of the BVerfG.

[30] BVerwGE 64, 274. The Court upheld the ban on grounds of Art. 1 I GG but in subsequent decisions preferred not to invoke this provision again. See T. Discher, "Die Peep-Show-Urteile des BVerwG" JuS 1991, pp. 642–648.

[31] As W. Schmitt-Gläser "Big Brother is watching you—Menschenwürde bei RTL 2", ZRP 2000, pp. 395–402 (with interesting arguments).

own will the people participating in the series. The key question is: Who is to decide on the content of human dignity? According to the *"Mitgifttheorie"* it depends upon a person's nature as it has been created and has developed because of the characteristics given by God or nature. Thus it would have to be assessed objectively (by the courts?) as to what is covered by "dignity". The *"Leistungstheorie"*, however, places emphasis on the individual's behaviour, i.e. the individual might define his own individual dignity. It has been argued that these theories do not necessarily contradict but complement each other.[32] It remains to be seen, what impact Article 1 I GG will have on future gene technology and cloning (or vice versa?).[33]

2.2 Article 2: Right to personal freedom (*Allgemeines Persönlichkeitsrecht*, Art. 2 I GG), right to life (*Recht auf Leben*), and physical integrity (*körperliche Unversehrtheit*, Art. 2 II GG)

Most often Article 1 I GG is connected to and discussed in the light of Article 2 I GG which concerns the right of the free development of personality. This right is a subjective right actionable on its own. It is a general right of freedom of action and personal development. The **scope of protection** within this freedom has been defined in the *horse-riding* case as "any form of human activity no matter how important this activity is for personality development".[34] This far-reaching interpretation of Article 2 I GG has its roots in the *Elfes* Decision from 1957:

BVerfGE 6, 32 Elfes

Wilhelm Elfes, a CDU-politician and opponent of chancellor Adenauer's policy of West-Integration and rearming West-Germany, had in the beginning of the 1950s established contacts with Eastern European politicians and attended various international conferences promoting a policy of German reunification. He did so by attacking the federal government's policy of the time. When applying for a passport the authorities denied this according to § 7 I a PassG (Law on Passports). This provision allowed for a rejection of the application if the applicant was likely to endanger important interests of the Federal Republic. He ultimately complained to the BVerfG on the grounds of violation of the basic right to freedom of movement (Art. 11 I GG). The Court denied the applicability of this provision as it literally only covered movement within the territory of Germany not outside of it. However, the Court held that as a subsidiary right he could invoke Article 2 I GG which as a general freedom of action included the right to leave the country. However, it is easier to limit the right under Article 2 I GG than the right under Article 11 I GG. Thus it posed no problems to the Court to hold § 7 I a PassG compatible with the constitution and reject the complaint.

---

[32] Pieroth and Schlink, above, n 3, p. 80.
[33] See M.T. Tinnefeld, "Menschenwürde, Biomedizin und Datenschutz" ZRP 2000, pp. 10–13: M. Herdegen, "Die Menschenwürde im Fluss des bioethischen Diskurses" JZ 2001, pp. 773–779.
[34] BVerfGE 80, 137, see above, sec. 1.1.2.

Its greatest use and influence has been in an unforeseen direction in the world of business for the economic development of legal persons, the joint stock company, and private companies, particularly with regard to trade development and contractual freedom.

Emphasis was put on a right to personality rather than a right to freedom of action as a society of multi media and electronic data processing developed. A need for privacy became apparent and a corresponding right was first developed by civil courts as a defence against yellow-press intrusion on celebrities' privacy.[35] Since then numerous decisions had to deal with a right to privacy, now rephrased as a general right to personality (*Allgemeines Persönlichkeitsrecht*).[36] One of the notorious ones being the *Census* decision (*Volkszaehlungsurteil*).

BVerfG 65, 1 Volkszählung (cont.)[37]

In 1982 a census law was passed by the *Bundestag* to prepare a census in April 1983. But in December 1982 the law was declared unconstitutional. It was hailed by many as the starting point of German data protection law.[38] Certainly its circumstances were remarkable as the judgment addressed about a thousand (!) constitutional complaints by citizens to the BVerfG.

The most disputed provision of the census law—apart from the fact that it was compulsory to take part in the census—was § 9 I. It allowed using the data obtained by the census to supplement all the data collections of registration offices. That way each administrative authority within the Federal Republic would have had wide access to personal data on each citizen. The complaints claimed a violation of the right to personality as derived from Article 2 I in connection with 1 I GG. The BVerfG agreed. It held that although it might be necessary for public planning and devising future policy to hold a census it must nevertheless respect the rights of human dignity and personality. A right to data protection called *informationelle Selbstbestimmung* ("informational self-determination") was established. The Court held that because of the wide-ranging possibilities of connecting data it should be within the individual's decision which of his data were to be processed. The individual needed to know who processed the data, when and for which purpose. Otherwise he would refrain from actions that were completely legal, but could entail disadvantages if circulated by administrative authorities (i.e. participation in demonstrations). The Court acknowledged limits to this right of self-determination, but stated that these limits had to be contained in a law and should not go beyond what was absolutely necessary. The disputed provision (§ 9) was clearly not necessary to obtain the goals of the census as not all administrative authorities needed all data. Thus the law was declared void.

---

[35] See the *Soraya*-case above, Chapter 2.
[36] For references see I. Richter, G.F. Schuppert, and C. Bumke, *Casebook Verfassungsrecht*, 4th ed. (2001: C.H. Beck, München), pp. 77–86.
[37] See above, Chapter 6, sec. 3.3.5.
[38] Peilert in Menzel, above, n 16, p. 344.

Limitations on the right to freedom of action and the right to personality are outlined in Article 2 I GG itself. They contain the rights of others, constitutional order, and the moral law. The constitutional order is now generally accepted to comprise the whole legal order. Therefore the rights of others (basic rights as well as rights under private law for example) are already included. Good morals or the moral law is already reflected in legal provisions such as §§ 138, 242 BGB. Thus the relevant limitation for this basic right is the constitutional order, meaning every existing legal provision—provided, of course, that it conforms to the constitution. Practically, this means the right to personality can be limited by an Act of Parliament as happened in the *Elfes* case or the *Census* case. But such an Act must conform to constitutional principles, namely the principle of proportionality—which it did not in the latter case. It is noteworthy that if Elfes had been allowed to base his case on Article 11 I GG, limitations would have met stricter conditions in Article 11 II GG.

Article 2 II GG guarantees the rights of life, physical integrity, and liberty and is really a precondition to Article 2 I GG. The scope of these rights is comparably easy to determine. The state is not allowed to take an individual's life, freedom, or hurt him. However, Article 2 II 3 GG allows limitations pursuant to a law. The relevant laws concerning physical integrity and freedom are the Criminal Code and Criminal Procedural Code. Such provisions must, of course, be constitutional, namely proportional. The death penalty could technically be introduced by law following Article 2 II 3 GG if it were not for Article 102 GG ("Capital punishment is abolished") and Article 1 I GG.[39]

An obligation on the state to take certain steps to protect the individual's life and physical integrity has already been mentioned in the *Schleyer* case.[40] It has also been emphasised by the BVerfG in its *abortion* decisions.[41]

Brief outline of BVerfGE 39, 1; 88, 203 Schwangerschaftsabbruch I, II

Article 2 II GG applies to all life including unborn children. Both before the reform of § 218 StGB and following the amendments consequent to the Unification Treaty, the BVerfG has been called on to consider the constitutionality of abortion provisions of the Criminal Code, the new § 218 a StGB. Its earlier decision had declared that the duty of the state was to protect life—by means that included criminal sanctions—but that in certain situations, abortion would be permissible without criminal sanction.[42] Any decision to abort an unborn child outside of the grounds stated was held to be

---

[39] According to general opinion the death penalty would violate the right to human dignity. See Pieroth and Schlink, above, n 3, p. 93.

[40] See above, sec. 1.1.1.

[41] For extensive coverage see Michalowski and Woods, *Constitutional Law* (1999: Dartmouth) pp. 135–146 and Dederer in Menzel, above, n 16, pp. 242–253.

[42] In the case of rape, a threat to the life or health of the mother, or where there was irreversible serious physical or mental injury to the unborn child.

unconstitutional.[43] In its second *abortion* decision the BVerfG, having to decide on another reform of § 218 a StGB,[44] accepted that, providing the mother has received extensive medical advice, a decision by her to have an abortion within the first twelve weeks of pregnancy should not be punished under criminal law, although preserving the unlawfulness of the action. As the original criminal sanctions had not achieved the aim of lowering the number of abortions and thus protecting unborn human life it was only logical now to allow other means of protection. However, as the Court was not satisfied with the provisions on counselling the pregnant mother it delivered guidelines for a future legislation—an action heavily criticized as overstepping its powers as a court. Furthermore, it seemed that unsatisfied players in the political arena more and more relied on the BVerfG to turn political defeats into constitutional law victories thus rendering the functioning of democratic decision-making questionable.

An obligation to protect bodily integrity was further discussed in cases of setting up nuclear power plants. Here not only the state's obligation of protecting the individual from harmful emissions was established but also the requirement of continuously improving precautions according to technological progress.[45]

2.3 Article 3: Equality before the law (*Gleichheit vor dem Gesetz*)

Article 3 I GG states "All people are equal before the law." This general right of equality is also inherent in a number of other rights, see Articles 3 II, 6 V, 33 I-III and 38 I 1 GG. The legislature and executive are required to apply the law equally to all persons. Article 3 I GG is not an absolute right but seeks to establish equal treatment under the law, based on the application of non-arbitrary criteria in determining what the legal rule should be, rather than the complete prohibition of any discrimination, whether or not justified.

The case-law of the BVerfG demands that essentially similar matters are to be treated equally, whereas essentially different matters will be treated differently.[46] However, this formula only gives vague guidelines in order to detect discrimination in breach of Article 3 I GG as it does not say what is essentially similar or essentially different. According to general opinion the following examination in three steps will help to assess whether a treatment is discriminatory:[47] first, the criteria of differentiation have to be assessed, then the aim pursued by this differentiation, and finally the relation between criteria and aim. If all these three aspects are compatible with constitutional law then a treatment, although differentiating, is not discriminatory.

---

[43] BVerfGE 39, 1.
[44] BVerfGE 88, 203.
[45] BVerfGE 49, 89 (Kalkar), see above, sec. 3.3.4.
[46] BVerfGE 49, 148,165.
[47] See Stein, above, n 12, pp. 390–393, 396–399.

Articles 3 III GG, for example, enumerates criteria which must never be considered as criteria of differentiation: sex, parentage, race, language, homeland and origin, faith, or religious or political opinions. A differentiation on these grounds will automatically be regarded unconstitutional.

The pursued aim must be one of general public interest as opposed to private interests (e.g. creating advantages for the ruling political party or members of the *Bundestag*). The general principles of state as examined in section 3 of Chapter 6 will serve as means to review the aim, of differentiation.

Finally, when looking at the relation of criteria and aim the principle of proportionality again becomes important. The criteria of differentiation must be adequate and necessary to obtain the aim pursued.

An example of the far reaching application of this provision concerns periods of notice in labour law (see further Chapter 9).

BVerfGE 82, 126 Kündigungsfristen von Arbeitern und Angestellten

Termination of labour contracts is regulated initially by § 622 BGB, which details the periods of notice required for the dismissal of the various categories of employees—it was previously two weeks for blue collar workers and six weeks for staff—both of which could be extended the longer the service of the employee. The preferential treatment of staff had remained the main difference of treatment between these two groups of employees, and the BGB had clearly supported the view that this was acceptable in law because staff workers had better qualifications and thus needed more time to find new jobs. It was argued these periods protected against unemployment. Furthermore, in the production sector more flexibility was needed than in other sectors.

It has always been possible for parties as a part of contractual freedom to negotiate individual periods of notice in contracts. In reality, though, most workers are subject to the industry or plant norm, whether they like it or not. In some circumstances periods more generous than the statutory minimum are agreed as the result of collective bargaining.

However, the distinction in periods required in this provision was challenged as contrary to Article 3 I GG, and § 622 BGB was held to be unconstitutional on the following grounds. The **criteria for differentiating** blue collar and white collar workers were constitutionally acceptable as they did not fall under Article 3 III GG and as the labour law courts had developed "subcriteria" sufficiently distinguishing these two groups. The Court also approved of the **aims of this differentiation** which were to create protection against unemployment and to ensure enough time to apply for new jobs. However, it held the criteria for differentiation in order to obtain these aims to be **inadequate and thus disproportionate**. Even if higher qualified workers needed more time to find a new job in reality staff workers were not necessarily better qualified than blue collar workers. It would thus have been more adequate to link the period of termination to qualifications than to affiliation to one of the groups. As far as flexibility in the production sector was concerned the Court held that the majority of workers were not necessarily occupied in the production sector. Hence the distinction of groups under this aspect was also inadequate. As a result, the *Bundestag* was required to introduce a legislative amendment to reflect this judgment within three years, which it did so in 1993, setting out periods of dismissal according to the amount of time served.[48]

It has to be noted that this idea of equal treatment is different from the concept of strict formal equal treatment as shown in the treatment of political parties. In these cases there is little room for differentiation.[49]

Article 3 II GG states that men and women shall have equal rights. This has been applied to provide that there shall be no discrimination on the grounds of sex unless objective biological or functional reasons exist, which warrant different treatment. The BVerfG nowadays consequently holds unconstitutional all provisions that are based on a traditional allocation of work between the sexes. Thus it scrapped the prohibition on women working at night.[50] See also the *Hausarbeitstag* decision, which concerned a law granting time off to women, living on their own, to do housework but which was not granted to men in similar situations. This was held to be unconstitutional.[51] Article 3 II GG has been applied most visibly to require equal pay, and § 612 II now requires equal pay for men and women.

The amended Article 3 II S. 2 provides for an obligation on the state to eliminate existing disadvantages based on sex. This has been implemented by so-called clauses of positive discrimination. According to these legal provisions in cases of equal qualifications of two applicants of different sex for civil service posts the woman had to be appointed, if women were under-represented in that area. Such clauses, however, have been held to breach Article 2 IV of the EC Directive (76/207) on Equal Treatment by the ECJ in the case of *Kalanke*, where the disadvantaged male applicant had challenged such a provision.[52] The ECJ disapproved of the absolute and unconditional preference for women, lacking possibilities to take into account the individual circumstances of each case. However, it approved of a similar provision in the *Marschall* case that included a so-called hardship clause.[53] There is now a considerable impact of Community law on this area, and many of the latest court decisions are the result of Community equal treatment legislation and its transformation into German law. One of the most recent examples of admitting women into a typical male domain is the case of *Tanja Kreil*.[54] The ECJ held that the German constitutional provision (Art. 12 a VI GG) was incompatible with the EC

---

[48] Refer to the revised § 622 BGB as amended by *Kündigungsfristengesetz* (KündFG) of 7 October 1993 (BGBl I S. 1668).
[49] See above, Chapter 6, sec. 3.2.3.
[50] BVerfGE 85, 191.
[51] BVerfGE 52, 369, 376.
[52] *Case C-450/93, Kalanke v Freie Hansestadt Bremen* [1995] ECR-I 3052.
[53] *Case C-409/95, Hellmut Marschall v Land Nordrhein-Westfalen* [1997] 1 CMLR 547.
[54] *Case C-285/98, Tanja Kreil v Bundesrepublik Deutschland* NJW 2000, p. 497f.

Directive (76/207) on Equal Treatment. The provision allowed access of women to jobs within the armed forces only in exceptional cases and under strict conditions.

As a result of judgments of the BVerfG, a number of general principles have been derived from the equality principle such as equal access to public benefits, especially in the field of education, the principle of tax equity,[55] and the equality of arms in legal procedure.[56]

2.4 Article 4: The freedom of faith, conscience, and creed (*Glaubens-, Gewissens- und Bekenntnisfreiheit*)

Article 4 I, II GG which guarantees freedom of conscience and other beliefs as well as undisturbed practice of religion offers a "uniform scope of protection" (*einheitlicher Schutzbereich*),[57] since freedom of religion could hardly qualify as "freedom" if only its belief in thought but not its practices (congregations, prayers, processions, rituals, etc.) were allowed. These rights have a longer history than some of the other liberal freedoms and are inseparable from the basic norms of the dignity of man and development of personality. The scope of protection covers not only each individual but also any religious or philosophical creed, no matter how big the religious group.[58] This obviously is not confined to Christian groups or the main world religions. Thus it is open to the person adhering to a specific belief to define which creed and behaviour this belief covers. Article 4 I GG must as a consequence also protect the freedom *not* to have a belief. It further covers the freedom to adjust one's life and general behaviour according to one's belief.[59]

As opposed to this individual basic right Article 4 I, II also (at least indirectly) offers a collective right of religious communities. Article 140 GG declares effective a few provisions of the former Weimar constitution (WRV) concerning "state church law" (*Staatskirchenrecht*). One of these provisions (Art. 137 III WRV) grants religious communities a right to self-determination (concerning, e.g. all the administrative side), which basically allows them to organize themselves without state interference. Religious communities can become bodies of public law such as, for example, the Catholic and Protestant Church. This will grant them certain privileges. That way the state acknowledges their important integrative function in social life. However, this will only be assumed if a certain degree of organization, support within the population, and "respect for the law" (*Rechtstreue*) can be shown.[60]

The acknowledgement of the Church as a corporate public body sometimes causes confusion because Articles 4 I, II GG and Article 140 GG in connection with

---

[55] BVerfGE 6, 70.
[56] BVerfGE 52, 131. The principle of the equality of arms is part of the expression *audi alterem partem* and seeks to ensure that both parties have equal opportunity to present their case and comment on the presentation of the other party's case. This principle is well recognized in civil law countries and will be familiar to those lawyers who have studied the ECHR, in particular Art. 6. For further explanation see J.E.S. Fawcett, *The Application of the ECHR*, 2nd ed. (1987), p. 154.
[57] Pieroth and Schlink, above, n 3, p. 122.
[58] BVerfGE 32, pp. 98,106.
[59] ibid.
[60] See Ehlers in Sachs, above, n 5, Art. 140, para. 20. Whether a certain degree of loyalty to the state is compulsory is disputed.

Article 137 I GG require the state to be religiously and ideologically neutral. The Churches, however, only have a certain independent status and some state privileges that can also be obtained by other religious groups if they satisfy the criteria mentioned. Thus the state in all public actions has to refrain from preferring one religion to another.

The latter aspect leads to the question of intrusion on Article 4 I GG which had to be discussed in the *Kruzifix* decision.

BVerfGE 93, 1 Kruzifix

According to a Bavarian law there had to be crucifixes within all Bavarian elementary schools. Several pupils and their parents who shared an anthroposophical belief felt that this violated their right to freedom of belief and upbringing of children. It was held that the freedom *not* to believe in the Christian religion was covered by the **scope of protection** of Article 4 I GG. Thus the state was not allowed to intrude on this freedom. The question now was whether the mere putting up of crucifixes constituted such an **intrusion**? Arguably, the pupils had their own beliefs already and were not forced by the teachers to believe in anything else. The crucifix did not have any missionary character according the dissenting opinions of three judges. The majority of the remaining five judges, however, ruled that it was an intrusion. It held that the crucifix had an "appealing" subliminal character apt to influence a child that has not yet completely formed its beliefs. Such an intrusion could, furthermore, **not be justified** by any other constitutional interests. Even if Article 7 I GG allowed for religious (especially Christian) education within schools this was not compulsory and left alternatives open to pupils of other beliefs. The crucifix, however, was omnipresent in school and could not be "evaded" by these pupils.

This decision was heavily disputed, as the general perception was that the Church historically had enjoyed a special protection, and even benefits from the state on the ground of representing the beliefs of the majority of the population. However, the decision was one of consequence in the light of the constitutional demand that the state is to be religiously and ideologically neutral.[61] In this context it is inevitable that a teacher of the Muslim faith must refrain from wearing her veil while teaching in a public school as this would amount to the same type of intrusion upon the children's religious belief.[62]

Article 4 I, II GG does not mention any possibilities of limiting this basic right. Thus the only limitations derive from conflicting constitutional law, i.e. interests or rights of constitutional rank. In the aforementioned case the Muslim teacher could try to invoke her rights under Article 4 I, II GG. But the limitations of these rights

---

[61] For background see Schulte zu Sodingen in Menzel, above, n 16, pp. 575, 576.
[62] As decided in *VG Stuttgart* NVwZ 2000, 959. For discussion see: Janz and Rademacher, "Das Kopftuch als religioeses Symbol oder profaner Kleidungsgegenstand?" JuS 2001, pp. 440–444.

are constitutionally justified by the constitutional requirement, that the state and its civil servants have to refrain from promoting any religious belief. A Muslim female pupil, however, who has to take part in joint sports classes with boys can successfully invoke Article 4 I, II GG.[63] In order to participate in these classes she would have to dispose of the veil. Here the only constitutional justification to force such participation could be the state's responsibility for school education (Art. 7 I GG). When balancing compulsory school participation and the pupil's right under Article 4 I GG it is likely that the state's interest in upholding the school order will suffer less than the pupil's interest in guiding her actions by her beliefs. A release from the class for these occasions would be a reasonable and proportional solution of the conflict. Thus both rights would be given their best efficiency (*praktische Konkordanz* or "Harmonizing").[64]

Article 4 III—a more specific provision than Article 4 I, II GG—which provides that no-one may be compelled to render military service involving armed combat against his conscience, is an example of where a general right is both limited and defined in respect of military service or the alternative public service (Art. 12a II GG).[65]

2.5 Article 5 I GG: Freedom of communication: freedom of expression, information, press, broadcasting, and film (*Kommunikationsgrundrechte*)

Article 5 provides no less than seven different basic rights of communication. Two of these concerning art and science are mentioned in Article 5 III GG and will be dealt with below. The other five are named in Article 5 I GG. As rights of communication they have been held to be of a pivotal character to a functioning democracy, as the participation of citizens in state affairs as a precondition requires sufficient information and open debate on politically, socially, and culturally relevant topics.

The right to express opinions orally, in writing or visually (*Recht der freien Meinungsäußerung*, Art. 5 I 1 GG) is applicable to every person. Its **scope of protection** comprises not only opinions but also the statement of facts, as the two are often not clearly separable. However, facts that are proven to be false are wrong information and thus not worthy of protection, such as, for example, the denial of the Holocaust.[66] Calls for boycotts are included by the scope of protection, as decided in the *Lüth* case.[67] Here the BVerfG has upheld Article 5 I GG for the free and open expression of views, as the basis and lifeblood of a pluralist society, and as a precondition to the democratic order of state, as noted above. The requirement to pay damages

---

[63] For this famous example see: Kahl, "Der praktische Fall: Koran und Schulsport" JuS 1995, S. 904–908 and BVerwGE 94, 82.

[64] See above, Chapter 6, sec. 2.2.2.

[65] Considered in BVerfGE 12, 45, BVerfGE 48, 127 and BVerfGE 69, 1 BVerfGE.

[66] BVerfGE 90, 241 (*"Ausschwitzlüge"*). This, however, is disputed, see Pieroth and Schlink, above, n 3, p. 134.

[67] BVerfGE 7, 198. See above, sec. 1.1.5 for details.

in civil law, it was argued, affected the freedom of opinion. Contrast this with the *Blinkfuer* case.[68] Here it was held that a boycott exerted by a dominating publisher threatening to exclude newsagents from supply of their products, if they did not stop circulating certain magazines, was not protected by Article 5 I GG. Even a boycott must reflect an intellectual contest of opinions rather than pure economic pressure based on a dominant position within the market.

The second right within Article 5 I GG is a reflection of the active right to express oneself. It is the right to freely obtain public information (*Informationsfreiheit*). It allows the individual access to all general sources of information (newspapers, broadcasting programmes, files, etc.). It usually refers to means of mass communication. It may also allow a foreigner access to special foreign programmes that can only be received via satellite dish and thus covers his right to erect the antenna.[69]

Further rights, the freedom of the press, and broadcasting (television and radio), mentioned in Article 5 I 2 GG, have been the subject of numerous constitutional actions. These have upheld, *inter alia*: the press as a constitutionally protected institution,[70] the right to protect sources,[71] the right to choose the content of the radio or television programme without interference from the state or other sources.[72]

Scope of protection for these mass media is wide as the BVerfG has acknowledged their outstanding importance as sources of information for a population that has to participate in the decisions of a democratic society.

However, differences between the freedom of the press and broadcasting have to be noted. Freedom of the press can be invoked by (private) publishers, editors and journalists against any actions of the state trying to interfere with the distribution of their print media at any level. Broadcasting, on the other hand, was originally not so much a basic right of private individuals as it was the task of public broadcasting companies.[73] Their right to rely on Article 5 I GG against the state was mainly based on the idea that their task served the public interest.[74] Thus they had to be granted a certain degree of independence from the state. Their inner structure had to reflect all interests of the pluralist society (*Binnenpluralismus*). Thus all groups (political parties, church, unions, etc.) had to be represented in the channels' committees making decisions on programmes and personnel. With the rise of cable TV and private channels Article 5 I GG has been given a new dimension. Terms of coexistence of private and public channels had to be determined (*duale Rundfunkordnung*). Private channels do not have to show the same balanced inner structure as public ones as long as the variety of channels in total reflects pluralist interest (*Aussenpluralismus*). Furthermore, there is no obligation to balance their programmes in the same way.[75] However, it follows that the public channels have to provide a basic service for the population covering all areas of interests (political

---

68 BVerfGE 25, 256.
69 See above, BVerfGE 90, 27 Parabolantennen, above, sec. 1.1.5.
70 BVerfGE 20, 175 (*Spiegelaffäre*).
71 BVerfGE 50, 234.
72 BVerfGE 59, 231 and 73, 118.
73 For details on this subject see Bethge in Sachs, above, n 2, Art. 5, paras 90–115.
74 BVerfG 83, 238, 295 (6. *Rundfunkurteil*).
75 BVerfG 83, 238, 297.

news, entertainment, culture, sports).[76] Their function is still to serve the public (*dienende Funktion*). The consequences become clear when looking at the fierce fights between private and public channels to obtain the broadcasting rights to football matches, especially in international competitions. Public channels must be able to provide a minimum coverage. Otherwise the less well-off spectators will be excluded from even basic information merely by not being able to afford pay-TV channels.

The final (less obvious) right in Article 5 I GG covers the freedom of films and protects against state interference in a way similar to the aforementioned rights.[77]

All the five above mentioned basic rights find their **limitations** in the provisions of general laws, especially for protection of the young and personal honour according to Article 5 II GG. The emphasis on general laws is a safeguard against specific laws that are directed only at suppressing free expression, the press, etc. The rights under Article 5 I GG thus can be limited wherever a law protects other rights. In the *Lüth* case the limitation was found in § 826 BGB, a tort provision also protecting the right to personality.[78] However, such limitations themselves have to be constitutional, i.e. they are limited by the constitution. One express limitation of the limitation is Article 5 I 3 GG, which claims that there shall be no censorship. This refers to pre-censorship by submission to state authorities for approval before expression and not post censorship, which may take the form of public or private prosecution or prevention, especially where other civil or basic rights are involved or may be breached. A general law providing for pre-censorship, however, would violate Article 5 I 3 GG and thus be unconstitutional. A good example of how the limitations of Article 5 I GG work is the *Lebach* case:

BVerfGE 35, 202 Lebach

In 1969 a raid on an armed forces base in the village of Lebach took place during which four soldiers were killed and arms and ammunition stolen. The criminals were apprehended and convicted. One of them, being an accessory to the crime, was only sentenced to six years' imprisonment. Shortly before his release the broadcasting channel ZDF was about to show a documentary play about the incident naming all the involved persons. The accessory obtained an injunction by a civil court against the broadcasting in order to protect his right to personality. The channel complained against the judgment and claimed under Article 5 I GG, freedom of broadcasting. Although the scope of protection was intruded on by the civil court's judgment this intrusion could be justified by general laws (Art. 5 II GG). The laws in question were private laws designed to protect personality. The BVerfG now had to decide whether the civil court had accurately interpreted the provision by taking into account the basic

---

[76] BVerfG 83, 238, 297/298.
[77] For details see Bethge in Sachs, above, n 2, Art. 5 paras 116–128.
[78] BVerfGE 7, 198. See above, sec. 1.1.5 for details.

> rights at stake. These were freedom of broadcasting, on the one hand, and a general right to personality (Art. 2 I, 1 I GG). On balancing these rights now the Court held that Article 5 I GG would be harmed less than Articles 2 I, 1 I GG if the broadcast went ahead. The main reason being that the person affected was to be released soon and his reintegration into society would be hampered severely, if his involvement in the crime was exhibited in the documentary. This would amount to an intolerable violation of his right to dignity and personality.

It is noteworthy that in 1996 another channel (*SAT 1*) attempted the broadcasting of a new documentary on the same subject. Again, the person affected obtained injunctions. This time, however, the constitutional complaints of the broadcasting channel were successful. It was held by the BVerfG that reintegration was no longer endangered, especially as the names were altered and that under these circumstances the right to personality had to stand back in favour of Article 5 I GG.[79]

2.6 Article 5 III GG: Freedom of artistic expression and science (*Freiheit von Kunst und Wissenschaft*)

Article 5 III serves to define the subjective rights involving the freedom of art, science, research, and teaching. These rights are not restricted by the limits of Article 5 II GG (!) as that section only applies to the first paragraph of the Article. Thus the only limitations here are (as in Art. 4 GG) rights and interests of constitutional rank. The *Mephisto* judgment above is seminal in this respect. In that case the general protection to personality was favoured over the specific right to the freedom of artistic expression of the publisher.[80] The scope of protection where art is concerned inevitably leads to fierce debates. It seems that the minimum requirement at least is that the person claiming Article 5 III GG is himself convinced that the work affected is art.[81]

2.7 Article 6: Marriage and family, children born outside marriage (*Ehe, Familie, Nichteheliche Kinder*)

This provides an institutional guarantee and individual rights for marriage, the family, and motherhood, (Art. 6 I, IV GG). For example, it was held that the authorities could not impose higher taxes on married couples than on unmarried couples whose tax was assessed separately.[82] The state is required not just to ensure none of its activities threaten the institutions of marriage and family but that it should

---

[79] Decision of 25th November 1999, see Cornils in Menzel, above, n 16, p. 224.
[80] For a recent review of Art. 5 and its case-law, see Grimm, NJW 1995, 1697–1705.
[81] For further information refer to Pieroth and Schlink, above, n 3, pp. 148–154.
[82] BVerfGE 6, 55.

positively encourage these important elements of society.[83] A recent example of the BVerfG attacking the inability of politicians (i.e. the legislature) to transform their declarations of "family friendly policy" into solid law is the 1998 decision *Familien-lastenausgleich*.[84] Here it was held that tax provisions not taking into account the additional effort of families raising children, which after all is of benefit to the whole of society, were contravening Article 6 I GG. The assessment of the obligation to create tax compensation was supplemented with detailed advice for future legislation. This of course again provoked discussion on the Court overstepping its powers.

In 2001 a new law introduced the *"Eingetragene Lebenspartnerschaft"* as a marriage-like institution for gay and lesbian couples allowing them certain privileges comparable to those of marriage. This law has been criticized as contravening Article 6 I GG and the protection of the institutions of marriage and family as it allegedly erodes their main core and structure.[85] It was challenged by the *Länder* Bavaria and Saxony before the BVerfG asking for an abstract review by an interim measure procedure.[86] The Court only decided on interim measures and rejected the application. On a balance of expected disadvantages it held that it would be less harmful to allow the law to enter into force than stop it. The final substantial decision, however, still has to be made.

2.8 Article 7: School education (*Schulwesen*)

This forms part of the social state and Article 7 I provides for state supervision of the education system. Although education is within the legislative competence of the *Länder* the federation provides framework regulations, the details of which are completed by the *Länder*. Private schools are assured by Article 7 IV but are subject to the regulation of the *Länder*.[87]

2.9 Article 8: Freedom of assembly (*Versammlungsfreiheit*)

Article 8 I provides for the right to peaceful assembly (without arms) in private and for public meetings. This right re-defines the individual right of freedom of expression but in a collective form. It is therefore considered to be also one of the communications rights. A distinction is made between public meetings held inside and those held under the open sky. The latter can be **limited** by law or pursuant to a law. In fact, according to the law on assemblies (*Versammlungsgesetz*)[88] they require forty-eight hours prior notification to the authorities, of the intent to hold the

---

[83] See generally, BVerfGE 29, 166, BVerfGE 28, 104, BVerfGE 40, 121.

[84] BVerfGE 99, 216.

[85] For two opposing views see: Beck, "Die verfassungsrechtliche Begruendung der eingetragenen Lebenspartnerschaft", NJW 2001, pp. 1894–1901 and Scholz and Uhle, "Eingetragene Lebenspartnerschaft und Grundgesetz", NJW 2001, pp. 393–400.

[86] BVerfG, 1 BvQ 23/01, 18 July 2001; see homepage of the Federal Constitutional Court: **www.Bundesverfassungsgericht.de/entscheidungen/qs20010718_1bvq002301.**

[87] BVerfGE 27, 195, BVerfGE 75, 40.

[88] Sartorius, No. 435.

meeting, failing which it may be banned. Note that a limitation is also contained in Article 8 I GG: "peaceful and without weapons". The right to private indoor meetings can be limited only by conflicting constitutional law, e.g. other basic rights.

The right to demonstrate derived from this Article was confirmed by the BVerfG in the *Brokdorf* judgment[89] concerning objections attached to a proposed demonstration against a nuclear power station. Limitations for reasons of public security or peaceful order would be acceptable providing each case was judged on its merits.

2.10 Article 9: Freedom of association (*Vereinigungsfreiheit*)

This reflects Article 5 and 8 GG and provides for the right to form societies and associations but not political parties, which are specifically catered for by Article 21 GG.[90] It is only available to Germans. A foreigner thus would have to base his right to form associations on Article 2 I GG. **Limitations** of this right are possible according to Article 9 II GG. This provision specifically prohibits associations whose activities or purposes conflict with criminal laws or the constitutional order, regulated by the Associations Act (*Vereinsgesetz*).[91]

Article 9 III GG protects the rights of collective action of individuals and collective action of associations (*Koalitionsfreiheit*) to secure and improve working and economic conditions. Article 9 III 2 GG clearly applies in the sphere of private relations to render void any agreement which restricts or seeks to impair the right given. This is an unambiguous example of the so-called *Drittwirkung* of the basic rights.[92]

2.11 Article 10: Privacy of correspondence, posts, and telecommunications (*Brief-, Post- und Fernmeldegeheimnis*)

Article 10 I GG is designed to protect the private or intimate sphere of communication. The **scope of protection** covers letters, anything else transported by the post (*Postgeheimnis*), and any sort of telecommunication: phone calls, faxes, e-mails, and communication via the Internet. Article 10 II allows **restrictions** pursuant to law. Examples can be found in the Criminal Procedural Code StPO (§§ 99 et seq.) and specifically in the "*Abhörgesetz*" (G 10).[93] If such restrictions (i.e. surveillance) are imposed for the protection of the free democratic basic order they need not be disclosed to the affected person. In other words, the affected person will not be able to challenge these actions in court. Instead, a committee of the *Bundestag* is to supervise the surveillance, e.g. phone tapping. However, the BVerfG held that where there is no further danger to the free democratic basic order the person must be told after the surveillance is completed.[94] At least he can subsequently have it

---

[89] BVerfGE 69, 315.
[90] See above, Chapter 6, sec. 3.2.3.
[91] Schönfelder, No. 425.
[92] Further details of Art. 9 III GG can be found in the section on labour law in Chapter 9.
[93] *Gesetz zur Beschränkung des Brief-, Post- und Fernmeldegeheimnisses* (G10), Sartorius No. 7.
[94] BVerfGE 30, 1 (*Abhörurteil*, G 10 I)

reviewed. This law was heavily disputed, as was the decision by the BVerfG review-ing and mainly upholding it as constitutional.[95] In the *Klaas* decision[96] the Euro-pean Court of Human Rights held that limitations based on Article 10 II GG and the G 10 to be compatible with the ECHR. Even the restricted access to courts was held to be compatible with Article 13 ECHR and the principle of effective remedies, since an independent supervising body (Committee of the *Bundestag*) existed.

Recently, the BVerfG has even upheld the 1994 amendment of the G10 law.[97] This amendment widened the scope of the federal intelligence service (BND) to allow phone tapping and extensive data transfer to other public bodies in cases of combating international and organized crime (before, it was state security only). In its 1999 decision, the BVerfG, however, only saw minor incompatibilities with the constitution.

2.12 Article 11: Freedom of movement (*Freizügigkeit*)

The guarantee of the freedom of movement is applicable only to German citizens. It allows them to visit and set up home anywhere in Germany without condi-tions.[98] Right of entry to Germany is guaranteed for Germans but not a right of exit, as seen in the *Elfes* decision.[99] Article 11 I GG can only be limited by law or pursuant to a law (Art. 11 II GG). That is only possible in a few cases of emergency, which are listed in Article 11 II GG. Thus the right is in fact very difficult to restrict. Here the consequences of whether to apply Article 11 I GG or Article 2 I GG as in *Elfes* become apparent. However, even if the right to leave Germany falls under Article 2 I GG that provision will have to be interpreted in the light of the EC rules on free movement (Arts 39–55 TEC) where these become applicable.

2.13 Article 12: Free choice of occupation or profession, prohibition of forced labour (*Berufsfreiheit*)

This is one of the outstanding provisions as far as it affects the individual's decisions on how to earn a living and build up an existence. It is only applicable to German citizens and applies to all occupations and choices of place of training and work.[100] All these aspects of occupation are closely linked so that it has been gener-ally agreed that this Article offers a uniform **scope of protection** against state inter-ference. As a consequence all these aspects are subject to the limitation clause of Article 12 I GG as opposed to only the practice of occupation and professions as the wording might suggest.[101] What sort of profession or occupation (*Beruf*) then is

---

[95] ibid.
[96] *Klaas v Federal Republic of Germany*, Series A. No. 28.
[97] BVerfGE 100, 313 (G10 II)
[98] BVerfGE 2, 266.
[99] See above under Art. 2.
[100] However, in the light of the non-discrimination principle of Art. 12 TEC and the provisions of free movement there are severe doubts as to its restrictions, see Tettinger in Sachs, above, n 2, Art. 12, para. 19.
[101] See Pieroth and Schlink, above, n 3, p. 199.

protected by Article 12 I GG? According to general opinion the definition of *Beruf* includes "any occupation followed for a certain period in order to create and maintain a living, provided it is not forbidden".[102] Thus thieves or drug dealers cannot invoke Article 12 I GG. However, prostitution has been recognized as a protected occupation under Article 12 I GG even if it is morally disapproved by large parts of the population.[103] This has now been given further support by a new law aiming at the protection of prostitutes, in force since the beginning of 2002.[104] Note that Article 12 I GG does not guarantee a right to work[105] nor a pursuable claim that the state provide work places although that remains an aim of the state.[106]

Limitations are possible by or pursuant to a law according to Article 12 I 2 GG which extends to all aspects of profession and occupation. Thus limitations can affect the practice of a profession or even an earlier stage, the choice of training (sometimes described as the *"How"* and the *"Whether"* of professional occupation). According to the "three steps doctrine" (*Drei-Stufen-Lehre*) of the BVerfG developed in the famous *Pharmacists* case, three different kinds of regulations (i.e. limitations) have to be distinguished:

(a) Step 1: Regulations of practice of occupation,
(b) Step 2: Subjective limitations of admissibility, and
(c) Step 3: Objective limitations of admissibility.

The least strict limitations on professions are regulations of practice of occupation as they do not affect the choice of a profession but merely the manner in which it is practiced, e.g. closing hours for pubs or shops, prohibition of advertising for lawyers and doctors and obligation for lawyers to wear gowns during court procedures.

Subjective limitations of admissibility subject the choice of a profession to subjective criteria inherent in the individual affected and usually within his sphere of influence, i.e. qualifications, abilities, experience, merits and also age.

Objective limitations of admissibility subject the choice of a profession to objective criteria that cannot be influenced by the individual, e.g. quotas for a certain profession in order to safeguard essential interests of society. This is the strictest form of limitation.

The stricter those limitations are the heavier is the burden for the state to **constitutionally justify** them. Such limitations, by law, must conform to constitutional principles namely the principle of proportionality as has been decided in the *Pharmacists* case.

---

[102] See, e.g. H.-W. Arndt and W.L. Rudolf *Öffentliches Recht* (1998: Vahlen, München), p. 128.
[103] Pieroth and Schlink, above, n 3, p.201.
[104] Gesetz zur Verbesserung der rechtlichen und sozialen Situation der Prostituierten Vom 20.12.2001, BGBl I 2001, 3983 (statute to improve the legal and social status of prostitutes).
[105] BAG, NJW 1964, 1921.
[106] BVerfGE 59, 231.

BVerfGE 7, 377 Apothekenurteil

Bavaria sought to restrict the issue of pharmacist licences to cases whereby they would be economically viable and cause no economic harm to nearby pharmacies. An applicant was denied a license. In holding this Bavarian restriction unconstitutional the BVerfG laid down general guidelines for the restriction of Article 12 I GG. Every individual has the right under Article 12 to take up any activity, which he believes himself to be prepared to undertake as a profession. However, where the state chooses to regulate this freedom it must consider the least restricting limitation in order to achieve the legislative aim. This means it must opt for the lowest possible "step". Thus the court held that **regulation of practice** (*step 1*) can be justified by **reasonable considerations of the public interest** (e.g. shop closing hours on Sundays). Limitations of choice of profession based on **subjective criteria** (*step 2*) can be only be justified by the **protection of specifically important public interests** (e.g. sufficient qualifications for certain professions such as doctors, lawyers, etc.). Finally, the strictest limitation on choice of professions, based on **objective criteria,** can only be justified by the need **to ward off grave dangers to an outstanding vital public interest** (e.g. quotas depending on demand). The Bavarian rule was held to be a third step measure, which could only be justified in a case of grave danger to an outstanding public interest. The argument that public health had to be protected from ruining competition between too many pharmacists was rejected. Less restrictive measures would have been possible (regulating the practice of the profession).

A further example is the *Numerus Clausus* case.[107] Up to the expansion of the universities in the sixties and seventies, the school leaving qualification, *Abitur* would secure entry. Higher requirements were applied by certain universities because of the pressure on places and facilities. This quota was upheld when absolutely necessary to allow universities to function properly and when based on objective criteria (e.g. grades) and not in case of a residence requirement in the *Land*.[108]

Article 12 II GG prohibits enforced labour, except as part of the civil service alternative to military service or those imprisoned by a court (Art. 12 III GG).

Article 12a GG concerns the regulation of military and public service (*Wehr- und Dienstpflicht*) but will not be examined here.[109]

2.14 Article 13: Privacy of the home (*Unverletzlichkeit der Wohnung*)

The scope of protection of Article 13 I GG ("The home is inviolable") applies to all persons and ensures a private and free environment in which personal develop-

---

[107] BVerfGE 33, 303.

[108] This is now generally governed by the University Framework Act (*Hochschulrahmengesetz* (HRG) of 9 April 1987, (BGBl I S. 1170), §§ 27–35. See also the later case concerned with the determination of the available or lack of further capacity in BVerfGE 56, 31.

[109] For further details see Pieroth and Schlink, above, n 3, p. 130.

ment is unhindered. The term "home" was held to include business premises, work rooms, garages, and hotel rooms.[110]

This right is subject to several limitations which are to be found in Article 13 II–VII GG. Article 13 II covers searches authorized by a judge. Details can be found in the Criminal Procedural Code (§§ 102–110 StPO). Furthermore, following an amendment Article 13 III–V GG now allows electronic surveillance (especially eavesdropping)[111] in order to prosecute serious crimes and avert acute dangers to public safety. Such measures, however, have to be authorized by one or more judges (see provision for details). Obviously, they have to meet constitutional standards such as proportionality. Finally, Article 13 VI GG allows limitations in order to protect the public or the life of an individual. The provision enumerates several examples. These restrictions, however, have to be based on a parliamentary law.

2.15 Article 14: Property, inheritance, expropriation (*Eigentum, Erbrecht, Enteignung*)

This provision is applicable to natural and legal persons and has proved to be a highly controversial right because of the very nature of property rights and the relationship with public law rights. The **protective scope** covers private property as an institution (*Institutsgarantie*) as well as the existence of the property rights of an individual (*Bestandsgarantie*), and the right to use the property as one wishes to (*Verfahrensgarantie*) in Article 14 I 1GG. It furthermore guarantees the right of inheritance. Paradoxically, although the constitution protects "property" its defin-ition is left to the legislative (Art. 14 I 2 GG). The BVerfG elaborated that property is everything that is defined by "the law" as property at a certain time.[112] The refer-ence is mainly then made to the Civil Code, the BGB, focusing on movable and immovable objects.[113] But the BVerfG has proceeded to include all rights with financial assets and rights in social security benefits.[114] Note that the right to carry on business (*Recht am eingerichteten und ausgeübten Gewerbebetrieb*) is viewed more sceptically by the BVerfG whereas the BGH[115] accepts it as a protected right **under private law** including amongst its typical elements market position and base of clients. Such factual conditions are not covered by Article 14 I GG.[116]

There are three kinds of **limitations** of the right of property. The **first** can be derived from Article 14 1 I GG: limiting the use of property. The laws mentioned there not only define property but by doing so they can also limit the rights of an owner (see §§ 903 et seq. BGB). The owner of a car, for example, cannot use his

---

[110] BVerfGE 32, 54; 76, 83. Compare this to the corresponding view of the European Court of Human Rights in *Niemitz v Germany* Series A, No 251, and the opposing view of the ECJ in *Hoechst AG v Commission*, Cases 46/87 and 227/88, ECR 2859.
[111] Known as "*grosser Lauschangriff*" or "*kleiner Lauschangriff*", the latter being less restrictive and only focusing on protection of undercover agents.
[112] BVerfGE 58, 300, 336.
[113] For the private law side of property see Chapter 10.
[114] BVerfGE 53, 257.
[115] BGHZ 23, 157.
[116] BVerfGE 77, 84, 118.

vehicle in any way he likes but has to follow the rules laid out by traffic laws. Such limitations, of course, have to be constitutional, namely proportional. In respect of its desired and sought-for neutrality the *Grundgesetz* tries to tread a middle course between outright capitalist property values and socialist requirements. This is exemplified by Article 14 II GG claiming that "property entails obligations. Its use shall also serve the public good". This is a special reminder to balance public and private interests proportionally in cases of conflict.

The **second possible limitation** is expropriation, meaning a complete withdrawal of the property. This is obviously the harshest restriction. It must be based on a Parliamentary law, which at the same time regulates nature and extent of compensation (Art. 14 III 2 GG). This provision is also known as *Junktimklausel*. Disputes on this will have to be decided by ordinary (civil) courts (Art. 14 III 4 GG).

The **third type of limitation** has caused much confusion for courts and academics and even greater despair for law students. How do we treat intrusions by the state that are neither legal expropriations nor legal limitations of the property's use? The intrusions in question are often real acts that happen to be detrimental to someone's property, for example building works on a street that cause a substantial loss of profits to the owner of a neighbouring pub or shop. It is not for this book to embark on a discussion of these "expropriating and similar intrusions" as they have been called. Suffice it to say though that in a landmark decision[117] the BVerfG held that the expropriation clause is not applicable in these cases as it only mentions expropriations based on a law regulating the compensation. In all other cases the individual cannot suffer intrusion on his property and subsequently demand compensation, but has to try to ward off the state's measures before the administrative courts.[118]

2.16 Article 15: Public ownership (*Sozialisierung*)

Article 15 GG provides for nationalization of land, natural resources, and means of production under the same requirements as Article 14 III 3, 4 GG. When creating the *Grundgesetz* the provision had been included on a proposal by the SPD who wanted to leave open the possibility of socialization. Therefore, if the political climate favoured greater socialization Article 15 GG would apply, subject to guarantees for compensation, but as yet it has not been used.

2.17 Article 16: Citizenship, extradition (*Ausbürgerung, Auslieferung*)

This provision seeks to outlaw arbitrary removal of citizenship and prevent any extradition of Germans, including those in transit from third states.[119] It was created as a response to the racially motivated removals of citizenship from German Jews under the Third Reich. Limitations concerning the citizenship thus can only

---

[117] BVerfGE 58, 300 (*Nassauskiesungsbeschluss*).
[118] For details refer to Pieroth and Schlink, above, n 3, pp. 230–235.
[119] BVerfGE 10, 136.

be based on law. A loss of citizenship against a person's will is only possible if he as a consequence does not become stateless.

Extradition of Germans is not possible at all, although it remains to be seen how Article 16 GG will be interpreted if a German is requested to be transferred to a court of an international organization, of which Germany is a part. Here Germany has possibly limited its sovereignty according to Article 23, 24 GG and thus Article 16 GG as well.[120]

2.18 Article 16a: Asylum (*Asylrecht*)

Article 16a I GG grants the right of asylum to all refugees who are victims of political persecution. This is the only basic right enacted exclusively in favour of foreigners previously in Article 16 II GG. It had been the subject of considerable debate in the early nineties in view of the numbers seeking asylum under this provision and the demands for a uniform European approach on granting asylum. Hence in 1993 Article 16a was introduced into the *Grundgesetz*.[121] Together with Article 13 GG (also newly amended) it stands out as a highly detailed provision. It has considerably expanded the previously simple statement now reproduced in Article 16a I and has introduced extensive and detailed rules into the *Grundgesetz* itself (Art. 16a II–V GG) severely restricting the basic right. Essentially, those entering Germany by way of another Member State of the EU or a third state applying international conventions on refugees, in other words so-called safe third states ("*sichere Drittstaaten*"), have no right to call on the protection offered by Article 16a GG. Which states exactly are safe states is assessed by federal law (Art. 16 a III GG). Further extensive and detailed rules, in particular dealing with the application process, are contained in a supplementary law, the *Asylverfahrensgesetz*.[122] This amendment of the basic right to asylum has been upheld by the BVerfG as constitutional.[123]

2.19 Article 17: Right of petition (*Petitionsrecht*)

Article 17 provides that everyone has the right to petition the appropriate agencies or parliamentary bodies to seek redress against perceived wrongs, in addition to all other rights such as normal law proceedings and the constitutional complaint. No particular form is required and there is no time limit. By providing this as of right it allows Parliament to hear what is happening and a Petitions Committee has been set up to consider applications.[124] About 12,000–14,000 petitions are received per year. A reply is constitutionally guaranteed but, outside of other more formal procedures, chances of a successful outcome are limited.

---

[120] See Pieroth and Schlink, above, n 3, p. 242.
[121] By the *Gesetz zur Änderung des Grundgesetzes* of 28 June 1993 (BGBl I S. 1002).
[122] *Asylverfahrensgesetz* (Sartorius No. 567).
[123] BVerfGE 94, 49.
[124] Further details are regulated in *Gesetz über die Befugnisse des Petitionsausschusses des Deutschen Bundestages* (Sartorius No. 5)

2.20 **Article 17a: The restriction of the basic rights for members of the armed forces and the alternative service in the civil sector**
2.21 **Article 18 and Art. 19 I–III** have been considered earlier[125]
2.22 **Article 19 IV: Procedural basic rights (*Prozeßgrundrechte*)**

Article 19 IV, 101–103 GG contain fundamental procedural rights that can be found in most legal systems adhering to the rule of law. As they are also basic rights an infringement of these rights can be challenged before the BVerfG by way of constitutional complaint.

2.23 Article 19 IV: Recourse to the courts (*Rechtsschutzgarantie*)

This provision is designed to provide a comprising recourse to the courts against measures of state authority infringing basic rights. It is applicable to all natural and domestic legal persons.[126] The term "state authority measures" basically covers all measures undertaken by the executive whether they are administrative or real acts. This is the main reason why there must be a system of administrative courts competent to review any administrative measures. Acts of the judiciary are excluded, in order to ensure legal certainty. Within the judicial system, of course, appeals are possible. However, in cases where the judiciary does not function as a decision-making body in legal disputes but rather acts in support of the executive effective legal remedies must be obtainable (for example, authorizations for searching houses or *Beschlagnahmungen*). Furthermore, acts of the legislature are not state authority measures in the sense of Article 19 IV GG. They may nevertheless be challenged by way of constitutional procedural law.[127]

Article 19 VI GG provides for effective legal remedies. This does not only include a general provision of a working court system but also an effective examination of the individual case concerning facts and the law. Thus even in cases where the state authority measure does not affect the individual anymore (for example, the search of the home has been concluded) he is still entitled to a judicial review where he could not have obtained a decision in time due to the nature of the measure.[128]

2.24 Article 101 I GG: Right to a lawful judge, prohibition of exceptional courts (*Recht auf den gesetzlichen Richter, Verbot von Ausnahmegerichten*)

Applicable to natural and legal persons alike, this provision guarantees a right to have one's case decided by an independent judge. This means that there must be general abstract rules within the judicial system to distribute cases to the different courts. That way arbitrary distribution and manipulation of who will decide a case

---

[125] See Chapter 6, sec. 5.2.4 and above, sec. 1.1.7.
[126] Whether foreign legal persons may rely on it is disputed, Krueger in Sachs, above, n 2, Art. 19, para. 114 with further references.
[127] See below, sec. 2.
[128] BVerfGE 96, 27.

should be prevented. This does not prohibit setting up distribution plans for certain chambers within a court (i.e. one chamber only dealing with commercial litigation, one with insurance law cases, etc.). However, these plans must be sufficiently abstract to guard against arbitrary allocation of an individual concrete case. As judges of the European Court of Justice are also recognized as legal judges in the sense of Article 101 I GG this provision is violated if a court of last instance arbitrarily refuses to obtain a preliminary ruling according to Article 234 II TEC. Such arbitrary refusal can be seen in the court's failure to take into account the relevance of an EC law question, its intentional departure from ECJ case-law, or its intention to rest the decision on a clearly less convincing opinion in EC law, if there is no ECJ case-law.[129]

Another consequence of this rule, based on experiences of the Third Reich, where courts such as the *Volksgerichtshof* were arbitrarily set up to "decide" on individual cases, is the ban of any exceptionally set up courts (*Ausnahmegerichte*) in Article 101 I 2 GG.

2.25 Article 102 GG: Abolition of death penalty (*Abschaffung der Todesstrafe*)

Rather a limitation on limitations than a basic right itself is the declaration of this short provision: "Capital punishment is abolished". It works as a limitation on the restrictions to the right to life and physical integrity possible under Article 2 II GG. Article 102 GG thus blocks a reintroduction of capital punishment by law. Even a constitutional amendment to eliminate the safeguard of Article 102 GG would, according to general opinion, violate the respect for human dignity (Art. 1 I GG) and thus infringe the eternity clause of Article 79 III GG.

2.26 Article 103 I GG: Right to legal hearing (*Anspruch auf Rechtliches Gehör*)

This provision, applicable to legal and natural persons, is directed at the courts, who have to give the parties to litigation sufficient opportunity to comment on the procedure.

2.27 Article 103 II GG: *nulla poena sine lege*

This classical right forbidding punishment for actions that have not been declared as a punishable offence beforehand is a concrete example of the general principle of non-retroactivity and legal certainty.[130] It has also been pointed out that legal problems in this context always arose in times of fundamental political changes. Another example of this is the case of former East German border troops shooting individuals who tried to flee to West Germany.

---

[129] BVerfGE 82, 159, 195.
[130] See above, Chapter 6, sec. 3.3.4.

BVerfGE 95, 96 Mauerschützen

East German border troops had been acting on a legal provision of East German law, which permitted the use of firearms and the shooting of fugitives. After unification, however, they were tried under West German law for manslaughter. The shootings had been lawful under the former East German law, so obviously the soldiers relied on the principle of *nulla poena sine lege*. The BVerfG, however, in a disputed decision, held that in cases of obvious and grave infringements of internationally recognized human rights such as this one there could not be any right to rely on the legality of the legal provision justifying the shooting. In other words, the soldiers could not expect provisions allowing the killing of fugitives, and thus basic right violations, to be "just" and "good law". The constitutional complaint of the accused soldiers therefore failed.

Thus in this case the Court made an exception of the *nulla poena sine lege* principle.[131] In a singular manner the Court had not relied on any written legal provision but ultimately rather on a principle of natural law as formulated by the academic Gustav Radbruch in 1946 as a response to the atrocities committed under Nazi law (*Radbruch'sche Formel*).[132] This principle claimed basically that where positive laws contradicted the idea of justice to an unbearable extent, these laws would have to give way to the idea of justice.[133] Originally, it was the Federal Criminal Court that had employed this principle[134] but the BVerfG took it over in the subsequent proceedings.

Furthermore Article 103 II GG entails a prohibition of analogy (*Analogieverbot*). This means that the wording of a criminal law provision may not be applied in an analogous way to the disadvantage of the accused. Otherwise the scope of application of such a provision would be unclear to the individual and legal certainty endangered.

2.28 Article 103 III GG: *ne bis in idem*

As another classical procedural right, the rule of *ne bis in idem*, forbids punishment for the same deed twice. This entails, for example, that once a person has been accused and tried for an offence but acquitted a reopening of the case is (generally) not possible.

---

[131] For discussion on this decision see Michalowski and Woods, above, n 3, pp. 357–360, with further references.
[132] See the article *"Gesetzliches Unrecht und übergesetzliches Recht"* of 1946, reprinted in G. Radbruch, *Rechtsphilosophie, Studienausgabe,* (1999: Hüthig/C.F. Müller, Heidelberg), pp. 211–219.
[133] Radbruch, above, n 132, p. 216.
[134] BGHSt 39, 1, 15 et seq.

3 The Federal Constitutional Court and constitutional procedural law

The *Grundgesetz* provides for a special court to settle disputes on constitutional law, the Federal Constitutional Court (*Bundesverfassungsgericht*). Its competences are outlined in Article 93 GG. Apart from that a special statute, the *Bundesverfassungsgerichtsgesetz* (BVerfGG),[135] serves as a legal source of constitutional procedural law.

3.1 The Federal Constitutional Court (*Bundesverfassungsgericht, BVerfG*)

Constitutional courts have existed in German history before but arguably none has been as powerful and respected as the BVerfG. The Holy Roman Empire of the German Nation could fall back on the *Reichskammergericht* or the *Reichshofrat* for constitutional disputes between the Emperor and the aristocracy. The Constitution of 1848/49 (*Frankfurter Paulskirchenverfassung*) aimed at establishing a constitutional court with wide-ranging powers similar to the US Supreme Court. The *Staatsgerichtshof* of the Weimar Republic, established in 1921, was designed to decide some but not all types of cases involving constitutional law issues, such as disputes between the Reich and the *Länder* or impeachment procedures against the *Reichspräsident*, the Chancellor or the ministers.[136] Its weak position and the following factual destruction of the Weimar constitution by the Nazis later supported the call for a strong guardian of the constitution. Thus in 1951 the BVerfG was established. Its main legal sources are Articles 92–94 GG and the BVerfGG.

The BVerfG consists of two senates each staffed with eight judges (§ 2 BVerfGG). The senates are responsible for different types of procedures, as defined by law. In exceptional cases the court will decide in plenary sessions to avoid discrepancies between the case-law of the senates (§ 16 BVerfGG). Half of the judges are chosen by the *Bundesrat* whereas the other half is elected by a twelve-member committee of the *Bundestag* representing its composition (§§ 6, 7 BVerfGG). Since in both cases a two-thirds majority is necessary for an appointment a candidate needs the support of both major parties. In practice, the parties divide the posts between themselves and agree to each other's suggestions. As a consequence, most judges are members of one of the two bigger parties. However, this does not mean that their decisions will be predictable. Judges of the BVerfG have been proven to show a healthy sense of independence in spite of party memberships or sympathies. Their term of office—twelve years, not allowing a second term—supports this independent position (§ 4 BVerfGG).

---

[135] Sartorius, No. 40.
[136] The latter was of small practical significance. Federal disputes, however, were quite important. The famous case of the *Preussenschlag*, which upheld the dubious dissolution of the *Land Preussen* by the government of the Reich, showed the court's lack of will and/or power to defend the republic against the totalitarian movement of the NSDAP. For details see C. Gusy, *Die Weimarer Reichsverfassung* (1997: Mohr Siebeck, Tübingen), pp. 209–223.

The BVerfG decides mainly disputes on constitutional law between constitutional organs, the federation and the *Länder*, but also reviews statutes. As an exceptional case the court hears constitutional complaints of individuals. Most of the procedures are listed in the catalogue of Article 93 I GG but some are found scattered across the *Grundgesetz* such as, for example, the party ban procedure in Article 21 II GG.

As a consequence, the role of the BVerfG is twofold: it is a court as its composition and procedures accord to the principles of independent courts. Furthermore, it is a constitutional organ on the same level as the *Bundestag* or the *Bundespräsident* because it derives its powers directly from the constitution and is independent from any other institution (unlike, for example, other courts which in some matters are subject to the orders of the federal ministry or *Länder* ministries of justice). Its political role is pivotal: its authority based on the interpretation of the constitution has long been accepted. But as most of its decisions have had a significant impact on highly political topics questions have arisen whether most important political decisions are gradually shifting from the *Bundestag* to the *Bundesverfassungsgericht*, as a lot of controversial legislative projects are often constitutionally reviewed at the instigation of the outvoted opposition.[137]

4 Constitutional procedural law (*Verfassungsprozessrecht*)

The main source of constitutional procedural law is the statute on the Federal Constitutional Court (BVerfGG). It first outlines general rules on court and procedure before turning to specific conditions for individual types of procedures. Decisions are taken by the majority of judges (§ 15 III 2 BVerfGG). Dissenting opinions are possible and will be published with the decision (§ 30 II BVerfGG). In cases of a draw a violation of the *Grundgesetz* or any other source of federal law cannot be assessed (§ 15 III 3 BVerfGG). Thus an application will fail. According to § 31 II BVerfGG the Court's decisions are attributed the force of law (*Gesetzeskraft*) which means that they are of general application (i.e. declaring a statute void). Interim measures such as injunctions are possible according to § 32 BVerfGG.

The procedures listed in Article 93 I GG cannot all be examined in this book. They include disputes between constitutional organs on the scope of their powers (*Organstreitverfahren*, Art. 93 I Nr. 1 GG)[138] and federal disputes such as those between the federation and the *Länder* on their constitutional relationship and competence (*Bund-Länder-Streit, Art. 93 I Nr. 3 GG).*[139] We will focus on the constitutional complaint and two procedures of judicial review of statutes.

---

[137] For discussion see Ipsen, above, n 11, pp. 220–223.
[138] Examples are the cases mentioned in Chapter 6: *Auslandseinsätze der Bundeswehr* (sec. 3.2.1), *Wüppesahl* (sec. 4.1.3) and *Bundestagsauflösung* (sec. 4.2.2.).
[139] Example: *1. Fernsehurteil* (Chapter 6, sec. 3.5.3 and sec. 3.5.4).

4.1 Abstract review of statutes (*Abstrakte Normenkontrolle*, Art. 93 I No. 2, §§ 13 No. 6, 76 et seq. BVerfGG)

This procedure allows the BVerfG—and only the BVerfG (!)—to review any legal provision (parliamentary statutes, delegated legislation, bye-laws) as to its compatibility with higher-ranking law. Thus federal law can be measured against the *Grundgesetz* whereas statutes of the *Länder* have to conform to any source of federal law. International treaties cannot be directly challenged but only by challenging the national statute implementing them.[140] The BVerfG may only act on applications. Such an application can only be made by the federal government, a government of one of the *Länder*, or a third of the *Bundestag* if there are disputes or doubts as to the compatibility of the provision in question with higher ranking law. If the Court holds the provision to be incompatible with the constitution or federal law then it will declare the provision void. This underlines the power of the BVerfG. Here the difference between the German and the UK constitutional systems becomes apparent. Unlike the UK Parliament the German Parliament (i.e. the *Bundestag*) is not supreme or sovereign. Its laws can be reviewed by the BVerfG. An unconstitutional provision will be declared void *ex tunc*, meaning as if it never entered into force.[141] In exceptional cases the Court will declare a law unconstitutional without declaring it void, for example if abolishing the provision altogether would create an even more unfair situation.

This procedure has often been used by the opposition parties in the *Bundestag* or governments of the *Länder* in opposition to the federal government on the basis of political disputes.[142] It has also been used by a government of one *Land* challenging legislation within another *Land* dominated by a different party.[143]

4.2 The submission procedure (*Vorlageverfahren, Konkrete Normenkontrolle*, Art. 100 I GG, §§ 13 No. 11, 80–82 BVerfGG)

This procedure occurs as a result of a question of the unconstitutionality of a statute which arises in the course of proceedings between parties. It is also referred to as the *Konkrete Normenkontrolle*, to test the validity of a normative law in a specific case. In other words, it is distinguished as a concrete review procedure from the abstract review procedure, because the question of constitutionality arises in a concrete case before a court. Usually this will happen when a court in a case has to apply a provision whose constitutionality is doubtful. If the court believes it unconstitutional and the result of the case depends on the provision then it must stay the proceedings and submit a question to the BVerfG (Art. 100 I GG). The constitutionality of other measures such as secondary legislation will be considered by the administrative courts. The BVerfG has the sole right to declare a statute void

---

[140] For, example, the Bavarian government challenging the implementing statute of the *Grundlagenvertrag* (Chapter 6, sec. 1.1).
[141] See § 79 BVerfGG for details.
[142] For, example *Grundlagenvertrag*, (Chapter 6, sec 1.1).
[143] For example *Ausländerwahlrecht* (Chapter 6, sec. 3.2.1).

(*Verwerfungsmonopol*) in order to guarantee legal certainty and limit the possibilities to interfere with the competence of Parliament. However, laws enacted before the *Grundgesetz* entered into force (*vorkonstitutionelles Recht*) may be reviewed by any court. Here the courts would not question the authority of the legislative of the Federal Republic of German but of its predecessors.

Like in the abstract review procedure the result of a finding of unconstitutionality by the BVerfG may result in the invalidation of a statute or alternatively a declaration that the provision in question is unconstitutional. The BVerfG will order that it is corrected or will request Parliament to correct the legal fault. The submitting court will then have to decide its case taking into account the decision of the BVerfG.[144]

4.3 Constitutional complaint (*Verfassungsbeschwerde*)

Article 93 I No. 4a GG provides that everyone is entitled to make a constitutional complaint to the BVerfG regarding alleged violations of their basic rights or their rights under Articles 20 IV, 33, 38, 101, 103, or 104 GG by the action of public authorities. This procedure has proved to be a valuable instrument for the protection and assessment of the scope of basic rights. It underlines the concept of the *Grundgesetz* regarding the citizen as an individual with subjective rights he can defend against unlawful state intrusion. The procedure is taken seriously by the citizens as the numbers of constitutional complaints show (some 5,000 each year), which make up about 96% of the court's workload.[145] Complaints to the European Court of Human Rights from Germany about human rights violations by comparison amount to about only 500 p.a.[146] Thus the constitutional complaint procedure could be regarded as having a "filtering effect" in favour of the ECHR.

The procedure's political significance cannot be overestimated, since even legislative acts may be challenged this way. A good example is the *Census* decision of 1983. The legal basis for an imminent census, as drawn up by the main legislator, the *Bundestag*, was successfully challenged by several citizens.[147]

As the constitutional complaint is a privileged process which could be the subject of abuse if used for spurious claims, it is subject to a number of preconditions before it can be set in motion (§§ 90 et seq. BVerfGG). Thus the complaint will first be examined as to its admissibility (*Zulässigkeit*) and then as to its merits (*Begründetheit*).[148]

The following preconditions will have to be fulfilled, if a constitutional complaint is to be held admissible:

---

[144] This procedure shows some similarities to mechanisms of the preliminary ruling procedure of the ECJ under Art. 234 EC, bearing in mind that the ECJ cannot declare a national statute void if it is incompatible with higher ranking EC law but merely request the submitting court to set aside this law in the concrete case. The national law remains still applicable in purely domestic cases where there is no conflict with EC law.

[145] Between 1951 and 1999 there have been 122,257 constitutional complaints. However, only 3,103 were successful (2.6%). See homepage of the *Bundesverfassungsgericht*: **www.Bundesverfassungsgericht.de/cgi-bin/link.pl?aufgaben.**

[146] See ECHR homepage, **www.echr.coe.int/eng/select%20folder.html**

[147] BVerfGE 65, 1seq. (*Volkszählung*); see above sec. 1.2, Art. 2 GG.

[148] This classical structure of examination is applicable to any action taken before most German courts whether in civil or administrative law cases.

4.3.1 *Capability to participate in the procedure (Beteiligtenfähigkeit)*

According to Article 93 I Nr 4a GG and § 90 BVerfGG "everyone" (*jedermann*) whose rights have been violated may lodge a constitutional complaint. This includes natural as well as legal persons as long as they are capable of holding the particular basic right they think to be infringed. Thus a foreigner would lack this capability in respect of a violation of typical "German" basic rights (e.g. Art. 12 I GG). A different matter is the question of capacity to take part in the procedure. This is relevant in cases of minors claiming an infringement of basic rights. Usually, participation in the procedure requires majority according to the civil code. However, in cases of constitutional complaints it depends on the minor's capacity to use his basic right. Thus if a minor is deemed capable to make his own decisions as to his religious freedom he may also try to defend them before the Constitutional Court.[149]

4.3.2 *Challenged act (Beschwerdegegenstand)*

The act challenged by the complaint can only be an act of the public authorities (*Akt öffentlicher Gewalt*). This includes all acts taken by the executive, judiciary, and legislature, in other words they mainly cover administrative acts, court decisions, and legislative acts.

4.3.3 *Locus standi (Beschwerdebefugnis)*

In order to have *locus standi* or a personal legitimacy to lodge the complaint the complainant must show the possibility of an incurred violation of his rights. It has to be evident that the complainant is personally (*selbst*) presently (*gegenwärtig*) and directly (*unmittelbar*) affected.[150] These criteria will exclude a number of possible complaints. The complainant will have to state a personal injury.[151] He cannot challenge acts that are no longer or not yet valid. Finally, he has to be directly affected. This means that where a statute is the basis of a restriction of his rights it depends on whether the restriction takes effect by the law itself or by an implementing administrative act.

Example: An amendment of the statute on assemblies offers the police the possibility to restrict gatherings in certain cases. Here it is not the law but the (implementing) police order which will in those individual cases restrict the freedom of assembly.

Rarely will statutes affect individuals. This is often circumvented where an applicant alleges damage as a result of judicial or administrative action based on an allegedly unconstitutional law. The law is therefore reviewed indirectly. In respect

---

[149] See above sec. 1.1.3.
[150] BVerfGE 1, 97.
[151] See the complaints in the *Maastricht* case above, in which only those relating to the personal right to vote in elections were held to be admissible. All others relating to general provisions of the Grundgesetz were held to be inadmissible. See Chapter 2.

of wrongs by an administrative authority the applicant must have been addressed personally.

4.3.4 *Exhaustion of remedies (Rechtswegerschöpfung)*

All other administrative and judicial remedies must first have been exhausted (§ 90 II 1 BVerfGG), but this requirement can be waived in exceptional cases, namely where the matter is of general importance or the consequences of the inevitable delay would be unduly severe (§ 90 II 2 BVerfGG). In general, however, the complainant must first have tried to obtain his remedy through the normal administrative and judicial channels including a request for a submission procedure. This principle serves to relieve the BVerfG and at the same time emphasize the authority of the specialized judicial branches. As a consequence, administrative acts will nearly always be reviewed by the administrative courts. A constitutional complaint will then mainly focus on the judicial decision of the administrative court of last instance upholding the original act. Thus most constitutional complaints challenge decisions of courts of last instance.

4.3.5 *Form and time limits (Form und Fristen)*

Constitutional complaints have to be submitted in written form (§§ 23, 92 BVerfGG). There are time limits of one month for complaints against administrative or judicial decisions and one year in the case of legislation (§ 93 I, II BVerfGG).

4.3.6 *Merits (Begründetheit)*

If all these conditions are met the complaint will be admitted. Now the merits will be considered (*Begründetheit*), here the BVerfG will examine whether the challenged act has indeed violated a basic right. As outlined before,[152] it will first assess the scope of protection of the basic right in question and whether it covered the complainant's claimed interests or activities. Then it will examine whether the challenged act intruded on this right at all and if so whether this intrusion was constitutionally justified. If the latter is not the case the complaint will be successful (*begründet*).[153] In such a case a challenged law will be declared void (§ 95 III 1 BVerfGG), a challenged decision will be quashed and the case will have to be decided again by the competent court taking into account the decision of the BVerfG (§ 95 II BVerfGG). If the BVerfG finds that the court of last instance relied on an unconstitutional law it will, furthermore, declare the law void (§ 95 II 2 BVerfGG). Where the BVerfG reviews merely the decision of another court it has to be pointed out that it only does so in respect of a violation of *specific* constitutional law. It will only examine whether basic rights have been sufficiently taken into account. It will not act as a "court of last instance after the court of last instance" (*Superrevisionsinstanz*). Thus it would not judge on the correct application of labour law by the Federal Labour Court but only on its impact on the basic right in question.

---

[152] See above sec. 1.1.6.
[153] Literally, "well-founded".

4.4 Constitutional courts of the *Länder*

Finally, the constitutional courts of the *Länder* have to be mentioned.[154] Their task, obviously, is to decide disputes on the constitutional law of the *Länder*, i.e. compatibility of laws of a *Land* with its constitution. They cannot review federal law. Otherwise the procedures are similar to the ones before the Federal Constitutional Court. Constitutional complaints as regards basic rights enshrined in the constitution of a *Land* are available in most *Länder*.[155]

FURTHER READING

Legislation

O. Akalin (ed.), *Law on the Federal Constitutional Court* (a translation of the BVerfGG), with an introduction by G. Wöhrmann (1982: Inter Nationes, Bonn).

Grundgesetz für die Bundesrepublik Deutschland, 1998, Bundeszentrale für politische Bildung, Bonn.

Verträge zur deutschen Einheit, Bundeszentrale fur politische Bildung (October 1990).

Books

H.-W. Arndt and W. Rudolf, *Öffentliches Recht*, 12th ed. (1998: Vahlen, München).

S. Aust, *Der Baader-Meinhof-Komplex* 2nd ed. (1997: Stern, Hamburg).

Bundeszentrale für politische Bildung (ed.), *Deutsche Verfassungsgeschichte 1849–1919–1949* 1989: Bonn).

E. Barendt, *An Introduction to Constitutional Law* (1998: Oxford University Press).

H. Barnett, *Constitutional and Administrative Law*, 3rd ed. (2000: Cavendish, London).

F. Becker, *Grundzüge des öffentlichen Rechts*, 6th ed. (1995: Vahlen, München).

P.M. Blair, *Federalism and Judicial Review in West Germany* (1981: Clarendon Press, Oxford).

P. Craig and G. de Burca, *EU Law*, 2nd ed. (1999:), pp. 349–357.

C. Creifelds, *Rechtswörterbuch*, 15th ed. (1999: C.H. Beck, München).

C. Degenhart, *Staatsrecht I: Staatsorganisationsrecht*, 15th ed. (1999: C.F. Müller, Heidelberg).

C. Gusy, *Die Weimarer Reichsverfassung* (1997: Mohr Siebeck, Tübingen).

K. Hesse, *Grundzüge des Verfassungsrechts der Bundesrepubik Deutschland*, 20th ed. (1999: C.F. Müller, Heidelberg).

J. Ipsen, *Staatsrecht I*, 11th ed. (1999: Luchterhand, Neuwied).

J. Ipsen, *Staatsrecht II*, 2nd ed. (1998: Luchterhand, Neuwied).

Jarass and Pieroth, *GG Kommentar*, 4th ed. (1997: C.H. Beck, München).

U. Karpen, (ed.), *The Constitution of the Federal Republic of Germany* (1988: Nomos Verlag, Baden-Baden), especially Karpen, Chapters 9 and 11, Giegerrich, Chapter 8 and Kunig, Chapter 10.

---

[154] They exist in most *Länder* except Schleswig-Holstein, which has transferred the competence to decide issues of constitutional law of the *Land* to the BVerfG according to Art. 44 of its constitution and Art. 99 GG.

[155] For details see Pestalozza, *Verfassungen der Deutschen Bundesländer*, 7th ed. (2001), pp. LXX–LXXII. See also Maurer, above, n 1, pp. 716–719 for the problems of conflicting competences and critical assessment of the *Honecker* decision.

H.W. Koch, *A Constitutional History of Germany in the Nineteenth and Twentieth Centuries* (1984: Longman).

D. P. Kommers, *Judicial Politics in West Germany: A Study of the Federal Constitutional Court* (1976: Sage).

D. P. Kommers, *Constitutional Jurisprudence of the Federal Republic of Germany* (1990: Duke University Press).

T. Maunz and G. Dürig (eds.), *Grundgesetz Kommentar*, Vol. 1–5 (2001: C.H.Beck, München).

H. Maurer, *Staatsrecht, München* (1999: C.H. Beck, München).

J. Menzel (ed.), *Verfassungsrechtsprechung* (2000: Mohr Siebeck, Tübingen).

C. Pestallozza, *Verfassungen der Deutschen Bundesländer*, 7th ed. (2001: C.H. Beck, München).

B. Pieroth and B. Schlink, *Staatsrecht II: Grundrechte*, 15th ed. (1999: C.F. Müller, Heidelberg).

G. Radbruch, *Rechtsphilosophie, Studienausgable* (1999: Hüthig/C.F. Muller, Heidelberg).

I. Richter, G.F. Schuppert, and C. Bumke, *Casebook Verfassungsrecht*, 4th ed. (2001: C.H. Beck, München).

M. Sachs (ed.), *Grundgesetz Kommentar*, 2nd ed. (1999: C.H. Beck, München).

Schmidt-Bleibtreu and Klein, *Kommentar zum Grundgesetz*, 9th ed. (1999, Luchterhand, Neuwied).

M. Schweitzer, *Staatsrecht III: Staatsrecht, Europarecht, Völkerrecht*, 6th ed. 1997, 15th ed. (1999: C.F. Müller, Heidelberg).

C. Starck, (ed.), *Main Principles of the German Basic Law* (1983: Nomos Verlag, Baden-Baden).

C. Starck, (ed.), *Rights, Institutions and Impact of International Law According to the German Basic Law* (1987: Nomos Verlag, Baden-Baden).

C. Starck (ed.), *New Challenges to the German Basic Law* (1991: Nomos Verlag, Baden-Baden), especially Ress, Chapter 5 and Götz, Chapter 6.

E. Stein, *Staatsrecht*, 16th ed. (1998: Mohr, Tübingen).

D. Willoweit, *Deutsche Verfassungsgeschichte*, 9th. ed. (1997: C.H. Beck, München).

Articles

P.-A. Albrecht and S. Kadelbach, "Zur strafrechtlichen Verfolgung von DDR-Aussenspionage" *Neue Justiz* 92, 137–147.

W. Czaplinksi, "The New Polish-German Treaties and the Changing Political Structure of Europe" (1992) 86 AJIL 163–173.

R. Dahrendorf, "A Confusion of Powers: Politics and the Rule of Law" (1977) 40 MLR 1–15.

T. Discher, "Die Peep-Show-Urteile des BverwG" JuS 1991, 642-648.

N. Foster, "The German *Grundgesetz* after the Unification Treaty of the Two Germanies" 1991 38 NILR 360–372.

J. Frowein, "Legal Problems of the German Ostpolitik" (1974) 23 ICLQ 105–126.

J. Frowein, "The Reunification of Germany" (1992) 86 AJIL 152–163.

K. Hailbronner, "Legal Aspects of the Unification of the Two German States" (1991) 3 EJIL 18–41.

R. Harvey, "Equal Treatment of Men and Women in the Work Place: The Implementation of the European Community's Equal Treatment Legislation in the Federal Republic of Germany" (1990) 38 Am J Comp L 31–71.

U. Karpen, "Freedom of Expression as a Basic Right: A German View" (1989) 37 Am J Comp L 395–404.

F. Mann, "The Present Legal Status of Germany" (1947) ILQ 314 reprinted in F. Mann, *Studies in International Law* (1973) pp. 634–659.

F. Mann, "Germany's Present Legal Status Revisited" (1967) 16 ICLQ 760–799.

B.S. Markesinis, "The Right to be Let Alone versus Freedom of Speech" (1986) Public Law 67–82.

A. Ogus, "The Federal Republic of Germany as sozialstaat: a British Perspective" 1990, Working Paper No. 3, University of Manchester, Faculty of Law, Manchester.

R. Piotrowicz, "The Status of Germany in International Law: Deutschland über Deutschland?" (1989) 38 ICLQ 609–635.

W. Schmitt-Gläser, "Big Brother is watching you—Menschenwürde bei" RTL 2, ZRP 2000, 395–402.

B. Simma and K. Volk, "Der Spion, der in die Kaelte kam" NJW 1991, 872–875, 874.

M. Singer, "The Constitutional Court of the German Federal Republic: Jurisdiction over Individual Complaints" (1982) 31 ICLQ 331–356.

M.T. Tinnefeld, "Menschenwürde, Biomedizin und Datenschutz" ZRP 2000, 10–13.

B. Vitanayi "Some Reflections on Article 25 of the Constitution of the German Federal Republic" (1978) 24 NILR 578–588.

8

Public law III

A General administrative law

1 Introduction

Public administration is not easy to define. It has often been referred to as that part of state activities that do not belong to the judicial, legislative, or governmental branch. Public administration deals with matters of the social community in the public interest.[1] The basic premises of administrative law in Germany show its close and strong connection to constitutional law. Constitutional requirements include that the exercise of all state authority must have a legal basis, that there is a clear distribution of administration competence and that the municipalities (*Gemeinden*) and have the right of self-government.[2] For the individual German administrative law is of interest when looking at the boundaries of public power and his ability to take legal action to nullify a decision affecting him. This is possible if the decision has infringed his rights and does not conform to either constitutional principles or statute. Furthermore, he might compel the public authorities to perform their obligations.

1.1 Different types of administration

There are numerous ways of distinguishing the types of administration. From the citizen's point of view the most significant ones are intervening administration (*Eingriffsverwaltung*) or service administration (*Leistungsverwaltung*). The classical nineteenth century type of administration has always been of an intervening character. It sought to ensure public order and safety. Thus it mostly dealt with police matters and restricted citizen's rights in the public interest. In modern social welfare states administration has an additional role. It provides services to the citizen in different forms, e.g. social security, running of hospitals, schools, public transport services, etc. It may also go beyond these basic services and offer benefits in very specific areas, i.e. by subsidizing parts of the economy or cultural projects.

Other forms of administration like planning administration (*Planungsverwaltung*) aim at steering developments in whole areas of social, cultural, or economic life,

---

[1] For discussion on definitions see H. Maurer, *Allgemeines Verwaltungsrecht*, 12th ed. (1999: C.H. Beck, München), pp. 2–6.
[2] Some of the constitutional impacts will be considered below in sec. 4.

often using instruments of an intervening or service character (i.e. prohibitions or subsidies). Finally, financial administration (*Abgabenverwaltung*) provides the state with necessary financial means by raising taxes or charges.[3]

1.2 Administrative law as part of public law

Administrative law has to be distinguished as part of public law from civil law. This is necessary for several reasons as some examples show: in cases of a dispute the distinction will decide which branch of the judiciary is competent to decide, as public law matters generally belong before the administrative courts (§ 40 VwGO) leaving private law matters to the civil courts (§13 GVG). The law on administrative procedure (*Verwaltungsverfahrensgesetz, VwVfG*) setting out general administrative rules is only applicable to administrative bodies if they are acting under public law. In cases where they are allowed to use private law instruments—e.g. a contract of sale to buy stationary—private law applies to them. Furthermore, state liability for damages caused by anyone exercising a public office[4] will depend on whether the tortuous act in question occurred in connection with a public duty. Thus this duty has to be one under public law if the claim under state liability is to succeed.

As a rule of thumb private law deals with the relations between citizens on an equal basis ("horizontal relationship") whereas public law deals with the (rather hierarchical) relation between state and citizen, in other words "vertical relationships".[5] However, this does not always help to accurately divide the numerous provisions into categories. Administrative rules may cover situations that do not involve the relation of state and citizen. Thus several rules and theories have been developed to provide a better distinction.[6] One of them suggests that public law comprise all legal provisions that address public authorities, thereby empowering and obliging only them. Thus public law is the specific law (*Sonderrecht*) of the state.[7] This seems to be a more favoured theory. However, the problems usually do not arise when characterizing a certain legal provision but rather when classifying an action. Here in each individual case the context will decide whether public or civil law rules apply to them.

BGH VersR 1979, 225 Dienstfahrt

In this case two civil servants—for simplification called *A* and *B* here—participated in a meeting on flight control matters which took place on the airport premises. In order to get there *A*—with approval of his superior—used his car offering *B* a lift. On their

---

[3] See also H.-D. Sproll, *Allgemeines Verwaltungsrecht* I (1997: C.H. Beck, München), pp. 17–20.
[4] Such claims are possible under § 839 BGB in connection with Art. 34 GG.
[5] This rule has been called *Subordinationstheorie.*
[6] For discussion on the various theories see Maurer, above, n 1, pp. 44–47.
[7] *Sonderrechtstheorie* or *Zuordnungstheorie*; Maurer, above, n 1, p. 45.

way back *A* negligently caused an accident during which *B* was seriously injured. When *B* claimed damages under state liability rules the main question to be decided was whether *A* had been acting "in the course of his duty". Participating in traffic, like the journey back from the meeting, is usually neither a matter of public or private law. However, participating in the meeting on flight control matters was a public law matter and thus within *A*'s official duties. The Federal Civil Court (*BGH*)[8] held that in cases where such journeys were so closely linked to the original official duty—the meeting—they had to be regarded as part of it. In this case—especially as *A* had used his own car with his superior's approval—this was accepted. The accident had therefore happened in the course of *A*'s duty. As a consequence state liability under public law was applicable.

1.3 Influence of European law

European Union law—to be exact European Community law—has a particularly strong influence on German administrative law.[9] As the EC may issue legal instruments within areas of its competence, such as for example agricultural policies, these have to be implemented by the administration. Where legal provisions are directly applicable, such as regulations (Art. 249 II TEC), they become national law and thus are applied by national administrative bodies. They must equally apply legal provisions that are not directly applicable, but have direct effect, such as directives (Art. 249 III TEC) under certain circumstances. Where they contradict national legislation the national authorities have to set aside the national law.[10] However, in cases not covered by EC law the national law still remains applicable. Finally, certain areas of EC law are administered by EC bodies themselves, such as for example procedures under competition rules (Art. 83 et seq. EC) by the European Commission.

1.4 General and specific administrative law

General administrative law (*Allgemeines Verwaltungsrecht*) comprises all the rules and provisions applicable to each area of administrative law and each administrative body. It comprises general principles, concepts, and legal institutions applicable to all spheres of administrative law, i.e. all special branches of administrative law (*Besonderes Verwaltungsrecht*) like laws on building, environment, police, public streets, local government, civil servants, and foreigners. This section will only deal with the general administrative law.

---

[8] Confusing as it may though for the distinction of public and private law, it has to be pointed out that state liability matters are decided by the civil courts (§ 40 II VwGO).
[9] For the impact of EC legislation on national administrative law see I. Richter, F. Schuppert, and C. Bumke, *Casebook Verwaltungsrecht*, 3rd ed. (2000: C.H. Beck, München), pp. 16–33.
[10] Case 103/88 *Fratelli Costanzo SpA v Commune di Milano* [1989] ECR 1839.

2 Sources of administrative law

The *Grundgesetz*, specific statutes concerning substantive law, court organization and procedure, decisions of the courts, administrative practices, and latterly European Community law, are all sources of administrative law.

2.1 The *Grundgesetz*

The *Grundgesetz* contains constitutional principles that specifically refer to administrative law such as the legality of administration (Art. 20 III GG), the distribution of competence between federation and *Länder* (Art. 83 et seq. GG), and the right of municipalities to self-governance (Art. 28 II GG).

2.2 Federal and *Länder* statutes (*Bundes- und Landesgesetze*)

Statutory law sources are federal law as well as laws of the *Länder*. As far as administrative law is concerned the federation has less legislative powers. Thus many laws dealing especially with the particular branches are laws of the *Länder* (such as, for example, the laws on policing, on building regulations, or self-governance of municipalities). The essential procedural principles have been codified and are contained in the Law of Administrative Procedure (*Verwaltungsverfahrensgesetz, VwVfG*) of 1976. Due to the federation's lack of legislative competence this could not be more than "sample legislation". However, the *Länder* copied it into their laws on administrative procedure thus ensuring uniform application throughout Germany. The Administrative Courts Act (*Verwaltungsgerichtsordnung, VwGO*) governs the procedure before the Administrative Courts, which form a separate hierarchy of courts.[11]

2.3 Delegated legislation (*Rechtsverordnungen*)

Another source of administrative law, provided for in Article 80 GG, is **delegated legislation**. According to this provision the federal government, ministers, and governments of the *Länder* can be empowered by Parliament under Article 80 *Grundgesetz* to produce statutory orders or Regulations (*Rechtsverordnungen*).[12]

2.4 Bye-laws (*Satzungen*)

A large variety of independent bodies established under public law exist, including the local executives in communes (*Gemeinden*), counties (*Landkreise*) and councils at all levels (*Räte* and *Kreistage*). Other autonomous bodies are the universities, professional bodies, broadcasting authorities and the Federal Bank. These are

---

[11] See above Chapter 3.
[12] For details see Chapter 6, sec. 4.5.1.

empowered by statute to produce **bye-laws** (*Satzungen*) which must also conform to the general principles. The bodies, which produce this form of law, are so disparate that no generally applicable description can apply. Communes and councils, which produce them, must be elected in applying the constitutional principles of democracy in general, direct, free, equal, and secret elections. *Satzungen* are also subject to general constitutional limits, basic rights, conform to federal and *Länder* legislation and require publication. *Satzungen* must therefore respect the limits of self-governance or self-administration set for the particular issuing body (regardless which particular body is concerned). They occupy the lowest level in the hierarchy of legal norms and must therefore comply with both their individual empowering statutory basis and any other higher form of law.

2.5 Administrative guidelines (*Verwaltungsvorschriften*)

Furthermore there are the **administrative prescriptions** or **guidelines** (*Verwaltungsvorschriften*).[13] These are general orders bearing an array of names—Decrees (*Erlasse*), Directives or guidelines (*Richtlinien*) and Service regulations (*Dienstvorschriften*)—given by higher authorities to subordinate authorities, usually regulating quite closely the organization and procedure of a subordinate. They constitute internal law. Thus they are not binding on the citizen and apply in respect of the internal administration only. However, in certain cases they may produce external effect. According to the case-law of the BVerwG such guidelines constitute external effect, if the administration has adopted a practice of handling cases on the basis of these guidelines. The principle of non-discrimination (Art. 3 I GG) demands that all similar cases are then treated in the same way. Thus the administration has bound itself (*Selbstbindung der Verwaltung*). The individual consequently has a claim to be treated according to the administration's practice based on the guidelines.[14] Sometimes even without an ascertained practice of administration administrative guidelines can produce external effect and thus be legally binding. This was decided by the BVerwG in the *Wyhl* decision concerning technical guidelines on admissible exposure to radioactive emission.[15]

The question of external effect of technical guidelines is also important in the context of European Community law:

Case C-361/88, Commission v Germany (*TA-Luft*), ECJ [1991] I-2567

According to Article 249 III EC EC Directives have to be transformed into national law leaving to the Member States the choice of form and method. The EC Directive 80/779 was designed to protect humans against lead and thus set limits for the content of lead

---

[13] See Maurer, above, n 1, pp. 598–620.
[14] E.g. BVerwGE 36, 323; 61, 15.
[15] BVerwGE 72, 300.

in air. In Germany the Directive was basically implemented by an administrative technical guideline (*TA-Luft*). The European Commission brought an action against Germany because of inappropriate implementation of the Directive. The ECJ agreed with the Commission. It held that the Directive was designed to protect and inform the individual as to his rights of protection against harmful lead content. As administrative guidelines in Germany did in general not produce external effect the individual could not rely on them. Thus this sort of implementation was held insufficient.

2.6 EC Law

The previous case shows that **European Community law** has to be kept in mind as a source of law affecting all areas of national law. Another classical example of how EC Law supplements and modifies national administrative law is the revocation of administrative decisions granting subsidies. Where such a subsidy falls under EC Law (Art. 87 et seq. EC) its revocation is not only subject to the national regulations (§ 48 VwVfG) but also Article 87 EC as interpreted by the ECJ.

3 Administrative bodies

Administrative law concerns, in its widest sense, the legal provisions and actions of public administration and the controls over the exercise of state power by the executive and other public bodies. These bodies comprise public authorities exercising administrative powers at all levels, including the federal administration, *Länder* administrations, and the levels of local administration (*Kommunen, Kreise, Gemeinden*). It is necessary to divide between the legal persons responsible for administration (*Verwaltungsträger*) and the organs that act for them.

Generally, there are two types of administration, direct and indirect administration of state. Direct administration of state (*Unmittelbare Staatsverwaltung*) comprises administration by authorities of either the federation or the *Länder*. Any decision taken by such authorities can only be taken in the name of one of them. The authorities cannot be bearer of rights or obligations as they are merely organs or instruments of the legal person they are acting for. These legal persons, the federation and the *Länder*, usually have a hierarchical three-rank system of administration, the highest level being the ministries. Whether the *Länder* or federation authorities are competent to act is determined by Articles 83–91 GG.[16] Furthermore, there are a few areas of joint administration (Arts 91, 91a GG).

Indirect administration of state (*Mittelbare Staatsverwaltung*) covers all areas of administration that the state has transferred to the competence of other independent legal persons. The most important ones are perhaps the communities

---

[16] See Chapter 6, sec. 4.5.2.

(*Gemeinden*). They constitute territorial legal entities (*Gebietskörperschaften*). Article 28 II GG grants them a right to self-government. Thus they are responsible for regulating and administrating typically municipal or local matters. Other independent legal persons established under public law often exercise specific functions, e.g. chambers of lawyers dealing with upholding the code of professional discipline of within legal professions. Examples of other legal persons (*juristische Personen des öffentlichen Rechts: Körperschaften, Anstalten* & *Stiftungen*) are: the universities, chambers of commerce, public savings banks, the public broadcasting authorities, or the various bodies in charge of national insurance, including state health schemes. In exceptional cases the state may engage even private persons (then called "*Beliehene*") to exercise certain tasks. A classical example is the *Technischer Überwachungsverein (TÜV)*, a private law association testing the safety of technical installations, machinery, and motor vehicles.

4 Basic principles of administrative law

Some basic principles can be found in the constitution (e.g. legality of administration), others are features of administrative law recurring in statutes and regulations (discretion and margin of appreciation) and finally some have been developed by the courts interpreting administrative law (principle of the "subjective public right").

4.1 Impact of constitutional law

Some provisions of the *Grundgesetz* specifically refer to the administration, for example, Article 20 III GG that declares the executive to be bound by law and justice. This principle of legality of administration has already been examined when looking at the *Rechtsstaatsprinzip*.[17] It basically means that any administrative action must be based on legislation. Administrative authorities are not allowed to make legally binding decisions solely based on their own power but need a legal basis. Without this no administrative action would be democratically justified. Furthermore, restrictive acts would contravene the basic right to free personal development (Art. 2 I GG).

Example: An administrative authority may only withdraw a driving license on the basis of an existing law. This would be § 3 I StVG (Road Traffic Act).

Articles 83 et seq. GG distribute the competence of administration between

---

[17] See above Chapter 6, sec. 3.3.3.

federation and *Länder*. As a general rule administration is a matter for the *Länder* unless the *Grundgesetz* states otherwise.[18]

Finally, the basic rights serve as protection against administrative actions unjustly restricting individual freedom. According Article 1 III GG they bind all state power including the executive.[19] It follows that where the administration acts in order to deliver public services it will be bound by basic rights, even if it chooses a private law structure, (e.g. privatization or outsourcing). Any evasion into private law (*Flucht ins Privatrecht*) is inadmissible.

Example: A municipality decides to run a swimming pool. Instead of running it directly under public law it sets up a private law company to do so. Conditions for use of the pool limiting access only to certain group of people would contradict the principle of non-discrimination under Article 3 I GG as the company is providing a public service on behalf of the municipality. Thus it is bound by Article 3 I GG.

4.2 Discretion (*Ermessen*)

In spite of being bound by the law administrative authorities are granted a certain degree of discretion (*Ermessen*) when making decisions. Thus some legal provisions will allow them discretion as to whether or how to react to certain situations.

Example: § 15 II VersG (law on assemblies) states: " The competent authority *may* dissolve an assembly, if it has not been notified . . . " This provision assumes a situation defined by clear facts: An assembly has not been notified, but takes place nevertheless. Whether the competent authority (police) now dissolves the assembly is left to their discretion. The authorities are closer to the individual situation. Whether dissolution of the assembly is necessary might be easier for the authority to decide than the legislature, for example because no danger emanates from the peaceful gathering in the particular case. Thus it is left to the authority to take the appropriate steps, if any.

Most legal provisions can be characterized as "if-then clauses". If a certain situation manifests, then a certain legal consequence follows. These legal consequences in administrative law include the authorities' competence to act. Discretion is provided for in the part concerning the legal consequence of the provision, in other words the "then"-side of the provision. However, some situations might only leave one possible option to act. Here discretion is reduced to that particular matter (*Ermessensreduzierung*).[20]

---

[18] See above Chapter 6, sec. 4.5.2.
[19] for basic rights see above, Chapter 6, sec. 5.
[20] BVerwGE 95, 15.

In the interest of limiting power there must of course be limits to this discretion. These limits are reached in the following cases of mistakes concerning discretion (*Ermessensfehler):*

(a) non-use of discretion (*Ermessensnichtgebrauch*),

(b) exceeding discretion (*Ermessensüberschreitung*), and

(c) misuse of discretion (*Ermessensfehlgebrauch*).

Examples: If in the above mentioned example, the police dissolved the assembly believing that this is a compulsory consequence prescribed in § 15 II VersG—in other words believing they have no other choice—this would be a case of **non-use of discretion**. **Exceeding discretion** would be the case if the police took actions not covered by the provision, such as taking down the details of all participants of the assembly or arresting them. A **misuse of discretion** would occur if the police make a decision not solely based on the purpose of discretion, i.e. in order to obtain personal benefits or out of other personal motives. This would be the case if the police dissolved the demonstration mainly in order to obstruct expression of a certain political opinion.[21]

When making a decision the authority has to choose the measure which least restricts the citizen's rights. In other words it is bound by the principle of proportionality.[22] Thus an inappropriate or unnecessary measure would not be covered by (i.e. exceed) their discretion. The same applies if on balance the citizen's basic rights are not sufficiently taken into account, e.g. Article 8 I GG in the above-mentioned example.

In all of these cases of mistakes concerning discretion the authorities' decision is unlawful and can thus be challenged before the administrative courts.

4.3 Margin of appreciation (*Beurteilungsspielraum*)

The principle of discretion is attributed to that part of the provision dealing with the legal consequences of a set of facts. The margin of appreciation (*Beurteilungsspielraum*) in contrast applies to the part of the provision setting out the facts as preconditions to legal consequences, in other words the "if"-side of the "if-then" clause. Here the legislative has used indefinite legal terms (*unbestimmte Rechtsbegriffe*) such as the "public interests", "sufficient reliability" (to run a commercial enterprise), or "against good morals". These terms grant the authorities an opportunity to judge for themselves whether the situation described in a provision is at hand or not.

---

[21] BVerwGE 26,135.
[22] See also above, Chapter 6, sec. 3.3.5.

Example: According to § 4 I No. 1 *GaststättenG* (law on pub licensing) the authorities have to refuse handing out a license if "there is evidence that the applicant does not possess **sufficient reliability** to run a commercial enterprise . . . ". It is left to the administrative authority to decide whether an applicant is reliable to run a business.

If the legislative grants administrative authorities this margin of appreciation, then the question arises whether the courts may subsequently review it.[23] The purpose of the margin of appreciation is that the authorities decide because they are more competent and closer to the relevant matters than the legislative and the judiciary. This purpose would be undermined if the courts had the last say. However, the Federal Administrative Court as well as the Federal Constitutional Court have decided that the administrative courts generally have the power and obligation to completely review administrative decisions. Otherwise the procedural guarantee of Article 19 IV GG and an effective protection of basic rights would be endangered. Nevertheless as an exception a few areas are excluded from "total review", such as decisions concerning exams (school exams and related decisions, state exams),[24] assessments of civil servants,[25] rating decisions by independent committees[26] or prognostic decisions of risks.[27] These types of cases usually deal with such highly complex matters that it is virtually impossible for the courts to completely comprehend the administrative decision.[28] However, the courts can review administrative decisions that are **based on** findings of an independent committee:

BVerwGE 94, 307 Weinprämierung

A dispute concerning the official rating of the quality of wine lay at the heart of this case. The plaintiff, owner of a vineyard, had applied for a specific rating ("*Auslese*"). According to § 12 *WeinG* (Law on Wine) a specific rating will only be given if the wine shows the **particular characteristics** of the aspired grading. Based on the findings of an expert commission, who had tested the vine, the authority only rated it "*Spätlese*", a lower grading. The plaintiff challenged this administrative decision. The Federal Administrative Court held that in general all indefinite terms were subject to judicial review. Here the relevant phrase was "particular characteristics". Although the Court admitted that the findings of the expert committee were highly complex and impossible to review, the **decision of the administrative authority** could be reviewed. It

---

[23] For discussion see H.-D. Sproll, *Allgemeines Verwaltungsrecht* II (1998: C.H. Beck, München) pp. 58–64 and Maurer, above, n 1, pp. 132–141.
[24] BVerwGE 8, 272; 99,74; BVerfGE 84, 34.
[25] BVerwGE 21, 127.
[26] BVerwG 91, 211.
[27] BVerwGE 97, 203.
[28] BVerfGE 84, 34, 50.

had not been the experts who had given the rating but the administration. Based on the experts' findings it had concluded that the wine did not show "particular characteristics" for the rating "*Spätlese*". Thus the plaintiff was entitled to judicial review and subsequently an independent opinion.

4.4 Subjective public right (*Subjektives Öffentliches Recht*)

The phrase "subjective public right" tries to emphasize the individual claims of the citizen against the state, namely the administration under public law. It points out that administrative law provisions are not only putting the administration under an obligation to act lawfully but also may give the citizen a corresponding right to demand certain actions, as the Federal Administrative Court pointed out at an early stage.[29] These claims are enforceable in court. But not every administrative law provision grants such subjective rights. A provision must be intended to serve (also) the interest of the citizen. This is unproblematic where a claim is expressly stated like in § 4 I BSHG (Federal law on social assistance) mentioning a "claim to social assistance". It is more difficult in areas regulating certain procedures. Here the provisions often have to be interpreted by the courts as to whether they convey individual rights. There is significant case law on building law and the question whether an individual can challenge an administrative permission to build granted to his neighbour.[30] In cases where discretion of the administrative authority is reduced to only one possible action, the citizen will correspondingly have a claim to this measure being carried out, provided it is designed to serve his interest as well.[31]

5 Types of administrative action

Administrative authorities may choose to act under private law in a few areas like when purchasing material for the administration, setting up commercial enterprises or even when delivering administrative services. This, however, is the exception. In most cases they will act under public law which offers several instruments or types of action such as the administrative act, regulations, public law contracts, plans, or so-called real acts. As the classical form of administrative action the "administrative act"—*Verwaltungsakt*—will be examined more closely.

---

[29] BVerwGE 1, 159. See above, Chapter 6, sec. 3.4.
[30] BVerwGE 52, 122. See also summary by Maurer, above, n 1, pp. 156–158.
[31] BVerwGE 11, 95.

5.1 The *Verwaltungsakt* (administrative act)

The classical instrument of administrative action, the *Verwaltungsakt*, has been translated as "administrative decision", "administrative act", or "administrative order". Here again it becomes apparent that exact translations of legal terms are often difficult if not impossible. In this case especially a translation itself is less helpful than an explanation of this instrument. We will thus adhere to the German term.

5.1.1 Definition

The *Verwaltungsakt* is defined by § 35 VwVfG as "*every order, decision or other sovereign measure (Maßnahme) taken by an authority for the regulation of a individual case in the sphere of public law and directed at immediate external legal consequence*".

This definition covers all sorts of administrative measures in everyday life, for example the granting of pub licenses, building permissions, permits of residence, tax orders, the withdrawal of licenses (e.g. driving licenses), etc. However, in order to qualify as a *Verwaltungsakt* all characteristics of § 35 VwVfG have to be fulfilled. A correct classification of an administrative measure is of vital importance for the individual in order to use the right procedural remedies against such a measure if it violates his rights.[32]

The first characteristic mentioned in § 35 VwVfG is a "measure to regulate" something (***Massnahme zur Regelung***). In other words it is a measure intended to bring about a legal consequence, thus distinguishing the *Verwaltungsakt* from other instruments such as mere communications, reports, or ratings.[33] Furthermore, the measure has to be taken by an "authority" (***Behörde***). This term is to be interpreted as wider than the one referring to authority in an organizational context.[34] Here an "authority" is any unit that fulfils tasks of public administration (§ 1 VwVfG). As a consequence this "functional" definition covers agencies or "*Beliehene*" that carry out tasks of administration.[35] The measure also has to be within the sphere of public law" (***auf dem Gebiet des öffentlichen Rechts***), meaning it must be based on a public law provision.[36]

The measure must be intended to regulate an individual case (***Einzelfall***). This is an important characteristic to distinguish the *Verwaltungsakt* from more general rules and decisions.[37] A *Verwaltungsakt* has individual and concrete effect: It addresses only one person (individually) and only one case (in concrete).

---

[32] Thus there is a specific procedure and legal action against detrimental *Verwaltungsakte*. See below sec. 6.

[33] BVerwGE 14, 323.

[34] See above, sec. 3.

[35] Ibid.

[36] For the distinction between public and private law see above sec. 1.1.

[37] A clear exposition can be found in H.D. Sproll, *Allgemeines Verwaltungsrecht* I (1997: C.H. Beck, München) 1997, pp. 234–244.

> **Example:** Citizen A wants to build a garage on his property and applies for a building permit. The authority refuses to grant this permit. The *Verwaltungsakt* (the refusal) affects only A and is only effective concerning this application. If he applied again, e.g. under different circumstances or after some time another *Verwaltungsakt* is necessary to deal with the request.

A statute or *Gesetz*, on the other hand, is applicable to an infinite number of persons (general) and an infinite number of cases (abstract).

> **Example:** The criminal legal provision on murder (§ 211) StGB is be applicable to each person and will also be applicable each time the same person commits the crime.

It becomes problematic where a measure has individual *and* abstract effect or is of general *and* concrete nature.

> **Example:** An authority issues an order to the company of a local factory to stop emitting coolant into a nearby river whenever the temperature of the river exceeds a certain limit. Here the measure is individual as it addresses only one person. However, it is effective for an indefinite number of cases (abstract), namely each time a certain temperature is exceeded.

It has been disputed how to handle these cases but general opinion seems to regard them also as cases of *Verwaltungsakt*.[38] Finally, a measure may have general and concrete effect if it addresses an infinite number of people but only a single case.

> **Example:** The police ban participation on a particular date in a particular place.

In these cases the measure will also be regarded as a *Verwaltungsakt* as they address one singular situation. The *Verwaltungsakt* will then usually be termed as a "general decision" or *Allgemeinverfügung* (§ 35 I VwVFG). The exact classification is important in order to distinguish the *Verwaltungsakt* from general and abstract legal provisions, as there are different procedures to challenge them. Classification is not always easy as the long dispute on traffic signs shows.[39]

---

[38] OVG NRW, OVGE 16, 289. See Sproll above, n 34, p. 239, for further references.
[39] See Maurer, above, n 1, pp. 184–186, 194–202.

Finally, a measure must have immediate external effect or external legal consequence (*Aussenwirkung*). This criterion serves to exclude any preparatory decisions within the administration, even if made by different authorities. Only a decision intended to be of direct legal consequence for the individual "outside" the administration can be regarded as *Verwaltungsakt*.[40]

5.1.2 Legal requirements for a Verwaltungsakt

There are a number of procedural and substantial requirements for a *Verwaltungsakt* to be lawful. If they are not fulfilled, they are unlawful and can be challenged. In extreme cases they are automatically void and need not be observed by anyone.

"Formal" requirements include matters of competence, form, and procedure. Thus only the competent authority is allowed to act. Form is regulated by §§ 37–39 VwVfG. A *Verwaltungsakt* can be oral, rarely so now, written, or in any other form as with automatic ticket machines. If written they must be signed, and the full reasons for it must be given, if oral, confirmation can be requested but all forms must be authorized. The content should be definite and certain. They must give consequences for failure to comply, including a statement of the legal remedies available and requirements and procedure to appeal against the decision. There are also several procedural requirements (§§ 11–13, 25–30 VwVfG), one of the most important being a right of a formal hearing of parties affected (§ 28 VwVfG). Other requirements are

(a) *The Informality Principle*: Especially when written, the decision should be simple and expedient to assist a quick decision (§ 10 VwVfG).

(b) *The Inquisitorial Principle*: The authority is obliged to seek all possible information which may affect the decision (§ 24 VwVfG) and the parties should, however, participate by producing relevant means of evidence, documents, or information (§§ 26 VwVfG)

(c) The authority is obliged to give all necessary and required information and advice on all aspects of the application and decision (§ 25 VwVfG).

(d) Parties have a right to inspect public records unless another's rights are affected (§ 29 VwVfG).

Finally, any *Verwaltungsakt* must comply with substantial law. Thus it must be based on a legal provision, which itself is constitutional (legality of administration) and it must not violate any law, including of course the basic rights. German terminology requires the *Verwaltungsakt* to be "formally and substantially lawful" (*formell und materiell rechtmässig*).

Administrative acts can order or prohibit certain action or impose a burden or affect rights. They may permit, alter, create, or withdraw rights, such as appointments, or create new legal positions or benefits such as in licensing laws or may define or re-define particular qualifications or characteristics in order to declare or

---

[40] BVerwGE 28,145; 60, 144. See also above, sec. 2.

confirm rights and duties, for example, citizenship. Thus the acts can be beneficial or disadvantageous.

5.1.3 *The binding effect of a decision*

The decision has a binding effect, which is to be obeyed by all until withdrawn or revoked by the authority or annulled under judicial review (§ 43 VwVfG). The effect of any decision is immediate when notified, unless it says otherwise and is directly enforceable. It is, however, suspended if any complaint is filed against it. There is a time limit in which to file complaints, the details of which must always be given. If the time limit expires or the party waives their rights or the remedy is exhausted, the decision is no longer subject to review. Under special circumstances the authority may be persuaded to re-open proceedings. Time limits and the reinstatement of proceedings are governed by §§ 31–32.

5.1.4 *Unlawful administrative acts (Rechtswidrige Verwaltungsakte)*

Different consequences may arise from unlawful administrative acts. Only basic traits will be described here. If the *Verwaltungsakt* suffers from an evident and grave breach of law then it will be void (*nichtig*) *ab initio* (§ 44 I VwVfG). This means that it never produced any legal effect. Therefore no one has to observe it. § 44 II VwVfG, furthermore, gives a list of cases in which such a breach will be assumed, e.g. where a written administrative act does not reveal the authority responsible or where an administrative act orders the individual to commit a crime, etc. On the other hand, some faults of the *Verwaltungsakt* are deemed negligible. Thus they will not render it unlawful if the authority remedies them in time, e.g. subsequently granting an omitted hearing or handing in the necessary reasons (§ 45 VwVfG).

Other unlawful administrative acts may be challenged by the individual and will ultimately be nullified by the courts. Otherwise the authority under certain circumstances can also revoke them. Procedural remedies against unlawful administrative acts will be considered below.[41]

5.1.5 *Repeal (Aufhebung)*

The repeal of administrative acts is an interesting topic to look at, because it shows the impact of constitutional law by means of the *"Rechtsstaatsprinzip"* and the principle of legitimate expectations as well as EC Law influences in the area of subsidies. Repeal (*Aufhebung*) refers only to administrative acts that have become valid, which is usually one month after publication to the addressee. By then the time limit for remedies has expired. However, the administrative authority may still repeal it. Conditions for this depend on whether it was a lawful (§ 48 VwVfG) or unlawful administrative act (§ 49 VwVfG) and subsequently whether onerous—such as an order to pay a fine or tax—or beneficial to the addressee—such as a permit to build or granting a licence or subsidies. Without going into detail it should be noted that from the individual's point of view legitimate expectations must be observed when repealing beneficial administrative acts. Thus it is within the

---

[41] See below, sec. 6.

discretion of the administrative authority to repeal[42] unlawful onerous acts (§ 48 I VwVfG), as it will not affect the addressees expectations in any harmful way. In a similar way administrative authorities may repeal lawful onerous acts (§ 49 I VwVfG).

Unlawful beneficial acts produce a conflict between two elements of the "*Rechtsstaatsprinzip*": legality of administration and legitimate expectations. They cannot be repealed if the addressee relied on them and his expectations were worthy of protection when balancing them against the public interest (§ 48 II VwVfG). In certain cases § 48 II VwVfG rejects such expectations, for example if the addressee induced the beneficial act by threat, bribes, or deception.

In the case of lawful beneficial acts it is even more difficult to repeal them as no conflict exists. Repeal might be necessary because the situation governing the act has changed substantially. But repeals of lawful beneficial acts are generally impossible, because legitimate expectations have an even greater weight. However, a list of exceptional cases allowing repeal is given in § 49 II, III VwVfG, an example being the use of subsidies for purposes other than they were intended for (§ 49 III No. 1 VwVfG). In some cases the addressee will have a claim to compensation (§ 49 VI VwVfG).

Finally, the impact of EC law in this area has to be mentioned. According to Article 87 I EC any state aid that might distort competition within the European Union by favouring certain undertakings, is incompatible with the common market and thus the EC Treaty. Consequently, if a Member State is planning to grant such aids, it must notify the European Commission according to Article 88. If a member state grants subsidies by an administrative act in breach of these EC provisions, the act will be unlawful in the sense of § 48 I VwVfG.

Case C-24/95 Rheinland-Pfalz v Alcan, ECJ [1997] I-1591

In order to prevent the closure of the aluminium works Alcan and the loss of many jobs the government of the Land Rheinland-Pfalz granted subsidies of 8 million DM by administrative act although the EC Commission had not yet approved of it. The Commission finally declared the subsidies incompatible with EC law. The government thus repealed the administrative act and demanded that the subsidies be paid back. Alcan challenged this before the national administrative courts claiming legitimate expectations under § 48 II VwVfG. In a preliminary ruling the ECJ finally had to decide on its interpretation. It held that when balancing the public interest against the individual interest of legitimate expectations, the procedure of Article 87 EC was of vital importance. This procedure had not been followed properly, since the government had granted the subsidies *before* having received the Commission's approval. As a consequence this administrative act had been unlawful. With the procedure still running Alcan had not been entitled to rely on the administrative act. Thus there was no legitimate expectation to be allowed to **keep** the paid subsidies.

---

[42] German terminology speaks of "taking back" unlawful acts (*Rücknahme*) but revocation of lawful acts (*Widerruf*).

The BVerwG seems to follow this line of interpretation of § 48 VwVfG when dealing with subsidies that are incompatible with EC Law.[43]

5.2 Public law contract (öffentlich-rechtlicher Vertrag, § 54 VwVfG)

Another instrument employed by the administration is the hybrid administrative contract or public law contract (öffentlich-rechtlicher Vertrag) § 54 VwVfG. It is used in place of a purely civil contract where the subject matter of the contract concerns the exercise of a public duty. Unless where stated otherwise (e.g. §§ 54–61 VwVfG), general principles of civil law apply (§ 62VwVfG). These contracts offer the authorities an opportunity to involve the citizen more actively. Instead of ordering him to do something using its hierarchically superior position (e.g. by using a Verwaltungsakt) the authority concludes a contract, based on two declarations of intent (Willenserklärungen) of equal weight, just as in private law contracts.[44]

Example: A owns a property in the city centre, on which he wishes to construct a building for giant cinema. He applies for a building permit. The authority rejects his application on the grounds that there is already a lack of parking spaces and the city centre would be overstrained. However, the authority could conclude a contract with A offering to grant the permit if in exchange he agrees to provide parking spaces on his property, e.g. by adding an underground car park.

5.3 Plan and planning

A plan (Plan) will emerge as a result of numerous public acts. The procedure of planning is relevant when realizing projects of huge territorial impact, especially in the areas of building law (municipal planning and development, e.g. § 8 BauGB), environmental law (e.g. building of nuclear power plants), or infrastructure (e.g. construction of highways). It provides for effective participation of the citizens affected mostly by granting rights to hearings.

5.4 Other instruments

Other instruments used by the administration are regulations and real acts (Realakte). Regulations (Rechtsverordnungen) can be issued by the federal government, one of its ministers, and governments or ministers of the Länder. They have to conform to the constitutional conditions for delegated legislation.[45] Realakte are acts not aimed at producing any legal effect. They include communications, warnings, or journeys using official vehicles.

---

[43] BVerwGE 92, 81.
[44] See below, Chapter 10 for details.
[45] See above, chapter, 6, sec. 4.5.1.

6 Enforcement by the authority

Where necessary an authority can enforce its own regulations without waiting for court decision by requiring a substitute action, where the first has not been performed, or by penalty in the form of fines (*Zwangsgeld*), both of which are rare. Policing laws even provide for the exertion of force.[46] The details are to be found in the Administrative Enforcement Act (*Verwaltungsvollstreckungsgesetz, VwVG*) or the relevant laws on specific law of administration, i.e. the laws on policing by the *Länder*.

7 Judicial review

The *Grundgesetz* gives the general right of judicial review under Article 19 IV. This is confirmed by the specific laws of procedure applicable before the various courts. Thus to challenge a tax assessment the law on procedure before financial courts, the *Finanzgerichtsordnung (FGO)*, applies. In the absence of specific allocations (*Spezialzuweisungen*) to courts dealing with particular public law matters (e.g. financial and social courts) the general rule of § 40 I VwGO applies, stating that all disputes of public law belong before the administrative courts. However, it will be remembered that most issues of constitutional law are exempted. They are decided by the Federal Constitutional Court (*BVerfG*).[47]

All procedures before the administrative courts are regulated by the *Verwaltungsgerichtsordnung, VwGO* (law on administrative procedures).

7.1 Informal remedies (*formlose Rechtsbehelfe*)

There are different remedies the individual can use against administrative actions. Informal remedies (*formlose Rechtsbehelfe*) are not restricted by form or time limits. The individual may use them to induce a review within the administration. That way he can draw the authority's attention to wrong decisions. Furthermore, he may allege insulting or degrading treatment by an official by complaining to the superior authority (*Dienstaufsichtsbeschwerde*).

7.2 Formal remedies: *Widerspruchsverfahren* (§§ 68–73 VwVfG)

Formal remedies mostly comprise actions before the courts. However, prior to certain types of court actions, the applicant must have exhausted the required administrative procedures (*Vorverfahren* or *Widerspruchsverfahren*) to try to resolve the problem (§ 68 VwGO). This applies to cases of challenging a disadvantageous administrative act or trying to obtain a beneficial one.

---

[46] see, e.g. §§ 57 et seq. NWPolG.
[47] see above, Chapter 6, sec. 6.

The procedure allows the authority to review the decision in question. This is achieved formally by the filing of a complaint, *Widerspruch*,[48] within one month of the decision (§§ 57–58 VwGO). If the authority does not accept the complaint it must reply formally or pass the matter to the higher administrative agency that will issue the reply (*Widerspruchsbescheid*). This must give reasons for the decision and the remedies available. The matter can proceed to court, within one month of the formal reply, if the complainant wishes. In the meantime the contested decision is suspended. It is disputed whether within this procedure the authority may also change its decision to the detriment of the complainant (*reformatio in peius*). General academic opinion and the BVerwG are in favour of it.[49]

7.3 Formal remedies: types of action

These are governed by § 42 et seq. VwGO and offer the individual different instruments in order to achieve different aims. Only four of them will be examined here.[50]

7.3.1 *Action to annul an administrative act (Anfechtungsklage, § 42 I VwGO)*

This is an action to quash an administrative act (*Verwaltungsakt*). It is roughly equivalent to annulment (*certiorari*) in the UK. The effect, if successful, is annulment *ab initio*. The court may also order how the decision is to be removed if already effected, or make a statement of the fact it was illegal, which will serve as the basis for damages where suffered. Using an example we will look at the different requirements of this action.

Example 1: Foreigner *A* has lived in Germany for twenty years, is married to a German, and has several children with her. The authority dealing with foreigners (*Ausländerbehörde*) sends him a deportation order, after he has caused an accident, hurting another person. The authority argues that this incident shows that his stay endangers public safety and order of the Federal Republic of Germany. Thus he has to be expelled according to § 45 I AuslG (*law on foreigners*). The deportation order fulfils all characteristics of § 35 I VwVfG and consequently has to be classified as *Verwaltungsakt*. *A* can try to have the *Verwaltungsakt* annulled under § 42 I VwVfG in order to be allowed to stay. However, he first has to exhaust the administrative "protest" procedure (*Widerspruchsverfahren*), giving the authority an opportunity to set right its decision. That way he could point out the significance of his long stay in Germany and his family ties. The authority might reconsider its decision and repeal its administrative act. Only if the authority upholds its *Verwaltungsakt* may *A* bring an action before the courts.

---

[48] Literally "objection" or "protest".
[49] For discussion see P. Hufen, *Vewaltungsprozessrecht*, 4th ed. (2000: C.H. Beck, München, pp. 144–148.
[50] For more details see Hufen, above, n 48.

As a classical type of action the *Anfechtungsklage* offers a good opportunity to look at the main procedural requirements to bring an action before the administrative courts. Similar to the structure of the constitutional complaint the requirements of admissibility will first be examined by the court before looking at the merits of the case.

(a) *Jurisdiction of administrative courts (Eröffnung des Verwaltungsrechtswegs, § 40 VwGO)*

Notwithstanding specific provisions according to the general rule of § 40 VwGO administrative courts are competent to deal with all public law disputes excluding those of constitutional law. Thus a classification as public law case as opposed to one of private law nature is required.

> In our **example** the dispute revolves around the law on foreigners which is a classic area of public law. The courts would thus have jurisdiction if *A* brought an action against the authorities.

(b) *Competent administrative court (Zuständigkeit des Verwaltungsgerichts)*

Local jurisdiction of the individual court is determined by §52 VwGO. As regards the correct instance (usually the *Verwaltungsgericht*) §§ 45–50 VwGO are applicable.

> The competent court in our **example** would thus be the *Verwaltungsgericht* within whose district the deportation order has been issued (§ 53 Nr.3 VwGO).

(c) *Capability to participate in proceedings (Beteiligtenfähigkeit, § 61 VwGO)*

Similar to the constitutional complaint the party bringing such an action before the administrative courts has to be capable of participating in the procedure. This capacity is generally granted to natural and legal persons. Furthermore, even administrative authorities may participate if the law of the particular *Land* allows so. This is remarkable because otherwise it is the legal person responsible for the particular authority that has to take the blame in proceedings, i.e. the federation or the *Land*.

> **Example:** As a natural person *A* is capable of participating in the procedure. Depending on the provisions of the particular *Land* he lives in he either has to bring the action against the authority that issued the deportation order or the *Land* itself.

(d) *Appropriateness of Action (Statthaftigkeit der Klage*, § 42 I 1 VwGO)
Here the court will examine whether in view of the objective of the plaintiff the right type of action has been chosen. In the case of the *Anfechtungsklage* obviously the aim must be to annul an administrative act. If the plaintiff aims at making an authority be obliged to issue an act he must choose a different type of action (*Verpflichtungsklage*).

For *A* this would be right type of action as he wants the deportation order annulled.

(e) *locus standi (Klagebefugnis*, § 42 II VwGO)
In order to have *locus standi* the plaintiff must present a case alleging the violation of a legally protected interest. The right must be one derived from a rule of law or statute in the individual's own interest. Most onerous administrative acts will somehow restrict an individual's personal freedom (Art. 2 I GG). Thus it is comparably easy to be attributed with *locus standi*. The administrative act does not necessarily have to be addressed to the applicant. There are circumstances in which third parties derive a right to review as a result of being affected by decisions addressed to others, such as in the cases of building and planning laws which may cause a nuisance or interference with the rights of third parties. There has, and continues to be a discussion of the rights of associations to bring actions especially in the area of environmental law where a community or general interest is often self-evident.

In *A*'s case the deportation order might infringe provisions of the law on foreigners which are designed for his protection, but possibly also his right to protection of marriage (Art. 6 I GG) and the right to personal freedom (Art. 2 I GG). At this point he does not have to prove the violation. It must merely seem possible to grant him *locus standi*.

(f) *Protest procedure (Widerspruchsverfahren*, § 68 VwGO)
The above-mentioned protest procedure has to be exhausted beforehand. Otherwise an action will only be admissible in exceptional circumstances.

In our case *A* must have exhausted this procedure with the authority that issued the deportation order before bringing an action to annul it.

(g) *Time limit, formalities, other legal protection*

The time limit for an action is one month beginning with posting of the reply to the protest (*Widerspruchsbescheid*, § 74 I VwGO). Generally a written form is required. For details see §§ 81 et seq. VwGO. Finally, there should be no simpler means of legal protection that the plaintiff could turn to instead (*Allgemeines Rechtsschutzbedürfnis*).

An admissible action will then be decided on according to §113 VwGO. If held to be unlawful and a violation of the plaintiff's rights, the court will annul the administrative act. When looking at the merits it will measure the administrative act against any source of higher law, especially the basic rights.

In the **example**, the Court would look at the formal requirements (*formelle Rechtmässkeit*) of the administrative act, i.e. did the competent authority act, did it use the right form and procedure and did it have a legal basis for acting?

Assuming these requirements were met then the Court will look at the legal basis of the administrative act (deportation order) which is § 45 I AuslG. It gives the authority discretion to expel a foreigner if his stay endangers public safety and order of the Federal Republic of Germany. Thus the provision provides for a margin of appreciation on the "if"-side and discretion on the "then"-side. As pointed out above both are subject to judicial review.

First the Court would examine whether A's stay constitutes a "danger to public safety". This will already be disputable given the reason of him negligently causing an accident. It is far more obvious in cases of foreigners committing serious crimes on intent. But when looking at the way the authority exerted its discretion, the Court would find for A. Here the authority had to take into account his rights as well and balance them against the public interest in a proportional way. In this case it seems that the authority did not take into account his family ties and the fact he has been living in Germany for twenty years. Here, § 48 AuslG has to be observed, granting special protection from deportation in cases where a foreigner is married to a German. The administrative act thus violated his rights under §48 AuslG, Article 6 I, 2 I GG. Consequently it will be annulled by the Court.

7.3.2 *Action to order an authority to issue an administrative act* (*Verpflichtungsklage* §42 I 2nd Alternative VwGO)

The action for the issue of a judgment compelling the authority to issue an administrative act is called the *Verpflichtungsklage*. This has a one-month time limit and is roughly equivalent to the UK action of *Mandamus*. If there is a discretion allowed the authority, the Court may give an advisory judgment (*Bescheidungsurteil*) on the limits of the discretion. Otherwise the Court will, if the applicants right is proved, require the authority to act in a particular way.

Example 2: *B* wants to tear down a 200 year-old mansion that stands on his property and replace it by a modern building, as its maintenance is too expensive. He applies for a permit to tear it down. The competent authority denies the permit because the mansion falls under the protection clauses of the *Denkmalschutzgesetz* (law on protection of historical monuments). After having gone through an unsuccessful protest procedure *B* can bring an action against the authority in order to finally obtain the desired administrative act, the permit. Formal requirements of admissibility would be similar to the ones of the action to annul an act. The only difference being the result. As he does not want an onerous act annulled but rather a beneficial act to be issued, the appropriate action is the *Verpflichtungsklage*, § 42 I 2nd alt VwGO. If considered admissible, the Court will examine the merits of the case. It will look at the relevant provisions of the law on protection of historical monuments taking into account his rights to property (Art. 14 I GG) and balancing it against his obligation to serve the public good under Art. 14 II GG. Thus if the denial was compatible with the above-mentioned law and the guarantees of Article 14 GG, the action will fail. However, *B* might still have a claim to compensation.

7.3.3 *Action to order a certain performance by the authority (allgemeine Leistungsklage)*

This type of action will serve to order an authority to take any "real action" desired by the plaintiff excluding administrative acts, which are dealt with by the *Verpflichtungsklage*. Such real acts (*Realakte*) include, for example, information, advice, or repair construction of streets. The procedural requirements are again similar to the ones of the *Verpflichtungsklage*. The action is not expressly mentioned in the VwGO but § 42 I 2nd alt. VwGO is applied in an analogous way. In order to have *locus standi*, the plaintiff will have to derive his claim for the desired action from a particular provision, in other words he will have to prove a "subjective public right".[51]

7.3.4 *Action for a declaration (Feststellungsklage, §43 VwGO)*

Finally, there is an action for a declaration (*Feststellungsklage*), under § 43 VwGO. It is an action for a declaration as to existence or non-existence of a legal relationship between the applicant and the authority. It may also be used to determine whether an action of an authority is null and void.

7.3.5 *Action to review bye-laws and regulations (Normenkontrolle, §47 VwGO)*

As opposed to the above actions dealing with individual decisions of the administration this action allows a review of general law provisions. Under § 47 VwGO the higher regional administrative courts (*Oberverwaltungsgerichte*) may review bye-laws and regulations below the *Landesgesetz* and also plans concerning town development. It has to be kept in mind, however, that review of other sources of law,

---

[51] See above, sec. 4.4.

namely parliamentary statutes, is reserved exclusively for the BVerfG. In order to have *locus standi* the complainant will have to show that the challenged provision infringes his rights or will in the near future do so (§ 47 II VwGO). This is interpreted widely. This procedure focuses on objective lawfulness. As a consequence the reviewed law will be annulled, if it contradicts any provision of higher law, no matter whether this provision was originally intended to protect the interest of the complainant or is just an objective right.

8 Claims for damages

Apart from claims that arise through contractual or delictual liability, liability is imposed initially by § 839 BGB personally on the official responsible for wilful or negligently caused damage. Article 34 GG, however, relieves the official of personal liability and imposes it instead on the state. Damages may be sought through the civil and not the administrative courts (§ 40 II VwGO). The law of state liability and especially the law of restitution in cases of restricting the right to property (Art. 14 I–III GG)[52] constitute an independent area of public law that cannot be examined in this book.[53]

FURTHER READING

Books

A. Bremer-Carias *Judicial Review in Comparative Law* (1989: Cambridge University Press, Cambridge).

F. Hufen, *Verwaltungsprozessrecht*, 4th ed. (2000: C.H. Beck, München).

International Institute for Legal and Administrative Terminology, *Allgemeines Verwaltungsrecht/General Administrative Law* (1987: Carl Heymanns Verlag, Köln).

König, von Oertzen, and Wagener (eds.), *Public administration in the Federal Republic of Germany* (1983: Kluwer).

F.O. Kopp and W.-R. Schenke, *Verwaltungsgerichtsordnung*, 12th ed. (2000: C.H. Beck, München).

H. Maurer, *Allgemeines Verwaltungsrecht*, 12th ed. (1999: C.H. Beck, München).

M. Nierhaus, "Administrative Law" in: Ebke and Finkin (eds.), *Introduction to German Law* (1996: Kluwer, The Hague), pp. 81–114.

I. Richter, F. Schuppert, and F. Bumke, *Casebook Verwaltungsrecht*, 3rd ed. (2000: C.H. Beck, München).

W. Schmitt Glaeser, and H.D. Horn, *Verwaltungsprozessrecht*, 15th ed. (2000: Boorberg Verlag, Stuttgart).

M.P. Singh, *German Administrative Law: in Common Law Perspective* (1985: Springer).

---

[52] See above, Chapter 6, sec. 5.5.
[53] Refer to Maurer, above, n 1, pp. 622–811.

H.-D. Sproll, *Allgemeines Verwaltungsrecht*, Vols I & II (1997 (1998): C.H. Beck, München).

P. Stelkens, U.L. Bonk and H. Sachs, *Verwaltungsverfahrensgesetz*, 6th ed. (2001: C.H. Beck, München).

P. van Dijk, *Judicial Review of Governmental Actions and the Requirement of an Interest to Sue* (1980: Sijthoff and Noordhoff, Alphen).

Articles

E. Denninger, "Judicial Review Revisited: The German Experience" (1985) 59 Tul L Rev 1013–1031.

E. Pakusher, "Administrative Law in Germany—Citizen v State" (1968) 16 Am J Comp L 309–331.

E. Pakusher, "Control of the Administration in the Federal Republic of Germany" (1972) 21 ICLQ 452–471.

H. Rupp, "Judicial Review in the Federal Republic of Germany" (1960) 9 Am J Comp L 29–47.

B Particular administrative law (*Besonderes Verwaltungsrecht*)

Amongst other topics in administrative law, the following legal topics are given particular treatment: civil servants (*Beamte*), foreigners (*Ausländer*), the police (*Polizei*), tax (*Steuer*), Community law (*Kommunalrecht*), building law (*Baurecht*), data protection (*Datenschutz*), and traffic law (*Straßenverkehrsrecht*). Social law, environmental law, and the law of economic administration are considered separately below. For the others topics the following list of books may be consulted for details, as they cannot be part of an introduction to the German legal system.

FURTHER READING

A. von Arnim, H. Büchner and K.H. Schlotterbeck, *Baurecht I*, 2nd ed. (1994: Kohlhammer, Stuttgart).

Achterberg, Püttner and Würtenberger (eds.), *Besonderes Verwaltungsrecht*, Vols I & II, 2nd ed. (2000: C.F. Müller, Heidelberg).

W. Brohm, *Öffentliches Baurecht*, 2nd ed. (1999: C.H. Beck, München).

C. Gusy, *Polizeirecht*, 4th ed. (2000: Mohr, Tübingen).

E. Schmidt-Assmann, (ed.), *Besonderes Verwaltungsrecht*, 11th ed. (1999: de Gruyter, Berlin).

H. Minz and P. Conze, *Recht des öffentlichen Dienstes*, 6th ed. (1993: Walhalla Verlag, Berlin).

Kodal and Krämer (eds.), *Strassenrecht* (1995: C.H. Beck, München).

U. Steiner, *Besonderes Verwaltungsrecht*, 5th ed. (1995: C.F. Müller, Heidelberg).

A. Mutius *Kommunalrecht*, 2nd ed. (1996: C.H. Beck, München).

W. Bamburger, *Ausländerrecht* (1995: C.H. Beck, München).

W. Dahm, *Beamtenrecht*, 2nd ed. (1993: Kohlhammer, Verlag, Stuttgart).

C Social law

1 Introduction

Social law is a part of public law because of its involvement in the relations between the state and citizen. The concept of social law has been widened over the years and there is considerable overlap with the areas of administrative law and labour law. Indeed following the completion of the tenth book of the Social Law Code in 1980 concerned with procedural law, it is subject to the Law on Administrative Procedure, see the section on administrative law above for more details on this law. Social law is widely regarded as one of the specialist areas of administrative law. It does, however, have its own hierarchy of courts regulated by the Social Courts Act. (*Sozialgerichtsgesetz* SGG).

2 Sources of social law

The appearance of the modern social state was brought about by the German emperor's request in 1881 to his *Reichskanzler*, Otto v. Bismark to establish through the *Reichstag*, a system of accident and illness insurance for workers. This was done and in 1883, compulsory illness insurance was introduced, followed in 1884, by accident insurance and in 1889, by invalidity and old age insurance legislation. These laws were consolidated in the 1911 Imperial Insurance Ordinance (*Reichsversicherungsordnung*: RVO). The period of the Weimar Republic saw the addition of unemployment benefit, but the largest impetus for the overall concept and provision of social law arises from the basic principles of state on which Germany is based and which are laid down in the *Grundgesetz*. For full details see Chapters 2 and 6. The requirement that the Federal Republic is a social state underpins the provision of social laws and the extensive involvement of the state generally in social welfare. The general requirements of Articles 20 (1) and 28 (1) *Grundgesetz* impose a legally binding obligation on the state for social welfare provision. As such, however, the obligation is not capable of translation into specific individual rights (see BVerfGE 39, 302, 315, which as in many other cases lays down that the principles of Articles 20 and 28 are there for the protection of socially weak and disadvantaged). The BVerfG has, however, declared social security claims to be legally protected property rights covered by Article 14 GG (BVerfGE 64, 87). Article 3 of the *Grundgesetz* has also been important in social law by removing unequal treatment in widows and widowers pensions and illness and accident insurance (BVerfGE 43, 213).

There are reference to social law in Article 74 *Grundgesetz* which catalogues the areas of concurrent legislative jurisdiction between the Federation and the *Länder*, however social law is predominantly federal law now, largely leaving the *Länder* to implement federal requirements with secondary legislation and by-laws.

A continuing aim of the legislature is the completion of the codification of social law (*Sozialgesetzbuch* SGB) which will be then the most important source of Social law. The decision to do this was taken in 1971 and codification commenced in 1975. This process is still going on with thirteen books planned so far and a number of extensive amendments of the existing books of the social law code to incorporate as special parts of the Code, the existing and previously applicable social law statutes including the Reich Insurance Code (*Reichsversicherungsordnung* RVO), the Federal Social Welfare Act (*Bundessozialhilfegesetz* BSHG) the Promotion of Employment Act (*Arbeitsförderungsgesetz* AFG), and the Employees Insurance Act (*Angestelltenversicherungsgesetz* AVG).

There are in addition a large number of Statutory instruments, administrative regulations and the *Länder* have passed numerous implementing regulations in the form of *Satzungen*. Finally there are the court decisions which have arisen mainly from the Federal and *Länder* Administrative and Social Courts.

3 The aims and basic principles of social law

One aim is that given by § 1 SGB, the putting into practise of the social state. The Code and BSHG further define the aims in the form of general principles of social law.

(a) *The Preservation of human dignity*. Any situation which threatens this must give rise to social aid which is provided to enable to beneficiary to live among non-receivers as equals.

(b) *Self help*. In theory, social aid is regarded as enabling someone to overcome or remove the situation which gives rise to the necessity for help so that it should not be needed and should therefore only temporary. Therefore social help should involve the participation of the recipient in achieving this goal.

(c) *The Principle of the individual case*. Although aid is normally given according to general standards, the law emphasizes that the individual case must be examined and help given according to individual circumstances and personality.

(d) *The Principle of aided need*. Reasons for a situation of need are irrelevant to the question whether help should be given, but in cases of self-induced need, aid may be less or its return may be demanded.

(e) *Consideration of wishes*. The recipient's wishes should be considered as long as they are appropriate and do not involve disproportionate expenses.

(f) *Immediacy*. As soon as the appropriate social body gets notice of the need, aid has to be given even without a formal application.

(g) *Preventative, after and family care*. Preventative aid should be given where early support will prevent or abolish the situation of need more efficiently, for example, the payments of debts or the premature payment of a pension. The form and measure of aid is not strictly defined by the legislature in order to be more flexible and to suit the needs of individual cases, such as whether a lump sum or periodic payments or whether specific aid is given or money targeted to particular items.

4 The administration and distribution of social aid

A wide variety of organizations are responsible for the administration and distribution of social security and other benefits involving both public and private organizations and termed collectively, *Versicherungsträgern*. These include the city, town, and district authorities, the state and private health insurance institutions (*Krankenkassen* and *Ersatzkassen* (§§ 143 et seq SGB V)), employers and public local bodies such as the Social Office (*Sozialamt* (§§ 9, 96 BSHG), and private bodies such as the churches and Red Cross (§ 10 BSHG). Paragraph 12 BSHG and §§ 18–29 SGB I give a list of all social welfare bodies. Details of the financing and further regulation can be found in §§ 86 et seq. SGB X.

Co-operation with other non-official organizations is encouraged to assist the needy rather than to save expenditure.

Information on Social security is handled by the Health Insurance Institutions (for example the *Allgemeine Ortskrankenkassen* AOK) and the state and Federal Insurance Authorities (*Versicherungsämter/Bundesversicherungsamt*) (see SGB IV §§ 91–94). Any changes in personal details must be notified to these offices. To administer the social security payments and health and accident insurances Germany has enacted a law requiring social security cards to be presented by employees to employers and to be presented and retained by social security and payments offices when benefits are received to try to prevent unlawful labour contracting.

5 Social welfare provision

SGB Book One deals with the general information and types of social rights available, general procedures to claim these and where advice and information can be obtained. The scope of what may be justifiably defined as coming within social law is extremely wide and has been divided by § 4 SGB I into four principles areas covering health and illness insurance now contained in SGB V, old age benefits under SGB VI, accident compensation in SGB VII (still under the RVO), unemployment benefits (by the AFG and SGB III) and social care provisions have now been consolidated in SGB Book XI.

Book Four contains the general rules on the social security system. Other books are expected to complete the details of this area of law by including the Educational Grants Act (*Bundesausbildungsförderungsgesetz* BaföG) in SGB II, child support in

SGB IX (presently BKGG) housing benefit in SGB X (Presently WoGG), youth welfare in SGB XI and re-ordering SGB X as SGB XIII.

Paragraphs 2–10 of SGB I contains the general rights which are available. This is criticized as being too general in that they do not give rise to positive rights which can be enforced and that it requires too much reference to the special parts of the code. They have thus only a clarifying function as to what social law is about and are not rights which can be enforced in the courts. Only specific rights provided by particular statutory provisions can be enforced in the social courts.

Paragraphs 13–15 SGB I provides the general duty to explain the available rights and duties under social law to the general population and to give advice and information to the individual.

Paragraph 31 SGB I states that any claims or rights or changes of rights are only valid through the medium of written law.

A distinction has to be made between a duty to give benefit and a discretionary benefit. The rules of discretionary benefit, § 39 SGB I, are subject to judicial review to ensure the level of standards that apply.

Paragraph 40 SGB I provides that a claim exists as soon as the conditions for it are present and not when the administrative decision has been made which merely confirms the existing right.

Generally, three forms of assistance are traditionally classified, and indeed noted in Article 74 (Nos 7, 10 and 12) GG, in the provision of social security. The first is social welfare (*Fürsorge/Sozialhilfe*) applying only to those with need. Within this first category, two kinds of aid are identified in § 1 BSHG—supplementary benefit and aid in special circumstances. The first secures the minimum necessary existence (*Lebensunterhalt*), for example, food, accommodation, clothing, hygiene and heating which can be divided into one-off payments and that required on a continuous basis (§§ 12 & 21 BSHG). The second kind includes special needs where there is a danger to health or in sickness, abortion, disabilities, social difficulties, hopelessness, or old age. The second category is state pensions provision (*Versorgung*) which are services generally provided not based on the individual or contributions from individuals and are available to general categories. These laws require no participation on the part of the recipients and includes the Federal Social Security Act (*Bundessozialhilfegesetz* BSHG) from 1961, now considerably amended and will be entirely incorporated into the Social Law Code in the near future, Provision for Children and youths (*Kinder- und Jugendhilfe*, now SGB VIII), the Housing Benefit Act (*Wohngeldgesetz* WoGG), the Federal Child Benefit Act (*Bundeskindergeldgesetz* BKGG), the Child Allowance Act (*Bundeserziehungsgeldgesetz*), Educational Grants Act (*Bundesausbildungsförderungsgesetz* BAföG), and the War Victims Benefits Act (*Bundesversorgungsgesetz*).

The third type, which is classified as the Insurance type, depends on contributions from the benefiting individuals and mainly consist of the various types of insurance schemes including Social Insurance (*Sozialversicherung*), Health/Illness Insurance (*Krankenversicherung*), Pensions (*Rentenversicherung*) and Personal Injury Insurance (*Unfallversicherung*). Unemployment benefit (*Arbeitslosengeld*) is also dependant on previous contributions and, as was the case in the UK until 1979, the level of benefit is dependant on the level of previous income, with recipients obtaining an amount up to 60% of the previous average net income (67 per cent for families with young children (§ 129 SGB III) with appropriate deductions for tax and insurance for a period between six to thirty-two months according to the time previously in employment (§§ 100 et seq AFG), after which it is replaced by unemployment assistance (*Arbeitslosenhilfe*) at a lower percentage of typical earnings (c. 50% or 57% with a child § 191 SGB III)). Within social insurance there is a further division into groups of profession which follow closely the division of the competences of the Unions. Despite the fact that they all rely on some form of contribution there is not necessarily a direct relation necessary between the contribution and the benefit.

6 Breaches of duty by social bodies

By an addition to the civil code delict provisions, § 839 BGB, a strict liability has been imposed on the state to compensate a person who has suffered as a result of a breach by an official of an official duty, for example giving false information or advice (Art. 34 *Grundgesetz*).

Paragraphs 60 et seq. SGB I require that the recipient of the benefit has a duty to assist the social body to provide help and a refusal may mean the temporary withholding of benefits.

7 Persons eligible for social assistance

The claimants are the usual categories such as the sick, old aged, invalids, disabled, blind, etc. There are specific rules in the BSHG for categories of persons in special circumstances such as German nationals abroad and foreigners seeking aid whilst in Germany, but not those who entered the country only for that purpose.

FURTHER READING

H. Becker, J. Heß and F. Wertheimer, *Grundwissen Recht*, Chapter 9 '*Sozialrecht*' (1999: Ernst Klett Verlag, Stuttgart), pp. 252–292.

H. Bley and R. Kreikebohm, *Sozialrecht*, 7th ed. (1993: Luchterhand, Neuweid).

E. Eichenhofer, *Sozialrecht*, 3rd ed. (2000: Mohr Siebeck Verlag, Tübingen).

W. Gitter, *Sozialrecht: ein Studienbuch*, 4th ed. (1997: C.H. Beck, München).

A. Ogus, The Federal Republic of Germany as *Sozialstaat*: A British Perspective', Working Paper No. 3, June 1990, University of Manchester.

F. Ruland, Chapter 7, '*Sozialrecht*' in E. Schmidt-Aßmann (ed.) *Besonderes Verwaltungsrecht* (1999: Walter de Gruyter, Berlin) pp. 727–825.

R. Waltermann, *Sozialrecht*, 2nd ed. (2001: Müller Verlag, Heidelberg).

D The law of economic administration (*Wirtschaftsverwaltungsrecht*)

1 Introduction

This area of law, also known as the law of public economy (*Öffentliches Wirtschaft-srecht*) and *Wirtschaftsverfassungsrecht*, is a recent development within the German legal system although many of the legal topics which fall within the umbrella of economic administration have quite distinct and older origins, for example, consumer protection law and the regulation of business activity. The concept is one barely recognized in common law, although without doubt the individual areas of law exist but are not classified in the same way. The area is basically concerned with the impingement of state on the economy, in other words the rules which have been created by the state to regulate economic affairs. Until recently this was regulated entirely by private law, notably the civil and commercial codes but this new body of law, concerned with the economy, stems from the public sector and thus is a mix of both public and private law concepts and elements. It can be defined extremely widely and thus incorporate anti-trust law, parts of criminal law, taxation, administrative law, trade and industry laws, and environmental protection and is made up of such a diverse number of laws and statutes affecting so many areas of the economy it appears at times to be pointless in classifying it as a separate topic. However, this has been done, and it is becoming a distinct and generally recognized area of study. For this section and generally, a narrower definition is preferred which does not annexe legal areas previously quite independent and covered elsewhere.

2 The scope of the law of economic administration

The most prominent areas of law in terms of legislation within this heading are environmental law and consumer law. Competition law and anti-trust law, which by definition would clearly belong to the law of economic administration, are not systematically considered under this branch of law as they pre-date the development of this legal area. They are also considered in German texts either separately, or generally with other private law or business matters, or with commercial law and company law. They will be the subject of only brief consideration in Chapter 11 because of the extensive coverage elsewhere, particularly as they are now widely superceded and supplemented by Community law.

The topics considered below are the general regulation of the economy, environmental law (considered below) and consumer law.

3 **The economic system**

There is no distinct economic system envisaged or required by the *Grundgesetz* and therefore compulsory in the German state. A middle path was chosen after the second world war between the problematic pure market economy, with no central planning, and the equally problematic pure State planned economy. The social market economy was chosen for Germany. The BVerfG has confirmed that the *Grundgesetz* does not require a specific form of economic system and it is economically neutral (see BVerfGE 4, 7 and BVerfGE 50, 290, the latter being the decision to affirm the constitutionality of the Co-determination Act when challenged by the employers' organization).

Whatever system is chosen, given the freedom allowed by the *Grundgesetz*, it must allow for the recognition and exercise of other basic rights guaranteed and upheld by the BVerfG. Despite the fact the *Grundgesetz* has not provided distinct and individual economic rights, they have nevertheless generally been recognized by the BVerfG as an extension of other basic rights in the *Grundgesetz* for the protection of human dignity. For further details on the specific rights see the section on basic rights in Chapter 7. These have been interpreted to apply within the economic sphere so that the general right to free development and action under Article 2 (1) *Grundgesetz* is translated into an economic basic right as the freedom to act economically (BVerfGE 4, 7). As with many of the basic rights, these are subject to limitations and restrictions. Providing the action is lawful and does not impinge or harm the basic rights of others it will be upheld.

Other articles of the *Grundgesetz* which have relevance and an impact on the law of economic administration are the following.

(a) Article 12, the freedom to choose a trade or occupation, which is however subject to significant restrictions on a number of grounds as can be seen on the "Apotheker Case", BVerfGE 7, 377 in which the relationship and ability of the legislature to impose on basic rights was discussed.

(b) Article 14, the right to own property is also circumscribed by law, both public law interests of other citizens and the state, including the right of the state under Article 15 *Grundgesetz* to nationalize private property and it is additionally closely regulated by the civil code. The consequence of the recognition and guarantee of private property is that the decision making in respect of the economy is not concentrated in the hands of the government or administration but amongst many.

(c) Article 3, equality before the law is also applicable to economic organizations as is Article 9, the freedom of association. Further details of the basic rights are noted in section A above.

(d) Article 109 in the chapter on fiscal administration imposes a duty on the federal and *Länder* budgetary authorities to have regard in their plans for the overall economic situation. Increasingly this Article is argued to justify intervention in the economy.

4 State promotion of the economy (*Wirtschaftsförderung*)

The government takes a part, albeit indirectly, in the promotion of the economy. The details of which are not entered into here but these includes various forms of financial assistance including grants, subsidies, credits, and tax advantages. Of the massive numbers of laws and regulations which apply in this area of law, only the most important and accessible will be considered here. To some extent the direction of regional development has been altered by unification and special assistance once necessary to promote investment in Berlin is no longer necessary. Most decisions are subject to the issue of an administrative decision and must be applied for by interested parties. A familiarity of the administrative legal procedures and actions is a useful asset in case of a suspected incorrect or harmful decision, considered further in the section on administrative law above. A statute which sets the overall direction of the economy is the Act promoting the stability and growth of the economy (*Gesetz zur Förderung der Stabilität und des Wachstums der Wirtschaft: (Stabilitätsgesetz (StabG))*[54]. This sets the aims of achieving price stability, i.e. no inflation, a high level of employment and free trade to promote a measured economic growth (see § 1).

As with other areas of law, further European integration will mean that EC law will also have an increasing impact in this area of law, particularly consumer protection considered below.

5 The general regulation of business

5.1 The Trade Act (*Gewerbeordnung* GewO)

The Trade Act is the basis of trade and industry legislation dating originally from 1891. It now acts as a residuary statute in that if not specifically catered for by other specialist laws applying, for example, to the railways or most professions, then the provisions of the GewO will apply providing the enterprise concerned can be classified as a business. It and the very many regulations issued under it are concerned with the basic licensing and setting up of businesses and not specific forms of registered companies covered by the specific acts and considered under company law. In it's latest form it dates from 1987 but has already been amended on a number of occasions. It is also considered, because of its regulation of employment

---

[54] Of 8 June 1967 (BGBl I S. 582).

relationships, in the chapter on Labour law. In the new *Länder* its application is governed by the provisions of the Unification Treaty (*Einigungsvertrag*) Arts 24 et seq, 105, 119b, and 120a et seq.

Allied to this area are laws applicable to associations (*Verbände*) which deal with the regulation of various forms of economic, trade, and industrial associations including chambers of commerce, agricultural associations, craft associations, employers associations, unions, and interest groups.

5.2 Particular trade law (*Besonderes Gewerberecht*)

Within the general legal regulation of business, a number of sections of the economy have been provided with rules particular to them. These include the provision of services in hotels and restaurants (*Gaststätten*), craftwork (*Handwerk*), the transport industry (*Verkehrsgewerbe*), the travel industry (*Reisegewerbe*) and markets, fairs and exhibitions (*Marktgewerbe*). Further details can be obtained from the books listed below.

There are in addition a number of statutory bodies which play an important role in the regulation of business, albeit self-regulation. Most notable amongst these are the chambers of industry and commerce (*Industrie- und Handelskammer*) and craftworkers chambers (*Handwerkskammer*).

6 Consumer protection law (*Verbraucherschutzrecht*)

The difficulty in defining an area of law called "consumer law" is deciding on its boundaries and although this is always a problem in that legal areas overlap to some degree with other areas, consumer law seems to want to select laws firmly established in other areas. To define it as laws in protection of the consumer means that the list of laws in the area would be extremely long. The notion of consumer law is in a way a distraction, not in terms of the actual laws which might appear in such a category as many of these provide and protect important rights but in terms of categorization. Defining the boundaries is an almost impossible task by either including all laws which impinge on consumer rights or in the negative all those that do not. It is regarded as a hybrid Public-private law, particularly as it contains many laws which should be considered as civil law subjects. Literature on the matter in Germany was mainly in the form of general legal advice books rather than textbooks devoted to consumer law.[55] The publication of a specific collection of consumers laws and a textbook has, however, now taken place, as noted in 'Further Reading'.

In 1975 there was a Consumer policy report by the Federal Government[56] which

---

[55] For example, E. Endriss, *Verbraucherrechte*, 1985, Dreisam Verlag, Freiburg, the subtitle of which is 'An Advice Book for everyday life'.
[56] Bericht der Bundesregierung zur Verbraucherpolitik, 1975.

helped to define its view of the scope of the area. Policy aims are defined to strengthen the consumers position in the market, provide more information and advice on market behaviour and movements, increase legal rights of redress, protection of health and ensuring supply and quality.

Other consumer laws largely concern product safety, packaging, content, labelling, pricing, information, weights and measures, especially in the area of food and pharmaceutical products. The EC has also made inroads into this area and in future German law will not be significantly different to other EC Member States' laws in many areas. Thus beside looking at the general categories and listing the most notable laws, no further inroads into this area of law will be made.

6.1 Safety legislation

Many of the laws in the area of safety legislation concern food production and aim to protect against health hazards. For example, the Food and Consumer Goods Act (*Lebensmittel- und Bedarfsgegenständegesetz LMBG*) of 1993[57] which applies to foods, cosmetics, tobacco, and other consumer products. It gives wide powers of delegation for further laws to be enacted by the responsible authorities and federal ministries. It includes in § 8 the prohibition of certain substances or additives considered dangerous and generally prohibits the manufacture or marketing of products which may cause impairments or injury to health from foodstuffs and goods in daily use. Similar laws in this category apply in respect of animal feeds, hydrocarbons in products, fertilizers, and pesticides. The European Community is probably now as responsible as the Federal Government for producing regulations in this area of law.

The EC case-law arising under Article 30 EC Treaty and from the case of *Cassis de Dijon* has also had a profound impact on German rules in respect of attempting to ban imports of goods not meeting German standards. Refer to EC law texts for further details.

The category also relates to Pharmaceutical products in which the major enactment is the revised Pharmaceutical Act (*Arzneimittelgesetz*) which provides for statutory approval of new products and stricter liability in delict.

The scope of laws in this area is very wide and further includes technical safety laws for the operation of chemical and nuclear plants, technical equipment safety laws, laws on the protection against hazardous substances, dangerous working materials and working conditions. All of which are as much to do with the protection of employees in the workplace as consumer protection although they do aim to protect both. The recently enacted Product Liability Act is considered below.

6.2 Identification and labelling

This category mainly comprises of safety legislation and applies particularly in respect of food labelling. The main act is the Food and Consumer Goods Act. Under

---

[57] Replacing the 1974 Act (BGBl I S. 1169).

this there have been a considerable number of regulations issued detailing the requirements and prohibitions with regard to product contents, additives and best by dates. Drugs are particularly stringently regulated with the requirement of use by dates. This category also includes weights and measures laws, requirements of clear weights on pre packaged goods, clear prices, and interest rates for purchases on credit.

6.3 Advertising legislation

Advertising is regulated initially by the Unfair Competition Act (*Gesetz gegen den unlauteren Wettbewerb*: UWG) which gives consumer associations the right to challenge deceptive advertising through the use of injunctions (§ 37). The LMBG was passed on 31 July 1986 (BGBl I S. 1169) amending a number of provisions designed to combat unfair selling practises and providing consumers with better remedies. It applies in particular to foodstuffs, cosmetics, pharmaceuticals and tobacco.

6.4 Sale of goods laws

This area of law has been considerably affected by the civil law reform which came into effect on 1 January 2002. The formally self-standing Statute, the General Conditions of Business Act (*Allgemeine Geschäftsbedingungengesetz*: AGBG) has now been incorporated into the BGB itself (§§ 305–310) along with a number of previous acts relating to consumer sales law. The Instalment Sales Act, otherwise referred to as the Consumer Credit Act (*Verbraucherkreditgesetz: VerbrKrG*[58]), can now be found reformulated in §§ 491–504 BGB. Previously, this Act allowed for a cooling-off period of one week for the consumer to revoke the agreement without penalty but this area of law has now been consolidated and codified to agree with doorstep sales contracts, previously governed by the *Haustürwiderrufsgesetz* (HaustürWG/HWiG) and distance sales, governed by the *Fernabsatzgesetz* (FernAbG)[59]. All contracts falling within these provisions can now be revoked up to two weeks after signing an agreement (see new §§ 355–359 in respect of revocation rights in consumer contracts). Consumer credit law protects consumers from excessive interest rates, regulated originally in the BGB § 138 II and surprise price increases are prohibited or subject to regulation by the AGBG but once again now within the BGB (see Chapter 10 for further details).

Also having its own applicable law are Insurance contracts in the Insurance Contracts Act (*Versicherungsvertragsgesetz*: VVG)[60] which applies in addition to the BGB and AGBG. The supervision of the insurance market and insurers is conducted by

---

[58] From 17 December 1990 (BGBl I S. 2840).
[59] 16 January 1986 (BGBl I S. 122 and 27 June 2000 (BGBl I S. 897) but now incorporated respectively in the BGB at §§ 312–312a and §§ 312b–312d.
[60] From 1908 (RGBl I S. 263) but considerably amended over the years and particularly of late.

the Federal supervision office with wide powers granted under the Insurance Supervision Act (*Versicherungsaufsichtsgesetz*: VAG).[61]

6.5 Warranty and liability legislation

This is provided initially by the Civil Code and the AGBG. The EC Directive on Product Liability[62] was not immediately transformed into German law because the government considered that the existing law contained both in BGB §§ 823 et seq and the UWG already achieved, and in fact exceeded, the aims of the Community law. However, following considerable debate the German Product Liability Act (*Produkthaftungsgesetz* ProdHaftG) of 15 December 1989 was enacted. It only relates to products of East Germany put into circulation from the date of unification. The law does not replace the civil code provisions but adds to the actions available.

Paragraph 1 imposes strict liability on a manufacturer of a defective product that kills of injures a person, or which damages property. Previously case law had reversed the burden of proof (see the section on BGB Book Two in Chapter 10).

As the law is substantially the same in Germany now as in other EC Member States, the further details of the ProdHaftG will not be considered here except in respect of the fact that the German legislation has introduced the defence of development risk in favour of manufacturers, whereby they are only expected to meet the standards applicable at the time of the introduction into the market of the product and not the subsequent improvements made since that date. Game and unprocessed agricultural products which were excluded from its scope, are now included in an EU-wide change to the Directive[63]. The German law was effective only from 1 January 1990 and not 25 July 1988 when required by the Directive.

BGB delictual remedies include non-material damages for pain and suffering and commercial property damages which are denied claims under the Act.

6.6 Other areas of consumer law

Rent contracts and travel / package tour contracts are also clearly placed in this area of law. The former is regulated by the BGB (§§ 564 et seq.) and the Rent Act (*Gesetz zur Regelung der Miethöhe*: MHG) and the latter by the BGB (§§ 651a et seq.), the latest version of which transforms the EC package tour Directive into amendments of the German law.

6.7 Enforcement

Enforcement is by three principle means: by governmental or local authorities supervising the application of legislation and standards; by court action by associ-

---

[61] See for further details on the reforms in this area of law, P. Mankowski, *Zur Neuregelung der Widerrufsfrist bei Fehlen einer Belehrung im Verbraucherschutzrecht* (2001) JZ 14, 745 et seq. and A. Alpmann-Pieper, *Express Reform des Schuldrechts: Das neue BGB*, 2nd ed. (2002: Alpmann und Schmidt, Münster).

[62] Council Directive 85/374, OJ 1985, L 210/29; Foster (ed.), *Blackstone's EC Legislation*, 6th ed., p. 453.

[63] New version of the German Statute from 1 December 2000 (BGBl I S. 1478)

ations of consumers, although class actions are only available in limited circumstances as allowed specifically by the Unfair Competition Act and the AGBG for unlawful standard form contracts. Thus most actions to defend consumers' rights and interests are undertaken by individuals before the civil courts.

Consumer organizations and advice centres[64] do exist which are able to give advice and information and the trade unions play quite a prominent role in this respect. As can be seen by their participation in dissemination of information on the law with the *Handbuch des Verbraucherrechts* (HdVR), Loose-leaf collection in two volumes edited by the Consumers Union (*Arbeitsgemeinschaft der Verbraucher*) and the German Federation of Trades Unions (*Deutscher Gewerkschaftsbund*).

FURTHER READING

Handbuch des Verbraucherrechts (HdVR), (loose-leaf collection of consumer protection laws), Luchterhand, Heidelberg).

P. Badura, Chapter 3, *Wirtschaftsverwaltungsrecht* in E. Schmidt-Aßmann (ed.) *Besonderes Verwaltungsrecht* (1999: Walter de Gruyter, Berlin), pp. 219–326.

G. Borchert, *Verbraucherschutzrecht* (1994: C.H. Beck, München).

Business Transactions in Germany (loose leaf) (M. Bender, New York and C.H. Beck, München) vol. I, ch. 19, by H. Hollman.

Droste, Killius & Triebel, *Business Law Guide to Germany*, 3rd ed. (1991: CCH Editions, Bicester), ch. 1 and 15.

W. Frotscher, *Wirtschaftsverfassungs- und Wirtschaftsverwaltungsrecht*, 3rd ed. (1999: C.H. Beck, München).

H. Jarass, *Wirtschaftsverwaltungsrecht*, 3rd ed. (1997: Luchterhand Verlag, Nuewied).

P. Kelly and R. Attree (eds), *European Product Liability* (1992:, Butterworths, London).

R. Stober, *Wirtschaftsverwaltungsrecht*, 10th ed. (1996: Kohlhammer, Stuttgart).

R. Weimar & P. Schimkowski, *Grundzüge des Wirtschaftsrechts*, 2nd ed. (1993: Vahlen Verlag, München).

R. Volhard, D. Weber & W. Usinger (eds.), *Real property in Germany: Legal and Tax Aspects of Development and Investment*, 4th ed. (1991: Knapp, Frankfurt).

E Environmental law (*Umweltrecht*)

Environment Law is a relatively new self standing area of German law and has been identified as a specialised form of administrative law. It incorporates legislation which existed prior to the present concerns and a new impetus of legislative activity over the last two decades. A considerable amount of the legislative activity in this area impinges on business.

---

[64] Each *Land* has set up a *Verbraucherzentrale* with a number of branches in the larger cities and towns.

Its importance was so highly regarded that in 1974 a Federal Environment Office (*Umweltbundesamt*) was established[65]. A Commission has been established for the codification of Environment law and the draft of the first book of the code has been completed[66].

1 **Sources**

Legislation in this area arises from three principal sources; national, European Community, and other international regulation.

Article 73 *Grundgesetz* provides exclusive competence to the Federation in the area of transport, Article 74 concurrent legislative competence of the Federation and *Länder* in many areas including civil and criminal law, notably waste removal, clean air maintenance and noise abatement (see paragraphs 11–24 of Article 74 in the Appendix at the end of the volume) and, under Article 75 it has framework competence in areas of the protection of the countryside, land distribution, regional planning and water supply.

Additionally, the environment is specifically referred to in the Unification Treaty, Chapter VII, Article 34. Paragraph 1 imposes a duty on the legislators "to protect the natural basis of man's existence, with due regard for prevention, the polluter pays principle, and cooperation, and to promote uniform ecological conditions of a high standard at least equivalent to that reached in the Federal Republic of Germany." This has now found expression in the introduction of an environmental protection principle (Art. 20a) to the *Grundgesetz* in 1994 and discussed in Chapter 6. These broad policy aims may be very difficult to translate into enforceable law and this problem is being tackled by the establishment of environmental standards to establish the link between law and application, to translate the vague legal notions into measurable applicable standards. Standards allow for easy application, they add to legal certainty and provide norms around which the facts of a case can be argued. Legislation therefore usually consists of two elements; the protection aim, which outlines the danger to be avoided and; the standard to be observed, the breach of which will give rise to liability.

Thus far the legislative activity can be divided into three phases:

(a) Pre-1970, when there was very little environmental legislation recognized as such. There existed, the provisions of the BGB for actions against nuisance and damages for pollution and a number of individual statutes applying in favour of environmental protection or licensing regulation for enterprises producing industrial pollutants, for example, the Water Management Act *Wasserhaushaltsgesetz* WHG from 1957.

---

[65] 1974 (BGBl I S. 1505).
[66] See the report and draft by M. Kloepfer, *Umweltgesetzbuch: Allgemeiner Teil, Forschungsbericht*, (1991: Umweltbundesamt, Erich Schmidt Verlag, Berlin).

(b) From 1971 an environmental policy was established which sought to tackle the problems of environmental pollution in a number of ways. By controlling the production of pollution directly and by indirect means such as tax incentives or penalties and by zoning laws.

(c) Finally, from 1980 a number of statutes under the banner of environmental law have been passed. The figure now stands in excess of twenty.

A fourth phase will be entered into, at some stage, with the current drafting of an Environmental Code. Any new national efforts, following the European Community single European Act, must be undertaken in conjunction with EC legislation on the matter. For example, the Environmental Impact Assessment Act (*Umweltverträglichkeitsprüfunggsgesetz* UVPG[67]) requires that any building or public works contracts subject to planning permission are considered in the light of the effect they will have on the environment. This is the direct transformation of the EEC Directive 85/337.

The legislative program has had the further consequence that there has been additional input from criminal and civil actions by third parties to enforce and police environmental matters.

As with other areas of public law concerned with the administration of laws, application is at the level of the *Länder* rather than the Federation. There is however a Federal Environment Ministry and the Federal Environment Office (*Umweltbundesamt*) responsible respectively for the issue of Regulations and the monitoring, reporting, and research into standards. The usual local authorities are responsible at the level of the *Länder*.

2 General principles

There are four leading general principles of environmental law which are recognized as broad political and legal principles.

2.1 The preventative or precautionary principle (*Vorsorgeprinzip*)

This principle has as its aim not only the prohibition of further damage by the prevention of pollution but also the improvement of the existing situation. Although somewhat vague it has nevertheless been incorporated into legislation usually in the opening paragraphs which outline the purpose and aims of the legislation (see § 1 BImSchG and § 1 WHG).

---

[67] 1990 (BGBl I S. 205).

2.2 The principle that the polluter pays (*Verursacherprinzip*)

This principle has a twofold aim. Not only does it seek to reduce the burden of the cost of remedying pollution that falls generally on society or producers or consumers but to positively punish those who cause pollution thus discouraging the worse offenders from future pollution. The problems are identifying or establishing conclusively who exactly is the polluter especially where the end result or damage is the cumulative result of many. In such situations the burden on individual actors may be reduced accordingly. This applies to both public and private polluters.

2.3 The co-operation principle (*Kooperationsprinzip*)

This principle is not so easy to translate into legislative requirements and is mainly applied in the procedural law by the involvement in standards committees. It seeks to involve the wider public in environmental protection.

2.4 The protection of the existing position principle (*Bestandsschutzprinzip*)

This more recently emerged principle seeks to ensure that there is no deterioration of the existing environment and to a large degree resembles the *Vorsorgeprinzip* but without the need to effect improvements. It can be found in concrete terms in § 8 BNatSchG which prevents avoidable damage to the environment, in particular areas of special importance such as moors, forestry, hills, cliffs, and similar features of the landscape which are more strictly protected (§ 20 BNatSchG), although in all cases exceptions for the overriding interests of society are allowed.

3 Principal legislative enactments[68]

3.1 The Water Resources Act (*Wasserhaushaltsgesetz*: WHG)[69]

This law and corresponding laws in the *Länder* were enacted to maintain, protect and improve clean water resources and applies in respect of surface, coastal or ground water. All use of public water requires approval (§ 2). Licences, required to release matter into water, are only granted on the basis that the release will not contaminate or affect the purity or the state of the water (§ 6). Similar requirements exist in relation to releases affecting ground water. In addition the BVerfG has extended the regime to privately owned water to limit the use of water in the public

---

[68] Since the first edition, these have been translated into English and can be found in G. Winter (ed.), *German Environmental Law* and also in Schlemminger and Wissel (eds.) both noted in further reading.

[69] Of 23 September 1986 (BGBl I S. 1529 as amended to 1992 (BGBl I S. 1564).

interest (BVerfGE 58, 300). Strict civil liability for damage can be imposed severally and jointly to companies or individuals who offend, under § 22 I, but the defence of *force majeure* is allowed.

The transportation or storage of substances hazardous to water are also regulated by the Statute (§ 19a-h). Particular areas in which there are water wells are identified and given a general and greater protection (§ 19).

As from 1981 water polluters have been required to pay an additional tax (*Abwasserabgabe*) depending on volume and noxiousness.[70]

Other important acts relating to water are: The Drinking Water Act *Trinkwasserverordnung* of 1986 and the Washing and cleaning Products Act (*Wasch- und Reinigungsmittelgesetz*) of 1987.

3.2 **The Federal Emissions Control Act (*Bundesimmissionsschutzgesetz*: BImSchG)**[71]

This Act applies to protect people, animals, vegetation, land, water, and the atmosphere from harm caused by all emissions including air pollution, noise, vibrations, light, heat, and radiation, § 1. Permits are required for the construction and operation of moveable and static facilities which are particularly apt to cause damage to the environment or pose hazards, impairments, or nuisance to the general public or surrounding area. All possible measures should be taken to reduce to a minimum such pollution and dispose of waste materials safely and properly.

There is scope under the act for the issue of Administrative Regulations for specific problems and areas and to lay down technical standards to which existing and new plants must adhere.[72] Additionally these list the types of operations which must apply for a permit. Other types of operation although not required to apply are still nevertheless subject to the general standards.

Companies which exceed a certain level of effluent discharge or emission into the air can be required under the WHG or BImSchG to appoint an Environmental Officer (*Umweltschutzbeauftragter*) whose duty it is to advise management on the environmental consequences of company action and policy (§§ 54–58).

3.3 **The Waste Act (*Abfallsgesetz*: AbfG)**[73]

This Act is the result of the serious waste disposal problems experienced in Germany. The Act imposes a duty on local authorities to provide facilities for waste disposal and a charge for the service provided can be levied under § 3. The facilities must be used by private parties and any other producers of waste products. Producers of industrial waste cannot dispose of it separately (§ 4). For dangerous waste,

---

[70] § 1 of the Waste Water Charges Act (*Abwasserabgabengesetz* AbwAG), 6 November 1990, BGBl I 2432.
[71] Re-enacted on 14 May 1990 (BGBl I S. 880). Further amended up to 1993.
[72] Technical directives relating to air pollution and noise abatement have been issued, TA-Luft and TA-Lärm.
[73] Of 27 August 1995 (BGBl I S. 1410) as amended to 1994.

defined by a regulation[74] under § 2 II of the Act, a waste disposal engineer or officer must be appointed by the company to oversee the storage and disposal of the waste and to inform the authorities of its existence.

A particular problem which the Act has tried to deal with is the transport and export of waste (*Mülltourismus*) both within Germany and outside by requiring domestic waste management (§ 2). Exception are allowed under § 13 by which the export of waste must be licensed. Previously, the Federal Republic's waste disposal problem was relieved by exporting huge quantities of waste to the DDR. Ironically, this problem Once again became a domestic problem when on Unification the disposal sites became a part of the Federal Republic. A new paragraph 9a was enacted to allow for time limits by which the existing sites in the new Länder are to be either cleaned up or closed down.

3.4 The Federal Nature Conservation Act (*Bundesnaturschutzgesetz*: BNatSchG)[75]

This is a framework law which is supplemented by individual laws of each of the *Länder*. It is designed to protect the natural environment and landscape (§ 1) and contains rules in respect of countryside planning (§§ 5–7), the designation of protected areas, national and nature parks (§§ 12–15) and for the protection of specific animals and plants (§ 20).

3.5 The Environmental Information Act (*Umweltinformationsgesetz*: UIG)[76]

This is the transformation of the Environmental Information Directive (90/313) into German law. It seeks to ensure public access to information on the environment held by public authorities. This statute is now backed up by the *Umweltstatistikgesetz* of 1994 (BGBl I S. 2530) and the EC prompted *Umweltauditgesetz* of 1995 (BGBl I S. 1591).

3.6 The Ozone Act (*Ozongesetz*: OG)[77]

This federal law on smog has been enacted. Rather than imposing speed restrictions on all cars or just those without catalytic converters, which were previous measures in some Länder, the Act allows area-specific bans from road use to be imposed on non-converter cars, when ozone limits have been reached. Exceptions are made for tourists, emergency services and necessity where no other alternative for trans-

---

[74] Verordnung zur Bestimmung von Abfallen. 24 May 1977, BGBl I 773.
[75] In the form re-enacted on 21 September 1998 (BGBl I S. 2995).
[76] 1994 (BGBl I S. 1490).
[77] Although referred as the *Ozongesetz* it is actually an amendment to the Federal Pollution Protection Control Act, § 40, (BGBl 1995 I S. 930).

port exists. The measure has already been criticized as unworkable and of limited application because of the number of exceptions possible.

3.7 The Federal Building Code (*Baugesetzbuch*: BauGB)

This restricts building to sites for which a development plan has been approved by the local authorities under local by-laws. The plan must conform to the general requirements of the federal legislation (§ 9).

3.8 The Packaging Act (*Verpackungsverordnung*: VerpackV)

This enactment of 12 June 1991 was designed to overcome the problems encountered in finding space for the disposal of waste products. Requirements include that packaging be kept to a minimum and should be made of reusable materials. The Act applies to the manufacturers of packing, and distributors of goods who use packing materials. Merchants and sellers are obliged to accept the return of packaging for re-use of re-cycling.

Specialized laws deal with the import, manufacture, use, and distribution of chemical substances, the Chemical Substances Act, (*Chemikaliengesetz* ChemG), and the use transportation, and disposal of radioactive substances by the Nuclear Substances Act (*Atomgesetz* AtG) and the Radiation Protection Regulation (*Strahlenschutzverordnung* StrSchV).

4 Liability and enforcement following environmental damage

4.1 Civil law

A claim under the delict rules of §§ 823 *et seq* BGB will lie as the result of death, personal injury or damage to property caused by direct of indirect environmental damage to the protected interests. The burden of proof has been reversed and now requires the defendant to show that no fault exists. See BGHZ 92, 143 and the section on BGB Book Two in the Capter 8 for further details.

Claims for nuisance under § 906 BGB and § 862 or interference under § 1004, apply in the case where an interference to the enjoyment of property is such that it is excessive and materially deprives the claimant of its use. The remedies are an injunction to restrict the emissions, where this is reasonable, or damages. No injunction is available against facilities which have been licensed under BImSchG, or where such pollution is considered normal for the locality.

A recent statute, the Environmental Liability Act (*Umwelthaftungsgesetz* UmweltHG) of 7 November 1990, provides for civil liability for death, injury, or property damage caused by an environmental effect and is similar, therefore, to the Product Liability Act (ProdHaftG) in the remedy provided. The statute lists in an appendix a number of types of operation which become strictly liable for damage arising from water, air or ground pollution. Like the product liability Act it does not replace the existing law, notably the civil code liabilities, but supplements them. The new law imposes only civil liability for breach of its provisions, but either jointly and severally and without fault.

Required elements are the operation of a facility named in the appendix, which lists ninety-sixardous facility, the effect of which is to cause environmental damage. The proof of causation is the most difficult obstacle to overcome but the Act contains under § 6 a presumption that if a particular facility is suited to the type of damage caused, it will be presumed to have caused the damage unless it can show otherwise, thus carrying the burden of proof of causation.

There are exclusions to the general strict liability imposed by § 1 on the basis of § 4, *force majeure*, and for insignificant damage or that to be expected in the locality under § 5.

Unlike the product liability Act considered, above there is no development risk exclusion which means that liability will lie according to the latest state of knowledge and not that applicable at the time of the erection of the facility. This in effect imposes a requirement to keep up to date with developments in environmental safety.

Paragraphs 8–10 provide damaged complainants with the right to obtain information from the operator of the facility and the authorities in respect of claims made. In this way the limited rights in German civil procedure law for the pre-trial discovery of information is circumvented.

4.2 Criminal sanction

The Act on Combating Environmental Criminality of 1980 (*Gesetz zur Bekämpfung der Umweltkriminalität*) codified the existing criminal sanctions for the protection of the environment and incorporated new ones within a new chapter of the Criminal code; Offences against the Environment, §§ 324–330d StGB.

Paragraph 324 StGB makes unauthorised pollution of public surface or ground water or high seas punishable. The maximum penalty is five years' imprisonment for wilful action and two years for negligent acts. Paragraph 325 creates an offence subject to imprisonment for anyone who is blameworthy for causing noise or a change in the natural composition of the air which endangers human beings, animals, plants, or objects of value. Paragraph 326 makes waste dumping outside of authorized sites and in an environmentally damaging manner punishable. Paragraph 327 applies to unlawful operation of atomic sites and waste disposal sites which require licensing and § 328 concerns the unlawful handling of nuclear materials. Paragraph 329 further protects environmentally protected areas, and § 330 increases the penalties of the above in the case of danger to life, limb, or to protected areas.

The main problem with criminal sanctions is that they apply to damage which has been committed and do not directly prevent damage, although the punishments may act as a deterrent on others.

4.3 Public law

Many of the *Länder* have their own public bye laws which permit the issue of orders requiring operators of facilities not to pollute or to clean up pollution where it has taken place, although increasingly these rules are provided on a federal basis to provide uniformity throughout Germany. Substantial fines may be levied in the event of non-compliance. These clean up orders may be specifically relevant in the new *Länder* and can apply to future owners of the facility.

5 Public enforcement of environmental law

Enforcement of environmental standards is usually commenced by the issue of a complaint notice sent to the company which if not acted on by the company will be followed by official orders requiring the company to stop the pollution or close down the facility entirely. Many of the above statutes contain powers for the local authorities and licensing authorities to inspect premises, conduct examinations and demand information with the sanction of fines for failure to comply (see inter alia, § 52 BImSchG, § 19 AtG, § 21 WHG and §§ 11 & 18 AbfG).

These orders are subject to judicial review in the Administrative courts (see the section on Administrative law above for general details). There are, however, further aspects of judicial review in respect of environmental issues which deviate from the general rules. The locus standi requirements have been relaxed in some Länder for third parties and citizens or associations, who have the right (*Verbandsklage*) to object an administrative decision and to obtain an administrative hearing. The particular laws grant either every citizen or the citizen whose interest is concerned, the right of participation, as opposed to the usual requirement that a legally protected interest be shown. Persons living in the area of an industrial establishment are granted a general right of locus standi. This allows third parties to either object to the severity of existing orders or to demand new ones. These actions are, however, limited to the circumstances where the legislation is held by the courts to be in the specific interest of third parties, which has proved to be rare, and the relaxation is therefore limited in effect. For example, the Atomic Energy Act (*Atomgesetz*) defines the area within which citizens have a protected right as within about 10 kilometres. In respect of general public facilities such as parks, landscape and rivers, it is for the public authorities to protect these and not individuals.

FURTHER READING

Books
B. Bender, R. Sparwasser & R. Engel, *Umweltrecht*, 4th ed. (2000: C. F Müller Verlag, Heidelberg).

H.P. Prumm, *Umweltschutzrecht* (1989, Metzner Frankfurt).

J. Salzwedel and W. Preusker, *The Law and Practice Relating to Pollution Control in the Federal Republic of Germany*, 2nd ed. (1982, Graham and Trotman for the Commission of the European Communities).

H. Schlemminger and H. Wissel (eds.), *German Environmental Law for Practitioners* (1996: Kluwer, the Hague).

R. Schmidt, *Einführung in das Umweltrecht*, 5th ed. (1999: C.H. Beck, München).

P. Storm, *Umweltrecht*, 6th ed. (1995, Erich Schmidt Verlag, Berlin).

G. Winter (Ed.), *German Environmental Law: Basic Texts and Introduction* (1994: Martinus Nijhoff/Graham & Trotman, Dordrecht).

Articles

R. Breuer, Chapter 5, *Grundlagen des Umweltschutzrechts* in E. Schmidt-Aßmann (ed.) *Besonderes Verwaltungsrecht* (1999: Walter de Gruyter, Berlin), pp. 461–625.

W.C. Hoffman, Germany's new Environmental Liability Act: Strict liability for facilities causing pollution, (1991) NILR, pp. 27–41.

9

Public law IV

A Criminal law

1 Introduction

Criminal law offences can be defined as those attracting penalties of a criminal nature and which leave a criminal record. They differ from minor offences (*Ordnungswidrigkeiten*) for which a fine is applied and which do not have the stigma of criminality, traffic offences being the clearest example of these. There is also a distinction to be observed between, which for the purposes of comparison can best be described as, felonies (*Verbrechen*) and misdemeanours (*Vergehen*) (§ 12 StGB).[1] Felonies in German law are classified as all those unlawful acts attracting a punishment of at least one year's imprisonment and misdemeanours a minimum of less than one year or alternatively punishment by fine. The category of misdemeanours is quite extended and includes criminal acts which would be regarded as serious crimes in other jurisdictions also, such as fraud and extortion.

The main sources of criminal law and the most important legislation in this area are: the Criminal Code (*Strafgesetzbuch*), the Juvenile Courts Act (*Jugendgerichtsgesetz*), and the Administrative Offences Act (*Ordnungswidrigkeitsgesetz*) which contains both substantive and procedural provisions. However, some criminal offences can also be found in other acts depending on their context, such as narcotics offences in narcotics law (*Betäubungsmittelgesetz*), violations of the arms law (*Waffengesetz*), or offences of illegal residence, which are dealt with in the law on foreigners (*Ausländergesetz*). Recently enacted, topical statutes include the statute on protection of embryos (*Embryonenschutzgesetz*) and the statute on transplantations (*Transplantationsgesetz*).

Dealing with the initiation, execution, and suspension of penalties is the Enforcement of Criminal Sentences Act (*Strafvollzugsgesetz StVollzG*) which concerns all aspects of the imprisonment, education and rehabilitation of offenders. The details of this statute will not be considered in this book.

Criminal law is divided into the substantive criminal law (*materielles Strafrecht*) which concerns the actual requirements and details of crimes which must be fulfilled before an act can be considered criminal and thus liable to a punishment, and procedural criminal law (*Strafverfahrensrecht* or *formelles Strafrecht*) which is

---

[1] All paragraph references will refer to the criminal code (StGB) unless otherwise stated.

concerned with the way in which the substantive criminal law is enforced. It thus deals with the organization, composition, and jurisdiction of the criminal divisions of the courts of ordinary jurisdiction and the organization of the Office of the Public Prosecutor. The applicable statutes are the Organization of the Courts Act (*Gerichtsverfassungsgesetz GVG*) and in respect of the process of the detection, prosecution, trial, and judgment, the Code on Criminal Procedure *(Strafprozeßordnung, StPO)*.

As with other areas of German law, an eye also has to be kept on the provisions of the *Grundgesetz* with which all laws in the sphere of criminal law must comply. In particular Article 103 (I and III) GG must be observed, which require that an action can only be punishable if it was an offence at the time it was committed, i.e. there is no retroactivity of law in criminal law and, there can be no double punishment (double jeopardy) for the same act.

2 History of criminal law

The first national German criminal code was the Carolingian penal code of 1532[2] which although being predominantly a code of criminal procedure contained also provisions on substantial criminal law. This was applicable throughout the empire and was the basis for the development of a common law in criminal law but, as with other laws, could be overruled by the territorially limited regional laws. It was therefore used only as a subsidiary law where the regional laws failed to give an answer. Notable amongst these are the Prussian Common Law Act of 1794 (*Preußisches Allgemeines Landrecht*) containing criminal provisions and the Bavarian penal code of 1813 (*Bayerisches Strafgesetzbuch*). The procedural provisions in the Carolingian penal code were supplemented by Imperial police ordinances (*Reichspolizeiordnungen*).

In 1871, the German empire adopted the Imperial Penal Code (*Reichsstrafgesetzbuch*) as a part of the process of the Unification of the State and German Law. This was largely based on the Prussian Penal Code and since its adoption had been severely criticized with an almost constant clamour for its reform and many false attempts to do so. Changes of criminal law carried out during the time of the Third Reich (1933–1945) were aimed at obscuring the line between repressive and preventive elements, thus creating a police state. They included, for example, the introduction of analogy in criminal law.[3] These changes were almost entirely repealed after the war. Finally, in 1975 a new general part was adopted and minor changes were made to the special part. This has now been re-issued to incorporate the many amendments since 1975 and stands in its latest form as of 1 April 1998.[4] It

---

[2] Die Peinliche Halsgerichtsordnung Karls V or in Latin the "Constiutio Criminalis Carolina".

[3] See H.L. Tröndle and T. Fischer, *Strafgesetzbuch*, 50th ed. (2001: C.H. Beck, München, Einleitung), para. 3.

[4] This 6. StrRG (= 6th reform of the Criminal Code) was mainly directed at harmonizing punishments, abolishing superfluous provisions, and simplifying law application. For critical comment and further references see H.L. Tröndle and T. Fischer, *Strafgesetzbuch*, 50th ed. (2001: München, Einleitung), para 14, 14a.

is now the present law for the whole of the unified Germany with a few exceptions as noted in the Unification Treaty.

Although there are no clear competences of the European Community to enact criminal laws, certain areas of EC law do provide for sanctions, namely within environmental law or regarding the fight against corruption and fraud affecting the EC's financial interests. Whether criminal sanctions concerning the latter subject can be based on Article 280 EC is disputed.[5] So far, any substantial criminal law will have to be agreed upon by using the mechanisms of unanimous decision-making within the third pillar of the European Union.

Due to the political changes within the last decade and the international community's growing willingness to provide effective protection of human rights on an international level, an international criminal law is about to emerge. Examples are the establishment of International Criminal Tribunals for the former Yugoslavia and Rwanda. The 1998 Statute of Rome establishing a International Criminal Court which, as opposed to the two courts mentioned above, is a permanent one, is designed to deal effectively with cases of genocide, war crimes, and crimes against humanity.[6] As a party to the Treaty, Germany is currently preparing a constitutional amendment (of Art. 16 II GG) to allow for the extradiction of German offenders to international courts.[7]

3 Structure of the criminal code

The code is divided into a General Part and a Special Part (*Allgemeiner und Besonderer Teil*). The general part contains the underlying assumptions of the code and the general rules applicable to all offences (§§ 1–79b). They include rules on the applicability of German criminal law (§§ 1–10), the general structure and forms of a criminal offence (§§ 13–37), the legal consequences of the offence (§§ 38–76a, e.g. forms of punishment and additional consequences), and limitation (§§ 78 et seq.). As the code is phrased very generally it is necessary for the judges to interpret quite widely the general and abstract terms in order to give them meaning in application. The special part, §§ 80–358, describes in detail individual offences and gives the statutory conditions which must be fulfilled to prove the offence and the punishment for breaches.

---

[5] see C. Waldhoff, in: C. Calliess and M. Ruffert (eds.), *Kommentar zu EG-Vertrag und EU Vertrag* (1999: Luchterhand, Neuwied), Art. 280, para. 3; Tröndle and Fischer, above, n 2, *Einleitung*, para. 16.

[6] The Convention has already been ratified by Germany. After having been ratified by 60 parties to the convention it will enter into force on 1st of July 2002.

[7] For more information see Tröndle and Fischer, above, n 2, *Einleitung*, paras. 17–18.

4 Applicability of German criminal law (§§ 3–9 StGB)

In general, the applicability of German criminal law is linked to the principle of territoriality (*Territorialitätsprinzip*), meaning that German law is applicable to all offences committed within the territory of Germany (§ 3) including German ships and areoplanes (§ 4). However, in certain cases the principle is extended. For instance, § 5 lists additional cases in which it is applicable to offences committed abroad. These offences are basically directed against German "objects of legal protection" (*Rechtsgüter*). Examples are crimes against the the German state itself (preparation of a military attack) or offences against criminal law designed to protect the environment when committed within the German exclusive economic zone, and also the abduction of a child by one parent to a different country ("legal kidnapping"). Furthermore, the catalogue of § 6 applies German criminal law to several internationally prosecuted crimes such as genocide or, slave trade. Finally, § 7 functioning as a subsidiary clause declares applicable German criminal law in those cases where the crime is committed against a German or by a German abroad if the crime is also an offence under the law of the scene of the crime. The same applies if the scene of the crime is not subject to any criminal law at all.

> **Example:** In the example of Satish stealing Nigel's pen in Nigel's office in Cardiff,[8] according to § 7 II No.1, German criminal law is applicable as the offender is German. This is not affected by the fact that the theft is also a crime by English law. Rather it enables the German state to ask for the offender's extradiction. An example of the second alternative mentioned would be if the theft had been committed by Satish in Antarctica. As the continent is not subject to any criminal law regime, but the offender is German, German law would be applicable.

5 Leading principles of German criminal law

5.1 The principle of legality (Gesetzlichkeitsprinzip)

This is the German version or understanding of the Latin maxims *nulla poena sine lege* and *nullum crimen sine lege*; no penalties without legislation and no crime without an offence, thus precluding retroactive criminal laws (§ 2 StGB). This principle is given absolute authority in Germany by its inclusion in the *Grundgesetz* Article 103 II and § 1 StGB. All other principles in criminal law essentially derive from this one. German law extends the principle to the requirement that there can be no crime or punishment without written laws. German customary law or common law

---

[8] See above, Chapter 2, sec. 3.2.

cannot be employed against offenders. There is then no possibility of a judge in Germany discovering an ancient crime to apply. The criminal code and additional legislation provide a definitive catalogue of both crimes and the preconditions for those crimes.

5.1.1 Ban on retroactivity (Rückwirkungsverbot)

The classic guarantee deriving from the principle of legality is the ban of retroactivity (Art. 103 II GG and § 2 StGB) It prohibits the retroactive application of a harsher law or penalty but also the retroactive creation of an offence.[9] The exception to the proscription of retroactivity is when it can be used in the defence of or to the advantage of the accused.

5.1.2 Ban on analogy (Analogieverbot)

In contrast to the position in civil law, if there is a gap in the range of legal crimes, it cannot be filled by way of analogy with another crime.[10] This is also allied with the principle of legal certainty. The exception to the proscription of analogy is when it can be used in defence of the accused. Quite how far interpretation of the law by reference to other sources resembles analogy, is clearly a debatable point.

5.1.3 Legal certainty (Bestimmtheitsgebot or Bestimmtheitsgrundsatz)

This principle is clearly recognized in the Anglo-American legal systems as either part of the rule of law or a part of the rules of natural justice. In German criminal law this is translated into the requirement that as far as possible a citizen must be able to predict with certainty what forms of conduct are to be classed as criminal and thus punishable and so act accordingly. This does not go as far, however, as to prohibit any interpretation of existing laws in order to determine their scope.[11]

5.2 The principle of the protection of legal rights (Rechtsgüterschutzprinzip)

The central element in the provision of a system of criminal law is the concern for the protection of legal rights or more accurately the "objects of legal protection" (Rechtsgüter)[12] in order to maintain the values of society.

5.3 The principle of guilt (Schuldprinzip)

The revised Criminal Code and thus the criminal legal system is based on the principle of guilt (normativer Schuldbegriff).[13] This view is underpinned by § 46,

---

[9] See Chapter 7, sec. 1.2 on Art. 103 II GG.
[10] See above, Chapter 2, sec. 3.3.
[11] See also below, Chapter 6, sec. 3.3.4 on constitutional frame of this principle.
[12] Such objects could be individual (life, property, self-determination) or collective ones (state as a whole, judicial system, objects of representation).
[13] As opposed to the psychological definition of guilt (psychologischer Schuldbegriff), that focused on intent and negligence as forms of guilt.

which states that the offender's guilt is the basis for the measurement of punishment. The principle of guilt therefore looks at the individual responsibility for a crime (*Vorwerfbarkeit des Handelns*), as highlighted by the Federal Court of Justice.[14] As each individual is regarded as a self-determined human being, he is capable of recognizing the rules of law and freely deciding whether he complies with them or not.[15] Thus guilt will always require the individual's capacity to recognize the unlawfulness of certain actions and the capacity to make his behaviour conform to this knowledge. Consequently, according to § 17, a deed committed by an unavoidable mistake as to its lawfulness is defensible as the offender is deemed to have acted "without guilt". Punishment is in fact only to be metered out when absolutely necessary and rehabilitation and prevention should be sought wherever possible. In line with this is the abolition of periods of imprisonment of less than one month (§ 38 II).

Paradoxically as it may sound, in German criminal law, guilt has both an objective and a subjective aspect. The objective aspect merely deals with the different forms of intent as to the committed crime in question. On a subjective level, however, the individual responsibility will be examined to determine the person's guilt.[16] Thus even cases of negligence, which may amount to criminal liablity, are based on the offendor's guilt, i.e. his responsibility or the reproach that *he could have acted diligently*. This will become more clear as we examine the "structure" of the criminal offence.

For the offender the principle of guilt has the following practical consequences: below the age of fourteen, criminal responsibility or capacity is excluded (§ 19), as it is with those suffering from mental disorders (§ 20). While legal persons are not capable of guilt and their representatives (managers, officers, etc.) are usually the ones prosecuted, legal persons themselves may be required to pay any fines levied (§ 30 OwiG).[17]

6 General concepts in criminal law

The general concepts are all those, which are derived, from the provisions of the general part of the Criminal Code (*Allgemeiner Teil*) §§ 1–79b.

---

[14] BGHSt 2, 194, 200.

[15] Although this is disputed by some academics, who argue that all human beings are not determined by themselves but by genetical concepts and their environment (*Indeterminismus*). Joecks, *Studienkommentar StGB* (1999: München), Vor § 13, Paras 55–56.

[16] See J. Wessels and W. Beulke, *Strafrecht Allgemeiner Teil*, 30th ed. (2000: C.F. Mü, Heidelberg), pp. 122–123.

[17] For further details see Tröndle and Fischer, above, n 2, Vor § 13, paras. 33–34a.

6.1 Forms of criminal offences

German criminal law distinguishes between different forms of committing a crime. They may be committed intentionally (*Vorsatzdelikte*) or negligently (*Fahrlässigkeitsdelikte, see* § 15). Additionally, the law differentiates between crimes of "commission" (*Begehungsdelikte*) and crimes of "omission" (*Unterlassungsdelikte* § 13), the latter covering cases where an individual failed to take a particular obligatory measure in order to avert certain damages, i.e. failure to assist in cases of accidents (§ 323a). The general "structure" of a criminal offence will first be considered in context with the intentionally committed crime (*vorsätzliches Begehungsdelikt*). Afterwards, modifications in the cases of crimes of negligence and "ommission" will be examined.

6.2 Structure of the criminal offence (*Aufbau der Straftat*)

Three essential elements must be present before an offence is committed. These are the physical and mental elements of an offence (*Tatbestand*), unlawfulness (*Rechtswidrigkeit*), and guilt (*Schuld*). If one fails, there has been no crime and there can be no punishment.

6.2.1 Tatbestand (the physical and mental elements of the offence)

The *Tatbestand* must meet the statutorily defined constituent elements of the particular offence and the offending act is defined as every deliberate physical behaviour which fits the statutory description of the offence. The offence elements are divided into objective and subjective aspects (*objektiver und subjektiver Tatbestand*). The objective aspects are the factual elements; what happened, the appearances, how the act is committed, which instruments are used. The subjective aspects are elements of the offence which belong to the mental reasoning of the offender. It is therefore at the subjective level that a discussion of intent takes place.

6.2.1.1 objektiver Tatbestand (objective, "physical", aspects)

These objective aspects focus on circumstances "physically" manifesting the offence or making it visible. They will include descriptive and normative aspects. Referring to the example of § 242 StGB[18] the elements "mobile" and "object" are easily ascertained and are thus descriptive aspects. By contrast the element "someone else's (object)" is normative, as it refers to the legal status of ownership which is not apparant to the eye but must be ascertained in accordance with the private law rules of the BGB. But it is not only the visible action and its circumstances that are covered by the *objektiver Tatbestand*. It is also at this stage that questions of causation are discussed. The following remarks on causation apply to negligently and deliberately committed offences alike. In order to show that the requirements of a particular offence have been fulfilled it is necessary to show that the act was caused by the accused. There has to be a fundamental connection between the act and the

---

[18] See also the example in Chapter 2, sec. 3.2.

result. Without going into the details of academic discussions on different theories of causation we will only look at the dominating opinion, which adheres to the theory of equivalence (*Äquivalenztheorie* also: *conditio sine qua non formula*). This theory holds that all acts which lead to the fulfilment of the requirements for an offence will satisfy causation and must be treated equally as causes for an offence.

The definition of the theory of equivalence goes as follows:

Every aspect or condition, that cannot be excluded from the chain of events without voiding the fulfilment of the offence, is considered a "cause" (*conditio sine qua non*).[19]

This causal character, however, cannot always be exactly determined.[20] In cases of alternative causation, the theory is extended.

Example: *A* and *B* independently spike *C*'s drink with deadly poisonous mixtures. After emptying his glass *C* dies. Here each of the two poisoning acts could be alternatively (mentally) substracted without reversing *C*'s death. In such cases, dominating opinion deems both alternative actions as causal.

If in this example only the combination of both mixtures becomes deadly, causation can be easily established according to the theory of equivalence (cumulative causation). It becomes more difficult where the cumulation of causes was not foreseeable.[21] The question of "reserve causes" or hypothetical causation became significant in one of the early BGH cases (1951):

BGHSt 2, 20 KZ-Fall

Due to an application by the accused, who had been a high ranking police officer in the Third Reich, three Jews had been deported to a concentration camp, where they had later died. He was charged with deprivation of liberty. The court of first instance (*Schwurgericht*)[22] acquitted him on the following grounds: the victims would in any case have been sent to the concentration camps—even without the plaintiff's application, as someone else would then have caused their deportation. Therefore his action

---

[19] "*Ursächlich ist jede Bedingung eines Erfolges, die nicht hinweggedacht werden kann, ohne dass der Erfolg entfiele.*" RGSt 1, 373, BGHSt 1, 332 as cited by Wessels and Beulke, above, n 15, p. 51.
[20] For detailed discussion of the following problems on causation see Wessels and Beulke, above, n 15, pp. 51–54.
[21] See below, this section.
[22] For the court structure see above, Chapter 3.

was not causal according to the theory of equivalence. The Federal Court of Justice (BGH) disagreed. It held the plaintiff's action could not be taken from the cause of events without leading to a different fate for the victims. Whether without his application the victims would have been deported or not was merely hypothetical. The court had to look at the actual facts. Allowing hypothetical aspects would, furthermore, permit any member of criminal associations to exculpate himself by pleading that another member would have fulfilled the offence if he had not committed it.

However, the theory of equivalence can lead to an unforeseeable liability for everyday actions. If, for example, the sale of a knife is used for a murder it is clear that the sale has helped cause the murder. If the act of sale were taken from the chain of events the murder would not have happened (at least not in this way). Fufilment of the offence would not have taken place. Obviously, such a broad view would unforeseeably make all sorts of actions causal to criminal offences at this level. In order to limit the effect of the theory of equivalence the dominating opinion examines whether the fulfilment of the cause could be "objectively attributed" to the cause in question (*objektive Zurechenbarkeit*).

Thus the following definition of *"Objektive Zurechenbarkeit"* restricts liability under the *conditio sine qua non formula*:

Fulfilment of an offence can only be objectively attributed to the offender's (causal) act, if the offender has created a legally relevant danger, that was subsequently realized in fulfilling the offence.[23]

According to this definition, atypical chains of causation cannot objectively be attributed to an act of the offender.

Example: *A* hits *B* severely hurting him. During the following drive to the doctor *B* is killed in an accident. *B*'s death was not foreseeable to *A*. *A* would only be convicted for grievous bodily harm.

Several categories of cases have been developed dealing with the question whether a legally relevant danger has been created by the offender. Apart from atypical chains of events, only two will be looked at here: cases focusing on the purpose of the relevant provision (*Schutzzweck der Norm*) and those of victims harm-

---

[23] See Wessels and Beulke, above, n 16, p. 57.

ing or endangering themselves (*Selbstschädigung und-gefährdung des Opfers*). The first category examines whether creating a certain legally relevant danger is disapproved of by law. However, not all violations of a legal provision will automatically lead to creating a legally relevant danger.

Example: A driver exceeds the speed limit in town *A*. Later on his journey a child unexpectedly crosses the street and is run over by him in town *B*. The driver acted diligently when in town *B* but he violated the Road Traffic Act in town *A*. It could be argued that he created a legally relevant danger in town *A*, which manifested itself in town *B*, because if he had observed the speed limit he would have reached the site of the accident a few seconds later. By then the child would already have crossed the street. This argument has to be rejected. Although he violated a legal provision (speed limit according to the Road Traffic Act) and although this was causal to the child's death it cannot be objectively attributed to him. In exceeding the speed limit the driver did not create a danger that the speed limit was designed to ban. The speed limit focuses on protection of other drivers and pedestrians within the concrete case (in town *A*) and not on preventing the driver reaching a certain point at a certain time. Otherwise one might as well accuse the driver of not having driven *fast enough* in order to have passed the site of the accident *before* the child crossed the road.

Thus the purpose of the provision (*Schutzzweck der Norm*) infringed has to be taken into account. The second category of cases mentioned will also limit an offender's liability even if his acts were causal. In these cases the offender participates in cases of victims harming or endangering themselves. Thus if a heroin addict gives one of his syringes to another addict and the latter does not survive his "shot" then the first addict is not guilty of (negligently) causing the other's death.[24] Although his action was causal in such a case, the victim knew about the dangers of his own actions (shooting heroin). The dominating opinion demands a certain degree of self-responsibility (*Prinzip der Eigenverantwortung*).[25] However, if the victim, unlike the participant, cannot clearly oversee the consequences of his actions, then the latter's acts will be deemed causal to the fulfilment of the offence.

6.2.1.2 *Subjektiver Tatbestand (subjective, "mental", aspects)*
The discussion of the subjective aspects commences with the question of intent. Paragaraph 15 states that intentional behaviour is punishable, whereas negligent behaviour will only satisfy the *Tatbestand* if included in the relevant substantive provision in the particular part of the code. Intent is defined as knowledge that the behaviour will have a particular result and the desire or will that this result should come about. This is the same definition as that used in German civil law.

---

[24] BGHSt 32, 262.
[25] Tröndle and Fischer, above, n 2, Vor § 13, para 19; Wessels and Beulke, above, n 16, p. 61.

Furthermore, the subjective elements must correspond with the objective elements. The offender must know and want the result as it is prescribed by the criminal code.

Knowledge, for example in the case of theft (§ 242), means that the offender must know that he is taking away something that doesn't belong to him. It is only necessary to show an abstract knowledge that the action undertaken is one which is desired. The knowledge of the unlawfulness of the action is not necessary, this is dealt with when considering guilt.

(a) Different categories of intent

Intent can be constituted in three different ways:

(a) As *Absicht* (also: *dolus directus 1. Grades*), an intensified form of direct intention, which may be equated with motivation whereby the offender wants a specific result,

(b) As *Direkter Vorsatz* (*dolus directus 2. Grades*), where the offender knows or expects the result of the action and wants this result, and

(c) as *Eventualvorsatz* (*dolus eventualis*), where the offender seriously expects the result often as a necessary intermediate step in order to achieve something else, although he does not necessarily wish this result.

The latter, especially, has to be distinguished from conscious negligence where although expected, the result is not desired and the hope is that it does not transpire.

Example: Driver *A* overtakes another car on a road at a place where it is difficult to see ahead. He hits and kills a cyclist coming towards him, whom he did not see. *A* knew that if someone was coming towards him on the other lane, he would hurt or even kill him by pursuing such a dangerous manoeuvre. Whether he had the intention of *dolus eventualis* or was rather consciously negligent depends on whether he was accepting this possible outcome as a necessary side effect or rather hoped that "nothing would go wrong". In the latter case (of conscious negligence) he would have refrained from the manouvre of taking over, had he known that there was a cyclist. If on the other hand he did not care about the cyclist but at any cost wanted to overtake, then he would have acted with intent (*dolus eventualis*).

In practice, however, this distinction is difficult to establish. The court thus will often look at the high probability of the result, which should have been foreseeable to the offender.[26] A case from 1989 will illustrate this:

---

[26] For discussion of the different theories see Wessels and Beulke, above, n 16, pp. 74–76.

BGHSt 36, 1 AIDS-Fall

In spite of having been warned by his doctor of the dangers of unprotected sexual intercourse, the accused, who was infected by the AIDS virus, frequently had sexual intercourse with several partners. None of them were infected. He was charged with attempted grievous bodily harm. The question raised now was whether the accused had acted with the intent of *dolus eventualis*. If not, then the accused would have had to be acquitted, as without actually having infected anyone he could not be charged with the negligent offence of GBH. The BGH held, that *dolus eventualis* still demanded the accused's knowledge of creating a serious danger to his sexual partners as well as wanting to create it. The Court had to find a way of distinguishing whether he had had sexual intercourse accepting that an infection of his partners was a possible result or whether he had done so genuinely hoping that there be no infection. As it is difficult to establish the accused's intent at the time of the act, the Court held it was legitimate to infer his intent from his knowledge. In this case his doctor had warned the accused about the dangers of unprotected sexual intercourse several times. In spite of this knowledge the accused carried on with his actions. As a consequence, the Court was allowed to infer intent in this case.

The problems of negligence will be dealt with when looking at this type of offence further below.

(b) Mistake

The criminal code distinguishes two kinds of mistake: § 16, mistake of fact relating to the elements of the offence (*Tatbestandsirrtum*) and § 17, mistake in law, meaning the offender does not know he is doing something that is "unlawful" (*Verbotsirrtum*). Other types of mistakes are not mentioned in the Code but have been developed as subcategories by academics and will be mentioned below. The question of mistake is dealt with when examing intent, unlawfulness, or guilt depending on the types of mistake, but also according to the different criminal law theories one adheres to. For simplicity's sake, we will only look at the dominating opinion in this introduction.

If an offender's mistake relates to the objective aspects (*Tatbestandsirrtum*, §16 StGB) of his actions, they might affect his intent and thus ultimately his liability. Thus if the offender mistakes one person or object for another *(error in persona vel objecto)* when committing an offence, the question arises whether he still acted with sufficient intent.

Example: *A* wants to kill *B*. He sets up an ambush, which a different person, *C*, enters. *A* mistakes *C* for *B* and shoots him. According to dominating opinion this mistake is irrelevant. The minute *A* was aiming at *C* he wanted to kill this particular person, which is sufficient for the offence of manslaughter (or even murder) according to §§ 212, 211.

Where objects and persons are confused however, the mistake is relevant. If *A* aims and shoots at a garbage bin, not knowing that a child has been hiding in there, he obviously had no intent of killing another person. He would, however, be charged with negligent manslaughter. Another problem of intent is the miscarriage of a criminal act (*aberratio ictus*). Here the action misses the person it is directed at but hits another person. In such a case the offender lacks the intent of, for example, killing the person he aimed at.

BGHSt 34, 53 Anfahr-Fall

When his former girlfriend was escorted home from a pub by a new suitor, the offender followed them by car. Seized by a fit of jealous rage he stepped on the accelerator directing the car at the other man. The latter managed to jump aside in time but the woman who had been standing behind him was hit by the car and killed. The Court held that the offender had not mistaken the persons but that this was a case of miscarriage of the criminal act or *aberratio ictus*. Thus the offender had to be convicted for attempted manslaughter of the man and negligent manslaughter of his former girlfriend.

Mistakes as to the unlawfulness will be considered below.

6.2.2 *"Unlawfulness" (Rechtswidrigkeit)*

This is the second of the three required elements to constitute an offence. Unlawfulness is usually defined as the actions that have breached social and legal norms, however there can be justifications whereby the apparent unlawfulness is adjudged lawful. Even where the elements of the statutory provision have been fulfilled there is no duty to abstain from conduct if there are grounds of justification present to negate unlawfulness. Only when there are no justifiable grounds can judgment on the legality take place. If unlawfulness is established, the final element, guilt or blameworthiness, must be considered.[27]

6.2.2.1 *Grounds for justification of the offence (Rechtsfertigungsgründe)*

These grounds can be derived either from the code or from customary law. In this book we can only focus on a few of them.[28]

(a) Self defence (*Notwehr*, §32)

According to § 32 StGB, the conditions for self defence are that there must be an attack, whether intentional, negligent, or unconscious, by a human, or an animal when ordered by a human, on a legal right of the defender or someone else, § 32. The attack must be present and unlawful. The defender must, furthermore, be aware of the situation of self-defence. His action of defence then has to be

---

[27] See below, section 6.2.3.
[28] For an overview see Wessels and Beulke, above, n 16, pp. 92 et seq. Further grounds of justification than those mentioned in this section—such as justifying conflict of duties (*Rechtfertigende Pflichtenkollision*)—cannot be examined here, refer to Gropp, below, n 32, pp. 211–218.

proportional in the sense that it should not be more harmful than is necessary.[29] It must be pointed out that any legal right of the attacked is capable of being defended under this provision. Frequent problems that arise in this context are the definition of whether an attack is indeed present and whether the defence action is necessary and proportionate.

An attack will be present, if it is about to be commenced, if it has started or continues.[30]

BGH NJW 1973, 255 Brusttaschenfall

Here it was held by the BGH that an attack is already present if the attacker reaches for his breastpocket in order to get out a loaded gun. Thus shooting the attacker was held to be a case of self-defence, even though the gun had not yet been in the attacker's hand. However, in that case the attacker had at an earlier point unsuccessfully tried to kill the accused by shooting him. Thus when the accused met the attacker for a second time he could infer that with reaching for the breast pocket an attack was about to commence.

When looking at proportionality and whether a defence action was necessary, one has to distinguish between two aspects: The action of defence must be necessary, meaning that the particular action taken is proportionate (*verhältnismässig*) or more accurate, necessary (*erforderlich*). Thus the use of firearms might be necessary in a situation of self-defence, but aiming at the attacker in order to kill him can only be the last resort. Proportionality requires the attacked to first threaten the use of the gun and then give warning shots.[31]

A second aspect is that in some cases it might be questionable whether any action of defence is necessary (*Gebotensein der Verteidigungshandlung*). In such cases of harmless attacks—i.e. by children—that can easily be dodged, society does not allow any action of defence. A defence action will, furthermore, not be tolerated if it is clearly out of proportion to the right endangered.

Example: Even if the only way for an old man to stop a boy stealing cherries from his garden, is to shoot him—i.e. because the old man is paralyzed and thus confined to a wheelchair—this action would not be allowed under § 32. The boy's life evidently outweighs the old man's interest in the property of cherries.

---

[29] See C.J. Hauf, *Strafrecht, Allgemeiner Teil*, 2nd ed. (2001: Luchterhand, Neuwied), pp. 29–37. More specifically Wessels and Beulke, above, n 16, pp. 101–110.

[30] Wessels and Beulke, above, n 16, p. 103.

[31] BGH NStZ 1987, 172.

The difference from the above-mentioned proportionality of means is that in our example the only effective action of self-defence is prohibited on grounds of proportionality, whereas in the previous settings proportionality allows the least harmful among several possible actions. However, these two categories may often be difficult to distinguish.[32]

BGHSt 26, 256 Boxer-Fall

The victim—*A*—had witnessed the accused, a semi-professional boxer, slapping and violently leading away a girl. He interfered, ordering the accused to let go of the girl. After the accused had told him to mind his own business, the victim attacked him. The accused easily pushed him back several times, repeating that he should leave them alone. In a fit of anger the victim charged the accused, repeatedly hitting him. The accused ducked and without success demanded the victim to stop. Finally, he knocked out the attacker by hitting him in the face. The attacker later died from the injury suffered. The court of first instance (*Schwurgericht*) had convicted the accused of *grievous bodily harm leading to death*. The BGH quashed the decision on the following grounds: although there was a situation of self-defence, the accused as a semi-professional boxer had control over it. Thus he was obliged to carefully choose his actions of defence, which he had done for some time. However, as the provocation went on, this restriction would not last forever. This had not been taken into account by the court of first instance. Thus the BGH handed the case back for a new trial.

It remains unclear from this decision whether this is a case where any sort of active defence was deemed to be unnecessary as the boxer (allegedly) was always in control of the situation or whether this was a case dealing with proportionality of the particular action of defence (the calculated swing at the attacker).

(b) Justifying necessity (*Rechtfertigender Notstand*, § 34 StGB)

Paragraph 34 requires that there must be a present danger to life, limb, liberty, honour, property, or other legal interest which in order to prevent it requires the committing of an offence not otherwise avoidable. The offence will not be unlawful if on a balance of interests the protected right is substantially more valuable than the interest infringed. The measures taken to avert the danger must be appropriate and be taken consciously. The main distinction from self-defence is that the action taken in order to protect one of the mentioned legal interests will be justified, even though it is not directed at *an unlawful attack* but *any sort of danger*.[33]

---

[32] Gropp, *Strafrecht Allgemeiner Teil*, 2nd ed. (2001: Springer, Berlin), pp. 191–194: Wessels and Beulke, above, n 16, pp. 106–109: Tröndle and Fischer, above, n 2, § 32, paras 12–20.

[33] Refer to Gropp, above, n 32, pp. 198–210; Wessels and Beulke, above, n 16, pp. 94–102 for more details.

Examples:
- a doctor exceeding the speed limit on a road in order to get to the victim of an accident in time
- shooting of an attacking dog that belongs to someone else
- confining a schizophrenic relative suffering from paranoid hallucinations to his room in order to protect him from harming himself[34]

Provisions in the Civil Code (BGB) acknowledge justifiying necessity in the special cases of destroying or damaging objects that can either be used to ward off a danger (§ 904 BGB) or that create a danger themselves (§ 228 BGB). These provisions—although provisions of private law—are move specific than the more general § 34 StGB.

(c) Justifying consent (*Einwilligung*)

This justification does not arise from the code but is recognized by the courts. A distinction has to be made between agreement (*Einverständnis*) which means that the constituent elements of the offence are not fulfilled (i.e. the agreement to sexual intercourse will not even create the objective aspects of the offence of rape) and consent (*Einwilligung*) justifying a conduct, which has already fulfilled the elements of the offence (*Tatbestand*) and thus removes the unlawfulness. In the latter case the legal interest affected must be at disposal in the first place. For example, it follows from the constitutional protection of human life and dignity (Arts 1, 2 GG), that no-one can renounce his right to life. Thus consenting to be killed could never justify the actions of the offender.[35]

If, however, the right concerned can be renounced, then the person whose right is being infringed must have the mental and legal capacity to waive the right and must do so consciously and of free will prior to the act, either expressly or impliedly. The latter concept of *Einwilligung* has been a source of debate especially in cases of consenting to bodily harm and consenting to medical treatment that involves measures affecting bodily integrity.

Cases of sado-masochism pose the problem of balancing between an individual's basic right to personal freedom (Art. 2 I GG) and the state's obligation to protect each individual's bodily integrity and dignity (Art. 1, 2 II GG).[36] As § 228 StGB states explicitly that consent will not be effective if it contravenes good morals, the question of how to define good morals arises. An early decision of the BGH, dealing with fencing bouts practiced in traditional student fraternities, suggests a restrictive interpretation of § 228 in favour of the offender.[37] No cases of "S-M" have been decided so far. Academic literature seems to be divided on this subject. Whereas the

---

[34] BGHSt 13, 197.
[35] However, suicide does not constitute an offence. See below, sec. 7.2.
[36] See also above Chapter 7, sec. 1.2, Arts 1 and 2.
[37] BGHSt 4, 24.

majority regard cases of S-M as contravening good morals,[38] a minority claims that this would fail to address social reality. The latter draws the line where consent is given to life-threatening, mutilating, dangerous injuries.[39] A clear infringement of § 228 entailing an invalid consent is the donation of organs in return for remuneration.[40]

Under German law a medical treatment or rather "intervention" (*ärztlicher Heileingriff*) fulfils the objective and subjective aspects of the offence (*Tatbestand*)[41] of bodily harm.[42] Thus the offence can only be justified by the consent of the patient. This consent must be made willingly in awareness of the risks of the treatment. As a result each medical doctor is obliged to sufficiently explain the risks and consequences of the treatment. Details will depend on each individual case.

BGH NJW 1978, 1206 Zahnarzt-Fall

A patient, having suffered from headaches for several years, demanded from the accused, a dentist, to extract all her teeth which had fillings. It was her firm belief that her headaches and the fillings were linked. The accused tried to convince her that an extraction of the teeth would not improve her situation, yet she insisted on the treatment. Ultimately, the accused yielded to her wishes and extracted all her teeth of the upper jaw. He was later charged with causing bodily harm. The BGH refused to recognize the patient's consent as justification. It held that this was a clear case of "lay ignorance" (*laienhafter Unverstand*). The accused knew all the time that an extraction of the teeth could not improve the patient's health in any way. The consent given by the patient was based on irrational assumptions and was thus invalid.

(d) Presumption of consent (*mutmaßliche Einwilligung*)

In some circumstances of necessity, where the owner of the endangered right cannot be consulted in time, preventative measures involving an offence will not be unlawful if it can be presumed that the owner would have consented had he known of the danger, especially in cases of medical aid for unconscious victims. Here priority will be given to the "probable" consent of the individual concerned. Thus a patient's precautionarily made instructions will be of importance.[43] Otherwise a consent will have to be based on a "common-sense" approach.[44]

The question of presumed consent is of paramount importance in cases of euthanasia, as a more recent case shows:

---

[38] *Stree* in A. Schönke and H. Schröder, *Strafgesetzbuch*, 26th ed. (2001: C.H. Beck, München) §228, para. 6 with further references.
[39] Fischer and Tröndle, above, n 2, § 228, para. 10 with further references. Judging from dominating opinion and the restrictive approach of the BGH towards §228 it is rather probable that the offenders in the case of *Brown* [1993] 2 All ER 75 would have been acquitted on grounds of justifying consent under German law.
[40] As manifested in §§ 17,18 TPG (Law on Transplants); Tröndle and Fischer, above, n 2, § 228, para. 10.
[41] See above, sec. 6.2.1.
[42] Tröndle and Fischer, above, n 2, § 223, paras 9–9v.
[43] See Wessels and Beulke, above, n 16, p. 117.
[44] BGHSt, 35, 246.

BGH NStZ 1995, 80 Behandlungsabbruchsfall

The accused, a medical doctor, had been treating a seventy year old patient since her heart attack. The attack had left her brain irreversibly damaged. Subsequently she was kept alive by being artificially fed. From 1990 she hardly reacted to anyone addressing her. Without any prospect of the patient's health improving, in 1993 the accused suggested to her son that her nourishment be reduced to tea, assuming that this would lead to a swift death. The son agreed remembering that eight years ago his mother had mentioned that she would never want to end up in a situation of being confined unconscious to a hospital bed. A nurse, having learned of this agreement, brought it to the attention of the authorities. Both were convicted for attempted manslaughter by the court of first instance. The BGH quashed the decision and handed it back to the court with the obligation to take into account the following aspects: in cases of fatally ill patients, who are no longer capable of making their own decisions, terminating life supporting medical treatment can be justified. It must, however, be based on the patient's presumed consent. Such a presumption will have to be subjected to strict conditions. Comments made by the patient previously, his religious belief, his personal values, and attitude towards life expectancy and pain will have to be taken into account. If no indication of these can be found then a decision based on general common sense may be taken albeit with caution.

6.2.2.2 *Mistake*

Mistakes as to unlawfulness have to be divided into mistakes relating to the existence or limits of a ground of justification (*Erlaubnisirrtum*) and mistakes relating to facts that would justify actions if they existed (*Erlaubnistatbestandsirrtum*). The first case is treated like a mistake in law and relates to individual guilt. Thus it will be examined when looking at guilt.[45] The *Erlaubnistatbestandsirrtum* is more difficult to deal with. Here the offender falsely assumes that a situation exists which allows him to take justified actions.

Example: *A* makes a sudden gesture in order to stretch. *B* sitting next to him mistakes the movement for an attack and swiftly knocks him unconscious. Thus *B* made a mistake relating to the situation but not to the general grounds of justification, because if his assumption had been right, then his action would have been justified (*Erlaubnistatbestandsirrtum*). By contrast, if *A* really had attacked him and *B* had assumed he was allowed to use any means of self-defence, i.e. clubbing *A* until he does not move anymore, then this would have been a mistake relating to the existence or limit of acknowledged grounds of justification (*Erlaubnisirrtum*).

---

[45] See below, next section.

A mistake as to the facts that would justify the offender's actions, did they exist is treated differently by different criminal theories.[46] Dominating opinion including the BGH treat it like a mistake of fact relating to the elements of the offence (*Tatbestandsirrtum*).[47] As a consequence, an offender making a mistake as to the circumstances, that would justify his action if they really existed, will be convicted for the negligently, rather than the intentionally, committed offence as the following case shows:

BGHSt 35, 246 Sterilisationsfall

Here two doctors during a cesarean operation discovered a deformation in the patient's abdomen. They came to the conclusion that another pregnancy would be fatal and thus assumed the patient's consent to sterilize her. Such a steriliation at a later time would have been significantly more dangerous. As the patient had not been aware of such a risk the doctors were accused of bodily harm. The BGH held that there was no justification of presumed consent and that the doctors had made a mistake as to the facts that would have justified their action. It was treated as *Erlaubnistatbestandsirrtum* and the accused were convicted of negligently causing bodily harm.

6.2.3 *Guilt (Schuld)*

The concept of guilt incorporates social responsibility and an offender is punished for violating the legal order against better understanding. Guilt applies at the level of whether the offender is personally liable for the unlawful conduct. Guilt, according to § 46 I, is the basis for punishment and is determined by the ability of the offender to choose between lawful and unlawful conduct. In individual circumstances guilt may be excused and there will be no punishment for the unlawful action.

6.2.3.1 *Capacity in guilt (Schuldfähigkeit)*

For guilt to be established there must be capacity for guilt. Paragraphs 19–21 provides details on excluded categories and the requirements for capacity. Paragraph 19 provides that children under the age of fourteen have no criminal capacity, those between the age of fourteen and eighteen are responsible according to the level of their individual maturity, § 3 JGG. Paragaraph 20 provides a rebuttable presumption of incapacity for those affected by mental disorder. This may be caused by different categories of mental illnesses but also by drunkenness or as a result of drugs. The BGH has accepted that in some cases of crimes being committed in a state of extreme emotion (*Affekt*), the offender has no capacity of guilt, because his emotional state has blacked out his capacity to rationally control his actions.[48]

---

[46] These cannot be examined here. Refer to Wessels and Beulke, above, n 16, pp. 145–151.
[47] See above, sec. 6.2.1.2(b).
[48] BGHSt 11, 20 (*Kartoffelschäler-Fall*).

This, however, has been restricted to exceptional cases and will depend on the individual circumstances.[49] Drunkenness presents the greatest problems in that there is no objective test as to what blood alcohol levels will result in incapacity for § 20. It must therefore always depend on individual tolerance although guidelines have been developed by the courts. However, drunkenness provides no excuse where the incapacitated state was self-induced, particularly where alcohol or drugs were taken with intent to provide courage to commit the offence. In such cases the courts achieve a just result by regarding the individual as unlawfully depriving himself of criminal capacity for guilt, as will be examined below.[50]

Paragraph 21 provides for diminished capacity, which if established results in a reduction of punishment as outlined in § 49 I.

Except in the above cases, capacity for guilt is presumed. A person must be of normal intelligence, have normal emotions and motivations and know that the conduct is offensive, i.e. unlawful. The offender does not have to know exactly what offence has been committed in a formal way but only that some offence may have been committed.

6.2.3.2 *Actio libera in causa*

Where an offender induces his drunkenness—and thus incapacity—prior to comitting an offence, his guilt will not be excluded under § 20 StGB. In such cases the act of self-inducing drunkenness itself will be part of the offence. Two categories of dealing with offences committed in a state of drunkenness have to be distinguished under German law:

(a) those falling under the principle of *actio libera in causa*, and

(b) those falling under the subsidiary rule of § 323a StGB (*Vollrausch*).

If the offender intentionally got drunk with the aim of later committing an offence while being in the state of incapacity, he will remain liable for the original offence in spite of § 20 but according to the principle of *actio libera in causa*.

Example: *A* wants to kill *B* but is afraid he might not have the courage to fulfil the deed. In order to overcome his scruples he gets drunk and then—in a state of incapacity—suceeds in killing *B*. As *A*'s intention covered getting drunk as well as killing *B* both actions were linked to each other by his intent. Furthermore, he had sufficient capacity of guilt the moment he started the chain of events (getting drunk). Thus he is liable for manslaughter (§ 212 StGB in connection with the principle of *actio libera in causa*).

This principle has been developed by customary law.[51] The element of guilt, which is missing at the time of committing the offence, is hypothetically brought forward

---

[49] See Tröndle and Fischer, above, n 2, § 20 para. 10b with further references.
[50] See below: "*actio libera in causa*", sec. 6.2.3.2.
[51] For details and different theories on *actio libera in causa* see Wessels and Beulke, above, n 16, pp. 127–130.

to the time the offender intentionally got drunk.[52] Dominating opinion states that committing the (whole) offence is actually commenced at this point.[53] At this time, however, the offender's intent must cover the whole chain of events. Thus he must intend to achieve the state of drunkenness and to commit a particular offence when being drunk. In other words, he must show "double intent" (*doppelter Vorsatz*).

To complicate things further, the principle of *actio libera in causa* has also been applied to cases of negligence: negligent *actio libera in causa* applies where the offender intentionally or negligently gets drunk and negligently ignores the danger of committing an offence while drunk. Most of these cases, however, can be covered by offences of negligence without resorting to the principle of *actio libera in causa*.[54]

In view of the phrasing of § 20 StGB, the principle of *actio libera in causa* is problematic. Paragraph § 20 expressly excludes guilt in cases of severe drunkenness. The exception of *actio libera in causa* is not mentioned anywhere within the Criminal Code. Thus arguably its application might contravene Article 103 II GG, the principle of *nullum crimen sine lege*.[55] However, it is argued that when enacting the Criminal Code the legislature was aware of this principle of customary law and seemed to tolerate it. Furthermore, it seems only logical to hold someone liable in spite of § 20 if he induces his drunkenness on purpose, in order to avoid capacity for his subsequently committed offences.[56] It remains nevertheless a disputed topic, especially since the 1996 decision of the 4th senate of the BGH, that had considerable practical effect:[57]

BGHSt 42, 235 Grenzübergangsfall

The accused, who had already been convicted for drunk driving several times, drove a truck from Germany to the Netherlands. Before looking for a hotel for the night he bought several alcoholic drinks in the early evening hours and began consuming them. Three and a half hours later he was severly drunk and steered his vehicle into another car at the German border checkpoint causing the death of two German customs officers. He was convicted of negligent manslaughter (§ 222), (intentionally) driving without license (§ 316) and (intentionally) endangering road traffic (§ 315c). His claim to be exempted from liabililty, under § 20 by reason of intoxication, was not accepted. Instead, he was convicted, applying the principle of *actio libera in causa*, by the court of first instance. The BGH partially quashed the decision. It held that the accused was indeed liable for negligent manslaughter but that the element of getting drunk already

---

[52] BGHSt 21, 381.
[53] *Tatbestandslösung*, see Gropp, above, n 32, p. 256; Tröndle and Fischer, above, n 2, § 20, para. 19a.
[54] As Wessels and Beulke, above, n 16, p. 128 suggest.
[55] See above, Chapter 7, sec. 1.2, Art. 103 II.
[56] Wessels and Beulke, above, n 16, p. 128.
[57] Tröndle and Fischer, above, n 2, § 20 paras 19–19b.

constituted the crucial negligent act. There was no need to employ the principle of *actio libera in causa*. As regard road traffic offences, the BGH delivered a landmark decision. The Court held that—at least as far as road traffic offences were concerned—the *actio libera in causa* principle can no longer by applied. It held that "transferring" the element of guilt to the time when the offender gets drunk, by claiming the offence hypothetically began at that time, is not acceptable where the offence concerned is clearly defined. In the cases of road traffic offences there are exact definitions of the commencing of the crime focusing on **driving** a vehicle instead of **causing the movement** of a vehicle. Only the latter would have allowed a more extensive interpretation of the commencement of the offence.

In a later decision, the 3rd senate of the BGH stuck to the principle of *actio libera in causa* as far as offences other than road traffic offences are concerned.[58] It remains to be seen whether *actio libera in causa* will remain an applicable principle in the long run.

Where committing a particular offence in the state of drunkenness was not intended by the offender and negligence as to that offence cannot be established, the subsidiary § 323a (*Vollrausch*) applies. Here the offender can be punished by fine or imprisonment up to five years, if he induces a state of his incapacity and later commits a deed for which he cannot normally be punished according to § 20. Thus § 323a imposes strict liability. Intentional or negligent links as to the subsequently committed crime need not be established.

6.2.3.3 *Grounds for excuse of guilt (Schuldausschließungsgründe/ Entschuldigungsgründe)*

Excuse is based on the consideration that although guilt exists there are certain mitigating or accompanying circumstances which reduce the level of guilt to that below meaningful or worthy punishment.

(a) Excessive use of force in self defence (*Notwehrexzeß*).
Paragraph 33 states that using excessive force in self-defence in order to prevent an attack on oneself or another person by reason of confusion, fear, or fright will not be punished. Thus if the attacked, out of sudden fear or confusion uses an unproportionally restrictive means of defence—i.e. shooting the attacker in the head where a shot at the legs would have been sufficient—the offence will be unlawful and unjustified but excusable. In other words, society does not approve of the action legally, but accepts grounds that may mitigate the offender's personal blame. The use of excessive force will, however, be problematic in cases where the attack is no longer clearly present, where the situation of self-defence has been provoked[59] or foreseen by the offender.[60]

---

[58] JR 97, 391.
[59] Wessels and Beulke, above, n 16, pp. 137–138.
[60] BGHSt 39, 133.

(b) Necessity as an excuse *(Entschuldigender Notstand)*.

In contrast to justifying necessity under § 34, necessity as an excuse (§ 35) does not require a balancing of values, but is restricted to the saving of life or limb or liberty. Even where all other elements of an offence are present, society may choose not to blame the person for the way he understandably felt forced to act and the guilty mind will be excused. This includes the situation where somebody is forced to commit an offence in order to avert danger to himself, his next of kin, or someone else close to him. The measure chosen must be the only possible way to save one's life, limb, or liberty.

Classical Example: The extreme case excusing the killing of another person has been illustrated by the case of two shipwrecked sailors clinging to the same plank. As the piece of wood can only support one person one of them knocks the other off the plank to save himself.[61]

The deed would clearly be unjustifiable. However, society would not under these circumstances blame the offender. His action will be excused. It is likely that this structure under German law, which splits a crime into three levels (aspects of the offence, unlawfulness, guilt) would, in a case like *Dudley and Stevens*[62] have led to an acquittal of the accused sailors. Their action of killing and eating the cabin boy while being shipwrecked and starving would most probably have been unjustified but excusable under German law. Thus a resort to pardon would not have been necessary.

A practical consequence of the division between justified and excused actions, on the other hand, is that in cases of excusing necessity, self-defence is admitted[63] whereas there can be no right to self-defence where an offence is justified and thus lawful. Contrasting § 35 with § 34 it therefore becomes clear that excusing necessity is far more restricted in its application than its "justifying" counterpart.

(c) Conflict of duties as an excuse *(Schuldausschließende Pflichtenkollision)*.

Where the offender has to choose between conflicting duties of the same value, as in the situation where two people are drowning but there is only the chance to rescue one, the offence of not saving the second will be excused but still remains unjustified, i.e. unlawful. This principle, sometimes also described as "extra-statutory excusing necessity" *(übergesetzlicher entschuldigender Notstand)*, is still very much debated. It seems to be confined to singularly exceptional cases such as the one concerning Nazi doctors, decided in 1953:

---

[61] As given by Wessels and Beulke, above, n 16, p. 134.
[62] *Dudley and Stephens* (1884) 14 QBD 273.
[63] Tröndle and Fischer, above, n 2, § 35, para. 9.

BGH NJW 1953, 513 Fall der Massentötung von Geisteskranken

Two doctors were accused of participating in the mass murder of mentally handicapped persons ordered by the Nazi regime in 1941. They were responsible for selecting persons from their asylums to be killed. Their defence was that keeping their posts as official doctors at the asylums and participating in the euthanasia programme was the only way to at least exert some influence in the selection process. That way, by selecting only as few potential victims as possible without arousing the suspicion of the authorities, they could save a substantial number of people. The BGH rejected this argument. It neither allowed it as justifying necessity nor as an excuse of conflict of duties by pointing out that there had been no real conflict of duties. There had been a no duty to remain as a doctor at the asylum. The Court drew special attention to other doctors in similar situations that had preferred to leave their posts rather than participate in the Nazi euthanasia programmes.

Some academics, however, do not as readily reject the idea of conflicting duties as an excuse in that particular case, but rather see it as a classical example for an excusing conflict of duties.[64]

6.2.3.4 *Mistake*

Mistakes in law are—according to dominating opinion—dealt with when examining the offender's guilt.[65] A mistake as to the law (*Verbotsirrtum*) is present when the offender is ignorant of the fact that his conduct constitutes an offence or that the offence does not count in the given circumstances or the scope of the provision. The crucial component of § 17 is that the lack of knowledge is unavoidable. This is judged from an objective viewpoint and thus becomes a very difficult test to satisfy.

Mistakes as to the existence of legally justifying or excusing grounds (*Irrtümer über Rechtfertigungs- oder Entschuldigungsgründe*) are treated as mistakes in law.[66] By contrast, mistakes as to factual circumstances that would excuse the offender's action, if they really existed, are provided for in § 35 II StGB. But here likewise it will be examined as to whether they were avoidable.

6.2.3.5 *Special elements of guilt (spezielle Schuldmerkmale)*

Finally, attention has to be drawn to special elements of guilt. These are additional elements that are mentioned in respect of particular crimes. They will appear in the relevant provisions. For example, § 211 StGB describing murder, does not only enlist the killing of another person as a constituting element of the crime but also morally corrupt motives[67] (*niedrige Beweggründe*) as particular elements of guilt (§211 II 1st category).

---

[64] See Hauf, above, n 28, p. 52; Wessels and Beulke, above, n 16, p. 139;
[65] Tröndle and Fischer, above, n 2, § 17, para. 2 with further references.
[66] See above sec. 6.2.2.2; see also Wessels and Beulke, above, n 16, pp. 153–154.
[67] This is the best translation that can be given for this which refers, for example, to racial hatred or greed or lust as the motive for the killing.

6.2.4 *Exemption from punishment (Strafausschließungs- und aufhebungsgründe)*

Even where all three elements of a crime are fulfilled (objective and subjective elements, unlawfulness, and guilt), an offender will not be punished in some circumstances because of personal exemption rules. Such rules that will exempt an offender *a priori* are, e.g. indemnity of a member of Parliament (§ 36 StGB)[68] or being a close relative in the case of obstruction of criminal justice (§ 258 VI StGB, *Strafvereitelung*). Furthermore, there are rules exempting the offender from punishment after having committed the offence, e.g. § 24 I StGB *(Rücktritt)* where an offender has gone beyond the attempt but deliberately abstains from the completion of an offence.

6.2.5 *Structure of the intentionally committed offence* (Struktur des vorsätzlichen Begehungsdelikts)

The following figure will outline the main elements of the structure of an offence and point out the classical problems:

I. Tatbestand

---

(1) objective elements of the offence (*objektiver Tatbestand*)

   (a) examining "factual" elements of case and of provision

   (b) problem of causation

(2) subjective elements of the offence (*subjektiver Tatbestand*)

   (a) intent covering all factual or objective elements of the offence including causation (= "acting knowingly and willingly")

   (b) distinguishing *dolus eventualis* from conscious negligence

   (c) problem of mistake as to objective elements of the offence = *Tatbestandsirrtum* § 16 (e.g. *error in persona vel objecto*)

II. Unlawfulness (*Rechtswidrigkeit*)

   (a) Existence of a situation giving rise to justifying grounds (i.e. situation of self-defence) = objective elements of justifying grounds

   (b) Problem of mistake concerning concrete situation = *Erlaubnistatbestandsirrtum* (treated at this point but analogous to an error according to § 16)

   (c) Mistake as to legally accepted grounds of justification (*Erlaubnisirrtum*) treated later when looking at guilt (like mistake in law, § 17)

---

[68] See also Chapter 6, sec. 4.1.3.

III. Guilt (*Schuld*)

(a) Capacity to be liable (problem of minors, mentally disturbed, § 20)

(b) Problem of intoxication and *actio libera in causa*

(c) Grounds excusing the offence (e.g. § 35)

(d) Mistake in law (§ 17) and mistakes relating to existence of legally acknowledged grounds of justification and excuse

---

IIII. Exemptions from punishment (*Strafaufhebungs oder—ausschliessungsgründe*)

(a) Personal *a priori* exemptions: e.g. § 36

(b) Personal exemptions granted *after* committing the offence (e.g. § 24)

6.3 Negligent offences (*Fahrlässigkeitsdelikte*)

The structure of negligent offences very much resembles that of intentionally committed ones. It is also split up into *Tatbestand*, unlawfulness, and guilt. However, when dealing with the subjective side intent is replaced by the phenomenon of "negligence" and the quality of guilt will be assessed according to the carelessness the offender displayed. Just like intent (or rather *Vorsatz*) negligence shows a double function: on the one hand, it shows a form or modus of action and, on the other, it defines a particular form of guilt.

In German criminal law, negligence is the unintended fulfilment of the constituent elements of an offence through neglect of the duty of care. The largest group of such offences arises from motoring. As a general rule it is stated in § 15 that negligence is not punishable unless clearly stated under the provisions of the appropriate offence. Although not defined by the code the jurisprudence recognizes conscious and unconscious negligence. The former has an awareness that an offence may be fulfilled but hopes it will be avoided whereas unconscious negligence has no awareness that either a breach of duty is occurring or that it is an offence.

6.3.1 Specific elements of negligence

Specific elements of negligent conduct are causation (*Erfolgsverursachung*) and the breach of an objective duty of care (*Objective Sorgfaltspflichtverletzung*). As they make out the "objective elements" of the offence, they are examined within the *Tatbestand*. A negligent offence is fulfilled, when a particular event (e.g. the killing of a person), provided for by the relevant provision (here § 222 StGB), has taken place. The principles of causation mentioned above apply when examining the link between the event and the offender's conduct. Furthermore, the offender must have breached an objective duty of care (e.g. breach of a road traffic safety provision). Only a breach of the particular duty of care aimed to protect a particular legal right can constitute the violation of the legal right. Therefore, just as in the case of causation of intentionally committed offences, we have to assess whether the result of the offender's conduct was "objectively attributable" to his actions.[69] In other words, where non-negligent conduct would have led to the same result, there is no wrong, as the following case might illustrate:

BGHSt 11, 1 Lastwagen-Fall

The accused, a truck driver, overtook a cyclist on a straight and clear road. However, when doing so he only kept a distance of 75 cm to the cyclist instead of the obligational 1–1.5 m. The latter obligation of keeping this sufficient space is set out by the road traffic regulation *(Strassenverkehrsordnung)*. The cyclist, in a sudden panic reaction, steered his cycle to the left and got caught under the truck's back wheels suffering fatal injuries. Subsequent examination of the body showed that the the cyclist had been severely drunk. The accused was charged with negligent manslaughter (§ 222). The BGH rejected the charge. The Court admitted that the accused's conduct was causal for the cyclist's death. However, it could not be excluded beyond reasonable doubt that the cyclist would have been killed in any case. Judging from his severe state of drunkenness and his sudden uncontrolled movement, it was highly probable that he would have been caught by the truck even if the accused had kept the correct distance. The danger that is created by breaching the particular duty of care has to manifest itself predominantly because of the accused's conduct. Here this was not the case.[70]

Thus the duty of care involves recognition of the danger to the legal right brought about by the actual conduct and alteration or ceasing of the conduct. The kind and extent of care to be shown is that of a thoughtful and responsible person in that particular situation. Special knowledge that leads to a greater awareness of a danger must be taken into account. At that point conscious and unconscious negligence have to be distinguished.

Unlawfulness *(Rechtswidrigkeit)* is also required as with intentional offences.[71] Finally, looking at the element of guilt, the offender must have been personally capable of foreseeing the danger. Physical and mental disabilities or defects, panic, or confusion can exempt the guilt.[72]

6.4 Offences of omission *(Unterlassungsdelikte)*

German criminal law distinguishes between "real" an "pseudo-omissions" *(echte und unechte Unterlassungsdelikte)*. Only few real omissions exist under the Criminal

---

[69] See above, sec. 6.2.2.1.
[70] This reflects the dominating opinion. For the dissenting opinion, that assumes an "objective attribution" where the offender merely enhances the risk *(Risikoerhöhungslehre)* see Wessels and Beulke, above, n 16, p. 226.
[71] See sec. 6.2.2 above.
[72] See further RGSt 30, 25 *(Leinenfänger-Fall)*.

Code. A classical example is § 323c imposing a specific duty to render assistance to those in need in cases of accident, common danger, or emergency.

On the other hand, § 13 StGB states that the commission of any crime that is statutorily defined can also take place through an omission. A pseudo-omission is the result of the failure to observe a legally demanded duty rather than simple passive non-action and consists of a result of some sort caused by the omission of the necessary and physically possible assistance.

6.4.1 *Objective and subjective elements of pseudo-omissions (Tatbestand)*

Again it is the phenomenon of *Tatbestand* that demands particular attention, whereas the elements of unlawfulness and guilt are not that different from those of intentionally committed offences.[73]

6.4.1.1 *Causation*

Objective elements of an offence of pseudo-omission include that the offender did not take an action in order to prevent the particular event, e.g. the killing of another person. However, it must have been realistically possible for him to take the required action.[74] Obviously, for example, an unconscious person cannot take any action. Furthermore, the omission must have been caused the result. Dominating opinion therefore applies a modified version of the above-mentioned[75] *condicio sine qua non* formula:

The omission of a specifically required action will be considered causal, if the required action cannot be hypothetically added to the chain of events without voiding the result.[76]

Such an assumption requires a "causation" beyond reasonable doubt.[77] Causation has to be limited however, according to the assessment as to whether the result was objectively attributable to the offender's omission. That will be the case only if the result reflects the realization of the particular danger created by the omission.

EXAMPLE: *A* watches his son fall into the water but does nothing to save him. The son, however, is rescued by another person. On his way to the hospital he dies, as the ambulance is smashed in an accident. This chain of events was not foreseeable. Thus the death of the son cannot be objectively attributed anymore to *A*'s omission.

---

[73] See above, sec. 6.2.
[74] Wessels and Beulke, above, n 16, p. 236.
[75] See sec. 6.2.1.1.
[76] Tröndle and Fischer, above, n 2, Vor § 13. Para. 20 with further references.
[77] RGSt 79, 49.

6.4.1.2 *Specific personal legal responsibility (Garantenpflicht)*

The element that distinguishes pseudo-omissions from the specific omission offences like §323c StGB is that of a specific personal legal duty of the offender to take action. Whereas in cases of an accident, any passer-by is under an obligation to render help (§ 323c), persons with a specific responsibility (defined as *Garantenstellung*) towards the victim are under a special obligation to avert harm from the victim. This explains why such a person, e.g. a father not saving his children, is liable for murder by omission (§§ 211, 212, in connection with § 13) rather than for failure to render assistance (§ 323c).

This legal duty (*Garantenpflicht*) can arise not just from the criminal code but may be contained in other acts of legislation such as the civil code family law which provides many duties to be fulfilled in respect of the duties of parents to look after and bring up children, duties between spouses, or the duties now recognized of fathers to their illegitimate children.[78] Generally, the specific legal duties to take action can arise from two categories:[79]

(a) the offender has a special duty of protection for certain legal interests (*Schutzpflichten für Rechtsgüter*),

(b) the offender is liable for certain sources of danger (*Verantwortlichkeit für Gefahrenquellen*)

The first category includes close personal links, usually arising between family members as mentioned above. Furthermore, close links within a special group can be established, e.g. where a group of people get together in order to overcome specific dangers like on traveling or research expeditions. Finally, the duty to protect can arise form voluntarily taking over responsibility, as happens in special professions, i.e. by taking over the tasks of a doctor, nurse, fireman, babysitter, etc. However, the following case shows that in particular circumstances the BGH agrees to exempt a doctor from his duty in spite of his special responsibility:

BGHSt 32, 367 Fall Wittig

Since the death of her husband "*Peterle*" the 76 year-old patient of the accused general practitioner, had repeatedly mentioned suicidal intentions. In vain, the accused had tried to get her to change her mind. As she was suffering from a hardening of her coronary blood vessels, he wanted to transfer her to hospital, which she resisted. When making a housecall in the evening a few days later he found her lying on the couch, unconscious. He found two pieces of paper, one addressed to him, imploring him not to take her to the hospital and another saying "*I want to join my Peterle*". The accused realized that the patient had taken morphium and sleeping pills and that it was impossible to save her life without severe damage ensuing. He did not take any action but

---

[78] see Chapter 10.
[79] For details see: Wessels and Beulke, above, n 16, pp. 239–244.

stayed with the patient until the following morning when at 7:00 o'clock he ascertained her death. The court of first instance acquitted him of manslaughter by omission. The prosecution, pointing out his special responsibility towards his patient, appealed. The BGH, however, upheld the acquittal. The Court acknowledged a situation where the doctor's duty (amounting to a *Garantenpflicht*) to save the patient's life conflicted with his duty to respect the patient's wishes. Furthermore, the Court recognized the accused's assumption that saving the patient's life was not possible without causing irreversible damage. It pointed out that the accused, instead of "taking the easy way out" by calling an ambulance to transfer her to intensive care, chose with respect to the human dignity of his dying patient to stay with her until death occurred. In these special circumstances, the Court held, the accused's decision could not be condemned.

The second category of specific legal duties aims at those who create dangers or have taken over responsibility to protect against certain dangers. Thus houseowners are legally obliged to ensure that dangers emanating from their property do not lead to the injury of others, e.g. removing unsafe parts of the building that might collapse close to a sidewalk. In the disputed "Compuserve" decision the liability of an internet provider for "a source of danger" was assumed, where hardcore child pornography was put onto the internet even though the provider's means of control were slight.[80] Teachers have a duty to keep a watch on the pupils while in school. Finally, anyone who has created a danger by "unlawful" conduct (*Ingerenz*) is under the same obligation. To be accurate, German law speaks of a conduct that is *"pflichtwidrig"* which includes not only unlawful (= *rechtswidrig*) conduct but also any conduct that would be socially inacceptable. Thus a pub-owner having provided a customer for several hours with alcoholic beverages and noticing the latter's severe drunkenness has a special duty to protect the him.[81] Such an "unlawful" conduct has also been assumed where a company endangered consumers by not calling back harmful products, here sprays for treatment of leather which caused severe injuries of the lungs.[82]

Finally, the subjective elements of offences of omissions include intent as well as negligence. Thus, the above said is applicable.[83]

6.4.2 *Unlawfulness and guilt in omissions*

There are justifications, one of which is a conflict of duty, whereby a more valuable right to be protected prevents action to protect a lesser right. The presence of danger and the necessary quick decision that has to be made allow for a much more

---

[80] *LG München*, NJW 2000, 1051.
[81] BGHSt 26, 35 (*Gaststättenfall*). In this case the drunk customer—hardly staying on his feet—had later been left by the pub-owner outside the pub on the sidewalk. He subsequently stumbled across the street and was run over by a car.
[82] BGHSt 37, 106 (*Lederspray-Fall*).
[83] For intent see sec. 6.2.1.2; for negligence see sec. 6.3.

lenient approach to mistake as a ground for the exemption of guilt under § 17. Due to the extraordinary situation normal rational behaviour cannot always be expected and unlawfulness or blameworthiness will be negated more readily than with normal offences.[84]

6.5 Attempt (*Versuch*)

The Criminal Code identifies five steps to the realization of an offence; the decision by the would-be offender (*Entschluss* or *Planung*), preparation (*Vorbereitung*), beginning of the accomplishment (*Beginn der Ausführung*), accomplishing the constituent elements of the act (*Vollendung des Tatbestands*), and the completion (*Beendigung*). The difference between the latter two is that some offences allow a distinction between accomplishing the elements of the offence and a later phase of completion. Thus a thief might have accomplished all elements of theft (§242 I StGB) by stealing something in a department store but will only have completed the offence when having left the store and secured his gains somewhere. This distinction is important in as far as qualifying elements may arise during the phase of completion and thus aggrevate the offender's guilt.[85]

The mere decision of a would-be offender without any manifestation is not a criminal offence. Attempt, on the other hand—usually coinciding with the beginning of accomplishment—is. The distinction between both preparation and attempt, and attempt and accomplishment, is important both for consideration of punishment and whether the ability to abandon the offence is still possible. Paragraph 23 I states that an attempt to commit a felony (*Verbrechen*) is always punishable whereas an attempt to commit a misdemeanour (*Vergehen*) is only punishable where specifically provided for in the code or other legislation (as, for example, attempted bodily harm, §223 II StGB = *versuchte Körperverletzung*). The reason given for the punishment of an attempt is that the offender, in showing hostility to the legal system, is guilty and should be punished. The punishment will be a mitigated version of the full punishment for the accomplishment of the offence (§ 49).

6.5.1 *Elements of the attempted offence*

An attempt is defined as involving the subjective elements of the *Tatbestand* (i.e. one of the forms of intent) but missing one or all of the objective elements required. Thus the main legal problem here revolves around defining, on the basis of objective criteria, when exactly preparation evolves into attempt.

Paragraph 22 states that there must be a direct move (*unmittelbares Ansetzen*) to accomplishment according to the offender's assumption. Again, different theories exist to define such a direct move. Dominating opinion within the academic world as well as the BGH demand, two elements: the offender must have started an action

---

[84] For details see Wessels and Beulke, above, n 16, pp. 246–248.
[85] See Wessels and Beulke, above, n 16, pp. 188–190.

of direct physical and temporal connection to fulfilling the offence[86] and he must in his own view have passed the stage of commencement, called *Schwelle zum "Jetzt-geht-es-los"* (threshold of "Here-we-go").[87] Mere acts of preparation will not suffice, e.g. bringing instruments and weapons to the place where the crime is to be committed later on. Preparation rather becomes attempt when the legal right to be violated is in danger according to the offender's assumption.

BGHSt 26, 201 Tankstellenfall

The accused had planned to rob a petrol station. Finding it empty they assumed that its proprietor was in the private house next to the petrol station, which they thought to be his home. They went over to the door carrying a gun, pulled down their masks, and rang the bell. Their plan was to immediately threaten and tie up the person answering the door. However, no one answered and after a while the accused left. The BGH upheld their conviction for attempted robbery. Although objectively the owner was not in immediate danger in the accused's view he was, because they believed him to be at home and believed that he would open the door as soon as they had rung the bell.

Contrast this case with the similar but still significantly different "Pepper-bag case":

BGH NJW 1952, 514 Pfeffertüten-Fall

The accused had planned to rob a courier taking wages to an enterprise. Sitting in a car with the engine running and armed with a bag of pepper they waited for him at the tram station he was bound to arrive at. Their plan was to throw the pepper into his eyes as soon as he alighted from the tram, then grab the wages and escape in the car. After having watched four trams go by the accused realized that their victim was not going to show up and left. Just as in the case above the BGH upheld the conviction for attempted robbery, finding that in the view of the accused the courier was already in immediate danger from the moment a tram stopped.

The latter decision has been criticized on the grounds that here even from the accused's view, the legal interest at stake was not yet endangered. Contrary to the offenders in the Petrol Station case, the accused had not seen themselves as having made contact with the victim yet. Neither had they entered his "sphere" nor the victim their's. That would only have been the case as soon as the victim had

---

[86] BGH NJW 1980, 1759.
[87] BGH NStZ 97, 83.

alighted from the tram.[88] The two cases illustrate the difficulties of defining the line between preparation and attempt.[89]

Furthermore, an attempted offence will only be punishable if the elements of unlawfulness and guilt are fulfilled, just as in fully accomplished offences.[90]

6.5.2 *Futile attempt (untauglicher Versuch) and imaginary offence (Wahndelikt)*

Paragraph 23 III considers the futile attempt (*untauglicher Versuch*) where the attempter has misconceptions about the ability to complete the act due to the nature of the object or the means of committing an offence. In such circumstances the court may mitigate punishment or not punish at all, especially if the offender acts out of foolishness (*grober Unverstand*), e.g. trying to bring about someone's death by superstitious means such as voodoo ceremonies. In general, however, a futile attempt will be punished in less obvious cases of lack of judgement because of the offender's open hostility towards the legal system. Such cases could, for example, include the offender's mistakes as to means (e.g. mistaking harmless sleeping-pills for poisonous ones) or objects of the offence (e.g. mistaking a corpse for a living target).[91]

A distinction also has to drawn between futile attempts and the imaginary offence (*Wahndelikt*) where persons think they are committing an offence which does not in fact exist (e.g. adultery, sodomy). Imaginary offences are not punished as attempts, since the offender does not negate an existing provision of the legal system.[92]

6.5.3 *Abandonment of an offence* (Rücktritt vom Versuch, § 24)

Paragraph 24 I 1 concerns the abandonment (*Rücktritt*) of an offence. Deliberate abandonment or active prevention of its accomplishment of the offence will remove the liability to punishment for the attempt. It is thus a reward for preventing the accomplishment of an offence. Dominating opinion regards punishment as unnecessary in these cases, as the offence has not been accomplished and the offender has finally shown his respect for the legal system or society.[93] Different rules apply depending whether the offence was attempted by a single offender (§ 24 I StGB) or several people acting jointly (§ 24 II StGB). A single offender can avoid punishment in two different ways according to the stage that of his actions have reached:

(a) if the attempt itself is incomplete (*unbeendeter Versuch*), the offender has to give up any further accomplishment of the offence in order to exclude himself from criminal liability (§ 24 I 1, 1st alternative StGB);

(b) if, however, the attempt is complete (*beendeter Versuch*), then the offender has

---

[88] See C. Roxin, *Höchstrichterliche Rechtsprechung zum Allgemeinen Teil des Strafrechts* (1998: C.H. Beck, München), pp. 184–185; Hauf, above, n 28, pp. 118–119; Wessels and Beulke, above, n 16, p. 193.

[89] For a summary of further decisions see Tröndle and Fischer, above, n 2, § 22 paras 11–12.

[90] See above, secs 6.2.2 and 6.2.3.

[91] Wessels and Beulke, above, n 16, p. 199.

[92] For details see Tröndle and Fischer, above, n 2, § 22 paras 49–55.

[93] For a summary of different theories on the grounds of removing criminal liability see Gropp, above, n 32 pp. 312–313.

to (actively) prevent the accomplishment of the offence to avoid punishment (§ 24 I 1, 2nd alternative StGB).

An attempt will be deemed "incomplete", if the offender thinks he has not yet done everything to complete the accomplishment of the offence. By consequence the attempt will be "complete" if the offender believes he has taken every action necessary to reach the desired result and thus the fulfilment of the offence.

Example: *A*, standing on a hill, plans to send a huge rock rolling down in order to hit and kill his enemy *B*. As long as he positions the rock aiming at the victim, his attempt is not yet complete, even from his viewpoint. However, as soon as he has set the rock in motion towards *B* he has done everything to complete the offence. In his view there is nothing more he can do now to achieve the result. Thus in the first case it is enough to abandon the rock unmoved on top of the hill to exclude punishment whereas in the second case he would have to actively prevent *B* from getting killed, i.e. by shouting and warning him or finding a way to stop or divert the rock.

If an attempt is complete but the offence is prevented by external factors the offender must have deliberately and genuinely tried to prevent the completion of the offence in order to escape punishment (§ 24 I 2StGB) as the following case illustrates:

BGHSt 33, 295 Schläfenschuss-Fall

Out of revenge for an bad deal with a salesman of used cars, the accused had planned to visit and shoot the latter in his office. He fired a shot at his victim's right temple. However, the salesman managed to raise his hand in time and tilt his head away. As a consequence the bullet—after having pierced his hand—entered his right eye went through it sideways below the brow, and exited before the bridge of his nose. Bleeding profusely, the wounded salesman cursed and yelled at the accused, who now realized what he had done. He left the office and encountered two of the victim's employees, who, attracted by the noise of the shot, were rushing to the office. He told them to look after their boss and left. The victim lost his right eye but survived. The accused was convicted of attempted manslaughter (*Versuchter Totschlag*). The BGH upheld the decision. It held that the attempt to kill the victim had been completed after shooting at the victim. Even though the accused had refrained from firing any further shots. The instant he had fired the shot, the accused had assumed that he had done everything necessary to kill the victim. Afterwards, the only way of avoiding punishment would have been to actively try to prevent the victim's death according to § 24 I 2 StGB. From his viewpoint the victim was still in mortal danger. Telling the employees to look after their boss was held to be insufficient as they had already been on their way. He would have had to play a more active role in rescuing the victim.

The accused's abandonment, whether it consists in abandoning further actions or preventing the result, must be deliberate. If guided by external factors the abandonment will not be regarded as deliberate. External or heteronomous factors would include the offender's fear of being discovered and prosecuted. Autonomous factors that constitute voluntariness, on the other hand, are, for example, pangs of conscience, shame, or pity for the victim. The so-called "**Frank-formula**"[94] helps to distinguish deliberate and unvoluntary abandonment according to the offender's view:

Frank'sche Formel

- Involuntary abandonment: "I could not achieve my aim, even if I wanted to."
- Deliberate abandonment: "I don't want to achieve my aim, even if I could."

Distinguishing autonomous and heteronomous reasons for abandonment in this context can be difficult. Without deciding on the case but referring it back to the court of first instance the BGH gave some guidelines in the "Lilo case":

BGHSt 9, 184 Lilo-Fall

The accused attacked the victim in order to rape her. While she had recognized him as an acquaintance he had not. After having dragged her off her bicycle and thrown her to the ground she cried out: "Herman leave me alone". Surprised, he answered "Lilo, it's you?" He went on to explain that he would not have attacked her had he recognized her and begged her not to call the police but to consider the embarassment for his family. He was charged with attempted rape. On the question as to whether he voluntarily abandoned the (incomplete) offence the BGH held, that if the accused had given up his plan because he feared prosecution that would constitute an external factor. His abandonment thus would be involuntary. If, on the other hand, he gave up because he was ashamed to rape the victim because he knew her that would be a deliberate abandonment. It was for the court of first instance though to determine his motives as a question of fact.

Where the offence was attempted jointly by several persons, § 24 II StGB offers a participant exemption from punishment in three different situations: He prevents the offence either by by giving up his (necessary) participation or by actively hindering the result to come about. Where the offence is not accomplished because of other factors he must at least seriously and deliberately have tried to prevent it. The

---

[94] Coined by the academic Reinhard Frank in the 1930's. Cited in Gropp, above, n 31, p. 309.

same applies where the offence is finally accomplished but without the participant's previous contribution. The latter alternative exceptionally allows exemption from punishment of a fully accomplished offence. Abandonment from a jointly committed attempt is thus more difficult, reflecting the increased danger emanating from crimes committed by groups of people.

According to § 24 StGB, as a consequence of abandonment, punishment will only be avoided for the attempted offence not for any other offences committed during the course of action.

6.6 Different forms of participation: *Täterschaft und Teilnahme*, §§ 25–31

German criminal law distinguishes between the principal offender (*Täter*) and participators or rather secondary parties *(Teilnehmer)* where there are two or more parties to a crime. Four types of primary participation or "principal offenders" are identified; the immediate perpetrator (*unmittelbarer Täter*), § 25 I 1, the perpetrator who acts through the agency of another (*mittelbarer Täter*), § 25 I 2, the accomplice, where two or more perpetrators work together (*Mittäter*), § 25 II, and the collateral perpetrator (*Nebentäter*). Two forms of secondary participation are identified by the code: § 26, instigation (*Anstiftung*) and § 27, aiding and abetting (*Beihilfe*).

6.6.1 *Täterschaft ("perpetration" or "principal participation"*, § 25 StGB)

The principal offender is the one who commits the crime by his own conduct, an instigator or aider participates in the act of somebody else. Whether one is a principal or participant is important for the constitutive elements of some offences where the act has to be done personally (*eigenhändig*), e.g. offences such as perjury, § 154 StGB. Distinguishing principal participation from mere secondary participation can be difficult and is mostly achieved by either employing the *Subjektive Theorie* (subjective theory) or the *Lehre von der Tatherrschaft* (theory of "Control over the crime"). For a long time the courts seemed to favour the first one by focusing on the offender's subjective perception of the offence: if he regarded committing the offence as "his own" deed (= acting with *animus auctionis*) he was classified as principal offender, whereas a person deeming the crime to be someone else's "project" (= acting with *animus socii*) would be treated as instigator or aider (subjective theory).[95] An illustrative case dealing with political murder was decided in 1962:

BGHSt 18, 87 Staschynski-Fall

The accused—Staschynski—had come to West Germany under orders from the Russian secret service, the KGB, to murder two exiled Russian politicians. He met the victims and killed them with a gun using poisoned arrows, just as he had been ordered. He later

---

[95] Since RGSt 2, 160; further references: Wessels and Beulke above, n 16, p. 162.

surrendered to the West German authorities. The BGH, relying on the "subjective theory", classified him as a mere accessory to murder instead of a principal offender. The Court reasoned that even though § 25 I 1 StGB classified as principal offender whoever committed the offence himself, one had to look at the accused's view of the offence. Staschynski had not wanted to commit the crime as "his own offence" but regarded himself as an "instrument" participating in an offence that was really committed by the KGB, the real principal offender "behind him". He had not believed in the ideological necessity of killing the politicians, as his subsequent surrender had shown. Instead, his fear of the "almighty totalitarian state" and the KGB had induced him to carry out the assignment.

This decision has been criticized by academics.[96] If the accused acted under duress it would have to be dealt with when looking at his guilt. Also, mitigating circumstances could have been invoked when administering the punishment. Staschynski's personal guilt, however, had nothing to do with the distinction between principal offender and secondary participant. After all Staschynski had still carried out all the main elements of the crime.

It seems that the BGH has now moved away from this strictly subjective approach and pays more attention to the idea of who is really in control of committing the crime (*Lehre von der Tatherrschaft*), in other words, who is a "key figure".[97] This theory has been dominating academic opinion for a long time now. Control over the crime may arise from control over the relevant act when committing it (*Handlungsherrschaft*), control by superior knowledge and intent as to the crime to be committed (*Willens- und Wissensherrschaft*), or in cases of jointly committed offences control over a contributing act that is necessarily causal for commission of the crime (*funktionelle Handlungsherrschaft*). Although the BGH has not adopted this theory, the Court takes it into account when looking at the offender's subjective perception of the crime.[98]

Distinguishing principal and secondary participation will become difficult in cases of "indirect" perpetration: the principal acting through another (*mittelbare Täterschaft*) arises in cases where the agent acts personally without the guilt or intention as the principal. Thus in some way the agent does not have sufficient autonomy of action to be blameworthy, although distinction from instigation can be very difficult here. Generally, an offender acts through another person when this person—albeit carrying out the act—does not fulfil all objective or subjective criteria of the offence (*Tatbestand*), for example when he does not act unlawfully or without guilt. Here the person carrying out the act might be regarded as an "instrument" more than an offender.

---

[96] See Gropp, above, n 32, p. 333; Roxin, above, n 88 p. 203.
[97] Wessels and Beulke, above, n 16, p. 161–162.
[98] BGHSt 37, 289; see also: Tröndle and Fischer, above, n 2, Vor § 25, para. 2a with further references.

> **Example:** *A* asks *B* to fetch him his coat, pointing at *C*'s coat. *B*—believing it is really *A*'s coat—does so. In this case *B* does not commit a theft because he does not fulfil the subjective criteria of the offence due to his mistake. The real offender is *A* who controls the whole situation.

The *Sirius* case, possibly the most famous case in German criminal law, gives an interesting example of the offender using an "instrument" person against herself (it also shows that reality supplies us with far more bizarre cases than any Law professor's fantasies could):

BGHSt 32, 38 Sirius-Fall

After having become acquainted with the witness in this case, the accused told her that he was in fact an inhabitant of the planet Sirius. He convinced her that he could help her lead a new and better life, if she got rid of her "old" body. He suggested she should drop a hairdrier into the water, when sitting in the bathtub. A new body would then await her in a "red" room in Geneva. There she would awake after her "seemingly accidental death". As she would need a lot of money for her new life he convinced her to take out a life insurance policy providing for the payment of 500 000 DM in case of accidental death, payable to the accused. He would then bring her the money to Geneva. The witness believed him (!) and dropped the hairdrier while switched on into the bathtub as instructed. However, she was not electrocuted due to the hairdrier malfunctioning. When calling the victim to check on her, the accused was surprised to find her answering the phone. For ten minutes he gave her advice on how to kill herself before abandoning the "hopeless" project. At no point had the witness regarded this action as a suicide ending her life but had firmly believed it would continue it in another body.

    The BGH upheld the accused's conviction for attempted murder. The main legal distinction to be drawn was whether the witness had attempted a suicide or not. In the first case the accused would not have been guilty at all as suicide is not punishable under German law. Furthermore, under German law aiding and instigating are offences that are strictly accessory to the main offence, in other words, no one can be guilty of aiding or instigating the commission of an offence if the main offence does not exist in the first place. The BGH took this to be a case of § 25 I 1, 2nd alternative StGB. The accused had used the witness as a "tool" against herself. The witness herself did not fulfil the subjective criteria (*subjektiver Tatbestand*) of the offence of attempted murder or rather suicide, because she did not think she would actually "kill" herself but merely dipose of her body in order to awake in a different one. The only person in full control of the crime, satisfying all elements of the offence (*Tatbestand*, unlawfulness and guilt) was the accused. He was clearly in a superior role to the witness, overseeing the situation. The fact that the witness believed in the accused's fairy tale, although she did not suffer from mental disorder, could not exonerate him.

Paragraph 25 II StGB mentions another form of principal participation, the joint participation of several accomplices (*Mittäterschaft*). The accomplice is one of two or more persons who act consciously and deliberately together. They are equal partners when committing the offence. Thus each one is punished as a principal offender. In general, this means that every action of each accomplice is also attributable to all others. This has lead to a logical but still surprising result in the following case:

BGHSt 11, 268 Verfolgerfall

Three accomplices had planned to burgle a shop. Each of them was armed with a gun. They had agreed to use them if in danger of being caught. After having broken into the shop they were discovered and fled. One of them mistook another for a pursuer and shot him, wounding him. Subsequently under §§ 22,23, 25 II, 211 StGB all of them—including the wounded accomplice—were convicted of attempted murder. The BGH reasoned that all the accomplices had agreed to use their guns in the case of being discovered. Thus an attempted murder by one accomplice was attributed to each of them. The fact that one accused made a mistake as to the object did not reduce his liability, as it did not matter which life he wanted to take.[99] The BGH went on to extend the irrelevance of mistake to all other accomplices including the unfortunate one who was in fact wounded, as his agreement covered the general intention to shoot any pursuers.

The line between being an accomplice or a mere secondary participant can be a difficult one to draw, as will be seen.[100]

Finally, collateral offenders (*Nebentäter*) act independently from each other. The punishment is the same, however, as for the offence itself and each is responsible for the whole act.

6.6.2 *Inciting (Anstiftung, § 26) and Aiding (Beihilfe, § 27)*

Inciting (*Anstiftung*, § 26) and aiding (*Beihilfe*, § 27) are the types of secondary participation defined by German criminal law. Both are dependant on a main

---

[99] See above: rules on *error in persona vel objecto*, sec. 6.2.1.2(b).
[100] See below, sec. 6.6.2.

offence having been committed (*Akzessorietät der Teilnahme*). Where there is no main offence to start with, a conviction for these two types of participation is impossible. Thus someone who incites or aids a third person to commit suicide will not be guilty of aiding or inciting, because committing suicide is not an offence punishable under German law.[101] However, the principle of guilt[102] allows the inciting or aiding participant to be punished in those cases where the main offender acted without guilt, but fulfilled all other elements of the offence, namely the *Tatbestand* and unlawfulness. As each individual is punished according to his "own" guilt, a conviction of the participants remains possible (see also § 29 StGB). Participation in an attempted offence is possible and punishable but has to be distinguished from "attempted participation" which is generally not punishable.

Inciting requires the intent to instigate[103] "someone else to commit an intentionally unlawful offence" (§ 26 StGB). "Instigating" in this context means to evoke another person's intent to commit an offence. There has to be "double intent" because apart from the intent to incite the instigator has to show an intent towards the main offence being committed as well. Attempted incitement of crimes, but not misdemeanors, is punishable (§ 30 I StGB).

Inciting, as a form of secondary participation, may be difficult to distinguish from cases where a person goes beyond mere inciting and can be regarded as an "indirect" perpetrator (*mittelbarer Täter*) in other words a primary participant (*Haupttäter*).[104]

BGHSt 40, 218 Fall des Nationalen Verteidigungsrats

The accused were former members of the East German National Defence Council and had participated in drafting official orders to prevent any escapes from the former East Germany across the border to the former West Germany. Any means including the fatal use of firearms had been authorized. During 1971 and 1989 seven people were shot by East German soldiers or killed by mines when attempting to escape from East Germany. After the soldiers had already been convicted of manslaughter[105] the accused in this case were convicted for inciting the killing by the court of first instance. The BGH quashed the decision and found them guilty for manslaughter as indirect perpetrators. The Court acknowledged that, in general, there cannot be an offender acting "behind" an offender. Either the person carrying out the act is fully responsible and in control, regarding it as his "own" deed—then any other participant can only be instigator or a collaborating accessory—or the person carrying out the act does not fully control it and views himself to be merely participating in someone else's offence and thus would only

---

[101] Tröndle and Fischer, above, n 2, Vor § 211, para. 10; BGHSt 24, 342.
[102] See above, sec. 5.3.
[103] The German definition uses the word *"bestimmen"* which cannot be acurately translated in this context.
[104] See above, sec. 6.6.2.
[105] See above, Chapter 7, Art. 103 II GG.

be a secondary participant. However, the Court held that this case was an example of the few exceptional cases of an offender acting indirectly behind the "direct" offender. This is possible where the indirect perpetrator's contribution will inevitably lead to fulfilment of the offence by way of the direct perpetrator's action because of the hierarchichal organization both perpetrators are members of. Even though the direct perpetrator will act fully responsibly, there is still room for liability of the indirect offender "behind" him. Such hierarchichal organizations would include organized crime groups as well as organizations of a state. The East German soldiers in question had already been convicted as principal offenders. Nevertheless, the members of the National Defence Council could also be convicted as offenders "behind" them for drafting the order to use firearms against fugitives.

The term "aiding" includes any physical or psycological support of committing the main offence. It is disputed whether this support must be causal for the main offence in the sense of the principle of *condicio sine qua non*.[106] Academics insist on a causal link as § 27 does not indicate any intention of the legislature to penalize any action that merely jeopardizes a legal interest.[107] However, the BGH takes a different view. According to case-law aiding does not have to be indispensable to the accomplishment of the offence.[108] Any act that can be classified as an action of support, be it a necessary cause or not, deserves to be punished.

Just as with inciting the aider must show "double intent". There must be an intention to aid and an intent covering the accomplishment of the main offence. Attempted aiding is never punishable, as the Criminal Code does not provide for it. However, aiding someone else who does not go beyond the stage of attempt in the main offence will be punished, provided the attempt of the main offence is punishable. Here the action of aiding is completed but the main offence is not.

Finally, under § 30 II StGB, conspiracy is punishable because of the perceived greater threat to the legal order when more than one person decides to commit an offence.

6.7 Legal consequences: punishment and other measures

Paragraphs 38–76a StGB contain the rules relating to the consequences of committing a criminal offence including the forms of punishment that are available. Here the "two-tier system"[109] of German criminal law becomes apparent. Apart from different measures of punishment (§§ 38–60) it provides for measures of "improvement and securing" (*Massnahmen zur Besserung und Sicherung*, §§ 61–70). The underlying aims of punishment provisions are that punishment should be

---

[106] See above, sec. 6.2.1.1.
[107] Tröndle and Fischer, above, n 2, § 27, para. 2; Hauf, above, n 28, pp. 97–98 with further references.
[108] E.g. BGH NStZ 85, 318.
[109] German term: *"Zweispurigkeit" des strafrechtlichen Rechtsfolgensystems.*

levied first of all according to the guilt of the offender (§ 46). Therefore penalizing an offender is a sanctioning measure focusing on his guilt whereas measures of improvement and securing place emphasis on his danger to society—no matter whether he acted with or without guilt. A mentally incapable offender will not be held guilty of an offence but still poses a threat to society. Thus the German criminal code provides for measures that protect society from him (measures of "securing" such as detention in mental asylums) but also aims at rehabilitation by measures of "improvement" (e.g. treatment in mental clinics).

German criminal law provides for two types of punishment: imprisonment (§§ 38, 39) and fines (§§ 40–43a). Capital punishment is prohibited by the *Grundgesetz*, Article 102. Life imprisonment was upheld as constitutional and not contrary to Article 1 GG as challenged in the "Life imprisonment" case.[110] Indefinite sentences, however, are not acceptable. Fines as a less drastic punishment have developed to be the main form of punishment. They are levied on the basis of a per day fine rate (§ 40 I StGB) but are set taking into account the economic and social circumstances of the offender. Additional punishment may include a ban from driving (§ 44) and since 1992, the penalty of paying a lump sum in offences related to organized crime and drug trafficking (§ 43a). In the latter case the additional penalty is designed to cut the profits of the offender from organized crime. Thus they are targeting his wealth in general (*Vermögensstrafen*).

Paragraphs 61–72 StGB give details of extraordinary measures for rehabilitation and security. Paragraph 61 et seq. provides for detention in a mental hospital, detention in drug addiction institutes, secure detention, probation, retention of a driving licence, and prohibition from work. The concept of improvement (*Besserung*) includes measures that encourage a dangerous offender to re-integrate normally into society and is not supposed be a form of punishment. Any measures applied must meet with the general requirement of proportionality (§ 62). The measures are determined by the trial court which heard the case. If criminal capacity is lacking, the Code of Criminal Procedure (StPO) provides that an expert must be present if such measures are contemplated (§§ 246a, 413 StPO). Any measures proposed take priority over the normal sentencing (§ 67 I).

In general, measures of rehabilitation favoured in the 1980s have, in the 1990s, given way to a more strict approach of punishment by imprisonment—especially where offences against the bodily integrity of persons are concerned.[111]

7 The individual or substantive offences

These are detailed in the Special Part of the criminal code (§§ 80–358). The Special Part organizes systematically the offences into groups and divides the offences into thirty sections which appear to be arbitrary, hence there has been a categorization

---

[110] BVerfGE 45, 187.
[111] Gropp, above, n 32, p. 531, with further references.

by academics onto two main groups: offences against the state and offences against the person. The latter is divided into offences against property of individuals (*Vermögensdelikte*) and offences against the person, i.e. liberty and health. The details go beyond the remit of this book and will only be considered where part of another subject such as environmental criminality in the section on the environment in Chapter 8 above.

B Criminal procedural law

1 Introduction

The criminal process is subject to extensive statutory regulation. The underlying aims of this legislation are to ensure that there can be an effective and complete enforcement of the substantive law for the punishment of offences but with provision to make sure there are adequate protections for the suspected individuals from repressive measures by the state and its enforcement and investigating authorities. As a consequence German criminal procedural law does not allow the establishment of truth at any cost. In this area of law especially, where state authorities can impose the most restrictive measures on an individual, his basic rights deserve the most effective protection. Criminal procedural law thus is always a "seismograph of constitutional law":[112] it will reflect the balance of interests between the individual and the state or the community. The German procedural system is characterized by its "inquisitorial approach" in which criminal prosecution is undertaken by a state service and the court is concerned more with an enquiry to determine the innocence or guilt of the accused rather than an adjudication of which of two parties has made a case for innocence or guilt as in the "adversarial tradition". However, the term "inquisitorial principle" can be misleading. The German term "*Inquisitionsprozess*" refers to the idea of the same state authority prosecuting and giving the decision in the case. Under German law this is not the case. Although a state authority is responsible for criminal prosecution, i.e. all aspects of enquiry, this authority is not the same as the one making the decision, as will be explained. This is another example of the difficulty in accurately translating legal terms.

---

[112] As pointed out by: C. Roxin, *Strafverfahrensrecht*, 25th ed. (1998: C.H. Beck, München), p. 9.

2 Historical aspects

Among several historical roots of and influences on German criminal procedural law the most noteworthy to point out are the Carolingian penal code (*Constituio Criminalis Carolinga*) of 1532 and the influences of English and French nineteenth century procedural law. The Carolingian penal code is an example of the reception of Roman law into German law. The previous system which had laid emphasis on private parties accusing an offender and the people participating in decision-making was replaced by a strict inquisitorial approach as it had been developed in medieval Italian cities. From now on criminal prosecution was undertaken by official authorities rendering the accused an almost defenceless object of investigation. Rules of evidence were restricted and formalized. Torture in order to extract confessions was still admissible but subject to the existence of suggestive pieces of circumstantial evidence.

The age of enlightenment which focused on the individual and developing individual rights in England and France had lead to procedural laws that took account of fundamental human rights. This eventually influenced the Criminal Procedural Code which was drafted for the second German Empire in 1877. The subsequent progress in protecting the fundamental rights of the accused during criminal procedure was reversed by the Nazi dictatorship with the establishment of the *Volksgerichtshof* for political offences as the outstanding example of perverted procedural law.[113] After the Second World War a new criminal procedure code re-established principles of fair trial in 1950. Several changes have been made to the StPO since then. Another good example showing how criminal procedure reflects the state of the constitution might be the amendment of 1974,[114] that allowed for a speeding-up of the procedure by abolishing the opportunities for the accused to delay, as well as a restriction of several rights of the defence attorney. It was passed as a reaction to procedural tactics of the defence lawyers in the *Baader-Meinhof* procedures against leading figures of the "RAF" terrorist group. The latest changes in order to combat organized crime included such measures as the heavily disputed bugging private homes (*"grosser Lauschangriff"*).[115] It remains to be seen what changes the terrorist attacks on the World Trade Center on 11 September 2001 will entail.[116]

---

[113] This court only served to deliver a "show-process". The outcome of the trial—conviction of the accused—was always certain before it had begun.

[114] *Gesetz zur Ergänzung des 1. StVRG* of 20 December 1974.

[115] *Gesetz zur Verbesserung der Bekämpfung der Organisierten Kriminalität* of 4 May 1998.

[116] For more details on history of criminal procedural law see Roxin, above, n 112, pp. 518–540.

3 Sources

Constitutional provisions enumerate general principles as well as fundamental rights of the accused in criminal proceedings such as independence of judiciary, right to a lawful judge, right to judicial hearing, *nulla poena sine lege, ne bis in idem,* and rights in cases of detention (Arts 97 I, 101 I, 103 I–III, 104 I–IV GG). The main source of law, however, is the Criminal Procedural Code (*Strafprozeßordnung StPO*) which contains rules regulating all aspects of proceedings including appeals, the rights of the suspected, the accused, the defence attorney, and the state attorney (*Staatsanwalt*), also referred to as the public prosecutor or state prosecutor. Further details can be found in Chapter 4. Other important sources are the "Organization of Courts Act" (*Gerichtsverfassunggesetz GVG*), and guidelines on criminal procedures and those entailing fines.[117] The latter comprise detailed regulations on the procedure restricting the scope of discretion of the state prosecution.[118]

4 Principal stages of procedure

Criminal procedure is divided into two main parts, the *Erkenntnisverfahren* and the *Vollstreckungsverfahren*. During the *Erkenntnisverfahren*[119] a case will either be closed or a court's decision reached. Once the decision has become absolute, i.e. allowing no further appeal, the procedure moves to the *Vollstreckungsverfahren*.[120] Here the decision will be enforced (e.g. the payment of fines) and its implementation monitored.[121] This book will only give an outline of the stages of the *Erkenntnisverfahren* at the court first instance and the possibility of appeals.

4.1 The pre-trial procedure

The preliminary investigation (*Ermittlungsverfahren* or *Vorverfahren*) is conducted in private by the state attorney usually with the extensive assistance of the police. This ends with either the closing of the case (*Einstellung*) when the state attorney considers there not to be grounds for a prosecution or with the laying of a charge before the appropriate court (*Anklage*).

---

[117] *Richtlinien für das Strafverfahren und das Bussgeldverfahren* of 1 January 1977.
[118] Other sources are noted in the section on criminal law above.
[119] Literally, "procedure of realization" or "discovery"; in other words, the procedure designed to find a decision as to facts and the law of the case.
[120] Literally, "enforcement procedure".
[121] Strictly speaking in cases of imprisonment the implementation of the decision constitutes a procedure different from the criminal procedure (*Strafvollzugsverfahren*) starting the moment the convicted begins his prison sentence. From now on provisions of the "Criminal Sentence Enforcement Act" (*Strafvollzugsgesetz StVollzG*) are applicable.

4.2 The interim proceedings (*Zwischenverfahren*)

The state attorney applies to the court responsible for the main proceedings to commence proceedings. The court determines the soundness of the evidence, factually and legally, and decides whether to proceed. If so, the process moves to the main proceedings.

4.3 The main proceedings (*Hauptverfahren*)

The court collects the evidence for itself and the main trial commences, culminating with the oral hearing in court, followed by the judgment.

4.4 Appeal

Lastly, the possibility of an appeal exists either on grounds of facts and law (*Berufung*) or exclusively on grounds of law (*Revision*).

5 Leading principles of procedural law

There is a significant number of underlying assumptions and requirements which have found expression in the German criminal procedure system. Some of these are general principles emenating from the principle of *Rechtsstaat*[122] to make state action predictable and safeguard the fundamental rights of the individual. Some can also be found elsewhere in the system of justice in Germany and in particular as principles of civil procedure as discussed in Chapter 5. Others are relevant only to the process of criminal prosecution. They all, in some way, regulate the conduct of the proceedings or lay down rights and duties of the various participants in the proceedings. Some find expression in specific Articles in the procedural code or other laws, whereas others are generally applicable. The provisions of the European Convention for the Protection of Human Rights are also capable of being taken into account in German procedural law. The principles of criminal procedural law concern the commencement of the procedure, handling of the procedure, and rules on evidence and on form.

5.1 Principles on commencing the procedure

5.1.1 *The principle of official duty (Offizialprinzip)*

This duty, imposed on the state attorney by §§ 151–152 and 160 StPO,[123] is to investigate whenever information is obtained about circumstances that might

---

[122] See Chapter 6, sec. 3.3.
[123] All paragraph references in this section of Chapter 9 will refer to the Criminal Procedure Code (StPO) unless otherwise stated.

suggest an offence has been committed. By regulating and undertaking the whole process of criminal investigation and prosecution, the state has deliberately stepped in to protect the weaker disadvantaged individual. The state represents the community and can prosecute, in most cases, without reference to the victim. However, this principle is restricted where offences require an application for prosecution by the victim (*Antragsdelikte*) like trespassing (§ 123 StGB) or where they require the authorization of a certain person in cases of political offences (*Ermächtigungsdelikte*).[124] In these two cases state prosecution is dependant on the application or approval. An exception from state prosecution and thus the principle of official duty is created by the private action procedure (*Privatklageverfahren*) according to §§ 374 seq StPO. These provisions allow the victim to bring a private action before the criminal courts but only as regards the few offences mentioned in § 374 StPO. These will be offences that predominantly concern the victim's interests and have less effect on the community's legal order.

5.1.2 *Principle of official accusation (Akkusationsprinzip)*

A system that gives the state the monopoly to prosecute criminal offences can either opt for an "inquisitorial" or an "accusatorial" procedure. The first one will allow a judge to undertake all preliminary investigations and decide the case. The "inquiring" judge will examine and decide throughout the procedure. The German system has opted for the accusatorial principle which underlies the division between the state attorney, police, and the court. Preliminary investigations and the accusation are in the hands of an autonomous authority: the state prosecution (*Staatsanwaltschaft*, § 152 I StPO). Although defined as a judicial authority it can neither be allocated to the executive nor the judiciary. It is an independent, hierarchically organized institution taking part in the administration of (criminal) justice (*Organ der Strafrechtspflege*).[125] Without an official accusation (*Anklage*) brought by a state attorney, a court has no right to bring charges itself and cannot consider an offence (§ 151 StPO). It is limited to considering the charges laid before it. As a consequence of the state prosecution's independence it is not bound by any case-law of the courts.

5.1.3 *The principle of compulsory prosecution (Legalitätsprinzip)*

This principle seeks to ensure that the law is impartially upheld and prosecutions are put into effect to do this. All participants in the criminal process are subject equally to the law and no arbitrary decisions should be reached either in the case or in the decision to prosecute. The state attorney has a duty to prosecute offences under § 152 II subject to a few exceptions and the duty to raise an official accusation before the court, if there is sufficient suspicion that an offence has been committed (*hinreichender Tatverdacht*) under § 170 I StPO. Where the decision not to investigate is taken the victim has the right under §§ 172 StPO et seq. to require the state

---

[124] E.g. the Federal President's approval in cases of disparagement of the Federal President (§ 90 StGB).
[125] See also the section on the *Staatsanwalt* in Chapter 4.

attorney to investigate and raise an official accusation (*Klageerzwingungsverfahren*). If he does not and his superior official also refuses, the victim can approach the *Oberlandesgericht* to review the decision.[126]

5.1.4 *The principle of expediency (Opportunitätsprinzip)*

This principle acts to restrict the principle of compulsory prosecution whereby the state attorney has the discretion not to prosecute. Paragraphs 153–154e allow the state attorney, with the consent of the court, to decide not to bring a charge where they consider this appropriate. This will be the case where the offence constitutes only a misdemeanour, where there would be only a small degree of guilt, and where there is no public interest in the prosecution (§ 153 I StPO). In some cases the state prosecution can link the abandonment of prosecution to certain conditions that will satisfy the interests harmed by the offence: e.g. remedying the harm done, payment of a lump sum of to charity, or rendering service for the benefit of the community (§§ 153a I No. 1–3 StPO). Although §§ 153 et seq. offer several opportunities to abandon prosecution, in practice this will mostly happen in cases of misdemeanours.[127] Special provisions allowing the prosecution to drop charges against "crown" witnesses providing information in cases of terrorist activities and organized crime existed from 1989 to 1999. However, they did not bring about the anticipated success in crime-fighting and were constantly criticized as an inacceptable breach of the principle of compulsory prosecution.[128]

5.2 **Principles concerning the implementation of the procedure**

5.2.1 *The principle of investigation (Untersuchungsgrundsatz or Ermittlungsgrundsatz)*

According to this principle the court is obliged to conduct its own investigation in the interim proceedings independent from the state attorney and the police and not to rely on the information and evidence supplied by the state attorney (§§ 155 II, 244 II and 264 II). Within the trial the court conducts the investigation and not the parties, therefore the court is free to do whatever it considers necessary to conduct the investigation and prosecution. It can verify all of the information given and seek more when and where it thinks fit. It is thus neither automatically bound by the accused's confession nor by the parties' motions to take evidence. The court is obliged to determine the truth of the matter and to find a defence for the accused if one exists, and to be sure that all necessary measures have been undertaken to reach a just and correct result. This accords with the principle of the dominion of the court over the proceedings. Criticism arose in recent years as to the practice of "deals" between the prosecution and the defence, such as submitting a

---

[126] In general, these procedures are not very promising. Whereas 600,000 cases are closed p.a. there are only 2,000 procedures instigated by victims to compel the state prosecution to raise a charge. In 1982 only eight of 1,792 procedures have been successful. However, their mere existence might induce state prosecution to carefully decide whether to close a case or not. See Roxin, above, n 112, p. 320.

[127] For more details on the principle of expediency see Roxin, above, n 112, pp. 86–92.

[128] W. Beulke, *Strafprozessrecht*, 5th ed. (2001: C.F. Müller, Heidelberg), p. 172.

confession concerning a main offence in exchange for the prosecution dropping charges for additional other offences. Such practices—it was argued—would keep the court from determining the truth. The case-law of the Federal Court of Justice suggests that the practice so far is still compatible with the principle of investigation.[129]

5.2.2 *The right to a judicial hearing* (Grundsatz des rechtlichen Gehörs)

This is one of the most fundamental rights for the suspect and includes the concept of "fair trial" and the equality of arms (*Waffengleichheit*). It is guaranteed by the constitution, Article 103 I GG and by Article 6, ECHR which is also a part of German law.[130] It guarantees the right to participate not only in the main proceedings, but also in the preliminary investigations and the interim proceedings. The rule itself is not stated expressly in the procedural code but the code does provide the right of the accused to comment after each statement made by a witness, or after the reading of a document to the court (§ 257 StPO) and the right for the defendant and attorney to examine witnesses (§ 240 II StPO). The BVerfG has held[131] that a decision of a court can only be reached if the participants in the trial have been given the opportunity to comment in an appropriate way and sufficient time to prepare to comment. This requires the provision by the prosecution of all the legal and factual evidences. Participation of the accused thus must be granted efficiently, e.g. by his right to a motion to take evidence in order to participate in determining the truth.[132] The principle of a fair trial has even been extended to take into account any wrongdoings by the police when rendering a judgment, e.g. where a police officer incited a person to commit a crime although the accused had not been inclined to commit it beforehand.[133]

5.2.3 *The unity of the main proceedings* (Einheit der Hauptverhandlung)

This attempts to ensure that the trial is dealt with as quickly as possible and in one piece, and that interruptions which would endanger this are avoided. Paragraph 229 provides that interruptions on specific grounds only are allowed, but for no longer than ten days each time or the proceedings must be re-commenced.

5.2.4 *The principle of concentration* (Konzentrationsmaxime/Beschleunigungsprinzip)

Closely related to the principle of unity of the main proceedings, this principle aims to keep the trial as short as possible. The criminal procedural code tries to keep this to a minimum by setting when breaks can be taken. It demands the avoidance of a protraction of the proceedings and the time limits for the various stages are shorter than in civil law. One of the main driving forces for this principle is Article 6 of the ECHR. Germany has been heavily criticized in the past for breaches of this by

---

[129] See Roxin, above, n 112, pp. 95–97 for details.
[130] see Chapter 2 on sources of German law.
[131] See, *inter alia*, BVerfGE 8, 89 and 9, 259.
[132] BVerfG NStZ 1997, 94.
[133] BGHSt 45, 321 following the ECHR case of *Texeira de Castro*.

the European Court on Human Rights for not conducting proceedings in a reasonable time.[134] Interruptions of the trial are therefore to be resisted.

Paragraph 212 et seq., considered below, provides for expeditious proceedings.

5.3 Principles concerning evidence

5.3.1 *The principle of immediacy (Unmittelbarkeitsgrundsatz)*

This requires that the proceedings are conducted as far as possible in person with the participants present the whole time. In practice, it is difficult to achieve. Paragraph 226 StPO stipulates that the main proceedings be held in the uninterrupted presence of the same judges who decide the case. Under §§ 226 and 227, a state attorney must be present the whole time as must a defence attorney but not necessarily the same ones. Although the accused should be present, it is also possible that pleas can be entered in his absence, for example for minor offences.

Paragraphs 250–251 StPO require that all evidence be heard in order to properly adjudge the credibility of the witnesses and evidence but allow for the possibility of hearsay evidence in exceptional circumstances.

5.3.2 *The principle of the unfettered consideration of the evidence or "free evidence" (Grundsatz der freien Beweiswürdigung)*

According to § 261 StPO the court will find evidence on the basis of its opinion freely formed within the main proceedings. Thus the court is not bound by strict rules of evidence such as the "ordeal by fire" in medivial times. By contrast the judge now must personally be convinced of the existence of the facts in question. However, this subjective assessment of the facts must be objectively convincing, e.g. to the other judges.[135] Thus the principle of "free evidence" does have limits. Other restricitions include the rule contained in § 274 StPO, which provides that violations of essential formal requirements within the main proceedings can only be proven by the protocol. The ban on using wrongfully obtained evidence (*Beweisverwertungsverbot*) constitutes another restricion on "free evidence".

5.3.3 *The principle of in dubio pro reo*

If at the end of the main proceedings doubt remains as to the guilt of the accused, he will benefit from this and thus cannot be found guilty. This principle is not expressly named in the Criminal Procedural Code but, according to general opinion, can be based on Article 6 II ECHR and § 261 StPO.[136]

---

[134] See *König v Germany* (1978) 2 EHRR 170 and the *Eckle v Germany* (1982) 6 EHRR 35 where periods of 10 and 17 years were involved!

[135] Roxin, above, n 112, p. 99.

[136] Roxin, above, n 112, p. 106.

5.4 Principles concerning the form of proceedings

5.4.1 *The principle of the Oral Proceedings (Mündlichkeitsgrundsatz)*

The principle requires all the evidence to be presented orally and that the decision of the court can only be reached if the evidence is heard (§§ 249 and 252–260 StPO). Thus the system in Germany is not a pure inquisitorial system which reduces all aspects into written form nor is it translated into the "day in court". Oral proceedings offer a better supervision of the criminal procedural system for the accused and the public—contrary to the written, secret proceedings that had been used in former times. The oral form is a much easier to understand and acceptable process for many members of society, hence the requirements of the code under §§ 249, 251 and 254 for the written statements, evidence, and files to be read out. There is also a requirement that particular aspects of the proceedings must be in writing, including the charge, the judgment, and the appeal (see §§ 199, 200 and 271–275 StPO).

5.4.2 *The principle of publicity (Grundsatz der Öffentlichkeit)*

Publicity of the proceedings is regarded as desirable to inform the public generally about the administration of justice and to dispel the myths about the law. Publicity acts as an example to discourage crime but may also have an adverse affect by providing information about law breaking and law avoidance. Publicity allows public inspection and criticism and so helps to bring about reform and the policing of the system. Publicity gives the accused innocent person the chance to openly clear his name or defend his position, it may, however, intimidate him and allow him to be subjected to the mercies of the press and to undermine his position in society even if only in his own eyes.

The basic regime of publicity is laid down in the GVG, §§ 169 et seq., that the proceedings are public except in prescribed circumstances. Paragraph 169 GVG does not include the admittance of radio or television within the basic definition of open publicity. In fact § 169 2 GVG prohibits expressly audio and visual recordings taken for public broadcasting during proceedings. Although it has been argued that the ban restricts the basic rights to freedom of expression, information, and freedom of the media (Art. 5 I GG) the BVerfG has upheld the ban as constituional[137] in the interest of the participants' independence during the procedure—especially in view of the scantily disguised main commercial interests of the media broadcasting from inside the court.[138] However, pictures may be taken in recesses if permitted by the judge and the usual forms of reporting are allowed, which involve the taking of notes and drawings.

Circumstances when it is considered that in the interests of justice, the parties, or witnesses that the public may be excluded are § 171a GVG, cases involving references to drug units or mental hospitals, § 171b I 1 GVG, the protection of privacy of

---

[137] BVerfG, ZUM 2001, 220.
[138] See also B. Kramer, *Grundbegriffe des Strafverfahrensrechts*, 4th ed. (1999: Kohlhammer, Stuttgart) pp. 240–241; Beulke, above, n 128, pp. 187–188; Roxin, above, n 112, p. 382.

personal matters, § 172 No. 1 GVG, reasons of state security or matters likely to endanger public order or offend public decency, § 172 No. 3 GVG and § 203 StGB, a breach of confidentiality, § 48 and 103 JGG, cases involving the interrogation and trial of persons under sixteen and, § 172 No. 4 GVG, witnesses under the age of sixteen.

6 The pre-trial preliminary investigation (*Vorverfahren*)

Pre-trial investigation extends from the first action by the police until either the bringing or dropping of proceedings by the state attorney. As soon as the state prosecution has a suspicion that a crime has been committed, it has to start investigations (§ 160 I StPO). According to § 163 StPO, the police are under the same duty. In practice, the police undertake an investigation, collect evidence and send the file to the state attorney as a closed file (*Schlußbericht*). This may be prompted by a public authority or by an individual but the state attorney's office, the police, the public authorities, and the courts are obliged to receive information (§ 158 StPO).

At this point the relationship between state prosecution and police has to be pointed out. Whereas the state prosecution is subject to orders of the ministry of justice of the relevant *Land*, the police is part of the hierarchy leading up the ministry of home affairs (of the relevant *Land*). This division is designed to limit the state prosecution's powers. However, § 161 StPO and § 152 GVG make it clear that where investigation in criminal proceedings are taken up the police are assistants to the state prosecution, receiving orders from them. It also has to be borne in mind that this is not the only function of the police. While they are acting in a repressive context when investigating criminal cases (on the basis of state prosecution's orders) they fulfil a preventive role when keeping up law and order, upholding public security or, in other words, preventing any disruptions of the peace. The latter classical tasks of policing are based on the policing laws of the *Länder* whereas competences of the police concerning investigation of criminal offences are based on the federal (!) Criminal Procedural Code. For these reasons it is important to exactly define what sort of action the police are taking.

Paragraph 152 II StPO provides that a *prima facie* suspicion (*einfacher Anfangsverdacht*) triggers the duty of the state attorney to act. The aim of these proceedings is the investigation of the facts or of an offence if one exists. Paragraphs 160–162 StPO emphasize the state prosecution's leading role in this phase.[139] These provisions give the state prosecution powers to take efficient measures during investigation such as ordering witnesses to appear for interrogation, demanding co-operation from other authorities, and the power to apply before the court for search warrants, confiscation, or reprimand.

---

[139] Thus the state prosecution is often defined as "Herrin des Vorverfahrens" ("Master of the pre-trial procedure").

6.1 The investigation (*Ermittlungsverfahren*)

Investigations are prompted by information supplied from the police or independent third parties (§ 158). Paragraph 161 permits the state attorney to collect the evidence from the police, to summon and interview the suspect (*Beschuldigter*), witnesses, and experts. The state attorney has the right to obtain the assistance of the police in the investigations and in fact the police usually do most of the factual work as auxiliary officers of state attorney's office under § 152 GVG.

The state attorney cannot bring a charge unless he has first undertaken his duty to investigate all complaints to see if a charge should be brought, including the search for evidence in favour of the suspect (§ 160 II). He then decides whether if at full trial a guilty result is probable. If probable he must proceed to prosecute and charges must be made (§ 170 I). The process then moves on to the interim proceedings (*Zwischenverfahren*). For some measures, the state attorney needs the co-operation of the court to keep the accused on remand for this period if the seriousness of the case warrants it.

According to the different stages of the procedure the suspect is referred to by different expressions. For the whole procedure—but mainly during the pre-trial procedure—he is named *Beschuldigter*, in interim proceedings he is referred to as *Angeschuldigter* (§ 157 1st Alt. StPO) and in main proceedings he becomes *Angeklagter* (= the accused) according to § 157 2nd Alt. StPO. For lack of better terms we will use the term "suspect" in this section for the expression "*Beschuldigter*".

6.2 Powers of state prosecution and police during pre-trial investigation

6.2.1 *The interrogation (Vernehmung)*

The interrogation of the suspect is regulated by §§ 133–136a StPO. These provisions only refer to interrogation by a judge but according to § 163a StPO they are applicable to interrogations by the police and the state prosecution as well.

The state prosecution—but not the police (!)—may order the suspect to appear before them for interrogation (§ 133 I and § 163a III 1 StPO), even though the suspect does not then have to make a statement. When interrogated by any of the above-mentioned authorities, the suspect first has to be informed of the charges brought against him (§ 136 I 1), that he has a right to remain silent (*Aussageverweigerungsrecht*, § 136 I 2), and to choose an attorney (§ 136 I 2). Any confessions or evidence obtained before the suspect's rights are read and charges are brought used to be admissible in court. The BGH for a long time regarded § 136 I StPO as a mere formality. This position has been reversed in a decision by the BGH, holding that failure to inform a suspect of the right to remain silent has the result that statements made cannot be used against him in criminal proceedings, unless it is proven that the suspect knew his rights anyway or unless his or her present attorney agrees to the use of the statement.[140] It has to be noted that spontaneously made statements to the police or the state prosecutor can be used in court, because no official interrogation has been started in these cases.[141] The suspect is not obliged to incriminate himself[142] nor to act as a witness against himself.[143] This goes beyond a right to silence because the right not to speak also has the effect of extinguishing the right to defend oneself. It is therefore the right not to enter a defence. However, should the suspect wish to speak, the same provision provides a right to be heard.

6.2.2 Illegal methods of interrogation (Verbotene Vernehmungsmethoden, § 136a StPO)

It follows from the idea of "fair trial" derived from the *Rechtsstaatsprinzip* (Art. 20 II, III GG) and Article 6 I ECHR that it is not admissible to find the truth "at any cost". Thus § 136a StPO contains a list of prohibited methods of interrogation and includes ill treatment, fatigue, deception, use of medicines or torture, and hypnosis. The list is exemplary rather than exhaustive. It exemplifies that the individual's right to form a free will may not be corrupted (*Freiheit der Willensentschlies-sung*) and thus emphazises his right to human dignity (Art. 1 I GG). Thus the use of lie detectors has been held to contradict the idea of § 136a StPO and Article 1 I GG as it undermines any possibility of the individual employing his free will. It thus makes him a mere object of state action and penetrates the core of human dignity.[144] The respect for human dignity also clearly forbids any form of torture. This term includes any kind of action inflicting physical or psychological pain, e.g. fake executions. The ban of "deception" as listed by § 136a poses problems as it interferes very much with criminological methods of investigating an offence. Thus it has to be interpreted restrictively.[145] Illegal deceptions include feigning non-existing facts such as claiming that the accessory has already been arrested and/or confessed to the crime. The BGH has also held that putting the suspect—while in remand—into a cell with another convict, who acts as a spy for the police and thus manages to get a confession, is not compatible with § 136a StPO.[146] A deception not intended by the interrogating authorities, however, does not fall under § 136a.

It follows from § 136a III 2 StPo that any statements gained in the above-mentioned way cannot be used in court. The causal link between the used method and the statement does not have to be proved by the suspect in such cases. It

---

[140] BGHSt 38, 214; 39, 349.

[141] Beulke, above, n 128, p. 57. However, in cases of first interrogations of a number of people by the police with the mere purpose of gathering some initial information on the case (*informative Befragung*), statements made by a subsequent suspect cannot be used if he has not previously been informed of his rights. In that case the suspect was induced by the state authorities to make the statement.

[142] BGHSt 14, 358; 56, 37.

[143] BGHSt 25, 325.

[144] BGHSt 5, 332. It seems that nowadays the main arguments against the use of lie detectors are their ineffeciency and their scientifically disputed reliability, see Beulke, above, n 128, p. 69.

[145] General opinion, see Roxin, above, n 112, p. 203; Beulke, above, n 128, p. 65 both with further references.

[146] BGHSt 34; 362. Strangely enough the Court held this to be an illegal method of "coercion" rather than deception.

suffices if such a link cannot be excluded.[147] It is disputed whether pieces of evidence found because of a statement that was gained by forbidden methods can be used in court or are inadmissible. The latter view, agreeing with the American "fruit of the poisonous tree doctrine", is taken by some academics who emphazise the aim of § 136a StPO to effectively ban the mentioned methods of interrogation.[148] This effect would be undermined if state authorities could rely on illegal methods in such cases. However, the BGH seems to allow a use of such evidence in most cases, arguing that one procedural mistake should not obstruct the whole procedure and that it is often difficult to prove whether the police would not have found the relevant piece of evidence anyway.[149]

Paragraph 136a III provides that evidence obtained by illegal methods banned by § 136a I is unlawful even where the suspect has consented to its use.

6.2.3 Coercive measures (Zwangsmittel)

Beyond the right to question the suspect, the state prosecution and police may employ more coercive measures (Zwangsmittel) to assist them during their investigation. These means usually restrict basic rights but have to be constitutionally permitted. When unconstitutional they will give rise to actions for compensation. The aim of the coercive measures is to secure the necessary evidence or to prevent further damage or injury occurring. Only some of these measures can be named here.[150] Note that most of them need to be authorized by a judge. The state prosecution or the police may only authorize them exceptionally in cases of emergency. They include arrest and detention, body and house searches (§§ 102–103), telephone tapping and interference with post (§100–101), and the right to seize property (§§ 94–95). Measures restricting the right to physical integrity include body search, taking blood samples (§ 81a), the analysis of an individual's DNA (§§ 81e–f) and taking finger prints (§ 81b). Note that correspondence between the suspect and the defence attorney are protected by the principle of legal privilege (§ 97). Paragraph 100c I StPO has introduced a legal basis for eavesdropping activities outside (*"kleiner Lauschangriff"*) and inside of private homes (*"grosser"* Lauschangriff). The latter can only be authorized by the chamber for state protection (*Staatsschutzkammer*) at the *Landgericht* (§ 100 d II StPO).

6.2.4 Pre-trial detention (remand) (Untersuchungshaft)

The classical restrictive measures to be pointed out are arrest and pre-trial detention. Remand is allowable under § 112 I on the conditions that there is a strong suspicion that the suspect has committed the offence (*dringender Tatverdacht*), and there is a legal ground for the arrest. Remand must not be disproportionate to the offence and the expected possible sentence. Alternative grounds for detention on remand are:

---

[147] BGHSt 5, 290.
[148] Roxin, above, n 112, p. 193; Beulke, above, n 128, p. 248.
[149] E.g. BGHSt 32,68.
[150] For further information see Beulke, above, n 128 pp. 112–134.

(a) the risk of flight and escape (§ 112 II 1 and 2),

(b) the risk of destruction or falsification of evidence (§ 112 II 3),

(d) the gravity of the offence (§ 112 III),[151] and

(e) the danger of the repetition of the offence (§ 112a).

Remand is limited to offences subject to a penalty in excess of one year, in other words crimes (*Verbrechen*). Paragraph 113 I states more precisely that offences with less than a possible six months' imprisonment or a fine will never give grounds for detention on remand in cases of a danger that the evidence will be destroyed.

A precondition for remand under § 114 is a (formal) warrant that has to list the suspect, the grounds for detention, and usually the facts that indicate these grounds and the suspicion. As a constitutional safeguard it can generally only be issued by a judge (Art. 104 II 1 GG). Usually, the state prosecution will apply for a warrant to the judge at the *Amtsgericht*, that has jurisdiction in the relevant case.[152]

The arrested person must be presented to a judge—at the latest one day after his arrest—to determine the legality of the pre-trial detention (§ 115 II StPO, Art. 104 III GG) and the detained must be informed of the right to a lawyer and the right not to speak (§§ 136–137). The judge now has a duty to inform the suspect's next of kin or person of confidence to ensure that the possibility of a defence is always secured (§ 114b I StPO). The judge will then interrogate the suspect and then decide whether the warrant remains in force. If there are no legal reasons to nullify the order, a judge must nevertheless refuse it if other measures are sufficient (§ 116), for example reporting to a police station. Bail (*Sicherheitsleistung*) is the most important substitute for remand but most applications for remand are granted and it is rare for bail to be granted in cases involving serious crimes (*Verbrechen*). A review of the detention can be requested at any time (§ 117) and the detained person can complain against the proportionality of the remand.

It is only with the permission the higher regional court (*Oberlandesgericht*) that remand can last longer than six months (§ 121 StPO). After six months this court has to automatically examine whether remand may continue. This will only be the case if one of the exceptional grounds listed in § 121 II StPO exist, e.g. extraordinarily complicated investigations that delay a final decision.

6.2.5 *Provisional arrest (Vorläufige Festnahme)*

Paragraph 127 StPO provides a power of provisional arrest in cases where somebody is caught red-handed and where there is a danger of flight or when the identity of the offender cannot be ascertained. This power of arrest is available under § 127 I 2 to all people (*"Jedermann"-Festnahmerecht*). The arresting person has a right to self-defence. The state prosecution and police are entitled to the same right under § 127 II StPO although in that case the conditions for an arrest (§ 112) must be fulfilled.

---

[151] Paragraph 112 III lists an exhaustive catalogue of relevant crimes including, for example, murder and manslaughter.

[152] However, after charges have been brought against the suspect a warrant can only be issued by the court that the charges have been brought before. For details see §§ 125 et seq. StPO.

Paragraph 128 provides that the police must present the detainee to a judge without delay in the case of provisional arrest. The judge then has to decide whether to set the suspect free or issue a formal warrant. The presentation should take place the next day at the latest.

The next part of the procedure would be the interim proceedings but because a defence attorney is mandatory in most cases this role will first be considered.

7 The role of the defence attorney (*Verteidiger*) during pre-trial investigations

7.1 Right to a defence attorney

The provision of an attorney is partly the reflection of the principle of equality of arms, where the suspect must be given the same chances in the proceedings as the state attorney. Furthermore, the principles of *Rechtstaat* and the respect for human dignity (Arts 1 I, 20 II, III GG) demand that the suspect is not treted as a mere object of the procedure but can actively participate, if necessary through his attorney. Thus § 137 I StPO allows a suspect to select an attorney of his choice at any stage of the proceedings. This may be, according to §§ 138 et seq., a full time attorney (*Rechtsanwalt*), an academic jurist teaching at a German university, or, under §§ 139 and 142 II, any law graduate who has already passed the first state exam and has completed at least fifteen months of the *Referendar* stage of his training.[153]

Paragraph 140 StPO lists the case groups requiring the presence of an attorney such as proceedings before the *Oberlandesgericht* or the *Landgericht* in the first instance (§ 140 No. 1), or where the suspect is accused of an offence punishable by not less than one year's imprisonment (= *Verbrechen*, § 140 No. 2). In these situations the case cannot proceed without an attorney. Therefore the court is obliged under § 145 to appoint one. If there are no prohibitive reasons the court will appoint an attorney admitted to a local court (§142 I 1). The defence attorney then has a claim for payment against the state for the fee (§ 97 BRAGO) and against the client only when the payment will not effect the situation of the client's family.[154]

According to § 1 BRAO, the defence attorney is "an organ of the adminstration of justice" (*Organ der Rechtspflege*). This entails independence from the client to the extent that the express wishes of the client can be disregarded and the attorney can pursue a line in court independent from the client except in the matter of an appeal (§ 297 StPO). However, if appointed by the client the attorney can be dismissed at any time but if appointed by the court, can only be dismissed by the court. The

---

[153] See Chapter 4 on legal education for further details.
[154] Details of the provision and the grounds for legal aid are contained in Chapter 5.

latter will only happen if the court is convinced that the basis of mutual trust between attorney and suspect has ceased to exist.[155]

7.2 Rights and duties of the defence attorney

Attorneys owe a duty to the court as organs of the court, but the duty to the client is such that even where the guilt is known the client must still be defended, although the ability to do so may be compromised by a client confession. The general tasks are to give any advice as to what the client may do, to introduce into the proceedings only matters which do not endanger the truth, but use anything correctly introduced by third parties. This obligation to help in determining the truth entails a duty not to falsify evidence. An attorney can refuse to give evidence on behalf of the client (§ 53 I 2 StPO).

The attorney has the right of access to read all the files of the state attorney and the court including the recordings of the interrogations of the police and state attorney in what therefore amounts to full pre-trial discovery (§ 147); but access can be denied where the investigations are not complete and premature access would itself endanger the success of the investigation (§ 147 II).

The defence attorney has an unfettered right of attendance in court and complete access between the attorney and client must be allowed (§ 148 I).

8 The interim proceedings (*Zwischenverfahren*)

These—termed in the StPO—as the decision concerning the opening of the main proceedings. Once the pre-trial investigation procedure has been terminated, the interim proceedings commence with the delivery to the court of the dossier of files by the state attorney with the accusation (§ 199 II). The court certifies the substantive and territorial competence of the court to try the alleged offence.

8.1 The choice of court

The choice of court is determined by the severity of the offence or group of offences and the decision of the state attorney as to the appropriate court (§§ 24–25 GVG). If the state attorney errs, it is a violation of the basic constitutionally guaranteed right to a lawful judge (Art. 101 GG) and is a ground for the revision of the judgment.

Minor offences are dealt with by a single judge in the *Amtsgericht* (§§ 24–25 GVG), when brought as private prosecutions or if a punishment of no more than two years' imprisonment is expected. There is a special juvenile chamber for minor offences also with a single professional judge.

More serious offences at first instance are heard before the *Schöffengericht*

---

[155] For details see Beulke, above, n 128, p. 83.

composed of one professional and two lay members (§§ 24–25 and 28–29 GVG) unless, four or more years' imprisonment is threatened, or detention in a mental hospital, or the case is of special importance. Furthermore, the lists of serious offences in §§ 74 and 120 GVG establish the *Landgericht/Oberlandesgericht* as courts first instance and thus limit the *Amtsgericht's* jurisdiction.

Special juvenile courts (*Jugendschöffengericht*) of the *Amtsgericht* for serious offenders have two lay members and one professional (§§ 33 and 40 JGG).

Serious crimes must go to a criminal chamber of the *Landgericht* at first instance (§ 74 II GVG) which is called *Schwurgericht*. The *Landgericht* sits as a *Große Strafkammer* with three professional and two lay members at first instance for serious crimes (§§ 74, 76 GVG). As a court of appeal the *Landgericht* sits as a *Kleine Strafkammer* with one professional and two lay members to hear appeals from the single *Amtsgericht* judge or the *Schöffengericht* (§§ 74, 76 II GVG).

A *Jugendstrafgericht* in the *Landgericht* hears the most serious offences and appeals from the *Amtsgericht* in juvenile cases.

Exceptionally, the *Oberlandesgericht* sits as a criminal senate of first instance for the most serious of criminal offences composed of five professional judges (§§ 120 & 122 GVG). Otherwise, the *Oberlandesgericht* acts as an appeal court with three professional judges for appeals from the small and large criminal chambers of the *Landgericht*.

Where a court comes to the decision that the case should be tried before a higher court, it is obliged to transfer the case (§ 270 I StPO).

8.2 Result of interim proceedings

The suspect is sent a copy of the charge (§ 201) and has two weeks in which to respond with applications for evidence or complaints. The court then decides whether to open or close the main proceedings (§§ 203–204). A decision in favour of proceedings will be taken when there is a high probability of a prison sentence but the court is not bound by the finding of the state attorney or the charges brought by the state attorney (§ 206). The decision is made only by the professional judges and there is no participation by the lay judges at this stage (§ 207). There is no right of appeal for the accused, but the state attorney can appeal under § 210 against a decision not to open the main proceedings.

Following the decision for the main proceedings, the court has to fulfil several administrative tasks such as the setting of a date and deciding which judge will sit (§§ 213 et seq.).

9 Structure of the main proceedings (*Hauptverfahren*)

The most notable element here is that the oral hearing is normally far shorter than in the UK.

9.1 **The role of the judge**

The judges have a major role in the conduct of the case (§ 238 I) and will be quite familiar with the facts and details of the case prior to the hearing and will have the case documents present.

The court has the task under §§ 238 and 243–244 to find out the truth of the matter before it. Its decision is based on a restricted set of questions, those necessary to find out whether the constituent elements of an offence have been fulfilled or not. The object of the evidence is to establish the internal and external facts of the case. The trial judge must take into account every possible interpretation of the facts and not just those presented to him by either the state attorney or the accused.

A judge's role is also to protect the accused, especially where the accused has no defence. In contrast, the state attorney has a very minor role in the main trial and is bound to seek justice rather than convictions. As such, he is under a duty to raise an objection if the court commits an error that is detrimental to the accused.

9.2 **The main proceedings: the oral trial (*Hauptverhandlung*)**

The structure of the oral trial is mapped out in § 243 StPO. The presiding judge will then ensure whether the accused, his attorney, all relevant evidence, and the witnesses are present (§ 243 I). The witnesses then must leave the room and wait outside to be summond for their testimony. After the charge is read out by the state attorney (§ 243 III), the accused can make a statement but has the right not to speak (§ 243 IV) which should not be prejudicial. Guilty pleas formally undermine the principle that it is for the court to decide on the guilt of the accused which should not be presumed without being proved. However, confessions of guilt are frequent but the trial nevertheless continues so that the court, in compliance with its duties, is itself convinced of the guilt of the accused. The court therefore examines and questions the accused (§ 238 I) and the witnesses, experts, and other information as it sees fit (§§ 243–4).

The personal circumstances of the accused and previous convictions can be raised (§ 249). Objectively, this may be regarded as prejudicing the innocence of the accused and resulting in the false view that civil law systems require innocence to be proved. The prosecution bear the burden of proof to establish guilt. Past convictions must have a direct bearing on present charge.

Now the hearing of evidence commences (§ 244 I). After each statement of evidence is heard the accused has the right to respond (§ 257 I) and question the witnesses (§ 240 II). After each piece of evidence is introduced, the defence attorney has a right to make a statement (§ 257 II). The defence attorney's right under § 239 to cross-examine witnesses and experts exists, just as for the state prosecutor, but these rights are generally less exercised in Germany than in the UK because it has largely been carried out by the judge already, which underlines the judge's leading role in the oral trial.

The hearing of evidence is followed by the state attorney's and the defence attorney's summing up. Then the judges will retire in order to reach a decision. Finally, they will conclude the trial by announcing the verdict.

The law of evidence will now be looked at in more detail.

10 The law of evidence

10.1 Principles of the law of evidence

These principles include the principle of investigation (*Ermittlungsgrundsatz*, §244 II StPO), the principle of immediacy (*Grundsatz der Unmittelbarkeit*, §§ 226, 250 StPO), the principle of evidence given orally (*Grundsatz der Mündlichkeit*), and the principle of the unfettered consideration of the evidence (*Grundsatz der freien richterlichen Beweiswürdigung*, § 261 StPO). Some of these principles have already been explained.[156] Paragraph 244 II clarifies that the court is not bound by motions of the parties to take evidence but has investigate the matter in any way it thinks necessary in order to find the truth (principle of investigation). Furthermore, all pieces of evidence introduced have to be given orally, e.g. documents have to be read out aloud, (e.g. § 249). This is meant as a safeguard against secrecy of the procedure.

The principle of immediacy (§§ 226, 250 StPO) demands that the deciding court hears evidence itself and that pieces of evidence must not be replaced by substitutes. For this reason, the questioning of witnesses in court generally has to be given priority above reading out a statement already made to the police (§ 250, 2 StPO). However, there are several exceptions to this rule.[157] Thus § 251 StPO envisages the possibility of allowing the use of statements, i.e. protocols of previous interrogations, to replace the questioning of the witnesses, experts, or other accused in extraordinary cases, such as death, illness, unknown residence, etc. In these cases all relevant parties—state prosecutor, defence attorney, and accused—must agree to the use of these protocols. Furthermore, it is essential that in the previous interrogation, which is to be read out in court, the questioned person had been effectively informed of his right to refuse to give evidence. The use of undercover police officers and informants has created difficulties. Their testimony is difficult to introduce to the court as their identity needs to remain secret. On the other hand, the court is obliged to hear their statements in court. Here different exceptions have been developed allowing for an indirect introduction of informants' or undercover agents' statements.[158] Videos of interrogations of witnesses can also replace a direct interrogations according to § 247a StPO. The new provision aims especially at the protection of abused children who should be

---

[156] See above, secs 5.3 and 5.4.
[157] Only a few of them are looked at here. For a detailed exposition refer to Beulke, above, n 128, pp. 203–221; Roxin, above, n 112, pp. 371–381.
[158] For details see Beulke, above, n 128, pp. 210–215.

spared numerous repetitions of interrogations that could otherwise cause or increase trauma.[159]

The principle of the unfettered consideration of the evidence means that there are no legal rules compelling the judge **how** to consider evidence and what emphasis to put on any particular piece of evidence (§§ 244 and 261), thus hearsay evidence may be acceptable. This may result from the fact that there is no jury to be influenced by possibly unreliable evidence. However, there is a fixed catalogue (*numerus clausus*) of **which forms** of evidence can be introduced, as will be considered now.

10.2 Forms of proof (*Beweismittel*)

Evidence may be heard from the suspect/accused (*Beschuldigter* §§ 136, 243 II, IV), witnesses (*Zeugen* §§ 48–71), experts (*Sachverständige* §§ 72–85), physical evidence (*Augenschein* §§ 86–93), and documents (*Urkunden* §§ 249–256).

Motions to give evidence (*Beweisanträge*) are means by which the state attorney and the suspect can help with the search for the truth by a motion specifically drawing the attention of the court to a particular item.

Paragraph 244 III–VI determines when evidence can be refused and names items which it is not necessary to prove as evidence. This includes expert evidence— when the court already considers it has the appropriate expertise, evidence obtained through a breach of the law, and immaterial evidence.

Paragraph 245 stipulates that present means of evidence should be treated preferentially because no effort in terms of time is necessary, therefore all the summoned witnesses and experts should be interrogated unless they fall into the categories of § 244 III–IV. This means that evidence which may not have been obvious from reading the files may be brought to light during the interrogation by the court or that which sheds new light on the trial or introduces new facts to lead to a different conclusion. Such evidence is not subject to the strict requirements of proof of indirect or external evidence.

10.2.1 The accused (*Der Beschuldigte/Angeklagte*)

The accused (*Angeklagte*) has the right to be heard in the trial and cannot be forced to give evidence against himself (§ 136). Paragraph 243 IV 1, provides that the accused must be informed that he does not have to give evidence and is entitled to remain silent. This may not be taken as evidence against him. The accused, having exercised the right to remain silent, can subsequently waive that right. Paragraph 244 I states that following the examination of the defendant other evidence can be heard.

10.2.2 Witnesses (*Zeugen*)

Witnesses are persons that are to give a statement in court about their perceptions of facts relevant to the case. This may include statements that have been made to

---

them by other persons—turning them into hearsay witnesses (*Zeugen vom Hörensagen*). They are required to appear in court when summoned subject, in the case of refusal, to fines or imprisonment (§§ 48, 51 StPO). There is a duty to tell the truth and to take an oath (§ 59) and a duty not to refuse to give evidence. Refusal would subject the witness to a fine or imprisonment (§§ 51 and 70). However, the court may in certain cases refrain from placing a witness under oath (§ 60 StPO). There is a right to refuse to give evidence on personal grounds (§ 52)—covering close relatives, spouses and fiancées—or on professional grounds (§ 53). The latter is applicable to members of the professions listed in § 53, such as defence attorneys, priests, doctors, and lawyers, covering everything communicated to them on the basis of their professional occupation. Furthermore, § 55 allows every witness to refuse to answer a particular question if this would entail their own prosecution for an offence. Before interrogation witnesses have to be informed of these rights. Afterwards they may be questioned by the judge, the state attorney, and the defence attorney (§ 240).

10.2.3 Expert witnesses (*Die Sachverständigen*)

Under §§ 73–74, the judge has the exclusive right to appoint expert witnesses which can be challenged by the state attorney and the accused, e.g. on grounds of interest. Their evidence is not, however, binding on the court.

10.2.4 Judicial inspections (*Augenschein*)

The court has the right to make judicial inspections under § 86 to acquaint itself with the crime. Inspections can be physical, the showing of videos, or the playing of tapes.

10.2.5 Documents (*Urkunden*)

Documents of any kind in writing, that can be read out aloud, are acceptable as evidence (§ 249 StPO).

10.3 The prohibition of evidence (*Beweisverwertungsverbot*)

There is a distinction to be made between prohibited evidence and prohibited use of evidence (*Beweis—und Verwertungsverbot*). This consists of the prohibition of certain subjects to be discussed when giving evidence (*Beweisthemenverbote*) and the prohibition of certain means or methods of obtaining evidence (*Beweismittelverbote und Beweismethodenverbote*). Just as for § 136a StPO,[160] the constitutional guarantee of individual rights and *Rechtsstaatsprinzip* (Arts 2 I, 20 III GG) demand that the ultimate proof of a person's guilt must come from legally admitted evidence and within limitations set by the law with regard to legitimate refusal of evidence of certain witnesses under §§ 53–54. A number of prohibitions on the use of evidence wrongly obtained are not mapped out by statute but have been developed by the case-law.

---

[160] See above, sec. 6.2.2.

Generally, such prohibitions can follow either from a breach of criminal procedural law provisions or from a breach of certain constitutional rights. This poses the problem of deciding when such a breach was grave enough to entail a prohibition of evidence. Where a procedural provision has been violated, general opinion will examine the "purpose of protection" intended by this provision (*Schutzzweck der Norm*). Thus if, for example, a witness has not been informed of his rights under § 52 StPO before an interrogation by the police, then a subsequent use of the statement in court is inadmissible, because the infringed provision (§ 52 StPO) was designed to protect the witnesses' rights, here to respect family ties with the accused.[161]

Where a breach of procedural provisions cannot be ascertained but there is an interference with constitutional rights, a solution must be found by balancing the interests at stake.[162] Examples concerning the right to privacy (Art. 2 I in connection with Art. 1 IGG) are the introduction of secretly made recordings and diaries. Recordings gained from eavesdropping activities are generally admissible if the procedure according to § 100c I No. 2, 3 StPO has been respected. Diaries have been prohibited as evidence although this has been qualified in the case of murder trials.[163] The BVerfG has developed three "spheres" of privacy to help the courts assess whether an intervention by the law enforcement authorities violated the citizen's right rendering the evidence thus gained inadmissible in court:[164]

(a) interventions in the "social sphere" (e.g. business contacts) are generally admissible (1st sphere),

(b) interventions in the "private sphere" (e.g. private talks held in public places) can be justified. However, here the interests at stake (including gravity of charge) have to be balanced,

(c) Interventions in the "intimate sphere" (e.g. bedroom conversation between spouses) cannot be justified.

Paragraph 252 StPO prohibits the introduction of evidence given by a witness during pre-trial proceedings, who in the main trial exercises his right to refuse to give evidence according to §§ 52–53 StPO. However, the BGH has held this ban to only be applicable to interrogations previously made by the police or the state attorney. The ban does not extend to previously made statements in the presence of a judge.[165]

Evidence obtained contrary to the provisions of § 136a, considered above, is clearly inadmissible.[166]

---

[161] BGHSt 11, 213; as it protects rights of the witness and merely as a "reflex" benefits the accused this has been termed as *Rechtskreistheorie* which can roughly be translated as the "doctrine of the rights' holder".

[162] For details see Beulke, above, n 128, p. 232–233.

[163] BGHSt 34, 397.

[164] BVerfGE 34, 238.

[165] BGHSt 2, 99.

[166] For details on prohibition of evidence see Roxin, above, n 112, pp. 178–195; Beulke, above, n 128, pp. 230–250.

11 The conclusion of the trial

After all the evidence has been heard the state attorney sums up, recommends a verdict, and applies for a certain sentence to the court. The defence attorney then sums up and enters the formal pleas for a certain judgment (§ 258). The state attorney can respond under § 258 II and finally the accused may make another statement. The judges retire to deliberate, governed by §§ 194 et seq. GVG. If not unanimous, a two-thirds majority is required (§ 263 I StPO). The court re-assembles and the presiding judge announces the verdict, the sanctions if found guilty (§ 260), and gives the grounds for the judgment (§§ 267–68). Unless already given, detailed reasons have to be added in written form within five weeks of the verdict (§ 275).

12 The accelerated procedure (*Beschleunigtes Verfahren*, §§ 417–420 StPO)

Paragraphs 417 et seq. provide for a form of accelerated proceedings but only in exceptional circumstances and only before the *Amtsgericht* and *Schöffengericht*. This can only be done on application of the state prosecution in cases of simple facts or clear evidence. This is provided to speed up the process in relation specifically to minor offences whereby the interim procedure is abandoned and the main trial is held immediately.

13 The summary procedure (*Strafbefehlsverfahren*, §§ 407–412 StPO)

This is provided by §§ 407–412 for minor offences (*Vergehen*) envisaging less drastic sanctions (as listed in § 407 II) and allows for a verdict without court appearance. The *Strafbefehl* can be described as a verdict in form of a written order issued by the relevant court, according to § 25 GVG the single judge at the *Amtsgericht* (*Strafrichter*). Once it cannot be appealed against, it takes the same effect as any judgment (§ 410 III). It is commenced by the state attorney who dispenses with the interim proceedings and presents the court with details of the proof of the offence and the desired sentence. The judge then has the following opportunities: he can refuse to issue the order because of a lack of suspicion (§ 408 II), he can issue the order if he agrees with the state prosecutor's opinion (§ 408 III 1), or he can call for an oral trial if he wants to deviate from the state prosecutor's proposition (§ 408 III 2). Once an order is issued and sent to the accused, the latter has two weeks in which to object and ask for an ordinary procedure (§§ 410 I, 411 I 2).

14 Means of legal redress (*Rechtsmittel*)

Every person who is the subject of a decision of a court which negatively affects their rights has a right to appeal against the disadvantageous decision (§§ 296 et seq). The means of legal redress are devided into two categories: ordinary means of legal redress (*ordentliche Rechtsbehelfe*) are those that will suspend the effect of the challenged decision (*Suspensiveffekt*) such as appeal, revision, and the complaint. They also have the effect of raising the procedure to a higher instance (*Devolutiveffekt*). Apart from these, the Code of Criminal Procedure also provides for extraordinary means of redress (*außerordentliche Rechtsbehelfe*), such as a re-trial (§§ 359 et seq.). These means can be employed—under exceptional circumstances—where a decision has already taken effect, thus they constitute the few exceptions where the effect of a decision can be subsequently voided (*Rechtskraftdurchbrechung*).

14.1 Common rules on ordinary means of legal redress

Under § 297, the defence attorney can appeal with the permission of the client and the state attorney also has the right to appeal under § 296 II which also includes the right to appeal in favour of the accused in order to ensure that an unsound conviction has a chance of being remedied.

Judgments can be entirely or partially appealed against and there is also the right to have the actions of the police and the state attorney reviewed in the courts. There is no specific form for an appeal provided it is in writing. Indeed, they do not even have to state first whether an appeal on facts and law (*Berufung*) or a revision is being made (§ 300). Only in the case of the *Revision* do reasons have to be given (§ 344 I). Appeals or revisions that have been lodged in favour of the accused must not result in an aggravation of the challenged verdict (§§ 331 I, 358 II). This prohibition, termed *Verbot der reformatio in peius*, is not applicable to complaints.

The right to appeal can be waived but the court has a duty to ensure that this right is not carelessly abandoned.

14.2 Forms of appeal

The process of appeal depends on in which court the case commenced and the type of appeal desired. For details on the courts involved and the members of the court see the sections on the courts and lay judges in Chapters 2 and 4.

14.2.1 The appeal on fact and law (*Berufung*)

An appeal on fact and law (*Berufung*, §§ 312–332) is possible against the decision at first instance of a single judge in the *Amtsgericht* and the *Schöffengericht*. The appeal must be in writing and the time limit of one week runs from the day of judgment (§ 314 I) and has to be adressed to the court that delivered the challenged decision (*iudex a quo*). It is not necessary to give any reason for the appeal which makes it a general right to have the judgment reviewed by a court with more members who take no notice of the previous decision.

The proceedings under §§ 323–326 involve basically a complete re-trial of the main proceedings unless the appeal has been restricted to particular aspects of the first trial (§ 327). The reports and much of the evidence can simply be read out under §§ 324–325. The principle of full investigation nevertheless applies and new evidence can be introduced (§ 323 III). The first summing up belongs to the party who made the appeal (§ 326).

Where the first instance court had acted without jurisdiction the case is sent to a new court with jurisdiction. If this turns out to be the appeal court itself it will hear the case at first instance.

14.2.2 *Revision of the law (Revision)*

The appeal for a revision of the law (*Revision*, §§ 333–358) is admissible against first instance decisions as well as against appeal decisions with a time limit of one week for the application (*iudex a quo*, § 341). One month after the application for the revision, the reasoning has to be submitted (§§ 344, 345). Revision is only available in fairly narrow circumstances involving questions of law, the right law, the correct application, the correct procedure, and the correct punishment by the lower court (§ 337 I and § 338). The pre-trial proceedings cannot be the subject of a revision and questions of fact are excluded. However, the term 'law' can be subject to a very wide interpretation and has included customary law, regulations, general rules of international law, rules of scientific experience, and logic. Violations of procedural law can generallly only be proven by the protocol of the main trial (§ 274). According to § 337, only those violations will be accepted as grounds for revision that were causal for the decision. Such reasons are described as relative grounds for revision (*relative Revisionsgründe*) and have to be proven. It is, however, sufficient to prove that it cannot be excluded that the verdict was based on the procedural breach. By contrast, § 338 gives eight absolute grounds for revision (*absolute Revisionsgründe*). Their existence will constitute a non-rebuttable assumption of causal link between the breach of law and the verdict delivered, for example lacking jurisdiction, participation of a prejudiced judge, and breach of the principle of publicity.

Where the state attorney applies for an appeal against acquittal, it can be rejected without main proceedings by the decision of the revision court when it considers the appeal as groundless (§ 349 II) because this appeal only asks for a judgment on the process for the benefit of the state attorney and to clarify a point of law for future reference. It leads only to a judgment without legal effect for any parties to help clarify the procedure and formalities.

The procedure according to § 351 is to receive the report of the reporting judge, to hear the applicant for revision and then the other side, and finally the accused has the last word before judgment. A simple revision can take place at the appeal court. If new evidence or submissions are to be heard the case must be referred to another, different lower court. In cases of successful revisions, the court will refer the case for a new decision back to the court of the previous instance, which is bound by any decision of the appeal court (§ 358).

14.2.3 *The complaint (Beschwerde)*

The complaint (§§ 304–311a) is a form of interlocutory appeal which has a wide application, since not only the suspect and the state attorney can make use of it, but it is also available to witnesses and victims (§ 304 II). There are several categories of complaints and they are possible at all stages of the criminal process, to cover all judicial decisions with the exception of the judgment itself against which either the appeal or the revision must be raised.

14.3 **The re-trial (*Wiederaufnahme des Verfahrens*)**

The aim of the retrial (§§ 359 et seq.) is to correct incorrect judgments that have already taken legal effect. As already metioned this is an extraordinary means of legal redress. It does not suspend the execution of judgment, unlike appeals. To stop this from being another general or extra last instance of "appeal" there is a definitive catalogue of grounds for a re-trial (§§ 359, 362). The grounds against the original conviction must be on one of those listed in the exhaustive catalogue, such as the use of faked or false documents, perjury on the part of one of the witnesses or experts, a breach of duty by the judge, or where the European Court of Human Rights has found a judgment to violate the European Convention of Human Rights (§ 359 No. 1–6). In practice, however, the most important reason is the introduction of new facts and evidence (§ 359 No. 5). A re-trial to the disadvantage of the accused is possible under similar conditions (§ 362 Nos 1–4) excluding the introduction of new evidence. There is no time limit but the petition must be signed by an attorney.

The procedure involves a consideration of admissibility (*Aditionsverfahren*, §§ 366–368), checking the substance of the claim (*Probationsverfahren*, §§ 369, 370) and the repeat of the main proceedings (§§ 370 II, 373). A complaint lies against the finding of inadmissibility under § 372.

FURTHER READING

Criminal law

German Criminal Law, Volume 1: *The Criminal Code and The Narcotics Law*, Translation by G. Harfst and O. Schmidt (1989: Harfst Verlag, Würzburg).

W. Gropp, *Strafrecht Allgemeiner Teil*, 2nd ed. (2001: Springer, Berlin).

C.J. Hauf, *Strafrecht, Allgemeiner Teil*, 2nd ed., (2001: Luchterhand, Neuwied).

W. Joecks, *Studienkommentar StGB* (1999: C.H. Beck, München).

C. Roxin, *Höchstrichterliche Rechtsprechung zum Allgemeinen Teil des Strafrechts* (1998: C.H. Beck, München).

A. Schönke and H. Schröder, *Strafgesetzbuch*, 26th ed. (2001: C.H. Beck, München).

H. Troendle and T. Fischer, *Kommentar zum Strafgesetzbuch und Nebengesetze*, 50th ed. (2001: C. H. Beck, München).

J. Wessels and W. Beulke, *Strafrecht Allgemeiner Teil*, 30th ed. (2000: C.F. Müller, Heidelberg).

Articles

G. Artz, "Ignorance or Mistake of Law" (1976) 24 Am J Comp L 646–679.

E. Binavance, "The Structure and Theory of the German Penal Code" (1976) 24 Am J Comp L 594–601.

A. Eser, "Justification and Excuse" (1976) 24 Am J Comp L 621–637.

G. P. Fletcher, "Criminal Omissions: Some Perspectives" (1976) 24 Am J Comp L 703–717.

J. Hall, "Comment on Error Juris" (1976) 24 Am J Comp L 680–689.

J. Hermann, "Sanctions: German Law and Theory", (1976) 24 Am J Comp L 718–736.

H.-H. Jescheck, "The Doctrine of *mens rea* in German Criminal Law—its Historical Background and Present State" (1975), 8 CILSA 112–120.

D. Oehler, "Revision of the Penal Code" (1976) 24 Am J Comp L 592–593.

D. Oehler, "Attempted Crimes" (1976) 24 Am J Comp L 696–702.

Criminal Procedure

German Criminal Law, Volume 2: *The Code of Criminal Procedure and The Youth Court Law* Translation by G. Harfst and O. Schmidt (1989: Harfst Verlag, Würzburg).

W. Beulke, *Strafprozessrecht*, 5th ed. (2001: C.F. Müller, Heidelberg).

E. Brießmann, *Strafrecht und Strafprozeß von A-Z*, 6th ed. (1995: Beck, DTV, C.H. Beck, München).

T. Kleinknecht and H. Meyer-Goßner, *Strafprozeßordnung*, 45th ed. (2001: C.H. Beck, München).

B. Kramer, *Grundbegriffe des Strafverfahrensrechts*, 4th ed. (1999: Kohlhammer, Stuttgart).

J.H. Langbein, *Comparative Criminal Procedure: Germany* (1977: West Pub).

C. Roxin, *Strafverfahrensrecht*, 25th ed. (1998: C.H. Beck, München).

R. Vogler, *Germany: A Guide to the German Criminal Justice System* (1989: Prisoners Abroad, London).

Articles

J. H. Langbein, "Controlling Prosecutors' Discretion in Germany" (1974) 41 U Chi L R 439–467.

D. W. Louisell, "Criminal Discovery: Dilemma Real or Apparent?" (1961) 49 Cal LR 56–103.

G. Schram, "The Obligation to Prosecute in West Germany" (1969) 17 Am J Comp L 627–632.

10

Private law I: the German Civil Code

A Introduction

The German Civil Code (*Das Bürgerliche Gesetzbuch BGB*) unified and codified civil law and is the most important source of private law. It provides the legal basis for all sorts of relationships between private individuals whether they concern areas of business and professions such as contracts of sale, service, lease, etc. or private areas of life like family law and law of succession. The code was devised at the time of the prominence of *laissez-faire* doctrines, and took over twenty years to complete, entering into force on 1 January 1900. The reception of Roman Law—especially concerning the law of obligations—and principles of Germanic Law concerning the law of property can be recognized as factors that have strongly influenced its character.[1] One of the underlying assumptions of the code is that individuals are regarded and mostly treated as equals, therefore the initial absence of social justice within its paragraphs is easy to understand. Over the years the code has had to fit in with changing social and economic circumstances and latterly the requirements of the *Grundgesetz*. This has proved to be more easily achieved than first envisaged because the BGB contains general interpretation clauses (§§ 138, 157 and 242,[2] discussed below) which have been applied with great effect to adapt the other more formal clauses of the code to suit the circumstances of the situation. The BGB is also subject to constitutional challenge and provisions of it have been held to be unconstitutional.

The BGB is described as the centre-piece of all legal education and is usually the first full course that the majority of German law students study. It is considered very abstract, very technical, and too steeped in the Roman juridical mould but nevertheless precise and consistent, especially in the use of legal concepts.

The Introductory Act to the Civil Code (*Einführungsgesetz zum BGB, EGBGB*) determines the relationship, status, and conflict of the rules of the BGB with other laws.[3] This is particularly important because of the influence that the BGB has on many areas of German law, including labour law, commercial law, company law,

---

[1] For historical details refer to Chapter 1.
[2] All paragraphs mentioned in this chapter without any further specification refer to those of the BGB.
[3] See also below, sec. H.

and particularly amendments made in respect of the property law rules in East Germany.

Book One, the general part, provides rules of general application for all of the books of the BGB and indeed, all areas of civil law, which are collected together and placed at the beginning of the BGB. This form of organization is not easy to work with and it can be difficult to see the relevance of the general rules until specific forms of legal transaction, contained in later books of the BGB, are considered, and it is usually necessary to refer back again to the general rules.

Other more specific areas of private law are not governed entirely by the BGB but regulated by special laws such as the Commercial Code (*Handelsgesetzbuch*) for commercial law, the law on limited companies (*Gesetz betreffend die Gesellschaften mit beschränkter Haftung*) and the law on joint stock companies (*Aktiengesetz*) for company law or the law on bills of exchange (*Wechselgesetz*), and the law on cheques (*Scheckgesetz*). These are laws which, to be fully understood in application, are dependent on the BGB for the basic principles. The law of agency, for example, is basically regulated by the BGB but is adjusted for application in the area of commercial law and specific forms of business organization such as partnerships and public and private companies. The basic rules for conditions of a valid contract establishing a company can only be found in the BGB. The relevant company law provisions will provide additional preconditions **only**. It is therefore essential that a basic knowledge and understanding of the BGB is achieved before the other specialist laws are considered.

Apart from the amendments made to the code in over 100 years of validity there have been specific laws enacted which have modified the application of the code. The most notable is the Standard Contracts Act (*AGB-Gesetz*) of 1976[4] but there are many more especially in the area of labour law, for example the Employment Protection Law. Other laws have been directly implanted into the code, for example the Package Tour Contracts Act (*Reisevertragsgesetz*) of 1979 incorporated into the BGB.

Regarded as the most fundamental change of the over 100-year-old code, a substantial and heavily debated reform of the law of obligations, entered into force on the 1 January 2002. Its aim was to implement EC law directives and at the same time simplify the law of obligations by codifying certain areas of developed caselaw. The results of this reform will be highlighted in their relevant context, namely when looking at the law of obligations.[5] A lot of the changes to the BGB were based on EC directives. Thus EC law with its aim of creating a common market and abolishing any restrictions to the four freedoms of movement of goods, persons, capital, and services has to be borne in mind as an important influencing factor in this area.

After 3 October 1990, the BGB replaced the East German civil code (*Zivilgesetzbuch ZGB*) in the new *Länder* of the former Eastern Germany according to Article

---

[4] Now incorporated into the BGB §§ 305–310.
[5] See below sec. C.

230 EGBGB. However, there are provisional regulations in Article 231 et seq. EGBGB.

This book can only give an introduction to the BGB. For more detailed information on this subject refer to the literature mentioned at the end of this chapter. Before we turn to the five different books of the BGB in particular we will have to first examine some aspects that are crucial for understanding the BGB:

(a) the structure (*Systematik*) of the BGB,

(b) "claims" (*Anspruchsgrundlagen*) as a methodical starting point for any solution of private law problems, and

(c) the freedom of contract (*Vertragsfreiheit*) and the principle of abstraction (*Abstraktionsprinzip*) as two major principles of private law.[6]

1 The structure of the BGB

The BGB is divided into five books. It follows a very "mathematical" approach: General rules applicable to all areas of the law precede the more specific rules. Thus, by analogy to multiplication in mathematics, the general rules are *placed* "before the brackets" as "common factors". The reason for this is to avoid needless repetition throughout the BGB.

As a consequence, Book One (§§ 1–240) deals with general concepts of law (*Allgemeiner Teil*) and definitions including amongst others: natural and legal persons, capacity, the legal transaction—especially the general preconditions for a valid contract, mistake, duress, and agency. These general concepts apply to all other books of the BGB and in many other legal areas unless specific rules apply to the exclusion of the general rules.

Example: Legal conditions for a contract of inheritance are found in the fifth book (Law of Succession). However, as this is still a specific form of a contract between at least two people based on their mutual agreement the general rules of contract, mapped out in Book One (General Part), are applicable in order to determine its validity. They are only supplemented by conditions of Book Five (§§ 2274 et seq.).

Book Two (§§ 241–853) deals with the law of obligations (*Schuldrecht*). This contains general concepts of obligations law up to § 432 and a special part (§§ 433–853). The special part contains rules for specific types of contract, such as sale, service, rent and also for non-contractual obligations, such as those resulting from unjustified enrichment and tort.

---

[6] For a more elaborate introduction refer to D. Leipold, *BGB I Einführung und Allgemeiner Teil* (1999: Mohr Siebeck, Tübingen) pp. 35–78.

Book Three (§§ 854–1296) concerns property law (*Sachenrecht*) and contains rules regarding possession as the factual control over an object, and ownership, the legal control over an object. It regulates in particular the acquisition and loss of ownership and the establishment of other property rights. It distinguishes between "movable objects" and "immovable objects" meaning estates. The latter might be comparable to "land law".

Book Four (§§ 1297–1921) deals with family law (*Familienrecht*) which has been subject to much amendment, particularly in the period following the Second World War. The values of the nineteenth century have been replaced with those of the second half of the twentieth century. The legal norms in family law cover the personal and economic position of the members of a family towards one another and towards third parties. Book Four can be separated into three parts: civil marriage §§ 1297–1588 (*Bürgerliche Ehe*); relatives §§ 1589–1772 (*Verwandtschaft*), and guardianship §§ 1773–1921 (*Vormundschaft*).

Book Five (§§ 1922–2385): The law of succession (*Erbrecht*) regulates the fate of property which the deceased has left. The law of succession is regulated by several laws, primarily the general law of succession found in the BGB which is divided into nine sections. The BGB regulates only the private law of succession and does not concern itself with the participation of the state in the matters of succession. Rules from other books of the BGB also apply where relevant, in particular those from property and family law.

2 Method of addressing private law problems: finding the claim (*Anspruchsgrundlage*)

The solution of private law problems is centred around finding a legal base that grants one party a claim against another (*Anspruchsgrundlage*). Paragraph 194 I BGB, which provides a general rule on lapse of time (*en passant*), gives a definition of the term "claim" (= *Anspruch*):

> "The *right to demand an action or omission from somebody else (claim)* is subject to lapse of time."[7]

Thus a claim covers any right to demand actions or omissions from another party and will be the basis of any civil action brought against that party. As a consequence, when solving a private law problem the first step to take is to find the relevant legal basis as created or declared by *statute*,[8] namely in the BGB.

---

[7] Paragraph 194 I BGB is the classical example of a "definition laid down by law" (*Legaldefinition*).
[8] As to contractual obligations, however, the contract itself is the legal basis, BGB provisions being declaratory.

Examples:

(1) *A* sells *B* his car but does not hand it over. *B* can now claim the transfer of the property of the car because of § 433 I 1 BGB, which states that where a contract of sale has been concluded the seller has to hand over the object of sale.

(2) *A* lends his book to *B*. Later a third person, *C* takes the book off *B* without him noticing it. If *A* demands back his book from *C* he cannot rely on contractual agreements between him and *B* as they have no effect on *C*. Here § 985 BGB gives *A* a claim against anyone who is in factual possession of the book on the mere basis of his ownership.

(3) After her divorce Mrs *A* raises her two-year-old son on her own but does not find the time to work in order to provide a living. Here § 1570 BGB constitutes the legal basis for her claim for maintenance against her former husband. It provides that a divorced spouse can claim maintenance from the other spouse if and in as far as he or she cannot be expected to find an occupation because he or she is taking care of the mutual child.

Once the relevant legal basis is found it will have to be examined as to its applicability, namely all the preconditions mentioned in the provision. Thus only if these conditions mentioned on the factual side of the legal basis (*Tatbestandsseite*) are fulfilled, will the legal consequences (*Rechtsfolgen*) amount to particular claim.[9] This means that in Example 1 all preconditions to a valid contract of sale will have to be examined. In Example 2, *A*'s ownership will have to be established. Example 3 demands that the marriage between Mrs and Mr *A* has been effectively divorced and that Mrs *A* is raising the mutual child and that as a consequence of this she cannot be expected to search for an occupation.

Thus no matter what eye-catching legal problems seem to present themselves in a case, the way to any solution has to start with the legal basis for a claim or several claims of the relevant parties in order to allow a structured approach.

Once it has been established that a claim has come into existence then all possible grounds for the extinction of the claim have to be examined. In Example 1, the claim under § 433 I 1 BGB might have entered into force but no longer exists if *A* has in the meantime handed over the car. Or the car might have been destroyed and can no longer be handed over. Thus performance is impossible and the claim is extinguished. However, there might be a secondary claim to compensation. Finally, a claim might still exist but might be not enforceable, for example because of lapse of time.

---

[9] See also above section on legal methods, Chapter 2, sec. 3.

3 Major principles

3.1 Freedom of contract (*Vertragsfreiheit*)

The BGB was produced in the era of classical individualism and *laissez-faire* which led to the presumption that the state should not interfere with the choice and rights of individual self autonomy. This meant a "hands off" policy by governments in respect of the arrangements and agreements that businessmen made. How they decided to formulate clauses in contracts was up to them because a contract represented the freely negotiated position of the two parties. Indeed, even following the Second World War, Article 2 I *Grundgesetz*, concerned with the free development of personality, applicable also to legal persons, seems to have supported this concept and to have given the nineteenth century development a twentieth century encouragement. However, this freedom was never absolute and limits have applied which can be seen most clearly in the area of labour law. While freedom of contract retains important ideological connections with the mixed market economy, some limits are imposed on this but not so as to totally destroy any idea of the freedom of contract, as can be seen in the importance placed on the intent of the individual in connection with the principle of abstraction in contract law, considered below.

The autonomy of the parties' will presupposes that there is an equality of bargaining power of the parties to a contract. In some contracts this is obviously and patently not so and sometimes the law may step in to protect one party. This has occurred more often, as with General Conditions of Business Act (*Gesetz zur Regelung des Rechts der Allgemeinen Geschäftsbedingungen AGBG*),[10] the equivalent of the Unfair Contract Terms Act in the UK.

Two different aspects of the freedom of contract are identified: the freedom to conclude contracts and the freedom to decide the content of contracts.

3.1.1 *The freedom to conclude contracts (Abschlußfreiheit)*

Theoretically, the freedom exists to decide whether and with whom a contract can be concluded. This right should not be limited to force a person to contract with others (*Privatautonomie*). It follows that it includes a right to discriminate. Where the right to conclude a contract is concerned Article 3 I GG (principle of non-discrimination) cannot be invoked by one party as the other party is a private person. Fundamental rights such as Article 3 I GG cannot be used horizontally between private individuals but only vertically—against the state.[11] It is, however, limited by a person's individual capacity, as discussed below, or less frequently restricted by statute, for example monopoly powers have no choice, they must supply gas, electricity, or train services (*Kontrahierungszwang*).

---

[10] Now incorporated into the BGB §§ 305–310.
[11] Note however, that there can be an indirect or "Third" effect of fundamental rights, see Chapter 7, sec. 1.5.

Paragraph 826, for example, is held to include a ban on rejecting contracts on racial grounds.

3.1.2 *The freedom to decide the content of contracts (Inhaltsfreiheit or Gestaltungsfreiheit)*

This aspect of the freedom gave the right to deviate from statutory proscribed forms of contract and to choose novel forms of contract or combine types of legal relations and types of contracts (also termed *Typenfreiheit*). An example of this can be found in the security rights developed for movable objects in property law, considered below. This right, however, is subject to general limits imposed both by the BGB and the constitution, especially where they concern legality and morality.[12]

There is today an increasing amount of control and management of many aspects of the economy by government. This arises from concerns for particular areas such as the environment or consumers and results in a considerable restriction in the freedom of parties to conclude contracts as they wish, for example the cartel and anti-trust laws forbid certain kinds of contract between businesses.

Paragraph 242 is another general clause which has been used very effectively to limit the excesses of contractual freedom. This requires all contracts to be performed "in good faith" (*nach Treu und Glauben*) and is considered in further detail below.

A further form of freedom which is often confused but also overlaps with the freedom of content of a contract, is that of the freedom of the form of the contract (*Formfreiheit*). In some circumstances a certain form of contract is imposed, such as in contracts for the purchase and sale of land or those involving gifts (see §§ 311b I and 518) which require notarial form. Other property law, family law, succession, and corporate contracts are also subject to the adoption of a particular form as determined by the relevant provisions. Examples are contracts for long term leases (§ BGB 550), guarantees (§ BGB 766), or the making of one's will (§ 2247) which all require a written form. Particular requirements concerning the written or notarial form are outlined by §§ 126–129.

3.2 **The principle of abstraction (*Abstraktionsprinzip*)**

The principle of abstraction is one of the most complicated and most important principles of German private law. It is the result of the adoption of very obtuse Roman legal principles of law into the German civil code and is an example of how logical analysis of the law breaks down a legal transaction into separate components. These components are independent from each other. As a consequence even if one of them is invalid the rest remains effective. Consider the following (classical) example:

---

[12] See, e.g. §§ 134 and 138 BGB. See also below.

> **Example:** *B* buys a newspaper from the vendor *V*. He hands over the money while V gives him the paper. This purchase which in other legal systems would be qualified as one transaction, in fact one contract (contract of sale), is divided into three different contracts under German law: an agreement to sell/purchase the newspaper (contract of sale, § 433 BGB), the transfer of property of the newspaper (contract of transfer of property, § 929 1st sentence BGB) and the transfer of the property of the money (again a contract of transfer of property § 929 1st sentence BGB).

Obviously, this artificial division of "one transaction" complicates its legal assessment at first glance. Indeed, only a few people in Germany (apart from the lawyers of course) would be aware of the fact that they were concluding three contracts instead of one in such a situation. Its purpose, however, will become apparent when looking at a third person's interest, for example, where a person sells something not belonging to him, the real owner still retains his ownership because a valid contract of transferring ownership does not exist. To elaborate on this, we will have to look at the special status ownership (*Eigentum*) has under German private law and the distinction between two different categories of transaction: *Verpflichtungs-* und *Verfügungsgeschäfte*.

3.3 Possession and ownership (*Besitz und Eigentum*)

German (property) law draws a distinction between mere factual possession and ownership. According to § 854 I BGB "possession" (= *Besitz*) describes the factual control over an object. Ownership (*Eigentum*, § 903 BGB), on the other hand, simply defines who is the legal owner or proprietor of the object. Possession and ownership may be held by the same person but this must not necessarily be the case.

> **Examples:** The tenant of a house will be in possession of the house but it is the landlord who (usually) is the proprietor or owner. If *A* lends his bike to *B* for a couple of days he does not cease to be owner. *B* is merely possessor of the bike. However, if *C* steals the bike from *B* he now becomes the possessor, as he has the factual control over the bike. This still does not affect *A*'s ownership.

The purpose of this distinction is to identify the rights between owner and possessor and to guarantee peace under the law. Thus the BGB assumes that a possessor has a right to the possession of the object in question and grants him several rights to protect his possession. In the above case *B* would have been entitled to defend his possession.[13] However, once *C* has stolen the bike, *B* cannot simply take it back

---

[13] See below, sec. E, on property law for details.

by force—unless *C* is caught red-handed—but has to resort to the courts. *C* is presumed to have a right to possession unless decided otherwise. That way peace under the law is ensured.

The presumptions of rightful possession have an impact on third parties. If the possessor transfers the object in question to a third party, that party will assume his right to do so. What now if the possessor had no right to possession or at least not a right to transfer the object that belonged to someone else?

Example: *B* steals *A*'s sculpture and sells it to *C*. Can *A* demand the sculpture back from *C*?

Paragraph 985 BGB provides the owner of an object with a claim against the possessor. The first thing to examine is whether *A* is still the owner of the object and *C* the possessor. Clearly *C* is now in possession of the sculpture. *A* used to be the owner. Now it has to be resolved whether his ownership could have been affected by the events leading up to *C*'s possession of the sculpture. Unsurprisingly, theft does not end *A*'s ownership. However, there was a transaction between *B* and *C*. As with the example under the previous section, the sale consisted of three contracts: the contract of sale—putting *B* under the obligation to deliver the sculpture and *C* under the obligation to hand over the money—and a contract transferring ownership of the sculpture from *B* to *C* as well as a contract transferring ownership of the money from *C* to *B*. As § 935 I BGB states that no ownership can be obtained over stolen goods, *C* has never become owner of the sculpture, even if he was in good faith. *A* is still the owner and can claim the sculpture back from *C* according to § 985 BGB.

For *C* this means that the contract of transfer of ownership of the sculpture was not effective. Due to the principle of abstraction this fault does not effect the validity of the other two contracts. There is still a contract of sale (which is purely obligatory) and a valid contract transferring the money from *C* to *B*. *C* will have to address this injustice by claiming compensation against *B* on the grounds of non-performance of the (still effective) contract of sale.

This case shows how the principle of abstraction protects the interests of the real owner not involved in the transaction. At the same time it leaves in force the contract of sale thus giving the damaged party a variety of claims because of non-performance against the breaching party.

3.4 *Verpflichtungs- und Verfügungsgeschäfte*: Two different categories of legal transaction

German private law distinguishes between two categories of legal transactions. Those that place an obligation on one or more parties are called *Verpflichtungsge-schäfte*[14] such as contracts of sale, contracts to provide services, and contracts of

---

[14] "transactions of obligation" (suggested translation).

lease or rent. Transactions that immediately affect a right or a legal position, on the other hand, are called *Verfügungsgeschäfte*.[15] The term *Verfügung* can be translated only inadequately as "disposal" in this context. It aims at including any action that **directly** transfers, releases, burdens, or varies a subjective right or legal position. Such a right can include the right of ownership of moveable or immovable things, or a claim. The division between these two categories is referred to as *Trennungsprinzip*.

EXAMPLES: *Verpflichtungsgeschäfte:*

(1) Carpenter C agrees to build a wardrobe for B within three months. This is a contract to provide services (§ 631 I BGB) placing C under the obligation to construct the wardrobe and deliver it to B transferring ownership to him. This has not affected C's position as owner of the material and ultimately the wardrobe. In order to transfer his ownership he has to conclude a different contract with B later on.

(2) A contract of sale creates the obligation for the vendor to hand over and transfer ownership of the object of sale to the buyer (§ 433 I 1 BGB) and the obligation for the buyer to accept the object and to hand over and transfer ownership of the money to the vendor (§ 433 II BGB). Note that at no point this contract affects the ownership of the object. The vendor is still the owner, albeit now under an obligation to transfer his ownership.

Verfügungsgeschäfte:

(3) A classical *Verfügungsgeschäft* is the **transfer** of a right, e.g. the transfer of property of the wardrobe in Example 1 or the transfer of the property of the object of sale in example 2). Such a transaction is a contract in itself, as you need an agreement by the involved parties to transfer the ownership (§ 929 S.1 BGB).

(4) Let us assume that in Example 1 B is not solvent. Thus B and C agree that instead of payment C will be entitled to B's new notebook as soon as the wardrobe is handed over. This agreement is a contract affecting, in fact **varying**, a subjective right: C's claim to payment has been changed into claim to the transfer of property of the notebook.

(5) If in Example 1 the carpenter—for whatever reasons—decided not to charge B and thus concluded a contract with B to waive his claim for payment, this would equally affect his subjective right, the claim. This is an example for the **release** of a right.

(6) Taking up a mortgage on a piece of land would be a **burdening** of the right, because the mortgage directly burdens the right to ownership of the piece of land. It is not as much directly linked to the owner but the rather the piece of land in question (!).

As already mentioned, the principle of abstraction allows *Verpflichtungsgeschäft* and *Verfügungsgeschäft* to exist independently of each other even though they are core

---

[15] Literally, "transactions of disposal".

parts of a something that appears to be one procedure such as the above-mentioned sale of the newspaper. However, the transaction creating the obligation (*Verpflichtungsgeschäft*) is the cause for the subsequent transfer of a right. Thus it is called *Kausalgeschäft* (causal transaction) whereas the transaction that actually affects the right in question is called *Erfüllungsgeschäft* (transaction of performance), as it performs the obligation agreed on earlier. The principle of abstraction now "abstracts" the causal transaction from the transaction of performance. As a consequence if the causal transaction is void—for whatever reasons—the transaction of performance is still valid.

Example: *A* has sold his car to *B*. He has also transferred the property to him. *B* has handed over the money and transferred its ownership. *B* now sells the car to *C* and transfers the ownership to him. If *A* now rescinds the contract of sale, say because of a mistake, it becomes void (§ 142 I BGB). However, *B* is still the owner of the car because the contract transferring the property of the car is not affected. *A* has merely got a claim against *B* to give back the car and transfer back its ownership, because of unjustified enrichment (§ 812 I 1 BGB).[16] The person benefiting from this is *C*. As *B* never lost his position as an owner he could legitimately transfer ownership to *C*. As a third person not informed of the transactions between *A* and *B*, *C* can rely on *B*'s ownership.

Thus the principle of abstraction helps to create legal certainty.[17]

B Book One: the general part

1 Introduction

Book One of the BGB deals with the general concepts of civil law which are not specific to certain forms of legal transaction found in the remaining books of the BGB such as contract of sale, rent, or aspects concerning delict and property amongst others.

2 *Rechtssubjekte* (holders of subjective rights)

In contrast to objects that are affected by legal transactions (*Rechtsobjekte*)—such as movable objects, immovable objects, or claims—*Rechtssubjekte* are persons (inter)-acting under the law through legal transactions, in other words by using rights

---

[16] The same applies to *B* as far as he is claiming his money back.
[17] Even though its complexity might create "uncertainty" as to the law among law students.

allocated to them by law. Thus *Rechtssubjekte* are holders or bearers of subjective rights.

2.1 Natural and legal persons (*Natürliche und Juristische Personen*)

Only natural or legal persons are capable of bearing subjective rights. The term "natural persons" (*Natürliche Personen*) includes all human beings. Legal persons (*Juristische Personen*) are certain associations of persons (e.g. limited companies) or even independently organized capital (such as foundations). The latter two gain legal capacity (*Rechtsfähigkeit*) through certain legal acts, whereas a human being will have legal capacity the moment he or she is born.

2.2 Different forms of legal capacity

The BGB differentiates between different levels of legal capacity, using the terms *Rechtsfähigkeit, Handlungsfähigkeit* and *Geschäftsfähigkeit* to convey different abilities in respect of legal rights and duties. *Rechtsfähigkeit* is the capacity to hold legal rights, i.e. to be legally capable. *Handlungsfähigkeit* is the capacity to perform legally relevant acts, that will result in the acquisition of rights or duties. A qualified form of this is the capacity to conclude legal transactions such as a contract, which is *Geschäftsfähigkeit* ("contractual" capacity[18]).

2.2.1 (General) legal capacity (Rechtsfähigkeit)

Paragraph 1 BGB states "the legal capacity of a human being begins at birth". Legal capacity does not actually determine the capacity to enter into binding contracts or liability for other actions. For these further definition is required. Legal capacity is the ability to be able to hold legal rights.

In certain circumstances babies may derive legal rights whilst in the womb. The BGH has awarded the unborn child legal capacity in certain cases of non-contractual liability according to § 823 I BGB: If through an action of a third person mother and unborn child are suffering damage, (e.g. car accident), then the unborn child is granted a claim for compensation independent of the mother's claim. As the wording of § 823 I BGB only awards such claims to "another person" affected by the tortious act this would only include live persons. Thus, when interpreting the provision, the BGH has considerably extended its applicability to unborn children, guided by the wide protective purpose of § 823 I BGB.[19] A further example exists in respect of the succession rights of an unborn child, also called the *nasciturus*, § 1923 II BGB. It allows for the legal fiction to regard the unborn child as already born at the time of succession—provided it is born subsequently. Thus the unborn child can already be regarded and thus treated as the successor, if his or her father dies before the child's birth.

---

[18] This term is somewhat inadequate because *Geschäftsfähigkeit* includes the ability to conclude any legal transaction, not only contracts and thus goes further than the English term purports. Consequently, we will stick to the German term in the course of this chapter.
[19] BGHZ 58, 48.

Legal capacity ends at death—as can be inferred from the succession provision of § 1922 I BGB, although as with birth the boundaries are not always so distinct. It seems that general opinion is favouring the medical definition of death demanding "brain death" or a stop of all brain activities.[20] In certain cases missing persons can be declared dead under the provisions of the Act on Missing Persons (*Verschollenheitsgesetz*). Such a declaration constitutes presumption of death that can however be rebutted, its purpose being a reversal of the burden of proof.

The BGB, furthermore, provides details of the legal capacity of legal persons (*juristische Personen*). These are contained in §§ 21–88 and include: the association incorporated by membership (*Verein*, §§ 21–79) and the foundation (*Stiftung*, §§ 80 et seq.) with legal capacity. Factually, most associations are those of a non-commercial interests (focusing on religious, cultural, or sports activities). The right to form associations is constitutionally guaranteed in Article 9 I GG. Associations gain legal capacity through official registration (§ 21). Without such registration an association is regarded as not having legal capacity (*nichtrechtsfähiger Verein* § 54). An example for the latter are political parties. Economic associations (§ 22) can be ignored here because most commercially guided associations are founded under specific private laws: The Share Act (AktG § 1 I 1) allows Public or Joint Stock Companies (*Aktiengesellschaften, AG*) and the Limited Liability Company Act (*Gesetz betreffend die Gesellschaften mit beschränkter Haftung*) allows private Limited Companies (*GmbH*) to have legal capacity and personality. In spite of their legal capacities these legal persons need natural persons to act for them, e.g. conclude contracts and manage their affairs, usually the executive committee for associations and the management for companies.[21]

2.2.2 The capacity to perform legal acts (Handlungsfähigkeit)

The capacity to perform legal acts is the ability to obtain rights, undertake duties, and incur liabilities and to enforce legal transactions or obligations. This is regarded as consisting of graduating degrees, the capacity to be held liable for the consequences of one's action when at fault, as in delictual liability, (*Deliktsfähigkeit*, §§ 827–829 BGB),[22] the power to undertake legally binding contracts or transactions (*Geschäftsfähigkeit*). A special form of the latter is the capacity to draw up one's will (*Testierfähigkeit*).[23] These capacities are initially dependant on age. As it is of fundamental importance to the forming of contracts we will now focus on *Geschäftsfähigkeit*.

2.2.3 The capacity to conclude legal transactions (Geschäftsfähigkeit)

The BGB provides the details of by whom and when this capacity can be exercised (see §§ 104–115). *Geschäftsfähigkeit* is the ability to give effective intent to conclude legal transactions.

---

[20] See, e.g. Heinrichs in O. Palandt, *Bürgerliches Gesetzbuch*, 61st ed. (2002: Munich), §1 para. 3; Brox, *Allgemeiner Teil des BGB*, 23rd ed. (1999: Cologne), p. 309; Leipold, above, n 6, p. 301.
[21] See Chapter 11 for details.
[22] See below, sec. D.
[23] See below, sec. G.

2.2.3.1 *Absence of capacity*

Geschäftsfähigkeit is not defined by the BGB but has to be inferred *e contrario* from those provisions that limit this capacity. As a consequence any person not falling under these provisions, that is §§ 104–113 BGB, has the capacity to conclude legally binding transactions. The purpose of §§ 104–113 is to protect those that cannot oversee the legal consequence of their actions from burdening themselves with any legal obligation. Thus § 104 denies *Geschäftsfähigkeit* to children under seven years of age (No 1) and to the insane (§ 104 No 2) and expresses this position as *Geschäftsunfähigkeit*. Any declaration of a will—and thus any transaction—undertaken by a child under seven is void *ab initio*. The same applies to declarations made by any person during phases of unconsciousness or temporary mental instability. Children will be legally represented by their parents according to the family law provisions of §§ 1626, 1629 BGB.

2.2.3.2 *Limited capacity (Beschränkte Geschäftsfähigkeit)*

Paragraphs 106–113 deal with the limited business capacity of children between the ages of seven and eighteen. Transactions carried out by them may in certain cases be valid, namely where there is parental approval (§§ 107 2nd–alternative 109) or where the transaction entails nothing but a legal advantage to these minors (§ 107 1st alternative). Again, the dominating concept of protecting minors (*Minderjährigenschutz*) becomes apparent: in both mentioned cases no further legal protection is needed.

Paragraph 107 states that if the transaction or rather the declaration of his will bestows only a legal advantage it is valid. Emphasis lies on the legal character of the advantage. Thus even concluding a contract entailing a highly economical benefit for the minor would be void, e.g. purchase of a valuable collector's stamp worth millions of *Euro* for a few *Cent*. The reason is that the entering into a contract of sale burdens a minor with a legal obligation which in our example is to transfer the property of his money. In other words, contracts can have both advantages and disadvantages. Whilst gaining a claim to certain goods (that is the transfer or ownership thereof) is an advantage, having to pay for them is a disadvantage (being the obligation to transfer ownership of the money).

Here the different categories of transaction have to be kept in mind: transactions of obligation (*Verpflichtungsgeschäfte*) are only of benefit to the minor if they place an obligation solely on the other party, such as a contract to give an estate of land to the minor. Here the minor receives a claim to transfer of ownership of the object in question.

Where a subjective right is affected directly by a contract (*Verfügungsgeschäft*) in favour of the minor (e.g. a contract transfering property or burdening a piece of land with a mortgage in his favour) the contract will also be valid as the minor acquires an additional legal position. Even where an estate is already burdened with a mortgage a contract to transfer ownership of that piece of land to a minor would still be advantageous to him, because the mortgage does not place an obligation on him directly. As a property related right the mortgage is primarily linked to the estate itself not to the owner of the estate. In its worst case the minor will only have to tolerate the enforcement of the mortgage affecting the estate whereas he himself is not placed under any new legal burden. He would not be liable personally.

General opinion even allows indifferent or neutral transactions to be valid. These are transactions without negative effect on the minor. Even if they do not entail a legal benefit he does not need any protection, as they do not produce a disadvantage either.[24]

Example: A minor takes part in a contract by determining the purchasing price of sale as impartial third person according to § 317 I BGB.

Another category of transactions with minors of this age group participating consists of contracts concluded with the parental approval (basically regulated by §§ 107 2nd alternative–109). The BGB distinguishes between prior approval (*Einwilligung*, § 183) and subsequent consent (*Genehmigung*, § 184) both of which are forms of assent (*Zustimmung*, § 182). If the minor concludes a contract without prior parental approval, its validity depends on the subsequent consent ratifying it (§ 108). Until then the contract cannot take legal effect. It is pending validity (*schwebend unwirksam*). This undesirable situation can be influenced by the other contracting or third party: if this party was not aware of the minor's lacking capacity, he is entitled to revocation (*Widerruf* § 109 I). Alternatively, the third party can ask the parents to give a decision on the matter of consent. If no decision is communicated to third party within two weeks, approval will be presumed to be rejected (§ 108 II) and the transaction cannot take any legal effect. Should the minor reach unlimited legal capacity during that time, his approval will replace that of his parents. Note that where subsequent consent is given, the contract will take effect from the moment it was concluded.

A special form of approval can be seen by the "provision on pocket money" (*Taschengeldparagraph*, § 110) whereby "means" (e.g. money) given by the parents to the minor is taken as a general agreement to purchase items which are normal for a child of that age in terms of subject matter and value. Purchasing a lottery ticket with pocket money would thus be covered by this provision. However, the sale of a car, won in the same lottery, would no longer be seen as "means" given to the minor even though the acquisition of the car was based on the pocket money. A contract of sale to be performed by the minor by paying with his pocket money in instalments is not covered by § 110 either.

Finally, the BGB allows minors between seven and eighteen years partial capacity (*partielle Geschäftsfähigkeit*), meaning that in certain areas their capacity will not be limited by their parents' consent. These are contracts concluded in pursuit of a business enterprise the running of which has the express approval of the parents or

---

[24] Brox, above, n. 20, p. 134; Leipold, above, n. 6, p. 97.

legal guardian (§ 112) and necessary contracts arising from a contract of employment which has been previously concluded with parental approval (§ 113).

3 The legal transaction (*Das Rechtsgeschäft*)

The concept of the legal transaction combines a number of principles such as contractual freedom, but is mainly built upon the declaration of intent (*Willenserklärung*) §§ 116–144. It requires at least one expression of intention which is sufficient to constitute a one sided legal transaction such as giving notice to terminate a contract of employment or the making of a will. Legal acts usually contain two or more intentions, as in the most common legal act, the contract. Neither the term *Rechtsgeschäft* nor *Willenserklärung* are explained by the BGB, although they are constantly used by it. They have been defined instead by academics—in a very abstract manner.

3.1 Declaration of intent (*Willenserklärung*)

An expression of intent or declaration of will encompasses any statements or action aimed to achieve a distinct legal outcome. It is the central term within the general part of the BGB as it constitutes the most important element of any legal transaction. Thus it has to be distinguished from other statements of purely social effects without legal attachments such as an invitation to dinner. In German law two aspects of intent are considered: the external or objective aspect (*objektiver Tatbestand*), which is the expressed declaration, and the internal or subjective aspect (*subjektiver Tatbestand*), which is what the person actually intended or desired.

3.1.1 Elements of the declaration of intent
The external or objective aspect is the actual manifestation of the will. It is the means used to express the declaration and may be written or spoken and can also include forms of meaningful conduct or movement, known as *konkludentes Verhalten*. This can therefore be regarded as a form of implied intent, which is equally as valid and binding as express intent under German contract law. The selection of goods in a supermarket and taking them to the check-out makes it clear that the buyer has expressed the intention to purchase.

The internal or subjective aspect is the actual intent or requirement or desire behind the expression, which cannot arise from an unconscious movement, such as somebody jerking their hand whilst asleep in an auction. There are three vital elements of this subjective aspect:

(a) *Handlungswille* (general intention to act),
(a) *Erklärungsbewußtsein* (conscious declaration of intent), and
(a) *Geschäftswille* (business intent).

The general intention to act is known as the *Handlungswille*, whereby the person must have intended to physically act, to make a movement. Thus the above-mentioned movement during sleep, for example, is not guided by this *Handlungswille* and therefore already lacks the first element of the subjective aspect of a declaration of intent.

The conscious declaration of intent (*Erklärungsbewußtsein*) is the realization that the action is committing the person to the specific act, in other words that it is of legal effect.

(**Classical text book**) **Example:**[25] *A* waves a hand to greet his friend *B* in a traditional wine cellar in Trier. At this time a wine auction is being held, which *A* has not realized. His movement is mistaken for a bid and accepted. *A* acted without legal intent because despite the intent to act there was no consciousness that the act had any further legal significance. Because of this lacking *Erklärungsbewußtsein* there would be no valid declaration. However, in such cases the interests of third parties have to be taken into account as well. Should *A* in this case be bound by his action?

This problem is heavily disputed by academics and the courts.[26] It seems that whereas some still demand an effective *Erklärungsbewußtsein* to constitute a legally binding declaration of intent the general opinion differentiates: if the mistake made by the person acting can be attributed to him, then he should be bound by it. For our example, this would have the following consequences: If the auctioneer was right to interpret *A*'s action as a bid then it will be regarded as an effective and binding declaration of intent—but it could be rescinded on the grounds of mistake. If the auctioneer, on the other hand, could have determined that *A* was a tourist and thus not acquainted with the local tradition of wine auctions being held in wine cellars then the action will not be regarded as a bid.[27] The BGH takes a similar view, as can be seen in the following case:

BGHZ 91, 324 (or NJW 1984, 2279)

Willenserklärung trotz fehlenden Erklärungsbewußtseins

In this case the plaintiff, a company producing sheds of steel, had demanded security from one of its clients. The client accepted a bill of exchange and agreed to arrange for security. A few days later the plaintiff received a letter from the defendant, a bank, referring to a guarantee they had taken over for the client. Two weeks later—after the

---

[25] See H.J. Musielak, *Grundkurs BGB*, 6th ed. (1999) p. 38 or Brox, above, n. 20, p. 74.
[26] See references made by BGH NJW1984, 2279 and Leipold, above, n. 6, pp. 170–171.
[27] Leipold, above, n. 6, p. 170, Brox, above, n. 20, p. 74.

plaintiffs had communicated to the defendant the outstanding debts of the client—the defendant sent a second letter denying that they had taken over any security. They explained that the first letter was based on a mistake: the responsible branch had referred to a guarantee which had previously been the object of negotiations but which had never come into existence. The letter had not been meant as a declaration to act as guarantor but had merely mentioned or referred to a security that in fact did not exist. Thus the defendant argued there had not been a conscious declaration of intent (*Erklärungsbewußtsein*) and consequently no valid offer to act as guarantor. The BGH disagreed. It held that *Erklärungsbewußtsein* is no absolute requirement for a valid declaration of intent. If the consciousness to make a legally effective declaration is lacking a valid declaration will still be assumed provided it can be attributed to the person acting, in this case the defendant. Even though they were not consciously making an offer any reasonable third person would have interpreted the first letter as an offer. The defendants thus were bound by their first letter. Although rescission of the declaration was now possible this would entail an obligation to compensate damaged negative interest of the claimants.

The final element of the subjective aspect of a declaration of intent is business intent (*Geschäftswille*) to conclude a particular contract and whose action is intended for this purpose. This might be missing where a person knows that his action constitutes a legally relevant action but is mistaken as to its particular effect.

Example: An employer signs a piece of paper thinking it to be an increase of salary for his employee when in fact it is a termination of the contract of employment. Here the intent to bring about a particular legal effect is missing (*Geschäftswille*). However, as the employer knew he was making a legally relevant decision here, he should have taken more care to study the paper signed. Thus he will be bound by his action.

Where there is a conflict and the subjective and objective elements of a declaration of intent do not correspond, as in the aforementioned case, the courts will often be required to interpret the facts. The BGB provides them rules of interpretation concerning declarations of intent and contracts. They will be considered below.[28]

3.1.2 The effectiveness of a declaration of intent (Wirksamwerden)

A distinction has to be drawn between declarations of intent requiring receipt (*empfangsbedürftige Willenserklärungen*) and those that need not be received (*nicht empfangsbedürftige Willenserklärungen*) by another party to become effective. The latter will become effective the moment they are made, such as testaments

---

[28] See below sec. 4. These rules of interpretation supplement those concerning the interpretation of statutes (considered above, Chapter 2, sec. 3.4.)

(§ 2247) because in this case no interests of third parties have to be taken into account.[29] Declarations that need to be received by another person, on the other hand, obviously have to be communicated to him. Oral declarations made towards persons that are present—including telephone conversations—pose less of a problem as long as there are no acoustic obstructions. Where written declarations are made to absent persons their interests have to be taken into account. Thus the declaration will only become effective if it has been received by the addressee (§ 130 I BGB). The term receipt (*"Zugang"*) does not require the addressee to actually have read the declaration. It rather demands that the person making the declaration has directed it to the addressee, that it reached the addressee's "sphere of control" (*Machtbereich*) and that the addressee could have been expected to take notice of it.

Example: *A* delivers a letter into *B*'s letter box at 10:00 p.m. Here *B* can only be expected to have taken notice of it the next morning. Thus the declaration will not be effective before that, unless *B* in fact finds and reads it before.

The use of electronic device (telex, e-mail) to transmit declarations also is covered by the rules of § 130 BGB.[30] The declaration will not take effect if it is revoked before or at least at the same time at which it is received (§ 130 I 2nd sentence).

Special provisions on revocation of declarations of intent protecting the consumer can now, after the *Schuldrechtsreform*, be found in the law of obligations.[31]

3.2 The "real act" (*Realakt*)

So-called "real acts" have to be distinguished from declarations of intent. Although they do not express an intention they may be necessary to bring about a legal effect.

Example: In order to transfer the ownership of a movable object § 929 (1st sentence) prescribes that the present owner has to hand over the object to the acquirer and both have to agree on the transfer of ownership. In other words, the contract to transfer ownership consists of two declarations of intent (an offer by the owner and an acceptance by the acquirer to transfer ownership) as well as a real act, the actual handing over of the object.

---

[29] However, other criteria may be required such as the form of writing or notarization, see also sec. G on succession.
[30] Leipold, above, n. 6, pp. 114–115.
[31] See below, sec. C.

3.3 The legal transaction (*Das Rechtsgeschäft*)

Legal transaction (*Rechtsgeschäft*) is the general term comprising all legal acts that bring about a legal consequence or effect. There are different categories of transactions. Their qualification may depend on how many persons are involved, whether they entail obligations (*Verpflichtungsgeschäfte*) or direct effects on a subjective right (*Verfügungsgeschäfte*), or whether they oblige only one or more parties.

The one-sided legal transaction (*einseitiges Rechtsgeschäft*) constitutes the simplest form. It consists of only one declaration of intent, such as a notice of termination of employment or the making of a will. No further elements are needed here. These transactions have to be divided into those requiring receipt and those that do not.[32] Two-sided legal transactions (*zweiseitige Rechtsgeschäfte*) require two declarations of intent, the most classical example being a contract between two parties. Finally, there are legal transactions concluded by more than two parties (*mehrseitige Rechtsgeschäfte*), such as company decisions (*Gesellschaftsbeschlüsse*) that are reached by an agreement of several partners.

Two-sided legal transactions entailing obligations can be subdivided into those that only entail obligations for one party, such as a contract to give something to someone (*einseitig verpflichtende Verträge*) and those that entail obligations for both parties, such as a contract of sale (*zweiseitig verpflichtende Verträge*).

The distinction between *Verpflichtungs- und Verfügungsgeschäfte* has already been explained.[33]

3.4 The contract (*Der Vertrag*)

A contract is defined as a legal act consisting of two or more declarations of intent, both corresponding with one another and aiming at bringing about a particular legal effect.[34] They are usually termed *Angebot* or *Antrag* and *Annahme* which corresponds with the English offer and acceptance.[35] A contract is therefore completed on the acceptance of an offer.[36] The position in German law is that offer and acceptance are both declarations of intent, offer being prior and acceptance being subsequent.

3.4.1 *Offer (Angebot)*

The offer is a declaration of intent which must be received by the other party. Under § 130 I, an offer only becomes effective when received by the other party, if not made in the presence of the offeree. Offers made in the actual presence of the offeree or to those in direct contact, i.e. by telephone, must be accepted immediately to remain effective (§ 147 I BGB). Any delay will cause the offer to lapse automatically. An offer has to contain all essential aspects of the desired contract.

---

[32] See above subsection 3.1.2, this section.
[33] See above, sec. A. 3.4.
[34] Heinrichs in Palandt, above, n. 20, Einf.v.§ 145, para. 1.
[35] Notwithstanding that there are some legal differences between the terms.
[36] Note that "**Consideration**" is not a requirement for a valid contract in German Law!

In other words, it must be phrased in such a way that it can be accepted by a mere "yes" of the other party.

Under § 145, whoever makes an offer capable of being accepted, is bound by the offer for the time specified in the offer (§ 148), or if no time is specified, is bound to keep the offer open for a reasonable time. This is defined under § 147 II as up to the time by which the offeror may expect an answer under ordinary circumstances.

Under § 147 I, an offer is open to immediate acceptance only by those to whom it is made if that person is either present or in contact by telephone. The result is that most "offers" in Germany are not offers but as with shop displays would be regarded as "invitations to treat". This is known in Germany under the Latin expression *invitatio ad offerendum*. Here the shopkeeper does not consider himself bound by the "invitation" made through his shop display or an advertisement as his capacity to conclude contracts will be limited by his stock.

However, in keeping with ideas of contractual freedom the offeror can avoid being bound to keep an offer open by including the word *freibleibend* (subject to change) or *widerruflich* (revocable) or *ohne Obligo* (without obligation). Any enquiries as a result or offers made by the other party to the invitation to treat would be treated as an offer.

The offer is extinguished if it has either been turned down, in which case this declaration must be received by the offeror, if the acceptance is not received in time (§ 146). The same applies in cases of an acceptance varying the original offer (= counter-offer) or late acceptance. Counter-offer or late acceptance will be treated as a new offers themselves (§ 150 I, II).

3.4.2 *Acceptance (Annahme)*

The rule is that acceptance, which is also a declaration of intent under § 130 in the same way as an offer, is effective on arrival, i.e. on receipt. Acceptance must be congruent with the offer in other words unreserved and unconditional. This is important where offers are left open for a reasonable time or in respect of posting. Therefore the German "posting rule" is that it is binding on receipt. This is interpreted to mean, in a business context, within the sphere of influence (*Machtbereich*) of the recipient and in respect of letters when it would be reasonably expected the letter would be collected from the mailbox.

Under § 130 I, an offer or acceptance will not be effective if a revocation reaches the other party before or at the same time. Therefore, if an offer or acceptance is to be effectively revoked, the revocation must arrive sooner than or at least simultaneously with the original.

Unless an offer is accepted in reasonable time the offer will be extinguished (§ 146). Acceptance is only possible by those to whom an offer is made (§ 147 I). A late acceptance is viewed as a new or counter offer, as are changes or additions (§ 150 II).

Problems exist with the battle of the forms, when firms accept by sending their own pre-printed acceptance form with different conditions which will be discussed when dealing with *Dissens*.[37]

---

[37] See below, sec. 3.4.4.

Apart from meaningful conduct, silence would not normally constitute an objective expression of intent with the exception of where it is a usual form of conduct between trading or business partners (§ 151) or in special cases of commercial relations under § 362 HGB.

Paragraph 151 outlines the situations on which the receipt of an acceptance is not necessary for the completion of a binding contract. Nevertheless some form of acceptance is still necessary. It will simply manifest itself in a different way. Examples are the booking of a hotel room by post or where acceptance has been waived by the offeror, such as with the order and dispatch of mail order goods without acknowledgement. Thus it is only the receipt of the declaration of acceptance that is omitted not the actual expression of intent itself, which, for example, is made clear by the hotel's reserving the hotel rooms through registering the booking or the use of the goods sent by mail.

Silence, in general, cannot constitute an acceptance. However, there are circumstances in which silence can be taken to be a valid declaration of intent particularly when concerned with previous practice, whereby a contract may arise by the acceptance of an offer without notification of acceptance. Silence in commercial law can be acceptable, see §§ 346, 362 HGB. These provisions of the commercial code provide for the applicability of customary law between merchants. The classical example here is the commercial letter of confirmation (*kaufmännisches Bestätigungsschreiben*). The terms of an orally concluded contract between merchants are usually summarized in a letter of confirmation by one party and sent to the other. If this letter contains variations from the original agreement but the other party fails to protest against it then silence will be classified as acceptance of this "new" offer according to customary merchant law.

Finally, auctions which are also an exception to the general rule are governed by § 156 whereby the fall of the hammer, the adjudication, is deemed to be the acceptance.

3.4.3 *"Factual contract"* (faktisches Vertragsverhältnis)

This concept has been invented in order to come to grips with the problem of people using public services without the intention to pay for it. It has been argued that this intention has been replaced by typical social conduct (*sozialtypisches Verhalten*) and that this factual contractual relationship (*faktisches Vertragsverhältnis*) dispenses with the need for the declarations and does not come within a true consideration of contract law. To some extent the courts followed this line of thought, as evidenced by the first of many parking place cases.

BGHZ 21, 319 Hamburger Parkplatz Fall

A car owner refused to pay for car parking in a new park with a car park attendant and said she had no intention of paying or forming a contract. The BGH held that a

> contractual relationship had nevertheless arisen through the actual parking of the car in the parking place, and despite the expressed intention. It was the factual relationship that was important to the forming of the contract rather than the subjective intention of the car owner. This would mean that revocation in such circumstances could not be effective.

Despite the more than fifty-year history, the idea of typical social conduct is still the subject of divided academic opinion, as to how it can be brought into line with the legal philosophy of the BGB. Another line of argument suggests that the acceptance and thus contract is formed from the meaningful conduct of parking the car as the true expression, despite the contrary stated expression. Thus the declaration of not wanting to pay for a service will be interpreted as incompatible with the actual conduct of, for example, parking the car in a public car park. Consequently it will be held to be a declaration to conclude a contract. The declaration of not wanting to do so will be seen as contravening principles of good faith. This school of thought seems to be the dominating opinion now.[38]

3.4.4 Lack of agreement in formation (Dissens)

Offer and acceptance must agree. Where there is a lack of agreement a distinction is raised between a conscious and unconscious failure to agree.

3.4.4.1 Open lack of agreement (Offener Dissens)

This is where the parties know they are not in agreement. The legal consequences of this depend on whether any agreement has been reached. If the lack of agreement is on fundamental points, the contract fails *ab initio*, if it is on side issues it will depend on the parties' intention whether the contract should go ahead or not. This intention has to be found by interpretation. As a rule, given in § 154 I, in cases of doubt no contract has been concluded.

3.4.4.2 Hidden lack of agreement (Versteckter Dissens)

This refers to a lack of agreement or ambiguity which the parties do not know about (§ 155). If the lack of agreement concerns fundamental aspects on which they can't agree, there is no contract. If it concerns secondary aspects, § 155 allows the contract to go ahead, but only if parties would have gone ahead even if they knew that the point was not considered. The latter provision thus manifests another rule of interpretation to help define the parties' previous intentions.

3.4.4.3 Battle of forms

Problems arise where one firm links its offer to its pre-printed terms and conditions (*Allgemeine Geschäftsbedingungen*) and the other firm accepts—but on its own terms and conditions. As this is a case of lack of agreement the contract will thus be interpreted according to the rule of §§ 154, 155. In such cases where the parties

---

[38] See Heinrichs in Palandt, above, n. 20, Einf.v. § 145 para. 25; Brox, above, n. 20, pp. 99–100; Leipold, above, n. 6, p. 86 with further references.

have performed and then discover a mistake in the conditions of the offer and the acceptance the courts will interpret the contract on the basis of the common ground and in cases of difference apply the provisions of §§ 133, 157, and 242 BGB, as discussed below.[39] The BGH has held that accepting the performance of a contract in such a case and afterwards claiming the original acceptance to be a counter-offer (§ 150 II) contravened the principle of good faith and was thus inadmissible.[40]

4 Interpretation rules (*Auslegung*)

German judges are able to rely principally on three general paragraphs—§§ 133, 157, and 242 in the BGB in order to define the exact content of legal transactions, including declarations of intent and contracts.

4.1 Paragraph 133

This provides that in the interpretation of a declaration the true intention shall be sought without the need to adhere to the literal meaning of the declaration. Paragraph 133 therefore looks at what was really intended and is thus a subjective interpretation and is supposedly the first test applied by the courts to the declarations of the parties. The classical example often employed is the *Haaksjöringsköd* case, decided by the *Reichsgericht* in 1920:

RGZ 99, 147 Haaksjöringsköd-Fall

The defendant had sold the plaintiff 214 barrels of *"Haakjöringsköd"*. Both parties believed this term to be the Norwegian word for whale meat whereas in fact it was shark meat. As a consequence shark meat was delivered to Hamburg. Upon its arrival it was confiscated by the authorities for which the plaintiff was poorly compensated. He then claimed the difference between the compensation awarded by the authorities and the price he had already paid from the defendant, because whale meat would not have been confiscated. Such a claim could only be made if the goods delivered were faulty (old §§ 459, 467). The defendant argued that this was not the case as he had supplied exactly what the term of the contract had described: shark meat. The RG rejected this. Employing § 133 it held that both parties although using the wrong term (*Haaksjöringsköd*) had referred to the same object, whale meat. Thus in fact a contract for whale meat had been concluded giving the plaintiff a claim to compensation.

---

[39] See Sec. 4.
[40] BGHZ 61, 282.

Thus a false description within the contractual agreement does not affect the declarations of intent and the contract if both parties were referring to the same meaning (*"falsa demonstratio non nocet"*).[41]

4.2 **Paragraph 157**

Paragraph 157 provides agreements shall be interpreted according to the requirement of good faith, common practice being taken into account. Paragraph 157 allows for more of an objective approach in that the court tries to ascertain what would be understood by the declaration and views the agreement as a whole. It is particularly useful to decide how the parties may have closed a gap in the contract had they known it was going to become an important issue. This is termed the "hypothetical intention of the parties" (*hypothetischer Parteiwille*).

Paragraphs 133 and 157 apply to the agreement and not the performance of a contract. The judicial construction is achieved by considering what the reasonable addressee would have understood. A three step process has been identified which involves, first, a subjective approach by looking at the words and intent of the contract and parties. If a solution still appears problematic the surrounding circumstances of the contract are taken into account and then finally the good faith of the parties and common practice are considered.

4.3 **Paragraph 242**

This is the general principle of good faith which appears in Book Two of the BGB and applies to the rules relating to the laws of obligations which if it were to be interpreted narrowly would only apply to requirements in the performance of a contract, for example the delivery of goods, or to conditions and not to the agreement. It has, however, been applied very generally throughout civil law. It provides that the debtor is bound to perform according to good faith (*nach Treu und Glauben*), regard being paid to common practice (*mit Rücksicht auf die Verkehrssitte*).

When the code was first introduced there was no case law to assist interpretation and only the code itself which, although comprehensive, lacked the flexibility required for many daily situations. Paragraph 242 was used to develop private law to suit the changing economic and social circumstances. Any difficulties encountered in trying to apply either §§ 133 or 157 could easily be overcome by a wider interpretation and application of the requirements of § 242. Its function thus became to justify in terms of the code the judgments of the German judiciary. Paragraph 242 became the way in which many notions of natural law, and the basic rights of the *Grundgesetz*, were able to enter civil law. The combination of § 242 with § 133 and § 157 applies the requirement of good faith to all aspects of the law of obligations. Paragraph 242 therefore comes close to resembling many aspects of equity and has been instrumental in developing general principles of law from

---

[41] Laterally "A false description does not harm".

actual cases, a form of deductive law developed in the face of inductive law. It has been applied as both a shield and a sword in the following ways.

4.4 The application of § 242

Paragraph 242 is employed by the courts to make sense out of contracts which would otherwise be unworkable or unfair or in some other way incomplete. It is used to interpret contracts and provisions of contracts, to expand them, to limit them or their application, and to correct them or re-construct them. The following categories are neither exhaustive nor definitive but are simply used as a convenient way of demonstrating the different uses of the same paragraph.

4.4.1 *The interpretation or expansion of contractual terms*

In case RGZ 131, 274, the plaintiff, a jeweller, had rented premises for ten years from the defendant landlord. The landlord then rented the adjoining premises to another jeweller. The court held that there existed an implied term or duty in the contract which prevented the landlord from renting to another jeweller. Thus the court clearly created new duties or obligations in the contract.

Another example or leading case is known as the *Venusberg* case[42] in which a seller who charged a very high price for a plot of land because of its exceptional view was prevented from building on an adjacent plot which he owned, because it would destroy the view from the first plot. This was despite the fact there was no actual term or duty existing in the contract to this effect.

In many cases duties of care, supervision, information, and explanation, amongst others, have been created.

4.4.2 *The reconstruction or correction of contracts*

Most of these cases took place in the hyperinflation years following the First World War, so it may be argued they are not representative or typical of the application of § 242. They do, however, demonstrate the lengths the courts were prepared to go to in order to ensure that good faith applied. During the hyperinflation years of the Weimar Republic many contracts for mortgages were reconstructed or revalued by the *Reichsgericht* so that they represented the original sale value, otherwise the seller would have lost out. For example, after 1923 the *Reichsgericht* revalued mortgage repayments to reflect the true value of the property rather than let it be paid for in inflated and almost worthless *Reichsmark*.[43] These cases are also considered to be a special category of cases that falls under collapse of foundations of the contract (*Wegfall der Geschäftsgrundlage*), considered below.[44]

The idea of reconstruction and correction has been taken over by the BGH in cases of long lasting contracts, for example where payments agreed upon by two

---

[42] RGZ 161, 330.
[43] RGZ 107, 78, 86.
[44] See section on law of obligations: sec. C.

parties in exchange for an *Erbbaurecht* (hereditary building right) no longer match the cost of living.[45]

4.4.3 *Limitation of general conditions of business*

A general rule, *contra proferentem*, applies in the absence of others, whereby ambiguous general conditions of business are construed against the party who seeks to rely on them.[46] However, with the General Business Conditions rules now incorporated into the BGB, considered below, § 242 does not have to be employed in this area anymore.

4.4.4 *Formal requirements*

Some contracts need to comply faithfully to requirements of form and will be void if they do not (§ 125). Paragraph 242 has helped to overcome the missing formal requirements and save a party from suffering particularly undue hardship from the failure of a contract. In the *Edelmann* decision,[47] an employee was promised a house as a Christmas bonus. No notarial authentication was made at the time, which is a normal requirement if a promise relating to real estate is to be enforceable, however the employee was assured nevertheless that the promise was good. When the employee claimed the conveyance of the house the defence was raised that the notarial authentication required by § 313 (now: § 311 b I) was missing. The *Reichs-gericht* held that the defence was contrary to good faith and allowed damages although not the conveyance. This idea of allowing validity of a contract in spite of the missing formal requirements under § 242 has been continuously upheld by the BGH in certain cases.[48]

4.4.5 *An equitable principle of justice*

Although not recognized as such, § 242 has been used in such a way as to reflect estoppel, i.e. where one party has acted in a way to produce in the mind of another a new legal situation, the first party cannot go back on this. If the appearance of new legal situation exists the courts will uphold this. The *Edelmann* decision could be seen as an example of this.[49]

5 Void legal transactions (*Nichtige Rechtsgeschäfte*)

The first book of the BGB provides for several rules declaring a legal transaction void *ab initio*. Thus a legal transaction, e.g. a contract, may be void because the law does not recognize the content or the form of certain transactions or because the declarations of will that constitute the transaction are defective. Another category

---

[45] BGHZ 94, 257.
[46] BGH DB 1975, 682.
[47] RGZ 117, 121.
[48] BGHZ 29, 6; 48, 396; 138, 339.
[49] For further details see Heinrichs in Palandt, above, n. 20, § 242 paras. 55–57.

already examined is that of void declarations of minors that equally render a legal transaction void.[50]

5.1 Breach of formal requirements (§§ 125–129 BGB)

Generally, there is no specific form to be chosen for the conclusion of a legal transaction. However, for a few transactions the BGB demands certain formal requirements, their purpose being either to warn the parties of the legal obligations they are about to enter into (*Warnfunktion*) or to provide evidence in cases of subsequent disputes (*Beweisfunktion*). A common form is the written form (§ 126) required, for example, for creating one's will (§ 2247) or contracts to stand as guarantor (§ 766). Furthermore, the parties are free to agree on a written form (§ 127).

Authentication (*Öffentliche Beglaubigung*) demands that the signature is witnessed by a notary (§ 129). This is necessary for official registration of associations (§ 77). The strictest form is that of documentation by a notary (*notarielle Beurkundung*, § 128) required, for example, where one party binds himself to dispose of or acquire a piece of land (§ 311 b I, 1st sentence) and for most contracts involving succession questions. If the formal requirement is not fulfilled the legal transaction is void *ab initio* (§ 125).

5.2 Breach of a law or good morals (§§ 134, 138 BGB)

General limits as to the contents of a contract are imposed by §§ 134 and 138 BGB. Paragraph 134 provides that contracts violating statutory prohibitions (*Verstoß gegen ein gesetzliches Verbot*) are void, such as a sale contract concerning stolen goods (receiving prohibited by § 259 StGB) or contracts to supply drugs or conspiracies or black market employment contracts.[51] This provision saves the legislator the effort of stating private law consequences in each and every prohibition within the German legal system.

Paragraph 138 I provides that contracts will be held to be void if contrary to public morals (*gute Sitten*). That will always be the case where the legal transaction contravenes "the sense of decency of all right and proper thinking persons".[52] This very general clause still remains difficult to apply and can only be done by reference to the different categories of cases developed by the BGH. Only, few examples can be mentioned here. Generally, contracts concerning the provision of services related to sexual activities, such as telephone sex, will fall under this clause.[53] However, the 2001 statute on prostitution takes some of these contracts out of the traditional area of application of § 138.[54] A contract for surrogate motherhood (*Leihmuttervertrag*) contravenes good morals if it renders the child a mere com-

---

[50] See above, sec. 2.2.3.
[51] BGHZ 85, 44. However, if one party to the contract was ignorant of the ban § 134 BGB does not apply and the contract remains intact (BGHZ 89, 369).
[52] This being only a rough translation of the BGH's classical formula: " . . ., *was dem Anstandsgefühl aller billig und gerecht Denkenden widerspricht.*", BGHZ 10, 228, 232.
[53] BGH NJW 1998, 2895.
[54] See above, Chapter 7, sec. 2, Art. 12.

mercial object of the legal transaction.[55] Equally void are oppressive contracts (*Knebelungsverträge*) restricting one party's economic freedom because of the other's powerful position. A classical example of this are long term contracts on the provision of certain goods (*Sukzessivlieferungsverträge*), such as contracts on beer between a brewery and a pub-owner binding the latter for an unreasonable period of more than fifteen years.[56] A loan contract was held to be contrary to Article 138 I because the disadvantageous effects were not fully explained to the borrower.[57] It would also be likely to breach Article 138 II. The standards of acceptable contractual behaviour may arise from the *Grundgesetz*, business, and trading customs. The indirect third effect (*Drittwirkung*) of the *Grundrechte* would be applicable here as in the *Soraya* case or the *Lüth* case.[58] A good example for this is provided in a case involving contracts enticing family members to grant security:

BVerfG NJW 1994, 36 Sittenwidrigkeit eines Bürgschaftsvertrags

The case that had to be decided on by the BVerfG in 1993 clarified the civil courts' obligations to account for basic rights such as Article 2 I GG when interpreting § 138 BGB. Here the complainant, a twenty-one-year-old daughter of a businessman, had signed a contract to personally grant security for her father's increased credit limit of 100,000 DM. At that time she had neither any professional education nor a regular job. When her father went bankrupt the bank claimed 100,000 DM from her according to the guarantee contract. As a consequence, she brought an action against the bank to declare the contract void. The case went through the levels of the civil courts hierarchy. Its final court, the BGH, declared the contract to be valid, relying mainly on the principle that anyone who is above eighteen should be aware of his legal acts and their legal and economic consequences. She complained against this decision claiming a breach of her fundamental rights, namely Article 2 I, 1 I GG (personal freedom) and the principle of the social state (Art. 20 I GG). The following decision of the constitutional court was significant, because there had already been several cases, in which family members without means had been induced to sign guarantee contracts without comprehending the legal implications. Several lower courts had then applied §138 BGB whereas the BGH had generally taken a restrictive approach which was not generally followed by all courts. Thus a decision was necessary. The BVerfG once again underlined the priority and impact of the *Grundgesetz* and its basic rights on other areas of law. It made clear that general clauses such as § 138 or § 242 served as "gateways" by which basic rights conveyed their core values into private law. Thus it was the role of the courts to take into account these rights when interpreting § 138 BGB. In the particular case that meant when examining the guarantee contract as to its compatibility with § 138 the civil

---

[55] OLG Hamm NJW 1986, 782.
[56] BGH NJW 1992, 2145.
[57] BGHZ 80, 153.
[58] See Chapters 2 and 7 for details.

courts should have given serious consideration to the complainant's right to personal freedom. Thus they would have had to examine whether there was an equality of bargaining power, resulting from the complainant's ability to oversee her actions. Here the complainant had clearly not understood that she would never be able to pay the guarantee and fulfil the contract given her means, education, and job perspectives. Furthermore, the bank—well aware of all of this—had not sufficiently warned her of the consequences. By neglecting these aspects the civil courts had breached Article 2 I GG indicating that the contract in fact should have been declared void according to § 138.

Paragraph 138 II provides specifically that contracts will be held to be void which exploit a weaker party or are contracts of a usurious nature. The kind of contracts which have fallen foul of this paragraph typically involve excessive interest charges,[59] long term contracts on fixed conditions, or non competition agreements. The latter are subject to additional specific laws in respect of companies and employment contracts in labour law.

5.3 Defect of declaration of intent (*Willensmängel*)

Willensmangel concerns situations in which the declared intent is defective in some way, where the objective expression fails to reflect subjective intention. According to the BGB there are two distinct groups of defective intent. First a group covered by §§ 116–118, where a party knew from the beginning there was a faulty declaration, in which case the BGB declares the contract to be null and void. Secondly, the group covered by §§ 119, 120 and 123, where mistake was only realized after the declaration of intent has been given by a party or in the case of deceit or duress, in which case the legal transaction is voidable and can be rescinded.

5.3.1 *Grounds for nullity*

5.3.1.1 *The mental reservation (Geheimer Vorbehalt)*
Paragraph 116 I provides that a mental reservation is to be disregarded and the declared intention is to be upheld to protect the other party who relied on the declaration. If, however, the other party knew about the reservation they are deprived of the protection given (§ 116, 2nd sentence) and the contract is void.

5.3.1.2 *The sham transaction (Scheingeschäft)*
Where both parties know of the agreed sham, the real agreement is that the declarations are sham although a legal transaction appears to exist. Therefore there is no real intent to transact and § 117 I renders the declared transaction void. The hidden transaction (*verdecktes Geschäft*), whereby a false transaction hides a real transaction—for example, the sale of an estate is made for €300,000 but the written

---

[59] See for e.g. BGH NJW 1980, 1155 involving an instalment payment scheme for goods which were overpriced and were subject to excessive interest rates.

notarized contract says €150,000 to save on taxes and notary costs, produces the result that the false transaction is rendered void by § 117 II. The hidden (real) transaction is also void due to lack of form (§ 311b I 1st sentence).[60]

5.3.1.3 *The false or joke declaration (Scherzerklärung)*

Under § 118, two preconditions must be fulfilled before this declaration is void. The joke must firstly appear to be a genuine declaration to the person to whom it is addressed but, secondly, the person who expressed it must have expected it to be received as a joke. The declaration is void and there is no contract. However, if the declaration is taken seriously by the other party, damages are payable under § 122 for any loss as a result of relying on it. A duty also exists, as soon as it is known that the other party has taken it seriously, to explain the true nature of the declaration. If there is a delay, the declaration will be held to be valid from the beginning (*ab initio*).

5.3.2 *Rescission of a declaration of intent (Anfechtung einer Willenserklärung)*

5.3.2.1 *Grounds for rescission (Anfechtungsgründe)*

Rescission is the remedy attributed to the second category of defective declarations. These are where mistakes, deceit, or fraud have been committed. German law allows greater freedom or grounds for rescinding and withdrawing from a contract, even when it is clearly the mistake of one party.

Here unlike in the cases of §§ 116–118 a valid contract came into existence. However, the result of a rescinded declaration of intent—and thus a rescinded contract since an essential element is missing—is that the legal transaction is deemed void *ab initio* under § 142 I, with the exception of long standing contracts such as employment contracts.

Rescission annuls one specific declaration of intent and thus only renders void the contract that was partly composed of this declaration. Thus if a declaration of a contract of obligation (*Verpflichtungsgeschäft*) has been rescinded, the contract of "disposal" or "performance" (*Verfügungs/Erfüllungsgeschäft*) still remains intact. Therefore any goods delivered or transferred are not automatically returnable and must be dealt with under the law of unjustified enrichment (§ 812).[61] Third parties acquiring rights in good faith are protected under provisions of the law on property (§ 932 et seq.) and § 142 II, unless they knew or should have known of the reason for a potential rescission.

Rescission is limited for reasons of legal certainty and good faith in legal relations to specific grounds (§§ 119, 120 and 123). The rules try to balance the interests of the protection of the trading partner who has trusted the declaration and the interests of the declarer who might suffer disproportionately from a mistake. It is not so

---

[60] However, this can be remedied by actually fulfilling the conditions of the contract on transferring the property which is the performing contract as opposed to the sale which is the mere contract of obligation (see above, sec. A. 3.2). Once the formal requirements of the performing contract—agreement and registering of the transfer—are fulfilled the breach of formal requirements of the contract of obligation are remedied (§ 311b 2nd sentence; see also BGH NJW 1980, 451).

[61] See also above, sec. A.3.2 on *Abstraktionsprinzip*.

important to stop any contract from being rescinded because there is the liability to pay damages under § 122 where loss is suffered as a result of rescission.

Omitted from the BGB is an answer for the misuse of the right to rescind where the rescinding partner benefits from the withdrawal from a contract despite having to pay damages to compensate under § 122. The amount is determined by the loss or expense incurred in connection with the formation of the agreement and does not therefore include loss of profits. This is known as the negative interest or breach of trust damages (*Vertrauensschaden*), considered in further detail below.

5.3.2.2 *Mistake*

Before examining the different types of mistake emphasis has to be put on the priority of interpretation. If by rules of interpretation (§ 133) the true meaning of the declaration can be assessed then there is no need for rescission in the first place.[62]

Paragraph 119 I distinguishes between mistakes as to the meaning or content of the declaration (*Inhaltsirrtum*) and mistakes as to the actual declaration (*Erklärungsirrtum*) although it is often difficult to distinguish between these in practice.

"Content mistake" (§ 119 I 1st alternative) occurs where the expressor has one thing in mind and the expression is correct as far as he is concerned, but it is not the same as that understood by the receiver. It is the unconscious ignorance of the real facts.

Example: A British exchange student asks for a portion of "Chips" in a German restaurant not knowing that in German the word "Chips" actually means crisps.

This type of mistake does not cover the situation where both parties have the same different view of what was meant. Here they are in agreement and so there is no need to rescind, as in the *Haaksjöringsköd* case.[63]

Errors of content lead to the examination of mistakes relating to identity, calculation, and mistakes in the law. Identity mistakes concern a declaration regarding a person or thing other than the one intended, e.g. where a bank mistakes a client applying for a credit, thinking him to be a wealthy lawyer instead of a impoverished student bearing the same name, which is a mistake as to the content of the declaration. Calculation mistakes are where the error is in the calculation which preceded the expression. The *Reichsgericht* had qualified such an error as error of content if the miscalculation was part of the declaration and thus obvious to the receiver.[64] The BGH has taken a more restrictive approach and does not accept miscalculation as a mistake of content. However, in certain cases the principle of good faith (§ 242) may oblige the receiver to draw the expressor's attention to the miscalculation.[65] Mistake as to the law, legality, or legal consequences does not

---

[62] BGH NJW-RR 1995, 859.
[63] See above, sec. 4.1.
[64] RGZ 105, 406 (*Rubel* case concerning a miscalculation based on the wrong exchange rate).
[65] BGHZ 139, 177 (= BGH NJW 1998, 3192).

include ignorance as to the true state of the law, which would not give rise to a ground for rescission under § 119 I.

Mistakes in the declaration, that is the actual communication, typically involve typing or writing errors of figures or misspelt words whereby the end result was not the one intended (§ 119 I 2nd alternative).

Under § 119 II, mistakes as to a characteristic (*Eigenschaftsirrtum*) concern the properties or qualities, the essential characteristics of a person or object. The concept of a characteristic is very wide. It has to be an implied condition of the contract or a fundamental basis of the agreement. Thus it will include all characteristics influencing value (*wertbildende Eigenschaften*). A characteristic is essential if it has an objective importance to a contract and must relate to either the object of purchase or person. A person's essential characteristics can be age, reliability, criminal record, or political views. This can lead to rescission in an employment contract where, for example, a cashier has a record of theft and the trustworthiness in such a position would be in doubt.

Essential quality has been defined by the courts to include only the factual and legal qualities of things which specifically characterizes them, not factors which only have an indirect effect on their value.[66] Mistake as to the value or the price of a thing will not lead to rescission unless it can be linked to an essential quality, such as a valuable painting.[67] Authenticity is thus regarded as an essential quality. Outside factors are not covered by § 119 II and cannot lead to rescission, e.g. as in motive mistake (*Motivirrtum*) where the reason for a purchase has fallen away. The purchase of a present for a wedding which does not take place would not be grounds to rescind the declaration.

Finally, § 120 concerns mistakes made during the delivery of the declaration (*Übermittlungsirrtum*) and relates to those things incorrectly said or written. A typical case is when an assistant or employer or other third party hears or writes something mistakenly and this is conveyed then to the other party. Such mistakes can be rescinded under the same conditions as in § 119. Alterations of the message during transmissions by electronic and mechanical delivery are covered by § 119.

5.3.2.3 *Deceit and duress*

A declaration given under deceit or duress can be rescinded providing certain criteria are met (§ 123 I). This underlines the importance the BGB attaches to the free formation of a person's will. In these two extreme cases the contract is not automatically rendered void. The law rather gives the "victim" a choice to either rescind the declaration and thus destroy the contract or to keep the contract in existence if that happens to be advantageous to him. Duress (*Drohung*) is defined as the threat of some evil, which the person making the threat has control over. The threat must be unlawful, for example the threat of violence is duress because it employs illegal means to obtain the declaration.

Deceit (*arglistige Täuschung*) is defined as the creation of a false impression or

---

[66] BGHZ 16, 54, 57.
[67] BGHZ 6, 371.

mistake in the mind of the other causing them to make the declaration in the form expressed. Deceit can be couched in positive terms as in giving false facts or in negative terms such as the suppression of the truth where a duty to inform exists. The latter can result from questions being asked, particularly so for the sale of used cars. It was held in there was a duty on the part of the employee of a car sales firm to inform purchasers about the accident record of a car.[68] Where inadmissible questions are asked knowingly given false information will not amount to deceit. This problem had to be addressed in cases of employment law where employers asked female applicants whether they were pregnant. Such a question was held to be inadmissible not only because of its intimate nature but also because it allows for an opportunity for discrimination against women. After the ECJ had held a rejection of an applicant because of her pregnancy to be discriminatory and contravening EC law the BAG drew the following consequences: questions as to the applicant's pregnancy where pointing at a probable rejection of the application and where thus discriminatory and inadmissible. Therefore there was no obligation for the applicant to respond truthfully. Thus deceit did not exist and § 123 did not apply in such cases. The employer could not rescind his declaration.[69]

Deceit has to be intentional, whereby the deceiver knows and wishes that the other party will make a declaration of intent to contract which he would not normally have made if not deceived. Intention is a necessary part and gross negligence would not satisfy.[70]

Rescission under § 123 gives rise to negative interest damages but damages may also be available under § 823 (delictual claim).

5.3.2.4 *The declaration of rescission under § 143*

A declaration of rescission, known as the *Anfechtungserklärung*, must be transmitted to the opposite party under § 143 to be effective. It does not have to be in writing and need not take any particular form. It must be clear to the other party what is demanded but does not need the agreement of the other party and it is not necessary to state the grounds.[71] § 142 provides that the effect of the rescission is that the declaration of intent is presumed void from the beginning (*ex tunc*).

Time limits for the declaration of rescission are governed by §§ 121 & 124. Rescission under § 119 and 120 must be declared as soon as (*unverzüglich*)[72] the knowledge of the mistake is known (§ 121 I).[73] In any case it is precluded ten years after the declaration has been made (§ 121 II). Rescission under § 123 must be declared within one year from the time the deceit is discovered or in the case of duress, when the duress ceases to be inflicted (§ 124). Again, after ten years following the original declaration of intent, rescission is no longer possible (§ 124 III).

---

[68] BGHZ 63, 382, 387.
[69] See BAGE NJW 1993, 1154.
[70] BGH NJW 1977, 1055.
[71] BGHZ 88, 240.
[72] Defined as *"ohne schuldhaftes Zögern"* in § 121, meaning without reproachable delay.
[73] BGH NJW 1968, 2099.

If a declaration has been rendered void under the rules on mistake, §§ 119 & 120 compensation is payable by the party rescinding, to place the damaged party in the position prior to the agreement, the negative interest (*Negatives Interesse* or *Vertrauensschaden*), but not to compensate what was promised if the contract was fulfilled, the positive interest (*Erfüllungsinteresse*). This includes expenditure costs but not profits that might or would have been made had the contract been performed.

If, however, the other party knew or was negligent of the fact that the contract should be rescinded or negated and did nothing, the liability to compensate does not arise (§ 122 II).

5.4 The concept and consequences of the void legal transaction

The nullity of a legal transaction stems either from the provisions of the BGB (for example, §§ 105, 117 I, 125, 134, 138) or from other statutes. Void contracts are unenforceable and the legal transaction is taken to have never existed at all (*null ab initio*). This nullity (*Nichtigkeit*) is final and a contract can only be reformed anew.[74] In specific circumstances the void transaction can be validated if void due to a lack of form (see § 311b I 2nd sentence, in respect of real property transactions, § 518 II concerning the validity of gifts, and § 766 for the form requirements of bailment contracts).

Although generally the entire contract will be rendered void, § 139 does allow partial nullity if the partners would have agreed to conclude the contract without the affected parts and the terms are capable of separation. A further exception allows the contract to be reformed anew if the parties faced with nullity would have concluded the contract in the same manner (§ 140).

A void declaration of intent can be confirmed as valid and will be regarded as a new declaration of intent (§ 141).

6 Agency (*Stellvertretung*)

The powers of agents and agency are dealt with in §§ 164–181. Generally, agency can be applicable to all legal transactions. Exceptions are made in cases of transactions that can only be concluded in person as in the formation of a will (§ 2064) conclusion of a contract of succession (*Erbvertrag* § 2274), such as or marriage (§ 1311 1st sentence). Agency allows for an effective conclusion of legal transactions by representation of the principal. It is especially relevant for compulsory representation of minors and legal persons, the latter obviously needing a natural person to act on their behalf. Thus the power to represent these two groups and the scope of agency in these cases are defined by law (*gesetzliche Vertretungsmacht*), e.g. §§ 1626, 1629 BGB (parents acting on behalf of their children) or § 26 II BGB

---

[74] BGH NJW 1985, 2579.

(representation of a registered association by its board members), § 78 AktG (representation of stock company by the board), and § 35 I GmbHG (representation of the limited company by its manager). Contrast this with cases of non-compulsory agency which can be chosen. The authority to act as an agent (*Vollmacht*) is bestowed by legal transaction (*rechtsgeschäftliche Vertretungsmacht*).

The general principles of agency are laid down in the General Part of the BGB and generally applicable to both mentioned categories of agency. An agency relationship consists of three main persons; the agent, who undertakes trade for other interests, the principal, for whom the agent gives his declaration, and the third party, with whom the agent concludes legal transactions.

An agent has to be distinguished from a mere messenger (as in § 120). The latter only transmits someone else's declaration of intent whereas the agent gives his own declaration thereby producing an effect for the principal. Therefore an agent requires at least limited capacity (§ 165) whereas even a minor without "contractual" capacity can act as a messenger.

6.1 Types of agency

Apart from a compulsory and optional agency the following distinctions can be drawn.

6.1.1 *Active and passive agency (Aktive und Passive Stellvertretung)*

Active agency under § 164 I provides that declarations of intent, e.g. an offer to conclude a contract, given by an agent on behalf of a principal, take effect as between the principal and the third party. For this to be valid the agent must deal in the name of the principal and the agent must have authority to do so. The latter is conferred upon him either by the relevant legal provision (§§ 1626, 1629 for the parents of a minor) or by legal transaction according to § 167 I.

Passive agency, under § 164 III, is where the agent, rather than making the declaration of intent, receives it from the third party, such as an acceptance of an offer.

6.1.2 *Direct and indirect agency (unmittelbare und mittelbare Stellvertretung)*

A direct agent deals with third parties in the name of the principal. An indirect agent deals in his own name but for a principal. However, only the economic result is directed at him. This form of agency, sometimes termed as *mittelbare Stellvertretung*, with an undisclosed principal, is not recognized by the BGB. In fact, the main characteristic of agency is missing: the legal consequence is that the principal is directly affected by the declaration of intent given by his agent. This is not the case where a front man or a commission agent (§ 383 HGB) concludes a contract as only they derive a claim from it. Therefore agency applies only where the agent has disclosed that a principal in fact exists and the agent is thus representing him. An exception is made in respect of cash transactions where there is no real need for disclosure of a principal to provide further protection to the third party. This is termed in German *"Geschäft für den, den es angeht"*, business for whom it concerns.[75]

6.2 Agency authority (*Vollmacht*)

Agency authority is affected by a one sided declaration of intent which must be received by the other. Agency can be issued either to the one being given the power (§ 167 I: the internal power of agency (*Innenvollmacht*)) or it can be issued to the third party (the external power of agency (*Außenvollmacht*)). According to § 167 II there is no particular form of agency and it can be created and revoked either orally or in writing. Exceptions are the power of attorney for legal proceedings or for the refusal to accept an inheritance (§ 1945 III). Generally agency authority will be effective for the time of the basic transaction it was affected for (§ 168 1st sentence). However, the power of an agent can be revoked at any time (§ 168 2nd sentence). The external agency authority can only be effectively revoked by notifying the third party (§ 170). Thus according to §§ 170–173 the principal inducing the third party to believe in a valid agency is bound by the "agent's" actions even if the agency authority was defective or has meanwhile extinguished provided the third party was in good faith. In these cases agency authority exists due to appearance (*Vollmacht kraft Rechtsschein*). Special cases are those of *Duldungs-* und *Anscheins-vollmacht* developed by the courts.

Duldungsvollmacht describes an agency authority that will be assumed if the principal knows about and tolerates the agent's actions on behalf of the principal although he does not have the authority to do so. If the principal does nothing to refrain the agent from acting and if a third party could rely on the agent's authority to act, then the principal will be bound by the agent's actions.[76]

If the principal did not know about the agent's behaviour but could have known it if he had acted diligently he might nevertheless be bound provided the third person in good faith could assume that the principal should have been aware of the agent's behaviour. Thus the apparent authority (*Anscheinsvollmacht*) of the agent has been negligently caused or at least not been prevented by the principal. It originated in his "sphere". Thus the BGH added this form of agency.[77]

6.3 The scope of agency powers

The powers of an agent may include:

(a) Special power for a single legal transaction (*Spezialvollmacht*),

(b) Type power, based on a group of legal transactions of the same type (*Gattungsvollmacht*),

---

[75] RGZ 100, 192, BGH NJW 1955, 590.
[76] For details see Heinrichs in Palandt, above, n 20, § 173 paras. 11–13.
[77] BGH NJW-RR 1986, 1169; NJW 1998, 1854.

(c) General power, based on all legal transactions of the grantor (*Generalvollmacht*),

(d) Collective powers of agency (*Gesamtvollmacht*) where more than one person deals on behalf of the principal, can also be given,

(e) Subordinate powers of agency (*Untervollmacht*) are also can be granted by the agent to sub agents.

6.4 Legal consequences of agency

Declarations made by the agent in the name of the principal have immediate legal effects for and against the principal (§ 164 I 1). The agent is under no liability and acquires no rights except where he has acted without authority. Thus where the agent acts with authority to acquire ownership of an object his declarations for the transaction of obligation (*Verpflichtungsgeschäft*) and the transaction of performance (*Verfügungsgeschäft*)[78] will produce immediate effect for the principal. Thus the contract of transferring ownership does not render him owner but the principal.

Where the agent does not make sufficiently clear that he is acting on behalf of a principal he himself will be bound by his declaration. Rescission according to § 119 I is precluded by § 164 II.

As the agent delivers his own declaration any defects or circumstances affecting this declaration will be relevant for the conclusion of the transaction instead of those of the principal (§ 166 I). Thus where good faith is an issue (e.g. § 932) it will be the knowledge of the agent rather than the principal that is relevant to decide the case. However, to prevent a misuse of this rule § 166 II provides that where the principal gave specific instructions to the agent he cannot later on rely on the agent's unawareness of certain facts that he himself knew. Otherwise it would be easy for a principal who is not in good faith to simply employ an unknowing agent to conclude a transaction that requires good faith.

6.5 Lack of authorization

An agent requires express authority for all transactions, however if the agent exceeds that authority a principal can ratify the unauthorized transaction or even an unauthorized agent (§ 177 I). Unauthorized transactions by an agent are temporarily ineffective until the principal approves them (§ 177 I). If not approved, the transaction fails. The third party may nevertheless withdraw from the transaction prior to ratification (§ 178).

Where the principal does not ratify, the third party can demand performance or damages from the agent under § 179. If the agent didn't know he lacked authority he must pay negative interest damages § 179 II, but is not liable if the third party knew or ought to have known that the agent lacked authority (§ 179 III 2).

---

[78] See above, *Abstraktionsprinzip*, sec. A.3.2.

6.6 Prohibition of self contracting (*Verbot des Insichgeschäfts*)

Paragraph 181 prohibits self contracting, meaning that the agent cannot act on two sides, either by concluding a contract for himself in person and acting as agent for the principal or by acting as agent for both contracting parties. Paragraph 181 makes an exception in those cases where the legal transaction in question is merely a performance of another contract e.g. a contract to transfer ownership in order to perform the obligations under a contract of sale. Furthermore, § 181 provides for the admissibility of self contracting where it has been authorized in law or by the principal(s).

This provision would put parents wanting to give presents to their under-age children in an awkward position. As they are acting on their behalf and as representatives and agents of their children (§§ 104 et seq., 1626, 1629) they would need assent from a neutral third party provided by the authorities each time they were to give something to their children and effectively transfer ownership thereof. Thus the courts have teleologically reduced the provision of § 181 to the following result: as § 181 is designed for the protection of the principal or represented person it is not applicable where a transaction entails a mere legal advantage for that person.[79] However, here the legal consequences will have to be carefully assessed.[80]

7 Limitation

Each claim is subject to limitation, as provided by § 194 I. Although technically it does not render the claim void limitation makes it unenforceable. It grants the person obliged by the claim a right to refuse performance (§ 214). The different periods of limitation, originally spanning from thirty years to six weeks in certain cases, have been changed by the 2001 reform of the law of obligations. They are partly regulated now by §§ 194–218. The general period of limitation is now three years (§ 195). However, there are numerous exceptions. Whereas § 197 allows for a long period of thirty years in specific cases such as several claims originating in the law of property, family, or succession law limitation periods vary between thirty and two years where claims of guarantee rights concerning sale are concerned (§ 438) or between five and two years concerning guarantee claims arising from contracts to deliver services (§ 634a).[81]

---

[79] BGHZ 59, 236 (= NJW 1972, 2262); BGHZ 94, 232.
[80] BGHZ 78,28 (= NJW 1981, 109).
[81] For substantial information on limitation refer to D. Leenen, *Die Neuregelung der Verjährung*, JZ 2001, 552–560; R. Zimmermann, D. Leenen, H.P. Mansel, W. Ernst, *Finis Litium? Zum Verjährungsrecht nach dem Regierungsentwurf eines Schuldrechtsmodernisierungsgesetzes*, JZ 2001, 283–287.

FURTHER READING

As with other chapters, a word or two of warning must be given here in respect of some of the English langauge works listed below. Older works continue to be listed, despite the fact that law reforms and amendments have overtaken them and they no longer represent an accurate statement of the law. However, they are still of some use to those readers who are unable to consult German texts. They are not, however, to be relied upon!

The German Civil Code, Translation and commentary by S. Goren, 2nd ed. (1995: Rothman/North-Holland Publishing Co).

Introductory act to the German Civil Code and Marriage Law of the Federal Republic of Germany, ed. by S. Forrester (1976: F. B. Rothman, South Hackensack, New Jersey).

1981 Supplement to the German Civil Code and the Introductory Act to the German Civil Code and the Marriage Law of the Federal Republic of Germany, (1982: F.B. Rothman).

P. Bähr, *Grundzüge des Bürgerlichen Rechts*, 10th ed. (2002: Vaheln Verlag, München).

W. Brehm, *Allgemeiner Teil des BGB*, 4th ed. (2000: Boorberg Verlag, Stuttgart).

H. Brox, *Allgemeiner Teil des BGB*, 23rd ed. (1999: Heymanns, Cologne).

W. Däubler, *BGB-kompakt* (2002: C.H. Beck, München).

N. Horn, H. Kötz, and H.G. Leser, *German Private and Commercial Law* (1982: Oxford University Press, Oxford).

M. John, *Politics and the Law in Late Nineteenth-Century Germany: The Origins of the Civil Code* (1989: Oxford Clarendon Press, Oxford).

P. Klink, *Gerichtsentscheidungen Zivilrecht I, BGB Allgemeiner Teil, Schuldrecht—Allgemeiner Teil* (1989: Verlag P. Klink, München).

P. Klink, *Gerichtsentscheidungen Zivilrecht 2; Schuldrecht: Besonderer Teil* (1989: Verlag P. Klink, München).

E. Klunziger, *Einführung in das Bürgerliche Recht*, 10th ed. (2001: Vahlen Verlag, München).

H. Köhler, *BGB Allgemeiner Teil*, 25th ed. (2001: C.H. Beck, München).

J. Kropholler, *Studienkommentar BGB*, 5th ed. (2002: C.H. Beck, München).

D. Leipold, *BGB I Einführung und Allgemeiner Teil* (1999: Mohr Siebeck, Tübingen).

H.J. Musielak, *Grundkurs BGB*, 6th ed. (1999: C.H. Beck, München).

O. Palandt, *Bürgerliches Gesetzbuch: Kommentar*, 61st ed. (2002: C.H. Beck, München).

M. Peltzer and P. Scesniak, *German Securities Act 1995* (O. Schmidt, Köln).

H. Schack and H-P. Ackmann, *Höchstrichterliche Rechtsprechung zum Bürgerlichen Recht*, 4th ed. (1997: C.H. Beck, München).

Articles

J.P. Dawson, "Effects of Inflation on Private Contracts: Germany, 1914–1924" (1933–34) 33 Mich L Rev 171–238.

J.P. Dawson, "Unconscionable Coercion: The German Version" (1976) 89 Harv L Rev 1041–1126.

W. Ebke and B. Steinhauer, "The Doctrine of Good Faith in German Contract Law" in Beatson and Friedmann (eds.), *Good Faith and Fault in Contract Law* (1995: Clarendon Press, Oxford), pp. 171–190.

C Book Two: the law of obligations: general part

1 Introduction

The law of obligations in the BGB lays the foundations for all aspects of legal relations between individuals involving their obligations to each other in civil law. Thus the founding, content, development, and ending of such legal relations are catered for by the law of obligations and the rules cover the equivalent of contract, tort, and quasi-contract (unjustified enrichment).

Book Two is divided into the general rules of the law of obligations (*Allgemeines Schuldrecht*) and specific forms of the most important and frequently employed obligational relationships (*Besonderes Schuldrecht*). It is concerned primarily with contractual agreements, the performance of them, and the consequences of their breach.

The law of obligations is also the starting point for the organization of business forms by providing for the partnership (*Personengesellschaft*), §§ 705 et seq.

The 2001 reform of the law of obligations (*Schuldrechtsreform*) entered into force on 1 January 2002. The following description takes it into account where appropriate in such a short introduction. For detailed information on this subject refer to the further reading mentioned at the end of this section.

2 The obligational relationship (*Das Schuldverhältnis*)— general principles

The fundamental basis for the organization of the rules in the BGB is the obligational relationship (*Schuldverhältnis*) which exists between a person entitled to demand a certain performance, called *Gläubiger*, and the corresponding party obliged to perform, described as *Schuldner*. To translate these terms as creditor and debtor would be misleading as they do not only cover an obligation concerning the loan of money. They are more abstract and refer to the right to demand or the obligation to provide any performance arising from the relationship in question, be it a contract of sale, a claim for damages arising from tort, or a claim based on unjustified enrichment. In the course of this book we will use the word "creditor" to describe the person entitled to demand a performance whereas the other side obliged to perform will be termed as "obligor". However, the somewhat inaccurate terminology must be borne in mind.

An obligational relationship in its original narrow sense (*Schuldverhältnis im engeren Sinne*) consists of one party that may demand and the other party that has to provide a performance, e.g. a seller's obligation of—and simultaneously the purchaser's right to demand—handing over the goods and transferring ownership thereof (§ 433 I). It therefore only covers the obligations of one side. However, in a broader sense an "obligational relationship" is sometimes referred to in order to describe the whole relationship between the two parties, thus including the obligations of all parties involved, e.g. the seller's and the purchaser's obligations (*Schuldverhältnis im weiteren Sinne*). It has to be borne in mind that in the latter case each party is the creditor in respect of their claim and at the same time the obligor in respect of their duty. It depends on the obligation one is looking at.

The duties in such a relationship of obligation are relative only to the parties and the particular type of obligation and contrast with absolute rights of ownership of property. In other words, whereas the rights and obligations can only affect the parties involved in this relationship (relative rights) a right arising out of property law will effect anyone (absolute right), e.g. the general right of the owner of an object to use it in whatever way he decides to and exclude others from its use (§ 903).

The first paragraph of Book Two (§ 241 I) provides that an obligational relationship entitles the creditor to claim a performance (*Leistung*) from the obligor. This may include a claim to refrain from action.

Paragraph 241 is a very abstract clause and to make sense, it must be applied to particular types of contract which appear in the second part of Book Two, for example, § 433 sale or § 535 rent. In a contract for sale the creditor, as purchaser, may demand the delivery of the goods and the transfer of ownership from the obligor as seller.

2.1 Types and the creation of obligational relationships

A contract or other legal basis is necessary for the creation of obligations:

(a) Contractually based obligations (*Vertragliche Schuldverhältnisse*) usually involve two sided agreements (*zweiseitig verpflichtende Rechtsgeschäfte*), but the BGB also recognises enforceable one sided agreements (*einseitig verpflichtende Rechtsgeschäfte*), such as a contract involving a gift (*Geschenk*, §§ 516 et seq.).

(a) Statute based obligations (*gesetzliche Schuldverhältnisse*) are those linking an obligation to a particular event defined by the law; the most important are: delictual acts (*unerlaubte Handlung*) under § 823 et seq., the equivalent of tortious liability; and unjustified enrichment (*Ungerechtfertigte Bereicherung*) the equivalent of quasi-contract, §§ 812 et seq.

As a consequence obligational relationships enter into force either with the conclusion of the contract (§ 311 I) or with the event described by the law in cases of statute based obligations.

3 Content of the obligational relationship

3.1 Primary and secondary duties (*Primär- und Sekundärleistungspflichten*)

The duty to perform (*Leistungspflicht*, § 241 I), arises directly from the agreement and is the primary duty, usually the whole object of a contract, e.g. the duty to deliver the goods and transfer ownership thereof and the duty to pay for them are primary duties under the contract of sale (§ 433 I and II). Secondary duties such as compensation arise in the event of a failure to perform the primary duty. The first has to be established to give rise to the second.

3.2 Main and ancillary duties (*Hauptleistungspflichten und Nebenleistungspflichten*)

Contracts usually define the main duties whereas ancillary duties may be express in the agreement or implied either by the BGB, the parties, or the court. In the absence of express ancillary duties, the provisions of the BGB apply unless overridden by the parties.

One of the most important duties which is imposed by § 242 of the BGB is the general duty to perform the obligation owed in good faith, discussed in further detail above. Paragraph 242 also can imply all manner of ancillary duties to ensure that the main obligation is performed in good faith.

Main duties are the purpose of the contract. Ancillary duties include duties of information or care (see § 241 II). They are usually dependant on the main duty in that they only serve to complete the main performance duty and have no purpose on their own. A house painter has an ancillary duty not to damage property, which alone would be senseless. There are some, however, which can be independent in that they can have their own purpose and are mainly found in the form of advice and information supplied subsequent to a contract of sale.

3.3 Performance of individual and generic obligations (*Gattungs- und Stückschuld, § 243*)

Specific or individual obligations (*Stückschuld*) are where the obligor has to deliver a specific item, e.g. a particular painting or antique. The duty to perform is then similarly specific.

Generic obligations (*Gattungsschuld*) are where objects are described only by a class, for example, sand or bricks or carrots. The purchaser is not concerned with individual items but is only concerned with obtaining the correct amount.

The quasi-generic obligation, where an obligation exists to deliver generic goods from a specific and limited supply, such as wines of a certain year or books of a particular title, is the most frequent type of obligation encountered. According to

§ 243 I the obligor of generic goods is required to deliver goods of an average type and quality.

In order to fulfil the obligation to supply generic goods, the debtor must prepare for delivery the amount required of the generic goods to be supplied under a specific contract. When it is designated, the debtor has fulfilled his obligation under § 243 II which is to prepare the goods for collection and not delivery, but in practice contracts extend to delivery.

When generic goods have been designated the obligation is limited to those goods (*Konkretisierung der Gattungsschuld*). A seller thus would only be under the obligation to sell the designated goods.

3.4 Time and place of performance (*Leistungsort und -zeit*, §§ 269, 270, 271)

Time and place of the performance are to be determined by the parties, if not, the rules of the BGB apply. Paragraph 269 provides that unless the parties agree, either expressly or impliedly, the place of performance (*Leistungsort*) shall be the residence of the obligor at the time of the obligational relationship entering into existence. For contracts of sale this means the place where the seller of the goods prepares the goods for collection or delivery. In other words, the purchaser (creditor as to the delivery of the goods) has to fetch the goods (*Holschuld*). However, the parties can agree on the obligor's duty to deliver the performance, e.g. sold goods to a certain place (*Bringschuld*). Finally, the term *Schickschuld* describes a duty of the creditor to send objects to an agreed place. In the latter case the place of delivery is called the *Erfüllungsort* and does not coincide with the *Leistungsort*, because the place of performance is actually where the creditor sends the goods on their way. In these cases performance by a third party is recognized as acceptable as the BGB recognized the standard business practice of the employment of transport firms (§ 267). This does not affect the place of performance or delivery or the passage of risk, which transfers to the buyer as soon as the goods are delivered to the transport firm or forwarder. An agreement that the seller will take over the costs of delivery, will not change the place of performance (§ 269 III). Unless agreed, delivery costs are borne by the buyer (§ 448 I).

Determining the place of performance is significant not only in order to clarify who is bearing the costs of delivery but also in order to allocate the risk of transport. For generic obligations this means that once the creditor has delivered the required amount of goods (e.g. forty kilos of carrots) out of his stock to the place agreed upon, he has designated them and thus done everything required for performance. As a consequence his obligation is restricted to these forty kilos of carrots. It does not extend to his stock anymore.

The time or due date of performance (*Fälligkeit*) is when the creditor can demand performance of the obligation. Paragraph 271 provides that if nothing regarding the time of performance has been determined or is clearly implied by the contract, performance can be demanded immediately by the creditor. If the obligor defaults on the time of delivery the creditor can claim compensation on grounds of delay. The consequences of a failure to deliver vary according to the type and subject matter of the contract, considered below.

The place of payment is determined by § 270 which provides that, unless agreed otherwise the debtor shall send money at own risk and expense to the seller's premises.

Paragraph 273 allows the obligor to withhold performance (*Zurückbehaltungsrecht*) if he has an enforceable claim against the creditor arising from the same relationship of obligation—until the other performance has been made—in order to enforce overdue claims arising from the agreement (see also § 320 in respect of mutual contracts).

3.5 Passage of risk in performance

The risk of performance, e.g. in the goods sold, passes when the obligor performs by preparing them for delivery (§ 269). The buyer is normally at risk during delivery or by refusing delivery. If, for example, the purchaser is late in accepting generic goods (*Gläubigerverzug*) that have been designated and they are damaged the obligor has no liability providing he has done all required of him (§§ 243 II). The risk passes to buyer on the transfer of possession of the goods and not whether or when the goods are actually transferred, i.e. delivered (§ 446).

3.6 Standard form contracts and general conditions of business (*Allgemeine Geschäftsbedingungen*, §§ 305–310 BGB)

This section is concerned with the judicial and statutory intervention to correct excesses arising from standard form conditions and contracts with general conditions (*Formularverträge* and *Allgemeine Geschäftsbedingungen, AGB*) and non negotiated contracts. It thus restricts the freedom of contract and the content of obligational relationships to protect the weaker party of a contract. The BGB assumes that parties, of equal strength, have the autonomy to create contracts as they wish. In real life this supposition is somewhat unrealistic. In a large majority of business contracts, the will of one party is often completely subjugated by the other party by use of standard contracts and business conditions. The ability of some parties to question conditions when these have been pre-set by the other party and when prices are also fixed is severely curtailed and the contractual freedom is almost entirely removed. Business was often able to pass on most of the risks and disadvantages to the consumer who was in a weaker trading position. The only choice was to buy or not to buy. The danger of misuse in which one party gets the benefit and the other interests are placed in weaker position or disadvantaged, was recognized by the courts and latterly the legislature.

At first the courts used general §§ 138 and 242. If the contract showed an abuse by the dominant party of the other the unfair clause would be struck out by the court. The leading example of this the following case:

BGHZ 2, 90

This concerned the purchase of bedroom furniture by a young couple from a discount store. When problems were discovered with the furniture the couple refused to pay the balance of the price payable until it was repaired. The contract of sale excluded all rights except the right of repair. The store was, however, unable to repair the furniture. The BGH decided that the purchaser should not effectively be denied of all rights when the only right available was useless. Therefore the clause was unfair and the consumers could return the goods.

Further consumer protection had subsequently been provided by the General Conditions of Business Act (*Gesetz zur Regelung des Rechts der Allgemeinen Geschäftsbedingungen, AGBG*) of 9 December 1976. The provisions were largely based on the results of court decisions but also applied to contracts between producers and merchants *inter se* despite the fact that normally under commercial law rules, it is assumed that they do not need such protection when dealing with each other. The 2001 reform of the law of obligations has incorporated them—together with several other private law acts—into the BGB in order to emphasize its initial purpose of a codification of all general principles of private law.

The provisions on standard contract terms (§§ 305–310) establish improvements in substantive rights and has in certain instances essentially altered the BGB in the core area of contractual freedom.

Paragraph 305 I provides a comprehensive definition of standard conditions as all contracts settled in advance for multiple use and presented by one party to the other party for assent. Paragraph 305 I 3 states that the Act does not apply to individually negotiated contracts whereby some of the terms are altered, however the remaining unaltered standard terms remain subject to the Act.

Section 2 of § 305 outlaws the "deem to know" clauses and prescribes that standard terms only become part of a contract where either express reference has been made to them and allows the other party reasonable opportunity to consider them and assent to them.

Special terms, even if oral, overrule standard terms (§ 305b).

Paragraph 305c I outlaws surprise or unusual clauses which cannot become part of the contract. Section 2 of the same provision provides a formulation of the *contra proferentem* rule whereby doubts in construing standard business conditions are to be resolved against the party applying such conditions. Paragraph 306 overcomes the harshness which sometimes results from the rule in § 139 BGB that renders the whole contract void if one part is annulled. The contract now remains valid apart from the offending clauses.

The general rule of § 307 AGBG essentially summarizes the rules of law established by case-law for the requirement of good faith and acts against clauses seeking to remove this requirement. The type of clause which would offend § 307 AGBG would be clauses seeking to exclude all liability for damage arising from the performance of a contract or all defects in a product. This provision will serve as a catch-all rule especially if §§ 308 and 309 are not applicable.

Paragraphs 308 and 309 combat inadmissible clauses by listing a catalogue of clauses such as, those not specifying a delivery date or those allowing for a price increase within four months. These paragraphs are not applicable to merchants.

Paragraph 310 defines the scope of application for §§ 305–309. According to § 310 I the protection for business contractors is reduced by excluding the application of §§ 305 II,III and 308 & 309 to business men and legal persons.[82] Furthermore, it is noteworthy that these provisions are not applicable to succession, family or company law or the law on partnerships. They cannot be applied to trade union agreements (§ 310 IV). However—and this marks a change—they are applicable to individual employment contracts under the new law.

Rules dealing with the procedural enforcement of these provisions (previously §§ 13–24a AGBG) are now found in the new Act on actions of injunction for the protection of consumers (*Unterlassungsklagegesetz*). They include such provisions as ex-Article 24a AGBG, introduced to implement the EC directive on the protection of consumers, extending their protection by applying the AGBG also to formulated terms that were only designed to be used once as well as to terms that were introduced by a third party.

Further private law Acts designed to protect the consumer have been incorporated in §§ 312–312d such as rules on "door step contracts" and in §§ 491–504, such as the law on consumer credits.

3.7 Third parties to contracts

In several circumstances, third parties can be involved in an obligational relationship of which only two shall be pointed out here. The contract beneficial to third parties (*Vertrag zugunsten Dritter*) basically entitles the creditor to demand performance to be made to a third party and at the same time gives this third party a right to claim the performance (§§ 328 I, so-called real contract beneficial to third parties).

Example: *A* concludes a contract for a life-insurance with an insurance company naming his wife as the beneficiary. This will generally entitle her to the payment of the insurance in case of her husband's death. Note, however, that § 331 I reserves a right of the insured to change or terminate the contract without possibilities of influence from the beneficiary.

In contrast to the aforementioned an "unreal" contract beneficial to third persons does not entitle the third party to claim the performance himself.

---

[82] See BGHZ 90, 273, 278.

> **Example:** *A* buys flowers for his fiancé and asks the flower shop to have them delivered to her.

Furthermore, § 414 et seq. allow for a change of the obligor if the creditor agrees to it, as the latter will usually have an interest in the obligor's solvency. A change of the creditor, however, does not need an authorization by the obligor as it is not in his interest whom he has to provide with the performance. All that is needed here is a contract between the old and the new creditor that the right to claim the specific performance is transferred from the former to the latter. This contract of ceding a right regulated in § 398 (*Abtretung*), is not a contract of obligation (*Verpflichtungsgeschäft*) but one of "disposition" (*Verfügungsgeschäft*) because it directly affects a subjective right. This has to be borne in mind with respect to the *Abstraktionsprinzip*.[83]

3.8 Extinction of an obligational relationship (*Erlöschen des Schuldverhältnisses*)

There are several reasons for the extinction of an obligational relationship the most usual being performance. If all goes well and performance is made, all obligations and duties are extinguished (§ 362), however under § 368 a duty to give a receipt remains. If a substituted article is accepted by the buyer in lieu of performance, this will also extinguish obligations (*Annahme an Erfüllungs statt* § 364).

> **Example:** *A* who owes *B* €1,000 instead offers him a painting worth the same amount which *B* accepts.

A different case is that of accepting an alternative performance or object "on account of fulfilment", i.e. with the promise to obtain satisfaction from the latter (*Annahme erfüllungshalber*).

> **Example:** *B* does not want the picture that *A* has offered him in the previous example but he promises to try and sell it in order to get his €1,000 before he turns to *A*.

In this case the obligational relationship still exists. It was not extinguished by the acceptance of the painting.

Obligational relationships may extinguish through set-off (§§ 387 et seq.) and deposit (§§ 372 et seq.). Conditions for a set-off (*Aufrechnung*) are that both parties

---

[83] See above, sec. A. 3.2.

owe each other the same type of performance (e.g. payments arising from different contracts) and that both obligations are due. The set-off has to be declared by one party (§ 388). The declaration then entails the extinction of the obligations of performance as far as they were congruent from the moment that both obligations faced each other and were fit for a set-off (§ 399).

If an obligor is unsure of the creditor, e.g. due to confusion over a contract of cession (§ 398) or if the creditor does not accept the performance he can still deposit it in order to extinguish his obligation. The deposit, however, can only be made at a public authority usually the *Hinterlegungsstelle* at the *Amtsgericht* and is only applicable to certain objects such as money or bills of exchange (§ 372).

Finally, the rules on rescission of a contract[84] (*Rücktritt vom Vertrag*) in § 346 et seq. provide for an extinction of the primary obligations of performance if one party has rescinded the contract.

4 Irregularities in performance

Breaches of contract or defective performance are termed irregularities in performance (*Leistungsstörungen*). The term irregularities under the new law now covers impossibility and delay of performances as well as "bad performance" such as the positive breach of a contract (*positive Vertragsverletzung*). Furthermore, the collapse of foundation of contract (*Wegfall der Geschäftsgrundlage*) and claims arising from pre-contractual relations (*culpa in contrahendo*) are now provided for. The latter three principles had been developed by the case-law of the courts as the original BGB had not accounted for them. The 2001 reform of the law of obligations has now introduced them to the BGB. This reform aimed to render the law on irregularities more consistent and clear by introducing a basic provision for liability in all cases of a breach as well as by streamlining the rules on limitation periods (especially with regard to the rights of secondary claims under the law on contracts of sale[85]).

4.1 Basic provision for liability: the new § 280 BGB

The central provision on liability and starting point for an assessment of damages for any irregularites in performance and thus breach of a contract is the new § 280. It entitles the creditor of an obligation to the compensation of damages he suffers as a cause of the obligor's breach of a duty under the obligational relationship (§ 280 I 1). However, the obligor can avert liability if he can prove he was not responsible for the breach (§ 280 I 2). Section 2 of § 280, furthermore, allows additional compensation for damages arising from a delayed performance, that is the

---

[84] Not to be confused with rescission of a declaration of intent (!), see sec. B. 5.3.4.
[85] See below, sec. D.

damages suffered although ultimately the performance was made. Section 3 clarifies that damages in lieu of performance can only be claimed under the specific conditions mapped out by §§ 281–283. The latter provisions deal with delay, bad performance (§ 281), breach of an ancillary duty (§ 282), and impossibility (§ 283). However, apart from claiming damages other remedies may be available for these irregularities, such as rescission of the contract, depending on the type of breach. We will first look at the classic, irregularity of impossibility.

4.2 Impossibility (*Unmöglichkeit der Leistung*)

Previous considerations of whether the impossibility of performance is initial or subsequent, whether it is objective or subjective, have been rendered irrelevant by the new law. (New) § 275—in a nutshell—defines several cases of impossibility and determines as a legal consequence of an impossible performance the obligor's release of the obligation. Under the conditions of § 280 he then may be liable to compensation. Where mutually obliging relationships are concerned the question arises what will become of the counter claim (e.g. the claim to payment if the goods to be delivered have been destroyed). This will be examined below.

Paragraph 275 now includes all cases of impossibility to render the obligatory performance. It does not matter whether this impossibility existed before the obligation entered into force (§ 311a) or subsequently. Furthermore, no distinction is made as to whether it is impossible for anyone to perform, such as where the car to be sold is destroyed (objective impossibility), or only impossible for the particular obligor in question, e.g. the car is stolen (subjective impossibility). In all cases—irrespective of the obligor's responsibility for the impossibility—the first legal consequence is the same: the obligor is freed from his obligation (§ 275 I). If the impossibility is in respect of a generic obligation (*Gattungsschuld*), the obligor is still obliged to perform or be responsible for non-performance according to § 276 (*Beschaffungsrisiko*),[86] even if faultless. Only the designation of generic goods into specific goods changes this (§ 243 II) as the obligation there has been limited to those goods.

Sections 2 and 3 of § 275 also include cases of factual impossibility and impossibility on account of "personal unreasonableness". Thus a performance demanding an unreasonable effort is considered a factual impossibility.

Example: The ring to be handed over to the creditor has sunk to the bottom of an ocean.

However, it does not cover economic impossibility such as sudden astronomical inflation or a rise in taxes or interest. This would be a case of collapse of the foundation of a contract.

---

[86] Previously regulated in § 279, which has now been repealed.

As opposed to the cases of § 275 I the legal consequence of factual impossibility mapped out in § 275 II is not an automatic release of the obligor but rather that he can refuse to perform. However, he has to raise this objection expressly if a court is to consider it (*Einrede*).

In addition to that § 275 III grants the obligor a right to refuse performance if it were unreasonable for the obligor to perform personally, such as in contracts of employment. Again, the obligor must raise this objection expressly.

Classical Example of personal unreasonableness: A singer refuses to perform because of a fatal illness of her child.

Note that in all these cases the obligor is freed from his responsibility or can refuse the performance "in as far as" it is impossible, thus allowing for partial impossibility (§ 275 I).

4.2.1 Secondary claims/duties in cases of impossibility

When looking at the secondary claims that now arise for the creditor § 275 does not generally point to the basic provision of § 280 but makes a distinction: in cases of initial impossibility § 311a BGB now is applicable (see § 275 IV). This is surprising as the idea of the 2001 reform was to streamline the legal consequences of any breach including any type of impossibility. According to § 311a where the performance of an obligation was already impossible at the establishment of the obligation the creditor may demand compensation for damages in lieu of performance. Alternatively, he can demand reimbursement of his expenses according to § 284. However, if the obligor can prove that he was not aware and could not have been aware of his impossibility then these rights are not available to the creditor.

As far as the performance was rendered impossible after the obligation was created, in other words in cases of subsequent impossibility, a reference to the basic rules of §§ 280 and 283 is made (§ 275 IV). Thus in these cases of impossibility the creditor may demand compensation if the obligor cannot prove a lack of responsibility (§§ 280 I, III, 283). Alternatively, under § 285 he can also demand whatever the obligor has received because of the impossibility, e.g. the premium of insurance for the destroyed car that can no longer be handed over (*stellvertretendes Kommodum*).

4.2.2 Impossibility and bilateral obligatory contracts

Where a performance becomes impossible and § 275 releases the obligor from his duty to perform the creditor has certain secondary claims, as we have just pointed out. But what happens to his own obligation in cases of a mutual obligational relationship (e.g. contract of sale)? Whether the creditor still has to perform his obligation here is determined by §§ 275 IV, 326. In these cases the general principle of § 326 I provides that the claim to the obligational "counter-performance"

(*Gegenleistung*) extinguishes. This is only logical as the two obligations in a mutu-ally obliging relationship have been created in respect of each other.[87] Objects already received will have to be exchanged again according to the rules of rescission of the contract (§§ 326 IV, 346 et seq.). However, where the obligor has been freed only partly from his obligation, e.g. because the obligation can be split into several units, the creditor possibly has no interest in receiving the rest of the performance under the valid part of the obligation. Thus he may rescind the contract as a whole (§§ 326 V, VI, 346 et seq.). The reform has introduced the possibility to demand compensation in cases of rescission as well. Thus they are no longer mutually exclusive (§ 325).

Where the creditor himself was responsible for the impossibility of the perform-ance by the obligor (opposite case of § 280 I) he still has to perform his obligation (§ 326 II). The same applies where the risk of the performance has shifted over to him, such as, for example, in cases where the seller has delivered the goods to a transport firm and thus done everything he was obliged to (§ 447). Note that § 447 is no longer applicable to the sending of consumer goods (§ 474 I).

4.2.3 *Passage of risk and Drittschadensliquidation in cases of § 447*

The case of § 447 gives rise to the question of what happens if the goods are des-troyed in transit due to negligence of the transport company. Here performance is impossible as the goods are destroyed and the obligor—the seller—has been freed of his obligation according to §§ 275 I. With the passage of risk (§ 447) he is entitled to the counter-performance. The creditor cannot claim damages according to §§ 280, 283 because the obligor is not liable in this case. Furthermore, the creditor has no claim against the transport company as no contractual obligations exist between them. The obligor (here the seller), on the other hand, has no claim against the transport company because he has not suffered any damage. Here the courts invented the principle of *Drittschadensliquidation*. The seller can claim damages from the transport firm for the damages caused to the third party. Afterwards the buyer (creditor) can demand the compensation received by the seller under § 285 (*stellvertretendes Kommodum*).[88]

4.3 **Delay (*Verzug*)**

This concerns the timely performance of the obligation and the consequences of a late performance.

4.3.1 *Obligor delay*

If the obligor fails to perform an obligation by the original date set he is in delay. This qualifies as a breach of his obligation under § 280 and will generally entitle the creditor to claim compensation if the obligor cannot prove that he was not res-ponsible. For the cases of delay § 280 II and III refer to two different provisions

---

[87] Such mutual agreements are described as *Synallagma*.
[88] See above, sec. 4.2.1.

providing the creditor with compensatory rights for two types of damages. On the one hand, he may demand compensation for damages in lieu of the performance (*Nichterfüllungsschaden*) under §§ 281, 286 I and, on the other, damages caused by the delay[89] in the meantime as *Verzögerungsschaden* (§ 286). In order to claim the latter first the conditions of § 286 must be fulfilled. The "breach" consisting in delay of the obligor according to § 286 I will occur if he fails to perform, the original performance was due and a reminder (*Mahnung*) has been given to him. There are, however, exceptions to the requirement of notice:

(a) where a set calendar date has been given or after which delivery would be of no use (§ 286 II No. 1),

(b) where the time of delivery can be determined due to linkage to a certain event (§ 286 II No. 2),

(c) where the obligor has seriously and expressly refused performance (§ 286 II No. 3) and

(d) where on a balance of the parties' interests an assumption of delay is justified, e.g. in cases of urgent repairs (§ 286 II No. 4).

According to § 286 III delay in money payments (*Entgeltzahlung*) does not require a reminder where a bill has been sent to the obligor. Here he will automatically be in delay thirty days after payment is due and he has received the bill. Consumers, however, have to be expressly warned of this consequence (§ 286 III 1, 2) otherwise it will not take effect. Interest rates for delay are at 5% above the base interest rate p.a. for consumers (§ 288 I), and 8% above the base interest rate p.a. for business transactions (§ 288 II).

Furthermore, the creditor may demand compensation of damages in lieu of performance under the conditions of §§ 280 I, III, 281. Again, § 280 is the starting point of the claim if there is a breach, here the delay according to § 281, and if the obligor cannot prove absence of liability. Paragraph 281 I adds conditions for the claim under § 280: the performance must be due and the creditor must have without success set a new time limit for the obligor to perform. Only then will he be entitled to claim damages according to § 280. However, setting a new time limit (*Nachfrist*) is not necessary where the obligor has seriously refused performance or where it is dispensable on a balance of the interests at stake (§ 281 II). Once the creditor has opted for damages (e.g. by bringing an action)—but only then—the (primary) obligation of performance has extinguished (§ 281 IV).

For bilateral mutually obliging agreements the following rules have to be observed: once the creditor has chosen to claim damages and thus rendered the claim for performance extinct, the obligor's claim for the "counter performance" extinguishes as well. Furthermore, the creditor may instead of or in addition to claiming damages (§ 281) rescind the contract under the conditions of §§ 323 I 1 et seq.

---

[89] E.g. costs for employing a lawyer to take pre-trial action.

4.3.2 *Creditor delay*

Delay by the creditor is dealt with in similar terms by §§ 293–299. A creditor will be in delay if he doesn't accept the performance of the obligor (§ 293). This will only apply if the obligor has attempted to effect the performance as agreed at the right place and at the right time or the performance must have at least been offered but refused (§ 294). Under § 295 an oral offer to perform is sufficient if the creditor has declared that he will not accept the performance. No fault is necessary on the part of the creditor to be liable if he has refused to perform.

Under § 297, the creditor is liable for delay as long as the obligor can effect performance and is also liable for delay if he accepts the offered performance but refuses to effect his own (§ 298).

4.4 Positive breach of obligation/contract (*Positive Forderungsverletzung/Vertragsverletzung*)

4.4.1 *Case-law development on positive breach*

Positive breach of obligation is now a well established category of irregularity in performance and has been incorporated into the BGB by the 2001 law reform. The claim under positive breach was a residual or subsidiary claim. It used to be only actionable if the irregularity was not actionable under any other basis of claim in the BGB. The relevance of the other categories, i.e. impossibility, delay, defect in goods, or fundamental breach had to be considered first. The claim for positive breach did not exclude claims under delict, which could be made at the same time.

Positive breach covers the situation where the obligor, by action or omission, fails to comply with a contractual duty which causes harm to the creditor—now especially protected under § 241 II. It had not been provided for by the BGB until the reform taking effect from January 2002. Thus previously the courts had to develop principles on how to deal with a positive breach of an obligation. The leading case on this is the original one considered by the *Reichsgericht* in 1902—in other words, 100 years before positive breach was finally regulated by law.

RGZ 54, 98 Gravel case

A gravel merchant contracted to supply gravel to a bridge builder. Payment was to be on basis of the size of bridge completed. The builder, however, also used gravel for the construction of the approach roads, thus falsifying the payment calculation. The court found that there had been no impossibility or delay in payment, nor any defect, but held a positive breach of contract had occurred and the supplier could rescind the contract.

This remedy has been applied in a variety cases. It applies not only to a breach of the principal duty of performance, but to all duties arising from the contract, the secondary or ancillary obligations. These include both express duties and those implied or construed by the court to protect the interests of the parties. It also applies to post contractual duties.

Whereas a defective performance in contract of sale or a fault in the objects of sale under the old § 459—now corresponding to the new § 434—would only be remedied by the rescission of the contract and the return of the money and would not compensate profits, positive breach may result in compensation for any consequent harm.

Further examples of claims under positive breach of obligation have occurred in a number of cases involving either the delivery of ill animals or poisonous fodder which caused consequential damage:

RGZ 66, 289 Poisonous Horse Fodder Case

A farmer delivered horse food to a stables. It contained a poisonous component and, as a result, two horses died. The farmer had complied with the requirements of the BGB and contractual obligations entered into in terms of the performance of the delivery, but had injured the property of the creditor. The horse owner could not claim against the farmer on the grounds of impossibility or delay. Performance was possible and the preconditions for delayed performance and rescission had not been met. (Old) § 459 et seq. would allow a claim for defective goods and impose liability for a defect in the quality of the thing but would award only the price of the fodder itself and not compensation for the harm caused. Neither would a claim under the old § 463 (lack of quality) compensate the damage. Positive breach of obligation would be the only basis of a contractual claim and was upheld in this case.

Other examples in the category of inadequate performance concern the delivery of contaminated fuel which ruined an engine,[90] wrongful treatment by a doctor, and wrongful advice from an attorney. Another category concerns ancillary duties, and is typified by the cases when damage resulted from a machine when operated incorrectly due to the absence of instructions or the supplying of incorrect instructions.[91]

Thus—abstractly phrased—the requirements are that a contractual duty, either a principal, secondary, express, or implied duty, must be breached, that the creditor has suffered damage as a result of the breach, and the obligor must be at fault.

4.4.2 *The consequences of a positive breach of contract* (now under §§ 241, 280, 281)

The case-law principles have been transformed into written law by the 2001 law reform. According to §§ 280 I, III, 281 any breach of an obligation by the obligor will entitle the creditor to compensation for damages, provided the obligor cannot prove absence of his liability and that the creditor has without success set a new time limit for proper performance (§ 281 I). This time limit is dispensable if

---

[90] BGH NJW 1968, 2238.
[91] BGHZ 47, 312; BGHZ 64, 46.

unreasonable under the circumstances of § 281 II, considered above.[92] Apart from damages the remedies of rescission of the contract (§ 323 et seq.) as well as termination, § 314 (in cases of permanent contractual relationships), are possible. The duty to fulfil ancillary obligations and thus respect the other party's interests, i.e. through careful performance, is manifested now in § 241 II.

4.5 Problems in pre-contractual relations (c.i.c.)

A category of claim exists which applies when liability arises in pre-contractual situations, known as *Verschulden bei Vertragsverhandlung* or *culpa in contrahendo* (c.i.c). This used to be neither a typical contractual remedy nor a delictual remedy. It is similar to positive breach in that it had to be developed by the courts but concerns pre-contractual as opposed to contractual relations. Both are, however, concerned with situations where damage has been suffered and a claim exists for compensation. As with positive breach, it was also a residual remedy, therefore a party had to determine whether it was excluded by the application of other claims.

The basis for allowing such a claim was that actions under contract and delict do not cover all the possible claims which can arise. In some situations there will be no contract in existence, and a claim in delict will be defeated on the basis that no fault exists in respect of the person who is capable of compensation. An example would be where the seller's assistant caused damage to a potential buyer during the test drive of a car. Paragraphs 823 and 831 would exclude liability in delict if the seller had no personal blame in employing a useless assistant. If a contract had existed § 278 would apply and include damage caused by sales assistants. Hence, an argument developed that by entering into pre-contractual discussions, a relationship akin to a contractual relationship comes into being. A duty therefore arises to take care of the other party because of the readiness to enter into contractual relations, and consequently a liability similar to contractual liability arises in the event of damage. The duties are not primary duties but the ancillary duties of care and loyalty.

The founding case for this remedy also arises from the *Reichsgericht*, the linoleum case:

RGZ 78, 239 Linoleumrollenfall

A woman was in a shop for the purpose of purchasing a roll of linoleum but was injured by the carelessness of an assistant. As a result, the purchase did not take place. The court granted her claim for damages in terms of pre-contractual contact, that contractual standards of liability could be applied when one was on the way to a contract. The customer had put herself under the protection of the shop in a contractual way, therefore a duty owed by the assistant was breached. Thus claims for damages under the principles of contract law rather than delict applied.

---

[92] See below, sec. C. 4.3.1.

Groups of cases have arisen from the court's acceptance of this rule which involve a breach of a duty of care as in the linoleum case above. They also include cases where there was no immediate intention to purchase. In the linoleum case the shopper had in fact already made purchases in the other departments of the store.

Ordinarily there would be no consequences when contractual discussions fail in business contracts, but the remedy could be applied by analogy to contractual preparations whereby somebody, through a readiness to contract, produces a situation of trust, which another may breach by the arbitrary breaking off of pre-contractual negotiations where the signing of a contract had been taken to be a mere formality or a certainty induced by the other party. The situation extends from the start of pre-contractual relations to the closing of the contract.[93]

These principles have now been incorporated into the BGB by the 2001 law reform: § 311 II clarifies that entering into contractual relationships by negotiation will already create a relationship of obligation in the sense of § 241. Thus the same remedies are available, e.g. compensation for damages according to §§ 311 II, 280 I, 282.

4.6 Collapse of foundation of contract, § 313 (*Wegfall der Geschäftsgrundlage*)

This concerns the consequences for the obligations of the parties in the event of a collapse of the contract or, to be more specific, of its base, known as *Wegfall der Geschäftsgrundlage*.

Where both parties are mistaken about the content or details of the agreement reached, general rules, especially the good faith paragraphs (§§ 157 & 242) have been employed. These cases involve the objective collapse of the foundation or basis of the contract. Whilst these are not terms or clauses of the contract itself nor motives they are the assumptions of the existence of fundamental circumstances which were the basis of the transaction by one or both parties.

Originally, the courts stood by the fact that the BGB had no specific solution for this problem. The view was adopted that this could not be considered as mistake under § 119 by both parties because it would be impossible to determine who made the mistake first and thus who should have the right to rescind and receive damages. Thus in 1920 a different approach was necessary to find a fair solution in a revaluation case.[94] A long term rental contract dating from 1912 provided for the supply of steam for heating purposes at a fixed price. The cost of the supply had risen. The *Reichsgericht* raised the price above that given in the contract otherwise, it held, it would be intolerable and a mockery of the principles of good faith, justice, and equity.

Cases involving the collapse of the foundation include lack of parity cases and frustration of purpose as in the case where a hall was booked to hear a recital by a

---

[93] See BGHZ 66, 51, BGH NJW 1962, 31, BGH NJW 1975, 1774, or where there was no sound reason to do so, BGH NJW 1980, 1684.
[94] RGZ 100, 129, 132.

contralto.[95] When she fell ill the contract collapsed and the court held it could be abandoned. In another case a person rented a boat house but shortly afterwards sailing on the lake was banned. The court allowed him to abandon the contract.[96]

The principle emerging was that where the preconditions for the contract can no longer be fulfilled and would lead to the collapse of the contract or would be grossly unfair to one party, the court will intervene. This has now been codified in § 313. The extent of the intervention is not usually to render the contract void but to adapt the original agreement or add to it or remove the original unfairness as the facts demand. This original principle of the courts trying to preserve the contract where possible as an alternative to rescission or nullity can now be found expressly in § 313 III.

4.7 Rescission, §§ 323–326, 346–349 (*Rücktritt vom Vertrag*)

In bilateral contracts a breach of an obligation by the obligor may—as has been already pointed out—entitle the creditor to rescind the whole contract. This is regulated in §§ 323–326, 346–349. According to § 323 I the creditor must first set a new time limit for performance if there has been no or only bad performance. If no performance is made he is then entitled to declare the rescission of the contract. The declaration (§ 349)—a declaration of intent requiring receipt—transforms the bilateral contract into a relationship obliging the parties to grant back the exchanged goods or services (*Rückgewährschuldverhältnis*, § 346). This means not only that received goods have to be given back but also any advantages gained from them (§ 347). Where this is not possible, in general, their value has to be replaced (§ 346). Another consequence of the declaration is the extinction of the primary obligations under the original contract. The right of rescission is precluded if the creditor was liable for the irregularities of performance of the obligor (§ 323 VI).

5 Assessing damages and compensation

We have referred to the claim of damages frequently especially in the context of § 280, the legal base for a claim for compensation in cases of a breach of an obligation. We will now briefly look at the provisions determining the damages suffered and liability. The BGB contains a complicated set of fault based rules for determining when and where compensation should be provided in the case of a breach or performance. In practice this is of less consequence for the parties, because insurance has been widely employed to allay the application of the law and has undermined the fault basis.

There is no definition of 'damage' in the BGB but the courts have defined damage as every disadvantage a person suffers as a result of action on property, belongings,

---

[95] OLG Bremen NJW 1953, 1393.
[96] BGH WM 1971, 1300.

or to a lawfully protected right. The level of compensation is the difference between the situation with the damage and the hypothetical situation if the damage had not taken place. The damage must have been caused by an action or omission carried out or omitted under a contract. This applies not only to the primary duty but to secondary duties.

There is a division between claims for compensation out of contract and arising from statute, as with delictual claims (§§ 823 et seq.) (*Schadensersatzansprüche aus Vertrag* and *aus Gesetz*). Only the contractual remedies will be considered here.

Compensation under §§ 249 et seq. is designed to make up for injury, initially by substitution or, when this is not possible, by money, the latter being by far the most usual form now. Compensation for non-physical damage is restricted to where provided for by statute (§ 253), for example as in § 847 in respect of pain suffered, and exceptionally where allowed by the courts.[97]

A distinction is drawn between breach of performance damage (*Schadensersatz statt Leistung*), the positive interest, which must compensate to the extent as if the obligations had been performed, and breach of trust damages (*Vertrauensschaden*), or negative interest, designed to put the person in the position he was in before the contract was concluded.

5.1 Types of damage

Damages are calculated by §§ 249–254:

(a) Direct damage is the actual impairment of the injured object or right, for example, the repair costs of a car involved in an accident,

(b) Indirect damage includes the further consequences of the original damage, the injuries causing a period of unemployment and loss of profit (§ 252),

(c) Material damage is any sort of damage which can be replaced naturally by a substitute or money. Non-material is that which cannot, for example, pain or loss of freedom (§ 253).

A breach of performance according to § 280 will under the conditions of §§ 281–283 lead up to compensation for non-performance to protect the positive interest including direct and indirect or consequential damage. With impossibility, specific performance is not available therefore the injured party can dissolve the contract, determine fault, and claim damages for non-performance (see §§ 280 and 249–252) for lost profit. The claim includes direct and indirect compensation. Damage caused by a breach of trust, as in rescission of a declaration of intent due to mistake, under § 122 harms a negative interest and the compensation is limited to direct damage. The remedy is therefore rather limited. As a result of rescission the contract disappears and therefore there must be a claim to pursue benefits already transferred.

---

[97] As in the *Ginsengwurzel* case, BGHZ, 35, 363 where compensation for pain was allowed for the damage to the general personality right.

5.2 Fault (*Verschulden*)

The liability to pay damages in the BGB has been strongly dependant on the actual fault of the debtor. This concept is thus very much tied to the principle of causation (*Kausalität*) in that compensation need only be paid for the damages which have resulted from the action of person at fault. There must be an appropriate link between the breach of the law and the resultant damage (*Adäquanztheorie*).

According to § 276 I 1 the obligor is responsible for the consequences occurring due to intentional and negligent conduct. Paragraph 276 II defines negligence as a failure to exercise ordinary care and mere or slight negligence may suffice. At the other end of the scale of personal fault is intentional fault or contractual misbehaviour. Intention has been interpreted by the courts as equal to knowledge combined with the desire to achieve the result and an awareness that the action or omission breaches a legal or contractual duty or obligation.

The perception of fault liability has been developed by the courts as an objective rather than a subjective concept and at times approaches strict liability which does not require personal fault on the part of the obligor. This concept is most clearly seen in § 278, the responsibility for those employed in the performance or execution of the contractual obligation. The obligor is automatically liable for such breaches and there is no investigation as to whether there was any real fault on his part. It is a primary and not a vicarious liability. The principle employed reflects the expansion of business by the use of assistants and imposes the risk of the use of assistants on the person who stands to profit from their use. The assistant should be carrying out the principal's work consistent with or under instruction to do so, express or implied. This contrasts greatly with the responsibility imposed in delict law where defences are allowed to the employer.

The failure to deliver generic goods incurs strict liability even where no personal fault exists on the part of the obligor, if he has taken over the risk to deliver (*Beschaffungsrisiko*). Previously regulated in the old § 279 this is now included in § 276 I.

Contributory negligence is regulated by § 254 whereby a contribution to the damage leads to a reduction in the compensation payable.

Fault liability can apply to protect third parties not privy to the contract known as *Vertrag mit Schutzwirkung für Dritte*. In a case where a heating engineer negligently allowed gas to escape from an installation which harmed a customer's child the child was allowed a contractual claim against the obligor (heating engineer).[98] This is not to be confused with contracts which were designed to benefit a third party, known as *Vertrag zugunsten Dritter*.[99] Under the former type of contract, the claim would arise as a result of a breach of secondary duties (*Verletzung von Nebenpflichten*).

Contracting parties are free to release themselves from any fault liability and often amend their contracts to exclude liability as permitted by § 276 I subject to

[98] BGHZ 61, 233.
[99] See above, sec. C. 3.7.

the general rules of the BGB—especially the rules on Standard Business Conditions (AGB) now found in §§ 305–310.

D Book Two: the law of obligations: special part

The special part of Book Two (§§ 433–853, *Besonderes Schuldrecht*) concerns the individual types of obligational relationships dealing with those established by contract or by law. Especially as regards contracts the legislator has provided rules for parties who have not, for whatever reason, formulated their own rules. Although contractual freedom is extensive, the general rules of the first book and obligations rules of the BGB must be observed, for example, excessive and unfair contracts or clauses are regulated by the general paragraphs previously considered, *viz.* §§ 134, 138, 157 and 242. Thus there are rules that can be altered by the contracting parties (*dispositives Recht*) and those that are mandatory (*zwingendes Recht*). The rules on areas such as unjustified enrichment (§§ 812 et seq.) and unlawful conduct (§§ 823 et seq.) cannot be altered by individuals.

The second book deals with over thirty particular forms of obligational relationships. As far as contractual obligations are concerned they can roughly be divided into those concerned with an assignment or transfer of objects and rights, for example, sale, exchange, gift, rent, hire, lease and loan, and those concerned with a service or activity, for example, contracts of employment, service, or association.

Not all contracts correspond exactly to the above and many are mixed contracts which overlap between categories. Additionally, new forms of business relations have come into being which were not envisaged at the time the BGB was drafted, such as factoring and franchising. The rules applicable are usually determined by the type of main obligation imposed by the agreement. In this section we will only give a brief outline of the law on contracts of sale, unjustified enrichment, and compensation under unlawful conduct.

1 Law on contracts of sale (*Kaufrecht*)

Paragraphs 433–479 contain the rules dealing specifically with contracts of sale. The general rules, previously discussed, applicable to contracts can be modified by the special rules applicable in this section, for example the rules on irregularities[100] can be modified by special rules on sale. The law on contracts of sale has been

---

[100] See above, sec. C.4.

substantially altered by the 2001 reform of the law of obligations with the aim of tying remedies in with the general principles of the law of obligations and of streamlining limitation periods.

The sale contract is a bilateral obligation whereby the seller binds himself to deliver the object and transfer ownership thereof to the buyer who is obliged to pay the price. Thus the contract of sale is only the obligating transaction (*Verpflichtungsgeschäft*) creating the rights and obligations for the parties. In other words, it refers only to the establishment of the principal duties or obligations, the promise to sell something in exchange for a promise to pay. The performance transaction or "transaction of disposal" (*Verfügungsgeschäft*) deals with the actual transference of the subject matter and money, and is further dealt with by the paragraphs on property law in the third book of the BGB.[101]

1.1 Duties of seller and buyer

The duties under the basic provision on the contract of sale (§ 433) apply to the sale of movable and immovable objects, and rights (§ 453) and also such "immaterial" objects as businesses or electricity. Paragraph § 433 I provides that the seller is bound to deliver the object and to transfer ownership thereof. Under § 433 II, the buyer is bound to pay the price and take delivery. The buyer can therefore demand the subject matter and the seller the price. The actual transfer of ownership is dealt with by the third book of the BGB (§§ 925 and 929) considered below. With the sale of rights, the seller is to transfer to the buyer the right and to comply with all necessary formalities in doing so. New sentence 2 of § 433 I clarifies that the seller has to deliver the object of sale free from defects concerning quality (*Sachmängel*) or legal title (*Rechtsmängel*). Therefore the latter rule implies that the seller warrants a good legal title in the subject matter, that he owned the goods in order to lawfully sell them and they are free from any third party interests. Ancillary duties arise either from statute (for example § 448, the duty to bear the costs of delivery) or from an interpretation of the contract itself,[102] in particular in the light of the principle of good faith under § 242.

The principal duties of the buyer are to accept delivery and pay the price (§ 433 II). There are ancillary duties concerning, for example, the costs of delivery (§ 448) and those arising from the interpretation of the contract.

1.2 Passage of risk

Additional rules for the passage of risk under sale are contained in §§ 446–47. Normally the risk in sale passes when the performance by the creditor is made. Paragraph 446 states that the risk of accidental damage passes to buyer at the time

---

[101] For explanation of the *Abstraktionsprinzip* see above sec. A. 3.2.

[102] Note that the duty to give information previously regulated in § 444 now follows from a generally acknowledged principle of ancillary duties. It is no longer specifically regulated by the law on contracts of sale. Compare, however, the new provisions on duties of information in the Introduction Act of the BGB: §§ 238–242 EGBGB.

of delivery, the physical transference of the thing and not necessarily the transfer of ownership. Paragraph 447 alters the above rule in respect of goods delivered to special instructions of the buyer and to a place other than the buyer's domicile (*Versendungskauf*). The buyer has the risk as soon as goods leave the seller and are in despatch, post or carriage. However, if the seller deviates from the special instructions of the buyer the risk remains with the seller. Furthermore, § 447 is not applicable to contracts where the seller is a consumer (§ 474 II).

Possession is the crucial factor in risk, particularly where legal ownership may be reserved by the seller. Paragraph 449 confirms that the seller may reserve title and, where he is not paid the BGB allows him to withdraw from the contract. He can claim damages (e.g. §§ 280 I, II, 286) or the return of the goods under § 985 or unjustified enrichment under § 812. In these circumstances the performance of the contract is suspended and the ownership in the goods is not transferred but retained by the seller. Further details of reservation of titles clauses can be found in the section on property law, below.

1.3 Remedies for delivery of defective goods (*Gewährleistungsrechte*)

Initially, there are the breaches for non-performance or bad performance (delay, impossibility, positive breach), discussed above. Where such irregularities arise the remedies mapped out by the general law of obligations are available, i.e. compensation, rescission of the contract, and reimbursement of expenses. However, the rules on contract of sale additionally provide for a specific type of bad performance: a "fault" of the object of sale, which may be a defect concerning quality (§ 434) or the legal title (§ 435). Here special rules on remedies apply. Conditions for claiming such remedies are that there is:

(a) a valid contract of sale,

(b) a reason for claiming remedies (e.g. a "fault"),

(c) no exclusion of the remedy by the law, and

(d) no obstacle as to the enforcement of the remedy claim by specific limitation periods.

The validity of the contract of sale depends on accordance with the principles under the general part of the BGB and the general law of obligations. The reason for claiming a specific remedy for fault is the seller's liability. It falls into two categories, liability for legal defects concerning warranties of title (*Rechtsmängel*) noted above, and defects in the quality of the goods (*Sachmängel*). However, the consequences for both types of fault under the new law are mostly the same.

1.3.1 *The seller's liability for a defect in quality (Sachmängelhaftung)*

(New) § 434 I provides that the object of sale is free from material defects (*Sachmängel*) only if it shows the negotiated quality at the time of the passage of risk. Where no specific quality has been negotiated section 1 of the provision defines that the object has to have the quality impliedly intended according to the specific purpose of the contract (§ 434 I No. 1) or "usual" quality that a buyer may expect under similar circumstances of an object of the type sold (§ 434 I No. 2).[103] Furthermore, characteristics of the object of sale announced in advertisements by the buyer or producer are part of its negotiated quality. If the quality of the object of sale thus does not correspond with the above defined criteria then there is a material defect or fault. Further faults are assumed in the cases of defective assembly of the object, defective assembly instructions (§ 434 II), and even the delivery of either the wrong object or too small an amount of the negotiated object (§ 434 III).

Liability is excluded by law where the buyer knew of the defect (§ 442) or generally in cases of public auctions (§ 445). Additionally, liability can always be excluded on the basis of contractual terms as long as they do not offend the general paragraphs of the BGB (e.g. § 444 malicious concealment of a fault or § 475 I, III concerning protection of consumers) or the rules on general standard terms, AGB (e.g. § 309 No. 8b).

1.3.2 Remedies (Gewährleistungsrechte)

The remedies for a breach of § 434 are described in § 437, which provides for compensation, rescission of the contract, or a reduction of the price paid or to be paid (Minderung). Before claiming any of these remedies the buyer has to try to obtain proper performance by setting a new time limit for the seller (Nacherfüllung, § 437 No. 1). According to § 439 the seller may choose between a removal of the fault or delivery of new goods without defect. If the time limit for this performance has passed without success § 437 provides for rescission or reduction (§ 437 No. 2) or compensation (§ 437 No. 3). Where the buyer chooses rescission the general rules on rescission of contracts become applicable (§§ 323 et seq., 346–349). In contrast to the previous law the buyer does not need an agreement of the seller anymore to reverse the contract of sale (previously Wandlung in old § 465). He merely has to declare the rescission, which nevertheless still requires receipt by the seller (§ 130 I).

The reduction in price (Minderung) is governed by § 441 and calculated on the basis of the market value of defective object. All other obligations under contract remain.

Finally, § 437 No. 3 allows for damages with reference to §§ 440, 280, 281, 283 and 311a. This means that where a demanded "new" performance (Nacherfüllung) is impossible the general rules on impossibility apply.[104] As delivery of too small an amount of the ordered goods qualifies as a defect as well, where the delivery of the missing amount is impossible this could be either a case of impossibility or bad performance. The question will have to be decided by the courts. In cases of delay § 437 No. 3 refers to § 280 and thus also to the general rules on delay (§§ 280 I, II, 286). Just as provided for by the general rules on delay and impossibility the

---

[103] Previous disputes about the definition of objective and subjective faults thus are now as obsolete as the distinction between a fault and the lack of a promised characteristic.

[104] See above, sec. C.4.2.

pre-condition of setting of a new time limit for a new performance before claiming damages can be dispensable in certain cases.[105]

In cases not dealing with impossibility or delay but rather a genuine defect in the quality of the goods (§ 434) the buyer may claim for the damage caused (§§ 440, 280, 281). This includes the reduced value of the goods, the costs of removing the defect, as well as direct losses, e.g. where the goods could have been sold to a third person with profit. Compensation for indirectly caused damages (*Mangelfolge-schäden*) is now available under §§ 440, 280 as well. These include such damages as physical injuries caused by the defective object and costs of medical treatment. Liability of the seller is essential in all of these cases but will be presumed—allowing him to prove otherwise (§ 280 I 2nd sentence). Where the primary obligations under the contract of sale have been performed but an ancillary obligation was breached (i.e. delivery and assembly of furniture is accompanied by damaging the buyer's flat) the general rules of positive breach are applicable.[106]

Previously existing special rules in respect of generic goods whereby further rights could be exercised by the buyer (Old § 480) are now abolished as § 437 no longer distinguishes between obligations concerning generic and specific goods but treats them equally.

1.3.3 *Breaches of duty by the buyer and remedies of the seller*

Payment is due when the seller is ready to perform unless contractually agreed differently. A breach of the duty to accept the goods or failure to pay provides the seller with a claim for the specific performance (*Erfüllungsanspruch* § 433 II). If the buyer delays in effecting performance the seller can demand compensation for damage under §§ 280, 286 I.[107] Complete failure to pay means the seller can rescind the contract or claim compensation for non-performance (§§ 280, 281, 323, 346–349).

1.4 **Limitation periods**

Claims for remedies under the law on contracts of sale, e.g. demanding new performance (*Nacherfüllung*) or compensation, are now subject to a general limitation period of two years (§ 438 I No. 3).[108] Exceptionally, claims in connection with the sale of new buildings are subject to a limitation period of five years (§ 438 I No. 2). Paragraph 438 I No. 3 concerns defects as to the legal title of the object of sale. Here a long limitation period of thirty years is applicable in correspondence with the period of the owner's claim against the wrongful possessor to hand back his property under § 985 (thirty years according to § 197 I No. 1).

---

[105] See above, sec. C.4.2.
[106] See above, sec. C.4.4.
[107] See above, sec. C.4.3.
[108] Note that the right to rescind the contract or declare reduction (§ 437 No. 2) are technically not claims in the sense of § 194 as a declaration by the buyer is necessary to bring about the legal consequences. Thus they are not directly subject to limitation. However, these rights are no longer enforceable if the primary claim to demand new performance (*Nacherfüllung* §§ 437 No. 1, 439) has lapsed.

Example: *A* has sold a sculpture to *B* which in fact belonged to *C*. *C* as the rightful owner has a direct claim against *B* to be handed back the sculpture under § 985. This claim will only lapse after thirty years. If *B* now had only a regularly limited claim against *A* for selling him this "legally" defective sculpture under § 438 I No. 3, his own claim would lapse after two years but for twenty-eight more years he would be threatened by *C*'s claim. As a consequence his claim has to have the same limitation period.

1.5 Consumer protection

In order to implement EC directive 99/44 on contracts of sale involving consumers the law reform introduced consumer protection rules in §§ 474–479. They are applicable only to contracts of sale with the consumer (defined in § 13) as buyer and the business man (defined in § 14) as seller. They, furthermore, only apply to sales of moveable goods. These rules cannot be altered by individual party agreements (§ 475 I 1). They generally aim at a better protection of the consumer where contracts of sale are concerned. Thus the general rule on passage of risk in § 447 is excluded (§ 474 III). Possibilities to reduce the limitation periods are restricted (§ 475 II). Paragraph 476 reverses the burden of proof in favour of the consumer: There is an assumption that the claimed defect of the object of sale existed at the time of passage of risk. The onus is thus on the seller to prove the contrary. Paragraphs 478 and 479 have now introduced a right of the seller to claim compensation against the responsible seller within the chain, i.e. the retailer or the producer.

2 Unjustified enrichment (*Ungerechtfertigte Bereicherung*)

This is a quasi-contractual claim which takes on particular importance as a result of the principle of abstraction. Paragraphs 812 et seq. provide that a person who, without legal right, has acquired something at the expense of another, is bound to return it to the party who has a just claim to it. The rules serve to eliminate the enrichment where a party has acquired goods under a contract which is subsequently nullified, probably their most important application. The balance is achieved whereby the one deprived can again possess the goods or obtain compensation as a substitute.

Paragraph 812 I incorporates two circumstances in which unjustified enrichment would give rise to a claim:

(a) the performance claim (*Leistungskondiktion*) where the enrichment is achieved by the performance of another (§ 812 I 1st sentence, 1st alternative),

(b) enrichment in other particular ways (*in sonstiger Weise*), where a party is enriched not through effort for example because actions of the enriched party directly intervening in the other's parties rights (§ 812 I 1st sentence, 2nd alternative).

Thus, to prove a case in § 812 I 1 1st alt., the following conditions must be fulfilled:

(a) someone must have obtained something,

(b) through the performance of another,

(c) without a legal basis.

If these conditions are fulfilled a relationship of obligation has been established by law (*gesetzliches Schuldverhältnis*), as opposed to contractual obligational relationships, with the enriched party being the obligor.

2.1 The enrichment of the obligor

The obligor must have obtained "something" and any sort of asset advantage or improvement can be considered. The acquisition of assets includes possession of actual things or personal rights such as property, claims, inheritance rights, or even access rights to a shop,[109] providing there is some value or the possession of something as in the use of an object or the release from the necessity to repay a debt. In such cases the debtor is released from an obligation.

An asset advantage can be saving money, for example, where payment for the cost of a flight from Hamburg to New York was demanded under § 812 I 2nd alternative when the defendant had smuggled himself aboard but was refused entry into America and had to be flown home on the next flight.[110]

2.2 The performance of the creditor

Performance, according to § 812 I 1 1st alternative, means a conscious and desired performance (BGHZ 40, 272). The performer must be aware of what is happening, which, for example, is not the case where transport services are provided to an undetected stowaway. The person making the claim must be the one who enriched the obligor. This latter requirement is the distinguishing factor from "enrichment in other ways".

2.3 The absence of a legal basis

The performance lacks legal basis when the transfer of the assets is not based on an objectively justified legal reason such as a contract of sale. It can occur by the collapse of the legal basis whereby the seller has delivered an object to the buyer to fulfil a contract which is void and payment has not been made.

---

[109] RGZ 146, 355.
[110] BGHZ 55, 128, 130.

Example: The seller of a car rescinds his declaration of intent, the offer to sell his car, according to § 119 I 1st alternative because he was mistaken as to the price. He had offered it for €3,000 instead of 5,000 as he had intended. His rescission now has rendered the offer void *ab initio* (§ 142) and thus has voided the contract of sale (missing offer). If in the meantime he has already handed over the car to the buyer and transferred the ownership thereof, then the buyer has received the performance without legal base (the contract of sale). Note that the rescission does not cover the offer to transfer ownership in the performing contract because here the seller was not under a mistake. At the time of handing over the car he wanted to transfer ownership.

A claim under § 812 I is excluded if the performer knew that he was not required to perform (§ 814) or if the performance was of a moral duty or one which is normally expected.

Paragraph 812 I 2 (1st alternative) considers the subsequent collapse of a legal basis which had existed, such as in the return of a stolen car after the insurance had paid up, thereby the basis for retaining the money has collapsed. When an agreed transaction does not achieve its aims, a claim may be made under § 812 I 2 after rescission by one party. However, a claim will not be successful if the performer knew from the outset that it was impossible to achieve or acted in bad faith (§ 815).

Paragraph 817 I governs claims for recovery of payments and deliveries made to fulfil prohibited or immoral acts. The requirements are that the obligor in accepting the goods has contravened a statutory prohibition. Claims on this basis may also be taken via § 812 I 1 if the cause has collapsed through the illegality. Paragraph 817 II states that if the creditor has knowledge of the illegality, the performance cannot be recovered.

2.4 Enrichment in other ways (§ 812 I 1 2nd alternative)

This concerns enrichment in different sorts of factual situations. Here the enrichment is not based on a performance but is often caused by the intervention of a third party, or it can be without any human activity.

Examples: *A*'s flock of sheep wander onto *B*'s land and feed on the grass/*C* steals *D*'s car/ *E* uses public transport services without paying for them.

In some way an advantage is enjoyed by someone of another person's objects or rights. Further examples of how enrichment may come about are the paying of the debtor's debts by a third party, repairing by accident goods which belong to another or, for example, *B* by mistake uses materials belonging to *A*, who owns the adjoining plot, to build a house. *A* is entitled, because of the change in the legal position of the enriched *B*, to the equivalent worth in money.

An important special case of enrichment is contained in § 816 I 1. Under property law it is possible for a person to acquire the rights in an object in good faith from a non-entitled third party (§§ 929, 932). Where the non-entitled person receives some form of payment for the goods, § 816 I guarantees a claim to enable the real entitled person to claim the payment made. If the transfer was a gift § 816 I 2 a claim lies against the receiver of the gift. Therefore this provision restricts the protection of third parties who acquired something in good faith, where they received it without any payment.

Where the performance is made to a non-entitled party, § 816 II provides a claim against this person. If a non-entitled party obtains rights which really belong to another, e.g. the true owner, the true owner can claim from this person any benefit received from the transfer or delivery of the rights or object.

2.5 Performance by a third party

In order to satisfy the requirements for a claim under the rules of unjustified enrichment there must be a performance relationship between the obligor and creditor which is not disturbed by third parties, agent, or assistants.

Occasionally a claim can exist against third parties, if the purpose of the performance directly relates to them. This would be the case when the obligor is not entitled to the performance. An obligational relationship between the performer and the third party must exist.

2.6 The scope of the obligation to return possession

Paragraphs 818 et seq. provide the details on the obligation to return following a successful § 812 action. If the claim succeeds, the enriched person must return the gain, provided it is capable of being returned. If the original is no longer in existence, the duty extends to surrogates. If the obligor is unable to return the object, compensation must be made to the value of the goods or the service received (§ 818 II). The enriched person also has to return profits made on the object. If the value has been lost and the enriched person is in fact no longer enriched the duty to return or make good lapses (818 III).

According to § 819, a stricter liability is attached to the obligor to look after the item, if he was aware of the absence of a legal ground or that the performance infringes a legal or moral rule or there is a claim pending and the obligor is still in possession of the goods (§ 819 II). Damage incurred before the obligor was aware of the obligation to return the object falls on the claimant whereas damage sustained afterwards falls on the enriched persons.

3 Tort law[111] (*Unerlaubte Handlung*)

In the German legal system the law on tortious acts (*Deliktsrecht*) is another form of obligational relationship which establishes a claim against another person. Thirty paragraphs deal comprehensively with this area of law, concerning mainly the liability arising from accidents. It is based largely on the objective of shifting, where possible, the cost of harm to those responsible and complements unjust enrichment by rectifying an unjust loss rather than eliminating an unjust enrichment.

The legislator has provided three paragraphs, §§ 823–4 and 826 which embrace most situations resulting in delictual liability. Liability arises as a result of injury caused in an unlawful and blameworthy manner which violates a legal interest of the victim (§ 823 I), by a contravention of protective law (§ 823 II), or by intentional unlawful damage (§ 826).

Each claim has the underlying theme that the wrongdoer has breached a duty, which in contrast to contract is not a pre-existing obligational relationship but only comes into being when the criteria of the relevant paragraph are fulfilled. This area of law also includes additional statutes which have imposed a delictual liabilities, for example, particularly dangerous activities, such as nuclear power stations. These often eliminate the fault basis of a claim and impose strict liability.

3.1 The duty to compensate for damage

Paragraph 823 I provides that a person is obliged to pay compensation for either negligently or intentionally violating the protected right of another. Three elements are required to establish unlawful conduct for the purposes of § 823 I. It must be established:

(a) that there has been an act that has violated an interest and caused damage,

(b) the violation of the right should be unlawful and not be justified, and

(c) it must be caused by either intentional or negligent fault.

3.1.1 The act causing damage

The act can be any type of conscious human behaviour which is usually in the form of a positive act by the wrongdoer that damages a protected right, but can also be caused by omissions where there has been a duty to act, for example the duty to clear snow from the steps of a shop so that customers will not slip.

There must be a causal connection between the act and the damage to the protected position, which is usually determined by a consideration of whether the act was an adequate cause of the damage (*Adäquanztheorie*). Only those circumstances that according to general life experience can be regarded as apt to cause damage will be deemed adequate. The detailed problems which arise in establishing causation can be found in the discussions noted in further reading at the end of the section.

---

[111] Or sometimes more readily understood as delict law.

3.1.2 *The rights protected*

The rights to be protected are those as stated by § 823 I including, life, body, health, freedom, and ownership of property. Additionally, harm to "other rights" is included but not defined. This has been held by the courts to apply to rights arising from property, such as future interest rights and intellectual property rights amongst others. There has been a particular development of rights protecting the personality which includes honour and extends to the personality of businesses. For example in the *Stern* case,[112] the *Stern* magazine published the transcript of a telephone conversation between two well known politicians and was held to have breached rights of personality. A very famous case involved the use of a picture in an uncomplimentary way of a brewery owner enjoying his favourite pastime of riding as the basis for promoting a potency drug, the *Herrenreiterfall*.[113]

In principle, pure economic loss or nominal damages are not covered by § 823 and compensation can only cover damage arising as a consequence of the injury itself. In the cases above this would be the costs of defending one's personality in the courts but the courts have nevertheless awarded money for pain and suffering, as established in the famous *Soraya* case.[114] The borderline between consequential and pure economic loss also causes difficulties in Germany.

The general concept of the business enterprise (*Gewerbebetrieb*) is protected by § 823.

Examples: of the extent of the protection of this right given by the courts include accidentally cutting off electricity cables during construction works and thereby causing a standstill in production of a connected business,[115] the blockade of a newspaper business by demonstrators in order to hinder the delivery of the tabloid newspaper '*Bild*',[116] and the go-slow by airplane pilots in 1973.[117]

3.1.3 *Unlawfulness*

In simple terms unlawfulness will be established when one of the protected rights is violated and there is no justification such as self-defence or consent. Latterly, the interpretation of this concept has established that the further requirement exists that an established duty needs to be breached to establish unlawfulness. Apart from the general duty imposed by § 276 to exercise ordinary care, increasingly the duty required to be shown is established by the courts and statute, as in the road traffic and product liability acts considered below.

---

[112] BGHZ 73, 20.
[113] BGHZ 26, 349.
[114] BVerfG 34, 269; see above, Chapter 2, sec. 3.4.
[115] BGHZ 29, 65.
[116] BGHZ 59, 30.
[117] BGHZ 69, 128.

3.1.4 *Fault*

The concept of fault includes intentional or negligent action. The definition of negligence is defined in § 276 as the exercise of care outside ordinary or reasonable care. Negligence generally has be proved by the plaintiff. However, there are exceptions in cases of product liability under the *Produkthaftungsgesetz*. Its principles had been established before through case-law starting with the Fowl Pest case:

BGHZ 51, 91 Hühnerpestfall

Following the Fowl Pest case the burden of proof is reversed in cases where injury has been caused by defective goods. In this case the sale of non sterile vaccine and use of it by a Vet who bought it, caused the death of 4,000 chickens. The plaintiff brought an action under § 823 I. It was held that where products were used according to their purpose and where they caused damage due to their defectiveness the manufacturers must prove there is no liability (i.e. intent or negligence) in. Thus the liability is not strict but the plaintiff need only show the defective product and the damage caused. If the defendant is unable to prove there was no fault on his part he is liable under § 823 I.

3.2 The infringement of a protective law

Paragraph 823 II provides that compensation is payable when a statute which serves to protect the rights of others is infringed. The clearest examples arise from the Criminal Code protecting the person (§§ 223 et seq. StGB), ownership (§§ 242 et seq. StGB), and numerous business and employment rights.

The provision also depends on the establishment of fault even where the particular statute does not. As with § 823 I, the burden of proof is reversed and fault is presumed unless disproved.[118] Paragraph 823 II includes compensation for pure economic loss only where the statute violated covered pure economic loss. The ambit of the statute, in terms of the persons protected and the type of harm prohibited, are restraining factors for the scope of compensation provided.

3.3 Intentional damage

Paragraph 826 is concerned with intentional damage contrary to public policy (*gute Sitten* = literally: "good morals"). The action must be intentional and negligence is insufficient. The courts have attempted to find categories for the wide variety of cases arising from this clause including procuring a breach of contract, behaviour contrary to public policy in the area of competition law including the misuse of monopoly position, boycotts, and dishonest competitive behaviour. Hence this also extends to cover economic loss providing it is contrary to public policy. The

---

[118] See BGHZ 51, 91, the Fowl Pest case.

intention required extends to envisaging some damage as a result of intended action if not the exact type and amount.

3.4 Other provisions of delictual liability

Paragraph 824 provides that compensation will be payable by those who spread lies or impair the credit standing or make it harder for another person to get credit.

Paragraphs 827 and 828 concern the reduction of responsibility in respect of certain persons. Under § 827, automatism as a result of mental disturbance would exclude liability unless brought on by one's own actions.

Under § 828 I, children under the age of seven cannot be held responsible. Between the ages of seven and eighteen the responsibility of the wrongdoer depends on awareness (§ 828 II). In such circumstance there is, however—under certain conditions—a liability of the children's guardian to compensate under § 832. If such a liability is excluded § 829 allows for the liability of a child if it would be equitable in the specific case.

3.5 Vicarious liability (*Haftung für den Verrichtungsgehilfen*)

Under § 831, there is a presumed liability for the employer, for employees who have unlawfully caused damage whilst carrying out delegated tasks. The employee must be undertaking work on the instructions of the employer and an exact definition of the tasks delegated is not necessary as long as the damage was caused whilst undertaking work within that sphere of activity. The presumption is that the employer has not watched over his employee closely enough. It does not extend to the subcontracting of the self-employed, as independent contractors are not considered employees. There is no need to look for an independent fault of the employee.

According to § 831 I 2, there is a defence, which is strictly interpreted, if the employer can show that sufficient care was exercised in selection of employee. If successful, the employer will not be liable. Alternatively, there is a defence on the grounds that no matter how carefully the assistant acted, the damage would have been caused in any case. In the area of product liability the courts have demanded a very high standard of employee selection so that the defence is very restricted.[119] An action may still lie against the employee under 823 I, if the employer rebuts the presumption of fault.

3.6 Strict liability (*Gefährdungshaftung*)

In certain circumstances the fault basis has been replaced by liability attached to lawful activities where the risk and potential damage to the public is very great. The scope of this liability has been provided for by the legislator in § 833 BGB and many special enactments. Only a few prominent examples will be considered here.

---

[119] BGH NJW 1973, 1602.

3.6.1 *Liability for animals (Haftung des Tierhalters)*

Paragraph 833 I imposes strict liability on the keeper of an animal for the harm it causes. There is a defence under § 833 II where an animal is used in the course of business as in a riding stable. There is no liability if the keeper exercised due care in supervising the animal or if the damage would have occurred in any event (§ 834).

3.6.2 *The Road Traffic Act (Straßenverkehrsgesetz)*

Paragraph 7 I of the 1952 Road Traffic Act (*Straßenverkehrsgesetz StVG*) renders the registered user or custodian of a car strictly liable for any damage to persons or property that arises through the operation of the vehicle. Liability is excluded in the case of unavoidable events but not defects or use (§ 7 II 2) and is also excluded where the accident is due to the action of a third party and the user of the car has acted with the relevant degree of care in regard to the circumstances. In the business context, where an employee is driving the owner's vehicle, a separate cause of action arises under § 7 StVG and operates against the owner of the vehicle.

3.6.3 *The Strict Liability Act (Haftpflichtgesetz)*

Strict liability for death or personal injury caused by operation of a railway is imposed by § 1 of the Imperial Compulsory Liability Act 1871 (*Reichshaftpflichtgesetz*). The Imperial Law of Liability was extended to cover installations for the transmission or supply of electricity or gas including cables and pipes. In 1978, the law was re-enacted in the Strict Liability Act (*Haftpflichtgesetz*) to extend to piped fluids, fumes, and gases. The only defence allowed is *force majeure*.

3.6.4 *The Air Traffic Act (Luftverkehrsgesetz) and Nuclear Energy Act (Atomgesetz)*

These Acts impose absolute liability on the operators of aircraft and nuclear power stations for all damage. Even *force majeure* is no defence.

3.6.5 *The Water Management Act and the Drug Act*

Two notable Acts, also mentioned in the section on the consumer law above, are the Water Management Act (*Wasserhaushaltsgesetz*) of 1957, which imposes strict unlimited liability on the pollution of water, including pure economic loss, and the Pharmaceutical Act (*Arzneimittelgesetz*) of 1976 in respect of drugs put onto the market by pharmaceutical companies.

3.6.6 *The Environmental Liability Act*

A recent addition to the statutes imposing strict, no fault liability is the Environmental Liability Act (*Umwelthaftungsgesetz*), noted above in the section on environmental law in Chapter 8. Operators of installations will even be presumed to have caused environmental damage if it is of the type to be expected from such an installation.[120]

---

[120] For further details refer to Chapter 8.

3.7 **Product liability**

Allied to the above but enacted for other reasons is the Product Liability Act of 15 December 1989 (*Produkthaftungsgesetz, ProdHaftG*). Prior to the enactment of this law the courts had imposed stricter liability for defective goods by reversing the burden of proof in the Fowl Pest case,[121] considered above. Paragraph 1 imposes strict liability on a manufacturer of a defective product that kills or injures a person or which damages property. This remedy only applies to product, put into circulation after the entry into force of the Act.[122]

3.8 **Buildings and occupiers' liability**

Paragraphs 836–838 guarantee claims for damage caused by unsafe premises, for example, the collapse of parts of a building. Those liable can be the owner, the former owner, the occupier, and those who take care of buildings. A defence exists, according to § 836 I 2, if it can be demonstrated that necessary care was taken to avoid the danger.

3.9 **Liability of the state**

Paragraph 839 allows a claim against the state, outside of those claims which are normally conducted by the administrative courts under public law. The civil law claim exists against the organs and officials of the state who in violation of a state duty intentionally or negligently cause damage. In the case of negligence the action only lies if no other is possible, for example, against the state itself. The state stands vicariously liable for the official under Article 34 *Grundgesetz* and will only have recourse against the official in the case of intent or gross negligence. If the state was at fault it will be liable to compensate.

3.10 **Compensation**

Compensation is determined by §§ 842–847 in respect of personal injury and §§ 848–851 for property damage and the general rules on obligations (§§ 249 et seq.).

According to § 842 the claim to compensation is designed to cover all the disadvantages the injured party has incurred.

Paragraph 843 provides for the periodic payment for the impairment of earning capacity and § 847 provides compensation for pain and suffering for injury and loss of freedom.

The basic position in respect of property damage is to make good the damage, in kind where necessary (§§ 848 and 249 et seq.).

If more than one person was involved in causing the damage, § 830 I holds all of them responsible to compensate. Paragraph 830 I 2 also provides for compensation

---

[121] BGHZ 51, 91.
[122] The further details and limitations of this Act are also considered in sec. D of Chapter 8.

to be levied in cases where the distinct individual cannot be determined but that the damage is self evident and a number of possible wrongdoers exist.

If the victim was also at fault, contributory damages are payable (§ 254).

3.11 Limitation periods

Paragraphs 195, 199 I set a limitation period of three years, running from the time the injured party and the wrongdoer are made aware of the damage. However this is subject to a maximum thirty year limitation running from the date the damage was caused to life, physical integrity, health and freedom (§ 199 II BGB). Where damages of property are concerned the maximum limitation period is ten years (§ 199 III BGB).

FURTHER READING

BGB 2002, *Sonderausgabe Schuldrechtsreform* (2002: C.H. Beck, München).

A. Alpmann-Pieper, *Express Reform des Schuldrechts: Das neue BGB*, 2nd ed. (2002: Alpmann und Schmidt, Münster).

H. Brox, *Allgeneines Schuldrecht*, 27th ed. (2000: C.H. Beck, München).

H. Brox and W-D. Walker, *Besonderes Schuldrecht*, 26th ed. (2001: C.H. Beck, München).

E. J. Cohn, *Manual of German Law*, Vol. I (1968: Institute of Comparative Law).

B. Dauner-Lieb (ed.), *Das Neue Schuldrecht* (2002: C.F. Müller, Heidelberg).

B. Dauner-Lieb (ed.), *Fälle zum Neuen Schuldrecht* (2002: C.F. Müller, Heidelberg).

H. Kötz and G. Wagner, *Deliktsrecht*, 9th ed. (2001: Luchterhand, Neuwied).

J. Kropholler, (Studienkommentar BGB), 5th ed. (2002: C.H. Beck, München).

B.S. Markesinis, *A Comparative Introduction to the German Law of Torts*, 2nd ed. (1990, Clarendon Press, Oxford).

D. Medicus, *Schuldrecht I: Allgemeiner Teil*, 12th ed. (2000: C.H. Beck, München).

D. Medicus, *Schuldrecht II: Besonderer Teil*, 10th ed. (2000: C.H. Beck, München).

O. Palandt, *Bürgerliches Gesetzbuch: Kommentar*, 61st ed. (2002: C.H. Beck, München).

D. Reinicke and K. Tiedtke, *Bürgschaftsrecht*, 2nd ed. (2000: Luchterhand, Neuwied).

D. Reinicke and K. Tiedtke, *Kaufrecht*, 6th ed. (1997: Luchterhand, Neuwied).

D. Reinicke and K. Tiedtke, *Kreditsicherung*, 4th ed. (2000: Luchterhand, Neuwied).

G. H. Treitel, *Remedies for Breach of Contract; A Comparative Account* (1988: Clarendon Press, Oxford).

Articles

T. Bennett, "Choice of Law in Claims of Unjust Enrichment" (1990) 39 ICLQ 136–168.

B. Dickson, "The Law of Restitution in the Federal Republic of Germany" (1987) 36 ICLQ 751–787.

C-W. Canaris, "Die Reform des Rechts der" *Leistungsstörungen*, JZ 2001, pp. 499–528.

W. Ebke and B. Steinhauer, "The Doctrine of Good Faith in German Contract Law" in Beatson and Friedmann (eds.), *Good Faith and Fault in Contract Law* (1995: Clarendon press, Oxford), pp. 171–190.

B.S. Markesinis, "An Expanding Tort Law—The Price of a Rigid Contract Law" (1987) 103 LQR 354–397.

U. Magnus, "Damages for Non-Economic Loss: German Developments in a Comparative Perspective" (1990) 39 ICLQ 675–683.

E Book Three: property law (*Sachenrecht*)

1 Introduction to the scope and sources of property law

German property law is found primarily in the third book of the BGB, §§ 854–1296 and is concerned with the designation of property, synonymously termed 'objects', to legal subjects who may be the owners or possessors of this property. The BGB contains rules regarding the possession, the factual control over an object, and ownership, the legal control over an object. It regulates the acquisition and loss of possession and ownership and the regulation of other property rights such as the rights of use and securities. Property law is divided into two main subject areas, movables (*bewegliche Sachen*) and immovables, otherwise referred to as real estate (*unbewegliche Sachen und Grundstücksrecht*). Each has a special set of rules applicable to it.

The basis of German property law arises from Roman law concepts of property but also includes concepts, German in origin, such as the land registration system (*Grundbuch*) as the means of lawfully acquiring and disposing of property.

Property law, as with the law of obligations, forms part of civil law proprietary rights. The concept of property is very wide. It includes rights concerned with the peaceful enjoyment of something without disturbance, in other words the law of nuisance. Provisions of public law also have a distinct impact and, as with other areas of law, the influence that the *Grundgesetz* wields is considerable. Thus, Article 14 I GG determines the scope of the protection of property within the relation between state and citizen. It grants a freedom of property but at the same time sets limits to it in order to render this freedom bearable to other members of society such as in Article 14 II GG.[123]

In addition, many administrative laws may supplement the restriction on the rights over property, e.g. building regulations (*Baurecht*) and zoning laws, amongst others. The transfer of ownership of real estate is strictly regulated as regards the requirement to register any legal changes in the Land Register (*Grundbuch*).

---

[123] For details see Chapter 7, Art. 14 GG.

2 Definitions and general principles of property law

2.1 Real rights (*dingliche Rechte*)

Rights concerned with property are characterized as real rights (*dingliche Rechte*) and they guarantee the holder of such rights the direct control over an object. Ownership is the most important of the real rights found in the third book of the BGB (§§ 903 et seq.).

The literal translation of *Sachenrecht* would be the law of "things" or "objects". The BGB in its general part defines *Sachen* as material (*körperliche*) objects in § 90. The term thus excludes immaterial rights, e.g. claims or intellectual property rights. Paragraphs 93–95 then distinguish between immovable objects which are real estates (*Grundstücke*) and their essential components, e.g. a house on the estate. Thus, the law on real estate is concerned with the rights attached to immovable property, the acquisition and transfer of title to land and buildings, the nature, establishment, and transfer of other rights in real estate, and security interests in real estate.

Moveable objects by contrast—known in common law jurisdictions as personal property—are those whose location can be altered.

Paragraph 93 clarifies that essential components of an object—whether moveable or immovable—cannot be subject to specific rights but only to those that apply to the whole object.

While animals are not objects, the rules on moveable objects, however, are applicable to them as long as this is compatible with the nature and the protection of animals (§ 90a).

2.2 Principles of property law

2.2.1 *Typenzwang* and *Typenfixierung*

In property law the owner of an object is considered as having a right of dominion over the object (*Herrschaftsrecht*) which can be upheld against everyone and is thus an absolute right protected by the laws of property and delict (§§ 823 et seq.). *Herrschaftsrechte* are restricted by law and standardized to a large degree and in order to be valid in relation to everyone, particular forms of right must be observed, thus there are a limited and distinct number of rights. This restriction is termed the *Typenzwang* and only the forms of right which have been established by law can be created and exercised. Secondly, a concept known as *Typenfixierung* determines that the content or substance of the right cannot be varied. Thus, due to these two requirements, the freedom of contract in property law is limited and property rights can only be established in the way provided for by statute. Property law is therefore a compulsory type of law in contrast with the freedom found in the law of obligations.

2.2.2 *The principle of absoluteness (Absolutheitsprinzip)*

This principle ensures that real rights are effective as against the whole world. They guarantee legal protection of the rights of dominion (*Herrschaftsrechte*). Thus they form the counterpart to relative rights that only exist in relation to one or few other persons, for example rights, i.e. claims, arising from an obligational contract and thus only binding the other contractual party.

2.2.3 *The principle of abstraction (Abstraktionsprinzip)*

Here the effect of the principle of abstraction has to be pointed out. Nullity of the obligational contract, i.e. a contract of sale, does not affect the contract to transfer the ownership of the sold goods.[124]

2.2.4 *The principle of public disclosure (Publizitätsprinzip)*

Real rights are open to public disclosure. Real rights over movables can be seen by the possession and real rights over real estate can be observed in the Land Register (*Grundbuch*). Thus possession, on the one hand, and registration in the *Grundbuch* are means of public disclosure. This principle has considerable effect because disclosure is the basis for the legal establishment of rights in property. Entries in the Land Register are a pre-requisite for the transference of the ownership in a real estate.

2.2.5 *The principle of certainty (Bestimmtheitsgrundsatz)*

When defining the content of a right under the rules of property law there might be some discretion for the parties in spite of the principle of *Typenzwang* and *Typenfixierung*.

Example: Although the general rules on mortgages are fixed by §§ 1113–1190 the amount of the mortgage has to be assessed in each individual case.

Thus, because of its absolute effect the exact content of the real right has to be clarified and certain. The same applies to the question of who the particular right is attached to.

2.2.6 *The speciality principle (Spezialitätsprinzip)*

This principle—connected to the principle of certainty (*Bestimmtheitsgrundsatz*)—means that real rights can only be established for certain individual objects and not for groups of objects described generically. Generic objects cannot be the subject of ownership rights because they lack certainty. The same applies to business as an commercial interest. Ownership can only relate to different specific objects, such as the real estate of the business, its trucks, its stationary, etc. but not the business as a whole, which includes such intangible interests as connections to clients and suppliers.

---

[124] See above, sec. A.3.4.

3 Possession (*Der Besitz*)

There are different types of possession governed by §§ 854–872 of the BGB. Paragraph 854 provides the basic definition that possession is the power of actual control over an object. The phenomenon of possession fulfils several functions. First, it serves to protect peace under the law. Whoever is in possession of an object will be deemed to be the rightful possessor and does not have to tolerate any intrusions. Second, it serves as a means of public disclosure. Thus the transfer of ownership of moveable objects has to be indicated by a transfer of possession (§ 929 1st sentence).

3.1 Direct and indirect possession

Direct possession (*unmittelbarer Besitz*) is the exercise of factual power over an object (§ 854 I) and (§ 872), if combined with the possession as owner, it is termed proprietary possession (*Eigenbesitz*). Indirect possession (*mittelbarer Besitz*), under § 868, is created through the establishment of a relationship allowing indirect possession (*Besitzmittlungsverhältnis*). This is where a person is allowed possession for a certain period of time as in a lease or a tenancy. The tenant has direct possession and the landlord indirect possession. The tenancy agreement allows the tenant to have possession for a certain period of time and then obliges him to return the use of the property. Here again the principle of abstraction underlines the distinction between two relationships: the obligational relationship between tenant and landlord under the tenancy agreement and the relationship of both parties to the object of tenancy marked by indirect and direct possession. A void tenancy agreement does not affect the positions of the parties as possessors. Direct possession of the tenant is not altered. However, if the obligational agreement allowing direct possession is void, then the owner, here the landlord, may claim back possession (§§ 812, 985).

Both parties, the direct and the indirect possessor are entitled to defend possession against intrusion from any third party (§§ 859, 869).[125]

3.2 Exclusive and joint possession

Exclusive possession (*Alleinbesitz*) is that envisaged by § 854 whereas joint possession (*Mitbesitz*) under § 866 is where more than one person share possession of an object. Joint possession can be further divided into the situation where all the joint tenants can exercise the factual dominion over the object but must take the others' views into consideration and referred to as *einfacher Mitbesitz*, and the "in common" type of possession (*gesamthänderischer Mitbesitz*) when the factual control can

---

[125] Although this is not expressly mentioned in relation to the indirect possessor it has been acknowledged by general opinion. See M. Wolf, Sachenrecht, 17th ed., (2001: C.H. Beck, München) p. 78.

only be exercised communally. Example of the first is the use of washing facilities in a block of flats and of the second is where access to a particular room or safe storage area is only possible if all those in possession exercise the right together by the use of several keys.

3.3 Complete and partial possession

Complete possession is the exclusive possession of the whole object. Partial possession is the case when a person has an incomplete possession, for example, of a flat in which he has possession of only some of the rooms and a share of others. Paragraph 865 states that even partial possession allows the possessor legal protection of the rights as contained in §§ 858–864.

3.4 The possessor's agent (*Besitzdiener*)

Possession can either be for oneself or for another. Paragraph 855 concerning the possessor's agent (*Besitzdiener*), states that a person is not a possessor if he exercises the factual control over an object for another in someone else's household, business, or in a similar relationship and in conjunction with certain instructions. This distinction is important when it comes to considering rights of prescription, considered below. A possessor's agent cannot become possessor when finding objects. In these cases possession is immediately established for the person he works for.[126] Paragraph 935 states that bona fide acquisition of ownership is not possible in the case of theft or loss from the owner, or from a possessor's agent if the object was lost by the possessor's agent.

3.5 The acquisition and loss of possession

3.5.1 *Acquisition of possession*

Direct possession is acquired by willingly obtaining the factual control over an object (§ 854 I). This does not require business capacity (*Geschäftsfähigkeit*).[127] The will to obtain possession must be indicated but need not be specific. Thus a bank note lost in a retail-market is in possession of the owner of the retail-market even if he does not know about it, because his will of possession extends to everything on the premises of his shop.[128] According to § 854 II possession can also be established through an agreement and the factual capacity of the new possessor to exercise control over the object. Indirect possession is acquired through the establishment of a legal relationship allowing such possession (§ 868). Paragraph 870 allows the indirect possession to be transferred to another if the other person is also assigned the right to the return of the object.

---

[126] BGHZ 8, 130.
[127] See the section on Book One of the BGB.
[128] BGHZ 101, 186.

3.5.2 *Loss of possession*

Direct possession comes to an end when the possessor of the factual power over an object voluntarily gives it up or loses it involuntarily (§ 856 I). Indirect possession comes to an end when the relationship allowing such possession ends.

3.6 The protection of possession

Possession strengthens the legal position of the person entitled by demonstrating the right to all others and guarantees defence claims (§§ 861–2). Possession is one of the rights recognized under the delictual rights of § 823 I. Legislative provisions protect the possessor against the loss of possession and disturbance to the control over an object. Whoever takes or disturbs the possessor's right to possession unlawfully and without his consent commits unlawful interference (*Verbotene Eigenmacht*) with possession as defined by § 858 I. Any possession acquired by these means is defective by virtue of § 858 II. Paragraph 859 I and II allows the possessor to reply to any such interference with force if necessary, to retain possession or defend against interference. With real estate the possessor can immediately displace the trespasser and regain control over the property (§ 859 III). This naturally has consequences for criminal law as it is a defence against charges for injury caused whilst retrieving or defending possession.

The right to retrieve possession by force is only granted where the intruder has been caught red-handed. Thus once the unlawful interference has been concluded the aggrieved party has to pursue its case before the courts. Under §§ 861–2, the possessor can apply to the court to regain possession from the person who has unlawfully interfered with it or to obtain an injunction requiring the person who interferes with possession to cease (§ 862 I). This system of protecting possession only in these cases again serves the idea of keeping the peace under the law. Once possession has been withdrawn from a person the new possessor can enjoy it, even if he has done so illegally. Even the thief can then use the rights under §§ 858 et seq. Questions of the legality of possession then have to be settled in court.

4 Ownership (*Das Eigentum*)

Ownership as the most important real right is dealt with in §§ 903 et seq. Whereas these provisions regulate the (horizontal) relationship between the owner and other private persons, the constitutional provisions of Article 14 I GG has to be kept in mind when looking at the (vertical) relationship between the owner as a citizen and the state.

Article 14 (1) 1 *Grundgesetz* guarantees a subjective right for the individual and an institutional guarantee as an objective right: "Property and the right of inheritance are guaranteed". The importance of the ownership of property has clearly been recognized by the BVerfG which upholds it as a constitutionally guaranteed right as a material basis for individual self-development.[129] As a subjective right it can be used against the state as a defence to any attacks on the individual rights to ownership. The institutional guarantee of Article 14 concerns the concept of property ownership itself and ensures that the state maintains the existing legal norms which allow and protect the legal basis, the rights, and the freedom of activity of property ownership.[130] This right is subject to a general restriction in Article 14 I 2 on the content and limit of the right according to statute. Article 14 II allows restrictions on the use of property in the interest of society which contrasts and corrects the individualistic approach of the property law rules of the BGB: "Property imposes duties. Its use should also serve the public goods".

Article 14 III allows for the expropriation of property in the interests of society, providing this is done according to the correct legislative procedures and adequate compensation is made. However, in compliance with the specific requirements of Article 14(3), expropriation (*Enteignung*) is only possible in the case of a specific and lawfully defined interest of the state.[131]

Article 15 *Grundgesetz* goes further and allows for the socialisation or nationalisation of property in the interests of society. The requirements of Article 14(3) also apply.

It has to be pointed out that the definition of ownership of property under the constitutional provisions of Article 14 is wider than that under the law of property under § 903. As an individual guarantee against state interference it covers all valuable positions or assets including, for example, pension rights.[132]

Paragraph 903, on the other hand defining ownership under private law restricts it to "objects" which in turn have been defined by §§ 90 et seq. in the general part of the BGB.[133] It defines ownership as the total legal control of an object and the freedom to do as one wishes with it, known as the freedom of disposition (*Verfügungsfreiheit*). There are a number of forms of ownership. Sole ownership relates to the ownership by one person. Joint ownership (*Miteigentum*) can be either of a precise fraction of a particular object in which each individual has an independent real right in the object which can be divided (see §§ 741 et seq. and §§ 1008 et seq.), or joint collective ownership (*Gesamthandeigentum*) where the individual shares cannot be separated (see §§ 719 I, 1419 I).

A special form of ownership is the trust property which is also recognized in German law (*Treuhandeigentum*). Here the owner under the trust property is obliged to use the property according to the purposes set out in the obligational agreement between him and the trustee. Examples are the administrative trust and the security trust.

---

[129] BVerfG 50, 290, 339; Wolf, above, n 3, pp. 16–17.
[130] For further details on the concepts of objective and subjective elements of basic rights see the section on the basic rights in Chapter 7 above.
[131] See BVerfGE 24, 367, 389 concerning the expropriation by the City of Hamburg of Dikeland following a flood in the City, noted by Kommers (1989) pp. 257–259. See also BVerfGE 50, 290, 339 and 68, 193, 222.
[132] BVerfGE 69, 272, 300.
[133] See sec. E.2.1.

Although § 903 itself states that the complete freedom to use one's property is subject to the provision that no other law or right stands in the way of this free use, ownership is subject to limits required in the interest of both society and, at times, the state, for example, Article 14 II GG. Paragraph 906 further requires that certain nuisances are tolerated which do not materially prejudice the use of land. Public law limitations include rules for the protection of the environment and in private law the interests of neighbours must be taken into account.

4.1 The acquisition and loss of ownership

There is a difference in the rules applicable, according to whether property is acquired or lost by operation of a statute or under a contractual agreement. Statute based reasons are where the acquisition and loss is determined without taking into consideration the wishes of the owner under the conditions imposed by the *Grundgesetz* and other public laws.

The acquisition of ownership through a legal transaction (*rechtsgeschäftlicher Eigentumserwerb*) or relinquishing of ownership are determined by the wishes of the owner as in a normal legal transactions. These transactions are transactions of disposition (*Verfügungsgeschäfte*) and are independent from the obligational transactions (*Verpflichtungsgeschäfte*), e.g. the contract of sale that form the legal cause for the transfer.[134] See §§ 873 et seq. and §§ 929 et seq. for the acquisition of land and movables respectively. In both cases the acquisition and loss are usually governed by the elements of bilateral legal agreement and transaction (§§ 873 and 929) which form a contract to transfer ownership. It is also possible for the right of ownership to be transferred in a one sided legal transaction, §§ 875, 928 and 959 dealing respectively with the cancellation of rights, the relinquishing of ownership, and the giving up of possession.

The rules for this are further divided into those applying to movables and real estate. For simplicity's sake the person transferring a right will be called the "transferor" (*Veräußerer*) whereas the person acquiring the right will be labelled the "acquirer" (*Erwerber*).

4.2 The acquisition and loss of real estate

A piece of land (*Grundstück*) is a defined plot of land which is registered under its own number in the Land Register (*Grundbuch*), regardless of the nature of the land and of what it actually comprises, i.e. bodies of water, buildings, etc. Objects which are firmly attached to the land such as buildings are deemed essential component parts (§ 94) of the land itself and, furthermore, structural elements of a building such as lifts are also a part of the land. The initial presumption of the BGB (§§ 93–4), states that essential component parts cannot be the subject of separate rights includes the rights of title over land and the buildings on it. Any rights therefore

---

[134] See also sec. A.3.4. on the *Abstraktionsprinzip*.

connected with the ownership of land are subject to this rule. However, there are exceptions created by statute which will be considered below.

4.2.1 *The freedom of disposition and protection of land*

Ownership of land gives the owner the full and exclusive right to possession which is unlimited in time. The rights according to § 905 extend to the air space above the land and the earth below. Owners can use land as they wish and can lawfully exclude interference by others under § 903, except at such heights and depths that they have no interest in them (§ 905 2nd sentence). Third party rights and public restrictions may, however, be applicable to curtail the full ownership rights otherwise enjoyed. Building, air traffic, and planning restrictions from public law may also limit and restrict the free use of land. The right is also subject to the limit that certain interferences must be tolerated and mainly relate to the so called neighbour rights—§ 906, for example, ordinary use of adjoining land which may give rise to gases, smells, smoke, noise, heat, or shocks, providing they do not materially prejudice the use of the land. Additionally, interferences which accord with local custom and which cannot be prevented except at unreasonable cost must also be tolerated. However, the owner can demand compensation if the interference is greater than normally to be expected. A landowner can prevent the installation on neighbouring land of works which will result in an unacceptable interference with the use of the landowner's own land (§ 907). Further details of permissible interferences are listed in §§ 908–923.

4.2.2 *The acquisition of land ownership*

Public policy requirements of certainty have provided stricter rules for real estate. Transfer of ownership of real estate is determined by a particular form of real estate contract in German law which has two components, governed by § 873, the agreement and the actual transfer known as the *Einigung* or *Auflassung* and the *Eintragung*. Paragraph 873 is applicable to any alterations concerning the right of property of a real estate, i.e. transfer of property or burdening the land with mortgage or a servitude and requires an agreement as to the alteration of the right and that these transactions are recorded in the Land Register (*Grundbuch*). For the transfer of ownership this means that it occurs with the agreement of the person entitled at the time to the ownership of the land and the other party to the registration of the new legal owner in the Land Register. A further requirement is imposed under § 925 that the agreement be declared and signed either in the presence of a notary or at the office of the Land Registry. No conditions or time limits can be imposed on the agreement (§ 925 II); otherwise the agreement is void. Furthermore, the obligational agreement (*Verpflichtungsgeschäft*) forming the cause for the transfer, e.g. a contract of sale has to be approved by the notary as well (§ 311 b I), thus confirming the correctness of both sides of the principle of abstraction.[135]

Tax laws apply to the transaction and, in addition, local authority laws may

---

[135] See above, sec. A.3.4.

require approval to be sought from the local authority in terms of building laws or use rights.

4.2.3 *The entry in the Land Register*

The system of property registration in Germany was introduced in 1897 by the Land Register Act (*Grundbuchordnung GBO*) and is regarded as being a particularly efficient and accurate form of land and property registration. The Land Register is operated by a special department (*Grundbuchamt*) at each *Amtsgericht* over its respective jurisdictional area. Only the existence of real rights (*dingliche Rechte*) directly affecting a right to a piece of land are entered into the Land Register. Obligational agreements that form the cause for the establishment of such rights, such as a contract of sale, are not directly connected with it and thus not entered.

Entries in the Land Register are divided into three parts in addition to their title and inventory. Part one lists the current and previous owners of land and buildings. The second part shows the rights of use in respect of land such as building rights, servitudes, usufructs, and land charges. The final part is concerned with land securities and their priorities. The Register shows the ownership under name and the legal basis of ownership, restrictions on land use, charges on the land, and mortgages and other security interests in the land and is therefore a reflection of the legal position of any plot of land in Germany.

The general principles relating to the Land Register reflect some of the general principles in property law. The publicity principles apply with limited effect in respect of the Land Register in that it is only open to public inspection by those who can show a legitimate interest (§ 12 GBO). The entries are *prima facie* evidence of the actual legal position. The principle of preciseness requires all entries to be precise and mandatory registration for all changes to the Register. The principle of consensus provides that the consent of the owner of the rights in the land is required before a change to this right can be registered (§ 19 GBO).

New entries into the Land Register are undertaken following an application (§ 13 GBO). The acquirer only becomes the owner as soon as the entry of change is made in the Land Register. The previous owner is simultaneously struck off the Register.

All rights concerning land must be registered so that the Land Register shows all real rights over property. Registration is also required for the creation of servitudes, rights of way, restrictive covenants, land securities, and mortgages. Any proposed change to the legal position of land and property must be entered in the Register before it can have legal effect. Without registration the legal transaction is not legally valid and the acquirer of the registered property does not become the new owner.

Changes which are not incurred by contract but made under public law do not need to be registered. They are nevertheless legally effective. These would be in respect of servitudes or covenants or pre-emption rights for conservation or preservation areas. The Land Register does not therefore cover everything, and additional enquiries must be made with local authorities to be certain of the ability of an owner to use land as desired.

The ranking of different rights entered into the Register affecting the same piece of land is dependant on the time of their entry. Thus rights entered at an earlier stage prevail over those entered at a later point in time in cases of conflict (§ 879). As a consequence the department responsible for the Land Register is obliged to strictly deal with all applications in the order they were made (§ 45 GBO).

4.2.4 The effect of entries to the Land Register

Only after registration of the alteration of the right in question will it become effective. Furthermore, according to § 891 I, if a right is registered in the Land Register in favour of a person, it is legally presumed that he is entitled to such a right; and if a right is cancelled, then § 891 II presumes the right no longer exists. The law allows a presumption that the registered details are correct, therefore according to § 892, a purchaser who acquires property from the person registered as the owner can rely on this unless he has positive knowledge that the transferor did not own the property or have the right to transfer it. Ownership will be assured even if the registered owner's own acquisition was defective. A good faith acquisition (*gutgläubiger Erwerb*) is therefore binding and free from all omissions or errors in the Register. Any unfairness created under this system may be resolved by the rules on unjust enrichment against the person who effected the transfer without good title and not the person relying on the Register.

In order to overcome difficulties created during the period between application and entry, for example the bankruptcy of a person in this period, § 878 provides that after the application for registration has been made, the agreement to transfer property by the transferor will not be ineffective if powers to make that agreement are no longer present, any difficulties can be resolved under unjust enrichment. The acquirer is also protected in that §§ 873 and 883 allow the transferor to approve the registration of a priority notice (*Vormerkung*) which secures the claim to the granting or lifting of rights attached to a piece of land and will be entered on the Register. According to § 883 II this has the consequence that a transaction which occurs after the entry of the priority notice in the Register will be ineffective against the acquirer, in so far as the acquirer can rely on the priority notice. In order for the owner to transfer it to a different party the third party has to get the agreement of the person in whose name the priority notice is entered (§ 888 I).

Paragraph 894 grants a claim to rectify the Land Register (*Grundbuchberichtigungsanspruch*) where there is a mistake, e.g. where contrary to § 45 GBO a right has been entered before a right that had been applied for earlier or where a right has been entered for the wrong person.

4.2.5 Ownership of a freehold apartment or flat (Wohnungseigentum)

As with the building lease rights established after the First World War to relieve the property shortage, measures were taken after the shortage of housing and accommodation following the Second World War. This resulted in a further significant change in the original rules provided by the BGB that a part, as opposed to the whole, of a building could not be owned, as in the case of apartment property. The reform of the law in 1951 altered this, and the Law Concerning the Ownership of Accommodation (the Condominium Act) (*Gesetz über das Wohnungseigentum und Dauerwohnrecht: WEG*) is now the basis for the legal ownership of an individual apartment. Special entries are made in the Land Register to show the sub-divisions of ownership of property.

The ownership of flats consists of individual absolute ownership of parts of a communal building with a co-ownership of the common property and facilities, such as the lifts, garaging, gardens, entrances, etc. (*Sondereigentum an einer Woh-nung*, § 1 II WEG). With industrial and commercial premises the concept of the private ownership is mirrored. Ownership in such circumstances includes add-itional duties as a result of the co-ownership of the common areas. Legally, owner-ship is created through the creation of a contract between the co-owners of the land or by the separation of existing ownership of the land.

4.3 The acquisition and loss of movable property

The transfer of ownership for movables under § 929 does not have to observe a specific form as is the case with real estate. It requires the agreement that ownership should pass (*Einigung*) and that delivery of possession to the acquirer should take place (*Übergabe*), the first element being a contract and the second one a "real act".[136] If the acquirer is already in possession then the agreement to transfer the ownership is sufficient.

An alternative transfer of possession can also take place through the legal instrument of the *Besitzkonstitut*, a constructive possession of movables based on agreement (§ 930). This is where the ownership is transferred to another party yet possession is retained by the first party as in the case of mortgages, debentures, and charges being created in favour of a lender. It is often used in the case of loans being raised on capital goods in a business, the factory owner retains the possession of the goods, usually real property or machinery, but the bank or lender is the owner of the goods. This is therefore the constructive use of possession of an object based on agreement which replaces the delivery of an object with a transfer of rights over it. This type of legal relationship provides that the new owner acquires indirect possession under § 868.

Another form of transfer under § 931 allows the transfer of ownership to be replaced by the assignment to the acquirer of the claim to the return of the object. The goods are retained by the third party and the claim for their return is transferred by the original owner.

4.4 Good faith acquisition

German law has adopted the principle that the acquirer can acquire ownership of property even in the situation where the transferor did not own the property.

---

[136] See also above, General Part of the BGB, sec. B.

Paragraphs 932–34 deal with the acquisition of objects which were in the possession of a party not entitled to transfer them. The true owner must bear the risk and recover loss under the rules of unjust enrichment from the bailee or transferor of the goods (§ 816). If, however, the objects have been taken from the owner unwillingly the owner should not have to bear the risk (§ 935).

4.4.1 *In relation to land*

In respect of the good faith acquisition of land, § 892 states that the content of the Register is regarded as accurate in favour of a person who acquires a right to land or a right to an interest in land. Good faith acquisition is excluded in two cases: when the acquirer acts in bad faith, i.e. with actual knowledge, and when an objection to an incorrect entry in the Register has been lodged, regardless of knowledge of this (§§ 899 and 894). The presence of gross negligence does not invalidate good faith because of the presumption of accuracy of the Register unlike the position with movables.

In the case of good faith acquisition, the true owner's title is extinguished (§ 936), therefore a claim under § 816, unjust enrichment, is the only recourse to get the proceeds of sale from the transferor.

4.4.2 *In relation to movables*

According to § 932, the acquirer can acquire ownership even if transferor did not own the goods. The presumption is that the acquirer must have believed the transferor to have been the owner and must obtain possession from the transferor. The BGB thus decides in favour of the acquirer in good faith as against the true owner in this collision of interests. Good faith is defined in the negative in § 932 II which states that the acquirer does not act in good faith when he knew or is grossly negligent in not knowing that the object did not belong to the transferor. Paragraph 933 states that the acquirer must still be in good faith when the goods are eventually given over to him. Under § 934, the assignment of the claim to return objects will be valid if the transferor was the indirect possessor. The acquirer in good faith must have obtained indirect possession from the transferor.

These "good faith" rules are not applicable if the object was stolen, mislaid, or lost (§ 935). In this case the legislature has decided in favour of the true owner whose interest in retaining ownership is regarded as higher than the trust of the bona fide purchaser, but § 935 II provides further exceptions for the acquisition of money and bearer bonds, negotiable instruments, and items obtained in a public auction which are, in turn, exempt from the application of § 935 I.

5 Acquisition of ownership by other means

Most other ways of acquiring ownership find their reasons in conditions laid down by statute (*Eigentumserwerb kraft Gesetzes*).

5.1 Appropriation (*Aneignung*)

Under § 958 I and II ownerless movables may be acquired through appropriation (*Aneignung*) unless prohibited or infringing third party rights. This is not a legal transaction merely the result of a physical act (*Realakt*). Ownerless objects are ones that do not belong to anyone and cannot be a part of land. They are abandoned objects, according to § 959, when the original owner has given up possession with the intention of giving up ownership as with, for example, the abandoning of a newspaper. Other seemingly abandoned objects may in fact be mislaid or lost and would thus fall to be included under § 935. There would be no acquisition in good faith in these cases.

5.2 Prescription (*Ersitzung*)

Under § 937 whoever has a moveable object in his own possession for a period of ten years acquires ownership of it. Good faith is assumed, in other words the lack thereof—excluding prescription—has to be proved by the party contesting the prescription (§ 937 II). As regards land, a person who is not the rightful owner of land but is nevertheless entered in the Register will obtain good title after the passage of thirty years, providing they have occupied it for this period and that no objection has been entered into the land Register (§ 900). Prescription will also apply where the possessor's agent (§ 855) had the object in possession on behalf of the possessor.

5.3 Union or combination (*Verbindung*)

Objects not separable without destroying or changing their character cannot be owned each as a separate object (§ 93). The consequence of this rule is that objects, although originally separate, which become a integral part of a greater object through some kind of process or mixture become irremovable and the new product becomes a separate object. The rules under §§ 946 et seq. determine who shall be the new owner.

5.3.1 Union of a movable with an immovable
In this case the moveable becomes an integral part of the immovable fixture of the land or property and according to § 946 the ownership of the land stretches itself to incorporate the new part, such as fixtures added to the structure of a house.

5.3.2 *Union of a movable with other movables*

Where a combination of objects become part of some other single whole, the previous owners become joint owners in the new object, with shares according to the value of the parts contributed (§ 947 I). If, however, one of the owners can be regarded as the owner of the main original part he becomes the owner of the new complete object and the others have a corresponding rights under §§ 1008 et seq. (§ 947 II).

5.4 Mixing (*Vermischung*)

A mixture of movables, e.g. storage of several amounts of wine produced by different vineyards in a joint wine tank, under the direction of § 948 follows the rules under § 947.

5.5 Manufacturing or processing (*Verarbeitung*)

Paragraph 950 provides that whoever produces a new object through the manufacture of one or more moveable objects becomes the owner of the finished product and extinguishes any existing or previous rights in the materials.

Example: *A* uses the canvas of *B* to paint a picture. By doing so he automatically becomes owner of the painting including the canvas.

The economic consequences of this are that any reservation of title clauses in the supplier's contract of sale are extinguished by operation of the BGB.[137] To avoid this a sole supplier whose goods make up a considerable value of the finished product may arrange for the manufacturer to promise to make the new product on his behalf.[138]

Those who have suffered a loss by reason of the provisions of §§ 946–950, can obtain compensation under § 951 I 1 in accordance with the rules on unjust enrichment as the provision refers to those rules.

5.6 Found objects

Paragraphs 965 et seq. provide that whoever finds a lost object has certain duties. The find, if worth more than ten Euro, must be advertised and the object must be kept in safe custody and surrendered to the loser. For thus doing so, compensation and a reward can be demanded from the owner. If under § 973 the owner does not come forward to claim the goods, the finder acquires ownership after six months after registration of the find with the police authorities.

---

[137] See, however, the comments on the Extended Reservation of Title Clauses (*Verlängerter Eigentumsvorbehalt*) below.
[138] See BGHZ 46, 117.

5.7 Separation of objects

A further special rule exists under § 953 to deal with the separation of objects in more parts such as in the produce of fruit from trees or the offspring of animals. It is provided that the new objects become the property of the person who is the owner of the main object known as the *Muttersache*. An exception is made where another, who is not the owner but entitled to use the main object, becomes the owner of the produce of the main object (§§ 954 et seq.).

5.8 Succession (*Gesamtsrechtsnachfolge*)

According to the laws of succession the heir takes the place of the testator and the inheritance is transferred to him under § 1922. The heir then automatically becomes the owner of all the objects which had once belonged to the testator. No legal transaction is needed, only the formality of changing the Land Register in the case of real estate to confirm the new owner's position.

6 The protection of ownership

Ownership, as noted, is protected as a basic right by Article 14 I *Grundgesetz*, subject to the limitations in the same Article. Private protection is also given under delict law (§ 823 I BGB). Two notable claims in property law serve to protect the ownership of an object: the claim for the return of property (*Herausgabeanspruch*, § 985) when property has been removed; and the claim to compel someone to refrain from an activity interfering with ownership (*Unterlassungsanspruch*, § 1004). These rights are supplemented by other property law, delictual and obligational rights.[139]

6.1 The claim for return (*Herausgabeanspruch*, § 985)

If an owner has been unlawfully dispossessed or is not in possession of his property, § 985 BGB provides that the owner can claim the return of an object from the possessor, unless the possessor can show an entitlement to possess it under § 986. Paragraph 985 applies where either the agreement or the performance elements of a contract are irregular and therefore void due to problems such as the lack of capacity. Claims are effective only against persons in actual possession. The claim when established obligates the possessor to prepare the goods for collection and to bear such necessary costs in doing so.[140]

The claim for return is barred according to § 986 I if the possessor can show that he is legally entitled to possession of the object. This is the case especially where an

---

[139] The additional property law rights are, *inter alia*, claims by owners against unlawful possession (§§ 987 et seq.), claims for damages (§§ 989–992), and claims for possession expenses against owners (§§ 994 et seq.).
[140] BGH, NJW 1988, 3264.

obligational agreement (*Verpflichtungsgeschäft*) between him and the owner allows him to possess the object, for example a tenancy contract. Only if the obligational agreement is invalid will § 986 no longer protect the possessor allowing the owner to claim back his property under § 985.

The claim for return is also valid against indirect possessors as well as direct possessors. The new owner can demand return of the indirect possession as a result of the assignment of the claim to return the object under § 870. It is only necessary to show the owner has lost possession against his will or that the present possessor did not have good faith when he acquired possession.

6.2 Rights under §§ 987 et seq. (*Eigentümer-Besitzer-Verhältnis*)

Paragraph 987 et seq. provide details of the compensation payable for the use of property by the possessor or if harm is caused whilst in possession, for example, they guarantee the owner a right to claim profits of the object and to claim compensation from the possessor. On the other hand, they also entitle the possessor to compensation for expenses incurred to maintain the object (§ 994). They are only applicable where there is a "§ 985 situation", in other words where the owner can claim back the object from the possessor (*Eigentümerbesitzerverhältnis* or *Vindikationslage*).

6.2.1 Rights of the owner

The claims under §§ 987 et seq. supplement the claim to return the object. The liability applies to possessors in good faith only from the date of proceedings under the claim where good faith on the part of the possessor is demonstrated (§§ 987–989). The owner's action for the return of his property is a procedural action and is effected as soon as the owner has made a complaint in court. From this point onwards the possessor is put on notice. Possessors in good faith must be prepared for the court to demand that they must return the object. From this point onwards they will then be obligated to return any profits made on the object (§ 987 I) and to pay compensation for any damage (§ 989).

Those acting in bad faith are liable from the beginning of possession (§ 990 I 1). Bad faith is defined under § 932 II as the situation whereby the possessor positively knows or is grossly negligent for not knowing that there is no entitlement to possession. Possessors who have acted in good faith but then realize the mistake are liable for the moment of realization (§ 990 I 2). From the commencement of proceedings or bad faith the possessor is liable to return all advantages of using the property (§§ 987 I and 990 I), for example, the produce of trees or offspring of animals. If, however, the possessor has failed to take advantage of the object, either negligently or intentionally, but could have done so, § 987 II renders him liable to pay compensation for the lost advantages. In respect of the possessor in good faith, § 993 I applies this liability from the date of proceedings or knowledge.

There is an increased liability in accordance with § 992 if the possessor has unlawfully interfered with the possession of another (§ 858) or acquired possession by the committing of a criminal act. In this case he doesn't even acquire any temporary protection and is fully liable for all damage even under delict rules (§§ 823 et seq.) including liability without fault (§ 848). This increased liability under § 992 is an exception to the general rule that claims under §§ 987 et seq. and those under delict law are mutually exclusive (see § 993 I).

6.2.2 *The claim for compensation for possession expenses* (*Verwendungsersatz*)

The good faith possessor can, before the commencement of the return action, demand compensation under § 994 I 1 for necessary expenses. These are all the necessary expenditures incurred in repairing, maintaining or improving property but excluding usual costs of maintenance during the use of the object. The latter are those incurred to maintain the object so that it continues to function in the way necessary for normal use (§ 994). Different rules apply to the liability for this item before and after the commencement of legal proceedings and for possessors in bad faith. Paragraph 994 II provides that after the commencement of proceedings for possession, the claimable necessary expenses must correspond with the interests and wishes of the owner.

The rights to claim expenses are limited to protect the owner from unjust claims or excessive claims. Under § 1001 I the possessor can only enforce his claim to which the owner has consented or when the owner has re-claimed possession of the property. Paragraph 1002 sets a limit for these claims for expenses following the return to the owner of one month for movables and six months in respect of land.

6.3 Interference with ownership (*Unterlassungsanspruch*)

Under § 1004, the owner of an object can demand an abatement of a nuisance to the enjoyment or the use of the object. This acts like an injunction. The interference must be unlawful, otherwise the owner is obliged under § 1004 II to tolerate it.

The interference can be caused by an action by someone known as the *Handlungsstörer* who positively creates the interference, for example, by dumping rubbish on land or where a person is responsible for the actions of third parties such as noise from visitors to a night club (known now as *indirekter Handlungsstörer*) or by a particular circumstance which could be controlled if desired, in which case the person responsible is known as the *Zustandsstörer*, for example, smoke or smells drifting into another's property.

6.4 Other claims under private law

Claims for compensation arising from an interference will be on the basis of delict law and § 823 I. Transfer to a non-entitled person may be remedied by the rules on unjust enrichment, and the loss of property due to processing or union can be rectified by the compensation claim under § 951. For details of all of the above, see the appropriate sections.

6.5 Judicial review

Procedural remedies against state interference with property is dealt with under public law. Thus any interference on the part of the administration which is also unfounded or in some way unlawful is actionable by either a declaration to set aside an incorrect order (*Anfechtungsklage*) or an action to compel action for the benefit of the complainant (*Festellungsklage*).[141] Furthermore, the constitutional complaint remains as a last resort in those cases where the courts have not interpreted Article 14 GG correctly and thus infringed the right to freedom of property.[142]

7 Other types of property rights

The courts have separated certain rights from the full legal rights contained in the concept of ownership. These are referred to as limited real rights (*beschränkte dingliche Rechte*). Two types are foremost: the rights of use, temporary possession, and enjoyment (*Nutzungsrechte*) and security rights (*Sicherungsrechte*).

Limited real rights enjoy the same defensive rights and rights to possession or recovery of the object as full legal rights of ownership. Paragraphs 1065 and 1227, referring to §§ 985 and 1004, are the founding paragraphs for such claims. The establishment and loss of these rights resemble the full rights of ownership, therefore the details will not be repeated here.

Other rights in respect of real estate focussing on enjoyment include, for example, servitudes (*Grunddienstbarkeiten*), defined in § 1018, personal servitudes (*persönliche Dienstbarkeiten* §1036), rights of pre-emption (*Vorkaufsrechte*), governed by §§ 1094–1104, and the usufruct (*Nießbrauch*)—the latter being applicable to land and movable objects (§ 1030), rights (§ 1060), and to personal property (§ 1085).[143]

8 Property finance and security (*Sicherungsrechte*)

Security can be established for movable objects, rights and land. The basic rules of security are to be found in Book Two BGB under §§ 455 et seq. in respect of security of title, and §§ 765 et seq., surety provisions. The rights can arise either in the form of contract as agreed by the parties or as a statute based right by operation of the law. In such cases the BGB and the HGB have defined when a lien over goods arises by operation of the law, for example, the right of a repairman who

---

[141] As discussed in detail in Chapter 8.
[142] For details see Chapter 7.
[143] For an introduction to these rights see Wolf, above, n 3, pp. 420–433.

effects repairs to a motor vehicle to retain possession of the vehicle until payment is received.

8.1 Security interests in land (*Grundpfandrechte*)

Security rights over land include mortgages, annuity charges, and land charges which are the most frequently used in the case of long term credit. The BGB recognizes three types of security interest: the mortgage (*Hypothek*, §§ 1113–1190), the land/rent charge (*Grundschuld*, §§ 1191 et seq.), and the annuity payment (*Rentenschuld*, §§ 1199 et seq.). All three allow the creditor to demand payment of money as a result of the land so charged and ultimately the creditor can enforce the debt by causing the sale or auction of the land (known as *Verwertung*, which can be regarded as a distinct and separate subject of study). The creditor has no right to take possession of the land. To be valid, all securities transactions in respect of land must be notarized and registered. The rules of good faith acquisition also apply to the existence and entry of securities. Therefore, whatever is recorded in the Land Register is what can be acquired in good faith, regardless of the actual situation.

8.1.1 *Mortgages* (*Hypotheken*)

These are used especially for the long term mortgage of buildings and house purchases. The mortgage is defined in § 1113 as a charge on an immovable object which secures the payment of a specified sum in favour of the holder of the charge. It is created as a real collateral right over land by agreement and registration in the Land Register (§ 873). The borrower retains ownership of the land so mortgaged but is additionally personally responsible for the repayment of the debt. Thus the creditor has a claim for payment of the loan under the obligational agreement as well as a real right of security linked to the land of the borrower. The mortgage is thus linked to the personal debt of the borrower (*Akzessorietät der Hypothek*). A mortgage certificate is then issued under § 1116 I, unless it is agreed that it is a registered mortgage (§ 1116 II). A mortgage limit of 60 % of the market value of the land for first mortgages would be the maximum that could be expected, although practice would suggest higher amounts.

Realization of the debt secured is achieved by writ of execution under § 1147 after judgment against the debtor has been made. Usually the mortgage agreement contains a clause allowing immediate issue of a writ on default of the debtor and a compulsory sale follows. It is not only the land which becomes liable but all other attachments which fall under the heading of mortgage—according to §§ 1120 et seq. all components and accessories, fixtures and fittings, claims to rent, and insurance claims in the case of damage. Paragraph 1181 states that the payment of the loan extinguishes the claim and mortgage. The deed must then be returned to the owner.

A mortgage does not restrict the use of land, and § 1136 provides that an agreement where the owner agrees not to transfer the land or not to encumber it further is void.

8.1.1.1 *Registered or book mortgage (Buchhypothek)*

The requirement to register in the Land Register makes the transference of the mortgage subject to the agreement of the parties named in the Register and thus the creditor is visible (§ 1116 II 1).

8.1.1.2 *Certified or letter mortgage (Briefhypothek)*

According to § 1116, only on receipt of a mortgage certificate does the creditor acquire the mortgage (§ 1117). The production of the certificate is necessary to assert rights in the mortgage (§§ 1160–61). The mortgage need not be registered in the Land Register.

8.1.1.3 *Transference of the mortgage*

A mortgage can be assigned under § 1153 I. A certified mortgage can only be assigned if in writing and transferred, but this can be replaced under § 1154 II by entry in the Land Register. The registered mortgage is transferred by agreement and entry in the Land Register.

8.1.2 The land charge (Grundschuld)

The land charge (which is more flexible than a mortgage) is used more for short to long term finance. It is defined in § 1191 and creates a charge on real estate for the payment of a definite sum of money. Paragraph 1192 refers back to the rules on mortgage. The borrower retains ownership, whereas the lender has a lien over the property. It differs from a mortgage in that it may exist without an underlying personal debt or claim. It gives the creditor the right to satisfy the claim by execution against the object on default under §§ 1147 and 1192. Land charges are legally independent of the borrower, and after the repayment of the loan can be retained independently on the Register in favour of the present or future owner to raise further finance, in which case they are known as *Eigentümergrundschuld*. Land-owners can themselves register a land charge in their own name for later assignment to a creditor for a loan. To finally extinguish these, they must be removed from the Land Register.

As with the mortgage they are available in certified (*Briefgrundschuld*) and registered forms (*Buchgrundschuld*). The certified form are more easily transferable by registration of the new holder whereas the registered land charges must be registered on transfer.

8.1.3 The annuity payment (Rentenschuld)

This is a type of *Grundschuld* under which land is charged with recurrent payments of a definite sum of money (§ 1199 I) at determined intervals. Rarely used these days, it was a form of spreading the payment of a capital sum in agriculture. Paragraph 1201 allows an early redemption of the debt by the owner. Repayment must be entered in the Land Register. It can, however, be used for the sale of property in exchange for the payment of a life long pension.

The priority of a security is based initially on the date it was registered, unless there is the agreement of all affected parties that a certain security should take priority, which includes the agreement of the previous prior holder.

8.2 Securities over movables

These are only initially regulated by the BGB, §§ 1204–1258 but also includes the right to realize a security on an unfulfilled debt (*Verwertungsrecht*).

8.2.1 Lien/pledge (Pfandrecht)

Paragraph 1205 requires the debtor to give the creditor immediate possession of the object to obtain security and is thus a pledge or pawn type of security, but is of little use in business because the use of the object must be surrendered and is understandably seldom used. They are, however, employed by the banks. In the case of a default of the obligation to repay, the *Verwertungsrechte* come into play to allow the creditor to realize the value of the goods under pledge by their sale, often by auction (§§ 1228 et seq.).

8.2.2 Lien of rights

The BGB, §§ 1273–1278, also allows for the creation of a lien over rights owned. If a debtor is a holder of certain rights he can use these as a means of security for a creditor. Paragraph 1280 requires that notice of the pledge is made to the debtor, unlike a full assignment of the debt under § 398 where notice is not required.

The rules provided by the BGB on *Pfandrecht* were seldom used in commerce because they were so restrictive, therefore commerce developed its own customary rules which have been recognized and confirmed by the courts. The general term applied to the form of security developed is security transfer (*Sicherungsübereignung*) or security title law or fiduciary transfer of title, which was nevertheless based on statutory provisions to enable the debtor to retain possession of objects to be secured, despite a transfer of title. Paragraphs 868 and 929 et seq. allow indirect or constructive possession of goods for another.

The development of ownership rights can be in the form of ownership transferred to a lender as security or ownership retained by a supplier as security, also termed, respectively, fiduciary transfer and fiduciary assignment.

8.2.3 Transfer of ownership

One form involves the transfer of ownership of an object but not the delivery of possession which is retained by the debtor. This involves a combination of indirect possession in terms of the bailment of objects for another party, §§ 868, and the agreement that the owner/creditor accepts the agreement of the debtor for the transfer of title and indirect possession instead of possession. If the debtor fails to repay the secured party can sell the object.

Under § 930 the title can be transferred by an agreement coupled with a custody agreement that the owner remains in possession of the goods whilst the purchaser has indirect possession. There is no need for public registration. Future assets can also be the subject of a transfer of title.

8.2.4 *Retention of ownership (Eigentumsvorbehalt)*

The second main form of security is that of reservation of title which is initially regulated by § 455 BGB. The delivery of property, under § 929 has taken place but the transfer of the ownership in the goods does not take place and ownership is retained by the vendor. The actual transfer of ownership is replaced by a conditional agreement to transfer ownership upon full payment of the object delivered. This form of retention has been developed in commerce in order to transfer some rights over the property to the purchaser earlier than at the stage of full ownership which, under reservation of title clauses, only takes place when payment for the goods is completed. This is to cover the situation where part payment has been made so that in the event of insolvency of either party the purchaser does not lose out. The greater the payment, the greater the interest of the buyer. These rights are termed inchoate ownership or equitable redemption (*Anwartschaft*) and are regarded as a step to full ownership. These rights can be transferred, inherited, assigned, charged, and acquired in good faith. Business can therefore use the rights as security to raise further credit.

One of the problems with such forms of security is that the objects secured, if stock in trade, are likely to change due to processing and the rules of the BGB would result in the loss of ownership and hence security on the part of the creditor. The need for additional forms of security led to the development of the processing clause, which allows ownership in the new or processed object to be acquired, and anticipatory assignment by which the debt or proceeds of the sale of the goods are acquired.

8.2.5 *Extended reservation of title (Verlängerter Eigentumsvorbehalt)*

This consists of the standard reservation of title clause combined with a additional processing clause by which the creditor allows the goods to be processed but acquires ownership rights in the processed goods. This is necessary for the security of the creditor due to the application of the rule under § 950 by which the ownership of the goods would be transferred to the possessor by reason of either the admixture of processing of the goods. A processing clause is the answer to this situation by which the supplier acquires joint ownership to the extent of the invoice price of the supplied goods.

Legally, this is achieved by the agreement between the parties that the ownership in the new product will be transferred to the creditor, known as the anticipatory transfer. The processor temporarily becomes the owner of the processed goods but by the agreement immediately transfers the ownership in them to the creditor.

8.2.6 *Anticipatory assignment*

Alternatively, there is the advance or anticipatory assignment of the proceeds or the future debt of the sale of the goods which extends the creditor's, usually a bank's, security. Goods subject to either transferred or reserved ownership, are sold and a right to the sale price is assigned in advance to the creditor. This is affected without notice to the future debtor/purchaser of goods. When processed the creditor normally loses ownership under § 950 but this is replaced by the advance assignment of debt.

Expanded security or reservation of ownership is achieved by agreement to use the secured property or rights as security to other outstanding or future debts. Claims against debtors can be further transferred to other creditors. This applies to present and future rights and is governed by the general rules of obligations BGB §§ 398 et seq.

For full details of this area of law, see Serick and/or Dickson et al., noted in further reading below.

8.2.7 *The problem of Globalzession*

Banks often demand as a security for a loan that the borrower assigns all of his existing claims arising from his business (*Globalzession*). As this would include a claim arising from the sale of processed goods it conflicts with the aforementioned processing clause (*Verlängerter Eigentumsvorbehalt*) in favour of a supplier. Based on §§ 185 II, 161 I general opinion applies the principle of priority (*Prioritätsgrundsatz*) in order to solve the conflict. This means an anticipatory assignment of all existing claims would void a later processing clause. Thus as far as the *Globalzession* includes the processing clause it is breaching good morals (§ 138) and therefore void, because otherwise the debtor would be always be induced to breach his contract with the supplier.[144]

FURTHER READING

Books

A. Anderson GmbH (ed.)., *Leasing in Germany* (1991: Neue Wirtschafs-Briefe, Berlin).

J.F. Baur and R. Stürner, *Lehrbuch des Sachenrechts*, 17th ed. (1999: C.H. Beck, München).

Dickson et al. (eds.), *Security on Movable Property and Receivables in Europe, National Report on Germany* by W. Rosener, (1988: ESC Publishing, Oxford), pp. 58–74.

J. Eckert, *Sachenrecht*, 2nd ed. (2000: Nomos Verlag, Baden-Baden).

H. Krause, *German Securities Regulation* (2001: Beck, Butterworth/Tolley, Stämpfli, München, London, Bern).

Peltzer and Scesniak, *German Securities Trade Act* (1995: O. Schmidt, Köln).

D. Reinicke and K. Tiedtke, *Kreditsicherung*, 4th ed. (2000: Luchterhand, Nuewied).

K. Schreiber, *Sachenrecht*, 3rd ed. (2000: Boorberg Verlag, Stuttgart).

G. F. Schuppert, "The Right to Property" in U. Karpen, (ed.), *The Constitution of the Federal Republic of Germany* (1988: Nomos Verlag), pp. 107–115.

K. H. Schwab and H. Prütting, *Sachenrecht*, 30th ed. (2002: C.H. Beck, München).

R. Serick, *Securities in Movables in German Law* (1990: Kluwer, Deventer).

R. Volhard, D. Weber and W. Usinger (eds.)., *Real Property in Germany: Legal and Tax Aspects of Development and Investment*, 4th. ed. (1991: Knapp).

---

[144] See BGHZ 55,34 and Wolf, above, n 3, pp. 319–321 for details.

M. Westerholt, in *Business Transactions in Germany*, LooseLeaf (M. Bender, New York and C.H. Beck, München), vol. I, ch. 14.

M. Wolf, *Sachenrecht*, 17th ed. (2001: C.H. Beck, München).

F Book Four: family law (*Familienrecht*)

1 Introduction

The family law book of the civil code (§§ 1297–1921) has been subject to considerable amendment, often the result of very diverse ideological premises, as influences and attitudes to personal relationships have altered over the years. In particular in the period following the Second World War, the nineteenth century values have been replaced with those of the second half of the twentieth century, especially those promoted by the *Grundgesetz*.

Therefore BGB provisions on family law have been subject to numerous changes, the most recent fundamental ones being the Child Law Reform Act, the Child Support Act, and the Formation of Marriage Act.[145]

The impact of constitutional law especially stems from Articles 6 and 3 II. Article 6 I *Grundgesetz* provides an objective guarantee to protect the institutions of marriage and the family against erosion by the state. This was confirmed by the Federal Constitutional Court[146] deciding that the provision guarantees the individual with a defence against measures of the legislature and executive which harm the institutions of marriage and the family. A duty is also imposed on the family to actively further the interests of these state guarantees.

Article 6 II GG provides that whilst the care and upbringing of children are the natural right and duty of the parents, the community nevertheless has a responsibility to keep a watchful eye on parents to ensure that they perform their duties. Article 6 V provides illegitimate children with the same rights as legitimate children.

Article 3 II *Grundgesetz* provides for equal rights for men and women and is supplemented by the Equal Rights Act (*Gleichberechtigungsgesetz*) 1957 which has led to amendment of family law provisions in the BGB.[147]

International Treaties ratified by Germany form additional important sources of family law apart from the constitutional provisions and legislation within the

---

[145] *Kindschaftsrechtsreformgesetz (KindRG)* of 16 February 1997, *Kindesunterhaltsgesetz (KindUG)* of 4 June 1998 and the *Eheschliessungsrechtsgesetz (EheschlRG)* of 4 May 1998.

[146] BVerfGE 6, 76.

[147] This section will only give a brief outline of some aspects of family law. For a concise introduction to this area see: p. Gottwald, D. Schwab, and E. Büttner, *Family and Succession Law in Germany* (2001; Kluwer, The Hague).

fourth book of the BGB. Most of them—especially the numerous Hague Conventions—deal with the protection of children and the conflict of laws in international cases dealing with family law issues.[148]

2 The scope of family law

The legal norms in family law cover the personal and economic positions of the members of a family towards one another. Book Four can be separated into three parts: civil marriage (§§ 1297–1588, *bürgerliche Ehe*); relatives (§§ 1589–1772, *Verwandtschaft*); and guardianship (§§ 1773–1921, *Vormundschaft*).

Family law rights, recognised by the *Grundgesetz* and the BGB, do not extend to cohabitation rights. In exceptional cases statutory provisions may be expressly applicable to unmarried couples as well. Additionally, the courts have allowed themselves to apply provisions aimed at married couples analogously albeit again only under exceptional circumstances as the legislature's aim and task to protect marriage according to Article 6 II GG has to be borne in mind. However, the new law on marriage-like institutions for gay and lesbian couples (*"Eingetragene Lebenspartnerschaft"*) provides an example for specific provisions on non-married couples. Other than that cases of dispute or dissolution of the personal relationship will be determined by the general rules of civil law.[149]

Family law disputes are handled by special chambers and senates of the ordinary civil courts and the rules for the procedure of family law matters are contained in §§ 606–644 ZPO as well as in the act on non-contentious matters (*Gesetz über Angelegenheiten der Freiwilligen Gerichtsbarkeit FGG*).

3 Matrimonial law (*Eherecht*)

3.1 Engagement (*Verlöbnis*)

The term "engagement" (*Verlöbnis*) describes the legal relationship between a man and a woman created by their mutual promise of marriage.

Although the breach of an engagement promise would not be actionable in the civil courts (§ 1297 I), it will give rise to a claim for compensation for breach of promise if no reason was given by the other party, (§ 1298). Damages would constitute the return of any gifts and limited compensation for expenses incurred with a view to the forthcoming marriage (§§ 1298 and 1301).

---

[148] For an overview of ratified conventions and treaties in this area see Gottwald, Schwab, and Büttner, above, n 147, para. 16. for more details on International Private law rules and international conventions on family law in Germany see B. von Hoffmann, *Internationales Privatrecht*, 6th ed (2000: München), pp. 264–333.

[149] For more details see Gottwald, Schwab, and Büttner, above, n 147, paras 134–139.

3.2 The act of marriage (*Die Eheschließung*)

This was previously largely supplemented by the Marriage Act of 1938/1946 (*Ehegesetz EheG*). Its rules, based on the principle of compulsory civil marriage (*obligatorische Zivilehe*), however have now been (re-)implemented in Book Four of the BGB (§§ 1303 et seq.) by the Formation of Marriage Act 1998.

Marriage can only be based on the principle of the free consent of both parties as follows from Article 6 I GG and § 1310 BGB. Thus it excludes any type of pressure or deceit or arranged marriages. The BGB assumes the concept of monogamy and the heterosexual basis of the relationship that marriage is the spiritual and physical partnership of a man and woman.[150]

Prerequisites to marriage are the capacity to marry (*Ehefähigkeit*, §§ 1303 and 1304), the absence of impediments to marriage (*Fehlen von Ehehindernissen*, §§ 1306–1308) and the compliance with formalities of marriage (*Beachtung der Formvorschriften*, §§ 1310–1312).

Capacity to marry is established on the attainment of the marriageable age (*Ehemündigkeit*) which is eighteen for both men and women (§§ 2, 1303 I), and business capacity, to be able to form legally binding contracts (§§ 104 et seq., 1304). The court can agree to the marriage of one of the parties who is at least sixteen as long as the other is over eighteen (§ 1303 II). The requirement of business capacity is imposed due to the far reaching legal consequences, responsibilities and duties of marriage. Hence couples who do not have business capacity cannot marry.[151]

There are restrictions on the scope of marriage and §§ 1306–1308 list impediments to marriage (*Ehehindernisse*) including, for example, marriage within the direct blood family or bigamy. As a specific rule § 1309 demands that foreigners, who are subject to the marriage law of their state of origin, to produce a certificate of their capacity to marry, issued by the competent authority of their state of origin.

Marriage is only legal in the eyes of the law when performed in the presence of a state official, the Registrar of the Registry Office for matters of personal status (*Standesamt*, § 1301 I). The two people marrying must both appear personally and simultaneously (§§ 1310 I, 1311), the presence of witnesses being optional (§ 1312 I 2nd sentence). Church ceremonies carry no legal consequences should they occur before the civil marriage.

3.3 Non-existent and voidable marriages (*Nichtehen und aufhebbare Ehen*)

Where the aforementioned conditions for marriage have not been complied with the marriage will generally be voidable by annulment of the court or in exceptional circumstances even non-existent. Thus a marriage lacking even the most basic

---

[150] Note, however, the new law on registered partnerships of homosexual couples, see Chapter 7, sec. 2 Art. 6 GG.
[151] See the sec. B on BGB Book One for further details on capacity.

prerequisites is non-existent (*Nichtehe*), i.e. where consent of one partner is missing or no registrar was present.[152]

Marriage can be annulled under §§ 1313 and 1314 if it suffers from defects present at the time of the marriage, in contrast to divorce, which is based on reasons that have arisen after marriage. Annulment (*Aufhebung*) will be effective for the future only from the moment on, that the court has delivered its decision (§ 1313). Grounds for annulment (*Aufhebungsgründe*) are breaches of formalities of marriage or absence of other prerequisites mentioned (§ 1314 I), e.g. the lack of capacity (§ 1303, 1304), bigamy (§ 1306), or due to the incorrect form of ceremony (§ 1311). Furthermore, § 1314 II lists additional reasons for annulment, for example threat or fraud used to induce a spouse to enter marriage (§ 1314 II Nos 3, 4). The consequences of annulment, i.e. concerning maintenance, splitting of pension funds etc., are similar to those of divorce. Paragraph 1318 I expressly refers to the provisions on divorce in its first section but also provides for modifications in section 2–5.

3.4 Legal consequences and the obligations of marriage

The act of marriage is considered to be for life and not to be dissoluble (§ 1353 I 1) and both partners are considered to be equal partners in a marriage. They are obliged to lend each other mutual support and respect. Thus § 1353 imposes a duty to create a marital fellowship to decide jointly on all aspects concerning the marriage, home, children, and to share or decide on the tasks to be undertaken and employment (specified by § 1356 I, II).

Both spouses are empowered to conclude contracts in order to satisfy the essential needs of the family (§ 1357). The spouses are jointly and severally liable for payment and able to demand performance. Paragraphs 1360–1360b require both parties to contribute to the maintenance of the family, depending on the position between the two in terms of occupation, or to provide subsistence when living apart (§ 1361).

3.5 Marital property (*Ehegüterrecht*)

The property of the spouses in marriage has also come under statutory reform, so that a more equitable division of property takes place if and when the marriage comes to an end (§§ 1363 et seq.). The statutory provisions can be excluded by contract by the partners (§ 1408), officially notarized (§ 1410) and registered (§ 1558). If there is no marital contract (*Ehevertrag*) the statutory marital property rules (*gesetzlicher Güterstand*) apply (§§ 1363 et seq.). Marital property can thus be organized as follows.

---

[152] Gottwald, Schwab, and Büttner, above, n 147, para 84.

3.5.1 *Community of surplus (Zugewinngemeinschaft)*

Despite the description, community of acquisition is in effect the legal separation of the property brought to and acquired by each partner during the course of the marriage (§ 1363). It does not, therefore, replace the individual ownership of property in a marriage but does impose restrictions under §§ 1365–1369 on the disposal of property, which is either considered as household goods (*Haushaltsgegenstände*) or as all or most of one partner's assets. Consent is thus required for such disposals, and if not forthcoming, renders the contract invalid (§§ 1365–1366).

If the marriage ends by divorce or annulment, an equalisation of acquisition (*Zugewinnausgleich*) must take place (§ 1378). This requires the division between the partners of the total increase in assets or acquisitions (*Zugewinn*) realized in the course of the marriage (§§ 1372 et seq.). Assets not separately listed at the start of the marriage are presumed to be assets realized in the course of the marriage. In the case of the death of one partner, the remaining spouse is entitled to half of the acquisitions realized in addition to existing rights in succession (§ 1371).

3.5.2 *Community of property (Gütergemeinschaft)*

This only applies if agreed to in a contract or covenant of marriage certified by a notary. All property, under § 1416, either owned or acquired, becomes by law joint marital property. However, some property can never be joint—for for example, those that cannot be transferred by legal transaction, such as usufrucht (§ 1417)—and other property can be subject to a reservation (*Vorbehaltsgut*, § 1418) made at the time of the covenant. These items remain the sole property of one spouse. In the case of divorce, there is an equal distribution of the surplus after all communal debts have been settled (§ 1478).

3.5.3 *Separation of property (Gütertrennung)*

This occurs where, at the time of the covenant, it is agreed and notarised that the property of the spouses should remain separate and that as a consequence there will be no equalisation of assets in the case of divorce (§ 1414).

3.6 Divorce (*Scheidung der Ehe*)

The law on divorce was altered by the reforming law in 1976[153] and reintroduced as §§ 1564–1568 of the BGB. The changes alter the ground for divorce from that of fault (*Schuldprinzip*) to the demonstration of an inevitable breakdown of the marriage (*Zerrüttungsprinzip*). Paragraph 1564 entitles both parties to make an application. The marriage has broken down, according to the paragraph, when the union for life is no longer in existence and it is not expected that the marriage partners will be able to recreate the fellowship they have lost (§§ 1564–1565). This is no longer present if one or both of the partners are not prepared or not in the position to lead a life together and their ideas and wishes of a matrimonial union are in conflict.

---

[153] Erstes Gesetz zur Reform des Ehe- und Familienrechts, 14 June 1976.

The change from the extremely damaging requirement to show fault, and the necessary imposition on the privacy of the partners, has led, under § 1566, to two non-rebuttable presumptions for the breakdown of marriage, which is demonstrated by periods of separation. If both partners want the divorce, then the marriage is presumed to have broken down if the couple have been living apart for a year (§ 1566 I). If only one partner wants the divorce, a period of three years applies before this presumption is fulfilled (§ 1566 II). The behaviour of the other partner is relevant only in cases where the separation has been for less than one year but the continuation of the marriage would cause unreasonable hardship for one or both of the parties (§ 1565 II).

Paragraph 1567 I defines separation as no longer sharing the fellowship of living together. The partners may share accommodation as long as they do not carry on a communal household and there no longer exists a personal relationship between them.[154] Divorce then follows unless there are special circumstances of hardship.

3.6.1 *Special circumstances (Härteklausel)*

Two reasons for the continuance of the marriage are provided by § 1568. First, if the divorce would not be in the interest of children under 18, it will not be allowed. However, the use of this in practice is very narrow and rarely used to deny a divorce. The courts require proof of the existence of very strong reasons, as in a case, where it was feared the child would take his life.[155]

Paragraph 1568 also protects the partner who does not wish the divorce for reasons of personal hardship. There must be exceptional hardship as a result of the divorce. Again, in practice, the application of this would be made only in the most extreme circumstances.[156]

The financial settlement after divorce will be according to one of the rules considered above in respect of marital property.

3.6.2 *Maintenance (Unterhalt)*

The previous requirement to pay maintenance was also based, to some extent, on fault, so that if one of the spouses were at fault he or she would not be able to claim maintenance. Employing the same philosophy as the rules on the equalisation of acquisitions gained during the marriage, are the new rules in respect of maintenance after the marriage has ended. The position now under §§ 1569–1573 is that divorced couples are responsible for their own maintenance unless a divorced spouse is prevented from earning by reason of bringing up children, or if they are too old or too ill to support themselves (§§ 1569–1572). Additionally, if one of the partners is not able to support him or herself in later life, especially where one partner has not worked in order to care for children or was ill, § 1587 establishes a right to one-half of the pensions of the other partner. Thus pensions are also subject

---

[154] BG NJW 1978, 1810.
[155] OLG Hamburg, Fam RZ, 1986, 469.
[156] An "unbearable life" was required by the OLG in Koblenz (NJW 1978, 54 et seq.).

to equal division (*Rentensplitting*) by the court and, where possible, will be maintained on the same basis as they were in marriage (§§ 1587 et seq.).

The rules introduced in 1976 are complex and have been subject to constitutional review.[157] The BVerfG, whilst basically approving them, subjected them to the requirement that new legislation be introduced for hardship circumstances. The changes are now contained in § 1579, in a so-called *negative Härteklausel*, which cancels or reduces the time and/or amount of support required according to the circumstances—for example, where the previous marriage was for a short time only, or where the recipient had failed in duties in the marriage, or obtained substantial property interests not shared by the other party or had acted unlawfully against the other party.

4 Relationship (*Verwandtschaft*)

According to the BGB § 1589 1st sentence, people are related to one another in "direct line" if they directly descend from distinct forebears. This relationship can also be created with adoption (below). Furthermore, persons not related in the direct line but who stem from the same third person (such as siblings) are described as being related in *Seitenlinie* (literally, "sideline" and understood as "once removed" in English) according to § 1589 2nd sentence. The BGB judges the closeness of the relationship to determine the legal relationship. The various degrees of proximity of actual relationship have legal consequences. One of the most important is the duty of maintenance between relatives who are directly related to one another, as with parents and children. This close relationship is also relevant to the statute-based rights in succession. The relationship may also excuse the necessity to give evidence in court actions and for other procedural laws and formalities.

4.1 The legal relationship between parents and children

The right of parental care enjoys special protection of the state in Article 6 II 1 GG. However, according to Article 6 II 2nd sentence GG the parent's right is also placed under the state's supervision and thus forms a constitutional basis to restrict the right in the interest of the child where necessary. Further specification of the relationship between parents and children have been left to family law provisions of Book Four of the BGB (§§ 1616–1698b). In order to correspond with the constitutional requirements of Article 6 V GG the legislature has sought to even out the legal position of illegitimate children in comparison with legitimate children. This has finally been realized by abolishing previous rules that were applicable only to illegitimate children (ex § 1705–1711) by the Child Law Reform Act of 1998. Thus now the general rules in Book Four of the BGB are applicable to children born in and out of wedlock (with only few exceptions such as §§ 1615l–1615o).

---

[157] BVerfGE 53, 257.

4.1.1 *Maintenance (Unterhaltspflicht)*

A general duty of maintenance between relatives in direct line is established in § 1601. Thus it exists between parents and children, grandparents and parents and works in both directions, where a person is unable to support himself (§ 1602 I). As regards maintenance claims of children both parents share the right and duty to provide maintenance for children until the child is no longer a minor. The rules regarding claims for maintenance for children born out of wedlock are slightly modified in §§ 1615l–1615o.

4.1.2 *Parental care (Elterliche Sorge)*

Parental care encompasses care for the child personally and for its property (§ 1626 I) and to be the legal representative of the child (§ 1629 I 1), the function of which is to protect the child and promote its development and welfare. In cases of joint parental care both parents act for the child. Decisions on parental care have to be taken jointly (§ 1627). Where a joint decision cannot be found the family court may upon application in certain fields transfer the competence of decision upon a sole parent (§ 1628). The law was amended to increase the competence of the family court to prosecute parents who injure the physical and spiritual welfare of their children through their behaviour, as contained in §§ 1666–67. On separation it is for the court to approve or decide which parent has the right and duty to take care of the child (§ 1671). Unless the individual circumstances dictate otherwise, this is to be shared.

4.2 Adoption (§§ 1741–1772)

This establishes a parent-child relationship between the child and the adoptive parents (§§ 1741, 1754). The child attains the legal position of a legitimate child (§§ 1754, 1767 II and 1770). Adoption only becomes effective by court order (§ 1752 I). At the same time links to the child's natural parents and relatives are severed (§ 1755).

5 Guardianship (*Vormundschaft*), curatorship (*Pflegschaft*), and care and control (*Betreuung*)

These forms of protection for persons who cannot care for themselves are governed by §§ 1773–1921. Guardianship (*Vormundschaft*, §§ 1773–1895) only applies to minors, i.e. orphans and can be arranged by the court § 1774. Care and control (*Betreuung*, §§ 1896–1908k) introduced by the Care and Control Act of 1990 is a new instrument only applicable to adults which due to physical or mental impediment cannot care for themselves. It has replaced the previously applicable guardianship. The difference is that now the protector—replacing the previous 'guardian'—is obliged to respect the protégé's interests by preserving as much self-determination as possible. General declarations of incompetence are thus no longer acceptable. Curatorship (*Pflegschaft*, §§ 1909–1921) in the context of family law resembles guardianship but differs in that it allows the curator only to take care of those affairs of the child that the parents or the guardian are restricted from handling themselves, i.e. because of conflict of interest or absence (§ 1909 I).[158]

FURTHER READING

1981 supplement to the German civil code and the Introductory Act to the German civil code and the Marriage Law of the Federal Republic of Germany, translated by Simon L. Goren (1982: Fred B. Rothman, Littleton, Col).

P. Gottwald, D. Schwab and E. Büttner, *Family and Succession Law in Germany* (2001: Kluwer, The Hague).

G. Langenfeld, *Der Ehevertrag*, 9th ed. (2001: C.H. Beck, München).

A. Lüderitz, *Familienrecht*, 27th ed. (1999: C.H. Beck, München).

H. Luthin, *Handbook des Unterhaltsrechts*, 9th ed. (2002: C.H. Beck, München).

E. Von Münch, *Die Scheidung nach neuem Recht*, 11th ed. (2002: C.H. Beck, München).

W. Schlüter, *BGB Familienrecht*, 9th ed. (2001: C.F. Müller, Münster).

D. Schwab, *Familienrecht*, 11th ed. (2001: C.H. Beck, München).

G Book Five: the law of succession (*Erbrecht*)

1 Introduction, sources, and scope

The law of succession is constitutionally guaranteed by Article 14 (1) *Grundgesetz*, and the general legal regime is found in the fifth book of the BGB which is divided into nine sections. The BGB regulates only the private law of succession and does not concern itself with any participation of the state in the matters of succession, notably in the area of tax. Rules from the other books of the BGB also apply where relevant, especially in the allied subjects of property law and family law.

Paragraphs 1922–2385 regulate the fate of property (*Erbschaft/Nachlaß*) which the deceased has left. Succession refers only to the death (*Erbfall*) of natural, and not legal, persons. The transference of property is characterized as the succession (*Erbfolge*); the deceased is referred to as the *Erblasser*.[159]

---

[158] For details see Gottwald, Schwab, and Büttner, above, n 147 paras 222–251.
[159] Again only a brief outline of basic ideas of the law of succession will be given. Refer to Gottwald, Schwab, and Büttner for more information on the law of succession in Germany.

2 **The basic principles of succession**

These basic principles underlie the law of succession in Germany:

2.1 **The principle of universal succession (*Gesamtrechtsnachfolge/ Universalsukzession*)**

The principle of universal succession, stated in § 1922 I, means that all the deceased's property passes in its entirety immediately on death to the heir or heirs. The term 'property' includes all rights and obligations. The passing of the estate includes liabilities as well as assets. Property which cannot be transferred includes strictly personal rights and duties of the deceased, such as the right to a name, personal user rights over property and the limited personal servitudes. In case of more than one heir, joint inheritance takes place (§§ 2032 et seq.).

2.2 **Automatic inheritance (*Vonselbsterwerb*)**

This means that a legal transaction is not necessary in respect of succession, for the totality or individual component rights or duties. According to § 1922 the transfer of property passes without the formalities of conveyance or acceptance in a particular form, or knowledge of the heir or the need for any action or cooperation by the heir.

2.3 **Capacity**

Any legal or natural person is capable of becoming heir (§ 1923 I) including a not yet born but already conceived baby (§ 1923 II).

2.4 **Testamentary and intestate succession**

Succession is usually in the form of the testamentary disposition (*testamentarische Erbfolge*), which, as a part of private law, allows the deceased to leave his property to whom he wishes, although this is subject to claims under the rules on compulsory portions (*Pflichtteil*) of the estate going to spouse and close family members. Paragraph 2302 guarantees the unlimited freedom to make wills (*Testierfreiheit*) and has its roots in the main underlying idea of the BGB to protect the free will (*Willensfreiheit*) of individuals.

Intestate succession (*gesetzliche Erbfolge*) will only occur if the deceased has not decided personally how to dispose of his property. Both forms can exist together, if only part of the estate has been willed. The transference takes place under the principles of universal and automatic inheritance. In the case of intestate succession the spouse and closest relatives will succeed the deceased. Succession of family (*Familienerbfolge*), given statutory authority by the legislature, recognizes that the family has earned a right to claim, at least, a certain proportion of the property of the deceased, as detailed below (§§ 1924 et seq.). Where no relatives exist the state will alternatively become the heir (§ 1936).

3 The acquisition of the inheritance

Paragraphs 1942–1966 (*Rechtliche Stellung des Erben*) concern the legal position of the heir including the acceptance or the disclaiming of the inheritance, relationship between heirs and liability for debts of the deceased.

3.1 Acceptance

The heir inherits on the death of the deceased even if he knows nothing about it whatsoever, and even if he cannot be identified and regardless of his own intentions in the matter. Paragraph 1950 prohibits either the acceptance or repudiation of only part of the inheritance—it must be all or nothing.

3.2 Repudiation of the inheritance

It is possible for the heir to disclaim the inheritance (*Ausschlagung*) but in the meantime he is still the heir. The deceased's assets and obligations pass directly to the heir on inheritance, and the disclaimer is the only way the heir can disburden himself of an overindebted estate, which should not be forced upon him against his wishes.

Paragraph 1942 I provides the right to disclaim. Under § 1943, once acceptance of the estate has occurred the acquisition of the estate is final and the heir loses the right to disclaim, although rescission of this decision is possible under §§ 1954–1957. The disclaimer is only effective under § 1945 I once it has been declared to the probate court (*Nachlaßgericht*) in the form of an officially authenticated written statement. The disclaimer must be made within six weeks of the heir learning of the inheritance (§ 1944 I). The consequence of the disclaimer under § 1953 is that the heir ceases to be the heir and the person next in line succeeds him, with retrospective effect, as if the first disposition had never occurred. The disclaimer can, however, be revoked within the six-week period (§ 1954 I).

Failure to disclaim by the end of the six-week period provided, is regarded by § 1943 II as an acceptance of the inheritance.

4 Rights and liabilities in succession

These are governed by §§ 1967–2031. As soon as the estate is transferred, the heir can enforce any claims or rights, including demands for the return of property. Paragraph 1967 I states as an initial position that the liability is unlimited, although it allows liability either to be regulated to impose unlimited liability of the heir's assets to satisfy the liabilities of the inherited estate, or to be limited to the available assets of the inherited estate.

5 Heirs

Heirs can be natural or legal persons but natural persons must be living at the event of succession (§ 1923 I). Legal persons must be in existence at the time of succession.

The status of the prospective heir or heirs is determined either by statute, in the case of intestate succession (*gesetzliche Erbfolge*), or by the intentions of the deceased, the testamentary succession (*gewillkürte Erbfolge*).

6 Intestate succession (*gesetzliche Erbfolge*)

Intestate inheritance, governed by §§ 1922–1936, occurs with the death of a person and the transference of the property as a whole to one or more other persons (§ 1922 I). Statutory intestate succession takes place in the absence of a will, if the testament proves to be invalid or if the heir named in the will disclaims the inheritance.

According to the BGB §§ 1924–1930, there are five mutually exclusive classes of persons and the surviving spouse (§ 1931) who are entitled to intestate succession. The first class includes the children and their children, the closer excluding the more remote. The second class includes the parents of the deceased and their issue. The third class includes the grandparents and their issue, the fourth class covers the great grandparents and their issue, and all other relatives constitute the fifth class.

If at the time of death the deceased has no heirs, then the revenue authorities in the *Land* of the legal residence of the deceased become the heir under § 1936.

A surviving spouse is entitled to one-quarter of the estate if there are any relatives in the first class, and to one-half if there are relatives in the second class but none in the first (§ 1931). If there are no relatives in the first or second classes, the surviving spouse receives the whole estate. The spouse will only succeed, however, if the marriage was valid at the time of the death and no proceedings for divorce had been filed, or there was no entitlement by the deceased to file for a dissolution of the marriage (§ 1933).

If the marriage was subject to the statutory property regime of the community of acquisitions, the spouse's part is increased by one-quarter to equalize the gain (§§ 1931 III and 1371). The special status of illegitimate children has now been abolished by the Child Reform Act 1997 thus granting them the same rights as legitimate children. Previously, they were only granted a monetary claim against the other heirs (ex-§ 1934d). Under the new law legitimate and illegitimate children become joint heirs.

7 Testamentary succession (*gewillkürte Erbfolge*)

The deceased can choose whom he wishes to inherit his property and disinherit a statutory heir through the means of a will (*ordentliches Testament*, § 1937), or an inheritance contract (*Erbvertrag*, § 1941). The drawing up of a will or an inheritance contract is governed by §§ 2064–2086 and §§ 2229–2264. The will is a one-sided declaration which until death is revocable, whereas the contract is concluded between the testator and heirs. If notarized and complying with formalities, this is binding on the testator who will then be restricted in the freedom to change the will.

7.1 The will (*Das Testament*)

To make a will requires the capacity to do so. This is denied to minors under the age of sixteen. Those over sixteen can make a will without the approval of their parents or guardians, but only in the form of an official will witnessed by a notary (§§ 2229 II and 2233 I). Paragraph 2229 III and IV states that those lacking legal capacity or the mentally handicapped are denied the capacity to make a will even with the consent of their legal representatives.

There are two main forms of the will and one or two variations.

7.1.1 *The private will (Das eigenhändige Testament)*

A person may write out and sign his own will, stating the date and place of writing (§ 2247). The testator takes the risk that his wishes may not be fully understood. This can be revoked at any time by the testator (§ 2253 I) drawing up another will revoking the first (§ 2254), or by destroying or changing the first testamentary document (§ 2255). Only hand-written testaments can be accepted, and not those typed or produced by other mechanical or electronic means.

7.1.2 *The public will (Das öffentliche Testament)*

This is an officially drawn-up document authenticated by a notary (§ 2232). This can be revoked by getting the return of the will (§ 2256) or by drawing up a new, contradictory will (§ 2258).

7.1.3 *The emergency will*

There is, additionally, the exceptional type of will drawn up in emergencies (*Nottestament*, §§ 2249–2251), which has virtually the same weight as the private will and is made by persons who are close to death and have previously made no other provision. The validity of such a will lapses after three months if the testator is still alive. It must be witnessed by three witnesses.

7.1.4 *The mutual will*

A further type of testament is known as the mutual will (*gemeinschaftliches Testament*), which is written and signed jointly by both spouses and provides for the agreed disposal of the assets (§§ 2265–2273). It can be revoked by both or one of the parties.

7.2 **The succession contract (*Erbvertrag*)**

Paragraphs 2274–2302 cover this form of disposition of property by agreement, which is binding on the testator and not revocable. These contracts can be concluded with any person and are not limited to spouses as is the case with the mutual testament. They can only be made in the presence of a notary. They do not restrict the disposal of the assets in the lifetime of the testator. They can be cancelled by a contract of rescission under §§ 2290 et seq.

7.3 **The ineffective or invalid will**

Wills will be declared invalid if they infringe certain statute-based formalities,— e.g., incapacity, or if they offend public policy or morals, or are in favour of a partner to a marriage which has subsequently been dissolved (§ 2077).

8 **Compulsory portion (*Pflichtteil*)**

Under §§ 2303–2338, the succession rights of the immediate family are secured by the institution of the compulsory succession. In the event that the spouse or close relatives have been either wholly or partially excluded from the succession by the deceased and there is no good reason for this exclusion, such as divorce proceedings by the spouse, the BGB secures certain rights in respect of the excluded members of the family.

The BGB provides that the children, parents and surviving spouse of the deceased have a statutory right of inheritance which cannot be curtailed by will, unless there has been an attempt by a particular relative to injure or kill the testator (see § 2333 for further grounds). These persons are not regarded as heirs but their claim is secured at one-half of the level of intestate succession and only as a monetary claim. If property has already been received, the balance is made up to the compulsory portion (§§ 2325–2326).

9 The execution of the estate

This is not usually carried out by an executor, although it is possible to appoint one. Normally the heirs are responsible for this task. Once the heir requests proof of succession, the court will issue a certificate (*Erbschein*, § 2353 et seq.). After the period has passed in which the heir may disclaim the inheritance, the certificate becomes conclusive of the entitlement as against third parties or for entries in the Land Register.

FURTHER READING

H. Brox, *Erbrecht* 19th ed. (2001: Carl Heymanns Verlag, Cologne).

R. Frank, *Erbrecht* (2000: C.H. Beck, München).

P. Gottwald, D. Schwab, and E. Büttner, *Family and Succession Law in Germany* (2001: Kluwer, The Hague).

K.-H. Gursky, *Erbrecht*, 3rd ed. (1999: Verlag R. v. Decker, C.F. Müller, Munich).

M. Harder and I. Kroppenberg, *Grundzüge des Erbrechts*, 5th ed. (2001, Luchterhand, Neuwied).

D. Leipold, *Erbrecht*, 13th ed. (2000: Tübingen, Mohr Siebeck).

W. Schlüter, *Erbrecht*, 14th ed. (2001: C.H. Beck, München).

H Private international law/conflict of laws

Only a few introductory remarks concerning private international law (*Internationales Privatrecht*) shall be made at the end of this chapter dealing with the German civil code.

Before applying German law to a case any lawyer will have to decide whether it is applicable in the first place. This will be increasingly difficult to answer the more connections a case has with different countries, for example in cases of cross-border contractual relationships or family law disputes between spouses of different citizenship. Guidelines in order to find the applicable law for private law cases are—as in every legal system—provided by private international law[160] (*Internationales Privatrecht*). Thus private international law is part of the national law designed to help the courts determine the applicable law in the relevant case. It has to be distinguished from international civil procedural law. The latter provides rules that

---

[160] Sometimes more accurately termed as the "Conflict of Laws"(*Kollisionsrecht*) since "International Private Law" is not a uniform global law, providing us with a substantial international provisions that solve all international private law cases. It merely explains which law is applicable, where several legal systems might compete to solve a case of cross-border importance.

determine which court has jurisdiction over a private international law case in the first place and which procedural rules are applicable. Private international law rules are only examined once the competent court has been determined.

As a general rule sources of international procedural law and private international law are found in international conventions or in national provisions but also in case law (*Richterrecht*). Conventions always take priority. Where they are not applicable or where there are none the national rules apply.

1 International civil procedural law (*Internationales Zivilverfahrensrecht, IZVR*)

A court dealing with a private international law case will first have to determine whether it has the jurisdiction to hear the case. Furthermore, one could argue that the relevant procedural law still has to be determined. However, it is generally acknowledged that the German courts will only apply German civil procedural law[161] according to the *lex fori*[162] principle. When determining whether the court faced with a case of private international law has jurisdiction for this particular case, the judge will first examine whether the country of his court is party to an international convention on international civil procedure and jurisdiction. The most important convention to bear in mind here is the European Convention on Jurisdiction and Enforcement of Judgments in Civil and Commercial Matters of 1968[163] (EuGVÜ) to which Germany as well as all the other EU Member States are parties to. A similar convention to help solve questions of jurisdiction and enforcement of judgments, the Lugano Convention on Jurisdiction and Enforcement of Judgments in Civil and Commercial Matters of 1988,[164] include the EU member states as well as the EFTA Member States. It is open to accession by other states as well. There are numerous conventions, especially in family matters,[165] dealing with jurisdiction, recognition, and enforcement of private law judgments. They cannot be examined or even named here. For more information refer to the further reading indicated at the end of this section.

If there is no relevant international convention then the court will turn to national rules on jurisdiction. Here the main principle is that local jurisdiction will indicate international jurisdiction. This means that where a national provision provides for the jurisdiction of one particular local court its international

---

[161] BGH NJW 1985, 552,553; B. von Hoffmann, Internationales Privatrecht, 6th ed. (2000: C.H. Beck, München) p. 62.

[162] Literally, "law of the court".

[163] *Brüsseler EWG-Übereinkommen über die gerichtliche Zuständigkeit und die Vollstreckung gerichtlicher Entscheidungen in Zivil-und Handelssachen vom 27. 9. 1968* (EuGVÜ), BGBl 1972 II, 774.

[164] *Luganer Übereinkommen über die gerichtliche Zuständigkeit und die Vollstreckung gerichtlicher Entscheidungen in Zivil-und Handelssachen vom 16.9.1988* (LugÜ), BGBl 1994 II, 2660.

[165] See P. Gottwald, D. Schwab,and E. Büttner, *Family and Succession Law in Germany* (2001: Kluwer, The Hague) p. 22–23.

jurisdiction for this case will be assumed—in the absence of international conventions.[166] The relevant German provisions will be found in the Civil Procedural Code (ZPO) §§ 12 et seq. generally and §§ 606a I, 640 a II for family matters.

2 International private law (*Internationales Privatrecht*)

If a German court has established its jurisdiction over a case of private international law it will have to assess which law is applicable. The case might have such strong links to a different country that the law of that state is applicable. In that case the German court would have to apply the law of that state—after having obtained expert opinion on the particular foreign law.[167]

Again the first source of law to look at for guidelines are international conventions. When dealing with cases of international contracts of sale the Vienna UN Convention on Contracts for the International Sale of Goods from 1980[168] (CISG) may be applicable. This convention ratified by Germany will take priority over any national rules. Instead of only giving guidelines as to which national law is applicable this convention creates new international rules on the law of contract where it is applicable. It thus consists of "substantial" law as opposed to those conventions that merely help solve questions of allocating the applicable national law. As a consequence before turning to German law on the contract of sales one should always check on applicability of the CISG in international sales of goods cases. Other examples of international conventions are those dealing with family law and the protection of minors in cross border family disputes, such as the numerous Hague Conventions,[169] for example the Hague Convention Concerning the Powers of Authorities and the Law Applicable in Respect of the Protection of Minors of 1961.[170] The latter convention—as opposed to the CISG—may serve as an example for an international convention not providing any new substantial law but rather setting up rules as to the applicable law in private international law cases.

Where conventions covering the relevant case of international private law do not exist the courts have to turn to national rules indicating the applicable law. In German law they can be found in the introductory act of the BGB (Art. 3-46 EGBGB). These provisions will then determine the applicable law for certain categories. Thus contractual obligations, for example, will be covered by the law of the state agreed upon by the parties (Arts 27, 28 EGBGB). In the absence of such an agreement Article 28 II EGBGB declares applicable the law of the state of domicile

---

[166] See B. von Hoffmann, *Internationales Privatrecht*, 6th ed. (2000: C.H. Beck, München), p. 73 with further references.

[167] Obtained for example, from the Max-Plack-Institut for Comparative and International law.

[168] *Wiener UN-Kaufrechtsübereinkommen über Verträge über den internationalen Warenkauf vom 11.4.1980* (UN-Kfr); BGBl 1989 II 588, amended in BGBl 1990 II 1699.

[169] See P. Gottwald, D. Schwab, and E. Büttner, *Family and Succession Law in Germany* (2001: Kluwer, The Hague), p. 22–23.

[170] *Haager Übereinkommen über die Zuständigkeit von Behörden und das anzuwendende Recht auf dem Gebiet des Schutzes von Minderjährigen vom 5.10.1961*, BGBl 1971 II, 214.

of the party rendering the specific contractual performance (i.e. the seller in cases of contracts of sale). However, there are exception clauses for contracts involving consumers and employees in order to protect them (Arts 29, 30 EGBGB). In cases of wrongful acts causing damages generally the law of the state will be applicable where the wrongful act was committed.

It has to be noted that these provisions may refer to either a foreign law as a whole system (*Gesamtverweisung*, Art. 4 I 1st sentence EGBGB) or only to its respective substantial law rules (*bedingte Verweisung*). In the first case a provision might refer to a whole foreign legal system including the foreign private international law rules. As a result those rules might refer the case back to German law which then will accept this reference and apply German substantial law (Art. 4 I 2nd sentence EGBGB). Where the German provision merely refers to substantial foreign law (*bedingte Verweisung*) that law will be automatically applicable (Art. 3 I 2 EGBGB).

It has to be emphasized the foreign law will not be employed by German courts where it contravenes the essential principles and values of German law, also termed as the *ordre public* (Art. 6 EGBG). This is especially the case where application of the foreign law in question would in the relevant case violate one of the parties' fundamental rights. As part of state authority the German courts are bound by the basic rights of the *Grundgesetz* (Art. 1 III GG) and thus could not apply such a law.[171]

FURTHER READING

P. Gottwald D. Schwab, and E. Büttner, *Family and Succession Law in Germany* (2001: Kluwer, The Hague).

B. von Hoffmann, *Internationales Privatrecht*, 6th ed. (2000: C.H. Beck, München).

R. Hüsstege, *Internationales Privatrecht*, 3rd ed. (1999: C.H. Beck, München).

J. Kropholler, *Internationales Privatrecht*, 3rd ed. (1997: Mohr Siebeck, Tübingen).

H. Schack, (ed.), *Höchstrichterliche Rechtsprechung zum Internationalen Privat- und Verfahrensrecht*, 2nd ed. (2000: C.H. Beck, München).

K. Siehr, 'Private International Law' in W. Ebke and M.W. Finkin, *Introduction to German Law* (1996: Kluwer, The Hague).

---

[171] See also the so-called "Spanierbeschluss", BVerfG NJW 1971, 1509 (= BVerfGE 31, 58).

Private law II: business and labour law

A Commercial law and the law of business association

1 Introduction

The principal source of law for these areas is statutory; for commercial law generally, the commercial code (*Handelsgesetzbuch*: HGB[1]) is applicable, and for the law
of business association, a number of additional statutes apply in respect of specific
business forms. Gaps left by these provisions will be filled by reference to either
newer statutes or by reference to the BGB, and less frequently to case law. Therefore,
it is necessary to be conversant with many of the provisions of the BGB which apply
to fill gaps in commercial law in specific instances and will be appropriately
discussed. The BGB provides the basic regime for legal persons under §§ 21–88
and for the establishment and conduct of the civil law partnership. In addition,
general principles, for example 'good faith' as contained in § 242, are also regularly
referred to in a commercial setting, as amplified in the section on Book One BGB
above. However, the greatest source of legislative change in these areas of law, and
one which is having similar effects in all member states, is the EC legislative activity
in respect of freedom of capital and undertakings and the harmonization of
company law.

The HGB, as the BGB, is a product of the codification of laws in the latter half of
the nineteenth century and so today does not accurately reflect the modern commercial environment, although its relevance is still surprisingly extensive. There is
now a number of areas of commercial law subject to legislative activity not covered
by the HGB, prominently, bankruptcy laws, competition laws, finance, insurance,
various aspects of labour law, and credit laws.

This section is divided into two parts, the first concerned with commercial law
and the second with the law of business association. The latter term is used in
preference to 'company law' because the German term for company, *Gesellschaft*, is

---

[1] Originally 10 May 1897 (RGBl 1897, 219) as of the latest amended to 10 December 2001 (BGBl I 2001,
3422).

a much wider concept and refers to any association, including partnerships and companies. The term is closer to the notion of an association or the French *société*. The scope and meaning of the term 'commerce' in German law is important, because different rules have been formulated and apply to commercial matters.

2 Commercial law

2.1 History

The Commercial Code was the result of the codification of commercial practice and the body of laws that had been developed in the latter half of the nineteenth century. The code entered into force at the same time as the BGB, on 1 January 1900. It has often been amended and variously increased and reduced in size on a number of occasions since its first appearance. In 1985 the HGB was subject to the largest revision for fifty years, due largely to the existence of and need to implement the 4th, 7th and 8th European Community company law directives. This meant the restructuring of the first two books and the creation of a new third book of the HGB. The pace of change has not slackened since the 1985 revision and there have been numerous further amending laws since then, which have imposed considerable alterations on numerous paragraphs of the code. In 1998, there was a further extensive revision of the code, in particular to the original central concept of the code, the merchant (*Kaufmann*), to the rules concerning business names, and to transport law.[2] Versions of the Commercial Code and discussions of it prior to 1998 are out of date and should be used only alongside a current text.

2.2 The structure of the HGB

The HGB is now divided into five books following the 1985 revision:

Book One (§§ 1–104) deals with the concept and status of the merchant, his activities and trading relations, employees and agents, and the commercial register.

Book Two (§§ 105–237) concerns a number of forms of business associations, notably partnerships, which are not covered by specific statutes.

A new third book (§§ 238–342a), concerns accounting provisions and business records, and is largely the result of the Community directives mentioned.

The fourth book (§§ 343–475) contains rules on particular forms of commercial transactions, such as sale and transport forwarding.

Book Five (§§ 476–905) is devoted to maritime and admiralty law and will not be considered here.

The details of what are now the most economically important and the most

---

[2] This latter area is not the subject of discussion in this introductory volume. The changes were effected technically by the *Handelsrechtsreformgesetz* (HRefG, BGBl I 1998, 1474) and the *Transportrechtsreformgesetz* (TRG) 1998.

popular forms of enterprise, the public and private companies, are not now regulated by the Commercial Code. Their regulation has largely been taken out of the code and provided for under separate statutes, which will be considered under the section on the law of business association below.

2.3 **HGB Book One**

The HGB commences with a pivotal concept in commercial law, whereby the applicability of this specific code to commercial transactions depends on the status of the party to an agreement. The Commercial Code distinguishes a particular person, legal or natural, to whom the epithet 'merchant' (*Kaufmann*[3]) is attached and thus separates these from persons to whom provisions of the BGB only apply. The consequence of this distinction is that specific rules apply in respect of merchants, therefore a definition of this concept is essential. Additional duties, such as the duty to register with the Commercial Register (*Handelsregister*) in the *Amtsgericht*, are applied to merchants. The HGB defines the circumstances when these rules apply.

Paragraph 1 I HGB[4] defines a merchant as a person who carries on a commercial enterprise, and remains unchanged by the 1998 revision. The second paragraph no longer lists a wide number of activities which, if conducted, will be deemed to be a commercial enterprise. The previous definitions of who or what constituted a merchant have been completely overhauled in the 1998 revision of the code. The definition of merchant now depends under § 1 II much more simply on the fact that a commercial business activity is being conducted. Such persons, natural or artificial, who undertake a large scale enterprise are automatically given the status of merchants (§ 1 II) and are now termed in German *Ist-Kaufmann*. Registration in the Commercial Register is merely declaratory (*deklaratorisch*) for this category of merchant. The recognized fact that business undertaking (*Gewerbe*) is not statutorily defined[5] means that other smaller business undertakings whose commercial activity may previously have been in question, may nevertheless now register in the Commercial Register regardless of the type of activity undertaken (§ 2). This category, whose registration in the Register is a constitutive act (*konstitutiv*) is now given the description of *Kann-Kaufmann*. Gone are the categories which by definition were required or should have had merchant status (*Muß- and Soll-Kaufmann*) and the further sub-divisions of those clearly merchants and those conducting a more limited commercial activity (*Voll- and Minderkaufmann*).

Share companies and limited liability companies are always merchants by compulsory registration in the Commercial Register, regardless of their activity (*Formkaufmann*). The relevant statutes confirm this status.

---

[3] And now that even German provisions are endowed with politically correct formulations see also *Kaufleute* or *Kauffrau/Kaufmann*.
[4] All future paragraph references will be to the HGB unless otherwise stated.
[5] But in the case-law defined as a profit oriented, self-standing economic enterprise (BGHZ 33, 321, 324 et. seq.)

Thus individuals, partnerships and private and public companies can be merchants. Historically, agricultural and forestry activities were excluded by § 3 but more recently the borderlines have become blurred and allied activities such as sawmills, slaughter houses, and vineyards are able to register as merchants (*Kann-Kaufmann*). The liberal professions and sporting or artistic persons are excluded unless constituted in a recognized business form and thus automatically considered to be of merchant status. The application of the merchant rules cannot be refuted once registration has taken place. Paragraphs 5 and 15 protect third parties in good faith from persons or associations who, either wilfully or negligently, makes themselves out to be a merchant. In these cases merchant liability is imposed on them by operation of the law. Notable exceptions from the status of merchant are the public utilities, such as the railway and Post Office, due to the overriding public interest element which imposes a special set of rules on them rather than by exclusion by reason of the trade or business undertaken (see § 452). It is likely that continuing privatization will, however, change this position.

2.3.1 *The Commercial Register (Handelsregister)*

The Commercial Register is an accurate record of commercial enterprise and is open to public inspection (§§ 8–16 HGB). It is administered by the *Amtsgericht* and divided into Part A for individuals and civil partnerships and Part B for limited liability companies and general and limited partnerships, which are required to apply for registration on establishment (§§ 106, 162). Registration takes place at the *Amtsgericht* where the association is to have its registered office (§ 13). Paragraph 29 requires every merchant to register the name of the firm and the location of the business. Branches must also be registered under the requirements of §§ 13–13c. Any changes in these particulars must be registered (see, *inter alia*, §§ 31–35 in respect of change of name). All submissions to the Register must be certified by a notary.

Powers of attorney given by the merchant are also required to be registered (§ 53).

Registration acts in general as evidence of an existing legal fact and not as the creation of rights. As with the Land Register, a presumption exists by reason of the judicial administration of the register as to its accuracy. See the section on property law in Chapter 10 on the BGB. Any registered facts can be asserted against third parties (§ 15 II), and third parties are entitled to assume that facts not registered do not exist (§ 15). It also means that incorrect entries can be relied on by third parties against the registered business associations. Registration also imposes the duty to maintain business records and accounts (§ 238).

2.3.2 *The firm name (Firma)*

This is used by merchants for all transactions, and they can sue and be sued under this name (§ 17 II). The choice of name was prior to the 1998 reform, heavily proscribed by the code under §§ 17–37. The amended §§ 18–19 now provide that the name should be suitable to the merchant and must inherently be able to distinguish the business. It must distinguish itself from similarly named firms in the same area (§ 30). The name when registered is legally protected under § 37, and both a fine and damages may be payable for any breach. The name must indicate the form of business, i.e. whether an OHG or a GmbH, so that third parties can determine the liability of the partners, company or members (§ 19).

2.3.3 Business employees

The HGB provided a legal regime for the employment of clerical personnel, which was defined to include most employees of merchants. This originally gave rise to distinct obligations in favour of merchants' employees in contrast to the employees of non-merchants. However, due to the application of a number of additional statutes and the extension by case law, the rules applicable are little different to those applicable to most employees. Of particular and remaining interest, however, are the provisions on loyalty, competition and the social care required of the merchant. For details refer to §§ 59–75h. Otherwise, refer to the section on labour law in this chapter.

2.3.4 Commercial agency

The BGB provides the basic regime and powers of agency (§§ 164 et seq.). The commercial power of agency is known as the *Prokura*. The *Prokurist* is the registered legal agent of the company, partnership or merchant (§ 53). Registration allows third parties to rely on the general scope of the power granted to *Prokuristen*. Paragraphs 49–50 define the scope of the power, which includes all judicial and non-judicial transactions relating to the operation of the business. The power to conduct land transactions, however, must be expressly conferred (§ 49 II). The powers cannot be limited in respect of third parties in good faith but can be limited internally (§ 50). These powers are non-transferable and can be revoked at any time. To be effective, a revocation must also be registered (§ 52). Agency law is also governed by the EC Directive of 18 December 1986 on Commercial Agents, which itself closely reflected the German law on the subject (§§ 52–53).

2.3.5 The business proxy (Handelsvollmacht)

A general non-registered power of attorney exists, the scope of which is determined by §§ 54 et seq. The powers granted are narrower than the *Prokura* and do not cover real property transactions, loans, bills of exchange, or judicial representation unless expressly granted. The statutory restrictions are valid against third parties; other restrictions on the powers granted are only valid if the third parties had not acted in good faith.

Paragraph 56 imposes statutory powers of agency on employees to the extent it is deemed customary for their position. Third parties may enforce wider rights if the appearance of them was not dispelled by the principal.

2.3.6 *Commercial agents (Handelsvertreter)*[6]

Commercial agents are independent and not employees of the merchant. The definition under § 84 is that of an independent contractor who is contractually obligated, permanently or on a fixed regular basis, to solicit sales for the account of and in the name of a principal. The independent status is determined by the ability of the agents to arrange their own activities and hours of work. Since statutory rules apply in favour of this agent for the payment of compensation in the event of the termination of the relationship, another form of sale has found favour. This is the appointed dealer or distributor, who buys the goods of the merchant but is nevertheless bound to a long-term relationship, usually a distribution agreement. These are not expressly governed by the HGB, although some rules may apply by analogy and they are subject to the general commercial and civil provisions and, latterly, Community law.

An agent may be considered to be a *Kaufmann* for the purposes of commercial law according to the revised §§ 1 and 2 of the code. Agents are not usually granted either a *Prokura* or a business proxy, and the role is generally restricted to that of securing orders for the principal, and known as a *Vermittlungsvertreter*. However, the code provides that commercial agents can have business proxy similar to that provided by direct agents under § 55, who can bind the principal to contracts either under direct instruction (as an *Abschlußvertreter*), or for those contracts made with third parties in good faith, despite the actual lack of power of the agent (§ 91 II).

The general duties of the commercial agent and principal are not significantly different from those of general agency, and often include just refinements or additional specific rules. Refer to the section on Book One of the BGB in Chapter 10 for the general regime.

Agents are paid on a commission basis, at least once every three months, regulated under §§ 86b–87c which, in the event of non-payment, gives the agent a right of retention over any goods of the principal held by the agent (§ 88a).

The agency agreement can be terminated by agreement or notice, the periods of which are specified in § 89 and cannot be altered even by the agreement of both parties. Termination without notice before this agreed date can only be for good cause (§ 89a). Typically, good cause would be along the lines of competing with the principal, giving away trade secrets or diverting trade. Compensation is payable according to § 89b in normal circumstances of termination for the advantage that the principal will continue to derive from the agent's previous efforts, but not where the termination is for good cause or where the agent terminates the agreement without giving reasons. The maximum payable is the average annual commission based on the last five years' payments (§ 89b II).

Paragraph 90 imposes an automatic prohibition of competition clause (restrictive covenant) on the agent, the scope of which is limited to the view of the prudent businessman as to what is covered, therefore contractual agreements need to clarify

---

[6] Agency law is also governed by the EC Directive of 18 December 1986 on Commercial Agents [1986] OJ L382 17 which itself close reflected the German law on the subject and which then further influenced German law on the subject.

this. They must nevertheless conform to § 90a in the content of the clauses and include reasonable requirements of the time and geographic area of their validity and the details of the payment of compensation. In any event, they are subject to a maximum period of two years (§ 90a).

2.3.7 *The distributor or appointed dealer (Vertragshändler/Eigenhändler)*

This is the favoured arrangement today, which is not subject to special provisions of the code. Appointed dealers are independent and buy and sell goods of the manufacturer in their own name. It is usual for an agreement to exist for a long-term arrangement of distribution, which will contain limits as to the other work the distributor can carry out in return for a protected territory for the dealer.

Some of the provisions relating to commercial agents apply by analogy to distributors, such as duties, termination and compensation for unjustified termination, but otherwise, as stated, these agreements lie outside of the rules of the Commercial Code and are subject to the general rules of the Civil Code. There are also the strict requirements of the Unfair Competition Act (*Gesetz gegen den unlauteren Wettbewerb*: UWG), the Competition Law (*Gesetz gegen Wettbewerbsbeschränkungen*: GWB) and Community competition laws. See the reading references at the end of the chapter.

2.3.8 *The commission agent (Kommissionär)*

This type of agent represents a half-way house between the commercial agent and a distributor. The commission agents acts like a commercial agent in respect of the relationship with the principal, but acts in his or her own name in dealings with third parties with whom direct contractual relations are made. The agent is paid commission by the principal, who also bears the costs of sales. The relationship can be for single transactions only (refer to §§ 400 et seq.).

2.3.9 *The commercial broker (Handelsmakler)*

A broker, according to the definition of the BGB § 652, is a person who intermediates in finding or negotiating agreements. A permanent arrangement is not envisaged. Under § 93 HGB, the broker must negotiate to earn a commission. His main duty is to supply a note of the details of the agreement. Further details and duties can be found in §§ 94 et seq.[7]

2.4 Book Two: partnerships under the commercial code

The forms of commercial partnership in the Commercial Code will be considered in the section on business association, below.

---

[7] There is a useful overview of commercial agency by Tscherwinka, 'Das Recht des Handelsvertreters' JuS 1991, 110.

2.5 Book Three: business accounts

The detailed requirements of the code for the maintenance and registration of business records and accounts are to be found in §§ 238–339. All registered businesses must maintain trading and financial records. Stricter requirements were introduced by the implementation of the Community directives by the *Bilanzricht-linien Gesetz* of 19 December 1985 (BGBI I S 2355 ff).

The German requirements contained in this book of the Commercial Code are now essentially the same as in other Member States, therefore, for details, see the 4th, 7th and 8th Community company law directives. The general principles and the essential rules can be obtained either by reading the directives themselves or by looking at the requirements of UK law on the subject. It is only if the exact German wording is required for a particular problem that consultation of the German texts will be required.

2.6 Book Four: commercial transactions

2.6.1 *Definition*

Paragraphs 343–372 contain the general provisions applicable to commercial transactions between merchants.

Paragraph 343 I defines commercial transactions as all transactions by a merchant relating to the operation of the merchant's business. Being so classified, these transactions are subject to the duties and obligations of merchants which differ from ordinary civil transactions. For example, the merchant standard of care imposed by § 347 is higher than that imposed by § 276 BGB.

If one party only is a merchant, it is presumed under § 344 that commercial provisions will apply to them unless it is provided that both must be merchants or the merchant is transacting in a private capacity. It may also be provided for by legislation that commercial rules will apply. Some rules apply only to merchants, such as the admissibility of higher interest payments for payment default under §§ 352–353 or the removal of the form requirements for guarantees under § 350. Further rules relate to the time, manner, and other details of performance (§§ 357 et seq.).

A particular concept of 'the commercial practice' is recognized by the code. 'Commercial practice' is defined under § 346 as the regular, standard, voluntary, and actual custom between or amongst merchants. For example, a commercial confirmation from one party to another will contain the first party's understanding of the agreement reached. If the second party does not respond to this, commercial practice dictates that the agreement will be on the terms of the first party. Both parties must be merchants, it must be clear there is an agreement and the confirmation must be in good faith. The concept of commercial practice is therefore a way in which commercial customs, although not legally binding rules, may nevertheless be incorporated into commercial law. This is also the way in which generally recognized international commercial rules are incorporated, such as the Incoterms of the International Chamber of Commerce.

Under the provisions of the BGB, silence cannot constitute an acceptance. However, § 362 I HGB provides that in transactions between merchants silence can be deemed to be an acceptance of an offer, i.e. where in the course of trading an immediate reply to an offer is not given, it is deemed to be an acceptance, as in the case of the failure to respond to a letter or the loss of a letter containing new terms or different conditions.

Paragraphs 355 et seq. provide for the offsetting of debts between merchants by the use and operation of current account agreements.

Paragraphs 363–365 concern merchant order papers, which operate like cheques but give rights over goods and not money.

Paragraphs 369 give a merchant a right, by virtue of an established claim for money, to retention of the debtor's movable goods and securities. With bilateral transactions this is stronger than the right under the BGB, and includes the right to retention of items not the subject of the claim. Transfers of the goods by the debtor are secured under § 372. These rules apply only between merchants. There must be direct possession, and indirect possession through an agent will not count.

2.6.2 Commercial sale (Handelskauf)

According to § 343 I, this is a transaction whereby the party is a merchant and it is within the operation of that business. Commercial sales do not relate to real estate, or rights and claims to real estate. Some of the provisions of the HGB apply to unilateral commercial sales. In the case of the non-acceptance of a delivery by a buyer, the merchant debtor has the right to deposit the goods in public warehousing and charge accordingly (§ 373). In the absence of information to the contrary, the transactions of a merchant are presumed to be commercial.

The requirement to perform on time can be tightened up in commercial agreements, or include at least the effective introduction of penalties for not performing by the agreed time (§ 376). The result is that the non-breaching party has the immediate right to rescind and claim damages for non-performance instead of having to set a further date before rescission can be effected as under the provisions of the BGB (see the section on Book Two of the BGB in Chapter 10).

Where both parties are merchants even stricter rules are imposed, e.g. the right to claim for defects after inspection. Paragraph 377 requires inspection and immediate protest, after which the right to protest is lost. The BGB gives the right to claim for hidden defects for up to six months despite the proper inspection of the goods at the time of delivery (§ 460 BGB). If only one of the parties to a transaction is a merchant, the transaction is governed by civil and not commercial rules.

Commission transactions are regulated by the provisions of §§ 383–406 which are relevant more for the banking and finance sectors.

The forwarding agent (§§ 407 et seq.) commercially undertakes to ship goods in his own name by means of a carrier. Whilst doing so he is under merchant standards of care and is liable for damage while in possession.

Warehousing (§§ 416 et seq.) involves a custody agreement with rights to expenses incurred in relation to the goods (§ 420). The warehousing agent has a statutory lien for payment (§ 421).

Commercial carriers under § 425 undertake to ship goods by land, rivers, or inland waterway. Liability is regulated by §§ 429–431. Carriers also have a statutory lien over goods in the event of non-payment.

Shipment by rail is subject to the special provisions of §§ 453 et seq. Basically, a stricter liability is imposed because of the monopoly position of the railways. Additionally, the Railways Regulations (*Eisenbahnverkehrsordnung*: EVO) contain the very many detailed rules relating to the carriage of goods by rail.

2.7 Commercial arbitration

Commercial arbitration is widely accepted and employed within the business community in Germany, and many disputes go before the Chamber of Commerce arbitration service (*Handelskammer*) or the German Arbitration Committee rather than the courts. Arbitration is chosen by the parties for varying reasons, e.g. lower costs, speedier dispute resolution, expertise of the arbitrators, or the secrecy of the proceedings.

The arbitration tribunal can be *ad hoc* or one of the permanent tribunals which exist, such as the International Chamber of Commerce, the London Court of Arbitration or those set up by the German Chamber of Commerce. The Hanseatic cities of Hamburg and Bremen are well noted for their arbitration chambers.

Although the state dispute resolution apparatus of the courts is replaced by arbitration, the state nevertheless has laid down some minimum standards which must also apply in arbitration (*schiedsrichterliches Verfahren*) in the Code on Civil Procedure (ZPO), 10th Book §§ 1025–1066.

The parties are free to decide whether to use arbitration and the scope of arbitration (§ 1029–1033). Arbitration agreements are subject to the general rules of the BGB applicable to contracts, such as § 138 BGB on public policy. The choice of law is up to the parties, but if none is chosen the rules of the ZPO apply. Current disputes and an agreement to refer future disputes to arbitration are acceptable under § 1030.

Under § 1031, the arbitration agreement must be an independent written document. Lack of form renders the agreement void unless both parties are merchants, in which case less formal agreements are acceptable if customary in the trade. An exception to this exists in respect of merchants' agreements to arbitration in the area of restrictive trade practices under § 91 GWB.

The procedure and evidence can be chosen subject to rules of the ZPO. Both parties must be given the right to present evidence orally or in writing. Under § 1042, it is not permitted to exclude legal representation by *Rechtsanwälte*, although the lesser qualified representatives, such as the *Prozeßagenten*, can be excluded from arbitration.

The rules of procedure can be decided in advance or determined by the arbitrator (§ 1042). Usually standard rules provided by arbitration institutions are employed, such as the Hamburg Friendly Arbitration Rules issued by the Hamburg Chamber of Commerce. There is no pre-discovery of documents in arbitration.

The award has the effect of a court judgment (§ 1055). There is no appeal against an arbitration award to the ordinary courts but the parties may expressly or impliedly agree to an appeal to a tribunal of second instance. Certain procedural rights are nevertheless preserved, the breach of which gives rights to apply to the courts to set aside the award (§ 1059). Judicial review of the award is possible for reasons including lack of due process, or violation of public policy or of the *Grundgesetz* or other statutes.

An award is only enforceable by the courts (§§ 1060 et seq.). The enforcement action can be the subject of appeals in the courts under the normal rules for appeal. The award is binding and has the effect of a final judgment.

Further details on the appointment of arbitrators and procedure can be found in references under 'Further reading' at the end of the chapter.

3 The law of business association

3.1 Introduction

The German definition of company law is considerably wider than the one employed in the UK, which applies quite narrowly to the regulation of particular forms of business enterprise; the public and private limited liability companies. Thus partnership law is excluded from the considerations of company law, although it may be the focus of comparison for some aspects.

In Germany, the definition of company law (*Gesellschaftsrecht*) includes any association by agreement to conduct joint pursuits, hence all forms of commercial and non-commercial enterprise come under this heading, as can be seen from the German texts on company law cited below. 'Company' is used, therefore, more in its literal sense in Germany.

Company law in Germany is governed by a number of principal enactments in the absence of a company code. Thus elements of the civil and commercial codes apply, as well as statutes on distinct business forms such as the Joint Stock Corporation Act (*Aktiengesetz*: AktG) and the Limited Liability Companies Act (*Gesetz betreffend die Gesellschaften mit beschränkter Haftung*: GmbHG). Additionally in this non-codified area, case-law has adopted a more important role.

The principal distinction in German company law is the division into partnerships which do not have legal personality, and corporations which are legal persons. The partnerships do, however, enjoy such legal rights concerning the name and the ability to sue and be sued in the partnership name as to render the absence of full legal personality almost inconsequential.

3.2 Partnerships

The Civil Code provides for a partnership, the partnership under civil law (*Gesellschaft des bürgerlichen Rechts*), under §§ 705 et seq. BGB, and for a non-profit making organization, the registered association (*eingetragener Verein:* e.V.), under §§ 21 et seq. and 55 et seq. BGB. The latter has legal personality, must consist of at least seven members and must deposit a set of articles. It is rare for this form to be used for commercial purposes.

The Commercial Code gives three further variations for commercial partnerships: the general partnership (*offene Handelsgesellschaft:* OHG) under §§ 705 et seq. BGB and §§ 105 et seq. HGB; the limited partnership (*Kommanditgesellschaft:* KG) under §§ 161 et seq. and §§ 105 HGB; and the silent partnership (*stille Gesellschaft*) under §§ 230 et seq. HGB. There is also the hybrid company/partnership, the GmbH & Co. KG and the new *Partnerschaftgesellschaft*[8] to consider.

3.2.1 *Partnership under civil law (Gesellschaft des bürgerlichen Rechts)*

Civil law partnerships, regulated by §§ 705 et seq. BGB, are non-commercial enterprises whose objects cannot be commercial,[9] and as such are not required to register in the Commercial Register. If the objects are deemed to be commercial as defined by the HGB, they must register as a commercial partnership, the OHG. The civil partnership is used fairly extensively in Germany as a means to organise the joint work or cooperation of persons or companies, either for projects of a short duration or to facilitate joint projects and most commonly is employed in joint building projects. It is also used in a wide variety of non-trade circumstances, such as associations of professional persons—lawyers, architects or doctors, although the new *Partnerschaftgesellschaft* has been established specifically for the use and purposes of these and other liberal professions. Public and private limited companies and other forms of partnerships can be members of a civil partnership.

Civil partnerships do not have legal personality, therefore any civil action must be in the name of all the partners unless a joint name for this purpose is formulated. They provide the model for the commercial partnerships. Formation under § 705 BGB is by agreement by the parties, whose contractual freedom, as with other agreements in German civil law, is constrained only by statutory provisions.

The rights and obligations of the members within a partnership are determined, *inter alia*, by §§ 706, 708–709, 711 BGB, and are to manage the partnership and vote in the meetings on an equal basis, unless the agreement specifies that voting is based on contributions (§§ 706–707 BGB). The sharing of profit and loss is equal

---

[8] Neither of the translations 'Partnership Partnership' or 'Partnership Company' make a great deal of sense so the original German will be used instead.
[9] In the sense that it would then be governed by provisions of the Commercial Code

unless agreed otherwise, usually according to contributions of the partners (§§ 721–722 BGB).

The level of the duty of care imposed by § 708 BGB is the same as would be observed in the conduct of the partners' own affairs. Partners are liable to each other for a breach of the partnership agreement.

Management and representation of the partnership to third parties under § 709 I BGB is joint unless otherwise agreed, and decision-making is by unanimity unless, under § 709 II, they decide to act by majority voting. Alternatively, one or more managing partners can be appointed under §§ 710 and 713 BGB, whose liability to the partnership is on the usual agency principles of the BGB, §§ 164 et seq. (refer to the section on BGB Book One in Chapter 10 for details). The partners not directly concerned with management have a right of information and inspection of the accounts under § 716 BGB.

As partnership is a personal matter, it is not transferable (§ 717 BGB).

Contributions made to the partnership become the assets of the partnership, the title to which belongs to all the partners jointly, and cannot be disposed of on an individual basis (§§ 718–719 BGB).

Liability to third parties is joint and several, and applies against partnership property and the partners' property unless excluded by agreement with the third party. Under § 859 ZPO, assets belonging to a civil law partnership can be attached by a claim only if the judgment is rendered against all the partners.

The dissolution of the partnership arises when the object for which it has been formed has been achieved, when the period agreed expires, or on the death or retirement of one of the partners (§§ 723–728 BGB). Liquidation rules for the distribution of partnership assets, or rules for the reforming of the partnership are contained in §§ 730–735 BGB. The rules for a change of membership are found in §§ 736–737 BGB.

3.2.2 *The general commercial partnership (offene Handelsgesellschaft: OHG)*

Paragraphs 105 et seq. HGB[10] state that a partnership formed under a common firm's name for commercial purposes, as defined by §§ 1–2 HGB, must register as a general commercial partnership in the Commercial Register. It is generally accepted that commercial purposes presuppose the making of profit. These partnerships are governed by rules agreed by the partners, in the absence of which the paragraphs of the HGB and the BGB apply. They are not a very popular form of association because of the unlimited liability of all members. They consist of two or more persons, natural or legal, who are general partners, and do not have a maximum number of participating partners.

Formation is by agreement which must be notarised, and the partnership must apply to the Commercial Register for registration (§ 106). Registration must include the names of the partners, and the partnership name and registered office address. The name is subject to the usual commercial rules discussed above. The legal start

---

[10] All § references now are to the HGB unless where otherwise stated.

date is given when the agreement of the partners is completed and the application to the Commercial Register has been accepted and the partnership registered (§§ 106 and 123 HGB).

The rights and obligations between partners are determined by the partnership agreement. Paragraphs 112–113 provide that the partners cannot compete with the partnership and cannot be partners of other partnerships undertaking similar business without the consent of the other partners.

Management is regulated by §§ 114–117, which provide that all the general partners are legal representatives of the partnership unless excluded and registered as so in the commercial register. Paragraph 115 allows all the partners to act individually on behalf of the partnership unless excluded by registered agreement. Internal restrictions can be imposed but do not have any effect on third parties dealing in good faith. Other general or specific agents or attorneys may be appointed, whose powers have been discussed above. In the case of partners who are not concerned in the running of the partnership, rights of information are guaranteed by § 118.

Profit and loss, unless otherwise agreed, is distributed according to contributions (§§ 120–121), but is in any case usually catered for in the agreement.

The OHG legally has the right to act in its own name and to acquire property, and thus has in effect a partial legal personality (§ 124). Partnership assets are in the firm's name and all partners are co-owners.

All the partners are jointly and severally liable to third parties (§§ 125–128) and cannot limit their liability. Even a partner who enters at a later date is liable for all previous claims by third parties, unless excluded by registered agreement (§ 130).

Actions by creditors should be taken against the partnership and all partners as co-defendants. Paragraph 129 allows defences to claims against the partnership and partners' assets, but only to the extent that they are defences based on the legal position of the partner as a member of the partnership and not personal defences. Claims cannot be made by third parties against members of the partnership to enforce judgments against the partnership (§ 129 IV).

The grounds of dissolution are contained in §§ 131–135. These include the expiry of the partnership agreement, by agreement of the partners, by application to the court for good cause, on the death or withdrawal of a partner, or bankruptcy.

Liquidation is administered by the partners themselves unless the agreement provides otherwise. The liquidators must be registered in the Commercial Register (§§ 145–158), and on dissolution the partnership name and details must be withdrawn from the register.

3.2.3 The limited partnership (Kommanditgesellschaft: KG)

The KG is governed by the agreement of the partners, in the absence of which §§ 161 et seq. and §§ 105 et seq. HGB apply.

This form of commercial enterprise is popular for small and medium-sized businesses but it does not have a good credit rating. The concept under § 161 allows limited liability of one or more partners. There must be at least one general partner, known as the *Komplementär*, and one limited partner (*Kommanditist*). There is no upper limit on the number of partners, who can be natural or legal persons. In this way a large number of limited partners can join as members and a considerable capital fund can be established.

Formation and registration is governed by § 162. The application to the Commercial Register must contain the name of the partnership, the details of those who are the limited partners, and the amount contributed by the partners.

Management is conducted by the general partner (§ 164). The limited partners are usually excluded by § 165 from the management of the business and have no power to represent the partnership (§ 170), unless this is agreed and registered. Even this would not remove the protection of limited liability as in limited partnerships in the UK. The limited partners have rights of information under § 166. The general partners require the consent of the limited partners to conduct transactions outside of the normal business range agreed by the partners.

The general partners are required to draw up annual accounts, and the distribution of profit and loss is determined by § 167, which applies §§ 120–121 (as in the OHG) unless alternative arrangements have been made by the partnership agreement.

The rules relating to the liability of the general partners to third parties and the dissolution of the partnership are the same as for the general commercial partnership. The liability of the limited partners is defined in § 171 and is confined to the amount of the contribution unpaid; where paid up there is no further liability.

3.2.4 *The silent or undisclosed partnership (stille Gesellschaft)*

The definition of this type of partnership (§§ 230–237 HGB), is found in § 230, which provides for an enterprise based on the provision of a loan of money to a business by an outsider. The undisclosed partner transfers money to the owner of the business and participates in the profit and, if agreed, the losses (§§ 231–232). The assets remain the property of the general partner. These partnerships usually consist of a financier and a proprietor, who may be natural or legal persons. The undisclosed partner does not have merchant status and has no influence in the management of the partnership, but has the right to inspect the books and to obtain copies of the annual reports (§ 233).

Formation is by agreement and the partnership must be registered as with other commercial partnerships, except that the details and the amount of the participation of the undisclosed partner need not be registered.

The general partner bears the liability to third parties. The liability of the undisclosed partner is limited to the extent of the transfer made. The agreement can include an internal restriction on the powers of the general partner but this would not restrict the liability to third parties.

Dissolution arises either by expiry of the agreement or by subsequent agreement, and on the retirement of one of the partners unless so excluded and registered. It is not automatic on the death of the undisclosed partner under § 234, which would normally be the case in other forms of partnership.

3.2.5 *GmbH & Co. KG*

This is a composite form of business enterprise whereby a GmbH acts as a general partner and natural persons are the limited partners, who are usually also the members of the GmbH. This means the management of the partnership can be put in the hands of the GmbH which would have professionals as business managers who are not involved in the financial aspects of the partnership. These enterprises are very popular because of the limit of liability of the natural persons. The liability of the GmbH as the general partner is unlimited.

Originally they were formed to obtain tax advantages, and the form was consequently confirmed as being legal by the *Reichsgericht* (RGZ 105, 101). The tax advantages previously enjoyed have now been removed by legislative reform and such enterprises are now used to limit and protect the liability of the natural members, and also to ensure the continuity of the partnership which otherwise would have to be dissolved on the death or exit of natural general partners.

Complications have arisen in respect of the decision-making and power of representation of the GmbH, and the relationship of the management of the private company to the natural limited partners. The management board is not responsible to the limited partners. In practice this does not present a problem, as the limited partners are usually also the members of the GmbH. Slight amendments have been made to the commercial code to take account of the fact that no natural members of these partnerships are subject to unlimited liability, and impose liability for transactions for stationary materials, capital replacing loans and overindebtedness.[11] The assets are jointly owned by the general and silent partners.

A recent development in respect of this type of business organisation is the judicial acceptance of limited companies registered in other jurisdictions as the general partner. As a consequence, establishing a business in Germany may be easier, but the companies may be exposed to full liability.

3.2.6 *The partnership for the professions (Partnerschaftsgesellschaften Angehöriger Freier Berufe)*

To cater for professionals, who previously were restricted to using the civil law partnership, a new form of partnership was introduced under the *Partnerschaftgesellschaftgesetz* (Part GG) of 25 July 1994 (BGBl I S. 1744). The civil law partnership was increasingly considered as unsuitable for the form of association and joint working which was taking place, especially between firms of lawyers (see the further details in respect of lawyers made in Chapter 4).

The new partnership is designed especially for the liberal professions and excludes, under § 1 I, those engaged in trade and commerce. Members can be natural persons only and not the associations of professions which have also found favour. A definitive list of professions is given in § 1 II. The partnership can carry its own name, be sued and sue, be bound in transactions with third parties and must be registered in the partnership register of the Commercial Register (§§ 2, 4, 5 and

---

[11] See §§ 125a, 129a, and 130a respectively, introduced by a law of 4 July 1980 (BGBl I S 836).

7). Partnership property, as well as the property of the partners, can be used to extinguish liability (§ 8). It remains to be seen whether this will prove to be popular.

B Company law (*Gesellschaftsrecht*)

1 The private limited liability company

In German law, the private limited liability company (GmbH) is an incorporated registered business enterprise which confers limited liability in favour of the members. It has legal personality and can therefore own property and sue and be sued in its own name. It acts through a management structure which is not necessarily made up of the membership. Its activities are not restricted to mercantile activities.

The GmbH is extensively used, and not just by smaller companies or those with few shareholders. The statistical year-books of the Federal Republic of Germany show that at the end of the 1990s there were over 800,000 a considerable number[12] of which about 25% were the general partners in the GmbH & Co. KG. The GmbH is the most popular choice for inward investment and the setting up of companies by foreign investors.

The private limited company in Germany is predominantly and extensively regulated by the GmbHG[13] but is also subject to the commercial and civil codes where appropriate. The GmbHG was enacted in 1892, ostensibly the first regulation in the world catering specifically for private limited companies. It was designed to avoid the often harsh application of the extensive and complex rules on public companies to smaller companies and in unfair circumstances, and also to avoid the complexities and restrictive membership rules of partnerships. The Act appears to have been copied in UK and in many other developed countries. The Act has been extensively amended, in particular in 1980 and 1985, both as a result of Community legislation, company law directives 1–4 and 7–8, and in order to effect general company law reform.

1.1 Formation

As a result of the reform of the law in 1980, the legality of one-man companies was statutorily recognised, and § 1 GmbHG now allows one person to act as founder and member of a private company[14] Companies in which the membership fell to one but which were not previously legally recognised are now allowed under § 5 III.

---

[12] Estimated at 15–20% by Grunewald, cited below, p. 308.
[13] *Gesetz betreffend die Gesellschaften mit beschränkter Haftung* of 20 April 1892 (RGBl 1892, 472), GmbHG as amended to 13 July 2001, BGBl IS. 1542.
[14] All §§ now refer to GmbHG unless otherwise indicated.

The legislation which also previously allowed a maximum of fifty members does not now reveal a maximum number.

One document, the *Gesellschaftsvertrag*, regulates the affairs of the company. This is the company contract and constitution which is the equivalent of the UK articles of association and memorandum combined, and it determines the level and extent of the regulation of the affairs of the company and the respective powers of management and shareholders (§§ 2–3). The establishment of the company would normally be in the form of a freely negotiated contract between the founders, or, in the case of a one-man business, a declaration certified by notarial deed (§ 2 I). The term 'the constitution' would be more appropriate but the most commonly translated term 'the articles' will be adopted here. The articles are more comprehensive and flexible than in the UK and allow the company to be formed for any purpose provided it is lawful (§ 1).

Paragraph 3 requires certain basic requirements to be stated in the articles, including the name of the *Firma* and its commercial domicile, the purpose of the enterprise, the amount of basic capital, the face value of the shares, the number of shares and the authorised directors. The name is subject to the general rules of the commercial code which require the name to derive either from the name of the shareholders or from the purpose or geographic origin of the company, as noted above. Paragraph 4 II also requires the name to indicate the company's limited liability by containing the words *Gesellschaft mit beschränkter Haftung* (or usually GmbH).

There must be at least one business director appointed (*Geschäftsführer*), for whom there is no share requirement. This appointment under § 6 can either be by the articles or by the general meeting. The director must be a natural person with full business capacity. Paragraph 45 allows the articles internally to limit the powers of the business directors but this has no effect on transactions with third parties in good faith (§ 37 II).

1.2 Capital

Share capital subscription under § 5 must be at least €25,000 of which at least 25% subject to an overriding minimum of €12,500 must be paid up before registration will be allowed by the court. In the case of one-man companies, the single member must give a security for the balance (§ 7 II), and in the case of wholly-owned subsidiaries, capital is usually fully paid up. Contributions in kind must be substantiated and will be checked by the registering court (§§ 5, 7, and 8).

1.3 Registration

Registration (§§ 7–11) takes place at the *Amtsgericht* of the legal residence, the registered office of the company. The registration has a constitutive effect in that it is the legal validation of the company (§ 11 I). The application for registration must notarised, usually done at the same time as the articles, and signed by all directors (§ 8 and § 12 HGB).

1.4 **Pre-incorporation status (vor-GmbH)**

Prior to the notarization of the articles, the members of the enterprise are treated in law as civil law partners with joint and several liability for pre-incorporation transactions, which is not disturbed by subsequent notarization or registration (NJW 1982, 932). If the shares have been subscribed to, the articles have been adopted and subjected to notarization but the company has not been registered, the company is known as a pre-company (*Vorgesellschaft*). The provisions of the GmbHG apply where relevant. Paragraph 11 II renders any person, including members of the board of management, who make contracts on behalf of the *Vorgesellschaft* fully personally liable for those contracts. The management are also liable for all acts of misconduct. On registration, the company automatically assumes the liability for transactions entered into prior to incorporation and the liability of those who transacted prior to incorporation ceases (see BGHZ 80, 129, NJW 1981, 1373). This includes liability imposed by § 11 II and personal liability.

Paragraph 13 provides that on registration the company acquires legal personality, limited liability of its members, and can sue and be sued in its own name.

1.5 **The rights and duties of shareholders (*Gesellschafter*)**

Shareholding (§§ 13 et seq.) must be of a minimum value of €100 value but divisible thereafter into €50 (§ 5). Share transfers or assignments are permitted under § 15 I but must be by notarial deed (§ 15 III–IV). This makes any transfer a formal and slow process, and as such demonstrates the clear distinction with public companies. The articles can and often do, impose further restrictions on share transfer and pre-emption rights for existing shareholders (§ 15 V). Share certificates are not required and not usually issued, and there is no registration of share transfers, although each year the share register must be updated and annually re-registered by the directors in the Commercial Register (§ 40).

Shareholders' liability is imposed not only to pay to the amount of the unpaid share subscription in the event of a call on it, but also to the proportionate extent of all the unpaid share capital of all other members who, for whatever reason, are unable to contribute to their subscribed amount (§ 24). Pre-incorporation losses have the effect of reducing the starting capital of a company before trading, and this is something legislation seeks to prohibit, therefore the shareholders remain liable to make good these losses for a period of five years after registration (§ 22 III).

The articles may allow for liability to be extended by way of supplementary contributions (*Nachschußpflicht*) in cases of call, or make members liable with a limit (§ 26) or they can be unlimited (§ 27). This form of achieving further contributions, which can also be paid back relatively easily, avoids the more cumbersome requirements for an increase and decrease in the capital of a company (§§ 30 and 55 et seq.). These are not subject to the demands of a liquidator unless the decision has already been taken in the articles to make the additional contribution, therefore it is best to decide on further contributions when the occasion demands.

Other provisions concerning share capital reflect those in the UK following the lead of Community law in respect of capital maintenance, payments of dividends only from profits, rules on the purchase of shares by the company itself and share redemption, as detailed under §§ 29–34 GmbHG. Paragraph 32a–32b GmbHG renders the shareholders liable for undercapitalisation, and any loans made to the company in such circumstances may not be repayable.

1.6 Management (*Geschäftsführung*)

The corporate management structure is regulated in the third part of the Act (§§ 35–52). It basically operates through the management board and, where determined in the constitution, by the general meeting of the company. There can also be an advisory board by choice or, if over 500 employees, by law[15]. The full details on co-determination will be considered below in the section on labour law. A GmbH is required by § 6 to have one or more business directors (*Geschäftsführer*), who must be natural persons. The day-to-day management rests with the director or, where more than one, the management collectively. Any change in the management must be registered in the Commercial Register (§ 39) and an annual list of directors must be submitted (§ 40). Where more than one director is appointed, they will usually be required to exercise power jointly and share joint responsibility, unless agreed differently and registered.

The power of the directors is legally to represent the company and, if a board, to do so jointly (§ 35). The details of a restricted scope of directors' authority must be registered, particularly if certain directors are given particular tasks to undertake (§ 10).

There is no limit on the external actions of the management under § 37 II, therefore the management will bind the company to third parties even for contracts the subject matter of which is outside the scope of the stated objects of the company. The directors will in turn be liable to the company as a result of any loss caused by those contracts. The management can be limited by either the articles or service agreements as to the scope of the activities they may carry out, but this restriction has no legal effect in respect of third parties (§ 37 II). They are required to consider the interests of the company, shareholders and employees in the exercise of their tasks.

The removal of directors is governed by § 38 and is permissible at any time, regardless of the existence of a service agreement, unless restricted by the articles. Damages may nevertheless be payable by the company for a breach of any service agreement. Paragraph 38 II allows the grounds of removal to be restricted and provides that the seemingly vague 'important grounds' clause (*wichtige Gründe*) must be included. The business directors are not subject to the usual labour law provisions on unfair dismissal and redundancy.

---

[15] Paragraphs 76–77 BetrVG. For further details, see the section on labour law below.

1.6.1 *Presentation of the accounts*

Paragraphs 41 and 42 concern the requirements for the pres-entation of the accounting books and the information which must be registered on an annual basis. This is a departure from the original, less restrictive disclosure requirements of private companies and results from the Community directives. Disclosure depends on the size of the enterprise divided into small, medium and large concerns by the Community 4th company law directive. Details can be found in the third book of the HGB especially §§ 267 et seq.

1.6.2 *Directors' liability*

Liability for damages for a breach of the directors' standard of care, or in the case of actions which exceed authority, is provided by § 43. The standard of care is that of an ordinary, prudent businessman. Additional duties can be established in the articles, service agreements and shareholders' resolutions, but would normally include the duties not to misuse power, not to conflict interests or to act in self interest, and not to compete with the company. Commentaries on the GmbHG will give the full scope of the duties. Any loans made to the directors require shareholder approval and that of the supervisory board, where present. No loans may be granted where the assets are needed to maintain the level of share capital (§ 43a).

1.7 General meetings

The general meetings (*Hauptversammlung*, §§ 45–51) usually decides on the appointment of the directors (§ 46), unless there are more than 2,000 employees when the supervisory board makes the appointments[16]. The general meeting is also responsible for broad instructions to the management, the approval of the annual accounts, use of profits, changes in capital, and alterations in the constitution of the company. Decisions are reached by a majority (§ 47) except in respect of an alteration of the articles where a majority of 75% of the votes cast and notarization are required (§ 53). The general meeting also determines the distribution of the profits subject to the limits written into the articles (§ 29).

Under § 48, resolutions reached by the shareholders do not need to be minuted or recorded in writing unless they are reached without holding a meeting and are unanimous, or if there is only one shareholder. A written decision of all the members will obviate the necessity of calling a general meeting and be legally valid (§ 48 II). German law does not have a requirement for a company secretary.

Minority rights may be established by agreement in the contract of association or failing that, a limited number of rights are provided by legislation. Under § 50, the shareholders of not less than 10% of the share capital have the right to demand that the directors call a general meeting. Extensive rights of the members to information at any time and the inspection of the books and company documents are given

---

[16] Paragraph 31 MitBestG.

under § 51 a–b, which rights are greater in private companies than in public companies.

1.8 The supervisory board (*Aufsichtsrat*)

Where the company has more than 500 employees a supervisory board is compulsory (see further the section on labour law, below). Paragraph 52 provides that a supervisory board may be set up on a voluntary basis and provides basic details unless regulated by the articles.

1.9 Alterations to the articles

Paragraphs 53–59 concern the amendment of the articles and share capital alterations. Paragraph 53 requires a three-quarters majority for any amendment except the members' increase in contribution, which requires unanimity. All amendments require the resolution and the registration to be notarized.

Paragraphs 55–58 concern the rules relating to the increase and decrease in capital, both of which must be registered. The capital cannot be reduced below the statutory minimum of € 25,000. Full accounting rules follow the requirements of Community law and are now contained in the third book of the HGB. They will not be considered here.

1.10 Dissolution and liquidation (*Auflösung*)

Dissolution (§§ 60–77), occurs on the expiry of the time agreed, by bankruptcy or by the resolution of a majority of 75% to dissolve the company at any time (§ 60 I). After this resolution the company can only conduct business necessary to achieve that aim. Paragraph 61 II allows 10% of the shareholders to bring dissolution proceedings with the approval of the court.

In cases of bankruptcy, an application can be made by any creditor to the court (§ 60 I (4)). The court then controls the proceedings.

Liquidation is normally carried out by the directors but § 66 II allows a 10% holding to apply to the court for the appointment of an independent liquidator. The dissolution must be entered in the Commercial Register (§ 65). A company remains a legal entity until all the assets have been distributed.

The final provisions in Part Six of the GmbHG concern duties imposed on directors, members of the supervisory boards and liquidators not to disclose trade secrets, and applies sanctions for breaches.

1.11 Company restructuring, mergers, and acquisitions

The merger or acquisition of a GmbH involves the purchase either of the share capital or of the assets of the company. Whichever method is used, the transaction to take over or purchase must be notarised and registered. All the employment contracts will be taken over by virtue of the civil code (§ 613a BGB).

The rules regulating company restructuring are now contained in the Transformations Act (*Umwandlungsgesetz*) of 28.10.1994 (BGBl I S. 3210), which in total provides 119 possibilities of changing the corporate structure in some way! All forms of mergers are catered for by the *Umwandlungsgesetz*, see §§ 4–48 for mergers involving a GmbH and §§ 123 et seq. for the division of a GmbH into two or more GmbHs. A GmbH can be transformed into all other forms of business enterprise under the provisions of §§ 190–302.[17]

The further details of mergers, divisions, transfer of assets between business forms and legal transformations are beyond the scope of this book but can be found in many of the titles listed under "Further reading" at the end of the chapter.

2 The joint stock corporation

The stock corporation (*Aktiengesellschaft*: AG) or, as it will be referred to, the public company has separate legal personality from its shareholders and is funded by a capital stock divided into shares (§ 1 AktG). These are, for the most part, publicly negotiable. It is deemed commercial because of its form and regardless of its activities (§ 6 HGB). The liability of the AG is restricted to its assets, and the liability of its shareholders is restricted to their contribution.

2.1 History

In Germany, the public company has followed a similar history and development to that experienced in the UK, where it also had seventeenth-century origins in the form of the trading corporations granted by government concession and was also the subject of some considerable abuse which resulted in government regulation.

It has not, however, proved as popular in the twentieth century in Germany as its equivalent in the UK and at the end of the 1990s there were only some 7,500 registered of which only c. 800 were quoted and publicly traded on the stock exchanges.[18] Much of the reason for this is the popularity of private companies, which were a much less regulated form of business enterprise with far lower disclosure and accounting requirements, at least prior to the requirements of the Community legislation. Although it is still the case that the scale of regulation continues to be considerable between the AG and the GmbH, the gap has closed recently. The extensive regulation of AGs can be seen in the fact that the law applicable, the *Atkiengesetz* (AktG),[19] has 410 paragraphs, many more than the

---

[17] For full details of the now quite extensive regulation of merger and transformation, which also owes a lot to the implementation of EC Directives, see Widman and Meyer, *Umwandlungsrecht*, vols I–V (1995: Stollfuß Verlag, Bonn), which may prove very useful (if not crucial).

[18] For further details, refer to Grunewald, cited below.

[19] Latest version from 6 September 1965 (BGBl I S 1089) as amended to 2001 (BGBl I S. 3822). All paragraph references will now be to this statute unless stated.

GmbHG. The rules were originally contained in the Commercial Code but were removed[20] as the law was subject to extensive revision and thus expansion.

The AktG also provides for the partnership limited by shares (*Kommanditgesellschaft auf Aktien*: KGaA), under §§ 278 et seq., discussed briefly below.

One of the reasons for the high level of regulation by the AktG is to protect the investing public who have less means of information and ability to protect their interests. Shares, recorded by stock certificates, are freely transferable without the need for notarial authentication, unless the articles of the company require the permission of the company to transfer.

2.2 Formation

The establishment and registration of an AG is a single but extensive process in which a number of requirements must be fulfilled. All the shares must be subscribed to in order to found the company and the company organs must be established. As with the private company, all of these requirements must be witnessed by a notary and registered (§ 23 I).

To establish a company there need now be only one or more founders, which is a significant amendment (introduced in 1994) to the previous requirement that there must be at least five founder incorporators (see the amended § 2). The minimum capital requirement now of an AG is € 50,000 (§ 7). This must be fully subscribed before the company can be registered and legally come into existence. However, only 25% need to be paid up before registration, in which case they must be registered shares (§§ 36a, 10 and 36), and in the case of a single founder, a security for the balance must be given (§ 36 II). A public offer is normally underwritten by the banks, who act as one of the founder members and who then conduct the sale of shares to the public. The shares can be for a minimum of € 1 and cannot be divided (§ 8). The founders are liable under §§ 46 et seq. for the correct formation and registration of the company. Following the initial foundation, the shares can be transferred to one shareholder, a situation approved by the Federal Court of Justice (BGHZ 21, 378).

A public company in Germany is required by law to have a three-tier constitutional structure for the conduct, management, and supervision of its affairs.

As with the GmbH, a single company contract (*Satzung*) regulates the affairs of the company (§ 23). The articles define the name, legal residence, the purposes, the capital and division into shares, the powers and meetings, and the existence and details of pre-incorporation contracts (§§ 23, 27 and 41). The name is governed by §§ 17–18 HGB, as discussed above, and by § 4 AktG, which also requires the word *Aktiengesellschaft* (or AG) to appear.

Paragraph 30 requires the founders to appoint a supervisory board (*Aufsichtsrat*) and the auditors for the first year. The supervisory board in turn has the task of appointing the management in the form of a management board (*Vorstand*) (§ 30 IV).

---

[20] Repealed by the BGBl I S 166, 30 January 1937.

Following these moves, a report must be drawn up under § 32 by the founders to be submitted for the approval of the supervisory and management boards (§ 33). The application can then be made to the Commercial Register (§§ 36 et seq.). This whole process, including the registration in the Commercial Register, must be notarized. Registration confers on the company legal personality (§§ 38 and 39). It is now able to acquire real and movable property.

2.2.1 Pre-incorporation liability

Pre-incorporation liability is determined by § 41 AktG. Incorporators are fully liable for transactions before the articles are notarised. Liability of individuals who have contracted on behalf of the *Vorgesellschaft* (pre-company) does not cease after registration, unlike the GmbH (§ 41 I 2). The extent of their liability differs according to opinion. Some argue there is full liability; others argue the incorporators are liable only to the extent of the subscribed capital, unless the company fails to come into existence in which case they will be fully liable. It is assumed that the distinction between the AG and the GmbH is the result of the concern for greater protection from liability for the shareholders of the AG. A clear ruling from the courts is, however, required to confirm this. Transactions prior to registration become the company's obligation only if accepted by the company (§ 41 II), which releases the incorporators' liability. Personal liability is likely to persist.[21]

2.3 The board of management (*Vorstand*)

The board of management (§§ 76–94) is responsible for the day-to-day running of the company and relations with third parties. It can consist of one or more natural persons (§ 76 III), unless the company has an initial capital of more than € 3 million when two directors are required (§ 76 II). As with the GmbH, there is no share qualification. Details of the members of the board must be registered and listed on letter headings (§§ 80 and 81). It is usual for one of the members in larger companies to be appointed as chairman.

The appointment of the directors by the supervisory board, on the basis of a simple majority, is for renewable periods of five years (§ 84). Dismissal is only for good cause as in gross breach of duty or incapacity, and can only be effected by the supervisory board (§ 84 III). Remuneration is governed by §§ 86 and 87 and must be reported in the annual report (§ 160).

Functions of the board are, amongst others, the day-to-day management of the business, the keeping of the accounts, and the presentation of the annual accounts and reports to the general meetings which it is required to convene. It has exclusive competence for these tasks. The directors have the power to represent the company in legal proceedings (§ 78), on a joint basis, unless otherwise ordered by the articles (§ 78 II).

The supervisory board cannot direct the management board but only supervise.

---

[21] See Heinemann, noted in 'Further reading' pp. 71–85.

However, certain transactions in respect of loans and property can be subject to the approval of the supervisory board (§ 111).

In relation to third parties, the ability of the management to bind the company cannot be limited (§§ 78 and 82). Paragraph 23 III 2 requires the articles to state the type of business which will be conducted by the company. This can internally restrict or prohibit the management from conducting certain types of transaction, or subject them to the prior approval of the supervisory board or the shareholders, but has no effect externally. If these restrictions are breached the company remains bound, but the business managers will be liable for damages.

Paragraphs 88 and 89 prohibit the management board members from entering into competition with the company, or from obtaining credit from the company unless with the approval of the supervisory board.

The board is required to inform the supervisory board of its activities and supply such information as required (§ 90), and is responsible for the company accounts (§ 91). The directors must call a general meeting when the capital of the company falls below 50% (§ 92).

Members are liable for damages caused by mismanagement and breach of duty, or breach of internal restrictions or breach of law (§ 93). The company can only waive liability after three years, and this waiver can be vetoed by a minority of the shareholders.

2.4 **The supervisory board (*Aufsichtsrat*)**

The supervisory board (§§ 95–116) is concerned with the appointment of the management board, the supervision of the same, and the approval of annual accounts and particular transactions determined by the articles.

The appointment is by the general meeting (§ 101) and, where applicable, under the provisions of the Co-determination Acts, as is discussed below. New companies do not have to appoint employee representatives to the supervisory board immediately but have a period of grace to do so (§ 30 I and II), except in the case of a takeover or merger (§ 31).

The number of members, who must be natural persons (§ 100), depends on the size of the company and varies from three to 21. There are detailed restrictions on the cross-membership of other boards of management and supervisory boards, particularly in respect of subsidiary and parent companies (§ 100). The appointment is for four years and is renewable (§ 102). Membership of both the management and supervisory boards is prohibited (§ 105).

The supervisory board has the rights under § 111, to inspect the accounts, to call a general meeting, and to appoint and dismiss members of the management board and obtain information. It has the power under § 112 to commence actions for breaches by the management on behalf of the company.

Under § 116, a duty of care and confidentiality is imposed, the breach of which renders the members liable for damages.

2.5 **The general meeting of shareholders (*Hauptversammlung*)**

The shareholders in general meeting and share rights are governed by §§ 118–141. The tasks of the general meeting are the election and removal of members of the supervisory board, the appointment of the auditors and determination of the distribution of the profits, amendment of the articles, increases to the share capital, and the dissolution of the company (§ 119).

An amendment of articles under § 179 requires the approval of a general meeting with a majority of at least three-quarters of the company's capital. Under § 181 all alterations must be registered in the Commercial Register and only become effective when so registered.

The technical details regarding capital increases and capital decreases under §§ 186 and 222 et seq. are also omitted from this section as these are also heavily proscribed by the implementation of the 2nd Community company law directive in 1978.

Meetings are normally called by the management board or by the supervisory board as noted above, or under § 122, whereby 5% of the shareholders may demand a general meeting. When called, a definitive agenda must be published (§ 124) which cannot be supplemented by new items. Shareholders are entitled to information at the general meeting from the management (§ 131). Resolutions are passed on the basis of a simple majority of the votes cast (§ 133) which may, however, be altered by the articles.

2.6 **Shares**

Shares are movable property and AG shares are freely transferable. They are largely bearer shares (§ 24) and are usually held by the banks and financial institutions. Alternatively, registered shares (§ 10) are issued which act and can be transferred like bills of exchange by endorsement. Banks and other institutions which hold shares exercise the voting rights on the instructions of, or on behalf of, the members. Detailed rules to ensure that the banks inform the shareholders of forthcoming meetings and give them the chance to state how their votes should be exercised are contained under §§ 128 et seq. Shares are held, for the most part, anonymously by the banks, which has been severely criticized, and future Community provisions in the 5th company law directive may alter this.

The company is able to issue non-voting preference shares under § 139, some with restricted transfer rights. However, all transfer rights cannot be removed entirely (§ 141).

Generally, the ownership of shares by the company is prohibited except in certain circumstances. For example, under § 71, up to 10% may be owned to help avert a serious detriment to the company as decided by the management. Further reasons are to hold them to transfer to employees, or if given to the company or acquired on merger.

2.7 Minority protection

Minority shareholder protection in German law is determined by statute. There is the right of 5% of shareholders to call a general meeting and, under § 122, to have items proposed by them included on the agenda.

The shareholders have the right to a special audit under §§ 142–147, whereby 10% may apply to the court to appoint auditors to investigate violations of the articles or law (§ 142 II).

The shareholders cannot sue in a derivative action, but where a minority of 10% believes breaches of duty by the management or supervisory board have been committed, it can require claims to be brought against the members of these boards (§ 147) and, if necessary, the appointment of special representatives to assert the claim against the supervisory or management boards. Should the action not be successful the minority is required to pay the costs.

Paragraph 120 gives a 10% minority the right to demand that in a vote to approve the actions of the members of the board, a separate vote is taken in respect of each individual board member.

German law also provides action to remedy the detrimental influence of a majority over a company. Paragraph 117 AktG initially provides for the liability of those who influence a company to its detriment. Any person who for personal reasons exerts influence on the general meeting, or intentionally causes a member of the management or supervisory boards to undertake a transaction to the detriment of the company or its shareholders, is liable to pay damages. Liability is also imposed on those who were influenced (§ 117 II).

2.8 Accounting provisions

As the German law on the preparation and submission of accounts follows that of Community law, no details will be provided here. The details in German can be found in Book Three of the HGB and throughout the AktG.

2.9 Dissolution (*Auflösung*)

Paragraphs 262 et seq. determine the grounds for dissolution. Reasons for dissolution of the company are the expiry of the period specified in the articles or by resolution of the shareholders. However, the application of the company in the course of bankruptcy proceedings is the most likely reason. The management must inform the Commercial Register of the decision to dissolve the company (§ 263).

Dissolution means the company is no longer able to carry on business, but it continues to exist as a legal person whilst being wound up. Liquidation then takes place, which is governed by §§ 264–273. The liquidators are usually the members of the management board, unless objected to by the supervisory board or the shareholders who may make application to the court for removal and the appointment of others (§ 265). The liquidators must be registered (§ 266). The rest of the procedure is similar to that in the UK and is also heavily influenced by Community provisions on the matter. The liquidators determine the assets and liabilities, make payments, and distribute any remaining to the shareholders, to whom a final report is presented before the company is struck off the Register and the company ceases legally to exist.

Insolvency is another area of law which, due to sheer volume, cannot be included in a book of this nature.

2.10 Acquisition and mergers

The acquisition of 25% or more of the stock of a company by another company must be notified to the company under § 20 AktG. These holdings must also be published in the *Federal Gazette* and in the annual reports of companies, thus ensuring public disclosure and information on the interlocking holdings and ownership of public companies. The relationship of the company to affiliated companies must also be notified (§ 312).

2.10.1 *Mergers (Verschmelzung)*

Mergers were governed by §§ 339–361 AktG, but these rules are now contained in the recently reformulated Transformations Act (*Umwandlungsgesetz*) of 28 October 1994 (BGBl I S. 3210), §§ 60–77. The concept of merger in German law envisages the takeover of the entire undertaking of one company by another. The company taken over is dissolved without being wound up and is acquired by the other company. The shareholders of the acquired company become shareholders of the acquiring company. This can be carried out in two ways: by the transfer of the assets and liabilities as a whole in exchange for shares in the acquiring company, or by the formation of a new company to which the assets and liabilities of the merging companies are transferred. Shares are then issued to the shareholders of the merged companies. In both cases, cash additions not amounting to more than 10 per cent of the nominal value of the shares can be made (§ 68 UmwG). This procedure also applies in cases where one of the companies is not an AG but a KGaA (§ 78 UmwG) or a GmbH (§ 46–59 UmwG).

The procedure briefly is that the companies involved enter a contract of merger, certified by a notary which must be approved by their respective general meetings (§§ 9–12 and 60–65 UmwG). The acquiring company must increase its capital and issue shares to be held by a trustee for the shareholders of the company to be dissolved (§§ 66–72). The acquired company is dissolved and the transfer of assets and liabilities takes place on the registration of these changes in the Commercial Register, duly notarized. The trustee then arranges for the exchange of share certificates.

The second procedure under § 73–77 UmwG, applies the relevant provisions of §§ 66–69 but can only take place if the merging companies have already been registered for a minimum of two years. In this case, the merger contract should contain the articles of the new company. Two merging companies will legally constitute the founding members of the new company. A trustee holds the new shares and the merging companies subscribe for the shares of the new company and appoint the supervisory board who appoints the management. The merging companies must then approve the merger contract and set up the new company. Upon registration of the new company, the transfer of assets and liabilities of the merging companies takes place and they are automatically dissolved, the shareholders acquiring the shares in the new company.[22] The further details of mergers or acquisitions can be determined from the specialist literature cited below.

2.10.2 *Transformations/conversions*

A public company can convert itself into a KGaA by altering its articles and recording the registration of the membership of a personally liable partner. Notarised re-registration must take place. A KGaA can transform into an AG or a GmbH (§ 78 UmwG).

3 Limited stock partnership/association limited by shares

The *Kommanditgesellschaft auf Aktien* (KGaA) is in effect the combination of a partnership and public company. It consists, in its intended form, of shareholders of a public company, of whom one or more members have unlimited liability and who are usually the managers. As such, then, it is similar to the limited partnership, the general partners of which are the managers (see §§ 278–290).

The shareholders with limited liability provide the capital and are governed by the AktG; whereas the relationship between the shareholders and the company to the general members, and the general members to third parties, is governed by the Commercial Code provisions on the KG (§ 278 II).

Paragraph 278 defines the KGaA as an association with legal personality and a capital divided by shares. There must be at least one general partner (*Komplementär*) with unlimited liability, the others are limited partners (*Kommanditaktionäre*). It was arguably intended that the unlimited partners should be natural persons, but it is now contended that[23] a GmbH can be the general unlimited partner, as in the GmbH & Co. KG but designated GmbH & Co. KGaA.

The general partners constitute the management, but can be required by the general meeting to seek approval for specified types of transactions (§ 285). The division of power between the boards and shareholders is much more flexible than in the AG.

Mergers of these companies are regulated by § 78 UmwG, but additionally require the approval of the unlimited partners.

Two other forms of organization which may be encountered are the cooperatives

---

[22] Full full details, refer to the reference work in n 21.
[23] By reason of a Supreme Court decision in BGHZ 134, 392.

(*Genossenschaften*: eG) which are like civil partnerships with legal personality but are not designed for profit-seeking enterprises but more for mutual cooperation, and insurance associations (*Versicherungsvereine auf Gegenseitigkeit*: VVaG) which spread the risk of insurance amongst themselves.

4 The law of groups of companies (*Konzernrecht*)

The problem, and thus control or regulation, of groups of companies was tackled in Germany far earlier than in other European countries. Germany has codified the law relating to groups of companies. In particular, problems arising from the responsibility of management in a subsidiary for decisions imposed on them by the parent company, and the lack of independence which results in the subsidiary, were considered. Detailed rules of the statutory regulation are to be found in §§ 291–328 AktG. It is from this base that the control and regulation of corporate groups proceeds with a definition of what constitutes dependency. From a determination of dependency, legal or factual group status can be assumed.

German law statutorily recognised the rights of parent companies to control subsidiaries but also ensured that minorities and the creditors of the subsidiaries were protected. This can be regarded as the provision of statutory rules for piercing the corporate veil (*Durchgriffshaftung*) in groups. As confirmed by the court, a parent company is liable for a subsidiary when it has instructed the directors to act (BGH NJW 1986, 188). The rules, however, relate predominantly to AG groups, and not to GmbH groups which have largely been left to the courts.

Connected and dominating enterprises are thus defined by the AktG, §§ 15–19. Associated enterprises under § 15 are those which arise when an enterprise holds a majority share in another, or controls, or is combined with, or mutually participates with other companies. Associated enterprises also include companies who are parties to contracts which involve any of the above concepts. There is a duty to inform imposed by § 20, where a holding of 25% or more in another company occurs. Furthermore, under § 90, the management of a public company must inform the supervisory board of the transactions of associated companies which may affect the company's own situation (§ 90 I 2).

Under § 131, shareholders have the right to information regarding legal and business relations with associated companies; the debts and liabilities of public companies and subsidiaries with each other must be shown in the annual accounts of the public company, as must the legal and business relations (§ 160).

Paragraph 16 defines a majority as a holding of more than 50% of the capital, or where the parent is entitled to the majority of the voting rights at the general meeting.

The definition of a dependent or dominating enterprise under § 17 is satisfied if one company can directly or indirectly influence the other. Dependence exists if one enterprise has the means to make the other comply with its wishes (RGZ, 167, 40, 49).

Groups of enterprises or combines are defined under § 18 as comprising companies either under a subordinate or vertical uniform management, or the uniform direction of legally independent enterprises. The former are subject to the AktG rules on groups, whereas the latter fall under competition law rules. Furthermore, the rules on group accounting become applicable under § 18 in the situation of the combine under uniform direction, whereby the parent company must prepare combined annual accounts (§§ 291–328).

Therefore, groups are not defined on the basis of an economic unit but on contractual and factual dependence or connection.

In cases of control which is exercised by virtue of a contract, the AktG provides that any control contracts should be subject to the approval of the shareholders and must be registered (§§ 293–294). The contract is legal where it provides protection to the shareholders and creditors of the subsidiary if damaged by the effects of the contract (§ 302). In other words, damage under the contract is legal if compensated. Breach of the contract by the parent will render the directors liable under § 309 to the subsidiary and its shareholders and creditors. Minority shareholders of the subsidiary are also protected, in that they can either obtain compensation for detrimental effects or force a sale of the shares at a fair price (§§ 304–305).

In relation to *de facto* rather than contractual control, § 311 makes it illegal to cause a dependent business to enter into transactions which are disadvantageous to it unless compensation is made either immediately or at the end of the financial year (§ 311 II). This applies where the majority power has been used to promote a single business policy. The dependent business may sue the parent for any detriment, and this claim may be brought by shareholders and creditors (§ 317 and § 309) should the compensation not be made.

In the case of linked firms, §§ 323–324 provide that if the parent has 100% control, it is liable for debts of the subsidiary. If 95% of the shares, it must compensate the minorities fairly (§ 320).

Paragraph 19 concerns mutual participation, i.e. cross-holding by two companies of more than 25% of the shares in each other. If independent, § 328 applies to the first company to register its holding in the other company. All rights attached to such shares are suspended until notice is given (§ 20 VII). Any company which has a notifiable cross-holding and is the subordinate company loses the right to exercise its share rights in the parent, but the dominating company retains its share rights. If both companies' holding is such as to enable them both to exert a controlling influence in each other, then both companies lose the right to exercise their shareholdings.

The above rules in respect of public companies do not apply to private companies except by analogy, which can only be determined by the courts. So far the courts have not gone as far with private companies as with dominant public companies to provide for compensation. Control is effected by the courts requiring good faith on the part of the directors of the controlling company, which may give rise to claims by the shareholders and creditors of the subsidiary should their instructions cause a breach. If either the management of a GmbH by a parent or the assets are treated in such a way as to remove the independence of the company, the parent company may be liable for the losses incurred by the subsidiary GmbH (see BGHZ 95, 330, '*Autokran*').

FURTHER READING

Please note that whilst there are a number of titles in this area of law which have been written in English, most of them are dangerously out of date but have been kept in the list of reading as they still serve the useful purpose of being an English language introduction into the German law and language of commercial and company law. They are not, of course, to be relied on any more as an accurate statement of the law.

Legislation and textbooks

The German Civil Code (as amended to 1993), translation and commentary by S. Goren (1995: Rothman/North-Holland Publishing Co., South Hackensack, New Jersey).

The German Commercial Code (as amended to 1 January 1978), translation and commentary by Forrester et al. and supplement to 1990 (1979: Rothman, Littleton, Colorado)).

Peltzer, Doyle and Allen, *German Commercial Code: Handelsgesetzbuch*, 3rd ed. (1995: Schmidt, Cologne).

The German Stock Corporation Act: bilingual edition with an introduction to the law by Schneider and Heidenhain (1996: C.H. Beck, Munich & Kluwer, The Hague.)

GmbH-law: German Law concerning the Companies with Limited Liability, German text with synoptic English translation and introduction by Müller, Meister and Heidenhaim, 5th ed. (1988: Fritz Knapp, Frankfurt).

GmbH deutsche-englisch, text and commentary by Peltzer and Brooks, 2nd ed. (1987: Verlag Dr Otto Schmidt, Cologne).

Baumbach and Hopt, *Handelsgesetzbuch: Kommentar*, 30th ed. (2000: C.H. Beck, Munich).

Baumbach and Hueck, *GmbH-Gesetz: Kommentar*, 17th ed. (2000: C.H. Beck, München).

A. Baumgarte, *German Agency Law*, 2nd ed. (1993: German Chamber of Industry and Commerce, London).

V. Beuthien, *Genossenschaftsgesetz mit Umwandlungsrecht Kommentar*, 13th ed. (2000: C.H. Beck, München).

M. Böcker et al., *Germany: Practical Commercial Law* (1992: Longman, London).

H. Brönner et al., *Die GMBH & Co. KG*, 8th ed. (1998: Haufe, Freiburg).

R. M. Buxbaum et al. (eds.), *European Business Law* (1991: de Gruyter, Berlin).

P. Bülow, *Handelsrecht*, 4th ed. (2001: C.F. Müller, Heidelberg).

Business Transactions in Germany (M. Bender, New York and C. H. Beck, Munich), vol. I, ch. 11 by M. Peltzer and C. E. Stewart and vol. I, ch. 13 by J. Schemding.

C.-W. Canaris, *Handelsrecht*, 23rd ed. (2001: C.H. Beck, München).

Droste, Killius and Triebel, *Business Law Guide to Germany*, 3rd ed. (1991: CCH Editions, Bicester).

Droste, *Mergers and Acquisitions in Germany* (1995: CCH Europe, Bicester, Oxford).

U. Eisenhardt, *Gesellschaftsrecht*, 6th ed. (1994: C.H. Beck, Munich).

V. Emmerich and J. Sonnenschein, *Konzernrecht*, 6th ed. (1997: C.H. Beck, München).

E. W. Erklentz, *Modern German Corporation Law*, vols I & II (1979: Oceana Publications, Dobbs Ferry, New York).

Glanegger et al., *HGB Kommentar*, 5th ed. (1999: C. F. Müller, Heidelberg).

O. Glossner, *Commercial Arbitration in the Federal Republic of Germany* (1984: Kluwer Law and Taxation, London).

B. Grunewald, *Gesellschaftsrecht*, 4th ed. (2000: Mohr, Tübingen).

M. Heidenhain and H. Schneider, *German anti-trust law: an introduction to the German anti-trust law with German text and synoptic English translation of the Act against Restraints of Competition*, 4th ed. (1991: Knapp, Frankfurt).

K. Heinemann, *Pre-incorporation Transactions* (1990: Carl Heymanns Verlag, Cologne).

H. Henze, *Aktiengesetz: Höchstrichterliche Rechtssprechung*, 4th ed. (2000: RWS Verlag, Köln).

P. Hofmann, *Handelsrecht*, 10th ed. (2000: Metzner, Frankfurt).

Horn, Kötz and Leser, *German Private and Commercial Law* (1982: Clarendon Press, Oxford).

U. Hübner, *Handelsrecht*, 4th ed. (2001: C.F. Müller, Heidelberg).

U. Hüffer, *Aktiengesetz Kommentar*, 3rd ed. (1997: C.H. Beck, München).

E. Klunzinger, *Grundzüge des Handelsrechts*, 11th ed. (2000: Vahlen, Munich).

E. Klunzinger, *Grundzüge des Gesellschaftsrechts*, 10th ed. (1999: Vahlen, Munich).

A. Kraft and P. Kreutz, *Gesellschaftsrecht*, 11th ed. (2000: Metzner, Frankfurt).

L. Michalski, *OHG-Recht Kommentar* (2000: Heymanns Verlag, Köln).

H. Oetker, *Handelsrecht*, 2nd ed., (1999: Springer Verlag, Berlin).

M. C. Oliver, *The Private Company in Germany*, 2nd ed. (1986: Kluwer, London).

G. H. Roth, *Handels-und Gesellschaftsrecht*, 5th ed. (1998: F. Vahlen, Munich).

K. Schmidt, *Handelsrecht Kommentar*, 5th ed. (1999: Heymanns Verlag, Köln).

F. Staubach, *The German Law of Agency and Distributorship's Agreements* (1977: Oyez Publishing, London).

W. Timm, *Höchstrichterliche Rechtsprechung zum Handels-und Gesellschaftsrecht: 75 Entscheidungen für Studium und Examen* (1995: C.H. Beck, Munich).

R. Volhard and A. Stengel, *German Limited Liability Company* (1997: John Wiley & Sons, Chichester, West Sussex).

c Competition law and anti-trust law

1 Introduction

The first edition of this work did not include these two connected legal topics, primarily because a considerable amount of information on them is available in English. However, as already indicated in Chapter 8, a brief introduction to the general principles and principal legal enactments may be useful and therefore should be given, along with references to some of the more accessible texts on the subjects, as noted in 'Further reading', to provide at least an overview of them. Both topics have been heavily influenced by Community law, but still reserve a core of legal rules of national law. They are sometimes grouped together under the umbrella title of *Gewerblicher Rechtsschutz*.

2 Competition law (*Wettbewerbsrecht*)

While in two articles (Arts 2 and 12) the *Grundgesetz* provides for personal and occupational freedoms, which have been interpreted as also applying to legal persons and especially to commercial organisations, these freedoms are subject to restrictions on the grounds of preserving fair competition. The (still) principal enactment for this area of law is the Unfair Competition Act (*Gesetz gegen den unlauteren Wettbewerb*: UWG), originally from 1909 but as amended to 1994.[24] The Act imposes quite a strict legal regime on the advertising and sale of products, and many of the practices which are fully accepted (if not found to be particularly desirable) in the UK and elsewhere, are contrary to the law in Germany.

2.1 The general prohibition

Paragraph 1 of the UWG is a far-reaching general clause which prohibits commercial action in competition contrary to good morals (*guten Sitten*). It was considered to be so wide and intrusive that it was even the subject of a constitutional challenge; it was, however, held to be constitutional by the BVerfG.[25] Anyone in breach of § 1 may be subject to injunction and may also be exposed to a liability to pay damages or to be fined. The standard of good morals has been interpreted widely by the courts by reference to trade practice and general opinion. Case law has played a very important role in the development of the understanding of the scope and effect of this provision. Five groups of cases of behaviour which will be considered contrary to good morals have been identified and categorised by Baumbach and Hefermehl, noted below. These are: entrapment of customers (*Kundenfang*); impeding free competition (*Behinderung*); exploitation (*Ausbeutung*); breach of law (*Rechtsbruch*); and disturbance of the market (*Marktstörung*). For example, telephone sales to private addresses are regarded as being contrary to § 1. A recent example of what might be considered disturbance of the market arose from the advertising campaigns of Benetton. The so-called "*Schockwerbung*" advertising campaign featured a picture of an oil covered duck swimming on a blanket of oil, depictions of child labour in the third world, and a naked human bottom with the words 'H.I.V. Positive' stamped on it. A public interest organization[26] sought an injunction against the adverts in *Stern* magazine, which featured them, and was successful before the *Landgericht*, whose decision was confirmed on a leap-frog

---

[24] RGBl S. 499 of 7 June 1909. Last amended 25 July, 1994 (BGBl I S. 1738)
[25] BVerfGE 32, 311.
[26] *Die Zentrale zur Bekämpfung unlauteren Wettbewerbs e. V.*

(*Sprungrevision*) appeal to the BGH which held all three pictures to be contrary to § 1. It had been noted[27] that the trend in the civil courts was to hold adverts which attempted to evoke an emotional reaction but in which the product held no connection to the content of the advert were likely to be held contrary to § 1. The case, however, came before the BVerfG[28] and without going into the public law issues to any extent,[29] the BVerfG held that other interests worthy of protection were also involved and that the freedom of expression under Article 5 GG could also be pleaded by *Stern*, despite not being the author of the adverts. Hence the BVerfG must balance the different rights involved and the crux of the matter was identified as being that the ban on using emotive material for advertising purposes was a restriction on the freedom of expression. According to the BVerfG, the BGH had got the balance wrong and had imposed its own interpretations on the meaning and effects of the adverts. The case may be a signal for a more tolerant interpretation of § 1 UWG when considering advertising. The unfair hindrance or obstruction of competitors has been held to be contrary to § 1 UWG. Unfair measures are considered to be boycotts, imitating competitors' advertising or products, and retail dumping. These practices may also constitute action breaching anti-trust law, noted below.

Further expression of the general clause comes in the form of rules prohibiting untrue and misleading statements (*irreführende Angaben*) in respect of the product on offer or those of competitors (§§ 3 and 6). This can include omissions where this would lead to a false view being taken of the product—for example, in cases where a purchaser would expect to be buying the latest model but is not informed that a newer model has, in fact, appeared on the market.[30]

Subjective value judgments are not considered to infringe § 3, as in the statement made in advertising baby milk, 'Mummy gives me only the best', which was held to be acceptable.[31] The restrictions on advertising are extremely finely tuned and any prospective campaign needs to be researched with considerable attention to the case law on the subject for examples of outlawed practices and statements which would offend the law.

Untrue advertising can attract a criminal penalty of up to two years' imprisonment under § 4 I UWG. Paragraph 5 extends the rules on misleading statements to pictures, which can also convey misleading impressions as to the history, origin, quality, etc. of a product. Direct comparative advertising of products and prices is now permitted following EC legislative and jurisprudential intervention in this area, providing that the advertisement is not misleading and that any comparison is fair.[32]

---

[27] See a case note on the Benetton advert case in JuS 2001, 12, 1169–1172.
[28] BVerfG, NJW 2001, 591.
[29] Such as, for example, the possible third effect (*Drittwirkung*) of basic rights in a civil law dispute between private parties, see Chapter 7 for details.
[30] BGH GRUR (*Gewerblicher Rechtsschutz und Urheberrecht*) 1982, 374.
[31] BGH GRUR 1965, 363.
[32] See, *inter alia*, EC Directives (84/450 misleading advertising, 97/55 comparative advertising, 98/43 tobacco advertising and 97/36 on television advertising). See also Cases C-34–36/95 *Konsumentombudsmannen (KO) v De Agostini (Svenska Forlag AB and TV Shop I Sverige AB* [1997] ECR I–3843.

2.2 Particular prohibitions

Sales are regarded as unlawful unless conforming to strict requirements. End of season sales can be held only twice yearly for twelve working days at the end of July and at the end of January (§ 7 III), and can include only specified products (see § 7 III 1). Anniversary sales (*Jubiläumsverkäufe*) can be held only every 25 years and clearance sales can also be held only for specific reasons, for example, where fire or storm has damaged business premises (§ 8 I). Unlawful, so-called 'special' sales are those which take place outside of normal selling conditions and which create the impression of a special advantages, usually of prices. It is not forbidden to reduce prices in the normal course of business; it is more the designation of 'sale' which offends the law. Following the repeal of the Free Gifts Regulation and the Rebate Act, discussed following, there is also now pressure for the special rules on sales to be repealed.[33]

The offering of inducements to customers' or suppliers' employees to purchase is prohibited (§ 12). Competitions run the risk of being regarded as inducements. After much internal criticism and also under pressure from EC statutory and case law, the German statutes regulating free gifts, offers, rebates, and discounts (the Free Gifts Regulation (*Zugabeverordnung*) and the Rebate Act (*Rabattgesetz*)) have been repealed[34]. The previous stricter German regime, which seriously impeded the giving of free gifts and discounts or two for one offers and the like, was regarded, amongst other considerations, as creating a disadvantage for German companies in the wider European free market. In particular, internet sales would have caused problems as suppliers are subject to the law of their own country regardless of where they supply[35]. German suppliers would, under the new EC E-Commerce Directive,[36] be subject to the stricter German law whereas suppliers to the German market from outside would not.[37] The grounds given by the government for reforms take account of the above but also cite the need to modernize consumer protection law to take account of the more sophisticated consumers today than in the 1930s when these laws were enacted. The German government was also aware that the laws were often ignored or were being applied in different degrees by different courts and in different areas. A clear overview of how these laws were applied or even should be applied had become impossible to discern. It also argued that the previous regime hindered innovation in marketing in such developments as power or community shopping. However, despite the repeal, advertising and marketing in Germany remains subject to the all encompassing Unfair Competition Act (UWG) and in particular §§ 1 and 3 which alone, have caught out new

---

[33] See K.-H. Fezer, '*Modernisierung des deutschen Rechts gegen den unlauteren Wettbewerb auf der Grundlage einer Europäisierung des Wettbewerbsrechts*' (2001) WRP 9 989–1022.

[34] Gesetz zur Aufhebung der Zugabeverordnung and Gesetz zur Aufhebung des Rabattgesetzes both from 23 July 2001 (BGBl I S. 1661 and 1663).

[35] In Germany this is known as the *Herkunftlandsprinzip*.

[36] Directive 2000/31 E-Commerce [2000] OJ L178/1.

[37] For further details, see J. Nordemann, *Wegfall von Zugabeverordnung und Rabattgesetz*, (2001) 35 NJW 2505–2512.

marketing arrangements such as power shopping[38]. The basic position now is that discounts and special offers and gifts are lawful, unless they offend the UWG, however a clear view of what marketing arrangements will be considered in breach of the UWG will only become clear after a considerable amount of case law has been decided. Furthermore, the Price Information Act (*Preisangabeverordnung*) remains in force and may itself catch pricing arrangements such as power-shopping where they are held to be unclear. Additionally, §§ 19 and 20 of the Unfair Competition Act (UWG) provide that market dominant enterprises may not apply discounts and gifts in such a way that they damage or discriminate against competitors or other markets players.

Industrial espionage and trade secrets are dealt with in §§ 17–20a.

2.3 Remedies

Remedies are left to civil action and not state enforcement. Organisations such as trade and consumer groups are given watch-dog rights, especially when the practice affects consumer interests involving §§ 3, 4, 6, 7, and 8 UWG. An organisation representing, and supported by, very many companies and the Chambers of Commerce undertakes numerous prosecutions in support of the law and consequently consumers. This is the *Zentrale zur Bekämpfung unlauteren Wettbewerbs e. V.*

Competitors have the right under § 13 to prevent a competitor, by injunction, from making misleading statements, especially, but not exclusively, in advertising. Injunctions are very often issued *ex Parte*. Damages may also be payable where the person making the statement knew, or should have known, that it was misleading. Buyers can also withdraw from a contract induced by untrue or misleading statements (§ 13a).

3 Anti-trust law (*Kartellrecht*)

The principal legislative enactment in this area outside of EC law (EC Treaty Arts 81 and 82) is the Act Against Restraints of Competition (*Gesetz gegen Wettbewerbsbeschränkungen*: GWB) from 1957[39].

Essentially, the relationship between European Community and national competition law was settled a long time ago in favour of giving EC law priority in this

---

[38] See the cases of LG Köln, *Sony v Powershopping.de*, Judgment of 25 November 1999, 31 O 990/99, JurPC Web-Dok 100/2000, *Volkswagen & Audi v Atrada.de*, LG Nürnberg, Judgment of 8 February 2000, 4 HK O 976/00, MMR 2000, 640, *Cnited v LetsBuyIt.com*, LG Hamburg Judgment of 13 October 2000, AZ 416 O 209/00 and *Sony et al. v Primus Online*, LG Hamburg judgment of 11 October 2000, AZ 33 O 180/00. For further details see D. Hoss, *Rabattgesetz und Zugabeverordnung—Die Rechtslage nach der Aufhebung* (2001) 19 MDR 1094–1100 and W. Berlit, *Auswirkungen der Aufhebung des Rabattgesetzes und der Zugabeverordnung auf die Auslegung von § 1 UWG und § 3 UWG*, (2001) WRP 4 349–354.

[39] In German it is also referred to as the *Kartellgesetz* and in English as the Law against Restrictive Trade Practices, it first entered into force 1 January 1958 and now stands as enacted on 26 August 1998 (BGBl I S. 2546).

area.[40] If the EC has approved an arrangement or indeed had come to a decision that there was an infringement, national authorities do not have the right to reverse this for their own territory. Only where the national authorities are concerned with a agreement affecting a market which is not a significant part of the EU, will the EC Commission have no interest and the national authorities have the full right to act without fear of being overruled by the EC Commission. Hence then national competition authorities have a restricted scope of jurisdiction if the matter concerns in any way Community competence, but this does not mean to say that there is no international competence of national competition law authorities.[41]

The rules seek to control two main areas, dealing with vertical and horizontal cartels and companies which abuse a dominant position. The latter area is also concerned with mergers.

Vertical agreements are those involving undertakings at different stages of the economic process, i.e. the production, distribution and marketing of products. For example, distribution agreements made between a manufacturer and a distributor or between the former or latter and retailers. Horizontal agreements are those made between undertakings at the same level of the economic process, involving for example, manufacturers between themselves or distributors between themselves.

3.1 Horizontal agreements between undertakings

The word 'undertakings' has been given a wide interpretation by the courts to include any person or organisation engaged in a commercial or business activity. According to case law the influence on the market achieved by the agreements needs to be substantial in order to offend the Act. German law has now been brought into line with EC law in that German law requires either an actual effect on the market or a potential effect.[42] Similar rules apply in respect of the definition of the relevant markets in order to demonstrate an effect. Again, like in the Community regime, practice guidelines have been issued by the enforcement authority, outlining the circumstances when action will not be taken by reason of their insignificant effect on the market.[43]

Where agreements are found to breach § 1 GWB, they are void, but if certain parts can be severed the remaining agreement may be maintained, where possible. Cartel agreements are also subject to administrative fines (§§ 32 and 81–86). Parties to an agreement may also expose themselves to civil liability (§ 33).

Paragraphs 2–8 and 26 GWB provide details of agreements which may be exempted and the procedure for application for exemption (§§ 9–10). Some gain automatic exemption upon notification, such as those meeting the criteria of being insignificant or purchasing co-operation agreements (§ 4). Others relating to

---

[40] In the case of *Walt Wilhelm v Bundeskartellamt* [1969] ECR 1.
[41] For details, refer to the appropriate sections of the books listed in 'Further reading.'
[42] See in respect of German law, BGH WuW/E 1976, 1458 (Fertigbeton) and the case of *Consten and Grundig v EC Commission* [1966] ECR 299.
[43] Pronouncement 57/80 (1980 BAnz 23 July 1980).

terms of sales (§ 2), or specialization agreements (§ 3) or small and medium-sized businesses (§§ 4 and 22 II) may be objected to, and some require express approval where they seek to control production (§ 6), or involve pricing arrangements (§ 5 II) or come within the catch all categories of §§ 7 or 8.

3.2 Vertical agreements

Vertical agreements are permitted unless they involve pricing, which is prohibited, or business terms (§ 14). For example, prohibited under § 14 is vertical price fixing, except in relation to books where price maintainence is acceptable for cultural reasons (§ 15). Paragraph 16 GWB outlines the types of agreements that the Cartel Office would declare invalid, typically involving market sharing, resale restrictions, distribution agreements, or those imposing unfair conditions on customers or distributors. Agreements can be notified to the authority for consideration.

Paragraphs 17–18 GWB are concerned with patents, licences and know-how agreements.

3.3 Dominant positions and mergers

The second main set of rules relate to dominant companies and mergers (§§ 19–23).

Those in either monopoly or oligopoly positions in the market are controlled by § 19 GWB. Here the attack is on the abuse of the position of dominance. Paragraph 19 sets out the circumstances in which dominance is achieved, largely relating to market share and access. Dominance can be shared by two or more enterprises (§ 19 II). As with EC rules, the relevant market must be defined with regard to the product, geography, and time. Abuse is defined by example in § 19 IV, including exploitation involving pricing, terms and conditions, and impeding competitors. Paragraph 20 provides further similar rules in respect of enterprises with a privileged competitive position. This category includes dominant enterprises and those in monopoly positions, who are prohibited from unfairly discriminating between customers or suppliers.

Mergers or acquisitions must be notified to the Federal Cartel Office (*Bundeskartellamt*) for review (§ 35–39). The 1998 reforms to this area of law have unfortunately seriously complicated the determination of whether a particular proposed merger meets the criteria for notification to such an extent that coverage in this short introduction is no longer possible. Reference to one of the books or commentaries below is now recommended.[44]

The notification requirement is removed where the turnover brings the matter within the jurisdiction of Community merger control. The *Bundeskartellamt* has the power to prohibit the proposed merger, or to exclude some parts of the business from merger or to require certain parts to be sold off after the event, and where the merger has already taken place to order its reversal (§§ 41–42).

---

[44] First enacted on 16 December 1980 (BGBl I S. 1) and last amended 22 December 1999 (BGBl I S. 2598).

Other rules relate to unfair pressure and coercion and boycott (§ 20–21). Allied areas of law, but beyond the scope of this volume, are Patent and Trade Mark law and Copyright law. The principal enactments governing these areas are the Patent Act (*Patentgesetz*) and the Copyright Act (*Urheberrechtsgesetz* UrhG[45]). For further details refer to the books listed below.

FURTHER READING

Baumbach and Hefermehl, *Wettbewerbsrecht: Kommentar*, 22nd ed. (2001: C.H. Beck, Munich).

R. Bechthold, *GWB: Kartellgesetz, Gesetz gegen Wettbewerbsbeschränkungen*, 2nd ed. (1999: C.H. Beck, Munich).

F. K. Beier, G. Schricker and W. Fikentscher, *German Industrial Property, Copyright and Antitrust laws*, 2nd ed. (1989: VCH, Weinheim).

W. Berlit, *Wettbewerbsrecht*, 3rd ed. (1998: C.H. Beck, Munich).

V. Emmerich, *Das Recht des unlauteren Wettbewerbs*, 5th ed. (1998: C.H. Beck, Munich).

V. Emmerich, *Kartellrecht*, 9th ed. (2001: C.H. Beck, Munich).

U. Gassner, *Grundzüge des Kartellrechts* (1999: Vahlen Verlag, Munich).

D. Hoffmann and S. Schaub, *The German Competition Law* (1983: Kluwer, Deventer) (Somewhat dated but still having its uses).

V. Ilzhöfer, *Patent-, Marken und Urheberrecht*, 4th ed. (2000: Vahlen Verlag, Munich).

Langen and Bunte, *Kommentar zum deutschen und europäischen Kartellrecht*, 9th ed. (2001: Luchterhand, Neuweid).

W. Nordeman et al, *Wettbewerbsrecht und Martienrecht*, 8th ed. (1996: Nomos Verlag, Baden–Baden).

M. Rehbinder, *Urheberrecht*, 11th ed. (2001: C.H. Beck, Munich).

Rüster (gen. ed.), *Business Transactions in Germany* (loose leaf) (M. Bender, New York and C.H. Beck, Munich), Vol. III, Chapter 32, 'Antitrust Law: Competitive Restraints' by J. Sedemund, Chapter 36, 'Antitrust Law: Merger Control' by M. Heidenhain, and Chapter 37, 'Competition Unfair Practices and Misleading Advertising' by J. Schmeding and C. Rohnke.

G. Schricker, *Urheberrecht, Kommentar*, 2nd ed. (1997: C.H. Beck, Munich).

K. Wenzel and E. Burkhardt, *Urheberrecht für die Praxis*, 4th ed. (1999: Schäffer-Poeschel Verlag, Stuttgart).

---

[45] First enacted on 9 September 1965 (BGBl I S. 1273) and last amended 16 July 1998 (BGBl I S. 1827).

D Labour law (*Arbeitsrecht*)

1 Introduction and history of German labour law

Modern German labour law arises from the era of industrialization in the nine-teenth century and liberalization of legal relations in the latter half of that century. The labour relationship was no longer viewed as based on the personal relationship which had arisen in the days of lord and serf and continued in the institution of master and servant, but under the influence of the civil law it adopted an individual approach. Thus the legal fiction of contractual equality between parties also applied to employment relationships.

As in the UK, the first collective organization and action by labour was disap-proved of by the ruling classes, and up to 1869 strikes, and even the persuasion to strike, were illegal. Any breach was punishable by imprisonment. Associations of workers and the unions, previously outlawed, were allowed to be established in this period. The Trade Act (*Gewerbeordnung*) of 1869 removed the ban on the freedom of association of trade unions and declared strikes to be lawful. However, persuasion to strike by intimidation or threat remained illegal, and a wide definition was given to these concepts such that strikes were seldom lawful. In an attempt to undermine the workers' and the labour associations' own efforts to organize themselves, worker representation was sponsored by the employers, but in a much weaker form. Limited forms of the representation of workers' views were first officially recognised by the Trade Act of 1891. This period also witnessed the establishment and growth of employers' organizations, partly as a counter to the workers' organizations.

In the period before and during the First World War the unions gained recogni-tion and status as a result of their support for the policies pursued by the govern-ment of the day, particularly in respect of the waging of war. Workers' committees were for the first time required by law in workplaces with over fifty employees which were considered vital for the war effort. These did not, however, involve the extensive rights of co-determination provided for today.

In the Weimar Republic the first significant provision of collective labour laws took place, including, in 1920 under the Works Councils Act (BetriebsräteG), the compulsory establishment of works councils for all workplaces with more than twenty workers, a feature which has been retained in the present system of indus-trial relations in Germany. There was even constitutional provision for the first time for the freedom of association and for the safeguarding and improvement of working and economic conditions, freedoms which have also found expression in the current constitution. A significant feature of the conduct of industrial relations of this time was the formalized agreements between unions and employers which covered c.75 % of the work force. The hierarchy of labour law courts was established in 1927, as was the first umbrella organization for the trade unions, the German Confederation of Trade Unions (*Deutscher Gewerkschaftsbund*: DGB). The economic recession and world slump in the 1920s and 1930s led to a dramatic fall in union membership and very high unemployment. The system of collective bargaining and the rigid positions adopted by the unions and management were partly blamed for the poor industrial and economic situation in Germany. Collective agreements were largely undermined by the issue of emergency decrees by the President. When Hitler came to power, the unions were banned and collective bargaining and works councils removed from the industrial scene by the Regulation of National Labour Act 1934.

The period following the Second World War introduced the social market economy. The reorganization of the German state allowed labour relations to be organised on a much more rational basis. The new constitution guaranteed individual and collective rights of organization. The unions, regardless of political outlook, were now organized under the umbrella of the DGB. Employers became members of an equivalent employers' organization, the Confederation of German Employers (*Bundesvereinigung der deutschen Arbeitgeberverbände*: BDA).

The civil law and the individualistic approach and assumptions of the Civil Code were recognized as not particularly apt in labour relations. Thus standard form labour contracts were balanced by the recognition and guarantee of the freedom of association of Article 9 (3) of the constitution. Legal approval of collective agreements had been given by the Collective Agreements Act (*Tarifvertragsgesetz*: TVG) of 1949, and the BVerfG later confirmed their binding effect on all parties. The Works Constitution Act of 1952 (*Betriebsverfassungsgesetz*: BetrVG) reintroduced the works council, so that the union and non-union forms of worker representation established before the war continued to be the dual approach to industrial relations after the war. Co-determination was introduced in both the private and public sectors.

Following unification, West German labour laws have been adopted by the former East Germany with only minor exceptions, as referred to in Article 30 of the Unification Treaty and applying mainly in respect of pensions and retirement.

German labour law is defined as the law of dependent labour; the law relating to the performance of labour for another in a relationship between the employer and employee and of the relevant collective agreements between these parties. As an area of civil law, there is no direct intervention by the state in the conduct of industrial relations. However, the state is very concerned with the protection of the employee (under the so-called *Schutzprinzip*) and recognizes that the employer and employee do not stand in equal relationship to each other. This has led to considerable regulation by the state in order to redress the balance and provide a counterbalance for the worker against the stronger position of the employer. Hence, there has been a considerable input of public law into an area of law which was originally regulated entirely within the civil law sphere. In particular, the collective laws provided have been held to be legally binding and enforceable by all parties. Labour law *per se* does not, however, apply to employment in the public service which has separate rules, noted below.

Many other rules have an effect on the employment relationship and industrial relations bargaining, in particular those relating to commercial, company and competition laws. Only those which are classified clearly in labour law are considered below.

2 Categories of labour law

There are four main categories into which labour law can be divided:

2.1 Individual labour law (*Individualarbeitsrecht*)

This general category of individual employment contract law concerns the relationship between the employer and the individual worker. It includes the rules on the formation of employment contracts, the rights and duties arising from them and their alteration and termination.

2.2 Worker protection laws (*Arbeitschutzrecht*)

These include the public law duties the state imposes on the employers. They set minimum standards to protect the position, jobs and welfare of the workers. Many rules are subject to criminal sanctions for breach. The public law intervention on behalf of the individual worker is very extensive, especially in relation to dismissal.

2.3 Collective labour law (*Kollektives Arbeitsrecht*)

This includes the collective agreements, their enforcement and legal effect, and industrial relations law, including the law of industrial disputes and strikes. Provisions also apply in respect of trade unions and employers' organisations. Private and public law collective laws include the rights of worker representation, the works councils and personnel councils in the public sector.

2.4 Procedural law

The last category concerns the procedural law applicable to labour law, which is mainly contained in the Labour Courts Act (*Arbeitsgerichtsgesetz*: ArbGG[46]).

---

[46] Originally from 1953, now in the form as of 2 July 1979 (BGBl I S. 1036) as amended up to 21 December 2000 (BGBl I S. 1983).

3 Sources of labour law

3.1 Constitutional law

Although there is no specific chapter or section in the *Grundgesetz* for labour or social law, the constitution is nevertheless important because of the general guidelines it provides for the organisation and conduct of state. In particular, Article 9 guarantees not only the individual right to the freedom of association but also the collective right to associate and reach agreements. Article 9 (3) imposes a duty on the legislature to provide a legal regime for the regulation of labour relations. This must be done, however, with one eye on civil law, which also regulates the individual labour contract.

Other relevant articles are: Article 3, the equal rights provision, which has been very important in labour law; Article 11, the freedom of movement to take up employment; and Article 12, the freedom to choose an occupation. Furthermore, the *Rechtsnormen* of Articles 20 and 28 for the social state mean that such laws as the Co-determination Act are not only promulgated in the first place but are supported by a duty imposed on the state to ensure they work effectively. The *Grundgesetz* has also proved important because of the fragmented nature of the other labour laws, making recourse to the provisions of the *Grundgesetz* necessary to fill gaps or overcome ambiguities and inconsistencies. This is reflected in the greater amount of case law in this area, noted below. There is also the influence and impact of international law, including the ILO Agreements ratified by Germany and in particular Community law, to consider. Community law has had a considerable impact in the area of equal rights, and in particular there have been many cases concerned with sex discrimination in employment, many of which originate in Germany.

3.2 Civil law

The labour relationship is initially regulated by the provisions of the BGB dealing with service agreements (*Dienstverträge*, §§ 611–630 BGB), of which the employment contract is one. The BGB rules apply to the extent that they are not supplanted by special statutory provisions, e.g., provisions of the HGB[47] which apply to the relationship between merchants and their employees.

In terms of specific statutory provision in labour law, there is an overwhelming number of individual statutes and regulations. The most notable of these is the Trade Act[48] (*Gewerbeordnung*: GewO), mainly concerned with employers' duties, details of which will be discussed where appropriate below.

---

[47] Commercial Code (*Handelsgesetzbuch*) of 10 May 1897 (RGBl S. 219) as amended up to 21 December 2000 (BGBl I S. 1983).
[48] Which is also referred to as the Industrial Code, originally from 1869 but now in the version published on 22 February 1999 (BGBl I S. 202) as amended up to 21 December 2000 (BGBl I S. 1983).

It has long been recognized that this is an area crying out for codification, but up to now attempts to do so have not met with success and have been abandoned. After seven years of work, the Commission set up in 1970 to produce a draft code presented it to Parliament. In 1982 the Commission was dissolved and its report finally rejected. However, Article 30 of the Unification Treaty now obliges the legislature to codify labour contract law, and in particular to ensure that the public law protective provisions are in agreement with Community law on the subject. To date, no progress in this direction is forthcoming.

3.3 Case-law

The fact that there is not a code or single comprehensive law means that a clear exposition of the general principles or an overview of labour law is extremely difficult to obtain. For this reason the principles are only discernible by looking at the application of labour law in case-law. So, despite the preponderance of individual statutes, labour law in Germany is incomplete without knowledge of the decisions of the labour law courts, and in particular the Federal Labour Court (*Bundesarbeitsgericht*: BAG). This makes it the area of law in Germany with the closest similarity to common law, where case law is needed to complete understanding of the law. If compared to other legal areas of civil law in the BGB, such as property or succession, labour law has been through what were revolutionary changes in the last century, and is still subject to rapid change to keep pace with the changes in economic and social relations in society. Hence many laws are outdated and not entirely relevant to the cases before the courts. In other instances legislative solutions have not yet been found or implemented to resolve new problems, such as decisions about compensation for those injured as an indirect result of labour disputes and the whole area of industrial disputes.

Although case-law is not recognized as a formal source of law in the German legal system, it is nevertheless generally observed in the area of labour law as binding law. The courts and BVerfG are often required to resolve inconsistencies and conflicts between the provisions of the BGB and the *Grundgesetz* as in the equal treatment case dealing with § 622 BGB, below. The BAG and other labour law courts have considerably developed the area of labour. In playing such a positive role they have fuelled the fire of the debate on the role of the judiciary in Germany (see the section on judicial law-making (*Richterrecht*) in Chapter 2).

It is very rare that customary law (*Gewohnheitsrecht*) acts as a source of labour law, due largely to the extent of the legislative and judicial intervention that have taken place in this area.

3.4 Contractual agreements

A further source of law is the agreements entered into by the parties to labour law contracts. These include the collective agreements, whose rules in favour of individuals are enforceable in the courts[49]. Difficulties arise in respect of the relationship between these rules, the applicable legislation and the case-law developed by the courts. Some agreements may in fact provide more or less generous provisions for staff, which presents the courts with the dilemma between observing the agreements freely entered into by the parties, applying the legislation which may help or restrict rights, or following case-law often relating to differing circumstances.

Similarly, the agreements between the works councils and the employers are also an alternative source of law and add to the minefield of rules in labour law. The agreements of the works councils are binding, and therefore have given rise to a considerable amount of case-law from their interpretation and often have to be considered in the light of the collective agreements negotiated independently.

There is, as previously mentioned, a considerable number of individual Acts, which makes an introduction to the area extremely difficult. Therefore, only the most important will be mentioned, and most without further comment where their subject matter is obvious.

4 Labour law institutions

Governmental institutions include the Ministry of Labour and Social Security, which exists at the level of the Federation and the *Länder* and is generally responsible for consideration of the possible changes in the law and the initiative for new laws. The Office of Labour Inspection (*Gewerbeaufsichtsbehörde*, § 139b GewO) is similar to the Factory and Health and Safety Inspectorates in the UK and is concerned with the supervision and control and health and safety of workers. The Employment Office (*Arbeitsamt*) and at the federal level the Federal Office of Employment (*Bundesanstalt für Arbeit*) are granted wide powers concerning the recruitment and training of personnel. They have the monopoly as the agency concerned with job placement, although this position is currently being challenged.

4.1 Unions and employers' associations

The unions were re-established after the war on an industry-wide basis and now play an important role in the conduct of industrial relations. There are sixteen unions and the umbrella organisation, the German Federation of Trade Unions (*Deutscher Gewerkschaftsbund*: DGB), which has as one of its principal duties the organisation and cooperation between unions. One of the results of this is the absence of demarcation disputes between unions because of their coherence, a

---

[49] As recognized by the Collective Agreements Act (*Tarifvertragsgesetz*: TVG) of 1949 but now in the version of 25 August 1969 (BGBl I S. 1323) which provides under § 1 that the agreements have the effect of laws (*Rechtsnormen*).

problem which often bedevilled union relations in the UK in the 1960s and 1970s. There is also the *Deutsche Angestelltengewerkschaft* (DAG) which is the union for the white collar workers and attracts membership from all areas of commerce and industry. The unions mostly have no legal personality but the rights they have to sue and be sued in their own name and to own property render this deficit almost meaningless.

There is a large number of employers' associations (over 700) which also have an umbrella organization, the Confederation of German Employers (*Bundesvereinigung der deutschen Arbeitgeberverbände*: BDA). These are also largely organized on an industry-wide basis, to reflect and assist negotiations with the unions.

4.2 The works council (*Betriebsrat*)

These were formally re-established under the Works Constitution Acts (*Betriebsverfassungsgesetze*: BetrVG) of 1952 and 1972, and operate at the plant or workplace level rather than the company level as with the supervisory boards, although there are also company or joint and group works councils (*Gesamtbetriebsrat und Konzernbetriebsrat*). They apply to workplaces with more than five employees over the age of eighteen and consist of representatives of the groups of employees. They do not involve the participation of managerial employees who, in companies with more than ten defined managerial employees, are entitled to elect a separate representative body. Details can be found in the Managerial Employees Committee Act (*Sprecherausschußgesetz*: SprAuG[50]). The scope of the involvement of the works councils will be considered below.

4.3 The supervisory board (*Aufsichtsrat*)

This operates on the level of the company or business enterprise and is an overview board. It is not concerned with the day-to-day running of the company but with the appointment and supervision of the management board. It must be established by law for companies with more than 500 employees under the Co-determination Act (*Mitbestimmungsgesetz*: MitbestG[51]) and voluntarily in smaller companies, considered below.

4.4 Labour law courts

There is a specialist hierarchy of labour law courts to deal with individual and collective labour disputes. See Chapter 3 for details.

---

[50] Of 20 December 1988 (BGBl I S. 2312) as amended up to 21 December 2000 (BGBl I S. 1983).
[51] Of 4 May 1976 (BGBl I S. 1153) as amended up to 28 October 1994 (BGBl I S. 3210).

5 Individual labour law

5.1 The employment relationship

An employment relationship under labour law is determined or defined initially by the classification of a particular person as a worker, and to do this various categories must be considered. The definition is important to decide the scope of protective rights which may be applicable and the rights of membership of the various forms of institutions involved in co-determination. The definition of who is an employed person has been held as one for the courts to decide and not the parties. Included are those who by reason of a contract perform a service (work) for another, incorporating those subject to civil law rules. Strictly considered, civil servants do not come within this definition since they are regulated by public law. Workers under labour law are also to be distinguished from independent agents as defined by the commercial code, considered above.

Workers can be classified by various means.

5.1.1 *Profession*

This may be determined either by the Trade Act (GewO), relating to all private businesses and generally to trade and commercial employees, except those falling under specialist laws relating to sailors, mining and agricultural employees, or those regulated by the commercial code (HGB), classified as business clerks (*Handlungsgehilfen*). The distinction was of more importance in the past because of the more favourable legal regime of the business clerks. Today, rights are interpreted equally in favour of all groups, as is increasingly being shown to be the constitutional requirement imposed by Article 3 *Grundgesetz*.

5.1.2 *The distinction between blue and white collar*

Here the distinction is along more traditional lines, between blue collar or shop floor workers (*Arbeiter*) and salaried staff, the white collar or office staff (*Angestellte*). A further sub-group of white collar workers is the managerial staff (*leitende Angestellte*). The 1984 Employees Insurance Act (*Angestelltenversicherungsgesetz*: AVG) for white collar workers (the RVO for blue collar workers) provides a rudimentary definition of categories of white collar workers and therefore, by elimination, defines blue collar workers.

The distinctions which arise as a result of the definitions were more significant for rights of participation in works councils and on the supervisory boards of companies. Additionally, they affect insurance, pension rights and wage guarantees in the event of sickness. The position and distinction of the managerial staff are still particularly strong in the above areas. The latest cases, however, point towards an abolition of such sharp distinctions as previously existed, the clearest example of which is the abolition of differing termination notice periods under § 622 BGB. The distinctions have been further eroded by the Works Constitution Reform Act of

2001 by the removal of the separate voting and representation rights for the two categories of Works Councils.[52]

5.1.3 *Executive or managerial staff (leitende Angestellte)*

This category, although clearly involving those who are employed by companies, is recognised as a distinct group within companies. Its members have now formed their own union, the Union of Managerial Employees (*Union Leitender Angestellter*: ULA). The clearest division of this group of employees can be observed in the provisions relating to representation on supervisory boards and works councils (§ 5 BetrVG) and the rules relating to overtime and dismissal.

5.1.4 *Board members (Organpersonen)*

These are persons who usually fall outside of the application of the specialist employment laws because they occupy the highest positions in companies as directors or partners of business enterprises. This category also includes the members of management and supervisory boards but only in that capacity and not in their capacity as employees where they are worker members. Where there are service contracts, usually between three to five years in length, they would be governed by the usual rules of either the civil or commercial code.

5.1.5 *Semi-independent workers/freelance workers*

Lastly there are the employee-like persons who occupy a half-way house between employees as such and independent contractors because they work for over 50% of their time under the instructions of one employer. This is a case law development to ensure that an increasing number of workers who would otherwise fall into the category of independent workers, and would therefore lose the benefits of many of the labour law protections, are not so prejudiced. Dismissal rights, however, do not apply to them. This group would include freelance workers and subcontractors on permanent contracts or long-time contracts with another party and subject to the direction of that party. Home workers would also be included here.[53]

5.2 The formation of contracts of employment

Employment contracts are initially subject to the general rules applying to civil law on service agreements (*Dienstverträge*, §§ 611–630 BGB).

Each employment relationship is governed by a contract which can be oral or in writing, although contracts of apprenticeship must be in writing. Many collective agreements additionally require written agreements. Freedom of contract generally allows the content of the contract to be decided by the parties, but in labour law there is strict regulation of certain aspects, e.g. under § 611a BGB there may be no

---

[52] 28 July 2001 (BGBl I S. 1852).
[53] And specifically catered for by the Home Working Act (*Heimarbeitsgesetz*: HAG) of 14 March 1951 (BGBl I S. 191) as amended up to 21 December 2000 (BGBl I S. 1983).

discrimination on the grounds of sex except where essential. Additionally, Community law applies in respect of nationality.

Statutory rules apply to fill gaps and overrule written and oral agreements where the contract is inconsistent with law. Additionally, any terms which have been agreed as part of a collective labour agreement between the union and the employer often determine the content of individual contracts, and agreements between the employer and the works council may also apply in individual contracts.

Contracts are usually concluded for an indefinite period, and the courts have viewed any contracts which have attempted to impose a fixed period with some suspicion and have often acted to protect the employee where contracts tried to avoid the application of dismissal legislation. Probation periods of up to six months maximum were legally permitted, after which employees would be able to obtain the protection of legislation in respect of unfair dismissals. After a number of periods of temporary measures[54] which allowed for fixed term contracts with no unfair dismissal rights, the German Parliament has now passed the Part Time and Fixed Term Contracts Act (*Teilzeit- und Befristungsgesetz*, TzBfG[55]) to regularize this area of labour law. The Act also transforms two EC Directives[56] on the same matters and applies to both private and public sector employment contracts. The Act sets out to ensure that there is no discrimination against part time and fixed contract workers in comparison with full time workers and to promote the establishment of part time working at all levels of the workforce. Employers are required to state in advertisements which positions are also suitable for part time appointment (§ 7 TzBfG). The Works Council is provided with supervisory powers over the advertising and appointment process (§§ 80 and 95 BetrVG). Workers in enterprises with more than fifteen employees are provided the right to claim a reduction in the number of hours worked under § 8 TzBfG unless business grounds apply to prevent any change. Part timers have the right to apply for full time or longer time positions (§ 9 TzBfG[57]). The new Act now makes it clear that employers can conclude fixed term contracts for existing positions with good cause up to a maximum of three contracts in two years (§ 14 I TzBfG). New fixed term positions do not need to be justified by good cause (§ 14 II).[58] The restrictions do not apply to the employment of workers who are over fifty-eight years old. Chain contracts (*Kettenverträge*)

---

[54] The Promotion of Employment Act (*Beschäftigungsförderungsgesetz* BSchFG) originally from 1985 for five years but extended to 2000.

[55] Or to give it, its full title, *Das Gesetz über Teilzeitarbeit und befristete Arbeitsverträge* of 16 November 2000 (BGBl I S. 1996).

[56] The Part time work Directive 97/81 [1998] OJ L14/9) and The Fixed Term Contracts Directive 99/70 [1999] OJ L175/43.

[57] For further details on the part time elements of the Act, see W. Hinrichs, *Neue gesetztliche Regelungen zur Teilzeitarbeit* (2001) AiB (*Arbeitsrecht im Betrieb*) 2 65–74.

[58] For further details in the good causes or other aspects of the new rules see, H. Nielebock, *Die neuen gesetzlichen Regelungen zur befristeten Beschäftigung* (2001) AiB (*Arbeitsrecht im Betrieb*) 2 75–82. See generally on the new Act, W. Hromadka, *Das neue Teilzeit- und Befristungsgesetz* (2001) NJW 6 400–405 G. Kleinsorge, *Teilzeitarbeit und befristete Arbeitsverträge—Ein Überblick über die Neuregelung* (2001) 55 MDR 4 181–186 and for an early view on how it appears to be working; D. Straub, *Erste Erfahrungen mit dem Teilzeit- und Befristungsgesetz* (2001) 18 NZA 17 919–927.

whereby a position is repeatedly re-offered only for fixed terms are no longer permitted (§ 14 II TzBfG). Collective agreements reducing or increasing the period for dismissal without grounds take priority over the provisions of the statute (BAG DB 1987, 2106 and now § 14 and § 22 TzBfG).

5.3 Works councils and hiring employees

If the enterprise has more than twenty employees, any decision to employ further workers must, if a works council exists, be notified to the works council under § 99 BetrVG. The position on offer and details of candidates must be given and its consent must be achieved. The works council can refuse consent on grounds of: an infringement of guidelines previously adopted as a result of the agreement between the works council and employer under § 95; resultant unfair treatment or termination of existing employees; disadvantage to the new employee, not properly classified positions or when not previously advertised within the works as demanded by the works council under § 93. If the 'works council objects to the engagement, the employer can apply to the court to obtain consent. This would be most rare and the works council often uses this veto power as a lever to obtain other benefits. The new individual rights created by the Part time and Fixed Term Contracts Act seem to have created uncertainties as to whether the Works Council has a say and indeed a veto in the change to the employment contracts in these cases.[59]

These rules do not apply to the appointment of managerial staff, therefore the definition of this category becomes crucial. In public companies and private companies with over 500 employees, the appointment of managers and directors is subject to the rules of the MitbestG and the BetrVG.

5.4 General terms of contracts

Paragraph 611 BGB is the basis of an employment contract which provides for payment for work performed. The scope of services is as the job description and working hours are as agreed, but may be subject to a collective agreement, or a works council if one is in place, § 87 BetrVG or the Working Time Act (*Arbeitszeitgesetz*: ArbZG).[60] Paragraph 611a BGB requires equal treatment in pay and treatment for male and female workers.

If not express, payment is implied under § 612 BGB, and payment by piece rates or by period is recognized (§ 614).

Paragraph 613 imposes the requirement to perform personally, i.e., the employment performance is not assignable unless this is expressly stated in the contract. Relocation to another works is possible but if in another town needs to be in the contract, otherwise the rules on constructive dismissal apply.

---

[59] See the comments above and for a detailed analysis, P. Schüren, *Die Mitbestimmung des Betriebsrats bei der Änderung der Arbeitszeit nach dem TzBfG* (2001) AuR (Arbeit und Recht) 9 321–325.

[60] Replacing the *Arbeitszeitordnung* and the provisions of the GewO dealing with Sunday and holiday working ArbZG of 6 June 1994 (BGBl I S. 1170) and amended up to 21 December 2000 (BGBl I S. 1983).

Paragraph 613a BGB provides for the survival of employment contracts in the event of a sale or transfer of the business. This is the transformation into German law of EC Directive 77/187. The new owner acquires by operation of law the rights and obligations of the previously existing employment relationships. If these are subject to a collective agreement, they must remain unaltered for at least one year. Even if there is only a sale of controlling shares or all the shares, or a transfer of all the assets, the protection of § 613a applies. The sale does not constitute a valid ground to terminate the employment relationship. However, a takeover of a company might well be followed by a restructuring of the business, in which case sufficient grounds for making redundancies for compelling business requirements are likely to arise, discussed below. A closure of a plant followed by a re-opening shortly afterwards would not avoid the application of § 613a.

Paragraph 615 concerns delay in performance. Impossibility which is not the fault of either side is a risk of business the employer must carry, which includes acts of God. Strikes elsewhere in the company, or even by other workers in supplying industries, which make work impossible will not oblige the employer to perform by the payment of wages. A refusal on the part of the employer to accept work will allow the employee to claim compensation instead.

Under § 616, payment must be maintained where employees do not perform for reasons beyond their control, of which illness counts as one. Additionally, the rules in HGB § 63 apply to commercial employees, and technical employees are covered by the GewO. These are supplemented by numerous laws now falling under the area of social law. See Chapter 8 for details.

Paragraph 618 requires that the employer ensures safe working conditions. However, the right to compensation for damage suffered as a result of a breach of the duty imposed by this paragraph has been almost entirely supplanted by the substitution of insurance claims against the employer's insurers. No fault need be shown on anyone's part. This has the unfortunate outcome that in cases of serious injuries, settlements are not likely to be as generous as under the normal delict rules. Pain and suffering are not included under the insurance scheme, whereas they would be under delict rules.

The Commercial Code provisions relevant to employment are contained in §§ 59–83. Most of these provisions reflect those of the BGB, but specifically in relation to commercial employees as discussed above. The BAG has extended these provisions by analogy to all workers—blue and white collar. Additionally, there are provisions on the prohibition of competition (§§ 60, 61 and 74 et seq.).

Paragraph 60 HGB prohibits working concurrently for another in the same line of business unless expressly or impliedly consented to, and § 61 provides that if the employee is in breach, the employer can claim either the remuneration or the profits from the transactions. Paragraph 74 HGB allows the parties to agree to a restraint of trade clause, otherwise known as a non-competition clause, following the expiry of the employment relationship. This is subject to a maximum period of two years, it must be justified as in the interest of the employer, and compensation is payable. Paragraph 75 gives details of the invalidity of agreements. For further details on the provisions, refer to the section on commercial law in this chapter.

Paragraph 622 BGB lays down the minimum periods of notice for employment contracts, supplemented now by the Protection from Dismissal Act (*Kündigungs-schutzgesetz*: KSchG[61]) discussed in further detail below.

The extensive duties of the employer and employees and the general conditions of employment are beyond the scope of this volume. Refer to 'Further reading' at the end of the section and to §§ 611 et seq. BGB.

In respect of the employment of German nationals in Germany by foreign companies, the applicable law need not necessarily be German if there is a genuine foreign legal connection. This would not be the case where a foreign company had a German subsidiary or branch which hired the employees, regardless of any provisions made in the contracts of employment. The employment must be directly by the foreign company. All public law statutes apply regardless, but civil laws, i.e. the BGB and HGB, can be excluded unless this is unfair.

5.5 Ending the employment relationship and dismissal

An employment relationship may come to an end by mutual agreement, lapse of time in fixed term contracts or termination by either of the parties. This must be in writing (§ 623 BGB). To be effective it must be received by the other party. Unless agreed under a contract of employment or a collective agreement or required by law, for example for dismissal without notice, reasons do not have to be given for termination.

Termination is regulated by §§ 622–628 BGB, which details the periods of notice required for dismissal, previously two weeks for blue collar workers and six weeks for staff, both of which are extended the longer the service of the employee. The BGB supported the view that different periods of notice were acceptable and to some extent reflected the individual bargaining strengths of the blue and white collar workers. This has been the legal regime which has been accepted and put into effect until recently. It has always been possible as a matter of course for parties to negotiate individual periods of notice and, of course, as a part of contractual freedom, to renegotiate longer termination periods (§ 622 V BGB). In reality, however, such freedom is only realised by higher management workers, and most workers are subject to the industry or plant norm whether they like it or not. In some circumstances periods more generous than the statutory minimum are agreed as the result of collective bargaining. Paragraph 622 BGB allows shorter periods to be concluded by the parties to collective agreements, subject to an absolute minimum of one month in respect of white collar workers. However, the distinction between blue and white collar workers was not eroded by negotiation.

Recently, however, the distinction in periods required in this provision has been challenged as unconstitutional and contrary to Art 3 (1) *Grundgesetz*. Paragraph 622

---

[61] Of 25 August 1969 (BGBl I S. 1317) as amended up to 30 March 2000 (BGBl I S. 333).

BGB was held as unconstitutional by the BVerfG in BVerfGE 82, 126, NJW 1990, 2246–2249. As a result the *Bundestag* introduced a legislative amendment to § 622 BGB to reflect this judgment.[62] The longer period of notice for staff has been extended to blue collar workers. This decision has consequences for unjust dismissal rights and all current dismissals, whereby insufficient or unfair notice periods may give rise to claims before the labour courts. There are also wider consequences for other areas of the employment relationship where differences in terms between white and blue collar workers exist, e.g. pensions.

Paragraph 626 I BGB allows either party to terminate the employment relationship with notice where the other party is responsible for a serious breach (*wichtige Gründe*) of the contract on important grounds. Under § 626 II, this must be effected by notice in writing and applies to all contracts of employment. Special reasons are required for extraordinary dismissals, which do not require any period of notice in circumstances where the party effecting the termination could not be expected to continue with the employment relationship until the expiry of the period of notice. The clearest examples of conduct to justify this would be criminal acts against the employer, such as theft, fraud or embezzlement. On one occasion the participation in a wildcat strike and subsequent refusal to return to work were held to be sufficient grounds for dismissal without notice (BAG NJW 1970, 487).

The BGB provisions have now been supplemented and amended by the Protection from Dismissal Act of 1969 (*Kündigungsschutzgesetz*: KSchG), which applies in favour of employees who have been employed for more than six months in firms with more than five employees (§§ 1 and 23)[63], with the exceptions for fixed term contracts noted above. It applies in cases of ordinary dismissal for which originally no reason was necessary (reasons were first required to be given by the Act reintroducing the works councils in 1920). The 1969 Act applies in respect of dismissals *per se* and to unilateral modifications of contract that are regarded and treated in exactly the same way as a termination of contract combined with a simultaneous new offer. This would be recognised and termed 'constructive dismissal' combined with re-employment in the UK.

For the dismissal to be acceptable or 'socially justified' in terms of § 1 II and III of the Act, the dismissal must be based either on personal grounds or on the conduct of the employee, or on compelling business requirements for not continuing the employment of the employee in question, in effect, redundancy for economic reasons. The term 'personal grounds' concerns mainly absences due to sickness, and dismissals for these reasons must be as a last resort. Repeated shorter absences are more likely to result in dismissal than one illness over an extended period.

Conduct covers a variety of reasons, from breach of conduct, working for a competitor, behaviour, lateness, or absenteeism. The employer is required to give written warnings to justify dismissals under this ground.

Compelling business grounds cover the usual sorts of reasons why redundancies

---

[62] The *Kündigungsfristengesetz* (KündFG) of 7 October 1993 (BGBl I S. 1668).
[63] And described as the "Double 6" formula.

are justified in the UK—poor company performance, plant closure, falling orders, economic downturn, rationalization, introduction of technology or materials shortages. Termination under this heading must be made on a social basis, i.e., how it affects particular persons, but also, where possible, on the basis of 'last in: first out'. The employer must also consider in cases of personality or economic reasons, whether under the circumstances it would be possible to transfer the employee to another position or to retrain him.

An employee has three weeks following dismissal to make an application to the Labour Court under § 4 I to challenge the dismissal. If this period expires without a claim being lodged, the dismissal is deemed under § 7 to be effective and valid.

Where works councils have been set up they play a significant role in the case of dismissal of employees. Paragraph 102 I BetrVG 1972 requires the works council be informed and its opinion heard on decisions to dismiss or transfer employees. Failure to comply renders the dismissal or transfer ineffective. The agreement of the works council is therefore required before the dismissal or transfer is lawfully valid. In the case of managerial employees, the works council need only be informed. The works council may, under § 103, object to the dismissal or transfer. If it does and the dismissal is actually made, the objection must be attached to the notice and may give grounds for an action for unjust dismissal before the Labour Court. An action by the employee to test the dismissal in the courts has the effect of suspending the dismissal. The employer need not continue to employ the worker, who can nevertheless be suspended on full pay.

Ordinary dismissal requires notice of one week to be given to the works council, whereas extraordinary requires three days, after which, silence on the part of the works council will be assumed by law to indicate approval. Under § 15 of the KSchG, works council members enjoy greater protection from dismissal.

Dismissals in relation to sales, takeovers, or business mergers are subject to the special rule in § 613a BGB, whereby the new employer takes on all the former obligations and duties of the existing contracts and individual and collective agreements. Dismissal in this situation by either the old or the new employers is ineffective, under § 613a IV, unless it comes with compelling business requirements in the case of a restructuring.[64]

6 **Worker protection laws**

Apart from the rules relating to dismissal considered above, there is a considerable number of special rules which exist in respect of all workers and other rules in respect of special categories of workers, e.g., pregnant women, those engaged in military and civil service, and the disabled.

---

[64] A good recent overview of this area of law can be found by H. Ehmann and H. Sutschet, *Die betriebsbedingte Kündigung* (2001) 23 Jura 3 145–153.

The Protection from Dismissal Act (KSchG) is the equivalent of the unfair dismissal provisions in the UK. The Act on Working Time (ArbZG) defines the regular working day as eight hours (§ 3 ArbZG) (forty in the week). The Act also regulates Sunday and holiday working and takes account of the EC Working Time Directive.[65] This is subject to collective agreements which can vary the actual time worked per day and week.

Young persons are protected mainly through the Youth Employment Protection Act (*Jugendarbeitsschutzgesetz*: JArbSchG)[66]. This prohibits the full time employment of any child under the age of fourteen or those who have not finished school, i.e., effectively sixteen. Those under eighteen can only work a maximum of forty hours per week over five days, nominally eight hours per day, and they are not allowed to work on Saturdays or Sundays subject to exceptions.

The Federal Vacation Act (*Bundesurlaubsgesetz*[67]) provides for a minimum of twenty-four paid working days' holiday per year, rising with long service and also longer for the under-18s. It is forbidden for workers to take on alternative work in this time or receive cash compensation in lieu, except in the event of termination of employment when it would be impossible to take the holiday due.

The Protection of Working Mothers Act (*Mutterschutzgesetz*: MuSchG[68]) and the Federal Parental Assistance Act (*Bundeserziehungsgeldgesetz*) provide protective rules and details of payments for mothers and fathers for absences due to pregnancy and after the birth of the child.[69]

The Sick Pay Act (*Lohnfortzahlungsgesetz*[70]) states that the benefit must be equivalent for blue and white collar workers.

The Disabled Persons Act (*Schwerbehindertengesetz*: SchwBG[71]) lays down a requirement that all employers with more than twenty in the workforce must employ a minimum of 5% disabled persons or, in penalty, pay contributions to a public fund for the rehabilitation of the disabled.

The EC will increasingly provide legislation and rules in this area, particularly in respect of Social Policy which has been accepted by Germany.

---

[65] Directive 93/104 [1993] OJ L307/13.

[66] Of 12 April 1976 (BGBl I S. 965) as amended up to 21 December 2000 BGBl I S. 1983) which takes account of the EC Directive on Young Workers 94/33 [1994] OJ L216/12.

[67] 8 January 1963 (BGBl I S. 2) as amended up to of 19 December 1998 (BGBl I S. 3843).

[68] Of 17 January 1997 (BGBl I S. 293) as amended up to 30 November 2000 (BGBl I S. 1638) and takes account of the EC Working Mothers Directive 92/85 [1992] OJ L348/1.

[69] This has now been amended and updated (latest 12 October 2000 and 30 November 2000 (BGBl I S. 1426 and 1638). For details see, B. Reinecke, *Elternzeit statt Erziehungsurlaub* (2001) FA (*Fachanwalt Arbeitsrecht*) 1 10–14.

[70] Of 27 July 1969 (BGBl I S. 946) as amended up to 20 December 1996 (BGBl I S. 2110).

[71] Of 26 August 1986 (BGBl I S. 1421) as amended up to 20 December 2000 (BGBl I S. 1827).

7 Collective labour law

As in individual labour law, the presence of a large number of statutes has not precluded extensive judicial development of the law.

As noted, Article 9 (3) *Grundgesetz* guarantees both the individual and collective right to associate. This has positive and negative aspects. The positive is the right to join and belong to a union; the negative aspect is the right not to join. The closed shop cannot be enforced by agreement between the union and employer or by pressure on the part of the union, and any attempted agreements are unlawful. The employers are similarly guaranteed the right to form employers' organizations.

The Collective Agreements Act (*Tarifvertragsgesetz*: TVG) defines who can make such agreements, their scope and legal effect. Paragraph 1 provides that the agreements can be applied as normative law in respect of the regulation, formation, content and termination of employment contracts. Other obligations which do not operate at the individual level of the worker only impose duties on the parties to the agreement. Paragraph 2 states the Act applies only in respect of unions on the side of the workers, but to single employers and organisations of employers on the other side. The agreements made apply in favour of all employers who are members of the employers' organization and all union members of the union. The agreements can also be binding in respect of non-union workers where agreed, and usually apply in favour of non-union members. This helps to discourage, or at least undermine, the ability of the employer to hire non-union labour at a lower rate.

It is argued that the negative aspect provides the right not to be discriminated against when the right not to join a union is exercised, i.e., to receive the benefits of a union negotiated pay rise even if not a member of the union. A case decided by the BAG to support this held there was no right to have collective agreements which give extra benefits only to union members (BAG NJW 1968, 1903 in respect of textile workers).

Collective agreements can apply to the employee-like workers (see above) but not to commercial agents.

Both the unions' and employers' umbrella organizations, the DGB and the BDA, could conclude agreements on behalf of their respective membership but this is not the case, and agreements are usually at the level of an industry or union in particular cases. Plant level bargaining and agreement in Germany are rare. The agreements have widened from the discussion and negotiation of wages and holidays, and now include most aspects of the employment relationship, including sickness benefits, retirement, pensions, hours and conditions.

Case-law has established that there are also implied fundamental duties in collective agreements. The obligation 'to keep the peace' (*Friedenspflicht*) exists, which, if breached by a wild cat strike action, will give rise to the liability to compensate. See case BAG NJW 1959, 356, involving metal workers in Schleswig-Holstein. The second duty is to carry out the contract, which, although self-explanatory, includes the notions that the parties must try to ensure the membership of unions and employers do nothing to breach the duty, and is known as the *Durchführungspflicht*, the breach of which can lead to injunctions or an early termination of an agreement and the justification of industrial action.

Paragraph 5 TVG provides that where 50% of the workers in an industry are covered by a collective agreement as union members, either the union or the employers' organization can apply to the Federal Minister of Labour who is empowered to extend the agreement to all employees and employers as the standard for all employees in the particular industry.

In contrast to the UK, the agreements can contain effective and enforceable no-strike clauses applicable to all aspects of the agreement or, if they wish, to all aspects of industrial relations between the parties. They are normally concluded for a specific period, or if indefinite, can be terminated by mutual agreement.

The right to promote union views and propaganda is also guaranteed by Article 9 (3) *Grundgesetz* and upheld, but is subject to limits. BAG NJW 1967, 843 guaranteed the right to distribute promotional material and information but outside working hours or during breaks.

7.1 Industrial conflict law

The rules on strike law are essentially those emanating from case-law, due to the fact that the legislature has not so far acted in this area.

Article 9 (3) *Grundgesetz* is taken as the basis for action undertaken in support of the workers' right to act collectively to improve working and economic conditions. The second sentence makes illegal measures designed to restrict or amend the constitutionally guaranteed right. However, the action in support of the right must be within the limits of legality and the constitution itself. Two leading decisions of the BAG in 1955 (BAGE 1, 291) and 1971 (BAG, NJW 1971, 1668) have determined that both strikes and lockouts are lawful if certain conditions are fulfilled. Strikes are lawful if they are conducted by a party to a collective agreement, that means a union, therefore the right is a collective right and not an individual right. Non-union members are, however, entitled to take part in the industrial action. Additionally, industrial action can only be held in respect of issues which are the subject of a collective agreement. They must be complementary to collective bargaining, which thus rules out political, protest or sympathy strikes. Wild cat strikes (BAG NJW 1964, 883) or strikes to show solidarity with sacked workers would not be lawful, regardless of their aims which may themselves be lawful and justified. Strikes in breach of the duty to keep the peace are also unlawful. Strikes must be last resort (*ultima-ratio*) and the decision to strike must be the result of a prior secret ballot (*Urabstimmung*), except in the case of the very short warning strikes (*Warnstreik*) of a few hours or a day in an individual plant to demonstrate the seriousness of the workers' demands. The warning strike has been used with great effect and confirmed by the BAG, NJW 1977, 1079.

A third, overriding criterion has been developed by the BAG on the legality of strikes; the action undertaken must also be proportional to the result to be achieved and not cause too much harm (see BAG Großer Senat NJW 1971, 1668). This would likely rule out strikes involving mass picketing as experienced in the UK from time to time. In case of a lawful strike the employer cannot sue; however, in the case of an unlawful strike a delict action lies against the union under § 823 BGB. As a part of the requirement of proportionality there is a duty to keep essential supplies and services going. Those employed in the public sector are governed by public law and are denied the right to strike.

Lockouts, although only rarely employed and usually only as a counter weapon to selective strike action by unions, have also been given judicial approval, but these must also be proportional. See BAG NJW 1980, 1642 and BVerfGE, NJW 1991, 2549. A lockout forces the union to pay strike pay (*Streikunterstützung*) to greater numbers of workers and thus depletes the strike fund. State benefit for locked-out strikers but not non-strikers has now been statutorily declared to be inapplicable under § 146 of the third book of the Social Code (SGB III).[72]

Lawful strikes and lockouts suspend the obligations of the employment contract which nevertheless continues. There is no need to pay remuneration, but equally the employer cannot demand services. There is no need on the part of the employees to perform services, and accordingly they cannot demand payment. Any strike by workers in a connected industry which forces employers to lay off workers will also relieve the employer of the obligation to pay wages to laid off workers. The strike is not a ground for a justifiable dismissal unless the strike is unlawful, when not only may dismissal be acceptable but damages may also be payable by the strikers.

7.2 Worker representation and co-determination

A very important area of law is concerned with the conduct of industrial relations through the rules on the representation of workers' views. These can arise either through contract as a part of a collective agreement or through statute. Historically, statutory intervention has a remarkably long record in this area and can be traced to the end of the last century, from the 1891 Trade Act, the 1919 Constitution of the Weimar Republic, Art 165, the 1920 Works Council Act, the 1937 Stock Corporation Act and the 1952 Works Constitution Act.

Worker participation (*Mitbestimmung*) in Germany finds expression in two main forms which were introduced at different times and for different reasons, although the end result is, of course, the greater involvement and say of workers in the organisation and, to varying extents, the decision-making in business enterprises.

7.2.1 Works councils (Betriebsrat)

The first works councils were provided by the employers, often to appease the workers' demand for their own, more powerful bodies for participation. The 1920

---

[72] Further details on this can be found in M. Lieb, *Arbeitsrecht*, 7th ed. (2000: C.F. Müller, Heidelberg), pp. 227–229.

Act confirmed the status of the works councils as independent of the unions, and this remains the case today. The aims and work of the works councils have at times become confused and combined with other objectives, such as the participation of workers in the management and decision-making in companies. Hence there is a considerable amount of legislation on the topic which can be overlapping.

The Works Constitution Act (*Betriebsverfassungsgesetz*: BetrVG) of 1952 provided the legal basis for the re-establishment of works councils following the Second World War. This was significantly amended and updated by the 1972 BetrVG and the Works Constitution Reform Act of 2001.[73] These Acts provide all the details on the setting up of the works councils and the rights of co-determination they enjoy. In brief, § 1 provides that membership is open to all employees over the age of eighteen in workplaces with more than five employees. The establishment of works councils is voluntary on the part of the employees and not compulsory. If the employees do decide to have one, the employer is prohibited from preventing it being set up. In practice they are the rule, especially in medium to large businesses, rather than the exception. In smaller enterprises they are the exception. The 2001 reform has given statutory status to the previous judicially sanctioned rule that the division of a company into a number of parts or the acquisition by a company of other still legally independent companies does not prevent a common works council being established to represent the whole structure where the personnel division caters for the group, thus recognizing the reality of the decision-making structure in the group as a whole.[74]

Paragraph 2 1972 BetrVG requires the employer and the works council to cooperate with each other in good faith, and with the trade unions and the association of employers, and to observe collective agreements. This amounts in law to a ban on strikes as a means to achieve the settlement of disputes by the works council. Disputes between the works council and the employer are resolved by the provision of a compulsory arbitration committee of workers' representatives, employers' representatives and a neutral chairperson.

Although legally independent of the unions, there is nevertheless a high degree of overlap and cooperation between the two bodies of worker representatives, largely because those active in trade unionism are often the same people who stand for election to the works councils.

Paragraph 5 (III) 1972 BetrVG defines rather loosely that those in leading managerial positions are excluded from any participation in works councils, but they are now allowed to set up their own representative body and are covered by specific legislation, the Managerial Employees Committee Act (*Sprecherausschußgesetz*).

Elected members are guaranteed paid time off work to attend to the duties of membership (§ 38 BetrVG). Larger workplaces with over 200 employees merit a

---

[73] Noted above, footnote 23.

[74] For further details on this and the other numerous changes to the Works Constitution Act, see P. Hanau, *Die Reform der Betriebsverfassung* (2001) NJW 35 2513–2519, H. Nielebock, *Neues Betriebsverfassungsgesetz* (2001) AiB (*Arbeitsrecht im Betrieb*) 8 441–448, and H. Reichold, *Die reformierte Betriebsverfassung 2001* (2001) 18 NZA (*Neue Zeitschrift für Arbeitsrecht*) 16 857–865.

full-time member or part time members who must be paid the same as equivalent colleagues, receive the same increases and benefits and be kept up to date with training. The 1972 Act increased the burden of the employers to pay for the training of worker members of the council to carry out their duties as council members, and to provide facilities and equipment for them including offices and personnel (§ 40 BetrVG) and modern IT and communications equipment.

The rights of the works council depend first on the size of the concern, but basically works councils have the right to company information but of most importance are rights of co-determination in the area of working conditions and social issues (§§87 et seq. BetrVG). These include such matters as hours of work, health and safety, form of payment, vacations, and accident and illness benefits. In matters of employment and dismissal matters (§§ 99 et seq.) they have rights of information from the employer regarding general personnel planning and to participate in the appointment of permanent employees. In businesses of over twenty workers, the council has rights in respect of individual personnel matters, as was considered above in respect of the employment and dismissal of employees. Under § 106, works councils in establishments with over 100 employees have the right to set up economic committees. In matters of operational changes, which includes closures, cutbacks, relocation and mergers, there is a duty under § 111 to inform the works council. In other areas not specifically covered by the provisions of the Act, there is a duty on the part of the employer to inform and try to accommodate the interests of the works council. However, at the end of day there is no veto on the part of the council.

Under §§ 111 and 112 the economic committees have the right to discuss the financial aspects of the reorganization of the business with the management, but this really boils down to working out the details in the event of redundancies. The council and employer can conclude binding and enforceable agreements in matters falling under the jurisdiction of the works council. However, collective agreements take precedence over the agreements of the works councils (§ 87 BetrVG), except in relation to economic matters under §§ 106–113.

The BetrVG only applies in the private sector, but it applies to all workplaces irrespective of nationality of the owning company and the choice of law applicable to the employment contracts (§ 130). In other words the provisions of the Act cannot be excluded. Further details can be found in the Act, English versions of which are listed in 'Further reading' below.

A similar federal law for the public sector only exists in respect of the federally-employed employees because of the lack of competence to legislate with effect over the publicly-employed staff of the *Länder*. The federal law, the Federal Staff Representation Act (*Bundespersonalvertretungsgesetz*)[75] (latest version of 1974), acts as a framework law for the *Länder* and has similar counterpart laws in the *Länder*. This provides for representation in the state administrative and public law bodies, which works in a similar way to the works councils.

---

[75] BPersVG of 15 March 1974 (BGBl I S. 693) as amended to 1994.

7.2.2 Supervisory boards and labour directors

The original provision for worker participation by the employers followed the practice of limited partnerships in the last century. They had grown very large and found it necessary to set up a small committee of persons to represent the limited partners to act as a supervising body over the activities of the managing partners. This practice spread to companies and led to the shareholder supervision of management. Worker participation in the supervisory board did not take place until 1922, much later than worker participation through the works councils. The 1922 legislation gave the right to the works councils to delegate one or two members with full voting rights to the supervisory board. Both were abolished by Hitler.

It had been proposed to de-industrialize Germany after the Second World War, but for various reasons this was not put into effect. Part of the lobby against this consisted of the coal and steel owners, who had secured the support of the relevant unions in exchange for greater rights of industrial democracy. At first the British issued special rules in their zone in 1947 following the voluntary agreement of the enterprises and unions in the iron and steel industry for the structure and control of companies, including equal representation of employees and shareholders and for worker directors. This was followed by legal requirements of worker participation in the supervisory board of companies in the Anglo-American bi-zone area of Germany.

The supervisory model chosen fits worker participation into the existing corporate form of public and private companies, rather than the establishment of a new or an additional forum as required in the case of the works councils.

The Coal and Steel Industry Co-determination Act (Montan-MitbestG) of 1951[76] provided the first national post-Second World War legislative provision in the steel and coal industries for worker representation on the supervisory board. Coal and steel producers with over 1,000 employees must have equal representation of shareholders and workers on the supervisory board with a neutral chairperson. Coal and steel manufacturing enterprises must also have a director responsible for personnel matters, known as the labour director (*Arbeitsdirektor*), who is appointed only with the approval of a majority of the workers' representatives on the supervisory board (§§ 12–13 of the Act). In 1956, the 1951 Act was extended to combined companies in the coal and steel industries.[77]

The BetrVG of 1952 extended the requirements of the 1951 Act to public and private companies with over 500 employees, whereby a supervisory board must be established with two-thirds shareholders' representatives and one-third employees' representatives (§ 76 BetrVG).

Paragraph 52 GmbHG allows private companies with fewer than 500 employees to decide to adopt a supervisory board. In these optional cases no worker directors need be appointed. Private companies with over 500 employers must have worker representation on the supervisory board.

---

[76] Of 21 May 1951 (BGBl I S. 347) as amended up to 9 June 1998 (BGBl I S. 1242).
[77] The Supplementary Co-determination Act of 7 August 1956 (*Mitbestimmungsergänzungsgesetz*) as amended up to 9 June 1998 (BGBl I S. 1242).

The Co-determination Act of 1976 (MitbestG)[78] was enacted to overcome some of the criticisms of the previous Acts and to extend the scope of employee representation and co-determination. It applies to all public and private companies with over 2,000 employees, who may be split up over a number of sites. It also applies to the GmbH & Co. KG. These companies are required to have equal shareholder and labour representation and a labour director. The size of the supervisory board depends on the size of the company involved. Of the employees' representatives, there must be at least one from managerial staff. A chairman, with casting vote, is appointed who is usually a representative of the shareholders. The labour director is appointed under this Act in the same way as any other director, that is by a simple majority of the votes of the members of the supervisory board and not by the approval of a majority of the worker representatives only.

This Act was challenged by industrial employers' federations who reacted strongly to its requirements. A constitutional complaint was lodged by the Confederation of German Industry (*Bundesverband der Deutschen Industrie*) on the basis that the Act undermined the system of collective bargaining previously established under Article 9 (3) *Grundgesetz* and it interfered with the right of private property (Art 14 *Grundgesetz*). Further, the combined effect of the works councils and the requirement of parity on the supervisory board was argued to lead to a bias in favour of the employees to the detriment of the shareholders' rights. In BVerfGE 50, 290, 366–78 (judgment given on 1 March 1979) the constitutionality of the supervisory board and the Act was confirmed.[79] The court ruled out any accumulation of co-determination by representation in the two bodies.

The rights and duties of worker representative members of the supervisory board are the same as those for shareholder members, further details of which can be found in the section on business associations above.

7.2.3 *Groups of companies*

As with other legal concerns in respect of groups of companies, the legislature has not provided a specific legal regime to cope with the factual and economic reality of corporate groups. The organization of business enterprise in this way has distinct consequences on the ability of workers to participate in the decision-making process in companies. The form and level of participation must coincide with the decision-making in the group concerned to be effective. Only to a limited, and not particularly effective, extent has the present legislation done this.

Where an enterprise has several plants, § 47 BetrVG provides that the works councils of the single plants can delegate representatives to a joint or company works council (*Gesamtbetriebsrat*). Paragraphs 54 et seq. BetrVG allow for the optional establishment by the joint works councils of a group works council (*Konzernbetriebsrat*) at the level of the controlling company of a group, but only grants limited powers to this body over social or personnel matters. The economic

---

[78] Of 4 May 1976 (BGBl I S. 1153) as amended up to 28 October 1994 (BGBl I S. 3210).
[79] BVerfGE, NJW 1979, 699, noted by Kommers, 1989, pp. 278–85. [1979] 2 EX 324–86.

committees have the right to be consulted on economic matters under § 106 which affect personnel. The establishment or reorganization of a group would arguably be such a situation.

The Co-determination Acts provide for the establishment of supervisory boards at the group level, but the definition of the group varies in the Acts and does not necessarily correspond with the reality of management and decision-making in particular groups. They often have no real say in dependent companies which still enjoy a significant degree of autonomy.

To alleviate the problems, the Federal Labour Court held in 1980 that a group works council can be set up in dependent companies or, in complex groups, several works councils may be set up where the decision-making power is located (BAG, 34, 230, 235).

In practice, the unions and groups of workers often make informal arrangements with the employers to overcome the absence of specific legislative requirements. It is clear that more thought and legislative action is required in this area.

8 Procedural law

The system of labour law courts was introduced in 1926 to deal with both individual and collective labour disputes. In the Federal Republic of Germany there are 123 labour law courts of first instance. Paragraph 2 ArbGG directs all disputes involving labour matters to these courts.

Representation by an attorney is not compulsory at the level of the local labour courts (§ 11 I ArbGG) but is allowed either by an attorney or a representative of either a union or employer organisation. Before the regional courts some form of representation is compulsory (§ 11 II ArbGG). Even when the worker is represented by a union official, this is invariably a qualified *Rechtsanwalt*. See the section on the courts and legal professions for more details on the labour law courts.

There is a statutorily provided procedure introduced for parties to collective agreements which provides that the parties may submit a dispute to arbitration (§ 4 and 101 et seq. ArbGG).

There are two forms of labour dispute. The first, like all civil disputes between parties and regulated as such, concerns disputes between the employer and employees, either individually or collectively. The second concerns judicial investigations. Most procedures are initiated by individual workers, and they typically involve dismissal disputes more frequently than anything else.

8.1 Individual disputes

If an individual disagrees with a normal or an extraordinary dismissal, a complaint may be filed with the labour court within three weeks of the dismissal. Labour law disputes consist of a two-step procedure. The first is a form of conciliation as part of an informal hearing (*Gütertermin*) and takes place very shortly after the filing of the action. This informal solution (§ 54 ArbGG), is first attempted by the judge who may inform the parties of the likely result if the matter went to a full hearing, hence most cases are settled at this stage. In the informal hearings only the professional judge, and not the two lay judges, is present.

If this step fails, the matter goes to trial before the labour court in full. The court is then obliged to decide the case and give judgment against one of the parties. A valid complaint by an employee upholds the right to continued employment, but if alternative employment has been found the winning employee may elect to disregard the judgment. Either party may elect before final judgment to apply for the termination of the employment relationship where dismissal is found to be unjust, and the employee can receive monetary compensation under § 9 KSchG. Considering the often very strained relations, this is the usual situation.

A significant feature is that the winning party cannot claim the costs of the case from the other party at first instance (§ 12a ArbGG). Each party bears its own costs. Legal aid can be provided by the court (§ 13).

An appeal only lies to the regional labour courts if the matter exceeds the value of €600 and covers questions of fact and law (§ 64 ArbGG). Only about 5 per cent of cases are appealed. A final appeal on matters of law only lies to the *Bundesarbeitsgericht* (§ 72 ArbGG) with compulsory representation by a lawyer (§ 11 II ArbGG). Again, only about 5 per cent of cases are appealed.[80]

8.2 Collective disputes

Collective actions include the actions and disputes between the parties to collective agreements and between the agreements between the works councils and employers. They also cover the industrial conflict actions discussed above. Additionally, disputes over the conduct of dismissals and redundancies are required to be notified to the state and federal labour offices. These are also defined and regulated by the KSchG.

8.3 Judicial investigation

The second type of procedure before the labour courts is a form of investigation procedure, known as the *Beschluß*, to establish general guidelines on co-determination amongst others (refer to §§ 80–98). Disputes involving court approval for the appointment or dismissal of an employee not given by the works council are also covered.

The courts of ordinary jurisdiction may also be involved if the rights of the supervisory board members are questioned, as this is regarded as part of company law and not part of the election process to the board which is governed by labour

---

[80] For a view of the limited changes to the *Arbeitsgerichtsgesetz* brought about the civil procedural reform in 2001, see J. Düwell, *Die Auswirkung der Reform des Zivilprozesses an die Verfahren in Arbeitssachen* (2001) FA (*Fachanwalt Arbeitsrecht*) 10 294–296.

law. The ordinary civil courts would also be concerned with membership rights of either the unions or the employers' organizations.[81]

FURTHER READING

Arbeitsgesetze, 59th ed. (2001: C.H. Beck, Munich).

Collection of Labour Law Statutes: Nipperdey I Arbeitsrecht (2001: C.H. Beck, Munich).

Co-determination in the Federal Republic of Germany: Co-determination Act 1976: Co-determination in the mining industry: Business Organisation Acts 1952 and 1972 (1991: Federal Minister of Labour and Social Affairs, Bonn).

Schneider and Kingsman, *The German Co-determination Act, the Shop Constitution Act and extracts from the Stock Corporation Act and the Shop Constitution Act of 1972* (1976: Knapp, Frankfurt am Main).

D. Belling and A. Luckey, *Höchstrichterliche Rechtsprechung zum Arbeitsrecht* 2nd ed. (2000: C.H. Beck, Munich).

B. Boemke, *Studienbuch Arbeitsrecht* (2001: C.H. Beck, Munich).

Brox & Rüthers, *Arbeitsrecht*, 14th ed. (1999: Kohlhammer Verlag, Stuttgart).

Business Transactions in Germany (M. Bender, New York and C.H. Beck, Munich), vol. II, ch. 28–30.

Droste, Killius and Triebel, *Business Law Guide to Germany*, 3rd ed. (1991: CCH Editions, Bicester), ch. 9.

W. Dütz, *Arbeitsrecht*, 6th ed. (2001: C.H. Beck, Munich).

Erfurter Kommentar zum Arbeitsrecht, (Dieterich, Hanau & Schaub Eds.) 2nd ed. (2001: C.H. Beck, Munich).

F. Gamillscheg, *Arbeitsrecht I*, 8th ed., (2000: C.H. Beck, Munich).

R. Großmann and F. Schneider *Arbeitsrecht*, 9th ed. with supplement (1999: Stollfuß Verlag, Bonn).

P. Hanau and K. Adomeit, *Arbeitsrecht*, 12th ed. (2000: Luchterhand, Neuweid).

G. Halback et al., *Labour Law: an Overview*, 4th ed. (1992: Federal Ministry for Labour and Social Affairs, Bonn). Although dated, this still provides an extensive overview in English.

W. Hromadka and F. Maschmann, *Arbeitsrecht, Band 1* (1998: Springer Verlag, Berlin).

W. Hromadka and F. Maschmann, *Arbeitsrecht, Band 2*, 2nd ed. (2001: Springer Verlag, Berlin).

M. Lieb, *Arbeitsrecht*, 7th ed. (2000: Müller, Heidelberg).

P. Pulte, *Individualarbeitsrecht* (1999: Fortis Verlag, Köln).

A Söllner, *Grundriß des Arbeitsrechts*, 12th ed. (1998: Vahlen Verlag, Munich).

M. Weiss, *Labour Law and Industrial Relations in the Federal Republic of Germany* (1987: Kluwer, Deventer).

M. Weiss, 'Germany', in R. Blanpain and T. Hanami (eds), *Employment Security: Law and Practice* (1994: Peeters Press, Leuven), pp. 139–58.

M. Weiss, 'Germany' in R. Blanpain (ed. in chief), *International Encylopaedia for Labour Law and Industrial Relations* (10 vol. loose-leaf work) (Kluwer, Deventer), vol. 5, pp. 1–190.

M. Weiss, *European Employment and Industrial Relations Glossary: Germany* (1992: Sweet & Maxwell, London).

R. Wörlen, *Arbeitsrecht*, 4th ed. (2000: Carl Heymanns Verlag, Köln).

---

[81] Further brief considerations of labour law court procedures can be found in most of the texts in the 'Further reading' below, but for those who require a complete and systematic coverage, the following should suffice: A. Ostrowicz et al., *Der Arbeitsgerichtsprozess* (2000: Erich Schmidt Verlag, Berlin).

APPENDIX

Extracts from the German Constitution[1]

CHAPTER I. Basic Rights

Article 1   Protection of human dignity

(1) The dignity of man is inviolable. To respect and protect it shall be the duty of all public authority.

(2) The German people therefore uphold human rights as inviolable and inalienable and as the basis of every community, of peace and of justice in the world.

(3)[2] The following basic rights shall bind the legislature, the executive and the judiciary as directly enforceable law.

Article 2   Personal freedom

(1) Everybody has the right to self-fulfilment in so far as they do not violate the rights of others or offend against the constitutional order or morality.

(2) Everybody has the right to life and physical integrity. Personal freedom is inviolable. These rights may not be encroached upon save pursuant to a law.

Article 3   Equality before the law

(1) All persons are equal before the law.

(2) Men and women have equal rights. The state shall promote the actual implementation of equal rights for women and men and take steps to eliminate disadvantages that now exist.

(3) Nobody shall be prejudiced or favoured because of their sex, birth, race, language, national or social origin, faith, religion or political opinions. No person shall be disfavored because of disability.

Article 4   Freedom of faith, conscience and creed

(1) Freedom of faith and conscience as well as freedom of creed, religious or ideological (*Weltanschauung*), are inviolable.

(2) The undisturbed practice of religion shall be guaranteed.

(3) Nobody may be forced against their conscience into military service involving armed combat. Details shall be the subject of a federal law.

---

[1] These are taken from the translation as supplied by the Press and Information Office of the Federal Government in Bonn and published in June 1994. It is to be noted that there have been considerable changes in the English versions from previous official translations, many of which appear only to be for stylistic reasons. It is to be further noted that the 1998 version supplied by the Press and Information Office in Bonn has changed yet again the words used, again seemingly for sylistic reasons only, for example American English spelling is now favoured (or should that be favored?). To save changing these again, for the purposes of providing helpful information in this volume, the updates and additions will be taken only from the 1998 version.

[2] As amended by federal law of 19 March 1956 (*Federal Law Gazette* I p. 111).

Article 5 Freedom of expression

(1) Everybody has the right freely to express and disseminate their opinions orally, in writing or visually and to obtain information from generally accessible sources without hindrance. Freedom of the press and freedom of reporting through audiovisual media shall be guaranteed. There shall be no censorship.

(2) These rights are subject to limitations embodied in the provisions of general legislation, statutory provisions for the protection of young persons and the citizen's right to personal respect.

(3) Art and scholarship, research and teaching shall be free. Freedom of teaching shall not absolve anybody from loyalty to the constitution.

Article 6 Marriage and family, children born outside marriage

(1) Marriage and family shall enjoy the special protection of the state.

(2) The care and upbringing of children are a natural right of parents and a duty primarily incumbent on them. It is the responsibility of the community to ensure that they perform this duty.

(3) Children may not be separated from their families against the will of their parents or guardians save in accordance with a law in cases where they fail in their duty or there is a danger of the children being seriously neglected for other reasons.

(4) Every mother is entitled to the protection and care of the community.

(5) Children born outside marriage shall be provided by law with the same opportunities for their physical and mental development and regarding their place in society as are enjoyed by those born in marriage.

Article 7 School education

(1) The entire school system shall be under the supervision of the state.

(2) Parents and guardians have the right to decide whether children receive religious instruction.

(3) Religious instruction shall form part of the curriculum in state schools except non-denominational schools. Without prejudice to the state's right of supervision, religious instruction shall be given in accordance with the doctrine of the religious community concerned. Teachers may not be obliged to give religious instruction against their will.

(4) The right to establish private schools shall be guaranteed. Private schools as alternatives to state schools shall require the approval of the state and be subject to *Land* legislation. Such approval shall be given where private schools are not inferior to state schools in terms of their educational aims, their facilities and the training of their teaching staff and where it does not encourage segregation of pupils according to the means of their parents. Approval shall be withheld where the economic and legal status of the teaching staff is not adequately secured.

(5) A private elementary school shall be approved only where the education authority finds that it meets a special educational need or where, at the request of parents or guardians, it is to be established as an non-denominational, denominational or alternative school and no state elementary school of that type exists locally.

(6) Preparatory schools (*Vorschulen*) shall remain abolished.

Article 8 Freedom of assembly

(1) All Germans shall have the right to assemble peacefully and unarmed without prior notification or permission.

(2) In the case of outdoor assemblies this right may be restricted by or pursuant to law.

Article 9   Freedom of association

(1) All Germans have the right to form associations, partnerships and corporations.

(2) Associations whose aims or activities contravene criminal law or are directed against the constitutional order or the notion of international understanding shall be banned.

(3) The right to form associations in order to safeguard and improve working and economic conditions shall be guaranteed to every individual and all occupations and professions. Agreements restricting or intended to hamper the exercise of this right shall be null and void; measures to this end shall be illegal. Measures taken pursuant to Article 12a, paragraphs (2) and (3) of Article 35, paragraph (4) of Article 87a or Article 91, may not be directed against any industrial disputes engaged in by associations within the meaning of the first sentence of this paragraph in order to safeguard and improve working and economic conditions.[3]

Article 10[4]   Privacy of correspondence, posts and telecommunications

(1) Privacy of correspondence, posts and telecommunications is inviolable.

(2) Restrictions may only be ordered pursuant to a law. Where a restriction serves to protect the free democratic basic order or the existence or security of the Federation or a *Land* the law may stipulate that the person affected shall not be informed of such restriction and that recourse to the courts shall be replaced by a review of the case by bodies and subsidiary bodies appointed by Parliament.

Article 11   Freedom of movement

(1) All Germans have the right to move freely throughout the federal territory.

(2) This right may be restricted only by or pursuant to a law and only where a person does not have a sufficient livelihood and his or her freedom of movement would be a considerable burden on the community or where such a restriction is necessary to avert an imminent danger to the existence or the free democratic basic order of the Federation or a *Land*, to prevent an epidemic, a natural disaster, grave accident or criminal act, or to protect young persons from serious neglect.

Article 12[5]   Free choice of occupation or profession, prohibition of forced labour

(1) All Germans have the right freely to choose their occupation or profession, their place of work, study or training. The practice of an occupation or profession may be regulated by or pursuant to a law.

(2) Nobody may be forced to do work of a particular kind except as part of a traditional compulsory community service that applies generally and equally to all.

(3) Forced labour may only be imposed on people deprived of their liberty by court sentence.

[Article 12a   Omitted]

Article 13   Privacy of the home

(1) Privacy of the home is inviolable.

(2) Searches may be ordered only by a judge or, if there is a danger in delay, by other authorities as provided for by law and may be carried out only in the manner prescribed by the law.

(3) If particular facts justify the suspicion that any person has committed an especially serious crime specifically defined by a law, technical means of acoustical surveillance of any

---

[3] Last sentence inserted by federal law of 24 June 1968 (*Federal Law Gazette* I p. 709).

[4] As amended by federal law of 24 June 1968 (*Federal Law Gazette* I p. 709).

[5] As amended by federal laws of 19 March 1956 (*Federal Law Gazette* I p. 111) and 24 June 1968 (*Federal Law Gazette* I p. 709).

home in which the suspect is supposedly staying may be employed pursuant to judicial order for the purpose of prosecuting the offence, provided that alternative methods of investigating the matter would be disproportionately difficult or unproductive. The authorisation shall be for a limited time. The order shall be issued by a panel composed of three judges. When time is of the essence, it may also be issued by a single judge.

(4) To avert acute dangers to public safety, especially dangers to life or to the public, technical means of surveillance of the home may be employed only pursuant to judicial order. When time is of the essence, such measures may also be ordered by other authorities designated by a law; a judicial decision shall subsequently be obtained without delay.

(5) If technical means are contemplated solely for the protection of persons officially deployed in a home, the measure may be ordered by an authority designated by a law. The information thereby obtained may be otherwise used only for purposes of criminal prosecution or to avert danger and only if the legality of the measure has been previously determined by a judge; when time is of the essence, a judicial decision shall subsequently be obtained without delay.

(6) The Federal Government shall report to the *Bundestag* annually as to the employment of technical means pursuant to paragraph (3) and, within the jurisdiction of the Federation, pursuant to paragraph (4) and, insofar as judicial approval is required, pursuant to paragraph (5) of this Article. A panel elected by the *Bundestag* shall exercise parliamentary control on the basis of this report. A comparable parliamentary control shall be afforded by the *Länder*.

(7) Interferences and restrictions shall otherwise only be permissible to avert a danger to the public or to the life of an individual, or, pursuant to a law, to confront an acute danger to public safety and order, in particular to relieve a housing shortage, to combat the danger of an epidemic, or to protect young persons at risk.

Article 14   Property, inheritance, expropriation

(1) Property and the right of inheritance shall be guaranteed. Their substance and limits shall be determined by law.

(2) Property entail obligations. Its use should also serve the public interest.

(3) Expropriation shall only be permissible in the public interest. It may only be ordered by or pursuant to a law which determines the nature and extent of compensation. Compensation shall reflect a fair balance between the public interest and the interests of those affected. In case of dispute regarding the amount of compensation recourse may be had to the ordinary courts.

Article 15   Public ownership

Land, natural resources and means of production may be transferred to public ownership or other forms of public enterprise by a law which determines the nature and extent of compensation. In respect of compensation the third and fourth sentences of paragraph (3) of Article 14 shall apply *mutatis mutandis*.

Article 16   Nationality, extradition

(1) Nobody may be deprived of their German citizenship. Loss of citizenship may only occur pursuant to a law, and against the will of the person affected only if they do not thereby become stateless.

(2) No German may be extradited to another country.

Article 16a   Asylum

(1) Anybody persecuted on political grounds has the right of asylum.

(2) Paragraph (1) may not be invoked by anybody who enters the country from a member state of the European Communities or another third country where the application of the Convention relating to the Status of Refugees and the Convention for the Protection of Human

Rights and Fundamental Freedoms is assured. Countries outside the European Communities which fulfil the conditions of the first sentence of this paragraph shall be specified by legislation requiring the consent of the *Bundesrat*. In cases covered by the first sentence measures terminating a person's sojourn may be carried out irrespective of any remedy sought by that person.

(3) Legislation requiring the consent of the *Bundesrat* may be introduced to specify countries where the legal situation, the application of law and the general political circumstances justify the assumption that neither political persecution nor inhumane or degrading punishment or treatment takes place there. It shall be presumed that a foreigner from such a country is not subject to persecution on political grounds as long as the person concerned does not present facts supporting the supposition that, contrary to the presumption, he or she is subject to political persecution.

(4) The implementation of measures terminating a person's sojourn shall, in the cases referred to in paragraph (3) and in other cases that are manifestly ill-founded or considered to be manifestly ill-founded, be suspended by the court only where serious doubt exists as to the legality of the measure; the scope of the investigation may be restricted and objections submitted after the prescribed time-limit may be disregarded. Details shall be the subject of a law.

(5) Paragraphs (1) to (4) do not conflict with international agreements of member states of the European Communities among themselves and with third countries which, with due regard for the obligations arising from the Convention relating to the Status of Refugees and the Convention for the Protection of Human Rights and Fundamental Freedoms, whose application must be assured in the contracting states, establish jurisdiction for the consideration of applications for asylum including the mutual recognition of decisions on asylum.

Article 17   Right of petition

Everybody has the right individually or jointly with others to address written requests or complaints to the appropriate agencies and to Parliament.

[Article 17a   Omitted]

Article 18   Forfeiture of basic rights

Those who abuse their freedom of expression, in particular freedom of the press (paragraph (1) of Article 5), freedom of teaching (paragraph (3) of Article 5), freedom of assembly (Article 8), freedom of association (Article 9), privacy of correspondence, posts and telecommunications (Article 10), property (Article 14), or the right of asylum (Article 16a) in order to undermine the free democratic basic order shall forfeit these basic rights. Such forfeiture and its extent shall be determined by the Federal Constitutional Court.

Article 19   Restriction of basic rights

(1) In so far as a basic right may, under this Basic Law, be restricted by or pursuant to a law the law shall apply generally and not merely to one case. Furthermore, the law shall specify the basic right and relevant Article.

(2) In no case may the essence of a basic right be encroached upon.

(3) The basic rights shall apply also to domestic legal persons to the extent that the nature of such rights permits.

(4) Where rights are violated by public authority the person affected shall have recourse to law. In so far as no other jurisdiction has been established such recourse shall be to the ordinary courts. The second sentence of paragraph (2) of Article 10 shall not be affected by the provisions of this paragraph.[6]

---

[6] Last sentence inserted by federal law of 24 June (*Federal Law Gazette* I p. 710).

CHAPTER II. **The Federation and the *Länder***

Article 20   Political and social structure, defence of the constitutional order

(1) The Federal Republic of Germany shall be a democratic and social federal state.

(2) All state authority emanates from the people. It shall be exercised by the people through elections and referendums and by specific legislative, executive, and judicial bodies.

(3) The legislature shall be bound by the constitutional order, the executive and the judiciary by law and justice.

(4)[7] All Germans have the right to resist anybody attempting to do away with this constitutional order, should no other remedy be possible.

Article 20a   (Protection of the natural bases of life)

Mindful also of its responsibility towards future generations, the state shall protect the natural bases of life by legislation and, in accordance with law and justice, be executive and judicial action, all within the framework of the constitutional order.

Article 21   Parties

(1) The parties shall help form the political will of the people. They may be freely established. Their internal organisation shall conform to democratic principles. They shall publicly account for the sources and use of their funds and for their assets.

(2) Parties which by reason of their aims or the conduct of their adherents seek to impair or do away with the free democratic basic order or threaten the existence of the Federal Republic of Germany, shall be unconstitutional. The Federal Constitutional Court shall rule on the question of unconstitutionality.

(3) Details shall be the subject of federal laws.

Article 23   The European Union

(1) With a view to establishing a united Europe the Federal Republic of Germany shall participate in the development of the European Union, which is committed to democratic, rule-of-law, social and federal principles as well as the principle of subsidiarity, and ensures protection of basic rights comparable in substance to that afforded by this Basic Law. To this end the Federation may transfer sovereign powers by law with the consent of the *Bundesrat*. The establishment of the European Union as well as amendments to its statutory foundations and comparable regulations which amend or supplement the content of this Basic Law or make such amendments or supplements possible shall be subject to the provisions of paragraphs (2) and (3) of Article 79.

(2) The *Bundestag* and, through the *Bundesrat*, the *Länder* shall be involved in matters concerning the European Union. The Federal Government shall inform the *Bundestag* and *Bundesrat* comprehensively and as quickly as possible.

(3) The Federal Government shall give the *Bundestag* the opportunity to state its opinion before participating in the legislative process of the European Union. The Federal Government shall take account of the opinion of the *Bundestag* in the negotiations. Details shall be the subject of a law.

(4) The *Bundesrat* shall be involved in the decision-making process of the Federation in so far as it would have to be involved in a corresponding internal measure or in so far as the *Länder* would be internally responsible.

(5) Where in an area in which the Federation has exclusive legislative jurisdiction the interests

---

[7] Inserted by federal law of 24 June 1968 (*Federal Law Gazette* I p. 710).

of the *Länder* are affected or where in other respects the Federation has the right to legislate, the Federal Government shall take into account the opinion of the *Bundesrat*. Where essentially the legislative powers of the *Länder*, the establishment of their authorities or their administrative procedures are affected, the opinion of the *Bundesrat* shall in this respect prevail in the decision-making process of the Federation; in this connection the responsibility of the Federation for the country as a whole shall be maintained. In matters which may lead to expenditure increase or revenue cuts for the Federation, the approval of the Federal Governments shall be necessary.

(6) Where essentially the exclusive legislative jurisdiction of the *Länder* is affected the exercise of the rights of the Federal Republic of Germany as a member state of the European Union shall be transferred by the Federation to a representative of the *Länder* designated by the *Bundesrat*. Those rights shall be exercised with the participation of and in agreement with the Federal Government: in this connection the responsibility of the Federation for the country as a whole shall be maintained.

(7) Details regarding paragraphs (4) to (6) shall be the subject of a law which shall require the consent of the *Bundesrat*.

Article 24   International organisations

(1) The Federation may by legislation transfer sovereign powers to international organisations.

(1a) Where the *Länder* have the right to exercise state powers and to discharge state functions they may with the consent of the Federal Government transfer sovereign powers to transfrontier institutions in neighbouring regions.

(2) With a view to maintaining peace the Federation may become a party to a system of collective security; in doing so shall consent to such limitations upon its sovereign powers as will bring about and secure a peaceful and lasting order in Europe and among the nations of the world.

(3) For the purpose of settling international disputes the Federation shall accede to agreements providing for general, comprehensive and obligatory international arbitration.

Article 25   International law and federal law

The general rules of public international law shall be an integral part of federal law. They shall take override laws and directly establish rights and obligations for the inhabitants of the federal territory.

Article 28   Federal guarantee of *Land* constitutions and local government

(1) The constitutional order in the *Länder* shall conform to the principles of the republican, democratic and social state governed by the rule of law within the meaning of this Basic Law. In each of the *Länder*, counties and municipalities the people shall be represented by a body elected by general, direct, free, equal and secret ballot. In county and municipal elections persons who are nationals of member states of the European Community, too, may vote and shall be eligible for election in accordance with, European Community law. In the municipalities the local council may take the place of an elected body.

(2) The municipalities shall be guaranteed the right to manage all the affairs of the local community on their own responsibility within the limits set by law. Within the framework of their statutory functions the associations of municipalities likewise have the right of self-government in accordance with the law. The guarantee of self-government shall extend to the bases of financial autonomy; these bases shall include the right of municipalities to a source of tax revenues based upon economic ability and the right to establish the rates at which these sources shall be taxed.

(3) The Federation shall ensure that the constitutional order of the *Länder* conforms to the basic rights and the provisions of paragraphs (1) and (2) of this Article.

Article 30 Powers of the Federation and the *Länder*

Except as otherwise provided or permitted by this Basic Law the exercise of governmental powers and the discharge of governmental functions shall be incumbent on the *Länder*.

Article 31 Precedence of federal law

Federal law shall override *Land* law.

CHAPTER III. **The *Bundestag***

Article 38 Elections

(1) The Members of the German *Bundestag* shall be elected in general, direct, free, equal and secret elections. They shall be representatives of the whole people; they shall not be bound by any instructions, only by their conscience.

(2) Any person who has attained the age of eighteen shall entitled to vote; any person who has attained the age of majority may be elected.

(3) Details shall be regulated by a federal law.

Article 45 The Committee on European Union

The *Bundestag* shall appoint a Committee on European Union. It may empower the Committee to exercise the *Bundestag*'s rights in relation to the Federal Government in accordance with Article 23.

CHAPTER IV. **The *Bundesrat***

Article 50 Functions

The *Länder* shall participate through the *Bundesrat* in the legislative process and administration of the Federation and in matters concerning the European Union.

CHAPTER V. **The Federal President**

Article 59 Representation of the Federation

(1) The Federal President shall represent the Federation in terms of international law. He shall conclude treaties with foreign states on behalf of the Federation. He shall accredit and receive envoys.

(2) Treaties that regulate the political relations of the Federation or relate to subjects of federal legislation shall required the consent or participation, in the form of a federal law, of the bodies responsible in such a case for the enactment of federal law. In the case of executive agreements the provisions concerning the federal administration shall apply *mutatis mutandis*.

CHAPTER VI. **The Federal Government**

Article 67 Constructive vote of no confidence

(1) The *Bundestag* may express its lack of confidence in the Federal Chancellor only by electing a successor with the majority of its Members and requesting the Federal President to

dismiss the incumbent. The Federal President must comply with the request and appoint the person elected.

(2) Forty-eight hours must elapse between the motion and the vote.

Article 68 Vote of confidence, dissolution of the *Bundestag*

(1) Where a motion of the Federal Chancellor for a vote of confidence is not carried by the majority of the Members of the *Bundestag* the Federal President may, upon the proposal of the Federal Chancellor, dissolve the *Bundestag* within twenty-one days. As soon as the *Bundestag* elects another Federal Chancellor with the majority of its Members it may no longer be dissolved.

(2) Forty-eight hours must elapse between the motion and the vote.

CHAPTER VII. Federal Legislation

Article 70 Legislative jurisdiction of the Federation and the *Länder*

(1) The *Länder* have the right to legislate in so far as this Basic Law does not confer legislative powers on the Federation.

(2) The legislative jurisdiction of the Federation and the *Länder* shall be governed by the provisions of this Basic Law concerning exclusive and concurrent legislation.

Article 71 Exclusive legislation of the Federation

In matters of exclusive federal legislation the *Länder* have the right to legislate only where and to the extent that they are explicitly empowered by federal law.

Article 72 Concurrent legislation of the Federation

(1) In matters of concurrent legislation the *Länder* have the right to legislate as long as and to the extent that the Federation does not exercise its legislative powers.

(2) The Federation shall have the right to legislate on these matters if and to the extent that the establishment of equal living conditions throughout the federal territory or the maintenance of legal or economic unity renders federal regulation necessary in the national interest.

(3) A federal law may provide that federal legislation that is no longer necessary within the meaning of paragraph (2) of this Article may be superseded by *Land* law.

Article 73 Areas of exclusive legislation

The Federation shall have exclusive legislative jurisdiction in respect of:

1.[8] foreign affairs and defence including the protection of the civilian population;
2. citizenship in the Federation;
3. freedom of movement, passports, immigration, emigration, and extradition;
4. currency, money and coinage, weights and measures, as well as standard time;
5. unity of the customs and trading area, treaties of commerce and navigation, freedom of movement of goods, as well as international trade and payments including customs and border protection;
6. air transport;
6a the operation of railways wholly or majority-owned by the Federation (federal railways), the construction, maintenance and operation of tracks of the federal railways as well as rates charged for the use of tracks;

[8] As amended by federal laws of 26 March 1954 (*Federal Law Gazette* I p. 45) and 24 June 1968 (*Federal Law Gazette* I p. 711).

7. postal and telecommunication services;
8. the legal status of persons employed by the Federation and federal public corporations;
9. industrial property rights, copyright and publishing;
10.[9] co-operation between the Federation and the *Länder* in
    (a) criminal police work,
    (b) safeguarding the free democratic basic order of the existence of the Federation or a *Land* (protection of the constitution) and
    (c) measures to counter activities in the federal territory which through preparations for or the use of force jeopardise the external interests of the Federal Republic of Germany, as well as the establishment of a Federal Criminal Police Office and international action to combat crime;
11. statistics for federal purposes.

Article 74   Areas of concurrent legislation
Concurrent legislative jurisdiction shall cover:
1. civil law, criminal law and penal measures, court organisation and procedure, the legal profession, notarial and legal advice services;
2. registration of births, deaths, and marriages;
3. association and assembly;
4. foreigners' residence and establishment;
4a.[10] weapons and explosives:
5. measures to prevent the transfer of German cultural property abroad;
6. refugees and expellees;
7. public welfare;
8. citizenship in the *Länder*;
9. war damage and restitution;
10.[11] pensions for war-disabled persons and dependants of war victims as well as assistance for former prisoners of war;
10a.[12] war graves and graves of other victims of war and despotism;
11. economic affairs (mining, industry, energy, crafts and trades, commerce, banking, the stock exchange system and private insurance);
11a.[13] production and utilisation of nuclear energy for peaceful purposes, construction and operation of installations serving such purposes, protection against hazards arising from the release of nuclear energy or from ionising radiation, and disposal of radioactive substances;
12. labour relations including works cbnstitution, industrial safety, labour placement, as well as social security including unemployment insurance;
13.[14] educational and training grants and promotion of research;
14. expropriation where applicable to the matters enumerated in Articles 73 and 74;
15. transfer of land, natural resources and means of production to public ownership or other forms of public enterprise;
16. measures to prevent abuse of economic power;

---

[9] As amended by federal law of 28 July 1972 (*Federal Law Gazette* I p. 1305).
[10] Inserted by federal law of 28 July 1972 (*Federal Law Gazette* I p. 1305) and amended by federal law of 23 August 1976 (*Federal Law Gazette* I p. 2383).
[11] As amended by federal law of 16 June 1965 (*Federal Law Gazette* I p. 513).
[12] Inserted by federal law of 16 June 1965 (*Federal Law Gazette* I p. 513).
[13] Inserted by federal law of 23 December 1959 (*Federal Law Gazette* I p. 813).
[14] As amended by federal law of 12 May 1969 (*Federal Law Gazette* I p. 363).

17.   promotion of agricultural production and forestry, food security, import and export of agricultural and forestry products, deep sea and coastal fishing and coastal preservation;

18.   real property transactions, land law and agricultural leases, as well as housing and land settlement;

19.   measures to combat communicable human and animal diseases that constitute a danger to public health, admission to the medical or ancillary professions, as well as trade in drugs, medicines, narcotics and poisons;

19a.[15]   economic viability of hospitals and regulation of hospitalisation charges;

20.[16]   protective measures in connection with the marketing of food, drink and tobacco, essential commodities, feedstuffs, agricultural and forest seed and seedlings, and protection of plants against diseases and pests, as well as the protection of animals;

21.   ocean and coastal shipping as well as sea-marks, inland navigation, meteorological services, sea routes and inland waterways used for general traffic;

22.[17]   road traffic, motor transport, construction and maintenance of roads for long-distance traffic as well as the collection of tolls for the use of public highways and the allocation of the revenue;

23.   non-federal rail-bound systems, except mountain railways;

24.[18]   waste disposal, air pollution control and noise abatement.

25.   state liability;

26.   human artificial insemination, analysis and modification of genetic information, as well as the regulation of organ and tissue transplantation.

Article 76   Bills

(1) Bills shall be presented in the *Bundestag* by the Federal Government, Members of the *Bundestag* or the *Bundesrat*.

(2) Bills of the Federal Government shall first be submitted to the *Bundesrat*. The *Bundesrat* is entitled to comment upon them within six weeks. Where in exceptional circumstances the Federal Government declares a bill to be particularly urgent it may refer it to the *Bundestag* three weeks after its submission to the *Bundesrat* even though it may not yet have received the latter's comments; upon receiving such comments it shall transmit them to the *Bundestag* without delay. In the case of bills to amend this Basic Law or to transfer sovereign powers pursuant to Article 23 or 24 the comment period shall be nine weeks; the fourth sentence of this paragraph shall not apply.

(3) *Bundesrat* bills shall be submitted to the *Bundestag* by the Federal Government within six weeks. In submitting them the Federal Government shall state its own views. If for important reasons, especially with respect to the scope of the bill, the Federal Government demands an extension, the period shall be increased to nine weeks. If in exceptional circumstances the *Bundesrat* declares a bill to be particularly urgent, the period shall be three weeks or, if the Federal Government has demanded an extension pursuant to the third sentence of this paragraph, six weeks. In the case of bills to amend this Basic Law or to transfer sovereign powers pursuant to Article 23 or 24 the comment period shall be nine weeks; the fourth sentence of this paragraph shall not apply. The *Bundestag* shall consider and vote on bills within a reasonable time.

---

[15] Inserted by federal law of 12 May 1969 (*Federal Law Gazette* I p. 363).
[16] As amended by federal law of 18 March 1971 (*Federal Law Gazette* I p. 207).
[17] As amended by federal law of 12 May 1969 (*Federal Law Gazette* I p. 363).
[18] As amended by federal law of 12 April 1972 (*Federal Law Gazette* I p. 593).

Article 77   The legislative process

(1) Bills shall be adopted by the *Bundestag*. After their adoption they shall be transmitted to the *Bundesrat* by the President of the *Bundestag* without delay.

(2) The *Bundesrat* may within three weeks of receiving the adopted bill demand that it be referred to a committee composed of Members of the *Bundestag* and the *Bundesrat*. The composition and proceedings of this committee shall be governed by rules of procedure drawn up by the *Bundestag* and requiring the consent of the *Bundesrat*. The Members of the *Bundesrat* on this committee shall not be bound by instructions. Where the consent of the *Bundesrat* is required for a bill to become law the *Bundestag* and the Federal Government may likewise request that it be referred to such a committee. Should the committee propose an amendment to the bill the *Bundestag* shall vote on it a second time.

(2a) Insofar as its consent is required for a bill to become law, the *Bundesrat*, if no request has been made pursuant to the first sentence of paragraph (2) of this Article or if the mediation proceeding has been completed without a proposal to amend the bill, shall vote on the bill within a reasonable time.

(3) In so far as its content is not required for a bill to become law the *Bundesrat* may, when the procedure described in paragraph (2) of the Article is completed, object within two weeks to a bill adopted by the *Bundestag*. The period for objection shall begin, in the case of the last sentence of paragraph (2) of this Article, on receipt of the bill as passed again by the *Bundestag* and in all other cases on receipt of a communication from the chairman of the committee provided for in paragraph (2) of this Article to the effect that the committee's proceedings have been concluded.

(4) If the objection was adopted with a majority of the votes of the *Bundesrat* it may be rejected by a decision of the majority of the Members of the *Bundestag*. If the *Bundesrat* adopted the objection with a majority of at least two thirds of its votes its rejection by the *Bundestag* shall require a majority of two thirds of the votes or at least the majority of the Members of the *Bundestag*.

Article 78   Passage of federal laws

A bill adopted by the *Bundestag* shall become law if the *Bundesrat* consents, does not request a referral as provided for in paragraph (2) of Article 77, does not enter an objection within the period stipulated in paragraph (3) of Article 77 or withdraws its objection, or if the objection is overridden by the *Bundestag*.

Article 79   Amendments to the Basic Law

(1) This Basic Law may be amended only by a law expressly modifying or supplementing its text. In respect of international treaties concerning a peace settlement, the preparation of a peace settlement, or the phasing out of an occupation regime, or serving the defence of the Federal Republic, it shall be sufficient, in order to make clear that the provisions of this Basic Law do not preclude the conclusion and entry into force of such treaties, to supplement the text of this Basic Law and to confine the supplement to such clarification.[19]

(2) Such law must be carried by two thirds of the Members of the *Bundestag* and two thirds of the votes of the *Bundesrat*.

(3) Amendments of this Basic Law affecting the division of the Federation into *Länder*, their participation in the legislative process, or the principles laid down in Articles 1 and 20 shall be prohibited.

Article 80   Delegated legislation

(1) The Federal Government, a Federal Minister or the *Land* governments may be

---

[19] Second sentence inserted by federal law of 26 March 1954 (*Federal Law Gazette* I p. 45).

empowered by law to issue statutory orders. The content, purpose and scope of that power shall be specified in the law. Statutory orders shall contain a reference to their legal basis. Where the law provides that the power to issue statutory orders may be further delegated another statutory order shall be required to that effect.

(2) Unless a federal law otherwise provides, the consent of the *Bundesrat* shall be required for statutory instruments issued by the Federal Government or a Federal Minister respecting fees or basic principles for the use of postal and telecommunication facilities, basic principles for levying of charges for the use of facilities of federal railways, or the construction and operation of railways, as well as for statutory instruments issued pursuant to federal laws that require the consent of the *Bundesrat* or that are executed by the *Länder* on federal commission or in their own right.

(3) The *Bundesrat* may submit to the Federal Government drafts of statutory instruments that require its consent.

(4) Insofar as *Land* governments are authorised by or pursuant to federal laws to issue statutory instruments, the *Länder* shall also be entitled to regulate the matter by a law.

CHAPTER IX. Administration of Justice

Article 92   Judicial power
Judicial power shall be vested in the judges; it shall be exercised by the Federal Constitutional Court, the federal courts provided for in this Basic Law, and the courts of the *Länder*.

Article 93   The Federal Constitutional Court, jurisdiction
(1) The Federal Constitutional Court shall rule:
1. on the interpretation of this Basic Law in disputes concerning the extent of the rights and obligations of a supreme federal institution or other institutions concerned who have been vested with rights of their own by this Basic Law or by the rules of procedure of a supreme federal institution;
2. in the case of disagreement or doubt as to the formal and material compatibility of federal or *Land* legislation with this Basic Law or as to the compatibility of *Land* legislation with other federal legislation at the request of the federal Government, a *Land* Government or one third of the Members of the *Bundestag*;
2a. in the event of disagreements whether a law meets the requirements of paragraph (2) of Article 72, on application of the *Bundesrat* or of the government or legislature of a *Land*;
3. in the case of disagreement on the rights and obligations of the Federation and the *Länder*, particularly in the implementation of federal legislation by the *Länder* and in the exercise of federal supervision;
4. on other disputes involving public law between the Federation and the *Länder*, between *Länder* or within a *Land*, unless recourse to another court exists;
4a. on constitutional complaints which may be filed by anybody claiming that one of their basic rights or one of their rights under paragraph 4 of Article 20 or under Article 33, 38, 101, 103 or 104 has been violated by public authority;
4b. on constitutional complaints by municipalities or associations of municipalities alleging violation of their right of self-government under Article 28 by a (federal) law; in case of violation by a *Land* law, however, only where a complaint cannot be lodged with the *Land* constitutional court;
5. in other cases provided for in this Basic Law.

Article 94   The Federal Constitutional Court, composition

(1) The Federal Constitutional Court shall be composed of federal judges and other members. Half of the members of the Federal Constitutional Court shall be elected by the *Bundestag* and half by the *Bundesrat*. They may not be members of the *Bundestag*, the *Bundesrat*, the Federal Government, nor of any of the corresponding institutions of a *Land*.

(2) The constitution and procedure of the Federal Constitutional Court shall be governed by a federal law which shall specify the cases in which its decisions have the force of law. Such law may make a complaint of unconstitutionality conditional upon the exhaustion of all other legal remedies and provide for a special admissibility procedure.

Article 100   Compatibility of legislation and constitutional law

(1) Where a court considers that a law on whose validity its ruling depends is unconstitutional it shall stay the proceedings and, if it holds the constitution of a *Land* to be violated, seek a ruling from the *Land* court with jurisdiction for constitutional disputes or, where it holds this Basic Law to be violated, from the Federal Constitutional Court. This shall also apply where this Basic Law is held to be violated by *Land* law or where a *Land* law is held to be incompatible with a federal law.

(2) If, in the course of litigation, doubt exists whether a rule of international law is an integral part of federal law and whether it directly creates rights and duties for the individual (Article 25), the court shall obtain a decision from the Federal Constitutional Court.

(3) If the constitutional court of a *Land*, in interpreting this Basic Law, proposes to deviate from a decision of the Federal Constitutional Court or of the constitutional court of another *Land*, it shall obtain a decision from the Federal Constitutional Court.

Article 101   Inadmissibility of courts with special jurisdiction

(1) Courts with special jurisdiction shall be inadmissible. Nobody may be removed from the jurisdiction of their lawful judge.

(2) Courts for specific matters may be established only by law.

Article 102   Abolition of capital punishment

Capital punishment is abolished.

Article 103   Court hearings, inadmissibility of retroactive criminal legislation and double jeopardy

(1) In court everybody is entitled to a hearing in accordance with the law.

(2) An act may be punished only if it constituted a criminal offence under the law before the act was committed.

(3) Nobody may be punished for the same act more than once under general criminal legislation.

Article 146   Validity of Basic Law

This Basic Law, which is valid for the entire German nation following the achievement of the unity and freedom of Germanyr shall cease to have effect on the day on which a constitution adopted by a free decision of the German people enters into force.

GLOSSARY

This glossary is intended to be an aid to reference and to act as a kind of German Index to the book. It will direct readers who wish to know about a given German **legal** term to the place in the book where this is discussed or placed in context, but which may not necessarily provide a translation, although in most cases it will. For the reason that this list was not intended to be a mini-dictionary, we eschewed the provision of simple, and thus sometimes misleading, translations into English. The terms are those taken directly from the text. Whilst this may not reflect German practice in the matter, by converting all terms in an index to nominative singular, it avoids the possible confusion which may arise by changing the spelling of the word. Singular and plural terms are included in the same entry, even if not expressly given in the glossary. The names of particular legislative enactments are included in the legislation list rather than here and the names of courts, institutions, particular named legal periodicals, and other proper nouns are included in the index for the most part.

Abitur 80, 81, 85, 232
Ablehnungsgesuch 126
Absatz 117
Abschlußfreiheit 369
Abschlußvertreter 487
Abschnitt 117
Absolutheitsprinzip 442
Abstraktionsprinzip 26, 366, 370, 394, 411, 422, 425
Abtretung 411
Abwehrrechte 205
Adäqaunztheorie 423, 433
Aktenversendung 20
Aktien 143, 365, 492, 505, 511
Aktiengesellschaft 376, 504, 505
Aktivbürgerrecht 206
Alleinbesitz 443
Allgemeine Geschäftsbedingungen 283, 386, 408

Allgemeinverfügung 260
Ältestenrat 182
Amtsanwalt 100
AmtsblattAmtsnotar 117
Amtsnotar 99
Analogieverbot 238, 299
Aneignung 453
Anfechtung 394
Anfechtungserklärung 397
Anfechtungsgründe 394
Anfechtungsklage 266, 267, 268, 458
Angebot 383
Angeklagter 347, 356
Angemessenheit 170, 171
Angestellte 220, 530, 531
Anklager 339, 341
Annahme 383, 384, 411
Anspruch 237, 367
Anspruchsgrundlagen 366, 367

Antrag 383
Anwaltskammer
Anwaltsnotar 99
Anwaltszwang 93, 110, 111
Anwartschaft 462
Äquivalenztheoric 302
Arbeiter 220, 530
Arbeitsamt 528
Arbeitsdirektor 544
Arbeitsgemeinschaft/en 84
arglistige Täuschung 396
Armenrecht 113
Arrest 350
Assessor 85, 86
Assessorenexamen 85
Asylrecht 235
Aufhebung 262, 467
Auflösung 503, 509
Aufnahmesperren 81
Aufsichtsrat 503, 505, 507
Augenschein 132, 357
Ausländerwahlrecht 155, 241
Auslegung 62, 387, 519
Auschlußvertreter 101
Ausschlagung 474
Aussenwirkung 261, 519
Baurecht 440
Beamten 99, 103, 272
Begründungen/Begründheldt 117, 242, 244
Behörde 259
Beibringungsmaxime 124
Beihilfe 330, 333
Beistand 128
Bereicherung 405, 429
Berichte 117
Berufsfreiheit / Beruf 230
Berufsrichter 69, 95
Berufung 71, 134, 340, 360
Berufungsinstanz 71
Berufungssumme 70
Beschaffungsrisiko 413, 423
Beschleunigungsprinzip 125, 343
Beschluß 547
Beschränkte dingliche Rechte 458
Beschuldigter 347, 356
Beschwerde 134, 362
Beschwerdeausschuß 72

Beschwerdebefugnis 243
Besitz 371, 443
Besitzdiener 444
Besitzkonstitut 451
Besitzmittlungsverhältnis 443
Besserung 335
Bestandsschutzprinzip 288
Bestimmtheitsgebot/
    Bestimmtheitsgrundsatz 166, 167, 299, 442
Beteiligtenfähigkeit 243, 267
Betriebsrat 529, 533, 541
Betreuung 471
Beweismittel 132, 356
Beweismittelverbote 357
Beweisthemenverbote 357
Beweisverbot 357
Beweiswürdigung 125, 344
Bezirksnotar 99
Binnenpluralismus 225
Briefgrundschuld 460
Briefhypothek 460
Buchgrundschuld 460
Buchhypothek 460
Bund 58, 175, 178
Bundesanwaltschaft 83, 99
Bundesgesetz/e 36, 58, 152, 213
Bundeskabinett 189
Bundesrechtsanwaltskammer 93
Bundesrichter 71
Bundesstaatsprinzip 153, 174
Bundestreue 178, 179
Bundeswehr 157, 178
Bürogemeinschaft 95
Culpa in contrahendo 412, 419
Deliktsrecht 433, 439
Deliktsfähigkeit 376
Demokratie (prinzip) 79, 153
Deutschenrechte 207
Deutschenspiegel 15
Dienstanweisungen/
    Dienstvorschriften 252
Dienstbarkeiten 458
Dienstverträge 526, 531
Diskontinuität 182
Diskussionsentwürfe
Dispositionsmaxime 124
Dissens 384, 386

Divergenzvorlage 41
Doppelcharakter/Doppelnatur (der
   Grundrechte) 208
Drittwirkung 209, 210, 299, 392, 517
Drohung 396
Durchgang (erster/politischer) 195
Drucksachen 117
Durchführungspflicht 540
Ehe 227, 465
Ehefähigkeit 466
Eheguterrecht 467
Ehemundigkeit 466
Eherecht 465, 468
Eheschließung 466
Ehevertrag 467, 472
Ehrenamtliche Richter 106, 107
Eigenbesitz 443
Eigenhändler 488
Eigenschaften 396
Eigenschaftsirrtum 396
Eigenstumserwerb 447
Eigentum 233, 371
Eigentümergrundschuld 460
Eigentumsvorbehalt 462, 463
Eingetragener Verein 160
Einheitsjuristen 88, 245, 343
Einigung 448, 451
Einspruch 195
Einspruchesgesetze 193, 195
Einstellung 339
Eintragung 448
Einwilligung 310, 311, 378
Endurteil 129, 133
Enteignung 233, 445, 446
Entscheidungen 112, 118, 479
Entwürfe 117
Erbfall 472
Erbfolge 472, 473, 475, 476
Erblasser 472
Erbrecht 233, 367, 472, 478
Erbschaft 472
Erbschein 478
Erbteilung 13
Erbvertrag 398, 476, 477
Erfolgsverursachung 320
Erforderlichkeit 170, 171, 308
Erfüllungsanspruch 428
Erfüllungsgeschäft 374, 394

Erfüllungsort 407
Erfüllungsschaden 411
Erkenntnisverfahren 339
Erklärungsbewußtsein 379, 380, 381
Erklärungsirrtum 395
Erlasse 252
Ermessen 255
Ermittlungsgrundsatz 342, 355
Ermittlungsverfahren 339, 347
Eröffnungsphase 128
Ersitzung 453
Erster Staatsexamen 84
Fachanwalt 96
Fachaufsicht 197
Fachhochschule 102, 103
Fahrlässigkeit 301, 320
Fälligkeit 407
Familienerbfolge 473
Familienrecht 367, 464, 468, 472
Festellungsklage 126, 270, 458
Festnahme 350
Firma 485, 499
Formfreiheit 370
Formularvertrage 408
Fraktion/en 183, 184, 185
Freibleiblend 384
Freischuß 85, 87
Freiheitsgrundrechte 205
Freiwillige Gerichtsbarkeit/
   Freiwilligengerichtsbarkeit 69, 141, 465
Friedenspflicht 539
Fürsorge/Fürsorgepflicht 173, 276
Gebührenvereinbarung 98
Gattungsschuld 406, 413
Gau 10
Geeignetheit 170, 171
Gefährdungshaftung 436
Gegenleistung 415
Gehör 126, 237, 343
Gemeinde 248, 251, 253, 254
Genehmigung 378
Generalstaatsanwalt 99
Gonossenschaft 512, 514
Gerichtsassessor 89
Gerichtsstandbarkeit
Gerichtsvollzieher 69, 135
Gesampthandeigentum 446
Gesamtbetriebsrat 529, 545

Gesamtrechtsnachfolge 455, 473
Gesamtvollmacht 401
Geschäftsbedingungen 369
Geschäftsfähigkeit 375, 376, 377, 378
Geschäftsführung 501
Geschäftsgrundlage 412, 420
Geschäftsordnung 182, 189
Geschäftsunfähigkeit 444
Geschäftswille 379, 381
Geschenk 405
Gesellschafter 143, 365, 376, 499, 500, 514, 515
Gesellschaftsrecht 492, 498
Gesellschaftsvertrag 499
Gesetz/Gesetze 6, 36, 38, 39, 40, 41, 49, 50, 51, 56, 63, 66, 68, 69, 70, 74, 75, 89, 91, 94, 112, 113, 114, 115, 116, 117, 119, 140, 141, 143, 150, 152, 163, 196, 219, 229, 235, 260, 280, 283, 284, 292, 338, 365, 409, 451, 453, 489, 492, 516, 518, 519
Gesetzblatt 117
Gesetzesbeschluß 195, 383
Gesetzesentwurf 194
Gesetzeskraft 41, 240
Gesetzeslücke 60
Gesetzgebung 37
Gesetzmäßigkeit 165
Gestaltungsfreiheit 370
Gewaltenteilung 164
Gewährleistungsrechte 426, 427
Gewerbe 26, 96, 484
Gewerkschaftsbund 523, 528
Gewohnheitsrecht 6, 36, 527
Gläubiger 404
Gläubigerverzug 408
Gleichberechtigungsgebot 464
Gleichheit/Gleichheitsgrundsatz 160
Gleichheitsgrundrechte/
   Gleichheitsrechte 205, 206
Globalzession 463
Grammatische Auslegung 61
Grundbuch 440, 447
Grunddienstbarkeit/en 458
Grundnormen 149
Grundpfandrechte 459
Grundrechte 56, 67, 150, 159, 164, 204, 205, 208, 392
Grundrechtsfähigkeit 208

Grundrechtsmündigkeit 208
Grundrechtsträger 207
Grundrechtsschranken 212
Grundrechtsverletzung 212
Grundrechtsverwirkung 202
Grundsätze 54, 96, 122, 123, 124, 126, 149, 344, 355
Grundschuld 459, 460
Grundstück 440, 441, 447
Gütergemeinschaft 468
Güterstand 467
Gütertermin 547
Gütertrennung 468
Gymnasium 80, 81
Habilitation 102
Haftung 96, 143, 365, 376, 436, 492, 498, 499
Handelsgesellschaft 45, 46, 153, 493, 494
Handelskauf 490
Handelsmakler 488
Handelsregister 70, 484, 485
Handelsrichter 70, 106, 515
Handelsvertreter 487
Handelsvollmacht 486
Handlung 405, 433
Handlungsfähigkeit 375, 376
Handlungswille 379, 380
Härteklausel 469, 470
Haupttermin 128, 131
Hauptverfahren 340, 353
Hauptverhandlung 125, 354
Hauptversammlung 502, 508
Hausarbeit 84, 85, 221
Haushaltsgegenstände 468
Herausgabeanspruch 455
Herrschaftsrecht 441
Herrschende Meinung 7, 122
Historische 62
Hoheitsrechte 49
Hochschullehrer 102
Homogenitätsgebot 175
Hypothek/en 459
Informationsfreiheit 225
Inhaltsfreiheit 370
Inhaltsirrtum 395
Inkompatibilität 186
Immunität 184
Innenvollmacht 400

Inquisitionsprinzip 337
Institutionelle Garantien 209
Interessenalge 60
Invitatio ad offerendum
Irrtum 318
Juristen 47, 100, 109
Juristenausbildung 83, 108
Justitiar 100
Kanzlei 95
Kartellrecht 519
Kauf/recht 424, 480
Kaufmann (Form 1st, Kann, Minder, Muss,
   Soll, Voll-Kaufmann) 483, 484, 485, 487
Kauselgeschäft 374
Kausalität 423
Kettenverträge 532
Klage/schrift 129, 268
Klagebefugnis 268
Kläger 128
Koalitionsfreiheit 229
Kollegialprinzip 188, 189
Kommanditgesellschaft 493, 495, 505, 511
Kommanditist 495
Kommanditaktionäre 511
Kommentar 43, 49, 79, 103, 119, 136, 147,
   205, 245, 246, 297, 363, 403, 439, 514,
   515, 522, 548
Kommissionär 488
Kommunalrecht 176, 272
Kommunen 253
Komplementär 495, 511
Kontrahierungszwang 369
Konzentrationsmaxime 125, 343
Konzernbetriebsrat 529, 545
Konzernrecht 512, 514
Kooperationsprinzip 288
Kooperationsverhältnis 54
Körperschaften 208, 254
Krankenkassen 275
Kreise 253
Kundennanfang 516
Laienrichter 69, 106
Länderblind 44
Landesanwalt 100
Landesgesetze 58
Länderverfassungen 58
Landesrecht 58, 177
Landesrechtsverordnungen 58

Lang dauernde Übung 39
Legalitätsprinzip 341
Lehrstuhl 102
Leihe
Leistung 405, 422
Leistungskondiktion 429
Leistungsort 407
Leistungspflicht 406
Leistungsstörungen 402, 439
Lesung/en
Lokalisierungsgebot/
   Lokalisierungsprinzip 93
Machtbalancierungmechanismus 164
Mahnbescheid 133
Mahnverfahren 133
Maßnahme 259
Menschenwürde 214, 216, 247
Mehrheitswahl 181
Minderung 427
Ministerialblatt 117
Mißtrauensvotum 187
Mitbesitz 443
Mitbestimmung 529, 533, 541
Miteigentum 446
Mittäter 330
Motivirrtum 396
Mülltourismus 290
Mündlichkeitsgrundsatz/
   Mündlichkeitsprinzip 124, 345, 355
Muttersache 455
Nacherfüllung 427, 428
Nachfrist 416
Nachlaß 472
Nachschußpflicht 500
Nebengesetz/e 117, 119, 363
Nebenpflichten 423
Nebentäter 333
Negatives Interesse
Nichtehelich 227
Nichtig/keit 398
Nießbrauch 458
Normenkontrolle 241, 270
Notar 88, 92, 98
Notstand 309, 317
Notwehr 307
Notwehrexzeß 316
Nur-Notar 99
numerus clausus 81, 82, 232, 356

Nutzungsrechte 458
Oberstaatsanwalt 99
Öffentliches Wirtschaftsrecht 33, 278
Öffentlichkeit 123, 345
Offizialmaxime 124
Offizialprincip 340
Ohne obligo 384
Opportunitätsprinzip 342
Ordnungswidrigkeiten 295
Organpersonen 531
Ortskrankenkassen 275
Ostpolitik 187, 246
Parlamentsvorbehalt 157, 165, 167, 196
Parteien 162
Parteienprivileg 160, 200
Parteienverbot 200
Parteifähigkeit 127
Partieherrschaft 122, 127
Partievernehmung 132
Patentanwalt 94, 101
Patentanwaltschaft 101
Personengesellschaft 404
Pfandrecht 461
Pflegschaft 471, 472
Pflichtteil 473, 477
Pflichtteilsrecht 13
Philogogische 61
Präjudizien 40
praktische Konkordanz 150, 151, 224
Prasidentenanklage 192
Prioritätsgrundsatz 463
Privatrecht 4, 139, 478, 479, 480, 481
Ptivatautonomei 369
Probezeit 89
Prokura 486
Prokurist/en 132, 486
Promotion 102
Prozeßagenten 89, 103, 110, 111, 492
Prozeßfähigkeit 127
Prozeßgarantien 206
Prozeßgericht 116
Prozeßgrundrechte 236
Prozeßkostenhilfe 113, 115, 135
Prüfungsrecht 191
Publizitätsprinzip 442
Randnummer 119
Realakt 264, 270, 382, 453
Recht 15, 34, 35, 39, 51, 56, 63, 64, 84, 117,
   120, 126, 139, 163, 169, 202, 208, 216,
   224, 231, 233, 236, 238, 242, 245, 254,
   258, 259, 272, 277, 369, 403, 409, 424,
   472, 493
Rechtmässig 261
Rechtsanwalt/Rechtsanwälte 84, 87, 88,
   92, 94, 98, 99, 101, 106, 108, 111, 128,
   129, 131, 132, 351, 491
Rechtsanwaltskammer 93
Rechtsaufsicht 197
Rechtsbeistand/Rechtsbeistände 89, 92,
   102, 103, 104, 110, 111
Rechtsberatung 102, 103, 109, 114
Rechtsfähigkeit 375
Rechtsfolge 368
Rechtsfertigungsgründe 307, 318
Rechtsgefühl 63
Rechtsgeschäft 379, 383, 390, 399
Rechtsgüter 298, 323
Rechtsgüterschutzprinzip 299
Rechtshängigkeit 129
Rechtsmängel 425, 426
Rechtsobjekte 374
Rechtspfleger 103, 108, 134, 351
Rechtsschutzgarantie 236
Rechtsprechung 41, 49, 67, 68, 75, 197,
   327, 362, 403, 481, 515, 548
Rechtsprechungsmonopol 66
Rechtssicherheit 166
Rechtssatz 59
Rechtsstaat 114, 115, 149, 154, 163, 173,
   197, 203, 212, 340, 351
Rechtsstaatprinzip 153, 154, 163, 164, 165,
   170, 172, 196, 254, 262, 263, 348, 357
Rechtstreue 222
Rechtssubjekte 374, 375
Rechtsverordnungen 36, 37, 58, 196, 251,
   264
Rechtswegerschöpfung 244
Rechtsweggarantie 172
Rechtswidrikeit 301, 307, 319, 321, 324
Referendar 85, 86, 351
Referendarexamen 83
Referendarzeit 85, 87
Rentenschuld 459, 460
Rentensplitting 470
Repetitor 87
Republik 154

Ressortprinzip 188
Revision 71, 134, 340, 360, 361
Revisionsinstanz 71
Richter 88, 106
Richterrecht 6, 29, 39, 479, 527
Richterwahlausschuß 89
Rücktritt 252, 412, 421
Rückwirkung 169, 319, 327
Rückwirkungsverbot 169, 170
Sachen 166, 167, 299, 440
Sachenrecht 440, 441, 463
Sachmängel 367, 440, 441
Sachverständiger 112, 132, 356, 357
Sammelblatt 117
Sammlung 7, 119
Satz 117
Satzung/Satzungen 6, 36, 37, 150, 251,
    252, 274, 505
Schadensersatzansprüche 422
Schiedsrichterliches Verfahren 491
Scheidung 472
Scheingeschäft 393
Scherzerklärung/geschäft 394
Schiedsgerichte 72
Schöffen 14, 69, 106
Schranken 211, 213
Schriftlichkeitsprinzip 124
Schuld 301, 313, 320
Schuldausschließungsgründe 316
Schuldfähigkeit 313
Schuldner 404
Schuldprinzip 299, 468
Schuldrecht 284, 366, 403, 404, 409, 424
Schuldverhältnis/se 404, 405, 411, 430
schwebend unwirksam 378
Sicherungsrechte 458
Sicherungsubereignung 461
Singularzulassung 93
Sozialamt 275
Sozialhilfe 276
Sozialstaat 173, 247, 277
Sozialstaatprinzip 153, 173, 174, 180
Sozialversicherung 276
Sozialversicherungsgesetzgebung 25
Sozietät 95
Sperrklausel 158
Spezialitätsprinzip 442
Sprungrevision 134, 517

Staat 163
Staatsangehörigkeit 207
Staatsanwalt/Staatsanwälte 87, 92, 99,
    339, 341
Staatsanwaltschaft 99
Staatsgewalt 48
Staatsrecht 46, 47, 65, 79, 140, 145, 147,
    148, 149, 152, 155, 159, 206, 208, 245,
    246
Staatssekretär 78
Staatsvolk 155
Stationen 85
Steuerausschuß 75
Steuerberater 101, 111
Stiftung/e 254
Stille Gesellschaft 496
Strafrecht 7, 119, 295, 300, 327, 362, 363
Strafsachen 118
Strafverfahrensrecht 295, 345, 363
Streitwert 112
Stuckschuld 406
Subsidiarität 154
Subsumtion 58, 59
Syndikusanwälte 100
Systematische 15, 62
Tatbestand 301, 304, 310, 311, 319, 320,
    325, 331, 379
Tatbestandsirrtum 306, 313
Tatbestandseite 368
Täter 330, 334
Teilhaberrechte 206
Teilnahme 330, 334
Teilrechtsbeistand 102
Teleogische Auslegung 62
Testament 476, 477
Testierfähigkeit 376
Testierfreiheit 473
Territorialitätsprinzip 298
Textbuch 116
Thing 10
Tierhalter 437
Trennungsprinzip 373
Treu und Glauben 370, 388
Treuhandeigentum 446
Typenfixierung 441, 442
Typenfreiheit 370
Typenzwang 441, 442
Übergabe 451

Überhangmandate 182
Überlassung
Übermaßverbot 170
Übermittlungsirrtum 396
überörtliche Rechtsanwaltssozietäten 95
Überprufungsphase 129
Übung 84
Umweltkriminalität 292
Umweltrecht 33, 285, 294
Umweltschutzrecht 33, 294
Ungerechtfertige Bereichung 405
Universalsukession 473
Unmittelbarkeitsgrundsatz 125, 344
Unmöglichkeit 413
Unterhalt 469
Unterlassungsanspruch 455, 457
Unterlassungsdelikte 301, 321
Untersuchungsausschuss 185
Untersuchungsgrundsatz 342
Untersuchungshaft 349
Urkunde 132, 356, 357
Urkundenprozeß 133
Verarbeitung 454
Verbände 281
Verbindung 453
Verbotsirrtum 306, 318
Verbraucherschutzrecht 281, 284
Verbrechen 69, 168, 295, 325, 350, 351
Verein 71, 229, 376
Vereinigungsfreiheit 229
Verfahrensrecht 7, 119, 84, 481
Verfassung 146, 175
Verfassungbeschwerde 242
Verfassungsfeindlich 201
Verfassungsorgantreue 190
Verfassungsprozessrecht 240
Verfassungsrecht 46, 151, 157, 245, 246
Verfassungswidrig 201
Verfügung 133, 373
Verfügungsfreiheit 446
Verfügungsgeschaft 373, 377, 383, 394,
    401, 411, 425, 447
Vergehen 69, 295, 325, 359
Verhalten 54, 178
Verhältnismaßigkeit 170, 308
Verhältniswahl 181
Verkehrssitte 38, 388
Verkündung 196

Verlöbnis 465
Vermischung 454
Vermittlungsvertreter 487
Vernehmung 347
Verordnung/en 6, 105, 150, 196, 290
Verordnungsblatt 117
Verpflichtungsgeschäft 372, 374, 377, 383,
    394, 401, 411, 425, 447, 448, 456
Verpflichtungsklage 268, 269, 270
Verrichtungsgehilfen 436
Versammlungsfreiheit 228
Verschmelzung 510
Verschulden 419, 423
Versicherungsverein auf
    Gegenseitigkeit 512
Versorgeprinzip 288
Versuch 325, 327, 328
Verteidiger 351
Vertrag 51, 53, 140, 264, 297, 383, 405, 410,
    412, 421, 423, 480
Vertragsfreiheit 366, 369
Vertragshändler 488
Vertragsverhandlung 419
Vertragsverletzung 39, 412, 417
Vertrauensschaden 395, 398, 422
Vertrauensschutz/prinzip 166, 167
Vertretungsmacht 398
Vertreter des öffentlichen Interesses 73, 100
Vertretungszwang 111
Verursacherprinzip 288
Verwaltung 165, 197
Verwaltungsakt 258, 259, 260, 261, 262,
    264, 266
Verwaltungshochschule 103
Verwaltungsordnung/en 37, 140
Verwaltungsvorschrift/en 37, 252
Verwandtschaft 367, 465, 470
Verwartungsrecht 140
Verwerfungsmonopol 242
Verwendungsersatz 457
Verwertung 459, 461
Verzögerungsschaden 416
Verzug 415
Völkerrecht 139, 169, 246
Völkerrechtsfreundlich/keit 43
Volksversammlung 10
Volljurist 83, 85
Vollmacht 399, 400

Vollrechtsbeistand 102
Vollstreckungsbescheid 133
Vollsrechungsverfahren 129, 339
Vonselbsterwerb 473
Vorbehalt 165, 393
Vorbehaltsgut 468
Vorbereitungsphase 128
Vorgesellschaft 500, 506
Vorkaufsrechte 458
Vorverfahren 19, 265, 339, 346
Vormerkung 450
Vormundschaft 367, 465, 471
Vorrang 165
Vorsatz 305, 315
Vorsitzender 70
Vorsorgeprinzip 287
Vorstand 505
Vorverfahren 346
Waffengleichheit 343
Wahlausschuß 93
Wandelung 427
Weistum 15
Werbeverbot 96
Wesentlichkeitstheorie 165
Wettbewerbrecht 283, 516, 518, 522
Widerruf/lich 263, 378, 384
Widerspruch 133, 266
Widerspruchsbescheid 266, 269
Widerspruchsverfahren 72, 265, 266, 268
Widerstandsrecht 199
Wiedervereinigungsgebot 146

Willenserklärung 264, 379, 381, 394
Willensfreiheit 473
Willensmangel 393
Wirksamwerden 381
Wirtschaftsförderung 280
Wirtschaftsprüfer 101, 109, 111
Wirtschaftsverfassungsrecht 285
Wirtschaftsverwaltungsrecht 4, 33, 278, 285
Witchtige Gründe 501
Wohnsitz 127
Wohnung 232, 451
Wohnungseigentum 450, 451
Zerrüttungsprinzip 468
Zeugen 112, 132, 356, 357
Zivilprozeßrecht 92, 136
Zivilrecht 7, 119, 403
Zivilsachen 118
Zollverein 24
Zugewinn 468
Zugewinnausgleich 468
Zugewinngemeinschaft 468
Zulässigkeit 242
Zurückbehaltungsrecht 408
Zuständigkeit 127, 267
Zustimmung 378
Zustimmungsgesetze 49, 193, 195
Zwangsgeld 265
Zwangsmittel 349
Zwangsvollstreckungsverfahren 69
Zwischenverfahren 340, 347, 352

INDEX

Abandonment of an offence 327–30
Abitur qualification 80–1
Abortion 218–19
Absoluteness principle 441
Abstraction 26, 370–1, 442
Academics 102
  legal opinions 121–2
  writings by 7
Accelerated procedure 359
Acceptance 384–5
Accessories 331
Accomplices 330, 333
Accounts 489, 502, 509
Accusation 341
Accused person, evidence from 356
Active agency 399
Administration 196–7
  administrative bodies 253–4
  legality of 165–6
  loyalty of civil service 201–2, 203
  types of 248–9
Administrative Appeal Court 73
Administrative courts 72–3, 107, 111, 267
Administrative guidelines 252–3
Administrative law 4, 140, 248–93
  action types 258–64
    administrative act 259–64
    other instruments 264
    planning 264
    public law contract 264
  administrative bodies 253–4
  basic principles 254–8
  constitutional law and 254–5
  damages claims 271
  discretion 255–6
  enforcement 265
  EU law and 250, 252–3
  general 250
  judicial review 265–71
  margin of appreciation 256–8
  as part of public law 249–50
  particular administrative law 250, 272–93
  sources 251–3
  subjective public right 258
  see also Economic administration law;
    Environmental law; Social law
Adoption 471
Advertising 283, 516–17
  attorneys 96–7
Agency 331–2, 398–402

  authority 400
  commercial 486, 487–8
  commission 488
  lack of authorization 401
  legal consequences 401
  possessor's agent 444
  prohibition of self-contracting 402
  scope of agency powers 400–1
  types of 399–400
Aiding 333, 335
AIDS/HIV 306
Air pollution 289
Analogies 59–61
  ban on 299
Animals, liability for 437
Annuities 460–1
Anti-trust law 519–22
Anticipatory assignment 462–3
Apartments 450–1
Appeals 70, 71, 72, 73, 74–5
  civil procedure 133–4
  criminal procedural law 340,
    360–1
  higher regional courts of appeal
    (*Oberlandesgerichte*) 41, 70
Appointed dealers 488
Appropriation of property 453
Arbitration 72, 491–2
Argumentum a fortiori 61
Arms control 295
Arrest, provisional 350–1
Artistic expression, freedom of 227
Assembly, freedom of 228–9
Association, freedom of 229
Associations 376
  see also Business associations
Asylum 235
Attempt 325–30
Attorneys 88, 92–8
  advertising 96–7
  disciplinary action 94–5
  fees 97–8, 112–13
  form of professional practice 95–6
  non-German 104
    from EU 104–6
  public authority attorneys 100
  reforms 94
  restrictions on professional practice 93–4
  rights of audience 92–3
  role of defence attorney 351–2

specialized 96
state *see* State attorneys
Auditors 101
Austria, codification in 22

Baden-Württemburg 175
Banning
  associations 201
  political parties 199, 200, 202
Basic rights 164, 204–38
  abolition of death penalty 237
  artistic expression and science freedom
    227
  assembly freedom 228–9
  association freedom 229
  asylum 235
  capacity 208
  citizenship 234–5
  communication freedom 224–7
  double character of 208–9
  ECHR and 213
  education 228
  equality before the law 219–22
  extradition 235
  faith, conscience and creed freedom
    222–4
  forfeiture 202
  general principles 205–13
  holders of 207–8
  human dignity protection 214–16
  judges 236–7
  legal hearing right 237, 343
  limitations 212–13
  marriage and family 227–8
  movement freedom 230
  nationalization 234
  ne bis in idem 238
  nulla poene sine lege (legality principle) 237–8,
    298–9
  personal freedom right 216–19
  petition right 235
  privacy of communication 229–30
  privacy of the home 232–3
  profession choice freedom 230–2
  property rights 233–4
  recourse to courts 236
  structure of 211–12
  third effect 209–11
  types of 205–7
Battle of the forms 384, 386–7
Bavaria
  appeal courts 71
  codification in 22
  legal aid in 114
  penal code 296

Berlin 175
  courts in 76
  legal aid in 114
Border guards 237–8, 334–5
Boycotts 224–5
Brandenburg 175
Brandt, Willy 187
Bremen, legal aid in 114
Broadcasting 177
  freedom of 225–6
Broker, commercial 488
Building 264, 291, 438
Bundesrat see Federal council (*Bundesrat*)
Bundestag see Federal parliamentary assembly
    (*Bundestag*)
Business associations 482, 492–8
  limited stock partnership 511–12
  partnerships 488, 492, 493–8
  see also Joint stock corporations; Limited
    liability companies
Business proxy 486
Bye-laws 251–2

Canon law 11, 17
Capacity 208, 375–9
  in guilt 313–14
  succession and 473
Capital, limited liability companies 499
Capital punishment (death penalty) 174, 218,
    237, 336
Care
  care and control 471–2
  duty of 320–1
Cartels (anti-trust) law 519–22
Case law 3, 6–7, 36, 39–42, 84, 527
Casebooks 120
Census 171–2, 217
Certainty 166–70, 299, 442
Chancellor
  appointment by president 186, 190–1
  powers 188–9
  removal 187
Charlemagne 12–13
Chemicals 291
Children
  adoption 471
  education 223–4
  guardianship 471
  illegitimacy 470
  legal capacity 208, 313, 377–8
  liability of 436
  parental relationship with 470–1
  unborn 207–8, 375
    abortion 218–19
Citation 117, 118

Citizenship 207, 234–5
Civil Code (BGB) 13, 23, 26–7, 29, 31, 143,
   364–481
  Book 1 (general part) 374–402
    agency 398–402
    holders of subjective rights 374–9
    interpretation rules 387–90
    legal transactions 379–87
    limitation 402
    void legal transactions 390–8
  Book 2 (law of obligations) 404–39
    assessment of damages and compensation
     421–4
    content of obligational relationship
     406–12
    contracts of sale 424–9
    general principles 404–5
    irregularities in performance 412–21
    tort law 433–9
    unjustified enrichment 429–32
  Book 3 (property law) 440–63
    definitions and general principles 440–2
    finance and security 458–63
    other property rights 458
    ownership 371–2, 445–58
    possession 371–2, 443–5
    protection of ownership 455–8
    scope and sources 440
  Book 4 (family law) 464–72
    care and control 471–2
    curatorship 472
    guardianship 471
    matrimonial law 465–70
    relationship 470–1
    scope 465
  Book 5 (law of succession) 472–8
    acquisition of inheritance 474
    basic principles 473–4
    compulsory portion 477
    execution of estate 478
    heirs 475
    intestate succession 475–6
    rights and liabilities 474–5
    sources and scope 472
    testamentary succession 473, 476–8
  finding the claim 367–8
  labour law and 526–7
  major principles
    abstraction principle 370–1
    categories of legal transaction 372–4
    freedom of contract 369–70
    possession and ownership 371–2
  private international law 478–81
  structure 366–7
Civil law systems 3

Civil (private) law 4, 139, 142–3
  see also Civil Code (BGB)
Civil procedure 122–35
  appeals 133–4
  civil law action 128–33
  enforcement of judgments 134–5
  environmental law 291–2
  general consideration of 126–8
  general principles 123–6
  special procedures 133
Civil service, loyalty of 201–2, 203
Coalitions 187
Codification 3, 5, 22, 33
  commercial requirements and 24–5
  criminal law 21, 296–7
  early codes 11
  Holy Roman Empire 15, 21
  natural law and 22–3
  twentieth century developments 27–9
  unification and 25, 26–7
Coercion, investigation and 349
Collective labour law 525, 539–46
Collusion (anti-trust) law 519–22
Commentaries 119
Commercial agency 486, 487–8
Commercial broker 488
Commercial law 4, 15, 143, 482, 483–92
  arbitration 491–2
  Book 1 484–8
  Book 2 488
  Book 3 489
  Book 4 489–91
  history 483
  structure of the Commercial code 483–4
Commercial lawyers 100
Commercial register 485
Commercial sale 490–1
Commercial transactions 489–91
Commission agency 488
Company law 4
  see also Joint stock corporations; Limited
    liability companies
Compensation
  assessment of 421–4
  duty to compensate for damage 433–5
  tort liabilities 438–9
Competition law 515–19
Competitions 518
Compulsory portion 477
Compulsory prosecution principle 341–2
Concentration efficacy principle 125
Concentration principle 343–4
Conflict of duties 317–18
Conflict of laws 478–81
Consent 310–12

Constitutional courts
    federal 7, 32, 39, 41, 76–7
    regional 77–8
Constitutional law 4, 139–40, 145–203
    administrative law and 254–5
    basic principles of state 153–81
        democracy 155–63
        environmental protection 180–1
        federalism 174–80
        republicanism 154
        rule of law/*Rechtstaat* 163–72, 254, 262
        social state principle 173–4
    complaints 242–4
    historical development 145–9
    international law and 152–3
    labour law and 526
    organization of the state 181–98
        federal council (*Bundesrat*) 192–4
        federal government 186–9
        federal parliamentary assembly (*Bundestag*)
            181–5
        federal president 189–92
        functions of the state 194–8
    procedural 240–5
    supreme position of 149–53
Constitutions
    content 148–9
    Federal Republic (*Grundgesetz*) 6, 32, 37, 43
        amendment 198–9
        basic rights under *see* Basic rights
        EU membership and 43, 44–56
        inconsistency with 39–40
        interpretation 150–2
        judiciary and 40
        priority of provisions 149–50
        protection of 198–203
        reunification and 147–8
        as source of administrative law 251
    Frankfurt Constitution (1849) 145, 204, 239
    regional (*Länder*) 149
    Second Reich 25, 145, 204
    Weimar Republic 30, 145, 146, 189, 204, 222,
        541
Consumer law 5, 281–5, 429
Contracts 372–3, 379, 383–7
    acceptance 384–5
    breach of 417–19
    collapse of foundation of 420–1
    correction of 389–90
    employment
        formation 531–3
        general terms 533–5
        termination 220–1, 535–7
    factual contract 385–6
    formal requirements 390

freedom of contract 369–70
    labour law 527–8
    lack of agreement in formation 386–7
    legal capacity 377–9
    main and ancillary duties 406
    obligations 405
    offer 383–4
    passage of risk in 408, 415, 425–6
    performance 406–7
        delay 415–17
        impossibility 413–15
        irregularities in 412–21
        time and place 407–8
    primary and secondary duties 406
    problems in pre-contractual relations 419–20
    public law contract 264
    rescission 394–8, 421
    sale 424–9
    standard forms 408–10
    succession contract 477
    third parties to 410–12
    void 391–2
Co-operation principle 288
Co-operatives 511–12
Corporations *see* Limited liability companies
Correspondence attorneys 95
Costs
    attorneys fees 97–8, 112–13, 128
    courts 111–12, 128
Courts 28, 66–78, 178, 197–8
    administrative courts 72–3, 107, 111, 267
    adoption of Roman law and 19–21
    arbitrary 237
    case law and 6–7, 36, 39–42, 84, 527
    choice of 352–3
    costs 111–12, 128
    decentralization 66–7
    federal courts 4–5, 67, 71–2, 73, 74–5, 76–7,
        197–8
    jurisdiction 127–8
    labour courts 73–4, 107, 111, 112, 523, 529
    new federal regions 67, 75–6
    officials 103
    ordinary jurisdiction 69–72
    recourse to courts 236
    regions (*Länder*) 67, 69–71, 73, 74, 75–6, 77–8,
        178, 197–8
    reports 117–18
    social courts 74–5
    specialization 67–75
    tax/revenue courts 75, 107, 111
    unification and 25–6
    see also Judiciary; *and individual courts*
Criminal courts
    lay judiciary 107

legal representation in 92, 110–11
local courts 69
regional courts 70
Criminal law 4, 141, 295–362
  applicability 298
  codification 21, 296–7
  general concepts 300–36
  history 21, 296–7
  leading principles 298–300
  public prosecutors 99–100
  retroactivity 167–9, 299
  structure of criminal code 297
  substantive 295
  see also Criminal offences; Criminal procedural
    law
Criminal offences 336–7
  attempt 325–30
  elements of the offence 301–7
    attempted offences 325–7
    negligent offences 320–1
    objective 301–4
    omission offences 322–4
    subjective 304–7
  environmental law 292
  exemption from punishment 319
  forms of 301
  guilt 313–18, 324–5
  intent 305–6
  justification grounds 307–12
  mistake 306–7, 312–13, 318
  negligence 315–16, 320–1
  omission offences 321–5
  participation forms 330–5
  structure of 301–20
  unlawfulness 307–13, 324–5
  see also Punishment
Criminal procedural law 295–6, 337–62
  appeals 340, 360–1
  history 338
  interim proceedings 340, 352–3
  law of evidence 344, 355–8
  leading principles 340–6
    commencing the procedure 340–2
    evidence 344
    form of proceedings 345–6
    implementation of the procedure 342–4
  main proceedings 340, 353–62
  means of redress 360–2
  pre-trial procedure 339, 346–52
    preliminary investigation 346–51
    role of defence attorney 351–2
  sources 339
Curatorship 472
Customary law
  Germanic tribes 10

Holy Roman Empire 14, 19
Salic Frank period 11, 12
as source of German law 6, 36, 38–9, 40
supersession by Roman law 19

Damage
  duty to compensate for damage 433–5
  intentional 435–6
Damages
  administrative law 271
  assessment of 421–4
Data protection 171–2, 217
Databases 120–1
Death
  death penalty 174, 218, 237, 336
  legal capacity and 376
Debts 133
Deceit
  in interrogation 348
  in legal transactions 396–7
Decentralization, court structure and 66–7
Defective goods 426–8
Defence attorneys 351–2
Delict (tort law) 433–9
Democracy 48, 155–63
  defence of 199–203
  elections 155–6, 158–9, 181–2
  militant/defensive 202–3
  status of political parties 159–63
Detention, pre-trial (remand) 349–50
Direct agency 399
Directness principle 125
Disciplinary action, attorneys 94–5
Disciplinary courts 72
Discretion, administrative law 255–6
Discrimination, gender 221–2
Distributors 488
Divorce 468–70
Dominant positions 521
Drugs and narcotics 295
Drunkenness 314–16
Duress 396

Economic administration law 4–5, 33, 142,
  278–85
Education 223–4
  basic rights 228
  legal education 80–8
  sex education 166
Elections 155–6, 158–9, 181–2
  Chancellor 186
  federal president 189
Electoral law 4
Embryos 295
Emergency will 476–7

Employers' associations 523, 524, 529
Employment 486, 530–1
  blue/white collar distinction 530–1
  contracts
    formation 531–3
    general terms 533–5
    termination 220–1, 535–7
  hiring employees 533
  worker protection 525, 537–8
  works councils 523, 524, 529, 531, 533, 541–3
Enforcement 134–5
  administrative law 265
  consumer law 284–5
  criminal law 295–6
  environmental law 291–3
Engagement 465
Environmental law 5, 33, 285–93
  general principles 287–8
  liability and enforcement following
      environmental damage 291–3
  principal legislative enactments 288–91
  public enforcement 293
  sources 286–7
Environmental protection 180–1
Equality before the law 219–22
Equivalence, theory of 302–3
European Coal and Steel Community (ECSC) 43
European Convention on Human Rights (ECHR)
      56–7, 152, 202, 213, 242
European Union/Community 3, 9, 33, 152–3,
      156
  administrative law and 250, 252–3
  anti-trust law 519–20
  attorneys from EU countries 104–6
  criminal law and 297
  environmental law and 287
  as source of German law 6, 36, 42–56
Euthanasia 311–12, 318
Evidence
  civil law actions 132–3
  criminal procedural law 344, 355–8
    forms of proof 356–7
    principles 355–6
    prohibition of evidence 357–8
  freedom of 125–6, 344
Execution of estate 478
Expediency principle 342
Expert witnesses 132, 357
Expropriation of property 234
Extradition 235, 297

Factual contract 385–6
False declaration 394
Family law 4, 464–72
  basic rights 227–8

care and control 471–2
curatorship 472
guardianship 471
matrimonial law 465–70
relationship 470–1
scope 465
Fault liability 423–4, 435
Federal Administrative Court 67, 73
Federal Association of Attorneys (BRAK) 93–4,
      96
Federal Constitutional Court
      (*Bundesverfassungsgericht*; *BVerfG*) 7, 32,
      39, 41, 76–7, 150, 151, 198, 239–40
  judiciary 91–2, 239
Federal council (*Bundesrat*) 192–4
  composition and procedure 192–3
  legislative process 194, 195–6
  nature 192
  tasks 193–4
Federal Court of Justice 41, 67, 71–2, 93
Federal courts 67, 71–2, 73, 74–5, 76–7, 197–8
  judiciary 89–92
Federal Environment Office 286, 287
Federal government (*Bundesregierung*) 186–9
  composition 186–7
  legislative process 194–6
  removal of government and chancellor 187–8
  tasks and organization 188–9
Federal Labour Court 67
Federal Ministry of Justice 78
Federal parliamentary assembly (*Bundestag*) 157,
      181–5
  elections 181–2
  legislative process 194–6
  organization 182–3
  status of members of 183–5
  tasks 185
Federal Patent Court 72
Federal president 189–92
  actions against 192
  appointment of chancellor and ministers
      186–7, 190–1
  duties of office 190–1
  election 189
  legislative process 196
  role of 189–90
Federal professional courts 72
Federal Social Court 67, 74–5
Federal Tax Court 67
Federalism 174–80
  competences in federation and regions 175–8
  Constitution and 175
  general principles 174
  relations between federation and regions 165,
      178–80, 197

Federation of German States (*Deutscher Bund*) 21, 22
Fees, attorneys 97–8, 112–13, 128
Finance and security
  property law 458–63
  security in land 459–61
  security over movables 461–3
Fines 336
First World War 28
Flats 450–1
Food labelling 282–3
Forced labour 232
Forfeiture of basic rights 202
Found objects 454
France
  codification in 3, 22
  Napoleonic period 21, 22
Frank-formula 329
Freedom
  artistic expression and science freedom 227
  assembly freedom 228–9
  association freedom 229
  choice of profession 230–2
  communication freedom 224–7
  of contract 369–70
  of evidence 125–6, 344
  faith, conscience and creed freedom 222–4
  movement freedom 230
  personal freedom right 216–19
Freelance workers 531
Futile attempt 327

Gaps and analogies 59–61
Gender, equal rights 221–2
General meetings
  joint stock corporations 508
  limited liability companies 502–3
German Democratic Republic (GDR; DDR) 145, 146, 365–6
  see also New Federal Regions
Germanic tribes 9–10
Good faith acquisition of property 451–2
Good faith requirement 388
Government and the state
  basic principles 153–81
    democracy 155–63
    environmental protection 180–1
    federalism 174–80
    republicanism 154
    rule of law/*Rechtstaat* 163–72, 254, 262
    social state principle 173–4
  economic administration law 4–5, 33, 142, 278–85
  Holy Roman Empire 13, 14, 175
  justice ministries 78

nationalization 234
organization of 181–98
  federal council (*Bundesrat*) 192–4
  federal government 186–9
  federal parliamentary assembly (*Bundestag*) 181–5
  federal president 189–92
  functions of the state 194–8
  public law and 4–5
  Second Reich 25
  Third Reich 31
  Weimar period 28–9
  see also Administration
Groups of companies 512–14, 545–6
Guardianship 471
Guilt 299–300, 313–18, 324–5

Hamburg, legal aid in 114
Hearsay 357
Heirs 475
Hierarchy of legal provisions 58
Higher regional courts of appeal (*Oberlandesgerichte*) 41, 70
Historical development 3, 9–34
  Charlemagne 12–13
  commercial law 483
  constitutional law 145–9
  criminal law 21, 296–7
  criminal procedural law 338
  customary law 10, 11, 12, 14, 19
  early development 9–10
  early modern times 16–21
  historical law school 22, 23–4
  Holy Roman Empire 12, 13–16, 17–21, 145
  joint stock corporations 504–5
  judiciary 14, 20, 26
  labour law 523–5
  middle ages 13–16
  natural law school 22–3
  post-medieval developments 21–7
  Salic-Frank period 10–12
  Second Reich 25–7
  twentieth century developments 27–34
  universities and 16–17, 18, 20–1, 27–8
  Weimar Republic 28–31, 40
Historical law school 22, 23–4
Hitler period (Third Reich) 31–2, 40, 57, 296, 338, 524
Holidays 538
Holy Roman Empire 12, 13–16, 145, 175, 296
  adoption of Roman law 17–21
Home, privacy of 232–3
Homosexuality, partnership rights 228, 465
Horizontal agreements 520–1

Human dignity protection 214–16
Hyperinflation 29, 64, 389

Illegitimacy 470
Imaginary offence 327
Immediacy principle 344
Imperial Council (*Reichhofsrat*) 76, 239
Imperial Court of Appeal (*Reichskammergericht*)
    16, 19, 76, 239
Impossibility 413–15
Imprisonment 336
    life sentences 215, 336
In dubio pro reo principle 344
Inciting 333–4
Indirect agency 399
Individual labour law 525, 530–7
Individualism 26
Industrial conflict 523, 540–1
Inflation 29, 64, 389
Information
    consumer law 285
    environmental 290
Inheritance *see* Succession and inheritance
Insurance 283–4
Insurance associations 512
Intent
    criminal offences 305–6
    declaration in legal transactions 379–82,
        383–5
        defect of 393–8
        interpretation rules 387–8
        rescission 394–8
    intentional damage 435–6
Interim proceedings 340, 352–3
International Criminal Court 297
International Criminal Tribunals 297
International law 4
    constitutional law and 152–3
    private 478–81
    as source of German law 43, 56–7
Internet 121
Interpretation
    constitution 150–2
    legal transactions 387–90
    statutes 61–4
Interrogation 347–9
Intestate succession 473–4, 475–6
Intoxication 314–16
Investigation 342–3
    pre-trial preliminary investigation 346–51
Invitation to treat 384

Joint stock corporations 504–11
    accounts 509
    board of management 506–7

dissolution 509–10
formation 505–6
general meeting 508
groups of 512–14, 545–6
history 504–5
mergers and acquisitions 510–12
minority protection 509
shares 508
supervisory board 507
Joke declaration 394
Journals 120
Judgments
    civil law actions 133
        enforcement of 134–5
Judicature law 140–1
Judicial review 164–5, 172
    administrative law 265–71
    property 458
Judiciary 6, 28, 197–8
    civil procedure 126–7
    Federal Constitutional Court
        (*Bundesverfassungsgericht; BVerfG*) 91–2,
        239
    Holy Roman Empire 14, 20
    lay judiciary 69, 91, 106–7
    local courts 69
    as profession 89–92
    right to independent judge 236–7
    role in trial 354
    unification and 26
Juries 106, 123
Jurisdiction of the courts 127–8
Justice ministries 78
Justification grounds, criminal offences 307–12
Juvenile courts 107

Kohl, Helmut 187, 188

Labelling 282–3
Labour law 4, 32, 142, 523–48
    categories 525
    collective 525, 539–46
    courts 73–4, 107, 111, 112, 523, 529
    history 523–5
    individual 525, 530–7
    institutions 528–9
    procedural law 525, 546–8
    sources 526–8
    worker protection 525, 537–8
    works councils 523, 524, 529, 531, 533, 541–3
Land charge 460
Land (real estate) 447–51, 452
    security in land 459–61
Land register 449–50
Länder see Regions (*Länder*)

Lawyers
  commercial lawyers 100
  patent lawyers 101–2
  public authority lawyers 101
  see also Attorneys
Lay participation in legal system
  judiciary 69, 91, 106–7
  juries 106
Legal advisers 102–3
Legal aid 113–16
  legal advice 113–15
  representation in court 113, 115–16
Legal capacity *see* Capacity
Legal certainty 166–70, 299, 442
Legal education 80–8
  criticisms 86–7
  part one examination 83–5
  part two examination 85–6
  reforms 87–8
Legal method 58–64
  gaps and analogies 59–61
  hierarchy of legal provisions 58
  statutory interpretation 61–4
  subsumption 59
Legal opinions 121–2
Legal positivism 24, 26
Legal professions 88–106
  academics 102
  auditors 101
  commercial lawyers 100
  court officials 103
  legal advisers 102–3
  notaries 98–9
  oversupply in 82
  patent lawyers 101–2
  public authority lawyers 101
  tax advisers 101
  see also Attorneys; Judiciary; State attorneys
Legal publications 116–21
  official publications 116–18
  private reporting and publication 119–21
Legal representation 92, 110–11, 128
  attorneys fees 97–8, 112–13, 128
  legal aid 113, 115–16
Legal transactions 379–87
  capacity to conclude 376–9
  declaration of intent 379–82, 383–5
    defect 393–8
    interpretation rules 387–8
    rescission 394–8
  interpretation 387–90
  real act 382
  types of 372–4
  void 390–8
    breach of formal requirements 391

breach of law or good morals 391–3
    consequences 398
    defect of declaration of intent 393–8
    see also Contracts
Legality of administration 165–6
Legality principle (*nulla poene sine lege*) 237–8, 298–9
Legislative process 47–8, 194–6
Legitimate expectations 167, 169
Lie detectors 348
Lien 461
Life sentences 215, 336
Limitation periods 168, 269, 402, 428–9, 439
Limited liability companies 484, 498–504
    accounts 489, 502
    alteration to articles 503
    attorneys as 96
    basic rights and 208
    capital 499
    combined with partnerships 497
    dissolution and liquidation 503
    formation 498–9
    general meetings 502–3
    groups of 512–14, 545–6
    as legal persons 375, 376
    management 501–2
    mergers and acquisitions 503
    pre-incorporation status 500
    registration 499
    restructuring 504
    shareholders' rights and duties 500–1
    supervisory board 503
Limited partnership 495–6
Limited stock partnership 511–12
Liquidation 503
Local courts (*Amtsgericht*) 69–70
Lockouts 541
Lower Saxony, legal aid in 114

Maintenance 469–70, 471
Management 531
    joint stock corporations 506–7
    limited liability companies 501–2
Manufacturing 454
Margin of appreciation, administrative law 256–8
Maternity protection 538
Matrimonial law 465–70
    basic rights 227–8
Media *see* Broadcasting; Press
Medical treatment, consent to 311
Mental reservations 393
Merchants 484
Mergers and acquisitions
    control of 521

joint stock corporations 510–12
limited liability companies 503
Military service 224, 232, 236
Minority protection, joint stock corporations
    509
Missing persons 376
Mistake
    criminal offences 306–7, 312–13, 318
    legal transactions 395–6
Mixing property 454
Morality 62
Mortgages 459–60
Movable property 451, 452
    security over movables 461–3
Movement, freedom of 230
Mutual will 477

Name of firms 485–6
Nationalism 26
Nationalization 234
Natural law
    natural law school 22–3
    as source of German law 57
Nature conservation 290
Nazi period (Third Reich) 31–2, 40, 57, 296, 338,
    524
Ne bis in idem 238
Necessity 309–10, 317
Negligence, criminal offences 315–16, 320–1
New Federal Regions (former East Germany)
    33–4, 147
    court structure in 67, 75–6
    waste disposal in 290
Notaries 98–9
Nuclear substances 291
Nulla poene sine lege (legality principle) 237–8,
    298–9

Oaths 132
Obligations 4, 404–39
    assessment of damages and compensation
        421–4
    content of obligational relationship 406–12
    extinction of obligational relationship
        411–12
    main and ancillary duties 406
    passage of risk in performance 408
    performance of individual and generic
        obligations 406–7
    primary and secondary duties 406
    standard form contracts 408–10
    third parties to contracts 410–11
    time and place of performance 407–8
    contracts of sale 424–9
    creation 405

general principles 404–5
irregularities in performance 412–21
    basic provision for liability 412–13
    collapse of foundation of contract 420–1
    delay 415–17
    impossibility 413–15
    positive breach 417–19
    problems in pre-contractual relations
        419–20
    rescission 421
    tort law 433–9
    unjustified enrichment 429–32
Occupiers' liability 438
Offer 383–4
Official accusation principle 341
Official duty principle 340–1
Omission offences 321–5
Opinion
    academic 121–2
    freedom of 224–5
Oral proceedings 124–5, 345, 354–5
Ownership 371–2, 445–58
    protection of 455–8

Packaging 291
Pandectist school 24
Parliament see Federal parliamentary assembly
        (Bundestag)
Parties to actions 124, 127, 132
Partnerships 488, 492, 493–8
Passive agency 399
Passports 216
Patent lawyers 101–2
Periodicals 120
Personal freedom right 216–19
Persons, natural and legal 375
Petition right 235
Planning 264
Plebiscites 155, 175
Pledge 461
Police 99–100, 339, 346
    pre-trial investigation 346, 347–51
Political parties 4
    banning 199, 200, 202
    in Bundesrat 193
    in Bundestag 183, 184–5
    coalitions 187
    elections and 158–9, 182
    federal president and 190
    status of 159–63
Polluter pays principle 288
Possession 371–2, 443–5
    acquisition 444
    complete and partial 444
    direct and indirect 443

exclusive and joint 443–4
loss of 445
possessor's agent 444
protection of 445
Posting rule 384
Powers, separation of 164–5
Precautionary principle 287
Precedent 6–7, 40–2
Pre-contractual relations 419–20
Pregnancy
abortion 218–19
maternity protection 538
Prescription of property 453
President *see* Federal president
Press, freedom of 225
Presumption of consent 311–12
Pre-trial procedure 339, 346–52
preliminary investigation 346–51
role of defence attorney 351–2
Preventative principle 287
Privacy
of communication 229–30
of the home 232–3
Private will 476
Privatization 191
Procedural law 4, 140–1
Processing 454, 463
Product liability 282, 284, 438
Profession 530
freedom of choice 230–2
Professional courts 72
Professional partnerships 497–8
Property law 4, 233–4, 440–63
appropriation 453
definitions and general principles 440–2
finance and security 458–63
security in land 459–61
security over movables 461–3
found objects 454
good faith acquisition 451–2
land/real estate 447–51, 452
security in land 459–61
manufacturing or processing 454
marriage and 467–8
mixing 454
movable property 451, 452
security over movables 461–3
other property rights 458
ownership 371–2, 445–58
protection of ownership 455–8
possession 371–2, 443–5
acquisition 444
complete and partial 444
direct and indirect 443
exclusive and joint 443–4

loss of 445
possessor's agent 444
protection of 445
prescription 453
real rights 440–1
scope and sources 440
separation of objects 455
succession 455
union or combination 453–4
Proportionality principle 170–2
Prosecution 341–2
public prosecutors *see* State attorneys
Protection of existing position principle 288
Provisional arrest 350–1
Prussia 25, 296
codification in 22, 23
Public authorities 4
attorneys 100
lawyers 101
Public business law *see* Economic administration
law
Public law 4–5, 139–42
environmental law and 293
see also Administrative law; Basic rights;
Constitutional law; Criminal law
Public prosecutors *see* State attorneys
Public will 476
Publications *see* Legal publications
Publicity, principle of 123–4, 345–6, 442
Punishment 335–6
death penalty 174, 218, 237, 336
exemption from 319
fines 336
imprisonment 336
life sentences 215, 336
ne bis in idem 238
nulla poene sine lege (legality principle) 237–8,
298–9

Radioactivity 291
Rau, Johannes 190
Real act 382
Real estate *see* Land (real estate)
Real rights 440–1
Redress, means of 360–2
Regional courts (*Landgericht*) 70–1
Regions (*Länder*) 175
administration and 196–7
Bundesrat and 192, 193
competences 175–8
constitutional procedural law 245
constitutions 149
court structure 67, 69–71, 73, 74, 75–6, 77–8,
178, 197–8
federal level and 165, 178–80, 197

judiciary 89–91
justice ministries 78
legal education and 80, 86
legislative role 47–8
Second Reich 25
Rehabilitation 336
Relationship 470–1
Religion, freedom of 222–4
Remand, detention on 349–50
Rent 284
Republicanism 154
Rescission 394–8, 421
Reservation of title 462
Retrial 362
Retroactivity 167–70, 299
Return, claim for 455–6
Revenue courts 75, 107, 111
Revenue law *see* Tax and revenue law
Revision of law, appeal for 361–2
Revolution of 1848 24–5
Rhineland-Palatinate, legal aid in 114
Rights
real rights 440–1
see also Basic rights; Subjective rights
Road accidents 437
Roman law 3, 4, 9, 10–11, 15, 16
adoption in Holy Roman Empire 17–21
historical law school and 24
natural law school and 22–3
Rule of law/*Rechtstaat* 163–72, 254, 262
judicial review right 172
legal certainty 166–70, 299
legality of administration 165–6
other elements 172
proportionality principle 170–2
separation of powers 164–5
see also Basic rights

Saarland, legal aid in 114
Sado-masochism 310–11
Safety legislation 282
Sale 283–4
commercial 490–1
contracts of sale 424–9
Sales 518
Salic-Frank period 10–12
Saxony
customary law 15
resistance to Roman law 19, 21
Schmidt, Helmut 187–8
Science, freedom of 227
Second Reich 25–7, 296
Second World War 3
Security *see* Finance and security
Self-contracting 402

Self-defence 307–9
excessive force in 316
Self-responsibility 304
Separation of objects 455
Separation of powers 164–5
Sex education 166
Sham transactions 393–4
Shareholders, rights and duties 500–1
Shares, joint stock corporations 508
Silence, acceptance and 385
Silent partnership 496
Social courts 74–5, 107, 111, 112
Social law 4, 32, 141, 273–7
administration and distribution of social aid
275
aim and principles 274–5
breaches of duty by social bodies 277
persons eligible for social assistance 277
social welfare provision 275–7
sources 273–4
Social security 25, 28, 173–4, 273–7
Sources of law 5–7, 36–58
administrative law 251–3
case law 6–7, 36, 39–42, 84, 527
Constitution of the Federal Republic
(*Grundgesetz*) 6, 37
criminal procedural law 339
customary law 6, 36, 38–9, 40
environmental law 286–7
European Union/Community 6, 36, 42–56
international law 43, 56–7
labour law 526–8
natural law 57
social law 273–4
statutes 6, 36, 37–8
Sovereignty 48
Speciality principle 442
Specialized attorneys (*Fachanwalt*) 96
State *see* Government and the state
State attorneys 99–100, 339, 340, 346
pre-trial investigation 346, 347–51
States (*Länder*) *see* Regions (*Länder*)
Statutes 3
commentaries 119
federation and regions and 177–8
legislative process 47–8, 194–6
obligations 405
official publication 117
priority of 165
private publication 119
review of 241
as source of German law 6, 36, 37–8
administrative law 251
statutory interpretation 61–4
submission procedure 241–2

Sterilization 313
Strict liability 436–7
Strikes 523, 540–1
Subjective rights 258
  holders of 374–9
Subsumption 59
Succession and inheritance 4, 13, 233, 472–8
  acquisition of inheritance 474
  basic principles 473–4
  compulsory portion 477
  execution of estate 478
  heirs 475
  intestate succession 473–4, 475–6
  property 455
  rights and liabilities 474–5
  sources and scope 472
  testamentary succession 473, 476–8
Summary procedure 359
Supervisory boards 503, 507, 529, 544–5
Surveillance 229–30

Tax advisers 101
Tax courts 75, 107, 111
Tax and revenue law 4, 141
  retroactivity 169–70
Taxation 227, 228, 289
Teleological reduction 61
Television broadcasting 177
Territoriality principle 298
Terrorism 206–7, 338
Testamentary succession 473, 476–8
Textbooks 119–20
Theft 59
Third Reich 31–2, 40, 57, 296, 338, 524
Thirty Years War (1616–1648) 16, 21
Tort law 433–9
Torture 348
Trade unions
  consumer rights and 285
  history of 523–4
Transactions
  commercial transactions 489–91
  legal see Legal transactions
Transplantations 295
Trials and hearings
  civil law action 128–33

criminal procedural law 340, 353–62
  accelerated procedure 359
  conclusion of trial 359
  form of proceedings 345–6
  oral proceedings 345, 354–5
  retrial 362
  summary procedure 359
  legal hearing right 237, 343
  see also Evidence; Pre-trial procedure
Trust property 446

Undisclosed partnership 496
Unfair dismissal 538
Unifications of Germany 24–7, 33, 66, 147–8
Unity of proceedings 125, 343
Universities 16–17, 18, 20–1, 27–8
  legal academics 102
  legal education in 80–8
Unjustified enrichment 429–32
Unlawfulness, criminal offences 307–13, 324–5
Usage 38

Vertical agreements 521
Vicarious liability 436
Void legal transactions 390–8
  breach of formal requirements 391
  breach of law or good morals 391–3
  consequences 398
  defect of declaration of intent 393–8
Voidable marriages 466–7

Warranties 284
Waste 289–90
Water resources 288–9
Weimar Republic 28–31, 40
  Constitution 30, 145, 146, 189, 204, 222,
    541
Westphalia, Peace of 21
Wills 476–7
  testamentary succession 473, 476–8
Witnesses 132, 356–7
Worker protection 525, 537–8
Works councils 523, 524, 529, 531, 533, 541–3
Written presentation 124–5, 129–30

Young workers 538